Rise Again

A Group Singing Songbook

Conceived, developed & edited by

Peter Blood &
Annie Patterson

Associate Editors:
Johanna Halbeisen & Joe Offer

Preface by Pete Seeger & Foreword by Billy Bragg

Cover art by Mary Azarian

Illustration by Annie Patterson, Meghan Merker & Mona Shiber

Acknowledgments

We could not have created this book without a tremendous community of hundreds of hard-working volunteers. We are grateful to our families & friends for your patience & support. We are deeply indebted to everyone who helped out. Unfortunately, we don't have the space here to thank all of you by name. A fuller list of our invaluable volunteers and contributors can be found on our website at www.riseupandsing.org/support/team.

Design, layout & formatting: Annie Patterson, Nicole Julius

Song licensing: David Dinan (with help from Peter Blood, Joe Offer & Johanna Halbeisen)

Music transcription for rounds: Joanna Katzen

File conversion & data management: Eric Lerner

Lead proofreader & publishing assistance: Mark Heiman

Lead chord checker: Paul Kaplan

Canadian coordinator (selection & permissions): Jack Cole

Proofing team: Honey Nichols, Pat Lamanna, Mark Mandel

Chord team: David Ahlfeld, Bob Cohen, Zack Danziger, Dan Grubbs, Jeremy Korr, Josh Korr, Jeff Lee, Karl Moore & Mike O'Leary

Non-English songs: Mary Dean, Jesse Greist, Paul Baker Hernandez, Linda Hirschhorn, Yosl Kurland, Dot Patterson Lin, Monique Palomares & Eduardo Reyes

Song genre assistance: Elias & Ian Blood-Patterson, Daryl Davis, Mary Flower, Sara Gowan & Bill Quern, Paul Landskroener, Bonnie Lockhart & Betsy Rose, Evy Mayer & Sol Weber, Kate Munger, Sarah Pirtle & Sally Rogers, Kathy & Marv Reitz, John Roberts, Claire Brandenburg Taylor, Jacqui Wallace

Original song selection committee: Dave Andrews, Greg Artzner, Joan Broadfield, Sallie Gordon, Johanna Halbeisen, Sam Hinton, Pat Humphries, Paul Klinkman, Jeremy Korr, John McCutcheon, Sonny Ochs, Faith Petric, Pete Seeger, Kevin Slick, Claire Brandenburg Taylor, Paul Tinkerhess, Anne Wright

Legal consultation, advice & support: Robert Meitus

Social media, promotion & outreach: Jaimé Morton

Personal support extraordinaire: Roger & Shirley Conant, Victoria Dickson, Ruth Hazzard, Mary Link, George Munger, Sarah Pirtle

We are deeply indebted to & thankful for all the talented songwriters who wrote the songs in this book. Please support them (& the thousands of other musicians writing & recording great songs today) by buying their music & going to their concerts. Help live music to flourish!

Traditional songs. There are many versions of almost every "traditional" song in this book. There is no "correct" version of any traditional song and the variants included here are in no way intended to be "definitive." For the most part, they were chosen because they are reasonably authentic versions that work well for group singing. Try researching different versions of a song you're learning and listening to a number of different recordings. Please don't use our books to tell another singer that she or he is singing the "wrong" version of a song! Songs in the public domain are indicated in this book with "Arr. © 2015 Hal Leonard Corporation." under the song. The publisher has copyright to this particular arrangement, but you do not have to get permission to record or reprint lyrics to the song itself. For any other song you must contact the copyright owner of the song for permission to use it in any way.

Songbook website. You can find a host of resources on the editors' website (see below) to help you use this book. These include: a searchable online song database with many more listings of composers and covers than those listed in the Artists Index in this book, links from songs to artist websites, tons of links to YouTube recordings of songs, more detailed instructions on how to use the book's chord system, a directory of sing-alongs & song circles, and much more. Please help us build the resources on this site, fix broken links, make corrections in the book, and post and update information on sing-alongs & song circles. Go to **www.riseupandsing.org**.

ISBN 978-1-4803-3189-1 spiral-bound (9 x 12)
ISBN 978-1-4950-3123-6 spiral-bound (7.5 x 10)
ISBN 978-1-4950-3124-3 paperback

Copyright © 2015 by HAL LEONARD CORPORATION

7777 W. BLUEMOUND RD. P.O. BOX 13819 MILWAUKEE, WI 53213

Visit Hal Leonard Online at www.halleonard.com

Preface

The older I get, the more I am convinced that if there's a human race still here in a hundred years, one of the main reasons will be that we found ways we can sing together. Different religions, different languages – the act of singing together makes us realize we're human beings. We can't put it in words. To a certain extent all the arts are important – the dancing arts! cooking arts! Humor arts! Sports!

But if we're still here I believe singing will be a main reason why. Not solo singing, singing *together*. Families can sing together. Strangers can sing together. People who think they hate each other can sing together.

And perhaps if we find the right songs, even people who are so filled with hate they are ready to pull the trigger on somebody – we can reach them too. Who knows?

—Pete Seeger , Beacon NY, February 2014

Foreword

I think Ol' Pete was on to something there with his plea for us to sing together. So many people interact with the world now through some kind of keyboard and screen, carrying their whole identity round with them on a silicon chip. The time we might have once spent socializing together we now spend online. If Woody were here, he'd wryly point out that you can experience a download, but you can't download an experience.

Maybe that's why more people are going to gigs than ever before. Live music offers something that you can't get on the internet – the sense of communion that comes from singing along to your favorite song knowing that everybody else in the room is feeling the same as you. Somehow singing the song takes you out of your shell and gives you permission to laugh or dance or cry or all three together. Most importantly, it gives you permission to share your emotions with everyone else, and to be lifted up and affirmed by their vocal responses.

That's the greatest kind of solidarity, the kind that makes you feel that you're not alone, that there are others who feel the way you do and are not afraid to show it. It's the kind of solidarity that recharges your batteries for whatever struggles you might face in your life – be they personal or political.

This collection is a celebration of that solidarity and an invitation to sing together. A wise person once said that the only bad thing you can do to a song is not sing it. So don't be shy, go right ahead – open up a page and sing together in the solidarity of song.

—Billy Bragg, Dorset, England, April 2015

for
Toshi Aline Ohta Seeger (1922-2013)
& Peter Seeger (1919-2014)

Thank you for your unwavering commitment
to our planet & the human race.

Introduction

We both grew up in singing families. Our first memories of our fathers were of them singing to us: "Sing a Song of Sixpence", "Sweet & Low", "The Caissons Go Rolling Along". Our families gathered to sing together while our moms played piano – hymns, unusual carols from around the world, old popular songs, Gilbert & Sullivan, *The Fireside Book of Folk Songs* and *The Messiah*. We sang with our families on car trips, around the campfire, and at family reunions.

The power of group singing shaped our formative years. For Annie this happened singing in choirs, musical theater and working at the A.R.E. Camp in Rural Retreat, VA. As a young woman Annie led singing at marches, sing-alongs, and coffee houses. She learned to play clawhammer banjo and quickly became immersed in the traditional music of Southern Appalachia. Hosting a weekly folk radio show called Homegrown on WXPN in Philadelphia exposed her to an expansive library of roots music by artists like Taj Mahal, Ry Cooder, Libba Cotten, and Ola Belle Reed.

In high school Peter led singing each Saturday night with fifty young people at the Friends Meetinghouse in Ann Arbor. He "cut his teeth" on Joan Baez, Peter Paul & Mary, and Pete Seeger. Taking part in voter registration in Mississippi & in the Poor People's Campaign Peter learned how freedom songs uplifted and sustained the Civil Rights Movement. He joined hundreds of thousands of people raising their voices with Phil Ochs, Pete Seeger, and others at the Washington monument protesting the Vietnam War. He sang with others at nonviolent sit-ins and spending time in jail as a result of those actions.

What we learned is: **singing makes a difference**. It deepens the bonds within families. It helps young people discover what they believe in and connect as a community of peers. Singing gives us courage to face hardships and discouragement, empowering us and moving us forward out of isolation.

And, time and again, song has played a central role in movements for fundamental change. African American slaves used song to maintain their sense of dignity and hope – and to plan escapes to freedom. Gospel music played a central role in the camp meetings and revival movements sweeping the US in the 19th century. Workers facing working conditions we can hardly imagine took African American spirituals and gospel songs and wrote new lyrics that fueled their struggle to build unions fighting for basic human rights. Later, many of these same songs were reworked further during the depression, in the Civil Rights movement, and in the antiwar and feminist movements of the 60's and 70's.

Although many great musicians have led audiences in song, Pete Seeger spent 75 years mastering this art. He got people singing who never thought they could sing. He got them singing in languages they had never even heard of. Pete & Toshi Seeger shared deep convictions about economic justice, racial and gender equality, peace, and the environment. Songs expressing these values filled Pete's concerts and Toshi's Hudson Clearwater Revival festivals. They reminded us that song has the capacity to reach hearts in ways words alone cannot.

Our world is facing a host of daunting challenges. Rather than despairing, let's focus on places where people are planting seeds of change. Pete & Toshi believed we can best address these problems by working both in our local communities and through building national and international movements for fundamental change. Our wish is that in small ways this book will open hearts and get us working together to heal this precious planet.

Use this book to…

…sing with each other – in your home, to your children, with your faith community, around the campfire or on the picket line. There are hundreds of monthly sing-alongs and song circles around the world where people gather to sing together with books like this one – or to teach each other songs without a book. Find one. Take a chance; try it out. If there isn't one, start one.

…make this your own book. Mark your favorite songs. Write in the keys and chords that work best for you.

…break out of your comfort zone. Dive into chapters with songs you've never sung before. Memorize some songs so you can put the book down. Learn songs you've never heard of from a friend, at a singalong, or online. And, above all

…keep strong your sense of pride, dignity, and joy. Don't let the past hold you down. Help create a healthy, peaceful, just world for ourselves and future generations. Singing together we can make our voices heard.

—Annie Patterson & Peter Blood
Amherst MA, May 2015

How to Use This Book

Here are some basics to get you started. Find more detailed instructions & examples at www.riseupandsing.org.

Locating Songs in the Book: Songs are grouped into chapters by song genre (e.g. Blues) or subject matter (Peace). Songs within each chapter are arranged alphabetically by title and the chapters themselves are arranged alphabetically. So if you remember (or can guess!) what chapter a song is in, you don't have to look it up in the book's Titles Index. In addition to the indices, see the lists of thematically-related songs at the end of each chapter or search the online song database at our website. Use the inside front cover to learn what kind of songs are in which chapters.

Format of Song Lyrics: Boldface lyrics indicate choruses, refrains, and other repeated sections of songs. Songs that are mostly boldface are called "zipper songs." Only 1 or 2 words (underlined & in regular type) are changed with new words "zipped in" for each successive verse.

(2x) or **(3x)** tells you to sing an entire line of the song 2 or 3 times, while **(x2)** or **(x3)** tells you to just repeat a word or phrase within the same line of lyrics.

(repeat) tells you to repeat a group of 2 or more lines of lyrics.

[Square brackets] indicate alternative lyrics for a given word or phrase.

(Parentheses) indicate an echo or other words that are sung with or complement the main lyrics.

The Chord System: We developed a unique short-hand chord system to fit 1200 songs in *Rise Up Singing*. This book uses the same system. It can be tricky at first: Don't get discouraged. Try learning the system with others.

Each **chord group**, separated by **slashes** (e.g. / C F C - /), corresponds to one line of lyrics in the verse or chorus. Chords before the 1st slash go with the 1st line of lyrics; chords between the 1st & 2nd slashes correspond to the 2nd line of lyrics, etc. (Note: In some songs, there are slashes in the middle of a line of lyrics, as well. This indicates the start of a new line of lyrics with its own corresponding chord group.)

Down arrows ↓ after a chord indicate bass runs. Small letters in parentheses after a chord show the bass notes you can play with the chord indicated.)

Parentheses around chords at the end of a chord line refer to minor variations at ends of verses or instrumentals. Square brackets within a chord line indicate alternate chords. If a whole chord line is in brackets, the song is usually sung a capella.

Where Each Chord Gets Played: Each chord represents the same number of **beats** (or "strums") **per chord** throughout a given song. However, how many beats a chord represents varies between different songs. In a given song each chord may represent 2, 4 or perhaps even 8 beats. In songs in waltz (3/4) time, each chord may represent 3 or 6 beats. When 2 **chords are squeezed** close together in a chord group (e.g. D G DA D), each squeezed chord gets half as many beats as the other chords in the song.

Chords fall on the main downbeats of the song. If there are "pickup notes" at the beginning of a line (think of the first 3 words in "This land is your land"), wait until the main downbeat ("your") to play the 1st chord of the chord group. In some cases pickup chords are shown in parentheses ( ) before the 1st chord group.

In songs with tricky rhythm, **underlined letters** in the lyrics indicate the syllables where the main beats fall ("The r<u>ai</u>n in Sp<u>ai</u>n falls m<u>ai</u>nly on the pl<u>ai</u>n.") These underlined syllables also show where a chord is meant to be played.

Repetition in Chord Lines: A hyphen / D - A D / means you repeat the previous chord (D). An empty space between 2 slashes /   / means you repeat the previous chord group, while singing the next line of lyrics.

(4x) means you play a chord group 4 times. Each repeat corresponds to one line of lyrics. x2 means you repeat 2 or 3 chords within the same chord group, while continuing to sing the current line of lyrics.

/ 1st / or / 2nd / means you repeat the same chords as the 1st or 2nd chord group of that line. / 1st 2 / means you repeat the chords used in the 1st & 2nd chord groups of that line.

/ " / or **"same as above"** means you use the corresponding chord group from the chord line directly above.

The **repeat sign** :‖ after 2 or more chord groups means you repeat those same chord groups for the next corresponding lines of lyrics. A double slash // (2 slashes close together) separates chords for the verse from those for the chorus when the chords for both the verse & chorus are shown in the same chord line.

For **songs with no chords** use the same chords & melody as the song directly above it.

Key: (↑2) before the 1st chord line means that you may wish to capo up two frets to make it easier to sing along. We've tried to pick keys that are easy to play & work best for group singing but the best key to play in may be too low for some singers. In the footnotes below a song, ↑3 means you can capo up 3 frets to play along in the same key with the recording indicated.

Sources for Tunes: Whenever possible, we list the original album on which the song was recorded by its songwriter. Where space allows, we also list recordings by other artists who have covered the song. You can often find recordings of a song on YouTube, Spotify, or other Internet music sources by searching for the song title and the name of one of the artists listed in the footnotes. For sources, "in" refers to CDs, YouTube videos & other recordings while "on" refers to songbooks, musicals & films.

Abbreviations in Footnotes:

adap = adapted / adaptation	**m:** = music composed by
alb = album	**orig** = original
alt = alternate / alternative	**trad.** = traditional
arr = arranged / arrangement	*RUS* = *Rise Up Singing*
Coll = Collected	**S** = songs, **SB** = songbook
conc = concert	**v.** or **vs.** = verse, **V.** = volume
DU = *Daily Ukelele*	**w:** = words (lyrics) by
DULY = *Daily Ukelele Leap Year Edition*	**YT** = YouTube (videos not from recordings)
fr = from	↑ = capo up (to play along)

WHATFG = *What Have All the Flowers Gone* – Pete Seeger's musical autobiography or double CD (Songs of Pete Seeger, Vol. 1).

*LS = you can access a leadsheet to the song via our song database at www.riseupandsing.org/songs

SO! refers to *Sing Out* magazine, which publishes *Rise Up Singing*. You can buy a leadsheet for any song that appeared in the magazine (www.singout.org)

Ballads & Old Songs

All Around My Hat

All around my hat I will wear the green willow
All around my hat for a twelvemonth & a day
And if anyone should ask me the reason why I'm wearing it
It's all for my true love who is far, far away

CG C - G / CG C CD G / - C F Am / CG C CG C

Fare thee well, cold winter & fare thee well, cold frost
Nothing have I gained but my own true love I've lost
I'll sing & I'll be merry when occasion I do see
He's a false, deluding young man, let him go, farewell he, & it's:

The other night he brought me a fine diamond ring
But he thought to have deprived me of a far better thing!
But I being careful like lovers ought to be / **He's a false…**

With a quarter pound of reason & a half a pound of sense
A small sprig of thyme & as much of prudence
You mix them all together & you will plainly see / **He's…**

   — trad. (English)

Arr © 2015 Hal Leonard Corporation. On Steeleye Span *All*...,

The Blacksmith

A blacksmith courted me 9 months. & better _
He fairly won my heart, wrote me a letter _
With his hammer in his hand, he looked quite clever _
And if I was with my love, I'd live forever _

Am G AmEm Am / / CD Em Am G / AmD Em CG Am

But where is my love gone with his cheeks like roses
And his good black billycock on decked round with primroses
I'm afraid the scorching sun will shine & burn his beauty
And if I was with my love I'd do my duty
   Strange news is come to town, strange news is carried
   Strange news flies up & down that my love is married
   I wish them both much joy tho' they can't hear me
   And may God reward him well for the slighting of me
"Don't you remember when you lay beside me
And you said you'd marry me & not deny me?"
"If I said I'd marry you, it was only for to try you
So bring your witness love & I'll not deny you"
   "Oh witness have I none, save God Almighty
   And may he reward you well for the slighting of me"
   Her lips grew pale & wan, it made her poor heart to tremble
   To think she loved a one & he proved deceitful
   — trad. (English)

Arr © 2015 Hal Leonard Corporation. On Planxty, Steeleye Span *Please to See the King*, & Deanta *Whisper of a Secret*.

Blow Away the Morning Dew

There was a shepherd's son, kept sheep upon a hill
And he walked out one May morning to see what he could kill
And sing blow away the morning dew, the dew & the dew
Blow away the morning dew, how sweet the winds do blow

D - A D / - Em D G // D - - G / D G DA D

He looked high, he looked low, he cast an under look
And there he saw a pretty fair maid a-swimming in a brook

"Cast over me my mantle fair & pin it o'er my gown
And if you will, take hold my hand & I will be your own

"If you come down to my father's house which is walled all around
There you shall have my maidenhead & 20,000 pounds"

He mounted on a milk white steed & she upon another
And then they rode along the lane like sister and like brother

As they were riding on alone, they saw some pooks of hay
He said "O is not this a pretty place for girls & boys to play?"

But when they came to her father's gate, so nimble she popped in
And said "There is a fool without & here's a maid within"

"We have a flower in our garden, we call it marigold
And if young men fail to when they can, they shall not
   when they're old"
   — trad. (English — Child Ballad #112)

aka "The Baffled Knight." Arr © 2015 Hal Leonard Corporation. On John Langstaff & Martin Best *Nottamun Town*, John Pearse Lost 1966 *Waldeck Audition*. In Cecil Sharp *Collection of Eng FS V2*, Coll Reprints fr SO! V7-12 & SO! 12.2.

Fear a Bhata

Fear a'bhata na ho ro eile (3x)
Mo shoraidh slan leat 'sgach ait an teid thu

(in 3/4) C G / Am Em / F CGF / CDmDm F

How often haunting the highest hilltop
I scan the ocean, a sail to see
Will it come tonight, love, will it come tomorrow
Will it ever come, love, to comfort me

They call thee fickle, they call thee false one
And seek to change me but all in vain
For thou art my dream yet thru the dark night
And every morning I watch the main

There's not a hamlet, too well I know it
Where you go wandering or stay awhile
But all its old folk you win with talking
And charm its maidens with song & smile

Dost thou remember the promise made me
The Tartan Plaid, a silken gown
That ring of gold with thy hair & portrait
That gown & ring I will never own

— trad. (Scottish)

Arr © 2015 Hal Leonard Corporation.On Silly Wizard *Caledonia's Hardy Sons* (17),
Capercaillie *The Blood Is Strong* (12), Bok Muir & Trickett *All Shall Be Well Again* (13).

Safe from Harm

Your mother is by your side, love
Keeping vigil through the storm love
She would carry you to the harbor
And there would keep you safe from harm
    There are angels come from heaven
    They have come while you were sleeping
    Healing hearts that have been broken
    Sowing seeds of love and kindness
There's confusion all around us
There is anguish and great sadness
Heaven help us heaven hold us
Heaven bless this hallowed ground
    So sleep now through the night love
    Peaceful dreams be yours tonight love
    There are wonders that await you
    In the morning comes the sun

— m: trad. (Scottish), new v. Anne Patterson

© 2005 Anne Patterson. Written as a lullaby for Patterson's niece at the time of
the Beltway Sniper attacks in Maryland, VA & DC in 2002. Anne Patterson *Meet
Me by the Moonlight*.

GET UP & BAR THE DOOR (John Blunt)

There was an old couple lived under the hill
Blunt it was their name-o
They had good beer and ale good to sell
And it bore a wonderful fame-o

`C - G C / C - F C /   / C - G C`

John Blunt and his wife they drank of the drink
Til they could drink no more-o
They both got tired and they went up to bed
But forgot to bar the door-o
    So they a bargain, bargain made
    Made it strong and sure-o:
    The 1st of them should speak the first word
    Should get up and bar the door-o
So there came travellers, travellers 3
Traveling in the night-o
No house, no home, no fire had they
Nor yet no candlelight-o
    They went to his cellar, they drank up his drink
    Til they could drink no more-o
    But never a word did the old couple speak
    For fear who should bar the door-o

They went to his larder, they ate up his food
Till they could eat no more-o
But never a word did the old couple speak
For fear who should bar the door-o
    They went upstairs, they went to his room
    They broke down the door-o
    But never a word did the old couple speak
    For fear who should bar the door-o
They hauled his wife all out of the bed
Laid her out on the floor-o
Then up got poor John Blunt in his bed
For he could stand no more-o
    Said "You've eaten my food and drunk all my drink
    Laid her out on the floor-o"
    "You spoke the first word John Blunt" she said
    "So go down and bar the door-o"

— trad. (Scottish — Child Ballad #275)

aka "Barring of the Door." Arr © 2015 Hal Leonard Corporation. This version on
Martin Carthy *Shearwater*. Also on Ewan MacColl *Ballads*, Silly Sisters *No More to
the Dance* & Jean Redpath *Skipping Barefoot*. In *SO!* 33:2.

GREENSLEEVES

Alas, my love, you do me wrong
To cast me off discourteously
For I have loved you well & long
Delighting in your company

(↑2)   `Am - G - / Am - E - / 1st / Am E Am -`

Greensleeves was all my joy
Greensleeves was my delight
Greensleeves was my heart of gold
And who but my lady Greensleeves?

`C - G - / Am - E - / 1st / Am E Am -`

I have been ready at your hand
To grant whatever you would crave
I have both wagered life & land
Your love & goodwill for to have
    I bought 2 kerchiefs for thy hands
    That were wrought fine & gallantly
    I kept thee both at board & bed
    Which cost my purse well favoredly
The petticoat of sendal white
With gold embroidered gorgeously
The petticoat of silk & white
And these I bought thee gladly
    My men were clothèd all in green
    And they did ever wait on thee
    All this was gallant to be seen
    And yet thou wouldst not love me
Ah, Greensleeves, now farewell, adieu
To God I pray to prosper thee
For I am still thy lover true
Come once again & love me

— trad. (English 16th c.)

Arr © 2015 Hal Leonard Corporation. 1st published as a broadside ballad
in London in 1580 & *Handful of Pleasant Delights* (1584). Recs by Loreena
McKennitt, King's Singers, etc.

The Gypsy Rover (Whistling Gypsy)

The gypsy [trav'ling] rover came over the hill
Down thru the valley so shady
He whistled & he sang til the greenwoods rang
And he won the heart of a la-dy

(↑2) C G C G / / C G Em Am / C F C F C G

Ah-de-do, ah-de-do-da-day / Ah-de-do, ah-de-day-de
He whistled & he sang…

She left her father's castle gate / She left her own fond lover
She left her servants & estate / To follow the **gypsy rover**

Her father saddled up his fastest steed
And he roamed the valleys all over
He sought his daughter at great speed
And the whistling **gypsy…**

He came at last to a mansion fine / Down by the river Claydee
And there was music & there was wine
For the gypsy & his lady

"He is no gypsy, my father" she said
"But lord of these lands all over
And I will stay til my dying day / With my whistling **gypsy…**

— w & m: Leo Maguire

© 1951 Walton's Piano & Musical Instrument Galleries. Copyright renewed. All rights controlled & administered by Box & Cox, Inc. There are many variants of this trad. English song (Child Ballad #200) incl adaps. by Woody Guthrie ("Gypsy Davy") & this one by Leo Maguire. In *SO!* 11.2. Recs by Clancy Bros., Tommy Makem, Limeliters. The word "Gypsy" is often used pejoratively to refer to Romany people. Some Roma organizations use the term. There is a huge amount of discrimination against Roma across Europe. During WWII they were sent to gas chambers along with Jews, Communists, gays, those w/ disabilities & others.

Henry Martin

There were 3 brothers in merry Scotland
In merry Scotland there were 3 _
And they did cast lots which of them should go
Should go, should go _
And turn robber all on the salt sea

Am - Em Am / - Dm E - / Am - - - / Dm E - / Am C G Am

The lot it fell 1st upon Henry Martin
The youngest of all the 3
That he should turn robber all on the salt sea / Salt sea…
For to maintain his 2 bros. & he
    He had not been sailing but a long winter's night
    And a part of a short winter's day
    Before he espied a stout lofty ship / Lofty ship…
    Come abibbing down on him straight way
Hullo! Hullo! cried Henry Martin
What makes you sail so nigh?
I'm a rich merchant ship bound for fair London Town…
Would you please for to let me pass by?
    Oh no! Oh no! cried Henry Martin
    This thing it never could be
    For I have turned robber all on the salt sea…
    For to maintain my 2 bros. & me
Come lower your tops'l & brail up your mizz'n
And bring your ship under my lee
Or I will give to you a full cannon ball…
And your dear bodies drown in the salt sea

O no, we won't lower our lofty topsail
Nor bring our ship under your lee
And you shan't take from us our rich merchant goods…
Nor point our bold guns to the sea
Then broadside & broadside & at it they went
For fully 2 hrs or 3
Til Henry Martin gave to her the death shot…
And straight to the bottom went she
    Bad news, bad news, to old England came
    Bad news to fair London Town
    There's been a rich vessel & she's cast away…
    And all of her merry men drown'd

— trad. (English — Child Ballad #250)

Arr © 2015 Hal Leonard Corporation. On *Joan Baez*. In *Coll Reprints fr SO V1-6*.

I Live Not Where I Love

Come all ye maids that live at a distance
Many a mile from off your swain
Come & assist me this very moment
For to pass away some time
Singing sweetly & completely
Songs of pleasure & of love
For my heart is with him all together
Tho' I live not where I love

C F C GC / FC - G / C F C GC / F - G C
F - - G / C - F G / "   /   "   /

When I sleep I dream about you
When I wake I find no rest
For every moment thinking of you
My heart affixed in your breast
Altho' far distance may be of assistance
From my mind his love to remove / Yet **my…**

All the world shall be one religion
Living things shall cease to die
If ever I prove false to my jewel
Or any way my love deny
The world shall change & be most strange
If ever I my mind remove / For **my…**

So farewell lads & farewell lasses
Now I think I've made my choice
I will away to yonder mountain
Where I think I hear his voice
And if he calls then I will follow
Tho' the world it be so wide / For…

— trad. (English)

Arr © 2015 Hal Leonard Corporation. On Steeleye Span *Live at a Distance, Jean Redpath, Mary Black Speaking w/ the Angel, Eddie & Finbar Furey I Live…, Maddy Prior & Tim Hart Celtic Love S*.

If I Were a Blackbird

I am a young sailor, my story is sad
For once I was carefree & a bold sailor lad
I courted a lassie by night & by day
But now she has left me & gone far away

Am Em G F / Am Em Am Em / C Em Am Em / 1st

Oh if I was a blackbird, could whistle & sing
I'd follow the vessel my true love sails in
And in the top rigging I would there build my nest
And I'd flutter my wings o'er her lily-white breast

Or if I was a scholar & could handle a pen
One secret love letter to my true love I'd send
And I'd tell of my sorrow, my grief & my pain
Since she's gone & left me in yon flowery glen

I sailed o'er the ocean, my fortune to seek
Tho' I missed her caress & her kiss on my cheek
I returned & I told her my love was still warm
But she turned away lightly & great was her scorn

I offered to take her to Donnybrook Fair
And to buy her fine ribbons to tie up her hair
I offered to marry & to stay by her side
But she said in the morning she sailed with the tide

My parents they chide me & will not agree
Saying that me & my false love married should never be
Ah but let them deprive me, or let them do what they will
While there's breath in my body, she's the one that I love still

— trad. (Scottish)

Arr © 2015 Hal Leonard Corporation. On Silly Wizard *Wild & Beautiful* (15), *Maggie Sand Susie Fair* (11). Female singers switch the gender: "I am a young maiden...in love w/ a lad / He courted me sweetly... etc."

LEATHERWING BAT

"Hi" said the little leatherwing bat
"I'll tell to you the reason that
The reason that I fly by night
Is because I've lost my heart's delight"
Howdy dowdy diddle-dum day (3x)
Hey le lee-lee lie-lee low

‖: Dm C / Dm F / - Dm / A* ADm :‖ (*extra beats on cho)

"Hi" said the blackbird sittin' on a chair
"Once I courted a lady fair
She proved fickle & turned her back
And ever since then I've dressed in black"
    "Hi" said the woodpecker sittin' on a fence
    "Once I courted a handsome wench
    She got saucy & from me fled
    And ever since then my head's been red!"
"Hi" said the bluejay & away he flew
"If I were a young man I'd have 2
If one were faithless & chanced to go
I'd add the other string to my bow"
    "Hoot" said the owl with head so white
    "A lonesome day, a lonesome night
    I thought I heard some pretty girl say
    'Court all night & sleep all day'"
"Oh no no" said the turtle dove
"That's no way to gain his love
If you want to gain your heart's delight
Keep him awake both day & night!"

— trad. (orig. English - later an Appalachian folksong)

Arr © 2015 Hal Leonard Corporation. Rec by Burl Ives (1941), Peggy Seeger, Luxon & Crofut, Smith Sisters, Pete Seeger, The Duhks, Bill Staines, Spider John Koerner, Peter Paul & Mary. In Lomax *Amer Bals & FS, SO* 42.2.

LILY OF THE WEST

When first I came to Ireland some pleasure for to find
It's there I spied a damsel fair most pleasing to my mind
Her rosy cheeks & sparkling eyes like arrows pierced my breast
They call her lovely **Molly-O** *[or Flora]*, **the Lily of the West**

Am CG F Am / C CG F Am /   / 1st

One day as I was walking down by a shady grove
I espied a Lord of high degree conversing with my love
She sang a song delightful while I was sore oppressed
Saying "I bid adieu to **Molly-O, the Lily...**"

I stepped up with my rapier & my dagger in my hand
And dragged him from my false love & boldly bid him stand
But being mad with desperation, I swore I'd pierce his breast
I was then deceived by **Molly...**

I then did stand my trial & boldly I did plead
A flaw was in my indictment found & that soon had me freed
That beauty bright I did adore, the judge did her address
"Now go, you faithless Molly..."

Now that I've gained my liberty, a-roving I will go
I'll ramble through old Ireland & travel Scotland o'er
Tho' she thought to swear my life away, she still disturbs
    my rest / I still must style her Molly..."

— trad. (Irish)

Arr © 2015 Hal Leonard Corporation. These lyrics on Chieftains *Long Black Veil* (w/ Mark Knopfler) & Dan Milner *Irish Ballads & Songs of the West*. U.S. version (also dating to mid 19th c.) on Joan Baez V2 & Chieftains *Further Down the Long Plank Rd* (w/ Roseanne Cash). In *Coll Reprints from SO!* V7-12.

MY LOVE IS LIKE A RED, RED ROSE

O my love is like a red, red rose that's newly sprung in June
O my love is like the melody that's sweetly played in tune
As fair art thou, my bonnie lass, so deep in love am I
And I will love thee still, my dear, til a' the seas gang dry

G↓ Em C D / G↓ Em CD G / Em CG G AmD / G CG D C

Til a' the seas gang dry, my dear & the rocks melt with the sun
And I will love thee still, my dear, while the sands of life shall run
And fare thee weel, my only love, & fare thee weel a while
And I will come again, my love tho' 't were 10,000 mile

— w: Robert Burns. m: trad. (Scottish)

Arr © 2015 Hal Leonard Corporation. Recs Andy M. Stewart, Jean Redpath, Karen Matheson, Eva Cassidy, Holly Tomas, Eddi Reader.

ONE MAN SHALL MOW MY MEADOW

One man shall mow my meadow
2 men shall gather it together
2 men, 1 man & 1 more
Shall shear my lambs & ewes & rams
And gather my gold together

C G C - /   / C - - - (extra beats v. 2&3) / F - - - / G - C -

3 men shall mow my meadow / 4 men shall gather it...
4 men, 3 men, 2 men, 1 man & 1 more / **Shall shear...**
5 men shall mow my meadow, 6 men shall gather...
6 men, 5 men, 4 men, 3 men, 2 men & 1 man & 1 more...

— trad. (English)

Arr © 2015 Hal Leonard Corporation. In Sharp *100 Eng FS*, *Revels Garland of S.* On Revels *Wild Mtn Thyme*, Alan Mills *One Man...*

POLLY VAUGHN

I shall tell of a hunter whose life was undone
By the cruel hand of evil at the setting of the sun
His arrow was loosed & it flew thru the dark
And his true love was slain as the shaft found its mark

(↑2) Am - Dm - - / Am ↓ F E - / 1st / Am ↓ F E Am -

**She'd her apron wrapped about her & he took her for a
     swan / And it's oh & alas it was she, Polly Vaughn**

C - - E - / Am ↓ F E Am - - -

He ran up beside her & found it was she
He turned away his head for he could not bear to see
He lifted her up & found she was dead
A fountain of tears for his true love he shed

He bore her away to his home by the sea
Cryin' "Father, oh father, I murdered poor Polly!
I've killed my fair love in the flower of her life!
I always intended that she be my wife

But **she'd her apron...** & **I took…"**

He roamed near the place where his true love was slain
He wept bitter tears, but his cries were all in vain
As he looked on the lake, a swan glided by
And the sun slowly sank in the grey of the sky

— trad. (English)

aka: Polly Von (or Wand). Arr © 2015 Hal Leonard Corporation. On Peter Paul & Mary *In the Wind*, Dillards *Back Porch Bluegrass*, Tia Blake *FS & Ballads*, Anne Briggs *A Collection*. In *Coll Reprints fr SO! V7-12*. There are many Irish recs of an older variant called *Molly Bawn*.

SAE WILL WE YET

Sit down here my cronies & give us your crack
Let the wind take the care of this life on its back
Our hearts to despondency we never will submit
For we've aye been provided for & **sae will we yet**

And sae will we yet (2x)
For we've aye been provided for & **sae will...**

G – D C / G – C D G / - - C D / G D C D //
G - D C / G D C D

So fill us a tankard of nappy brown ale
It'll comfort our hearts & enliven the tale
For we'll aye be the merrier the longer that we sit
For we drank together many's the time & sae will we yet

Here's a health to the farmer & prosper his plough
Rewarding his faithful toils all the year thru
For the seed-time & harvest we ever will get
For we've lippen'd *[trusted]* aye to Providence & **sae...**

So fill up your glass, let the bottle go roun'
For the sun it will rise, tho' the moon has gone down, and
Tho' the room be rinnin' *[spinning]* round about, it's time
     enough to flit
When we fell we aye got up again & **sae…**

— Walter Watson

Arr © 2015 Hal Leonard Corporation. Watson was a Scottish poet who lived in Chryston, 1780-1854. On Tony Cuffe *Sae...* & Bok Muir & Trickett *And So Will We Yet*. "Crack" is Scots dialect for entertainment, "flit" means leave.

SEARCHING FOR LAMBS

As I walked out one May morning
One May morning betime
I met a maid from home had strayed
Just as the sun did shine

Dm - / - C / Dm - / Am Dm

What makes you rise so soon, my dear
Your journey to pursue?
Your pretty little feet they tread so sweet
Strike off the morning dew

I'm going to feed my father's flock
His young & tender lambs
That over hills & over dales
Lie waiting for their dams

O stay, O stay, you handsome maid
And rest a moment here
For there is none but you alone
That I do love so dear

How gloriously the sun doth shine
How pleasant is the air
I'd rather rest on a true love's breast
Than any other where

For I am thine & thou art mine
No man shall uncomfort thee
We'll join our hands in wedded bands
And a-married we will be

— trad. (English)

Arr © 2015 Hal Leonard Corporation. In Cecil Sharp *100 Eng FS & Garland of S*. On Steeleye Span *Tempted & Tried*, June Tabor *Aqaba*, John Renbourn *Ship of Fools*, Vaughan Williams *2 Eng FS*.

THERE WAS A PIG WENT OUT TO DIG

There was a pig went out to dig
Chrismas Day, Chrismas Day
There was a pig went out to dig
On Chrismas Day in the morning

(↑4) Am - - - / Am E Am E / 1st / Am E Am -

There was a cow went out to plough...
There was a sparrow went out to harrow...
There was drake went out to rake...
There was a crow went out to sow...
There was a sheep went out to reap...
There was a minnow went out to winnow...

— trad. (English)

Arr © 2015 Hal Leonard Corporation. In Revels SB & Jean Ritchie *FS of the So. Appalachs*. On Revels *Child's Xmas Revels*, Jean Ritchie *Carols for All Seasons*, Sharon Lois & Bram *Fam Xmas*. Choral arr by Percy Grainger.

THE THREE RAVENS

There were 3 ravens sat on a tree
Down a down, hey down, hey down
They were black as black might be / **With a down**
The one of them said to his mate
"Where shall we our breakfast take?"
With a down, derry, derry, derry down, down (↑2)

Am↓F E / /Am↓F Dm / C - E - / / 1st / Am Dm E Am

Down in yonder green field / **Down a down...**
There lies a knight slain under his shield / **With a...**
His hounds they lie down at his feet
So well they do their master keep / **With a down, derry...**

His hawks they fly so eagerly / **Down a down...**
No other fowl dare him come nigh / **With a...**
Down there comes a fallow doe
As heavy with young as she might go / **With a down, derry...**

She lifted up his bloody head / **Down a down...**
And kissed his wounds that were so red / **With a...**
She got him up upon her back
And carried him to the earthen lake / **With a down, derry...**

She buried him before his [the] prime / **With a down, derry...**
She was dead herself ere evening [evensong] time / **With a...**
God send every gentleman
Such hawks, such hounds & such leman / **With a down...**

— trad. (English)

Arr © 2015 Hal Leonard Corporation. On Peter Paul & Mary *Live Conc*. Rec by Loreena McKennitt, Mary Hopkin. In *Fireside Bk of FS*.

THE WIND & RAIN (Twa Sisters)

There were 2 sisters came walkin' down the stream
    O the wind & rain
The older one pushed the younger one in
    Cried o the dreadful wind & rain

(in C) G - C - / F C G - / 1st / Dm - F G - - -

Johnny gave the youngest one a gay gold ring / **O...**
Didn't give the other one anything / **Cried o the...**

So she pushed her into the river to drown...
Watched her as she floated down...

She floated til she came to the miller's pond...
Cried "Father o father, there swims a swan"...

The miller pushed her out w/ a fishing hook
Drew that fair maid from the brook

Then out of the woods came a fiddler fair...
He plucked 30 strands of her long yellow hair...

Made a fiddle bow of her long yellow hair... / **Made a...**
He made fiddle pegs of her long finger bones... / **Made...**

He made a little fiddle of her long breast bone...
The sound would melt a heart of stone...

The only tune that the fiddle would play was "O..." (2x)

— trad. (English — Child Ballad #10)

Arr © 2015 Hal Leonard Corporation. On Crooked Still *Shaken by a Low Sound*. Jerry Garcia *Almost Acoustic* & *Shady Grove*. Altan *Local Ground*. Gillian Welch & Dave Rawlings sing on *Songcatcher: Music fr & Inspired by the Motion Picture* (re a musicologist collecting folklore in the Appalachian Mtns).

YE BANKS & BRAES (Banks o' Doon)

Ye banks & braes o' Bonnie Doon
How can ye bloom sae fresh & fair?
How can ye chant, ye little birds
And I'm sae weary, fu' o' care!
    Ye'll break my heart, ye warbling birds
    That wanton thru the flow'ring thorn
Thou mind me o' departed joys
Departed, never to return

(in 3/4) C G C G / C F C G / 1st / C F G C /

- - - - / - - - G / 3rd & 4th

Oft I have rove by Bonnie Doon
To see the rose of woodbine twine
And ilka bird sang of its love
And fondly sae did I o' mine
    Wi' lightsome heart I put a rose
    Full sweet upon the thorny tree
But my false lover stole my rose
And ah, she left the thorn wi' me

‖: C G C F / C F Dm G / C G C F / C F G C
C - - - / - - F G / " / " /

— w: Robert Burns (1791), m: trad. Scottish ("Caledonian Hunt's Delight")

Arr © 2015 Hal Leonard Corporation. Jean Redpath S of *Robt Burns V2* (I.13), Holly Thomas *My Love Is Like a Red Red Rose* (II.19), Madeline Cave *Away to the Westward*. "Ilka" means "every" or "each one".

There are many versions of almost every song in the **Ballads & Old Songs** chapter (& of many songs elsewhere in this book). The ones here should in no sense be considered the authoritative or most authentic version. See comments in the introduction about how we chose songs & how the versions here should be regarded. This chapter contains trad. songs from the Brit. Isles along with a few 18th or 19th c. composed songs such as those of the great Scots poet, Robert Burns.

Additional trad. songs from England, Scotland & Ireland can be found in **Good Times** (bawdy songs), **Pub Songs**, and **Seas & Sailors**. **Freedom** includes 3 trad. Irish liberation songs: The Foggy Dew, The Minstrel Boy, and Wearin' of the Green.

Others include **Lullabies**: Dream Angus, **Old-timey**: The Cuckoo (an Appalachian variant of a very old English song), **Outdoors**: Hal-an-Tow, **Peace**: Bonnie Light Horseman, Johnny Has Gone for a Soldier (Shule Aroon), **Rich & Poor**: Dives & Lazarus, Time to Remember the Poor, and **Work**: Byker Hill.

AIN'T NOBODY'S BUSINESS

Champagne don't drive me crazy / Cocaine don't make
  me lazy / **Ain't nobody's business but my own**
Candy is dandy & liquor is quicker / You can drink all the
  liquor down in Costa Rica / **Ain't nobody's business...**

C - / F - / C - G - / 1st 2 / C G C -

You can ride a great big pink Cadillac to church on Sunday
You can hang around the house with your old lady on Monday
Ain't nobody's business...
Man I don't care what in the world that you do
As long as you do what you say you going to / **Ain't...**

(bridge) Now, I know some of you cuties, you real fine cuties
You go stepping downtown just to hang around
Standing on the corner so the fellows will stare & say:
"O, ain't she sweet?"

E7 - / Am - / D7 - / G -

You can walk downtown in your birthday suit / I can see you
  coming out of the Bank of America with a whole lotta loot...
Now you know that cocaine's for horses now it ain't for men
The doctors said it'll kill me but they didn't say when...

(bridge) Now you know sometime I put on my straw hat &
  my stripe pants & my spats baby
You know & I go trucking downtown
Standing on the corner so the fellas can stare & say:
(spoken) "Hey man, ain't you the bro. in the '57 Mercury with the
  turnpike skirts & chrome reverse wheels, the whitewall tires &
  running lights, with 4 on the floor, 745 hp & a big stereo?"

   — w & m: by Clarence Williams, James Witherspoon, Porter Grainger,
       Robert Prince.

Arr © 2015 Hal Leonard Corp. Orig version ("Tain't Nobody's Bizness If I Do") by
Porter Granger & Everett Robbins in 1922, rec by Ann Meyer. Adap. by Jimmy
Witherspoon '47. Many variants. The above version is per rec by Taj Mahal on
Satisfied & Tickled Too ('76). In *Real Blues Bk*

ALABAMA BOUND

I'm Alabama bound (I'm Alabama bound) **(2x)**
And if the train don't stop & turn around
I'm Alabama bound (I'm...)

E - - - / A - - - / E - - - /   /

Oh don't you leave me here **(echo) (2x)**
But if you will go anyhow
Just leave a dime for beer **(echo)**

Elder Green is gone **(2x)**
He's way 'cross this country, sweet gal
With his long clothes on

Oh, the preacher preached **(2x)** / The sister turned around **(2x)**
Yes the deacon's in the corner hollerin' "Sweet gal / **I'm...**"

The preacher's in the stand **(2x)** / Passing his hands around **(2x)**
Saying "Bros. & sisters, shoot your money to me / **I'm...**"

You oughta be like me **(2x)**
You can try your good high test whiskey, boys
And let that King Corn be

   — w & m: Huddie Ledbetter

aka "I'm..." TRO © 1963 (renewed) Folkways Music Publishers, Inc., New York,
NY. Hoffman composed this as a ragtime piano piece in 1909. This version is per
Leadbelly & Seeger. Also rec by Papa Charlie Jackson, Odetta, Arlo Guthrie, The
Charlatans. In *Leadbelly SB*. "King Corn" refers to moonshine.

BABY WHAT YOU WANT ME TO DO

Got me running, _ got me hiding _
Got me run-hide, hide-run, **anyway you want to**
Let it roll, _ yeah yeah / Yeah, _ _ _ you got me
Doin' what you want me, so baby why you want
To let go? _ _ _

E - - - / - - E E7 / A - - - / E - - - / B7 - A - / E - - B7

Going up, going down
Got me up-down, down-up, **anyway…**

Got me peeping, got me hiding
Got me peep-hide, hide-peep, **anyway…**

   — w & m: Jimmy Reed

© 1959 (renewed) Conrad Music (BMI) & Seeds of Reed Music (BMI). Conrad
Music & Seeds of Reed Music administered by BMG Chrysalis. On his *At Carnegie
Hall*. This tune was used by Lorre Wyatt for his Clearwater anthem "Sailing Up,
Sailing Down" in *RUS*.

BEFORE YOU ACCUSE ME
(Take a Look at Yourself)

Before you accuse me, take a look at yourself (2x)
You say I've been spending my money on other women,
  you've been taking money from someone else

E A E - / A - E - / B7 A E (EB7)

I called your mama 'bout 3 or 4 nights ago **(2x)**
Your mother said "Son, don't call my daughter no more!"

Come back home baby, try my love one more time **(2x)**
You've been gone away so long, I'm gonna lose my mind

   — w & m: Ellas McDaniels ("Bo Diddley")

© 1957 (Renewed 1985) EMI Longitude Music. On B-side of "Say Bossman" (1957)
& on his *Bo...* On Clapton *Journeyman* (1989) & *Unplugged* (1992) & Creedence
Clearwater *Cosmo Factory* (1970). In *Real Blues Bk*.

BRING ME A LI'L WATER SYLVIE

Bring me li'l water, **Sylvie**
Bring me li'l water **now**
Bring me li'l water, **Sylvie**
Every little once in a while

C - / - G / C F / C G C

Don't you see me comin', **Sylvie**?
Don't you see me comin' **now**?
Don't you see me comin', **Sylvie**
Every little once in a while

Bring it in a bucket, **Sylvie**... / Bring it in ... **now**? / Bring it ...
See me come a-runnin' / See me comin' now...
Sylvie come a-runnin' / Sylvie comin' now...

   — trad. (African-American)

Arr © 2015 Hal Leonard Corporation. Also spelled "Silvy." As sung by Leadbelly. In *Leadbelly SB & Coll Reprints fr SO! V1-6*.

CAKEWALK INTO TOWN

**I had the blues, so bad one time, it put my face in a
   permanent frown**
**You know I'm feeling so much better, I could cakewalk
   into town _**

C - F - / C G C -

I woke up this mornin' feelin' so good, you know I_lay back
   down again _
Throw your big leg over me mama, I might not feel this good
   again _

My baby, O my baby, I do love the way she walks
And when the girl gets sleepy, I love the way she baby-talks_

Now work done got scarce, honey, (aw!) & work it done got hard
I spend my whole day stealin' chickens, Mama, from the rich
   folks' yard _

I want to go on a picnic in the country Mama (aw!) & stay all day
I don't care if I don't do nothing, just while my time away _

   — w & m: Taj Mahal

© 1972 (renewed 2000) EMI Blackwood Music Inc. & Big Toots Tunes. All rights controlled & administered by EMI Blackwood Music Inc. On his *Recycling the Blues & Like Never Before*.

CORRINA, CORRINA (trad.)

Corrina Corrina, where ya been so long? **(2x)**
Haven't been no lovin' since you been gone

G - - - / C - G - / D7 C G -

Corrina Corrina, where'd you stay last night?...
Come in this mornin', the sun was shinin' bright

I met Corrina 'way across the sea...
She wouldn't write no letter, she didn't care for me

I love Corrina, tell the world I do...
Just a little bit of lovin', let your heart be true

Goodbye, Corrina, it's fare you well...
When I'll come back here, can't anyone tell

   — trad. (blues)

Arr © 2015 Hal Leonard Corporation. As rec by Armenter "Bo Carter" Chatmon in 1928. On YT (13). In *Coll Reprints fr SO! V7–12* (Mark Spoelstra version).

CORRINA, CORRINA (Dylan)

Corrina Corrina, gal, where you been so long? **(2x)**
I been worryin' about you, baby, baby, please come home

E - A B7 A E - - - / A - - B7 A E - - - / B7 - A - E - - -

I got a bird that whistles, I got a bird that sings **(2x)**
But I ain't a-got Corrina, life don't mean a thing

Corrina Corrina, gal, you're on my mind **(2x)**
I'm a-thinkin' about you, baby, I just can't keep from crying

   — w & m: Bob Dylan

© 1962, 1966 Warner Bros. Inc. Copyright renewed 1990, 1994 Special Rider Music. Reprinted by permission of Music Sales Corporation. On his *Freewheelin'*... ('63 ↑↑).

CROSS ROAD BLUES (Crossroads)

I went to the crossroad, fell down on my knees **(2x)**
Asked the Lord above "Have mercy, save poor Bob, if you please"

A D A - / D7 - A - / E D7 A -

Mmm, standin' at the crossroad, I tried to flag a ride
Standin' at the crossroad, I tried to flag a ride
Didn't nobody seem to know me, everybody passed me by

Standin' at the crossroad, baby, risin' sun goin' down **(2x)**
I believe to my soul now, poor Bob is sinkin' down

You can run, you can run, tell my friend, Willie Brown **(2x)**
That I got the crossroad blues this mornin' Lord, babe I'm sinkin' down

I went to the crossroad, mama, I looked east & west
I went to the crossroad, baby, I looked east & west
Lord, I didn't have no sweet woman, babe, in my distress

   — w & m: Robert Johnson

© (1978), 1990, 1991 Standing Ovation & Encore Music (SESAC). Under license from the Bicycle Music Company. On his orig rec in 1936, Elmore James (as "Standing at the...", '54), Clapton *What's Shakin'* ('66) & Cream *Wheels of Fire* ('68). In *Real Blues Bk*. Myth is that this song is about the place where Johnson sold his soul to the devil in exchange for his musical genius.

DEEP ELEM BLUES

If you go down to **Deep Elem** put your money in your shoes
The women in **Deep Elem** got them Deep Elem Blues
Oh sweet mama, your daddy's got them Deep... Blues (2x)

E - /   / A - E - / B7 - E -

Once I had a girlfriend, she meant the world to me
She went down to **Deep**... now she ain't what she used to be

Once I knew a preacher, preached the Bible thru & thru
He went down to... now his preaching days are thru

When you go down to... to have a little fun
Have your $10 ready when the police man comes

When you go down to... put your money in your pants
'Cos the women in... they don't give a man a chance

When you go down to... put your money in your socks
'Cos the women in... they'll throw you on the rocks

   — trad. (blues)

Arr © 2015 Hal Leonard Corp. The title of the tune refers to "Colored Red Light District" in downtown Dallas, TX known as "Deep Ellum." Orig rec by Cofer Bros as "The Georgia Black Bottom" on OKeh Records. Rec by Grateful Dead.

Diddie Wa Diddie

There's a great big mystery & it sure has worried me
It's diddie wa diddie (2x)
I wish somebody'd tell me what diddie wa diddie means!

C - - C7 / F - C - / G F C(F C)

I went out & walked around, somebody yelled
   "Look who's in town / **It's diddie wa diddie...**"

Had a little girl about 4 ft. 4, said:
   "Come on Papa & give me some more of your..."

I went to church, put my hat on the seat,
   a lady sat on it, said you sure is sweet / Oh **diddie...**

I said, Sister, I soon be gone,
   just give me that thing you sittin' on / My...

Then I got thrown outta church, 'cos I
   talked about diddy wah diddy too much / Oh...

— w & m: Blind Blake

Arr © 2015 Hal Leonard Corporation. This 1928 song is often confused with a later completely different song by Bo Didley. Covered by many artists often as "Diddy Wah Diddy." On Leon Redbone *Double Time*, Ry Cooder *Paradise & Lunch* (as "Ditty..."), Chris Barber *One of Your Smiles*. In *Blues Bag*.

Don't Ever Let Nobody Drag Your Spirit Down

_You might slip, you know you might slide
_Stumble & fall by the roadside, but
Don't you ever let nobody_drag your spirit down _
Remember we're walkin' up to heaven,
   _don't let nobody turn you round _

Em - / - - / A - Em - / B7 A Em -

_Walk with the rich,_walk with the poor
_Learn from everyone, that's what life is for / **Don't you let...**

_Some say yes, _some say no
_Some people wait & see which way the wind gonna blow...

_Well I might say things sound _strange to you
_And I might preach the gospel, I believe it's true
I can't let nobody drag my spirit down, yes
I'm walkin' up to heaven,_won't let nobody turn me round

— w & m: Eric Bibb and Charlotte Hoglund

© 2006 Bug Music Ltd. All rights administered by BMG Rights Management (US) LLC. On his *Sisters & Brothers* w/ Maria Muldaur.

Fishin' Blues

Bet you goin' fishin' all of the time
Baby goin' fishin' too
Bet your life that your sweet wife
Gonna catch more fish than you

D - / G D / 1st / E A

Many fish bite if you got good bait
Here's a little tip that I would like to relate:
Many fish bite if you got good bait
I'm a-goin' fishin', yes I'm goin' fishin'
And my baby's goin' fishin' too

D - / G D / - - / D G D G / D A D

10

I went on down to my favorite fishin' hole
Baby grab me a pole & line
Throw my pole on in caught a 9 lb. catfish
Now I brought him home for suppertime, provin' / **Many...**

Baby bro. 'bout to run me out of my mind
Sayin' "Can't I go fishin' with you?"
I took him on down to the fishin' hole
Now what do you think that he did do?

(as refrain) Pulled a great big fish out the bottom of the pond
Now he laughed & jumped 'cos he was real gone
Many fish bite… (as last 3 lines of refrain)

D - / G D / - - / D G D G / D A D

Put him in the pot, Baby, put him in the pan
Honey, cook him til he's nice & brown
Make a batch of buttermilk hoecakes, Mama
Then chew them things & chomp 'em on down, singin'...

— w & m: Taj Mahal

© 1972 (renewed 1999) EMI Blackwood Music Inc. & Big Toots Tunes. All rights controlled & administered by EMI Blackwood Music Inc. On his *Giant Step*.

Hesitation Blues

Lord, I'm standing on the corner with a dollar in my hand
Lookin' for a woman who's looking for a man
Tell me how long do I have to wait
Can I get you now or must I hesitate?

Am E Am E / Am E Am C7 / F - C - / G FG C C(G)

Well, the eagle on the dollar says, "In God we trust"
Woman says she wants a man, but wants to see a dollar 1st

Ain't never been to heaven, but I've been told
St. Peter taught the angels how to jelly roll

Well, a nickel is a nickel & a dime is a dime
I got a house full of children, not one of them mine

If the river was full of whiskey & I was a duck
You know I'd swim to the bottom & never come up...

— w & m: Billy Smythe and J. Scott Middleton

Arr © 2015 Hal Leonard Corp. This is WC Handy adap, as above by Dave Van Ronk, Janis Joplin on *Pearl*, Hot Tuna, etc. Jelly Roll Morton rec from 1920's has different chords & raunchier lyrics. adap. fr trad. tune

How Long Blues

(How Long, How Long Blues)

How long babe how long
Has that evenin' train been gone?
How long, how how long, baby how long?

E E7 / A - / E B7 E(B7 E)

I stood at the station, watched my baby leavin' town
Blue & disgusted, nowhere could peace be found / **For how...**

I can hear the whistle blowin' but I cannot see no train &
It's deep down in my heart baby, there lies an achin' pain...

Sometimes I feel so disgustin' & I feel so blue
That I hardly know what in this world baby just to do...

And if I could holler, like I was a mountain jack
I'd go up on the mtn & I'd call my baby back / But for **how...**

And someday you gonna be sorry that you done me wrong
But it will be too late, baby, I will be gone / For <u>so</u> **long, so…**

My mind gets a ramblin', I feel so bad
Thinkin' about the bad luck that I have had / For **how…**

> — w & m: Leroy Carr

©1929, 1941 Universal Music Corp. Copyright renewed. Orig rec 1928. Also rec by Doc & Merle Watson, Count Basie, BB King, Eric Clapton, Odetta, Del McCoury.

I BELIEVE I'LL DUST MY BROOM

I'm goin' get up in the mornin', I believe I'll dust my broom **(2x)**
Girlfriend, the black man you been lovin', girlfriend, can get my
    room

E - E7 - / A7 - E - / B7 A7 E (EB7)

I'm gon' write a letter, telephone every town I know…
If I can't find her in West Helena, she must be in East Monroe I know

I don't want no woman wants every downtown man she meet…
She's a no good doney, they shouldn't allow her on the street

I believe, I believe I'll go back home…
You can mistreat me here, babe, but you can't when I go home

And I'm gettin' up in the mornin', I believe I'll dust my broom…
Girlfriend, the black man you been lovin', girlfriend, can get my room

I'm gonna call up China, see is my good girl over there…
If I can't find her on Philippines island, she must be in Ethiopia
    somewhere

> — w & m: Robert Johnson (1936)

© (1978), 1990, 1991 Standing Ovation & Encore Music (SESAC). Under license from the Bicycle Music Company. Also rec by Elmore James, Howlin' Wolf, "Doney" is blues slang for a woman of low character.

I'VE GOT WHAT IT TAKES
(But It Breaks My Heart To Give It Away)

Oh stingy Ginny saved up all her pennies,
    straight to the bank she would go
The sharks would have their hands around her,
    but none could get her dough
Ginny's fellow was a slick high yeller,
    sent away to jail one day
He cried for bail then turned real pale when I heard Ginny say

G DG GD G / GE7 DB7 E7A D7 ://

I've got what it takes but it breaks my heart to give it away
It's in demand, they wants it every day
I've been saving it up for a long, long time, to give it away
    would be more than a crime
Your eyes may roll, your teeth may grit, but none of my
    money will you git

G A7D7 G - / - A7 D - / G7 - E - / A7 - D7 -

You can look at my bank book, but I'll never let you feel my purse
'Cos I'm a woman, believes in safety 1st (safety 1st)
Said "If you want my money, here's my plan: I'm saving it
    up for a real good man
I've got what it takes but it breaks my heart to give it away"

G A7D7 G - / G7 - CE7 Am / C7 - G E7 / G A7D7 G -

> — w & m: Hezekiah Jenkins and Clarence Williams

© 1929 Universal Music Corp. & Great Standard's Music Publishing Co. Copyright renewed. All rights for Great Standard's Music Publishing Co. administered by the Songwriters Guild of America. Rec by Bessie Smith (1929).

IN THE EVENING (When the Sun Goes Down)

In the ev'ning **(x2)**, Mama, when the sun goes down
In the ev'ning, Baby, when the sun goes down
Well, ain't it lonesome **(x2)**, Babe, when your lover's not
    around **when the sun goes down**?

A A7 / D - A - / E - AE A

Last night I laid a-sleeping, I was thinking to myself **(2x)**
Well, one of the things that's why the one that you love will mis-
    treat you for someone else / **When the sun…**

The sun rises in the east & it sets up in the west
The sun rises in the east Mama & it sets in the west.
Well, it's hard to tell **(x2)** which one will treat you the best
    when…

Goodbye, old sweethearts & pals, yes I'm going away
But I may be back to see you again some ol' rainy day
Well, in the evening **(x2)**, Babe, when the sun goes down,
    when…

> — w & m: Leroy Carr

©1935 Universal Music Corp. Copyright renewed. Recs by Leadbelly, Big Bill Broonzy, Ray Charles, Pete Seeger. In Seeger's *Where Have All the Flowers Gone* (w/ an additional v.).

IN THE JAILHOUSE NOW

I had a friend named Ramblin' Bob who used to steal, gamble & rob
He thought he was the smartest guy in town
But I found out last Monday that Bob got locked up Sunday
They've got him in the jailhouse way downtown

C - - - / - - F - / - - - - / D - G -

He's in the jailhouse now (2x)
I told him once or twice to quit playin' cards & shootin' dice
He's… / Yodel-ay-hee

C - F - / G - - - - / C - / F - - - C - - G - C -

He played a game called poker, pinochle, whist & euchre
But shootin' dice was his greatest game
Now he's downtown in jail, nobody to go his bail
The judge done said that he refused the fine / **He's in…**

I went out last Tuesday, met a girl named Susie
I told her I was the swellest man around
We started to spend my money then she started to call me honey
We took in every cabaret in town

(last cho) We're in the jailhouse now **(2x)**
I told the judge right to his face, we didn't like to see this place
We're in…

> — w & m: Jimmie Rodgers

© 1928 Peer International Corporation. Copyright renewed. In film *O Brother Where Art Thou?* & *SO!* 40:1.

IT'S NOBODY'S FAULT BUT MINE

Nobody's fault but mine **(2x)**
If I die and my soul be lost / Nobody's fault but mine

Am E Am - / Am - E - / Am - Dm - / 1st

I had a mother who could pray **(2x)** / If I die & my soul...
I had a mother who could sing **(2x)** / If I die...

(orig. Johnson lyrics) **Nobody's fault but mine (2x)**
If I don't read my soul be lost / Nobody's fault...
Now I have a Bible in my home **(2x)** / If I don't…
Father *[Mother]* taught me how to read **(2x)** / If I don't read…

— w & m: Blind Willie Johnson

© 1927, 2005 Sweet Roll Songs (a wholly-owned division of Delta Haze Corporation). Copyright renewed. Orig rec by Johnson in 1927. Above is per Nina Simone *And Piano*. Also on Abigail Washburn *S of the Traveling Daughter*, Willie Nelson, Led Zeppelin, Grateful Dead. Blinded as a child, Johnson sang this as a warning to those who learned to read, but concerned themselves too much with earthly matters.

KANSAS CITY

I'm going to Kansas City, Kansas City here I come (2x)
They got a crazy way of loving *[They got some crazy little*
women] **there & I'm gonna get me some** *[one]*

C - - - / F - C - / G F C -

I'm gonna be standing on the corner, 12th St. & Vine
With my Kansas City baby & a bottle of Kansas City wine

(bridge) Well I might take a train, I might take a plane, but
If I have to walk, I'm going just the same / **I'm going to...**

C - / | F - C - / G F C -

I'm going to pack my clothes, leave at the break of dawn **(2x)**
My old lady will be sleeping & she won't know where I'm gone

(bridge 2) 'Cos if I stay with that woman, I know I'm gonna die
Gotta find a brand new baby & that's the reason why / **I'm...**

— w & m: Jerry Leiber & Mike Stoller

© 1952 Sony/ATV Music Publishing LLC. Copyright renewed. All rights administered by Sony/ATV Music Publishing LLC, 424 Church Street, Suite 1200, Nashville, TN 37219. Orig rec Wilbert Harrison (1959). In *SO!* 41-1, *Blues Bag*.

MY BABE

My baby don't stand no cheatin', **my babe**
Oh yeah she don't stand no cheatin', **my...**
Oh yeah she don't stand no cheatin', she don't stand none
   of that midnight creepin' / **My babe, true little baby...**

E A E - / | - - B7 / E E7 A - / E B7 E -

My babe, I know she love me... / Oh yes, I know she loves...
Oh yes, I know she love me, she don't do nothin' but kiss
   & hug me / **My babe, true little...**

My baby don't stand no cheatin'... / Oh no, she don't stand...
Oh no, she don't stand no cheatin', ev'rything she do she do so
   pleasin' / **My babe, true...**

My baby don't stand no foolin'... / Oh yeah, my baby don't...
Oh yeah, she don't stand no foolin', when she's hot there ain't no
   coolin' / **My...**

— w & m: Willie Dixon

© 1955 (Renewed 1983) Hoochie Coochie Music (BMI)/Administered by Bug Music, Inc., A BMG Chrysalis Company. Above is from orig 1955 rec by Little Walter. Other recs by Dixon, Lou Rawls, Chuck Berry, Coasters, Everly Bros. Based on trad. gospel song "This Train."

PAPA'S ON THE HOUSETOP

Mama made Papa be quiet as a mouse
So Papa climbed up on the top o' the house
Made a lot o' whoopee, made a lot o' noise
Stood up an' cheered with the rest of the boys

C - / | | F - / G G C

Baby's in the cradle, brother's gone to town
Sister's in the parlor, tryin' on a gown
Mama's in the kitchen, messin' all aroun'
Papa's on the housetop, won't come down

The blues they come **(2x)**
Nobody knows where the blues come from
The blues they go **(2x)**
And everybody's happy when the old blues go

Papa saw a chicken out in the yard
Picked up a rock and hit him hard
Hit him hard, killed him dead
Now the chicken's in the gravy & the gravy's on the bread

Hush-a little baby, don't you cry
Blues gonna leave you by & by
Papa came in, sure was sore
Put the baby in the cradle & the blues outdoor

— w & m: Leroy Carr

Arr © 2015 Hal Leonard Corporation. Orig rec by Carr 1930. Other recs Tim & Maggie O'Brien, Butch Thompson.

SEE SEE RIDER (C.C. Rider)

See see rider, see what you done done **(2x)**
You made me love you, now your gal *[man]* done come

E - - E7 / A7 - E - / B7 A7 E -

I'm goin' away, Baby, I won't be back til fall **(2x)**
If I find me a good man *[gal]*, I won't be back at all

I'm gonna buy me a pistol just as long as I am tall
Gonna kill my man & catch the "Cannonball"
If he don't have me, he won't have no gal at all

See see rider, the moon is shining bright **(2x)**
If I can just walk w/ you, everything's gonna be all right

See see rider, where'd you stay last night?
Came home baby, sun was shinin' bright
Your hair was all torn & your clothes didn't fit you right

— w & m: Ma Rainey

© 1943, 1944 Universal Music Corp. Copyrights renewed. 1st 3 v. are orig rec by Gertrude ("Ma") Rainey in 1924; last two are various artists. Similar recs by Ray Charles, Grateful Dead, Chuck Willis, Elvis, Big Bill Broonzy.

SITTING ON TOP OF THE WORLD

Was all the summer & all the fall
Just tryin' to find my little all & all
But now she's gone, I don't worry
I'm sitting on top of the world

E - - E7 / A - E - / | - - B7 / | A B7 E - - -

Was in the spring, one summer day
Just when she left me, she'd gone to stay

Needn't have come here runnin', holdin' up your hand
Can get me a woman, quick as you can a man

It have been days, I didn't know your name
Why should I worry & prayer in vain

Goin' to the station, down in the yard
Gonna get me a freight train, work done got hard

The lonesome days, they have gone by
Why should you beg me, & say goodbye

— w & m: Walter Jacobs & Lonnie Carter

© 1930 (renewed) Edwin H. Morris & Company, a division of MPL Music Publishing, Inc. Orig rec by Mississippi Sheiks, rec Shreveport LA in 1930 for Okeh Recs.

SWEET HOME CHICAGO

Oh, baby don't you want to go? (2x)
Back to the land of California to my sweet home, Chicago

E A E - / A - E - / B7 A E (EB7)

Now, 1 & 1 is 2, 2 & 2 is 4
I'm heavy loaded baby, I'm booked, I gotta go,
Cryin' baby, honey **don't you want to go…**

Now 2 & 2 is 4, 4 & 2 is 6
You gonna keep on monkeyin' 'round with your friends boy,
You gonna get your business all in a trick / Cryin' baby honey…

Now 6 & 2 is 8, 8 & 2 is 10
His wife, she trick you 1 time, she sure gonna do it again
I'm cryin' hey, baby, **don't you…**

I'm going to California, some passing in my byway
Somebody will tell me that you need my help some day
Cryin' hey hey, baby…

— w & m: Robert Johnson

© (1978), 1990, 1991 Standing Ovation & Encore Music (SESAC). Under license from the Bicycle Music Company. Many recs incl John Hammond, Luther Allison, Clapton, Taj Mahal, Dave Bromberg, Robt Lockwood, Keb' Mo', Fleetwood Mac & Blues Brothers. (Johnson presumably had enough knowledge of geography to suggest that the "California" in this song refers to a mythical paradise!)

THAT'S ALL RIGHT

That's all right now Mama, that's all right with you
That's all right now Mama, any way you do
But that's all right, that's all right
That's all right now Mama, anyway you do

A - / - A7 / D7 - / E D7 A -

Well my Mama she done told me, Papa told me too
The life you're living, son, now women be the death of you

Baby, 1 & 1 is 2, 2 & 2 is 4
I love that woman but I got to let her go

Babe, now if you don't want me, why not tell me so
You won't be bothered with me 'round your house no more

— w & m: Arthur Crudup

© 1947 (renewed) Unichappell Music Inc. & Crudup Music. All rights administered by Unichappell Music Inc. Rec by Elvis, Canned Heat, Carl Perkins, Ricky Nelson, Jerry Garcia, Paul McCartney.

THE THRILL IS GONE

The thrill is gone (x2) away
The thrill… baby, **the thrill…** away
You know you done me wrong baby & you'll be sorry someday

Am - - - / Dm - Am - / F E Am -

The thrill is gone, it's gone away from me
The thrill… (x2) away from me
Altho' I'll still live on, but so lonely I'll be

The thrill… it's gone away for good
The thrill… baby, it's gone away for good
Someday I know I'll be open-armed baby just like I know a good man should

You know I'm free, free now baby, I'm free from your spell
Oh I'm free, free, free now, I'm free from your spell
And now that it's all over, all I can do is wish you well

— w & m: Roy Hawkins & Rick Darnell

© 1951 Universal Music-Careers. Copyright renewed. Rec by B.B. King (12), Jerry Garcia & David Grisman, Aretha Franklin, Luther Allison.

WHY DON'T YOU DO RIGHT

(Get Me Some Money, Too!)

You had plenty money, 1922
You let other women make a fool of you
Why don't you do right like some other men do?
Get out of here & get me some money too

I: Dm - / - - / Gm - Dm - / A7 - Dm -

You're sittin' down wonderin' what it's all about
If you ain't got no money, they will put you out

If you had prepared 20 yrs ago
You wouldn't be wanderin' now from door to door

I fell for your jivin' & I took you in
Now all you got to offer me's a drink of gin

II: Em↓ C B7 / / C Am D B7 Em - / /

— w & m: Joe McCoy

© 1941, 1942 Edwin H. Morris & Company, a division of MPL Music Publishing, Inc. Copyright renewed 1969, 1970 Morley Music Co. Rec by Harlem Hamfats, Lil Green (I) in 1941 & Peggy Lee (II) in 1942.

WOMEN BE WISE

Women be wise, keep your mouth shut
Don't advertise your man
Don't sit around gossiping
Explaining what your good man really can do
Some women now days, Lord, they ain't no good
They will laugh in your face, they'll try to steal your man from you
Women be wise… / Don't…

C A7 / D G C / 1st / D G / C C7 / F Adim (or D7) / 1st 2

Your best girlfriend, she might be a highbrow
Changes clothes 3 times a day
But what do you think she's doing now
While you're so far away?
She's lovin' your man in your own damn bed
You better call for the doctor, try to investigate your head…

Women… / Now don't sit around girls, telling all your secrets
Telling all those good things he really can do
'Cos if you talk about your baby, you tell me he's so fine
Honey I might just sneak up & try to make him mine…

— w & m: Sippie Wallace

© 1982 Sippie Wallace Productions LLC. Copyright renewed. On her *Woman…, Sippie & Blues Legend.* On Bonnie Raitt. In *SO!* 38:1.

You Got to Move

You got to move (2x)
You got to move, child, you got to move
But when the Lord gets ready
You got to move

D - / G D / - A / D -

You may be high, you may be low
You may be rich, child, you may be po'

You see that woman that walk the street
You see the policeman out on his beat

— w & m: Fred McDowell & Gary Davis

There are many versions of the songs in the **Blues** chapter. Blues is the root source for much jazz, rhythm & blues, reggae and rock & roll. You can find heavy blues elements, for example, in much of Elvis Presley's material, Rolling Stones, Grateful Dead & many other "popular" artists, so see **British Invasion, Jazz, Motown, Rock Around the Clock** & **Surfing USA** for blues-influenced songs.

Find additional blues songs in **Freedom**: Black, Brown & White, **Good Times**: Wang Dang Doodle, You Gotta Know How, **Rich & Poor**: Strange Things Happening In the Land, **Time**: Travelin' Shoes, **Travelin'**: Mystery Train.

BRITISH INVASION & ROCK

Across the Universe

Words are flowing out like endless rain into a paper cup
They slither wildly as they slip away **across the universe**
Pools of sorrow waves of joy are drifting thru my opened mind
Possessing & caressing me

(↑2) C Em - - / Dm - G - / 1st / Dm Fm - -

Jai Guru Deva - Om
Nothing's gonna change my world (4x)

C - - - Dm - ‖: G7 - - - / F - C - :‖

Images of broken light, which dance before me like / A million eyes, they call me on & on **across the...**
Thoughts meander like a restless wind inside a letter box
They tumble blindly as they make their way **across...**

C Em - - / Dm - G - / 1st / Dm - G -

Sounds of laughter, shades of life are ringing thru my opened ears
Inciting & inviting me
Limitless undying love, which shines around me like a million suns / It calls me on & on **across...**

C Em - - / Dm Fm - - / 1st / Dm - G -

— w & m: John Lennon and Paul McCartney

Alison

Oh it's so funny to be seeing you after so long, girl
And w/ the way you look I understand that you are not impressed
But I heard you let that little friend of mine
Take off your party dress
    I'm not going to get too sentimental
    Like those other sticky valentines
    'Cos I don't know if you've been loving somebody
    I only know it isn't mine   **(in C)**

F - C - / F - Em AmG / F - Em Am / Bb - Gsus G
F - Em AmG /   /   "   /   "   /

Alison / I know this world is killing you
Oh Alison / My aim is true

F - C - / F G Em AmG / 1st / F G C -

Well I see you've got a husband now
Did he leave your pretty fingers lying in the wedding cake?
You used to hold him right in your hand
I'll bet he took all he could take
    Sometimes I wish that I could stop you from talking
    When I hear the silly things that you say
    I think somebody better put out the big light
    'Cos I can't stand to see you this way

— w & m: Elvis Costello

ALL MY LOVING

Close your eyes & I'll kiss you, tomorrow I'll miss you
Remember I'll always be true
And then while I'm away I'll write home every day
And I'll send all my loving to you

(↑3) A₁ₙ D G Em / C Am F D / 1st / C D G -

I'll pretend that I'm kissing the lips I am missing
And hope that my dreams will come true / **And …**

All my loving I will send to you
All my loving, darling I'll be true

Em Gaug G - /   /

(tag) All my loving **(x3)** I will send to you

— w & m: John Lennon and Paul McCartney

AS TEARS GO BY

It is the evening of the day
I sit & watch the children play
Smiling faces I can see, but not for me
I sit & watch as tears go by

C D F G /   / F G C Am / F - G -

My riches can't buy everything
I want to hear the children sing
All I hear is the sound of rain falling on the ground / **I sit…**

It is the evening of the day / I sit & watch the children play
Doin' things I used to do they think are new / **I…**

— w & m: Mick Jagger, Keith Richards & Andrew Loog Oldham

BABY NOW THAT I'VE FOUND YOU

Baby, now that I've found you
I won't let you go, build my world around you
I need you so, baby even tho'
You don't need me, you don't need me

C - Bb - / F - Fm - / C - D - / Dm7 - Dm G

Baby, baby when first we met
I knew in this heart of mine
The love we had could not be bad
I'd play it right and bide my time
Spent my lifetime looking for somebody
To give me love like you
Now you tell me that you want to leave me
But darling, I just can't let you

C Dm7 C Dm7 (4x)   A Em7 / A Em A / G Dm7 / F F G

— w & m: Tony Macauley & John MacLeod

BUILD ME UP, BUTTERCUP

Why do you build me up (build me up), **Buttercup, baby**
Just to let me down (let me…) **& mess me around**
And then worst of all (worst…), **you never call, baby**
When you say you will (say…) **but I love you still**

C - E7 - / F - G - :|

I need you (I need…) **more than anyone, darlin'**
You know that I have from the start
So build me up (build…), **Buttercup**
Don't break my heart

C - C7 - / F - Fm - / C - G - / F - C (G7)

"I'll be over at 10" you told me time & again
But you're late, I wait around & then
I run to the door, I can't take any more
It's not you, you let me down again

C G Bb F / C - F - :||

(bridge) (Hey hey hey) **Baby baby, try to find_**
(Hey hey hey) **A little time & I'll make you mine**
(Hey hey hey) **I'll be home, I'll be beside the phone**
Waiting for you (ooh-oo-ooh **x2**)

Dm - G - / Em - A - / F - D - / G - - -

To you I'm a toy, but I could be the boy you adore
If you'd just let me know
Altho' you're untrue, I'm attracted to you all the more
Why do I need you so? / (Hey hey hey)…

— w & m: Tony Macauley and Michael D'Abo

CAN'T BUY ME LOVE

(intro) Can't buy me love, _ love _
Can't buy me love _

Em Am Em Am / Dm G7

I'll buy you a diamond ring, my friend, if it makes you feel all right
I'll get you anything, my friend, if it makes you feel all right, 'cos
I don't care too much for money, money can't buy me love

C - - - / F7 - C - / G F7 - C

I'll give you all I've got to give, if you say you love me too
I may not have a lot to give, but what I've got I'll give to you
I don't care too much for money, money can't buy me love

Can't buy me love, _ everybody tells me so
Can't buy me love, no no no, no

Em Am C - / Em Am Dm G

Say you don't need no diamond rings & I'll be satisfied
Tell me that you want the kind of things, that money just can't buy
I don't care…

(tag is as intro but ending:) Dm G C -

— w & m: John Lennon and Paul McCartney

EVERY BREATH YOU TAKE

Every breath you take, _ every move you make _
Every bond you break, every step you take, **I'll be watching you** _
Every single day, _ every word you say _
Every game you play, every night you stay, **I'll be...**

(↑6) D - Bm - / G A Bm - / 1st / G A D -

Oh can't you see, _ you belong to me? _
How my poor heart aches _ w/ every step you take _

G - D - / E - A -

Every move you make, every vow you break
Every smile you fake, every claim you stake, **I'll...**

(bridge) _Since you've gone I've been lost without a trace,
   I dream at night, I can only see your
Face I look around but it's you I can't replace,
   I feel so cold & I long for your
Embrace — I keep crying baby, baby, please! _

Bb - C - /   / Bb - D -

Every move you make, every vow you break
Every smile you fake, every claim you stake, **I'll...**

— w & m: Sting

© 1983 G.M. Sumner. Administered by EMI Music Publishing Ltd. On Police *Synchronicity* & Gloria Gaynor *The Power of...* Sung w/ Phil Collins at Live Aid 1985.

FIELDS OF GOLD

You'll remember me when the west wind moves
Upon **the fields of barley**
You'll forget the sun in his jealous sky
As we walk in **fields of gold**

Em - C - / - - G - / 1st / C D G -

So she took her love for to gaze awhile / Upon **the... barley**
In his arms she fell as her hair came down / Among... **gold**

Will you stay with me, will you be my love /Among... **barley**
We'll forget the sun in his jealous sky / As we lie in... **gold**

See the west wind move like a lover so / Upon...
Feel her body rise when you kiss her mouth / Among...

(bridge) _ I never made promises lightly
_ And there have been some that I've broken
_ But I swear in the days still left
We'll walk in **fields of gold** (2x)

C - G - /   /   / C D G - /   /

Many yrs have passed since those summer days / Among...
See the children run as the sun goes down / Among...

— w & m: Sting

© 1993 Steerpike Ltd. Administered by EMI Music Publishing Ltd. On his *10 Summoner's Tales* (17), Eva Cassidy rec solo (12) & w/ Michael Bolton; Lauren Dawes *For Eva*.

A GROOVY KIND OF LOVE

When I'm feeling blue, all I have to do
Is take a look at you, then I'm not so blue
When you're close to me, I can feel your heart beat
I can hear you breathing in my ear
Wouldn't you agree, baby you & me / Got a groovy kind
   of love? (groovy kind of love), **we've got a groovy...**

(↑2) G D / G C / Am Bm / C D // G D / G (D) G (D)

Anytime you want to you can turn me onto
Anything you want to, anytime at all
When I taste *[kiss]* your lips, ooh I start to shiver
Can't control the quivering inside / **Wouldn't...**

When I'm feeling blue, all I have to do
Is take a look at you, then I'm not so blue
When I'm in your arms, nothing seems to matter
My whole world could shatter, I don't care...

— w & m: Toni Wine and Carole Bayer Sager

© 1966 (renewed 1994) Screen Gems-EMI Music Ltd. All rights in the U.S. & Canada controlled & administered by Screen Gems-EMI Music Inc. Rec by Mindbenders in 1965 (12) & by Phil Collins in 1988. In *Daily Ukelele*.

HEY JUDE

Hey Jude, don't make it bad / Take a sad song & make it better
Remember to let her into your heart
Then you can start to make it better

C - G - / G7 - C - / F - C - / G7 - C -

Hey Jude, don't be afraid / You were made to go out & get her
The minute you let her under your skin
Then you begin to make it better

_And anytime you feel the pain, hey Jude, refrain
Don't carry the world upon your shoulder
_For well you know that it's a fool who plays it cool
By making his world a little colder

C7 - F Am Dm F / G7 - C - :‖ (C7 G - G7 -)

Hey Jude, don't let me down / You have found her, now go & get her
Remember to let her into your heart
Then you can start to make it better

So let it out & let it in, hey Jude, begin
You're waiting for someone to perform with
And don't you know that it's just you, hey Jude, you'll do
The movement you need is on your shoulder

(repeat v.1 change to:) Remember to let her under your skin...

(tag) Nanana na ‖: C - Bb - / F - C - :‖

— w & m: John Lennon and Paul McCartney

© 1968 Sony/ATV Music Publishing LLC. Copyright renewed. All rights administered by Sony/ATV Music Publishing LLC, 424 Church Street, Suite 1200, Nashville, TN 37219. On Beatles' *Hey Jude* (15).

I ONLY WANT TO BE WITH YOU

I don't know what it is that makes me love you so
I only know I never want to let you go
'Cos you've started something, oh can't you see?
That ever since we met you've had a hold on me
It happens to be true / I only want to be w/ you

G - Em - /   / C D C D / 1st / C - D - / C D G -

It doesn't matter where you go or what you do
I want to spend each moment of the day with you
Oh look what has happened with just one kiss
I never knew that I could be in love like this
It's crazy but it's true / **I only want to be with you**

(bridge) You stopped & smiled at me
And asked if I'd care to dance
I fell into your open arms
And I didn't stand a chance (now listen honey)

Cm - / G - / D - /A7 D

I just want to be beside you everywhere
As long as we're together, honey, I don't care / **'Cos you've...**

I just want to be beside you everywhere
As long as we're together, honey, I don't care / **'Cos...**

(tag) I said no matter, no matter what you do
I only want to be with you

C - D - / C D G -

— w & m: Mike Hawker & Ivor Raymonde

I SAW HER STANDING THERE

Well, she was just seventeen, you know what I mean
And the way she looked was way beyond compare _
So how could I **dance with another** _
When I saw her standing there

E7 - A7 E7 / - - B7 - / E E7 A C / E7 B7 E7 -

Well she looked at me & I, I could see
That before too long I'd fall in love with her / She wouldn't...

(bridge) Well my heart went boom when I crossed that room
And I held her hand in mine

A7 - - - / - - B7 - A7 -

Whoa we danced thru the night & we held each other tight
And before too long I fell in love with her
Now I'll never...

— w & m: John Lennon and Paul McCartney

I STILL HAVEN'T FOUND
WHAT I'M LOOKING FOR

I have climbed highest mountain, I have run thru the fields
Only to be with you **(2x)**
I have run, I have crawled, I have scaled these city walls
These city walls, only to be with you
But I still haven't found what I'm looking for (2x)

G - - - / C - G - :|D C G - /   /

I have kissed honey lips, felt the healing in her fingertips
It burned like fire, this burning desire
I have spoke with the tongue of angels, I have held the hand of a devil
It was warm in the night, I was cold as a stone

I believe in the kingdom come, then all the colors will bleed into one
Bleed into one, well yes I'm still running
You broke the bonds & you loosed the chains, carried the
    cross of my shame
You took the blame, you know I believed it

— w & m: U2

I WILL

Who knows how long I've loved you
You know I love you still
Will I wait a lonely lifetime?
If you want me to, I will

C Am Dm G / C Am Em C7 / F G Am C7/ F G C -

For if I ever saw you
I didn't catch your name
But it never really mattered
I will always feel the same *(this line:* F G C C)

(bridge) Love you forever & forever
Love you with all my heart
Love you whenever we're together,
Love you when we're apart

F G Am - / F G C - / F G Am - / D - G G7

And when at last I find you / Your song will fill the air
Sing it loud so I can hear you / Make it easy to be near you
For the things you do endear you to me
Oh you know, I will / I will

C Am Dm G / C Am Em C7 / F G Am C7 /   /   /
F G Ab - - - / C - (F Em Am - F G C)

— w & m: John Lennon and Paul McCartney.

I'M HENRY THE EIGHTH, I AM

I'm Henry the 8th I am / Henry the 8th I am, I am
I got married to the widow next door
She's been married 7 times before
And every one was a Henry (Henry!)
She wouldn't have a Willy or a Sam (no Sam!)
I'm her 8th old man named Henry / Henry the 8th I am!

G - / C CG / - - / A D / G D / C G / GD C / AD G

(tag) H! E! N-R-Y! / Henry (Henry!) Henry (Henry!)
Henry the 8th I am, I am / Henry the 8th I am!

G - / G Em / GD GE / AD G

— w & m: Fred Murray & R.P. Weston (1910)

IF I FELL

(intro) If I fell in love with you would you promise to be true
And help me understand
'Cos I've been in love before & I found that love was more
Than just holding hands

Abm G / F#(Gb) Ebm / Abm G / Am D

If I give my heart to you, I must be sure
From the very start that you would love me more than her

GAm Bm Am D / GAm Bm Am D G

If I trust in you, oh please don't run & hide
If I love you too, oh please don't hurt my pride
Like her 'cos I couldn't stand the pain & I
Would be sad if our new love was in vain

GAm Bm Am D / / G7 - C Cm / - G D

So I hope you see that I would love to love you
And that she will cry when she learns we are
Two — 'cos I couldn't stand the pain & I
Would be sad if our new love was in vain

(tag) So I hope... / ...we are / Two — if I fell in love w/ you

GAm Bm Am D / / G Cm G (Cm G)

— w & m: John Lennon & Paul McCartney.

© 1964 Sony/ATV Music Publishing LLC. Copyright renewed. All rights administered by Sony/ATV Music Publishing LLC, 424 Church Street, Suite 1200, Nashville, TN 37219. On Beatles *Hard Day's Night* (17) & in film *Across the Universe* (in G as above).

JULIA

(intro) Half of what I say is meaningless
But I say it just to reach you, Jul-ia ("a" falls on 1st beat of next line)

(↑2) C Am Em - / C Am Em G

Julia, Julia / Ocean child, calls me
So I sing a song of love Julia
Julia, Julia, seashell eyes / Windy smile calls me
So I sing a song of love, Julia

C Am Gm - / A - C Fm / C Am Em G /

1st 2 / C Am Em G C -

(bridge) Her hair of floating sky is shimmering
Glimmering in the sun

Bm - C - / Am7 Am6 Em ↓

Julia, Julia / Morning moon, touch me
So I sing a song of love, Julia

C Am Gm - / A - C Fm / C Am Em G C -

When I cannot sing my heart / I can only speak my mind, Julia
Julia, sleeping sand / Silent cloud, touch me
So I sing a song of love, Julia

(tag) (*hums*) __ Calls me
So I sing a song of love for Julia / Julia, Ju-_ lia _

Gm - A - C Fm / C Am7 G C / G C Em G Cmaj7 -

— w & m: John Lennon & Paul McCartney.

©1968 Sony/ATV Music Publishing LLC. Copyright renewed. All rights administered by Sony/ATV Music Publishing LLC, 424 Church Street, Suite 1200, Nashville, TN 37219. On Beatles *White Album*. Written for Lennon's mother who was killed by a drunk driver when he was 17.

MRS BROWN YOU'VE GOT A LOVELY DAUGHTER

Bbm

Mrs Brown, you've got a lovely daughter
Girls as sharp as her are something rare
But it's sad, she doesn't love me now
She's made it clear enough, it ain't no good to pine

CEm DmG x2 / / Am C Am C / Am C - G

She wants to return those things I bought her
Tell her she can keep them just the same
Things have changed, she doesn't love me now
She's made it clear enough, it ain't no good to pine

(bridge) Walkin' about even in a crowd, well
You'll pick her out makes a bloke feel so proud

(Bb) Eb Gm Ab Bb / F#(Gb) Bbm Bb G

If she finds that I've been 'round to see you
Tell her that I'm well & feelin' fine
Don't let on, don't say she's broke my heart
I'd go down on my knees but it's no good to pine

— w & m: Trevor Peacock.

©1965 (renewed) Unichappell Music, Inc. & Songs of Universal. All rights administered by Unichappell Music, Inc. Rec by Herman's Hermits. In *DULY*.

OB-LA-DI, OB-LA-DA

Desmond has a barrow in the market place
Molly is the singer in a band
Desmond says to Molly "Girl, I like your face"
And Molly says this as she takes him by the hand

C - G - / - - C - / - - F - / C G C -

Ob-la-di ob-la-da life goes on brah
La-la how the life goes on (repeat)

‖: C - G Am / C G C - :‖

Desmond takes a trolley to the jewellers store
Buys a 20 carat golden ring (golden ring?)
Takes it back to Molly waiting at the door
And as he gives it to her she begins to sing

(bridge) In a couple of yrs they have built a home sweet home
With a couple of kids running in the yard
Of Desmond & Molly Jones

F - - - C - - -/ F - - - / C - G -

Happy ever after in the market place
Desmond lets the children lend a hand (arm! leg!)
Molly stays at home & does her pretty face
And in the evening she still sings it with the band

(tag) And if you want some fun, take ob-la-di bla-da Am - G C

— w & m: John Lennon & Paul McCartney.

© 1968 Sony/ATV Music Publishing LLC. Copyright renewed. All rights administered by Sony/ATV Music Publishing LLC, 424 Church Street, Suite 1200, Nashville, TN 37219. On Beatles' *White Album*.(in Bb ↑0). Mainly Paul.

(I Can't Get No) SATISFACTION

I can't get no satisfaction (2x) (3rd cho: "girl reaction")
'Cos I try & I try & I try & I try
I can't get no (2x)

(↑4) G - C - / / G D7 G C / G F G F

When I'm drivin' in my car & the man comes on the radio
He's tellin' me more & more about some useless information
Supposed to fire my imagination, **I can't get no** _
Oh no no, _ / **Hey hey hey,** _**that's what I say** _

G F G F /   /   / G (tacet) / G F G F

When I'm watchin' my TV & a man comes on & tells me
How white my shirts can be but he can't be a man 'cos he doesn't smoke
The same cigarettes as me, **I can't no / Oh no no...**

When I'm ridin' round the world & I'm doin' this & I'm signin' that
And I'm tryin' to make some girl, who tells me baby, better come
    back maybe next week
Can't you see I'm on a losing streak, **I can't...**

— w & m: Mick Jagger & Keith Richards

© 1965 (renewed) ABKCO Music, Inc., 85 Fifth Avenue, New York, NY 10003. On
Rolling Stones' *Out of Our Heads* (14). About advertising & commercialization.

WILD WORLD

_Now that I've lost everything to you
You say you wanna start smth new
And it's breakin' my heart you're leavin', baby I'm grievin'
_But if you wanna leave, take good care,
I hope you have a lot of nice things to wear,
But then a lot of nice things turn bad out there _

Am D7 G / C F / Dm E - / 1st 2 / Dm E G7

Oh baby, baby, it's a wild world
_It's hard to get by just upon a smile _
_Oh baby… / _I'll always remember you like a child, girl_

C G F - / G F C - / 1st / G F C DmE

_You know I've seen a lot of what the world can do
And it's breakin' my heart in two
Because I never wanna see you a sad girl, don't be a bad girl
_But if you wanna leave take good care
I hope you make a lot of nice friends out there,
But just remember there's a lot of bad & beware _

— w & m: Cat Stevens

© 1970 Cat Music Ltd. and BMG Rights Management (UK) Ltd., A BMG Chrysalis
Company. Copyright renewed. On his *Tea for Tillerman*.

YOU WON'T SEE ME

When I call you up, your line's engaged
I have had enough so act your age
We have lost the time that was so hard to find
And I will lose my mind if **you won't see me** (echo)
You won't...

C D7 F C /   / C F Fm C / - D7 FC C / FC C

I don't know why you should want to hide
But I can't get thru, my hands are tied
I won't want to stay, I don't have much to say
But I get turned away & **you...**

(bridge) Time after time you refuse to even listen
I wouldn't mind if I knew what I was missing

Dm Fm G C / D7 - G -

Tho' the days are few, they're filled with tears
And since I lost you, it feels like yrs
Yes it seems so long, girl, since you've been gone
And I just can't go on if...

— w & m: John Lennon & Paul McCartney

© 1965 Sony/ATV Music Publishing LLC. Copyright renewed. All rights
administered by Sony/ATV Music Publishing LLC, 424 Church Street, Suite 1200,
Nashville, TN 37219. On Beatles *Rubber Soul* (in Bb).

YOU'VE GOT TO HIDE YOUR LOVE AWAY

Here I stand head in hand, turn my face to the wall
If she's gone I can't go on, feeling 2 foot small
Everywhere people stare each & every day
I see them laugh at me & I hear them say:

(in 3/4) DA CD G CG / DA CD G CG A :‖ (A)

Hey you've got to hide your love away (2x)   D G A (↓) :‖

How can I even try, I can never win
Hearing them, seeing them, in the state I'm in
How could she say to me, love will find a way
Gather round all you clowns, let me hear you say:

— w & m: John Lennon & Paul McCartney

© 1965 Sony/ATV Music Publishing LLC. Copyright renewed. All rights administered
by Sony/ATV Music Publishing LLC, 424 Church Street, Suite 1200, Nashville, TN
37219. On Beatles *Help!* (15)

YOUR SONG

It's a little bit funny this feeling inside
I'm not one of those who can easily hide
I don't have much money but boy if I did
I'd buy a big house where we both could live

C F G Em / Am ↓ F - / C G E Am / C Dm F G

If I was a sculptor, but then again, no
Or a man who makes potions in a travelling show
I know it's not much but it's the best I can do
My gift is my song & this one's for you   (C Dm F C)

And you can tell everybody this is your song
It may be quite simple but now that it's done
I hope you don't mind (x2) **that I put down in words**
How wonderful life is while you're in the world

G Am Dm F /   / Am ↓ F - / C Dm F G

I sat on the roof & kicked off the moss
Well a few of the verses well they've got me quite cross
But the sun's been quite kind while I wrote this song
It's for people like you that keep it turned on

So excuse me forgetting but these things I do
You see I've forgotten if they're green or they're blue
Anyway the thing is what I really mean
Yours are the sweetest eyes I've ever seen

— w & m: Elton John & Bernie Taupin

© 1969 Universal/Dick James Music Ltd. Copyright renewed. All rights in the US &
Canada controlled & administered by Universal-Songs of PolyGram International,
Inc. On *Elton John* (13).

This chapter contains British rock songs beyond "British Invasion"
songs thru the mid '90's. See also **Country:** First Cut is the Deepest,
Earthcare: Where Do the Children Play, **Family:** Father & son,
Good: Quinn the Eskimo, **Peace:** Peace train, Peace love &
understanding, **Time:** Tears in heaven, **Millennial** chapter. More
Cat Stevens listings in Artist Index.

Country

Always On My Mind

Maybe I didn't love you / Quite as often as I could have
And maybe I didn't treat you / Quite as good as I should have

D – A – / Bm D G – / 1st / Bm D E –

If I made you feel 2nd best / Girl, I'm sorry I was blind
You were always on my mind (2x)

G – D – / G D Em – / A BmA D – / G A D (GA)

And maybe I didn't hold you / All those lonely, lonely times
And I guess I never told you / I'm so happy that you're mine

Little things I should have said & done
I just never took the time / **You were always...**

(bridge) Tell_me__ / _Tell me that your sweet love hasn't died
And give me___ / Give me one more chance_to keep you satisfied, I'll keep you / Satisfied___

D A Bm D / G D Em GA / 1st / G D Em A / D – – –

— w & m: Wayne Thompson, Mark James & Johnny Christopher

Blame It on Your Heart

You've got a thing or 2 to learn about me baby _
'Cos I ain't taking it no more & I don't mean maybe _
You don't know right from wrong, well the love we had is gone, so

G – – – / – – D – / – – – –

Blame it on your lying, cheating, cold dead-beating, two-timing
Double-dealing, mean mistreating, loving heart _

D – – – / – – G –

Well all I wanted was to be your one & only
And all I ever got from you was being lonely
Now that dream is laid to rest 'cos you have failed the test, hey...

(bridge) Are you headed for a heartache? (oh yeah!)
Gonna get a bad break (oh yeah!)
You made a bad mistake (oh yeah!)
Well you're never gonna find another love like mine

C – / G – / A – / D –

Someone's gonna do you like you done me, honey
And when she does you like she'll do you, it ain't funny
You'll need some sympathy but don't be calling me, hey...

— w & m: Harlan Howard & Kostas

Bless the Broken Road

I set out on a narrow way many years ago
Hoping I would find true love along the broken road
But I got lost a time or 2, I wiped my brow, kept pushing thru
I couldn't see how every sign pointed straight to you

CF GAm FG C / / Am G FC DmG / 1st

Every long-lost dream led me to where you are
Others who broke my heart, they were like northern stars
Pointing me on my way into your loving arms
This much I know is true, that
God blessed the broken road that led me straight to you

F C G C / F Am DmC G / F C G Am
DmC F – / CF GAm FG C

I think about the years I spent just passing thru
I'd like to have the time I lost & give it back to you
But you just smile & take my hand, 'cos you've been there,
 you understand
It's all part of a grander plan that is coming true

(tag) Now I'm just rolling home into my lover's arms
This much... / That God blessed the broken road...

F C G Am / DmC F – / CF GAm FG C

— w & m: Marcus Hummon, Bobby Boyd & Jeff Hanna

Cold, Cold Heart

I tried so hard, my dear, to show that you're my every dream
Yet you're afraid each thing I do is just some evil scheme
A memory from your lonesome past keeps us so far apart
**Why can't I free your doubtful mind & melt your cold,
 cold heart?**

D – – A / – – – D / – – – G – / A – – D

Another love before my time made your heart sad & blue
And so my heart is paying now for things I didn't do
In anger, unkind words are said that make the teardrops start
Why can't I...

You'll never know how much it hurts to see you sit & cry
You know you need & want my love, yet you're afraid to try
Why do you run & hide from life, to try it just ain't smart...

There was a time when I believed that you belonged to me
But now I know your heart is shackled to a memory
The more I learn to care for you, the more we drift apart...

— w & m: Hank Williams

CRAZY

Crazy, I'm crazy for feeling so lonely
I'm crazy, crazy for feeling so blue
I knew you'd love me as long as you wanted
And then someday you'd leave me for somebody new

C A7 Dm - / G - C(Edim DmG) / 1st / G - C(F CC7)

(bridge) Worry, why do I let myself worry
Wondering what in the world did I do?

F - C - / D7 - G7 -

Crazy for thinking that my love could hold you
I'm crazy for trying & crazy for crying, I'm crazy for loving you

C A7 Dm - / FEm DmA DmG C

— w & m: Willie Nelson

THE FIRST CUT IS THE DEEPEST

I would have given you all of my heart
But there's someone who's torn it apart
And (s)he's taking almost all that I've got
But if you want, I'll try to love again
Baby I'll try to love again but I know
The first cut is the deepest, baby I know / The first cut...

D A G A (4x) D G A - // 1st / /

'Cos when it comes to being lucky (s)he's cursed
When it comes to lovin' me (s)he's worst
But when it comes to being loved (s)he's 1st — that's how
   I know / **The first cut...**

D A G A / D G A G / 1st // / /

I still want you by my side
Just to help me dry the tears that I've cried
'Cos I'm sure gonna give you a try
And if you want, I'll try to love again
But baby, I'll try to love again, but I know / **The first...**

— w & m: Cat Stevens

FOLSOM PRISON BLUES

I hear the train a comin', it's rolling round the bend
And I ain't seen the sunshine since I don't know when
I'm stuck in Folsom prison _ & time keeps draggin' on _
But that train keeps a-rollin' _ on down to San Antone _

G - / - G7 / C - G - / D7 - G -

When I was just a baby my mama told me "Son
Always be a good boy, don't ever play with guns"
But I shot a man in Reno just to watch him die
When I hear that whistle blowing, I hang my head & cry

I bet there's rich folks eating in a fancy dining car
They're probably drinkin' coffee & smoking big cigars
Well I know I had it coming, I know I can't be free
But those people keep a-movin' & that's what tortures me

Well if they freed me from this prison, if that RR train was
   mine / I bet I'd move it on a little farther down the line
Far from Folsom prison, that's where I want to stay
And I'd let that lonesome whistle blow my blues away

— w & m: John R. Cash

THE GAMBLER

On a warm summer's evenin' on a train bound for nowhere
I met up with the gambler, we were both too tired to sleep
So we took turns a-starin' out the window at the darkness
Til boredom overtook us & he began to speak

C - F C / - - - G / 1st / F C G C

He said "Son, I've made my life out of readin' people's faces
And knowin' what their cards were by the way they held their eyes
So if you don't mind my sayin', I can see you're out of aces
For a taste of your whiskey I'll give you some advice"

So I handed him my bottle & he drank down my last swallow
Then he bummed a cigarette & asked me for a light
And the night got deathly quiet & his face lost all expression
Said "If you're gonna play the game, boy, ya gotta learn to play it right

**"You got to know when to hold 'em, know when to fold 'em
Know when to walk away & know when to run, you
Never count your money when you're sittin' at the table
There'll be time enough for countin' when the dealin's done**

C - F C / F C - G / C F C F C / C F C G C

"Every gambler knows that the secret to survivin'
Is knowin' what to throw away & knowing what to keep
'Cos ev'ry hand's a winner & ev'ry hand's a loser
And the best that you can hope for is to die in your sleep"

And when he'd finished speakin', he turned back toward the
   window / Crushed out his cigarette & faded off to sleep
And somewhere in the darkness, the gambler he broke even
But in his final words I found an ace that I could keep

— w & m: Don Schlitz

GUESS THINGS HAPPEN THAT WAY

Well you ask me if I'll forget my baby
I guess I will someday
I don't like it but I guess things happen that way
You ask me if I'll get along
I guess I will someway
I don't like it but I guess things happen that way

A D / / A E A (E) / 1st 2 / A E A A7

God gave me that girl to lean on
Then he put me on my own
Heaven help me be a man
And have the strength to stand alone / I don't like it...

D A / E A :‖ A E A (E)

You ask me if I'll miss her kisses
I guess I will, everyday / **I don't...**
You ask me if I'll find another
I don't know, I can't say / **I don't...**

— w & m: Jack Clement

HELP ME MAKE IT THROUGH THE NIGHT

Take the ribbon from your hair, shake it loose & let it fall
Layin' soft upon my skin like the shadows on the wall
Come & lay down by my side til the early morning light
All I'm takin' is your time, **help me make it thru the night**
I don't care what's right or wrong, I don't try to understand
Let the devil take tomorrow, Lord, tonight I need a friend
Yesterday is dead & gone & tomorrow's out of sight
And it's sad to be alone, **help...**

C - F Dm / G - C - :‖ F - C - / D - G - / 1st 2

— w & m: Kris Kristofferson

HEY, GOOD LOOKIN'

Hey hey, good lookin', whatcha got cookin'?
How's about cookin' somethin' up with me?
Hey, sweet baby, don't you think maybe
We could find us a brand new recipe?
I got a Hot Rod Ford & a $2 bill & I know a spot right over the hill
There's soda pop & the dancin's free, so if you wanna have fun
    come along with me

Hey hey, good lookin', whatcha got cookin'?
How's about cookin' somethin' up with me?

(11) G - - - / C D G (D) :‖ C G C G / C G A D / 1st 2

I'm free & ready, so we can go steady
How's about savin' all your time for me?
No more lookin', I know I've been tooken
How's about keepin' steady company?
I'm gonna throw my datebook over the fence &
    find me one for 5 or 10 cents
I'll keep it til it's covered with age 'cos I'm writin' your name
    down on every page / **Hey good lookin'...**

— w & m: Hank Williams

I WALK THE LINE

I keep a close watch on this heart of mine
I keep my eyes wide open all the time
I keep the ends out for the tie that binds
Because you're mine, I walk the line

(D - - -) A7 D / / G D / 1st

I find it very, very easy to be true
I find myself alone when each day is thru
Yes, I'll admit that I'm a fool for you / **Because...**

(G - - -) D G D G / C G D G

As sure as night is dark & day is light
I keep you on my mind both day & night
And happiness I've known proves that it's right...

(C - - -) G C G C / F C G C

(in G as v. 2) You've got a way to keep me on your side
You give me cause for love that I can't hide
For you I know I'd even try to turn the tide...

— w & m: John R. Cash

I WILL ALWAYS LOVE YOU

If I _ should stay _
I would only be in your way _
So I'll go _ but I know _
I'll think of you each step of the way _ and

G - - - / Em ↓ C D :‖

I _ will always / Love you - I will always / Love you _ _ _

G Em C D / G Em C D / G (C G -)

Bittersweet _ memories _
That's all I am taking with me _
Goodbye, _ please don't cry _
We both know that I'm not what you need, _ but...

And I hope life _ will treat you kind _
And I hope that you have all that you ever dreamed of _
And I wish you joy _ & happiness _
But above all of this, I wish you love _

— w & m: Dolly Parton

JACKSON

We got married in a fever, hotter than a pepper sprout
We've been talkin' 'bout Jackson, ever since the fire went out
I'm goin' to Jackson, I'm gonna mess around
Yeah I'm goin' to Jackson, look out Jackson town

`C - - - / - - - C7 / F - C - / F G C -`

Well go on down to Jackson, go ahead & wreck your health
Go play your hand you big-talkin' man & make a big fool of your-
   self / Yeah, go to..., go comb your hair!
Honey, I'm gonna snowball Jackson, see if I care

When I breeze into that city, people gonna stoop & bow (hah!)
All them women gonna make me teach 'em what they don't know
   how / I'm goin' to..., you turn-a loose-a my coat
'Cos I'm goin'..., "Goodbye" that's all she wrote

But they'll laugh at you in Jackson & I'll be dancin' on a Pony Keg
They'll lead you 'round town like a scalded *[orig. scolded]* hound
   with your tail tucked betw your legs
Yeah, go to Jackson, you big-talkin' man
And I'll be waitin' in Jackson behind my Jaypan Fan

We got... / ...out / I'm goin' to Jackson & that's a fact
Yeah we're goin' to Jackson, ain't never comin' back

   — w & m: Billy Edd Wheeler & Jerry Leiber

JOLENE

Jolene (x4) / I'm begging of you please don't take my man
Jolene (x4) / Please don't take him just because you can

`Am C G Am - / G - Am - :‖`

Your beauty is beyond compare w/ flaming locks of auburn hair
With ivory skin & eyes of emerald green

`Am C G Am / G - Am -`

Your smile is like a breath of spring, your voice is soft like
   summer rain / And I cannot compete with you, Jolene

He talks about you in his sleep & there's nothing I can do
   to keep / From crying when he calls your name, Jolene

And I can easily understand how you could easily take my man
But you don't know what he means to me, Jolene / **Jolene...**

You could have your choice of men but I could never love
   again / He's the only one for me, Jolene

I had to have this talk with you, my happiness depends on you
And whatever you decide to do, Jolene / **Jolene...**

   — w & m: Dolly Parton

LOVE & HAPPINESS

Here's a wishing well, here's a penny for
Any thought it is that makes you smile
Every diamond dream, everything that brings
Love & happiness to your life

`D - G - / A - D - :‖`

Here's a rabbit's foot take it when you go
So you'll always know you're safe from harm
Wear your ruby shoes when you're far away
So you'll always stay home in your heart

You will always have a lucky star that shines because of
   what you are
Even in the deepest dark because your aim is true &
If I could only have 1 wish, darling, then it would be this
Love & happiness for you

`G - D - / E - A - / G - D - / A - D -`

Here's a spinning wheel, use it once you've learned
There's a way to turn the straw to gold
Here's a rosary, count on every bead
With a prayer to keep the hope you hold

   — w & m: Emmylou Harris & Kimmie Rhodes

MOVE IT ON OVER

Came in last night at half past 10
That baby of mine wouldn't let me in
So move it on over (move it on over) **(2x)**
Move over little dog 'cos a big dog's moving in

`C - / - C7 / F - / C - / G7 - C -`

She's changed the lock on our front door
And my door key don't fit no more
So get **it on over** (move it...) / Scoot it **on over** (move...)
Move over skinny dog cause a fat dog's moving in

This dog house here is mighty small
But it's better than no house at all
So ease **it on over...** / Drag **it on over...**
Move over old dog cause a new dog's moving in

She told me not to play around
But I done let the deal go down
So pack **it on over...** / Tote **it on over...**
Move over nice dog cause a mad dog's moving in

She warned me once, she warned me twice
But I don't take no one's advice
So scratch **it on over...** / Shake **it on over...**
Move over short dog cause a tall dog's moving in

She'll crawl back to me on her knees
I'll be busy scratching fleas
So slide **it on over...** Sneak **it on over...**
Move over good dog cause a mad dog's moving in

Remember pup, before you whine
That side's yours & this side's mine
So shove **it on over...** Sweep **it on over...**
Move over cold dog cause a hot dog's moving in

   — w & m: Hank Williams

OKIE FROM MUSKOGEE

We don't smoke marijuana in Muskogee
We don't take our trips on LSD
We don't burn our draft cards down on Main St.
'Cos we like livin' right & bein' free

C - - - / - - G - / - - - - / - - C -

We don't make a party out of lovin'
But we like holdin' hands & pitchin' woo
We don't let our hair grow long & shaggy
Like the hippies out in San Francisco do

And I'm proud to be an Okie from Muskogee
A place where even squares can have a ball
We still wave Old Glory down at the courthouse
And white lightnin's still the biggest thrill of all

Leather boots are still in style for manly footwear
Beads & Roman sandals won't be seen
And football's still the roughest thing on campus
And the kids here still respect the college dean

And I'm proud to be an Okie...
And white lightnin's still the biggest thrill of all (2x)
In Muskogee, Oklahoma, USA

— w & m: Merle Haggard & Roy Edward Burris

PANCHO & LEFTY

Living on the road my friend
Was gonna keep you free & clean
And now you wear your skin like iron
And your breath is hard as kerosene
You weren't your mama's only boy
But her favorite one it seems
She began to cry when you said goodbye
And sank into your dreams

C - / G - / F - / C G / F - / C F / Am Dm G G / F Am

Pancho was a bandit, boys
His horse was fast as polished steel
He wore his gun outside his pants
For all the honest world to feel
Pancho met his match you know
On the deserts down in Mexico
Nobody heard his dying words
Oh but that's the way it goes

All the federales say
They could have had him any day
They only let him hang around
Out of kindness I suppose
F - / C F / Am Dm G G / F Am

Lefty he can't sing the blues
All night long like he used to
The dust that Pancho bit down south
Ended up in Lefty's mouth
The day they laid poor Pancho low
Lefty split for Ohio
Where he got the bread to go
There ain't nobody knows

All the federales say / We only let him slip away / **They...**

The poets tell how Pancho fell
And Lefty's livin' in a cheap hotel
The desert's quiet & Cleveland's cold
And so the story ends we're told
Pancho needs your prayers, it's true
But save a few for Lefty too
He only did what he had to do
And now he's growing old

All the federales say / They could have had him...
They only let him go so long / **Out of kindness I suppose**

(last cho) A few gray **federales say** / They could...
They only let him go so wrong / **Out of kindness...**

— w & m: Townes Van Zandt

PLEASE HELP ME, I'M FALLING
(In Love With You)

Please help me I'm falling in love with you
Close the door to temptation, don't let me walk thru
Turn away from me darling, I'm begging you to
Please help me I'm falling in love with you

G GC G - / C G A D - / G - C - / G D G -

I belong to another whose arms have grown cold
But I promised forever to have & to hold
I can never be free, dear, but when I'm with you
I know that I'm losing the will to be true

Please help me I'm falling & that would be sin
Close the door to temptation, don't let me walk in
For I mustn't want you but darling I do / **Please...**

— w & m: Don Robertson & Hal Blair

RING OF FIRE

Love _ is a burning thing _ / And it makes _ a fiery ring _ _
Bound _ by wild desire _ / I fell into a ring of fire _ _

G GC G - / G GD G - / 1st / G DG G -

I fell into a burning ring of fire
I went down, down, down & the flames went higher
And it burns, burns, burns / _ The ring of fire (x2)

D - C G / / G - GC / G GD G -

The taste _ of love is sweet _ / When hearts _ like ours meet _
I fell for you like a child _ _ / Oh _ but the fire went wild _

— w & m: Merle Kilgore & June Carter

© 1962, 1963 Painted Desert Music Corporation, New York. Copyright renewed. On Anita Carter *Folk S Old & New* (orig rec) & Johnny Cash *Ring...*

THE RIVER

You know a dream is like a river, ever changing as it flows
And the dreamer's just a vessel that must follow where it goes
Trying to learn from what's behind you & never knowing what's
    in store
Makes each day a constant battle just to stay betw the shores

C - FC / F Am Dm G / C - Am F / C - G C

But **I will sail my vessel til the river runs dry**
Like a bird upon the wind these waters are my sky
I'll never reach my destination if I never try
So I will sail my vessel til the river runs dry

Too many times we stand aside & let the waters slip away
Til what we put off til tomorrow has now become today
So don't you sit upon the shoreline & say you're satisfied
Choose to chance the rapids & dare to dance the tide /
    And **I...**

(bridge) And there's bound to be rough waters & I know
    I'll take some falls
But with the good Lord as my captain, I can make it thru them all
Yes **I will sail...**

Am F C F / Dm C F G

— By: Garth Brooks & Victoria Shaw

©1989 w & m: Universal Music-MGB Songs & Major Bob Music Co., Inc. On his *Ropin' the Wind* (12).

THAT'S THE WAY LOVE GOES

I've been throwing horseshoes over my left shoulder
I've spent most all my life searching for that 4-leaf clover
Yet you ran with me chasing my rainbows
Honey I love you, too **& that's the way love goes**

D Am G A / G D E A / 1st / G D A D

That's... babe, that's the music God made
For all the world to sing, it's never old, it grows
Losing makes me sorry, you say "Honey, now don't worry"
Don't you know I love you, too **& that's...**

— w & m: Lefty Frizell & Sanger Shafer

©1973 w & m: Peer International Corporation & Sony/ATV Music Publishing LLC. Copyright renewed. All rights on behalf of Sony/ATV Music Publishing LLC. Administered by Sony/ATV Music Publishing LLC, 424 Church Street, Suite 1200, Nashville, TN 37219. Rec by Frizzell (†2), Johnny Rodriguez ('73), Connie Smith ('74), Merle Haggard ('84, 11).

WALKING AFTER MIDNIGHT

I go out walking after midnight
Out in the moonlight just like we used to do
I'm always walking after midnight searching / For you

C - C7 - / F - - C / C - F(7) G / C - - (G7)

I walk for miles along the hwy
Well that's just my way of saying I love you / **I'm always...**

(bridge) I stopped to see a weeping willow, crying on his
    pillow / Maybe he's crying for me
And as the skies turn gloomy, night winds whisper to me
I'm lonesome as I can be

F - - - / C - C7 - / 1st / C - G -

I go out walking after midnight
Out in the starlight just hoping you may be
Somewhere **a-walking after midnight searching / For me**

— w: Don Hecht, m: Alan W. Block

© 1956 Sony/ATV Music Publishing LLC. Copyright renewed. All rights administered by Sony/ATV Music Publishing LLC, 424 Church Street, Suite 1200, Nashville, TN 37219. Orig rec by Patsy Cline. Also rec by Doc Watson, Kelly Clark, Cowboy Junkies.

YOUR CHEATIN' HEART

Your cheatin' heart will make you weep
You'll cry & cry & try to sleep
But sleep won't come the whole night thru
Your cheatin' heart will tell on you
    When tears come down like falling rain
    You'll toss around & call my name
    You'll walk the floor the way I do / Your...

C F / G C :‖ F C / D7 G7 / 1st 2

Your cheatin' heart will pine some day
And crave the love you threw away
The time will come when you'll be blue / **Your...**

— w & m: Hank Williams

© 1952 Sony/ATV Music Publishing LLC. Copyright renewed. All rights administered by Sony/ATV Music Publishing LLC, 424 Church Street, Suite 1200, Nashville, TN 37219. Reportedly about his 1st wife Audrey Sheppard & written while he & his fiancée were driving fr Nashville to Shreveport in 1952.

There is a lot of overlap of early country with old-timey and bluegrass (Bill Monroe), so see also **Old-Timey & Bluegrass** chapter. Additional **Country** songs can be found in **Farm & Prairie, Gospel** and **Travelin'**.

Others include **Blues**: In the Jailhouse Now, **Dreams**: If I Had a Boat, **Good Times**: Down at the Twist & Shout, Jambalaya, **Healing**: Mercy Now, Wide River to Cross, **Home**: My Tennessee Mtn Home, **Hope**: Why Walk When You Can Fly, **Lullabies**: Dreamland.

Dignity & Diversity

All welcome here regardless of race, gender, religion, or economic status.

ANNIE

Annie's up at 7 on a work day
Brewing up a cup of peppermint tea
Gathering her papers & lesson plans
She grabs her keys

C - G - / Am D G D / Bm - Em C / G - D -

    Teaching arithmetic & Africa
    Geology & girls' basketball
    All the kids in her class will tell you she's the best
    But she's heard other teachers in the hall saying:

G D C D / Em - C - / Am D Bm Em / A - D -

"What are we going to do about Annie?
Pretty girl like her shouldn't be alone
If she took our advice, dressed up real nice
She'd find a man to take her home"

G D C D / Em D C - / Am D Bm Em / C D G -

Mondays come questions of couples
Where & with whom did you go?
Avoiding the personal pronoun
She hopes it doesn't show
    Shopping with her lover in the city
    2 women holding hands don't get a stare
    If the kids at school knew, what would they do
    Would they hate her? Why should they care? Tell me:

Never getting too close to a student
Never letting out too much of her life
Keeping her delights & disappointments
Tucked out of sight
    Annie takes herself to the Christmas party
    The principal whispers with a smile
    "You're vivacious & bright, if you play your cards right
    There're some men here tonight worth your while"
      Thinking:

Work that you love is hard to come by
The kids she could never bear to lose
So she makes conversations out of silences
And half-truths
    But at night by the fire with her lover
    She looks out at the wind-driven snow
    And imagines the day when she'll look in their faces
    And tell everybody she knows — she'll tell 'em

(final cho) Don't you worry about Annie
She don't lie awake & pine
Got love to fill her heart, flowers growing in the garden
Annie's doing just fine
    — w & m: Fred Small

AT SEVENTEEN

I learned the truth at 17 — that love was meant for beauty queens
And high school girls with clear skinned smiles who married
    young & then retired
The valentines I never knew, the Friday night charades of youth
Were spent on one more beautiful — at 17 I learned the truth
And those of us with ravaged faces, lacking in the social graces,
Desperately remained at home inventing lovers on the phone
Who called to say "Come dance with me" & murmured vague
    obscenities / It isn't all it seems at 17

C - Dm7 - / G7 - C - :‖ Eb - Dm7 G7 / Cm Fm Cm Fm /
Ab G7 Cm Fm / Dm7 - G7 -

A brown eyed girl in hand-me-downs whose name I never
    could pronounce
Said "Pity please the ones who serve, they only get what they deserve
The rich-relationed hometown queen marries into what she needs
With a guarantee of company & haven for the elderly"
Remember, those who win the game lose the love they sought to gain
In debentures of quality & dubious integrity
Their small town eyes will gape at you in dull surprise when
    payment due
Exceeds accounts received at 17

To those of us who knew the pain of valentines that never came
And those whose names were never called when choosing sides
    for basketball
It was long ago and far away. The world was younger than today
When dreams were all they gave for free to ugly duckling
    girls like me

We all play the game & when we dare, we cheat ourselves
    at solitaire
Inventing lovers on the phone, repenting other lives unknown
That call & say "Come dance with me" & murmur vague obscenities
To ugly girls like me, at 17
    — w & m: Janis Ian

BIG ITALIAN ROSE

She was riding on the airline leafing thru their magazine
They said "We'll fly you to the homeland that you have never seen"
Smiling tourists in the picture back in sunny Italy
Said she, "These pretty people don't look anything like me!"

D - A - / G D A - / G - D - / A - GA D

"I'm a big Italian woman & I want the world to see
All the big Italian women who look just like me
You can take your slender models & their 5th Ave clothes
But you'll never find a flower like the Big Italian Rose!"

D - G D / D - A - / D D7 G - / D - A D

Well the more she thought about it, the more it made her mad
How they make you feel so ugly, they make you feel so bad
Sell you junk food & booze then make you diet til you're dead
She sat & wrote a letter & this is what it said:

"Well, I'm nearly 57, my hair is turning gray
The dress I wore at 20 I cannot wear today
Just an ordinary woman & it sure would make me glad
Just for once to see someone like me in your ad"

3 weeks later came an answer, from NY it was sent
Said "We'd like to take your picture for our next advertisement"
Soon magazines across the nation in a prominent place
Showed a big Italian woman with a smile on her face

    — w & m: Fred Small

THE CHRISTIANS AND THE PAGANS

Amber called her uncle, said "We're up here for the holiday
Jane & I were having Solstice, now we need a place to stay"
And her Christ-loving uncle watched his wife
   hang Mary on a tree
He watched his son hang candy canes all made with Red Dye No. 3
He told his niece "It's Christmas Eve, I know our life
   is not your style"
She said "Christmas is like Solstice & we miss you & it's been awhile"

G C Am D / / / Em C Am D - / 1st / /

So the Christians & the Pagans sat together at the table
Finding faith & common ground the best that
   they were able
Just before the meal was served, hands were held
   & prayers were said
Sending hope for peace on earth to all their gods & goddesses

G C Em D / / Em C Am D / Em C Am D G - - -

The food was great, the tree plugged in, the meal had gone
   without a hitch
Til Timmy turned to Amber & said "Is it true that you're a witch?"
His mom jumped up & said "The pies are burning"
   & she hit the kitchen
And it was Jane who spoke, she said, "It's true,
   your cousin's not a Christian"
"But we love trees, we love the snow, the friends we have,
   the world we share
And you find magic from your God & we find magic everywhere"

So the Christians... / And where does magic come from?
   I think magic's in the learning
'Cos now when Christians sit with Pagans only pumpkin pies are
   burning

When Amber tried to do the dishes, her aunt said "Really,
   no, don't bother"
Amber's uncle saw how Amber looked like Tim & like her father
He thought about his brother, how they hadn't spoken in a yr
He thought he'd call him up & say "It's Christmas & your daugh-
   ter's here"
He thought of fathers, sons & brothers, saw his own son tug
   his sleeve, saying
"Can I be a Pagan?" Dad said "We'll discuss it when they leave"

So the Christians...
Lighting trees in darkness, learning new ways from the old &
Making sense of history & drawing warmth out of the cold

    — w & m: Dar Williams

THE COLORS OF EARTH

Tell me the names of the colors of earth:
The purple of eggplant, the purple of peach
The green & the gray of the rocks on the beach
The sun on the mountain in the morning

G - C G / C G C D / 1st / C G D G

Who can count all **the colors of earth?**
Each color is different, each color is true
We are made of the colors of earth
And I love the colors that made you

When I look in the eyes of my friends
I can see topaz, I can see sky
The green & the gray of the sea rolling by
And the dazzling brown river in the morning
    We are made of **the colors of earth...**

When I look at the hands of my friends
I can see chestnut, I can see corn
The color of wheatfields & a dappled brown fawn
And the rain-kissed black trees in the morning
    We are made of **the colors...**

Earth that I love, do you know how I feel?
How much I love sea shells, how much I love stones?
When I walk barefoot in the fields all alone
I sing out a song to the morning
    Who can count all **the colors of earth?...**

    — w & m: Sarah Pirtle

COURAGE

A small thing once happened at school
That brought up a question for me
And somehow it forced me to see
The price that I pay to be cool
Diane is a girl that I know
She's strange, like she doesn't belong
I don't mean to say that that's wrong
We don't like to be with her, though

G↓ - - - / Am D Am D / Am - D - / G - - - :‖

  And so, when we all made a plan
  To have this big party at Sue's
  Most kids in the school got the news
  But no one invited Diane

 C - G - / / G↓ Em - / A - Am D

The thing about Taft Junior High
Is secrets don't last very long
I acted like nothing was wrong
When I saw Diane start to cry
I know you may think that I'm cruel
It doesn't make me very proud
I just went along with the crowd
It's sad, but you have to in school
  You can't pick the friends you prefer
  You fit in as well as you can
  I couldn't be friends with Diane
  'Cos then they would treat me like her

In one class at Taft Junior High
We study what people have done
With gas chamber, bomber & gun
In Auschwitz, Japan & My Lai
I don't understand all I learn
Sometimes I just sit there & cry
The whole world stood idly by
To watch as the innocent burn
  Like robots obeying some rule
  Atrocities done by the mob
  All innocent, doing their job
  And what was it for? Was it cool?

The world was aware of this Hell
But how many cried out in shame?
What heroes & who was to blame?
A story that no one dared tell
I promise to do what I can
To not let it happen again
To care for all women & men
I'll start by inviting Diane **(last v:)** Am D G -

 — w & m: Bob Blue

DON'T PUT HER DOWN
(You Helped Put Her There)

You pull the string, she's your plaything
You can make her or break her, it's true
You abuse her, accuse her, turn around & use her
Then forsake her any time it suits you

(in 3/4) A E D A / - - E - / D - A - / A E A -

**Well there's more to her than powder & paint
Than her peroxided, bleached out hair
Well if she acts that way, it's 'cos you've had your day
Don't put her down, you helped put her there**

E - D A / D A E - / D - A - / A E A -

She hangs around playing the clown
While her soul is aching inside
She's heartbreak's child 'cos she just lives for your smile
To build her up in a world made by men

At the house down the way, you sneak in your *[& you]* pay
For her love, her body, her shame
Then you call yourself a man, you say you just don't
 understand
How a woman could turn out that way

Well there's more to her than powder & paint
Than the men she picks up at a bar
Well if she acts that way...

 — w & m: Hazel Dickens

FOR THE MOTHERS

I sing for the mothers <u>all over the earth</u>
For their power, _ for their love _
I ache for the mothers <u>all over the earth</u>
For their sorrow, _ for their love _
May their broken hearts be cradled _
May their righteous anger be heard _
  I pray for justice & healing for_ all of the mothers / <u>All</u>
  <u>over the earth</u> _

(↑3) Am - Em Am / C - G E / 1st / C E Am -
C - G - / Dm E Am - / Am - Dm - / E - Am -

I sing for the mothers of soldiers at war...
I sing...who grieve for the child
  ...who live w/ regret
  ...who are finding their voice
  — w & m: Betsy Rose

HERE'S TO THE MEN

Here's to the men with the vision to see
With equality everyone gains, so
Here's to their courage & here's to their truth
And their part in the breaking of chains-oh

(in 6/8) C G C F / C - - G / 1st / C - G C

Boys are brought up from the time they are small
To believe that they've got to be tough
And they're taught not to cry & they're trained not to feel
For they're told that it's womanish stuff
    And they're taught on the TV that women exist
    For the pleasure & service of men &
    They see in their schools that the men are in charge
    So they're taught this again & again, so...

C F C - / F C G - / C G C F / C G C -
C - F C / F - G - /   "   / C G C G

And as they get older they learn from their friends
The terrible power of names
And the ones they hate most are the ones they'll be called
If they don't play the old macho games
    So it's only the wise who consider the cost
    And only the brave who can change
    For the wise & the brave know that for the applause
    They give half of themselves in exchange, so

The customs of centuries die very hard
But we still look in hope for the time
When equality's not just in charters & laws
But entrenched within everyone's mind
    Still the internal struggle's the hardest of all
    It's the fight to be all we can be
    But when women & men join as allies & friends
    We'll find truth can set all of us free, so

— w & m: Eileen McGann

© 1987 Eileen McGann/Dragonwing Music (SOCAN). www.eileenmcgann.com. On her *Elements*.

HOME IS WHERE THE HEART IS

On the corner there's this nice man
His name is Mark, he's always smiling
He's got this mom who comes on Wednesdays
In the evening with soup so steaming
He shares his house with his friend Martin
They're not brothers, they're not cousins
My little girl wonders all about these men
I take hold of her hand & I begin

A - / - - D - :‖ (3x) / E - / D -

Home is where the heart is _ _
No matter how the heart lives _ _
Inside your heart_where love is, _ that's
Where you've got to make yourself _ / At home _ _ _

A - / D E / A - / D E / D -

Thru the yard live Deb & Tricia
With their tools & ladders & their room addition
My kid yells over "Are ya having a baby?"
They wink & smile, they say "Someday maybe"
But thru their doors go kids & mommies
Funny how you don't see the daddies go in
My little girl wonders 'bout this house with no men
I take hold of her hand...

'Round the corner, here comes Martin
He's alone now, he tries smiling
He roams around his well-stocked kitchen
He knows that fate will soon be coming
My little girl wonders where will he live / **I take...**

Martin sits & waits with his window open
His house is empty, his heart is broken
We bring him toys & watercolors
He loves to hear my little baby's stories
She's the gift I share, she's his companion
She's the string on the kite, she guides him into the wind
My little girl wonders who will care for him
<u>We</u> **take hold of** <u>his</u> **hand, we begin** *[Let's begin now]*...

— w & m: Sally Fingerett

© 1990 Green Fingers Music. 4 Bitchin' Babes (Fingerette w/ Christine Lavin, Megon McDough, Patty Larkin) *Buy Me, Bring Me, Take Me, Don't Mess My Hair*, PP&M *Lifelines*, Holly Near & Ronnie Gilbert *This Train Still Runs*, David Grisman *Home*..., In *SO!* 37:4.

I AM A ROCK

A winter's day
In a deep & dark December
I am alone
Gazing from my window to the streets below
On a freshly fallen silent shroud of snow
I am a rock, I am an island

(↑5) G - - - / C - G - / Am D C G / Am Bm x2
Am C D - / G - D - G - - -

I've built walls
A fortress deep & mighty
That none may penetrate
I have no need of friendship, friendship causes pain
It's laughter & it's loving I disdain / **I am a rock...**

Don't talk of love
Well I've heard the word before
It's sleeping in my memory
I won't disturb the slumber of feelings that have died
If I never loved I never would have cried / **I am ...**

I have my books
And my poetry to protect me
I am shielded in my armor
Hiding in my room, safe within my womb
I touch no one & no one touches me...

(tag) And a rock feels no pain / & an island never cries

Dm G C - / /

— w & m: Paul Simon

© 1965 Paul Simon (BMI). On Simon & Garfunkel *Sounds of Silence*.

I Kissed a Girl

Jenny came over & told me 'bout Fred
"He's such a hairy behemoth" she said
"Dumb as a box of hammers
But he's such a handsome guy"
And I opened up & I told her 'bout Larry
And yesterday how he asked me to marry
I'm not giving him an answer yet / I think I can do better

G - / C - / Am - / G - :‖

And we laughed, _ compared notes _
We had a drink, we had a smoke, she took off her overcoat _
I kissed a girl (2x)

Em - Am - / Em - Am C / G C↓ Am D - /   /

So she called home to say she'd be late
He said he worried but now he feels safe
"I'm glad you're with your girlfriend / Tell her hi for me"
Then I looked at you, you had guilt in your eyes
But it only lasted a little while
And then I felt your hand / Above my knee

And we laughed at the world
They can have their diamonds & we'll have our pearls / **I...**

(bridge) Well I kissed a girl, her lips were sweet
She was just like kissing me
I kissed a girl, won't change the world
But I'm so glad **I kissed a girl**

F - / C - / D - / D - G -

(tag) I kissed a girl for the 1st time
I kissed a girl & I may do it again / I kissed a girl **(2x)**
I kissed a girl her lips were sweet, she was just like kissing me
(But better!) I kissed a girl
I kissed a girl, won't change the world but I'm so glad I
Kissed a girl for the 1st time I kissed a / Girl

G C↓ Am D (9x)

— w & m: Robin Eaton & Jill Sobule

© 1995 Left Right Left Music (ASCAP), administered by Bug Music and Warner-Tamerlane Publishing Corp. On *Jill Sobule*.

Let It Go

(intro) The snow glows white on the mountain tonight, not a
   footprint to be seen
A kingdom of isolation & it looks like I'm the queen
The wind is howling like this swirling storm inside
Couldn't keep it in, Heaven knows I tried

Em C D AsusAm / Em C D AsusA / 1st / Em D A -

Don't let them in, don't let them see, be the good girl you always
   have to / Be — conceal don't feel, don't let them know
Well now they know!

D - C - /   / C -

Let it go (x2) Can't hold it back anymore
Let it go (x2) Turn away & slam the door
I don't care what they're going to say
Let the storm rage on, the cold never bothered me anyway

G D Em C /   / Bm Bb C -

It's funny how some distance makes everything seem small
And the fears that once controlled me can't get to me at all
It's time to see what I can do to test the limits & break thru
No right, no wrong, no rules for me — I'm free!

Em C D Am / Em D Asus A / D - C - /   /

Let it go (x2) I am one with the wind and sky
Let it go (x2) You'll never see me cry
Here I stand & here I'll stay
Let the storm rage on

(bridge) My power flurries thru the air into the ground
My soul is spiraling in frozen fractals all around
And one thought crystallizes like an icy blast
I'm never going back, the past is in the past!

C - - - /   / D - - - / E Cmaj7 D Am (C)

Let it go (x2) & I'll rise like the break of dawn
Let it go (x2) That perfect girl is gone
Here I stand in the light of day
Let the storm rage on! / The cold never bothered me anyway

G D Em C (3x) / Cm Bm Bb - / C -

— w & m: Kristen Anderson-Lopez & Robert Lopez

© 2013 Wonderland Music Company, Inc. Sung by Idina Menzel in the 2013 film *Frozen* (11).

Let My Stomach Be Soft & Round

When a tire is flat, we don't like that
A singer singing flat is not where it's at
No one likes flat feet or beer without the fizz
So tell me what good a flat stomach is?

G D A D / G D A - / 1st / E - A -

Let my stomach be soft & round
Round, round, soft & round
Feels so phony to work at being bony
And hard as the cold, cold ground, oh
Hard as the cold, cold ground

D - G D / G D A - / D - G - / D A D A / D A D -

Now once upon a time when humans were new
No one seemed to care what shape they grew
Along came fashion & it became a sin to be
A little too thick but never too thin
   There were whale bone corsets to hold the body in
   They squeezed all your insides up to your chin
   In our enlightened times we're not so dumb as that
   A surgeon cuts you open & vacuums out the fat
I once ate only carrots and lost 6 pounds
But when I gave up carrots, I gained back 10
Then I lost 20, gained back 28
Great thing 'bout dieting, you put on weight
   So I gave up on diets & Nautilus machines
   I'm living with the code that's in my genes
   Be I plump or thin, whichever way I'm built
   Bring on the chocolate cheesecake, to hell with all the guilt!

— w & m: Grit Laskin

© 1986 Grit Laskin/Strutting Day Music. On his *A Few Simple Words, These Times*.

MEAN

You with your words like knives
  (& swords & weapons that you use against me)
You have knocked me off my feet again
  (got me feeling like I'm nothing)
You with your voice like nails on a chalkboard
  (calling me out when I'm wounded)
You picking on the weaker man _

(↑4) Am G F - (4x)

(bridge 1)
_Well you can take me down _with just one single blow _
But you don't know what you don't know

G - C F G - / F -

Someday I'll be living in a big ol' city
And all you're ever gonna be is mean _
Someday I'll be big enough so you can't hit me
And all you're ever gonna be is mean, why you gotta be
So mean? _ _ _

C G Am F / C G F - :‖ C - (Bb C C)

You, with your switching sides
  (& your wildfire lies & your humiliation)
You have pointed out my flaws again
  (as if I don't already see them)
I walk with my head down trying to block you out
  ('cos I'll never impress you)
I just wanna feel okay again _

(bridge 2)
_I bet you got pushed around, _somebody made you
Cold (but the cycle ends right now 'cos)
You can't lead me down that road (& you don't know what you
  don't know) / Someday...

G - C F / G - / F - - -

(bridge 3) And I can see you yrs from now in a bar
_Talking over a football game with that same big loud opinion but
_Nobody's listening — washed up & ranting about the
Same old bitter things _
Drunk & grumbling on about how I can't sing
  (but all you are is)

G - / C F G - / C F G - / F G F - / G - F - (tacet)

(tag) Mean _ _ all you are is
Mean (& a liar & pathetic & alone in life &)
Mean & mean & mean & mean but / Someday...

C G Am F (3x)

    — w & m: Taylor Swift

NAMES

A patchwork of thousands of precious names
There must be someone that you know
Woven together in a quilted frame
Names the loved ones won't let go

(↑2) G D C G / C G D - / 1st / C D G -

And I know that my name could be there
And I feel the pain & the fear
And as human love & passions do not make us all the same
We are counted not as numbers, but as names

D - GC G / / C D G Em / C D G -

We grieve for the lovers & the families
And I pray they'll meet again some day
But until that time I will carry the flame
As the numbers grow we'll not forget their names

A lover, a carpenter, a father, a friend
A sister, a minister, a mom
Each quilted piece holds a memory
Each memory helps us to go on

    — w & m: Cathy Fink

THE ONES WHO AREN'T HERE

I'm thinking about the ones who aren't here
And won't be coming in late
Home all alone & the family
And won't be coming out tonight
Wish I could know all the lovers
And friends kept from gathering
I think of you now the ways you could go
We're all of us refugees

(in 3/4) D G / D DDmaj7 GEm / 1st 2 / A D /
G A (Em) / D G / DA D

Telling myself & the family
My friends & the folks on the job
One by one & it's never been easy
And me & everyone changed
The hugs & the tears when they show you their hearts
And some never speak again
Every pot off the wheel can't bear the kiln
And every love can't bear the pain

So let's pass a kiss & a happy sad tear
And a hug the whole circle round
For the ones who aren't here, for the hate & the fear
For laughter, for struggle, for life
Let's have a song here for me & for you
And the love that we cannot hide
And let's have a song for the ones who aren't here
And won't be coming out tonight

    — w & m: John Calvi

THE POWER OF LOVING YOU

You're gay, I'm straight — I think you're great
I think you're so strong
If I had a million yrs to spend
I could not have done what you've done
 Yeah I'm straight it's fate I'm trying to relate
 But I'm feeling like a fool
 I'm trying to find how I can show
 My love & respect for you

C G F G / C - F - / - - C - / - - G - // 1st 3 / G - C -

So I'll raise my voice clear & loud
It's time I stood up it's time I spoke out
Against the silence & fear around
And for your love that's true

Am G C F / Am G C - / 1st / C - G -

But I'm the one who held my tongue
I never knew quite what to say
I figured you were doing fine
I thought I'd stay out of your way
 But silence is a barbed wire kiss
 My lips are bleeding red
 So I open my mouth it's time I say
 Those words I never said

(final cho) And **so we'll raise our voices clear & loud**
We'll sing for your courage we'll keep singing out
And speak up for you, gay & proud
We'll **sing for your love that's true**
For the power of loving you

Am G C F / Am G C - / 1st / C - G - / - - C -

 — w & m: Kristina Olsen

1993 Take A Break Publishing. On her *Love, Kristina*.

ROSA'S LOVELY DAUGHTERS

Who's that walking miles for water
Who's that sweat-shoppin' all day long
In the hot south, in the cold north
Who are these so proud & strong?

D - - - / G - D - / - - - / D A D -

From the workbench in the back room
From the benchmarks upon the bed
From the mad mothers to the peace campers
Who are these seeing red?

These *[we]* are Rosa's lovely daughters, these *[we]* are no
 man's blushing brides
These *[we]* are Rosa's... & they *[we]* will not be denied!

D - - - / G - D - / 1st / D A D -

Well the fathers handshake their bargains
And their good wives stand around & they weep
But their hearts sing when they're dancing
They *[we]* are no man's to give or to keep
 They are skewed, slewed, stewed & awkward
 They are clumsy like a clown
 But these are wildfire in the backyard
 And the big white house is a-burning down

Wearing trousers or short skirts (as we please!)
We'll walk at night together in the middle of town
We are free spirits taking back the night back
We are wildfire across dry ground!

 — w & m: Robb Johnson

© 1987 Moose Music. On his *Margaret Thatcher: My Part in Her Downfall* (17), Leon Rosselson & Robb Johnson *The Liberty Tree*, Roy Bailey *Women of Steel: the Album*, Janet Russell *Celebrating Subversion: The Anti-Capitalist Roadshow*. Rosa refers to Rosa Luxemburg (1871-1919), a German revolutionary Marxist economist & activist. Tune is adap from "Will the Circle Be Unbroken."

SEASONS OF LOVE

525,600 minutes
525,000 moments so dear
525,600 minutes
How do you measure, measure a year?

(↑4, in D) G2 F#m Em7 D (4x)

In daylights, in sunsets,
In midnights, in cups of coffee
In inches, in miles, in laughter, in strife
In 525,600 minutes
How do you measure, a year in the life?

(bridge) How about love? (3x)
Measure in love
Seasons of love (x2)

C G - D / / / C - - A / G F#m Em7 D

525, 600 minutes
525,000 journeys to plan
525,600 minutes
How do you measure the life of a woman or a man?

In truths that she learned or in times that he cried
In bridges he burned or the way that she died
It's time now, to sing out tho' the story never ends
Let's_celebrate remember a year in the life of friends_

(as bridge) Remember the love! (oh you got to, you got to
 remember the love)

Remember... (you know that life is a gift from up above)
Remember... (share love, give love, spread love)
Measure in love (measure, measure your life in love)
Seasons of love (measure your life (x2) in love) (2x)

 — w & m: Jonathan Larson

©1996 Finster & Lucy Music Ltd. Co. All rights controlled and administered by Universal Music Corp. In *Rent*.

SENSITIVE NEW-AGE GUYS

Who like to talk about their feelings?
   Sensitive New-Age Guys
Who knows if you kiss a booboo it will start healing?...
Whose dream car is a hybrid station wagon?...
Whose favorite song is "Puff the Magic Dragon"?...

(↑2) Cmaj7 Edim Dm G / C Em Dm G :‖ (4x)

   Who like to cry at weddings?
   Who think that football is so very upsetting?
   Whose favorite place to hang out is a shopping mall?
   And at the movie "Castaway" cried for Wilson the volleyball?
   (Ooh...)

F - Fm - / C E7 A7 - / D7 - - - / G7 - - - (C Am Dm G)

Whose last names are hyphenated?...
Who walked out of Long Dong Silver, a movie they hated?...
Who prefers clothing styles understated?...
Who thinks a full head of hair is overrated?...
   Who think that red meat is disgusting?
   Who's into UFO's, channelling & dusting?
   Who believes us when we say we have premenstrual syndrome?
   Who doesn't mind if we get all the attention?

Who likes music that's repetitious?... **(repeat)**
Who used to be wild men but now are calm?...
Who now call their wives "Mom!"?...
   Who carries the baby on his back?
   Who thinks the Dalai Lama is on the inside track?
   Who sings on singalongs even when they
   Can't stand stupid singalong songs?

— w & m: Christine Lavin and John Gorka

SISTERS ARE DOIN' IT FOR THEMSELVES

Now there was a time when they used to say, that
Behind every "great man," there had to be a "great woman"
But in these times of change you know that it's no longer true
So we're comin' out of the kitchen 'cos there's smth we forgot to
   say to you (we say)

(↑3) Dm DmA Dm DmA (3x) (v2: 7x) Dm DmA A C

Sisters are doin' it for themselves
Standin' on their own 2 feet & ringin' on their own bells
Sisters are doin' it for themselves

F GA Dm - / / /

Now this is a song to celebrate
The conscious liberation of the female state!
Mothers, daughters & their daughters too
Woman to woman we're singin' with you
   The "inferior sex" has got a new exterior
   We got doctors, lawyers, politicians too
   Everybody take a look around
   Can you see **(x3)** there's a woman right next to you

(bridge) Now we ain't makin' stories & we ain't layin' plans
'Cos a man still loves a woman & a woman still loves a man

Bb - G - / Bb - G A

— w & m: Annie Lennox & David Stewart

TREE OF LIFE

Beggar's Blocks & Blind Man's Fancy
Boston Corners & Beacon Lights
Broken Stars & Buckeye Blossoms
Blooming on **the Tree of Life**

(↑2) A G / - D :∥

Tree of Life, quilted by the lantern light
Every stitch a leaf upon the Tree of Life
Stitch away, sisters / Stitch away

G D / / A G / D -

Hattie's Choice (Wheel of Fortune) & High Hosanna (Indiana)
Hills & Valleys (Sweet Wood Lilies) & Heart's Delight
   (The Tail of Benjamin's Kite)
Hummingbird (Hovering Gander) in Honeysuckle (Oleander)
Blooming on **the...**

We're only known as someone's mother
Someone's daughter or someone's wife
But with our hands & with our vision
We make the patterns on **the...**

— w & m: Eric Peltoniemi

TRUE COLORS

You with the sad eyes, don't be discouraged
Oh I realize, _ it's hard to take courage
In a world full of people, you can lose sight of it all
And the darkness inside you can make you feel so small

Am G C - / F - Am G / C Dm Em F / Am G F C

But **I see your true colors shining thru**
I see your true colors & that's why I love you
So don't be afraid to let them show your
True colors, true colors are / Beautiful like a rainbow

F C G - / F C F G / F C F Am / F C F C / Dm - Am -

Show me a smile then, don't be unhappy
Can't remember when I last saw you laughing
If this world makes you crazy & you've taken all you can bear
You call me up because you know I'll be there / And **I see...**

— w & m: Billy Steinberg & Tom Kelly

WALK A MILE

I want to walk a mile in your shoes (2x)
I want to know what you think & what you feel
So I really want to walk a mile in your shoes!

C - F C / - - G - / F G Am F / C - G C

Remember that fight that we had?
Why did we both have to lose?
It's because we both walked away mad
Instead of walking a mile in each other's shoes!

C - F - / C - G - / 1st / C - G C

You hear how the world is a mess
Whenever you turn on the news
But all countries could have happiness
If they'd be walking a mile in each other's shoes!

Tempers start to cool down
A frown turns into a smile
Anger cannot be found
When you're wearing their shoes
And you're walking that mile!

— w & m: Jan Nigro

© 1987 Janimation Music. On Vitamin L *Walk a Mile*, Bill Harley *Big Big World*, Tom Pease *Wobbi-Do-Wop*. In *SO!* 37.2. Nigro is the brother of Laura Nyro.

WALKING ON MY WHEELS

Walkin' on my wheels, walkin' on my wheels
People let me tell you just how good it feels
I'll go anywhere if I've got my chair
Watch me now, I'm walkin' on my wheels

C - F C / F C D7 G / C C7 F - / C Am G C - (v: C - G C)

My name is Terry & I'm 9
Take a look at this amazing chair of mine
Silver & black & the wheels go round
Just a little push & I really cover ground
    Why don't my legs work? I don't know
    Something happened to 'em, very long ago
    But I work out every day & my arms are strong
    They're just the thing for rolling me along
Every day when I go to school
I ride in a van that's really cool
The lift takes my chair right down to the floor
Help me w/ the strap & I'll race you to the door
    Wasn't it funny when the substitute teacher
    Asked us to name that silly-looking creature?
    I raised my hand & she nearly dropped her chalk
    She thought I couldn't think just because I couldn't walk
Can you come on over? Ask your folks
We can use the computer or just tell jokes
And later on, I can come to visit you
If your bldg has a ramp, so my chair can visit too
    My friend Jack rides a chair like me
    But he's really, really old — I think he's 23
    He can shoot a basketball just like Dr. J
    And last week he started teaching me to play!

— w & m: Mark L. Cohen

© 1993 Dan Robert Allshouse DBA Childsong Music. Bob Reid *Marz Barz*, Fink & Marxer *Nobody Else Like Me*. Teaching Tolerance *I Will Be Your Friend*. In *SO!* 35.2.

WE ARE FAMILY

We are family, I got all my sisters with me
We are family, get up everybody & sing (repeat)

A G D F (4x)

_Ev'ryone can see we're together as we walk on by
_And we fly just like birds of a feather, I won't tell no lie
_All of the people around us they say "Can they be that close?"
_Just let me state for the record:_we're giving love in a family dose

A EmD A EmD (4x)

_Living life is fun & we've just begun to get our share of this
    world's delights
_High hopes we have for the future & our goal's in sight
_No we don't get depressed, here's what we call our golden rule
_Have faith in you & the things you do, you won't go wrong: this
    is our family jewel

— w & m: Nile Rodgers and Bernard Edwards

© 1979 Sony/ATV Music Publishing LLC and Bernard's Other Music. All rights on behalf of Sony/ATV Music Publishing LLC administered by Sony/ATV Music Publishing LLC, 424 Church Street, Suite 1200, Nashville, TN 37219. All rights on behalf of Bernard's Other Music administered by Warner-Tamerlane Publishing Corp. Rec by Sister Sledge, Spice Girls & The Chipmunks.

WE WON'T HOLD BACK

Oh you can't hold back the mighty wind when it blows
You can't hold back a surging river when it flows
And you can't hold back the budding flower of a rose
You can't hold back the heart of love when it grows

(↑3) G C G C G / C G D G(C G) :‖

We won't hold back, we're moving on
There's a force of love that is pure & is strong, so
Be we straight or be we gay, we have the right to wed today
We won't hold back, the time has come, we're moving on

Em - Bm - / C G D - / G Am7 G C / G D G -

Oh, you can't hold back justice & dignity
You can't hold back equality
And you can't hold back the need for family
You can't hold back he & he or she & she

And you can't hold back the natural power of the sun
You can't hold back as it shines bright on everyone, &
You can't hold back these times of change once they've begun
You can't hold back the vote of victory once it's won

— w & m: Ruth Pelham

© 2011 Ruth Pelham Music

The **Dignity & Diversity** chapter contains songs on equal rights for women, men, LBGTQ & other groups, songs on empowerment & pride in self. See **Friendship**, **Healing**, & **Hope**.

See also: **Blues:** Women Be Wise, **Country:** Mean, **Faith:** Come Ye Thankful People (alt. lyrics), Miriam ha-neviah, They'll Know We Are Christians (alt. lyrics), **Family:** Coloring Outside the Lines, **Freedom:** Something Inside So Strong, **Good Times:** YMCA, Your Disco Needs You, **Lullabies:** Love Makes a Family, **Millenial:** Perfect, **Play:** What I Am, **Rich:** When the Rain Comes Down, **Struggle:** We Can Move Mtns, **Trav:** Freeborn Man (on Travellers).

Dreams & Mystery

ALL THAT IS GOLD

All that is gold does not glitter
All who wander are not lost
The old that is strong does not wither
Deep roots are not touched by frost

(in 3/4) D G D A / D G A D :|

From the ashes a fire shall be awoken
A light from these shadows shall spring

G - - - D - - - / G - - - D - (A -)

Those who bring peace shall not grow weary
Tho' the road be long they will find rest
Often the silence speaks the loudest
The unclenched fist is still the best

Those who seek truth shall not be sorry
Those who hope shall find new sight
Happy are those who show mercy
A candle shines the brightest light

— w & m: Brooks L. Williams

Some lines based on a poem by J.R.R. Tolkien © 1992 Brooks L. Williams. On his *Back to Mercy* & Grace Notes *Red Wine & Promises*.

BOX OF RAIN

Look out of any window, any morning, any evening, any day
Maybe the sun is shining, birds are winging, no rain is falling from
   a heavy sky
What do you want me to do, to do for you to see you thru?
For this is all a dream we dreamed, one afternoon long ago

D Am Em C G - / D Am Em G A -

D G Am EmD D - / C D Am G - *   *(varies on later v.)

Walk out of any doorway, feel your way, feel your way like
   the day before
Maybe you'll find direction, around some corner, where it's
   been waiting to meet you
What do you want me to do, to watch for you while you're sleeping?
Well please don't be surprised when you find me dreaming too

(last line:) Am C G D

Look into any eyes you find by you, you can see clear to another day
Maybe it's been seen before thru other eyes on other days while
   going home
What do you want me to do, to do for you, to see you thru?
It's all a dream we dreamed one afternoon long ago

(last line:) C Em D G

Walk into splintered sunlight, inch your way thru dead
   dreams to another land
Maybe you're tired & broken, your tongue is twisted with
   words half spoken and thoughts unclear
What do you want me to do, to do for you to see you thru
A box of rain will ease the pain and love will see you thru

(last line:) Am C G D -

Just a box of rain, wind & water
Believe it if you need it, if you don't just pass it on
Sun & shower, wind & rain
In & out the window like a moth before a flame

G - Am Em / C A D - / G Am - Em / G D Em A -

And it's just a box of rain, I don't know who put it there
Believe it if you need it or leave it if you dare
And it's just a box of rain or a ribbon for your hair
Such a long long time to be gone & a short time to be there

D Em G D / - Bm G A / D Em G D / Em - G D -

— w: Robert Hunter, m: Phil Lesh

© 1970 Ice Nine Publishing Co., Inc. Copyright renewed. All rights administered by Universal Music Corp. On Grateful Dead, *American Beauty, The Best of.*

EL CONDOR PASA

I'd rather be a sparrow than a snail
Yes I would, if I could
I surely would -

Am C / - - / Am -

I'd rather be a hammer than a nail / **Yes I would...**

(bridge) Away, I'd rather sail away
Like a swan that's here & gone
A man gets tied up to the ground
He gives the world its saddest sound, its saddest sound

F - / C - / F - / C - Am -

I'd rather be a forest than a street...

I'd rather feel the earth beneath my feet...

— w: Paul Simon, music arr. by Jorge Milchberg & Daniel Robles

© 1933, 1963, 1970 Edward B. Marks Music Company and Jorge Milchberg. English lyric © 1970 Paul Simon (BMI). Tune based on trad. Andean folk tune. On Simon & Garfunkel's *Bridge Over Troubled Waters* (17).

DAYDREAM

What a day for a daydream
What a day for a daydreamin' boy
And I'm lost in a daydream
Dreamin' 'bout my bundle of joy

 And even if time ain't really on my side
 It's one of those days for taking a walk outside
 I'm blowing the day to take a walk in the sun
 And fall on my face on somebody's new mowed lawn

C - A - / Dm7 - G7 - :‖ F D7 C A7 / / / G - - -

I've been havin' a sweet dream
I've been dreamin' since I woke up today
It's starring me in my sweet dream
'Cos she's the one that makes me feel this way

 And even if time is passin' me by a lot
 I couldn't care less about the dues you say I got
 Tomorrow I'll pay the dues for dropping my load
 A pie in the face for being a sleepy bull toad

(whistle first 4 lines) And you can be sure that if you're feelin' right
 A daydream will last along into the night
 Tomorrow at breakfast you may prick up your ears
 Or you may be day dreamin' for a thousand yrs

  — w & m: John Sebastian

© 1966 w & m: Alley Music Corp and Trio Music Company. Copyright renewed. All rights for Trio Music Company administered by BMG Rights Management (US) LLC. On The Lovin' Spoonful *Daydream* (11) & Art Garfunkel *rec*.

DAYDREAM BELIEVER

If I could hide 'neath the wings of the bluebird as she sings
The 6 o'clock alarm would never ring
But it rings & I rise, rub [wipe] the sleep out of my eyes
My shavin' razor's old [cold] & it stings

C Dm Em F / C Am D7 G / 1st / CAm DmG C -

But cheer up, Sleepy Jean, ah what can it mean
To a daydream believer & a homecoming queen?

FG Em FG AmF / C F CAm D7 (G)

You once thought of me as a white knight on his steed
But now you know how funky [happy] I can be & our
Good times start & end without dollar one to spend
But how much, baby, do we really need? / So cheer up...

  — w & m: John Stewart

© 1967 (Renewed 1995) Screen Gems-EMI Music Inc. Rec by Monkees ('67) & Anne Murray ('79). Stewart wrote the song shortly before leaving the Kingston Trio. RCA requested changing "funky" to "happy" for Monkees rec.

DIRE WOLF

In the timbers of Fennario, the wolves are running round
The winter was so hard & cold, froze 10 ft 'neath the ground
Don't murder me, I beg of you, don't murder me
Please, don't murder me

D - F C / - - - D // C D GG7 C / D C G -

I sat down to my supper, 'twas a bottle of red whiskey
I said my prayers & went to bed, that's the last they saw of me
Don't murder...

 When I awoke, the Dire Wolf, 600 lbs. of sin, was
 Grinning at my window, all I said was "Come on in"...

  Em D GF C / - - - D

The wolf came in, I got my cards, we sat down for a game
 I cut my deck to the Queen of Spades, but the cards were all
  the same... (as v. 3)

In the backwash of Fennario, the black & bloody mire
The Dire Wolf collects his dues, while the boys sing round
 the fire...

  — w: Robert Hunter, m: Jerry Garcia

© 1970 Ice Nine Publishing Co., Inc. Copyright renewed. All rights administered by Universal Music Corp. On Grateful Dead *Reckoning & Workingman's Dead* (15).

DO YOU BELIEVE IN MAGIC

Do you believe in magic in a young girl's heart?
How the music can free her whenever it starts
And it's magic if the music is groovy
It makes you feel happy like an old time movie
I'll tell you about the magic & it'll free your soul
But it's like trying to tell a stranger 'bout rock 'n' roll

C - F - (4x) Dm Em F Em / G - - -

If you believe in magic don't bother to choose
If it's jug band music or rhythm & blues
Just go & listen, it'll start with a smile
It won't wipe off your face no matter how hard you try
Your feet start tapping & you can't seem to find
How you got there so just blow your mind

If you believe... come along with me
We'll dance until morning til there's just you & me
And maybe if the music is right
I'll meet you tomorrow sorta late at night
We'll go a dancin' baby, then you'll see
How the magic's in the music & the music's in me

(tag) Yeah! Do you believe / In magic? (Yeah!)
Believe in the magic of a young girl's soul
Believe in the magic of a rock 'n' roll
Believe in the magic that can set you free / Ohhh!
Talkin' 'bout magic (Do you believe like I believe)
Do you believe in magic? (Do you... etc.

F - - - / C - - - / F Em F Em (3x) G - - -
‖: F - - - / C - - - :‖

  — w & m: John Sebastian

© 1965 Alley Music Corp. and Trio Music Company. Copyright renewed. All rights for Trio Music Company administered by BMG Rights Management (US) LLC. On Loving Spoonful *Do You*...(in B 111).

FOLLOW THAT DREAM

If your heart is restless from waiting so long
If you're tired & weary & you can't go on
If a distant dream is callin' you
Then there's just one thing you can do

(↑2) G - - - / - - Em - / Am - C - / G Em D -

Follow that dream wherever it may lead
Come on follow that dream to find the love you need
Come on follow that dream

C GD C / GD C GD C / GD G -

Now I've been searching for a heart that's free
Searching for someone to search with me
I need a love, a love I can trust
Together we'll search for the things that come to us

In dreams, wherever they may be / **Come on...**

Now every man has the right to live
The right to a chance, to give what he has to give
The right to fight for the things he believes
For the things that come to him in dreams

— w: Fred Wise, m: Ben Weisman

HALLELUJAH

I've heard there was a secret chord
That David played & it pleased the Lord
But you don't really care for music, do ya? _
It goes like this: the 4th, the 5th
The minor fall, the major lift
The baffled king composing Hallelujah _

C Am / | / F G C G / C F G / Am F / G E Am -

Hallelujah (4x)

F - / Am - / F - / C G C - - -

Your faith was strong but you needed proof
You saw her bathing on the roof
Her beauty in the moonlight overthrew you
She tied you to a kitchen chair
She broke your throne & she cut your hair
And from your lips she drew the Hallelujah

Baby I've been here before
I know this room, I walked this floor
I used to live alone before I knew you
I've seen your flag on the marble arch
Love is not a victory march
It's a cold & it's a broken Hallelujah

There was a time when you let me know
What's really going on below
But now you never show it to me, do you?
And remember when I moved in you
The holy dove was moving too
And every breath we drew was Hallelujah

Maybe there's a God above
But all I've ever learned from love
Was how to shoot at someone who outdrew you
It's not a cry you can hear at night
It's not somebody who has seen the light
It's a cold & it's a broken Hallelujah

You say I took the name in vain
I don't even know the name
But if I did, well really, what's it to you?
There's a blaze of light in every word
It doesn't matter which you heard
The holy or the broken Hallelujah

I did my best, it wasn't much
I couldn't feel, so I tried to touch
I've told the truth, I didn't come to fool you
And even tho' it all went wrong
I'll stand before the Lord of Song
With nothing on my tongue but Hallelujah

— w & m: Leonard Cohen

I'M A BELIEVER

I thought love was only true in fairy tales _
Meant for someone else but not for me
_ Love was out to get me, _ that's the way it seemed
_ Disappointment haunted all my dreams

G D G - / | / C G C G / C G D -

**Then I saw her face, _ now I'm a believer _
Not a trace _ of doubt in my mind _
I'm in love, _ I'm a believer! I couldn't leave her
If I tried**

G C G GC G / | / G C G F / D -

I thought love was more or less a giving thing
Seems the more I gave the less I got
What's the use in tryin? All you get is pain
When I needed sunshine I got rain

— w & m: Neil Diamond

IF I HAD A BOAT

**If I had a boat, I'd go out on the ocean
And if I had a pony, I'd ride him on my boat
And we could all together, go out on the ocean
Me upon my pony on my boat**   (↑4)

F F maj7 C F F maj7 C / F F maj7 C Am G / 1st / C G C -

If I were Roy Rogers, I'd sure enough be single
I couldn't bring myself to marrying old Dale
It'd just be me & Trigger, we'd go riding thru them movies
Then we'd buy a boat & on the sea we'd sail

C - F C / - - G - / 1st / C G C -

The mystery masked man was smart, he got himself a Tonto
'Cos Tonto did the dirty work for free
But Tonto he was smarter & one day said: "Kemo Sabe,
Kiss my ass I bought a boat, I'm going out to sea" (C - G C)

And if I were like lightning, I wouldn't need no sneakers
I'd come & go wherever I would please,
And I'd scare 'em by the shade tree & I'd scare 'em by the light pole
But I would not scare my pony on my boat out on the sea

— w & m: Lyle Lovett

LOOKING OUT MY BACK DOOR

Just got home from Illinois, lock the front door, oh boy!
Got to set down, take a rest on the porch
Imagination sets in, pretty soon I'm singin'
Doo doo doo, lookin' out my back door

(↑3) G - Em - / C G D - / 1st / C G D G

There's a giant doing cartwheels, a statue wearin' high heels
Look at all the happy creatures dancing on the lawn
A dinosaur Victrola list'ning to Buck Owens / **Doo doo...**

Tambourines & elephants are playing in the band
Won't you take a ride on the flyin' spoon? Doo doo doo
A wondrous apparition provided by a magician / **Doo...**

D - C G / G Em D - / G - Em - / C G D G

(as v 3) Tambourines & elephants...
Bother me tomorrow, today I'll buy no sorrows / **Doo...**

(as v 1) Forward troubles Illinois, lock the front door, oh boy!
Look at all the happy creatures dancing on the lawn
Bother me tomorrow, today I'll buy no sorrows / **Doo...**

— w & m: John Fogerty

THE MOUNTAIN

I was born in a forked-tongued story
Raised up by merchants & drugstore liars
Now I walk on the paths of glory
One foot in ice, one in fire

(↑3) Em D G Asus2 / / / Em D Em -

I see **the mountain, the mountain comes to me**
I see **the mountain & that is all I see**

Cmaj7 D Cmaj7 D Em (D CD Em) (2x)

Some poor prophet comes, some find solace
Some lay him down in a junkyard bay
Some will chase us & some will call us
Gone, gone, gone in a day / Gone to **the mountain...**

Miller take me & miller grind me
Scatter my bones on the wild green tide
Maybe some roving bird will find me
And over the water we'll ride / Over **the mountain...**

Some build temples & some find altars
And some come in tall hats & robes spun fine
Some in rags, some in gemstone halters
And some push the pegs back in line / I see **the mountain...**

— w & m: Dave Carter

MR TAMBOURINE MAN

Hey Mr Tambourine Man, play a song for me
I'm not sleepy & there is no place I'm going to
Hey Mr Tambourine Man, play a song for me
In the jingle jangle morning I'll come followin' you

(in D) G A D G / D G A - / 1st / D G A D

Tho' I know that evenin's empire has returned into sand
(*1x:) Vanished from my hand
Left me blindly here to stand but still not sleeping
My weariness amazes me, I'm branded on my feet
(*1x:) I have no one to meet
And the ancient empty street's too dead for dreaming

G A D G / D G *(repeat 1-4x as indicated) / D G A - :||

Take me on a trip upon your magic swirlin' ship
(*3x:) My senses have been stripped
　　　My hands can't feel to grip
　　　My toes too numb to step
Wait only for my boot heels to be wanderin'
I'm ready to go anywhere, I'm ready for to fade
(*1x:) Into my own parade
Cast your dancing spell my way, I promise to go under it

Tho' you might hear laughin', spinnin' swingin'
　　madly across the sun
(*2x:) It's not aimed at anyone
　　　It's just escapin' on the run
And but for the sky there are no fences facin'
And if you hear vague traces of skippin' reels of rhyme
(*3x:) To your tambourine in time
　　　It's just a ragged clown behind
　　　I wouldn't pay it any mind
It's just a shadow you're seein' that he's chasing

Then take me disappearin' thru the smoke rings of my mind
(*4x:) Down the foggy ruins of time
　　　Far past the frozen leaves
　　　The haunted, frightened trees
　　　Out to the windy beach
Far from the twisted reach of crazy sorrow
Yes, to dance beneath the diamond sky with one hand waving free
(*4x:) Silhouetted by the sea
　　　Circled by the circus sands
　　　With all memory & fate
　　　Driven deep beneath the waves
Let me forget about today until tomorrow

— w & m: Bob Dylan

OH RIVER

Oh river take it on down / Take it on down (x2)
Oh river take it on down / Take it on down to the sea

C Am / F G / C Am / F G C

Someday I will fly so high
I will walk barefoot on the sky

Em Am / Dm F G

Someday I will dance so fast
The future will start to look like the past

(bridge) Here we are to celebrate love
A family is gathered around
In a time when war is raging / Love is so profound

Dm - / Am - / F - / G -

Someday I will sing so high
The birds will look up & wonder why
— w & m: Holly Near

© 2004 Hereford Music. On her *Show Up.*

THE RAINBOW CONNECTION

Why are there so many songs about rainbows
And what's on the other side?
Rainbows are visions, but only illusions
And rainbows have nothing to hide
So we've been told & some choose to believe it
I know they're wrong, wait & see
Someday we'll find it, the rainbow connection
The lovers, the dreamers & me

(in 3/4)   G Em C D (3x)   G Em C -
Cmaj7 - - - / Bm - - - / Am D Bm E / Am D G -

Who said that every wish would be heard & answered
When wished on the morning star?
Somebody thought of that & someone believed it
Look what it's done so far
What's so amazing that keeps us star-gazing
And what do we think we might see? / **Someday...**

(bridge) All of us under its spell
We know that it's probably magic

I: Am D G / C G D -

II: D Em G / C Bm Am D (Dsus D)

Have you been half asleep & have you heard voices?
I've heard them calling my name
Is this the sweet sound that calls the young sailors
The voice might be one & the same
I've heard it too many times to ignore it
It's something that I'm supposed to be...
— w & m: Paul Williams and Kenneth L. Ascher

© 1979 Fuzzy Muppet Songs. I: Kermit the Frog in *The Muppet Movie* (12). II: Willie Nelson on Sesame Street video (in B 19).

RATTLIN' BONES

Smoke don't rise, fuel don't burn, sun don't shine no more
Late one night, sorrow come round scratching at my door
But I cut my hands & break my back draggin' this
** bag of stones**
Til they bury me down beneath the ground w/ the dust &
** rattlin' bones**

Em - Bm Em / / / Em - BmD Em

Left my home & left my love caught on a rusty nail
Devil rose up, heavy with gold my soul's not for sale
Then a holy man in a hse of God, he offered me a bk of prayer
And when I left my home I left my love, I left my faith back there

Shuttin' my eyes & hang my head, darkness makes no sound
Climb it up, bottom there, earth's on the way back down
When a sadness falls on the morning bird, wonder what
   the day will bring
But I'm shuttin' my eyes & hang my head, at least that bird can sing
— w & m: Shane Nicholson & Kasey Chambers

© 2008 Universal Music Publishing MGB Australia & Mushroom Music Pty. Ltd. All rights for Mushroom Music Pty. Ltd. administered by BMG Rights Management (US) LLC. On their *Rattlin'...* (11)

TANGLEWOOD TREE

Love is a tanglewood tree
In a bower of green in a forest at dawn _
Fair while the mockingbird sings
But she soon lifts her wings & the music is gone _
   _ Young lovers in the tall grass with their hearts open wide
      When the red summer poppies bloom _
But love is a trackless domain
And the rumor of rain in the late afternoon _

(↑2) Am D Am / D Am G Am (GEm) :|

G C G C / Em Bm C - / 1st 2 as above

Love is an old root that creeps
Thru the meadows of sleep when the long shadows cast
Thin as a vagrant young vine
It encircles & twines & it holds the heart fast
   Catches dreamers in the wildwd with the stars in their eyes
      And the moon in their tousled hair
But love is a light in the sky
And an unspoken lie & a half-whispered prayer

(bridge) _ I'm walkin' down a bone-dry river
   but the cool mirage runs true
_ I'm bankin' on the fables of the far, far better things we do
_ I'm livin' for the day of reck'nin countin' down the hrs
_ I yearn away, _ I burn away, _ I turn away the fairest flower of
   love, 'cos darlin'

Em C G D / Em C G A / C Em CD G / C D C D

Love is a garden of thorns
And a crow in the corn & the brake growing wild
Cold when the summer is spent
In the jade heart's lament for the faith of a child
   My body has a number & my face has a name
      And each day looks the same to me
But love is a voice on the wind
And the wages of sin & a tanglewood tree
— w & m: Dave Carter

© 2000 David Robert Carter (BMI), administered by Tracy Grammer Music. On his & Tracy Grammer's *Tanglewood Tree.*

TIME IN A BOTTLE

If I could save time in a bottle _
The 1st thing that I'd like to do _
Is to save every day til Eternity passes
Away, just to spend them with you _

(in 3/4, ↑5) Am ↓ - - (G#,G,F#) / Dm - E -
Am ↓ F Dm / Am Dm E -

If I could make days last forever
If words could make wishes come true
I'd save every day like a treasure & then
Again, I would spend them with you

But there never seems to be enough time to do the things
you want to do / Once you find them
I've looked around enough to know that you're the one
I want to go / Thru time with

A ↓ - - (G#,G,F#) / D A Bm E :|

If I had a box just for wishes
And dreams that had never come true
The box would be empty except for the memory
Of how they were answered by you

— w & m: Jim Croce

THE UNICORN

A long time ago, when the Earth was green
There was more kinds of animals than you've ever seen
They'd run around free when the Earth was being born
But the loveliest of 'em all was the unicorn

D - Em - / A7 - D - / D D7 G - / D - A7 D

> **There was green alligators & long-necked geese**
> **Some humpty backed camels & some chimpanzees**
> **Some cats & rats & elephants, but sure as you're born**
> The loveliest of all was the unicorn

D - Em - / A7 - D - / D D7 G - / D - A7 D

Now God seen some sinnin' & it gave Him pain
And He says "Stand back, I'm going to make it rain!"
He says "Hey Bro. Noah, I'll tell you what to do
Build me a floating zoo & pick some of them

> **Green alligators... / Some humpty... / Some cats...**
> Don't you forget my unicorn"

Old Noah was there to answer the call
He finished up makin' the ark just as the rain started fallin'
He marched in the animals 2 by 2
And he called out as they went thru:

> "Hey Lord I got your **green...** / **Some humpty...**
> **Some cats... elephants** but Lord, I'm so forlorn
> I just can't see no unicorn!"

And Noah looked out thru the driving rain
Them unicorns were hiding, playing silly games
Kickin' & splashin' while the rain was pourin'
Oh them silly unicorns!

> **There was green alligators & long-necked geese**
> **Some humpty backed camels & some chimpanzees**
> Noah cried, "Close the door 'cos the rain is pourin'
> And we just can't wait for no unicorn!"

The ark started moving, it drifted with the tide
Them unicorns looked up from the rocks & they cried
And the waters came down & sort of floated them away
And that's why you never seen a unicorn to this very day

> You'll see **green alligators & long-necked geese**
> **Some humpty backed camels & some chimpanzees**
> **Some cats & rats & elephants but sure as you're born**
> You're never gonna see no unicorn!

— w & m: Shel Silverstein

UNICORNIO

Mi unicornio azul ayer se me perdió
Pastando lo dejé y desapareció
Cualquier información bien la voy a pagar
Las flores que dejó no me han querido hablar

C - Em A / Dm DmG C - / Em - F A / Dm - Em DmG

Mi unicornio azul ayer se me perdió
No sé si se me fue, no sé si extravió
Y yo no tengo más que un unicornio azul
Si alguien sabe de él, le ruego información

/   "   /   "   /   "   / Dm DmG C -

Cien mil o un millón yo pagaré
Mi unicornio azul se me ha perdido ayer / Se fué

Am - Ab - / C Am Dm G / C (- Em - / F D7 Gsus G)

Mi unicornio y yo hicimos amistad
un poco con amor, un poco con verdad
Con su cuerno de añil pescaba una canción
Saberla compartir era su vocación

Mi unicornio azul ayer se me perdió
y puede parecer acaso una obsesión
Pero no tengo más que un unicornio azul
Y aunque tuviera dos yo solo quiero aquel

Cualquier información la pagaré / **Mi unicornio...**

— w & m: Silvio Rodrigues

VINCENT (Starry Starry Night)

Starry, starry night, _paint your palette blue & gray_
Look out on a summer's day with eyes that know the darkness
  in my soul
Shadows on the hills, _sketch the trees & the daffodils_
Catch the breeze & the winter chills in colors on the
  snowy linen land

(↑2)   (F) C - Dm - / F G C :‖

Now I understand _what you tried to say to me_
And how you suffered for your sanity & how you tried to
  set them free - they would not listen
They did not know how; perhaps they'll listen now _

Dm G C ↓ / Dm G Am (tacet) / D7 DmG C -

Starry... flaming flowers that brightly blaze
Swirling clouds in violet haze reflect in Vincent's eyes of china blue
Colors changing hue, morning fields of amber grain
Weathered faces lined in pain are soothed beneath the
  artist's loving hand

(bridge) For they could not love you but still your love was true
And when no hope was left in sight on that starry, starry night,
  you took your life as lovers often do,
But I could've told you, Vincent, this world was never
  meant for one as beautiful as you

Am G C ↓ / Dm Fm C A7 / Dm F G C(F C)

Starry... portraits hung in empty halls
Frameless heads on nameless walls with eyes that watch the
  world & can't forget
Like the strangers that you've met, the ragged men in ragged clothes
The silver thorn of bloody rose lie crushed & broken on the
  virgin snow

(final cho) Now I think I know **what you...** / **...free**
They would not listen, they're not listening still
Perhaps they never will
  — w & m: Don McLean

WHEN YOU WISH UPON A STAR

When you wish upon a star, makes no difference who you are
Anything your heart desires will come to you
If your heart is in your dream, no request is too extreme
When you wish upon a star as dreamers do
  Fate is kind, she brings to those who love
  The sweet fulfillment of their secret longing
Like a bolt out of the blue, fate steps in & sees you thru
When you wish upon a star your dreams come true

(↑4) CA Dm G AdimC / CAdim Dm DmG C :‖

Ddim C DdimG AdimC / Am AbD D7 Fm G / as above

  — w: Ned Washington, m: Leigh Harline

WONDERING WHERE THE LIONS ARE

Sun's up, uh huh, looks OK
The world survives into another day
And I'm thinking about **eternity**
Some kind of ecstasy got a hold on me

(↑2) D - - - / G - - - :‖ (3x)

I had another dream about lions at the door
They weren't half as frightening as they were before
But I'm thinking about **eternity** / **Some kind of...**

Walls windows trees, waves coming thru
You be in me & I'll be in you
Together in **eternity** / **Some kind of...**

Up among the firs where it smells so sweet
Or down in the valley where the river used to be
I got my mind on **eternity** / **Some kind of...**

And I'm wondering where the lions are (echo) (6x)

Em7 - - - / D - - - :‖ (4x)

Huge orange flying boat rises off a lake
Thousand-year-old petroglyphs doing a double take
Pointing a finger at eternity
I'm sitting in the middle of this ecstasy

Young men marching, helmets shining in the sun
Polished & precise like the brain behind the gun (should be!)
They got me thinking about **eternity** / **Some kind of...**

Freighters on the nod on the surface of the bay
One of these days we're going to sail away
Going to sail into **eternity** / **Some kind of...**

And I'm wondering...
  — w & m: Bruce Cockburn

The **Dreams & Mystery** chapter contains songs of the imagination.
See also: **Faith, Lullabies.** Others include: **British Invasion:** Across
the Universe, **Earthcare:** Gentle Arms of Eden, My Roots Go
Down, **Faith:** Let the Mystery Be, **Farm:** Ghost Riders in the Sky,
Golden: Swinging on a Star, **Love:** If You Could Read My Mind
Love, Love Minus Zero, **Musicals:** I Dreamed a Dream, **Outdoors:**
California Stars, Cassiopeia, **Rock:** All I Have to Do Is Dream.

Earthcare

BLACK WATERS

I come from the mountains, Kentucky's my home
Where the wild deer & black bear so lately did roam
By cool rushing waterfalls the wildflowers dream
And thru every green valley, there runs a clear stream
Now there's scenes of destruction on every hand
And there's only black waters run down thru my land   (in 3/4)

D - A D - /   / G - - D - - / - - A - / D - G - / 1st

Sad scenes of destruction on every hand
Black waters, black waters, run down thru my land

G - - D - - - / - - A D - - -

O the quail, she's a pretty bird, she sings a sweet tongue
In the roots of tall timbers she nests with her young
But the hillside explodes with the dynamite's roar
And the voice of the small birds will sound there no more
And the hillsides come a-sliding so awful & grand
And the flooding black waters rise over my land

In the rising of the springtime we planted our corn
In the ending of springtime we buried a son
In the summer come a nice man saying "Everything's fine
My employer just requires a way to his mine"
Then they tore down my mountain & covered my corn
Now the grave on the hillside's a mile deeper down
And the man stands & talks with his hat in his hand
As the poisonous water spreads over my land

D - A D /   / G - - D / - - A - /
D - G - / D - A - / D - G - / 1st

Well I ain't got no money & not much of a home
I own my own land, but my land's not my own
But if I had 10 million, somewheres thereabouts
I would buy Perry County & I'd run 'em all out!
Set down on the bank with my bait in my can
And just watch the clear waters run down thru my land!

(last cho) Well wouldn't that be just like the old Promised Land?
Black waters, black waters no more in my land!

— w & m: Jean Ritchie

BLUE BOAT HOME

Tho' below me I feel no motion, standing on these mountains & plains
Far away from the rolling ocean, still my dry land heart can say
I've been sailing all my life now, never harbor or port have I known
The wide universe is the ocean I travel
And the earth is my **blue boat home**   (in 3/4)

C FG CAm GC /   / EmAm DmG x2 / CG AmG / CF CG C -

Sun, my sail & moon my rudder as I ply the starry sea
Leaning over the edge in wonder, casting questions into the deep
Drifting here with my ship's companions all we kindred pilgrim souls
Making our way by the lights of the heavens
In our beautiful **blue**...

I give thanks to the waves upholding me, hail the great
    winds urging me on
Greet the infinite sea before me, sing the sky my sailor's song
I was born upon the fathoms, never harbor or port have I known
The wide universe is the ocean I travel / & the earth is my...

— w: Peter Mayer, m: "Hyfrydol" by Rowland Huw Prichard (1830)

CALL ME THE WHALE

Call me the whale, for that's what I am
And that's what I aim to be
You may call yourselves the kings of the land
But I am the king of the sea, **brave boys**
Yes, I am the king of the sea

G - - - /   - - D - / G - CD / GCD - / GDG -

You came after me in your matchstick boats
With your harpoons poised for the kill
When I looked you in the eye I never saw you cry
But I know that I gave you a chill, **brave boys** / I know...

But I didn't ever mean you any harm, brave boys
When I sent you to the bottom with my tail
I only meant to show you that you should been at home
Instead of on the ocean chasing whales...

But you never got the message, so more and more you came
Til I ran out of places to hide
When your boats got so big that I could not bring you down
Then I knew you had turned the tide, **brave boys** / I know...

Now you hunt me down in your factory ships
And you never even touch me with your hands
In the morning I am playing with my babies in the waves
In the afternoon I'm packed into your cans...

You've gotten so efficient with your instruments of death
That by now I'm barely alive
But if you treat each other the way you've treated me
I think I'm going to survive, **brave boys**
Yes I think I'm going to survive

— w: Paul Kaplan; m: trad. ("Greenland Fisheries")

GENTLE ARMS OF EDEN

On a sleepy endless ocean when the world lay in a dream
There was rhythm in the splash & roll but not a voice to sing
So the moon shone on the breakers & the morning
    warmed the waves
Til a single cell did jump & hum for joy as tho' to say (in G ↑2)

DC G DC G / CG CG Am C / 1st / CG CG Am D

This is my home, this is my only home
This is the only sacred ground that I have ever known
And should I stray in the dark night alone
Rock me Goddess in the gentle arms of Eden

G - CG G / CG Em D - / G - CD EmC / G CD G -

Then the day shone bright & rounder til the 1 turned into 2
And the 2 into 10,000 things & old things into new
And on some virgin beachhead 1 lonesome critter crawled
And he looked about & shouted out in his most astonished drawl

Then all the sky was buzzin' and the ground was carpet green
And the wary children of the woods went dancin' in betw
And the people sang rejoicing when the fields were glad with grain
This song of celebration from their cities on the plain

Now there's smoke across the harbor & there's factories on the shore
And the world is ill with greed & will & enterprise of war
But I will lay my burdens in the cradle of your grace
And the shining beaches of your love & the sea of your embrace

— w & m: Dave Carter

© 2001 David Robert Carter (BMI). Administered by Tracy Grammer Music. On his
Drum Hat Buddha (w/ Tracy Grammer 15), Priscilla Herdman *The Road Home* (11),
Joe Uveges *When Freedom Calls*, David Rogers *S of the New West*.

HABITAT (Have to Have a Habitat)

Habitat, habitat, have to have a habitat (3x)
You have to have a habitat to carry on!

(↑2) C Am F G / / / G - - C

The ocean **is a habitat, a very special habitat**
It's where the deepest water's at, it's where the biggest mammal's at
It's where our future food is at, it keeps the atmosphere intact
The ocean **is a habitat we depend on!**

The forest **is a habitat, a very special...**
It's where the tallest trees are at, it's where a bear can
    scratch her back
It keeps the ground from rolling back, renews the oxygen, in fact
The forest **is a habitat we...**

The river **is a habitat, a very...**
It's where the freshest water's at for people, fish & muskrat
But when people dump their trash, rivers take the biggest rap
The river **is a habitat...**

People are different than foxes & rabbits
Affect the whole world with their bad habits
Better to love it while we still have it
Or rat ta-tat-tat, our habitat's gone!

— w & m: Bill Oliver

© 1980 Bill Oliver. On his *Texas Oasis, Audubon Adventures, Have to Have a...* &
Magpie *Circle of Life*. Both play in G (17). In *For the Beauty of the Earth*.

HARD RAIN'S A-GONNA FALL

Oh where have you been, **my blue-eyed son?**
Oh where have you been, **my darling young one?**
I've stumbled on the side of 12 misty mountains
I've walked & I've crawled on 6 crooked highways
I've stepped in the middle of 7 sad forests
I've been out in front of a dozen dead oceans
I've been 10,000 miles in the mouth of a graveyard

A - D A - / - - - E - / D - E A (5x - 12x as needed)

And it's a hard & it's a hard / It's a hard & it's a hard
And it's a hard rain's a-gonna fall

A - E - / A - D - / A - E - A - - -

Oh what did you see, **my blue-eyed son?** / Oh what... **one?**
I saw a newborn baby with wild wolves all around it
I saw a highway of diamonds w nobody on it
I saw a black branch with blood that kept drippin'
I saw a room full of men with their hammers a-bleedin'
I saw a white ladder all covered w water
I saw 10,000 talkers whose tongues were all broken
I saw guns & sharp swords in the hands of young children...

And what did you hear, **my blue-eyed...?**
I heard the sound of a thunder, it roared out a warnin'
Heard the roar of a wave that could drown the whole world
Heard one hundred drummers whose hands were a-blazin'
Heard 10,000 whisperin' & nobody listenin'
Heard one person starve, I heard many people laughin'
Heard the song of a poet who died in the gutter
Heard the sound of a clown who cried in the alley...

Oh who did you meet, **my...?** / Who...?
I met a young child beside a dead pony
I met a white man who walked a black dog
I met a young woman whose body was burning
I met a young girl, she gave me a rainbow
I met one man who was wounded in love
I met another man who was wounded w hatred...

Oh what'll you do now...?
I'm a-goin' back out 'fore the rain starts a-fallin'
I'll walk to the depths of the deepest black forest
Where the people are many & their hands are all empty
Where the pellets of poison are flooding their waters
Where the home in the valley meets the damp dirty prison
Where the executioner's face is always well hidden
Where hunger is ugly, where souls are forgotten
Where black is the color, where none is the number
And I'll tell it & think it & speak it & breathe it
And reflect it from the mountain so all souls can see it
Then I'll stand on the ocean until I start sinkin'
But I'll know my song well before I start singin'...

— w & m: Bob Dylan

© 1963 Warner Bros. Inc. copyright renewed 1991 Special Rider Music. Reprinted
by Permission of Music Sales Corporation. On his *Freewheelin'*. Rec by Baez, Seeger,
Leon Russell, Edie Brickell, Staple Singers. In *Coll Reprints fr SO! V1-6, SO!* 12:5.

Hey Little Ant

(Kid:) Hey, little ant, down in that crack
Can you see me? Can you talk back?
See my shoe, can you see that?
Well, now it's gonna squish you flat!

C - F C / - F G - / 1st / C F G C

   (Ant:) Please, oh, please, do not hurt me
   Change your mind & let me be
   I'm on my way home with a crumb of pie
   Please don't hurt me, don't make me die
(Kid:) Anyone knows that ants can't feel
You're so tiny, you don't look real
I'm so big & you're so small
I don't think it will hurt at all
   (Ant:) Well, you're a giant & giants can't
   Know how it feels to be an ant
   Come down close, I think you'll see
   That you are very much like me
(Kid:) Are you crazy — me, like you?
I've got a home & a family too
You're just a speck that runs around
No one will care if my foot comes down
   (Ant:) Oh, big friend, you are so wrong
   My nest-mates need me 'cos I am strong
   I dig our nest & feed baby ants, too
   I must not die beneath your shoe
(Kid:) But, my mother says that ants are rude
They carry off our picnic food
They steal our chips, our bread crumbs too
It's good if I squish a crook like you
   (Ant:) Hey, I'm no crook, kid — read my lips
   Sometimes ants need crumbs & chips
   One single chip feeds our whole town
   You must not let your foot come down
(Kid:) But, all my friends squish ants each day
Squishing ants is a game we play
They're looking at me, they're listening too
They all say I should squish you
   (Ant:) I can see you're big & strong
   Decide for yourself what's right & wrong
   If you were me & I were you
   What would you want me to do?
Should the ant get squished? Should the ant go free?
It's up to the kid not up to me
We'll leave that kid with the raised up shoe
What do you think that kid should do?

   — w & m: Phillip Hoose & Hannah Hoose

I Am a Dolphin

I am a dolphin, rollin' in the sea
My passion is to live & to live I must be free
I am traveling, rollin' in the sea
I am bound for home in the bay of Waikiki

D - - G / - D A D : D - - - G / - D A D

**Will I ever make it home home home? Jumpin' in the foam
Swimmin' in the blue briny ocean**

I swam with the tuna, rollin' in the sea
When they came for the tuna, they also came for me
They cast their nets o'er the side, rollin' in the sea
They missed me by a yard, but they caught my family

I saw a mighty tanker, rollin' in the sea
That ship had sprung a leak that was spreading rapidly
I swam around the oil slick, rollin' in the sea
I swam the other way just as fast as I could flee

I smelled a stinking garbage barge, rollin' in the sea
It carried all the poisons for a poisonous industry
The poison & the garbage were rollin' in the sea
They dumped it o'er the side where it almost strangled me

I saw a brutal whaling ship, rollin' in the sea
They'd shot another whale who was dying helplessly
In rage, I breached above the waves, rollin' in the sea
I dove beneath the waves just before they shot at me

At last I saw my friendly bay, rollin' in the sea
My spirits were restored, but it still occurred to me
That I am a dolphin, rollin' in the sea
My passion is to live & to live I must be free

(last cho) <u>How did</u> **I ever make it home, home...?**

   — w & m: Jay Mankita

In My Bones

There once was a time when people were gentle
We talked to the trees & were never alone
And all that we owned were our baskets & digging sticks
I still remember it in my bones

[D A - - / D A D A / D - G A / A D Bm -]

And sometimes we quarreled & then we forgot it
For all to keep living we needed each one
And all that we owned was the skill in our fingers / **I still...**

We never had locks, so our lives were not hidden
Our tears & our laughter were shared all around
And all that we owned were our dreams & our stories / **I...**

   — w & m: Nancy Schimmel

It Really Isn't Garbage Till You Throw It Away

It really isn't garbage til you mix it all together
It really isn't garbage til you throw it away
Just separate your paper, plastic, compost, glass & metal
And then you get to use it all another day

A - D7 - / A - E7 - / 1st / A - E A

There's garbage in the kitchen, garbage in the basement
Garbage in the bathroom, yes, & in the backyard too
Sometimes it seems to me that we're burying our future
That stinking pile of trash gives me the garbage blues, but

Don't put it in a landfill, it gets in your drinking water
It hurts the fish & beaches if you dump it in the sea
Reduce, reuse, recycle's the solution to pollution
Don't count on someone else, it's up to you & me, because

Now there are some folks who say we really ought to burn it
It's so convenient, makes new jobs & electricity
But if you're gonna burn it, then you know you're gonna
   breathe it
And what to do with what is left, there's no guarantee, but

Now all of this can only work if everybody does it
So always pay attention when you go to the store
Encourage businesses that try their hardest to recycle
Don't buy it unless it's been something somewhere before

— w & m: Dan Einbender

Just One Earth

I am Fukushima, I gave so you could see
I gave my land, my people & my houses by the sea
I gave my farms, my cattle, my flowers & my ferns
I gave it all so everyone could learn

(↑2) C - G - / - - C - / - - F - / Dm - G -

It's just one earth, just one sea
Just one sky, over you & me
Just one chance, the world around
Shut them down, shut them down, shut them down (2x)

C - G / F G C - / Am - F Dm / C G Am F / C G C -

I am 3 Mile Island, I'm wounded & I'm sore
You can hear me calling by the Susquehanna shore
My song sends out a warning, to stir the deaf & dumb
I tell of all the danger yet to come

I am Chernobyl, my song is not my own
I'm a million missing voices from the great exclusion zone
Our melody is drifting, 'cross the flat lands of Ukraine
That may seem far away, but just the same...

— w & m: David Bernz

Lambeth Children

50 children sitting in the trees
50 children swingin in the breeze
Up in the branches & off their knees
Hooray for the Lambeth children-o (2x)

C - G - / / Am C Dm - / G - C - / G - - C - - -

11 fine maples growing in a row
The road to be widened doomed them to go
But 50 kids of Lambeth cried "No, no!" / **Hooray...**

The men with the chainsaws all stood around
'Cos the kids were in the trees & they wouldn't come down
So the lumberjacks packed up & went back to town...

Roads we've enough & roads everywhere
Roads for the cars we can very well spare
But long live the maple trees, green or bare...

Lambeth town in Ontario
That's where the maple trees stand in a row
That's where the loveliest children grow...

— w & m: Malvina Reynolds

Letter to Eve

Oh Eve, where is Adam, now you're kicked out of the
   garden? **(2x)**
Been wandering from shore to shore, now you find there's
   no more / **Oh, pacem in terris, mir, shanti, salaam, hey wa**

(↑5) Am - - - / - - - E / Am - Dm F7 / Am - Am E Am

Don't you wish love, love alone, could save this world
   from disaster? **(2x)**
If only love could end the confusion or is it just one more
   illusion? / **Oh, pacem…**

If you want to have great love, you got to have great anger **(2x)**
When I see innocent folk shot down, should I just shake my
   head & frown? / **Oh, pacem...**

If you want to hit the target square, you better not have
   blind anger **(2x)**
Or else it'll be just one more time, the correction creates
   another crime / **Oh, pacem...**

Oh Eve, you tell Adam, next time he asks you **(2x)**
He'll say, "Baby it's cold outside, what's the password to
   come inside?" You say / **"Oh pacem...**

Oh Eve, go tell Adam, we got build a new garden **(2x)**
We got to get workin' on the bldg of a decent home for all o'
   God's children / **Oh, pacem...**

If music could only bring peace, I'd only be a musician **(2x)**
If songs could more than dull the pain, if melodies could
   break these chains / **Oh, pacem...**

Oh pacem... (2x) / 4,000 languages in this world means the
   same thing to every boy & girl / **Oh, pacem...**

— w & m: Pete Seeger

LIVE LIKE A PRAYER

Born in the Rockies_of high mountain streams
Runnin' down the valleys,_the ocean in its dreams
Great Blue Heron___graces the shore
The water rushing before _
Don't dam the river, **leave the** river **alone**
Don't dam the river, **for the** river **is a home**
Don't dam the river, **let the** river **survive**
The river, the river **is alive**

Am - - - / Dm - - Am / 1st / Em - Am - :‖

Feel the current rising toward the Great Divide
Blessed by the lightning & the green forests wide
Alpine meadows, the golden eagle flies
The mountains touching the sky
Don't mine the mtn, **leave the** mtn **alone**
Don't mine... **for the** mtn **is a home**
Don't... let the mtn **survive** / **The** mtn... **is alive**

The desert's waiting, red rock canyon walls
Hot sun is beating & one coyote calls
Sagebrush fragrant in the stillness of the heat
Desert fires burning, burning a steady beat
Don't pave the desert, **leave the** desert **alone...**

Tall grasses waving miles across to sky
Broad fields remembering the buffalo hunter's cry
Song to season, circles by the stream
Sweetgrass burning, the breeze fresh & clean
Don't plow the prairie....

Feel our Mother hurting, know that scars are done
Breathe in your courage 'cos a struggle has begun
Live like a prayer now, in praise of one
We are, we are all alive _

Live like a prayer now, deep in your heart
Live like… for we are all a part
Live… if we want to survive / We are, we are all alive

— w & m: Elena Holly Klaver

© 1991 Dawn Wind Music (BMI). On her *Live Like a Prayer* & Magpie *Seed on the Prairie*. In *SO!* 33:2. These lyrics have been slightly adap. by Magpie and Kim & Reggie Harris.

LIVING PLANET

If all the world were peaceful now & forever more
Peaceful at the surface & peaceful at the core
All the joy within my heart would be so free to soar
And we're living on a living planet, circling a living star
I don't know where we're going, but I know we're going far
We can change the universe by being who we are
And we're living... star

Am - - - ‖: Am - - E - / Am - - - / - - AmEm Am :‖

If all the world knew justice now & forever more
Justice at the surface & justice at the core...

If all the world knew freedom now...

If Mother Earth were honored now &… / Honored at the…
I don't know where…but I know we've gone too far
We can heal this planet by changing the way we are
Time to heal this living planet

— w & m: Jay Mankita

© 1988 Jay Mankita. On on his *Jay Mankita & Sing Down Trouble*, Magpie *Living Planet & Spoken in Love* (w/ Kim & Reggie Harris), Emma's Revolution *Roots, Rock & Revolution*. In *SO!* 35:2, *For the Beauty of the Earth*. New v. is by Magpie. *LS.

LOCALLY GROWN

If I were an apple I'd be very unhapple
Traveling 4,000 miles or more
From far off Tasmania in a shipping contain-ia
To a shelf in a New Jersey store
   Why should I be tortured when some New Jersey orchard
   Would be totally thrilled to the core
   To pick me & crate me & load me & freight me
   Not 4,000 miles, but 4!
An apple should be not far from the tree
Where it ripens in the fall
Locally grown & locally eaten
Is globally good, good, good for us all

C - F - / C A7 Dm G / C - F - / C G C -
‖: F - C - /   "   /   "   /   :‖

If I were a berry I expect I'd be very
Contrary & hardly inclined
To get shipped out from Chile to a store in North Philly
Hey I'd have to be out of my mind
   It seems paradoxic & carbon dioxic
   That we force all our food to commute
   Wasting gallons of fuel which we know isn't cool
   For people or planets or fruit
A berry is fine not far from its vine
Near the farmer's market stall
Locally grown...

So when you're walking the aisle past a beautiful pile
Of the fruit you might want to take home
Do not buy for your table til you check out the label
And determine how far it did roam
   Aside from the karma of helping the farma
   Who lives in your county or state
   There is one more good reason to buy what's in season
   The taste is incredibly great!
So keep buying foods from your regional dudes
Keep your carbon footprint small
Locally grow...

— w & m: John Forster & Tom Chapin

© 2011 Limousine Music Co. (ASCAP) & the Last Music Co. (ASCAP). On his *Give Peas a Chance*.

LOW TO THE GROUND

We stand on the edge of a cliff in the deepest night I've ever seen
People looking for light, people who cherish a dream
But the light's shining out from our eyes & the dream's
   resting deep in our souls
If it's magic we're needing to keep us from falling, it's magic we've
   already know

(↑3) G Em Am7 D (4x)

It's music that keeps us alive, it's dancing that sets our
   hearts free
It's children remember the laughter in life, it's animals
   teach us to see
Stay low to the ground, live close to the earth
Don't stray very far from your soul, it's simple things show
   us the reason we're here
And it's simple things keeping us whole

G Em Am7 D (4x) AmD G -

Tell me the place you were born, the lives your ancestors led
The ground that surrounded the people you love, the streams
   from which you were fed
It's the wind that carries the seed & the seed that carries the song
The food that we're eating is rooted in soil & it's soil that is keeping
   us strong

The temples are falling around us, we stand strong & fierce
   where they've been
I never have seen a holier sight than a person who sings in the wind
Our blood is the river of life, our joy is the sun on the land
All of the love that is inside this heart is more than one person
   can stand

— w & m: Libby Roderick

MAHOGANY TREE

When you see, when you see the mahogany tree
Oh tell me what do you see?
When you see... tree / In the rainforest of Mexico

C - - F / G - - - / 1st / G - C -

"I see" said the farmer "my calendar tree
Mahogany flowers speak to me
When the blossoms fall & the petals are torn
I know that it's time to plant the corn"

C - F G / - - C - :‖

"I see" said the great bird "my butterfly tree
The food in her branches speaks to me
I will feast on the moths that hide at the top
While the monkeys howl & the raindrops drop"

"I see" said "the logger, a money tree
The promise of lumber speaks to me
This could bring a big price at the company town
Move the bulldozers in & we'll cut it right down!"

"I see" said the banker "a furniture tree
The shine of the wood speaks to me
On the 44th floor this will make a fine desk
Move the bulldozers in & I'll see to the rest"

"Stop!" said the child "it's my grandmother tree
I've always known she can speak to me
She lives in the Mayan memory
As a tree of life for my family

Come around, come around the mahogany tree
To cut her down you'll have to pass by me
I stand in a circle with my family
Protect the rainforest of Mexico"

— w & m: Sarah Pirtle

MAKE IT, MEND IT

Growing up in hard times on the wrong side of the tracks
Means you're often taking short cuts & you're always looking back
But tho' you're running barefoot chasing dreams down
   dead end streets
You remember what your Momma said about the way to
   make ends meet

Ya gotta make it, mend it, wear it out, make it do or do
   without (2x)

G - - - / C G F G / F - G - / F G D G ‖ F - G - / /

Now when my old man learned his trade they made things that
   would last
They would temper future vision with a knowledge of the past
If smth broke or wore out, well you know they'd feel no shame
For they took pride in using skills to make it good again

Now the watchword is disposable & plastics rule the day
And if something now gets broken, you can only throw it away
But when the wells all dry up & the mines are all worked out
Well you'll see this house start falling, hear the poor &
   hungry shout

Now politicians tell you they're both green & left or right
They can see the problem clearly, they can understand our plight
But if greed's the only motive, a chance for all to fill their purse
How can things *[you know things can't]* expand forever, you
   know that bubble's got to burst!

— w & m: Lester Simpson

MY DIRTY STREAM (Hudson River Song)

Sailing up my dirty stream
Still I love it & I'll keep the dream
That some day, tho' maybe not this year
My Hudson River will once again run clear

D - - - / Em - D - / 1st / Em A D -

    She starts high in the mountains of the north
    Crystal clear & icy trickles forth
    With just a few floating wrappers of chewing gum
    Dropped by some hikers to warn of things to come

    D - - - / Em - A - / 1st / Em A D -

At Glens Falls 5000 honest hands
Work at the Consolidated Paper Plant
5 million gallons of waste a day
Why should we do it any other way?

    Down the valley one million toilet chains
    Find my Hudson so convenient place to drain
    And each little city says "Who, me?
    Do you think that sewage plants come free?"

Out in the ocean they say the water's clear
But I live right at Beacon here
Halfway betw the mountains & sea
Tacking to & fro, this thought returns to me:

    (reprise v 1) Sailing up my dirty… / Still I… / That someday…
    My Hudson River & my country will run clear

    — w & m: Pete Seeger (1961)

MY GRANDDAUGHTER'S WEDDING DAY

This is the country where I was born
And this is where I will remain
And I'll raise my children in the gathering storm
As the wheat fields ripple in the acid rain

(in 3/4 ↑3) G - - - / - - C - / - - D G / Am - D -

They called my mother crazy
For wanting to raise her kids in a place
Where birds can still fish from the rivers
Where something still remains
That can teach us how to distinguish ourselves
From all these machines that we've made

G - C - / Am - D - / Em - - - / D - - - /
Em D G C / Am - D -

And I know they'll call me crazy
They say we have nothing to fear
But what is this world gonna look like / In another 50 yrs?

G D Em C / / Am - F - / Em - D -

And I want to live a long life / & when my hair is grey
To be able to gather wildflowers
On my granddaughter's wedding day

G - C - / / / D C G -

(as v. 1) They call my mom an environmentalist
And they say it like it's a disease
Because they believe the American dream
Is that everyone ought to be free

G - - - / - - C - / - - D G / Am - D -

To destroy whatever they want to destroy
But why is it crazy to say
I just want to be able to breathe the air / On my…?

G - C - / / / D C G -

On… (2x) / I just want to be able to breathe the air / On…

C - F - / Em - D - / G - C - / D - G -

(as v. 1) This is the country where I was born
Genetically modified waves of grain
And I'll pay my taxes for nuclear missiles
As shopping malls blossom like weeds in the rain

G - - - / - - C - / - - D G / Am - D -

They'll say not to worry / Nature can always adapt
But why are we in such a hurry
To tear down the beauty and build all this crap?

G D Em C / / Am - F - / Em - D -

And I know that it's easy to forget in this country
But wouldn't you trade it all away
For the promise of gathering wildflowers / On **your**…?
And I want to live a long life / And when my hair is grey
To be able to gather wildflowers / On my…

‖: G - C - / / / D C G - :‖

    — w & m: Polly Fiveash

MY ROOTS GO DOWN

My roots go down, down to the earth (3x)
My roots go down! (1st verse & cho)

I: D - / G D / - D A / D -

I am a wildflower reaching for the sun (3x) / **My roots…**
I am a pine tree on a mountainside…
I am an ancient redwood tree…
I am a willow swaying in the storm…
I am a mtn strong & still…
I am a waterfall skipping home…
I am the river running to the sea…
I rise w/ the voice of every living thing…

II: (↑2) C - / F C / C F G / C - //
CF C / F C / Am F G / C -

    — w & m: Sarah Pirtle

ONE DRUM

Life unfolds around me
I can choose which path I take
_Will it be darkness again?
Or a brilliant life I make?

G D Em C (4x)

_We are standing on the shoulders of giants
We are standing in the shelter of ancients
We are speaking the truth of the people_

G C Em / C G / C Em C

We are marching to the beat
Of one drum, _one drum_

G C Em C / /

Wey hey ah-hey, wey hey ah-ey
Wey hey ah-hey, ah _ (repeat)

G C Em C (4x)

__Come here in many forms_
Embrace the sounds you make
We'll speak here in many tongues
_Join the circle with your mask down, you will see
The plans you make
We are standing…

(bridge) _Time & circumstance_
Will bring me down,_bring me down_
But there's a time for recompense & a time
To break_new ground,_new / ground! **We are…**

Am - C - / G - D - :‖

— w & m: Leela Gilday

© 2006 Leela Gilday. On her *Sedzé* which won the 2007 Juno Award for aboriginal rec of the yr. Album title means "my heart" in North Slavey language. Gilday was raised in Yellowknife in Canada's Northwest Territories.

PANNING FOR GOLD

I saw God by the river panning for gold
I saw God by the river weary & old
**He said "Son, I used to know where I put things,
   I used to know"**

(↑2) **G↓ Em G DC / G C G D // EmC G CD G**

I saw God in the forest teaching Tai Chi
To the trees in the wind & bowing to the seas

I saw God on the mountain tearing at the sky
I saw God on the mountain with tears in his eyes

(as cho) "I could have shown you all the beauty in the world
But now I need you to show me"

— w & m: Ben Sollee

© 2008 Pubblast Songs (BMI) and Lawrence Graefenburg Music (BMI). On his album *Learning to Bend.*

PRAISE BOGS (Ecology Doxology)

Praise bogs from whom all waters flow
Praise bugs above & frogs below
Praise lily pads & all, by luck
Who bloom *[thrive]* while rooted in the muck

**DDAGD DAD-- / DDDABm GDA--
DADAD GABm-- / DDDAG DAD--**

— w: Paul Tinkerhess, m: trad hymn ("Old Hundredth" 16th c.)

© 2000 Paul Tinkerhess.

ROCKIN' IN A WEARY LAND

Sing me an old song, mother & child
She rocks the babe safe in her arms thru the hard & hungry night
Earth is the mother, we are her young
Each day she rocks us dancing
From darkness into light (x2)

(in G) C - G - / DC DG GF D / 1st / DC DG / G C D G

**We're rockin' in a weary land, rockin' in a weary land
May love guide each & every hand
Rockin' in a weary land (x2)**

G - - C / EmC DG / G C D G

We've been shortsighted, done so much harm
The land stripped bare, the poisoned air. Some cry progress,
   some cry in pain
Wild geese are flying, springtime returns
The breeze blows without anger / The sun shines without blame…

A crack in the pavement, a wildflower breaks free
Lifts golden blossoms to the sun, roots run deep in mother earth
May we learn to treasure every gift we receive
The changing dance of each new day / The miracle of birth…

— w & m: Lorraine Lee Hammond

© 1987 Lorraine Lee Hammond/Snowy Egret Music (BMI). On her *Beloved Awake* & Priscilla Herdman *Darkness into Night.*

SING FOR THE CLIMATE (Do It Now)

We need to wake up, we need to wise up
We need to open our eyes & do it now now now
We need to build a better future
And we need to start right now

Em - / - B7 / Am Em / B7 Em

We're on a planet that has a problem
We've got to solve it, get involved & do it now now now
We need…

Make it greener, make it cleaner
Make it last, make it fast & do it now now now / We…

No point in waiting or hesitating
We must get wise, take no more lies & do it now now now /…

— w: Nic Balthazar & Stef Kamil Carlens, m: trad. (Italian "Bella Ciao") arr: Stef Kamil Carlens

© 2012 Belgian Climate Coalition. Sing for the Climate took place in Belgium in Sept 2012. 80,000 Belgians sang "Do It Now" in 180 town squares. YT video is Dm (11). "Bella Ciao" is a women's activist song, in *RUS.*

SOLARTOPIA

Was there an Adam, was there an Eve?
Or did we evolve from what we conceived?
Either way we got what we needed
When the sun shone down on a Garden of Eden

(in Am) C Dm / Am E / 1st / C E

Doncha know we're gonna have a Solartopia
Solartopia, Solartopia
Doncha know we're gonna have a Solartopia
All over God's green world

Am - / D Am / - - / DEm Am

Well we bit that apple & the Garden was lost
So we had to work, to pay the cost
And so we went digging, into the ground
And started to burn many things we found, but...
    We multiplied, we needed more
    The rich got rich, the poor got sore
    The fuel ran scarce, the price jumped high
    And so we gave nuclear power a try, but
But the nuclear plants were built in haste
With too many risks & no place for waste
And so from Seabrook to Shoreham town
We have to shut those nuke plants down, but
    Now we're fighting wars over oil & gas
    No matter who wins, it will not last
    The earth is scarred, the planet is warming
    Don't you think that all of it's a great big warning
We'll learn to power houses & cars
With the light that's made up in stars
It's a gift to share that's always been given
It falls down to Earth like rain from Heaven

    — w & m: Pete Seeger, Harvey Wasserman & David Bernz

SULPHUR PASSAGE

Come you bold men of Clayoquot
Come you bold women
There is a fire burning on the mountain
The sting of smoke blowin' in the wind

D - - C / D - C G / D - - - / - - A D

Hear the blast of the whistle
Hear the snarl of the chain
Hear the cracking in the heartwood
Hear it again & again & again

D - - C / D - C G / D - - - / - - G A D

No pasaran! Megin River
No pasaran! Clayoquot River
No pasaran! Sulphur Passage

D - A - G - A - (3x) **(D - - -)**

There is a valley torn asunder, there is a mtn stripped to bone
Grove of spruce, stand of cedar, the ancient garden sacked & burned
Come you bold men of Clayoquot, come you bold women
There is a cry deep within the forest, hear the whisper in the wind
Hear the breath in the cedars, the sighing in the salal
The beating deep within the forest, the grouse, the thrush,
    the Great Horned Owl
We'll stand with these cedars, stand with these balsam groves
Stand with the heron, the cougar, the otter, like the tree by the
    water, we shall not move

    — w & m: Bob Bossin

THERE GOES THE MOUNTAIN

There goes the mountain, father of fir trees
Home for the grizzlies under its snow
Shorn of its timber, torn by the monsters
Taken by truckloads to the great plains below

(in 3/4) FAm Am FAm Am / G - Am - :|

And there goes the mountain, the avalanche maker
Heaven's caretaker, breeder of streams
There goes the mountain, maker of thunder
Torn down for the plunder, remembered in dreams

F - Am - / D - Am - / 1st / D F Am -

There goes the mountain, greeter of sunrise
Giant by starlight the highest & best
The roar of the engines, the first in its lifetime
Will take what man values & spit out the rest

Lord of the highlands, home for the eagle
Catcher of snowfalls for millions of yrs
Bleeding in mudslides robbed of its insides
Prey to the skills of the bold engineer

    — w & m: Tom Paxton

THERE'LL COME A DAY

There'll come a day when our rivers will run again
    pure on their way
There'll come a time when we'll cherish the life
    in our oceans & bays

(in 3/4) C F C F / /

Let the light (echo) **shine out upon the land,**
    let the love (echo) **flow out of everyone**
And the way (echo) **will break upon the darkness of the**
    storm / There'll come a day! (There'll...) **(x2)**

Em Am Em Am / Em DmF G - / C F C F

...day when the wheels of war will evermore stand & decay
...time when the hunger in the youngest eyes will no longer stay

...day when the strong will no longer make the weaker ones pay
...time when the homeless will have a safe warm place to stay

...**day** *when all the armies will lay down their guns*
And on that day we'll know that the war has finally been won

I'll bet you didn't know when you came here tonight
  that you could all sing so well
Well the world doesn't know, it's within our hands
  to make this globe a heaven or hell

...**day** *when justice & truth will rule all we will say*
...**time** *when everywhere, everyone will stand up & say:*

— w & m: Robert Killian

© 1979 Wingsongwon Music. On *Fast Folk* 1:2, Pete Seeger *Tomorrow's Children* (12). In *For the Beauty of the Earth* & *SO!* 29:4. v.4 Paul Kaplan, v.5 Pete Seeger.

THIS PRETTY PLANET

1. This pretty planet spinning thru space
  You're a garden, you're a harbor, you're a holy place
2. Golden sun going down, gentle blue giant spin us around
3. All thru the night safe til the morning light

D Em A GD

— w & m: John Forster & Tom Chapin

© 1988 Limousine Music Co. (ASCAP) & the Last Music Co. (ASCAP). On Chapin's *This Pretty Planet* & *Rounds Galore & More V2*. In *Rounds Galore* & *Children for a Friendly Planet*.

TWO HANDS HOLD THE EARTH

My head is in the sky, sky, sky
My feet are on the ground, ground, ground
And what about my blood? It's from the sea
And what about my bones? Like the mtns be
And my hands, oh my hands
I believe with my hands I could hold this land
My two hands hold the earth **(2x)**

[C - / / C G C / / C F C **(4x)**] (a capella)

— w & m: Sarah Pirtle

© 1980, 1988 Discovery Center Music (BMI). On her *Two Hands Hold the Earth*. In her *Linking Up*. *LS.

WATER

Water, water everywhere & not a drop to spare
Water in the ground, water in the air
Tho it may evaporate it never goes away
It snows on top the mountain, melts & flows into the bay

D - **(4x)**

Animals need water, people need it too
Keep it clean for me & I'll keep it clean for you (repeat)

‖: A G / D - :‖

Now you can take a shower in it, you can wash your hair
You can wash your clothes or wash your teddy bear
Really clean water is gettin' pretty rare
If we want to save it, people have to care!

Now water is rain, water's a flood
Water turns dirt into mud
Sometimes water's blue, sometimes water's green
Sometimes water's dirty & sometimes water's clean

Now they say the ocean's filling up with stuff like DDT
It shows up in the fish & then in you & me
If we drink too much of it we'll wind up in bed
If we drink enough of it we might wind up dead!

— w & m: Bob Reid

© 1985 Bob Reid. On his *...w/ Abracadab* & Magpie *Circle of Life* (as "Animals Need Water"), Two of a Kind *Friends*.

WE BELONG TO THE EARTH

We belong to the earth
We all belong to the earth
It's not that she belongs to us
It's we belong to her (2x)   (↑2)

G - Em - / C - - - / G D Em C / G - Em C / G D G -

A strand in a web are we
A strand in a web I believe
To own it we cannot dare to dream
It's a web that we didn't weave **(2x)**

In sun & in wind & in rain
Is a seed of what will be
It awakens a power that grows down below
It courses thru you & thru me **(2x)**

And when our spirits take flight
And we lay our bodies down
Our ashes may be carried away on the wind
But return to the birthing ground **(2x)**

— w & m: Greg Artzner & Terry Leonino ("Magpie")

© 1994 Greg Artzner & Terry Leonino. On their *Seed on the Prairie* & *Spoken in Love* (w/ Kim & Reggie Harris). In *SO!* 39:4. *LS.

WHERE DO THE CHILDREN PLAY

Well I think it's fine, _ building jumbo planes _
Or taking a ride _ on a cosmic train _
Switch on summer from a slot machine, yes
Get what you want to if you want, 'cos you can get anything

D G D G (4x)

I know we've come a long way, we're changing day to day
_But tell me, where do the children play?

Em A Em A / Em A D (G D G)

Well you roll on roads over fresh green grass
For your lorry loads pumping petrol gas
And you make them long & you make them tough
But they just go on & on & it seems that you can't get off

D G D G / / / C G C G

Well you've cracked the sky, scrapers fill the air, but
Will you keep on bldg higher til there's no more room up there?
Will you make us laugh, will you make us cry?
Will you tell us when to live, will you tell us when to die?

D G D G / / C G C G / /

— w & m: Cat Stevens

The **Earthcare** chapter contains songs on care for the environment. See also: **Hope, Outdoors.** Other songs on this subject include: **Faith:** Swimming to the Other Side, **Family:** Bless This House, **Funny:** Why Am I Painting the Living Room?, **Gospel:** Let the Sun Shine Down on Me, **Home:** River that Flows Both Ways, **Play:** I Had an Old Coat, **Struggle:** God's Counting on Me, **Travelin':** Bicycle Song.

Faith

AMAZED

May I stay amazed for all of my days
And all of the ways of the world's turning
Amazed at what I've got, not what I've not
All soon forgot in the world's turning

A - D A / D A - B7 E / A D - A / D A E E A

— w & m: Linda Hirschhorn

BREATHING IN, BREATHING OUT

Breathing in, breathing out (x2)
I am blooming as a flower, I am fresh as the dew
I am solid as a mountain, I am firm as the earth
I am free

C - - - / Dm G - C / Em Am Dm G / C - - -

Breathing in, breathing out (x2)
I am water, reflecting what is real, what is true
And I feel there is space, deep inside of me
I am free (x3)

— w: Thích Nhất Hạnh, m: Betsy Rose

EARLY IN THE MORNING

Well early in the morning, about the break of day
I ask the Lord, "Help me find the way!"
Help me find the way to the promised land
This lonely body needs a helping hand
I ask the Lord to help me please / Find the way   (↑5)

GC G x2/ Bm - Am D / GC x3 G /
Em - A / G Em Am D / " /

When the new day is a-dawning, I bow my head in prayer.
I pray to the Lord, "Won't you lead me there?"
Won't you guide me safely to the Golden Stair?
Won't you let this body your burden share?
I pray to the Lord, "Won't you lead me please / Lead me there?"

When the judgment comes to find the world in shame
When the trumpet blows won't you call my name?
When the thunder rolls and the heavens rain
When the sun turns black, never shine again
When the trumpet blows, won't you call me please
Call my name!

— w & m: Paul Stookey

Esa Einai (Psalm 121)

Esa einai el heharim / Me'ayin me'ayin yavo ezri (**repeat**)
Ezri me'im Hashem / Oseh shamayim va'aretz (**repeat**)   (↑3)

Am DmAm (2x) / Dm G E Am / Am Dm G Am / F G Em Am

I will lift up my eyes unto the mountains
From whence (x2) will my help come?
My help cometh from the Lord / Who created heaven & the earth

— w & m: Shlomo Carlebach

© 1959 (renewed) Rabbi Shlomo Carlebach (BMI). Used by permission of the Estate of Rabbi Shlomo Carlebach.

The Gift of Love

Tho' I may speak with bravest fire / And have the gift to all inspire
And have not love, my words are vain
As sounding brass & hopeless gain

D G D - / Bm Em A - / D G Bm G / A - D -

Tho' I may give all I possess / And striving so my love profess
But not be giv'n by love within
The profit soon turns strangely thin

Come, Spirit, come, our hearts control
Our spirits long to be made whole
Let inward love guide every deed / By this we worship & are freed

— w & adap of English melody: Hal H. Hopson ("The Water is Wide")

© 1972 Hope Publishing Company, Carol Stream, Il 60188. From 1 Cor. 13:1-3.

Give Thanks to Allah

Give thanks to Allah for the moon & the stars
Praise him all day for what is & what was
Take hold of your iman, don't give in to Shaitan
O you who believe, please give thanks to Allah

G - - D / C G - D / 1st / C G D G :‖

Allahu Ghafur, Allahu Rahim
Allahu yuhibo el Mohsinin
Hua Khalikuna, Hua Razikuna
Wahuwa 'alaa Kulli shayin Qadeer

Allah is Ghafur, Allah is Rahim
Allah is the One who loves the Mohsinin
He is our Creator, he is our Sustainer
And he is the One who has power over all

— w & m: Zain Bhikha

© 1994 Zain Bhikha Studios, South Africa. iman=faith, ghafur=forgiving, rahim=merciful, yuhibo el mohsinin = loves those who help others.

Gotta Serve Somebody

You may be an ambassador to England or France
You may like to gamble, you might like to dance
You may be the heavyweight champion of the world
You may be a socialite with a long string of pearls

(↑2) A [Am] - (4x)

But you're gonna have to serve somebody, yes indeed
You're gonna have to serve somebody
Well, it may be the devil or it may be the Lord
But you're gonna have to serve somebody

D7 - / A [Am] - / E7 D7 / A [Am] -

You might be a rock 'n' roll addict prancing on the stage
You might have drugs at your command, women in a cage
You may be a businessman or some high degree thief
They may call you Doctor or they may call you Chief

You may be a state trooper, you might be a young Turk
You may be the head of some big TV network
You may be rich or poor, you may be blind or lame
You may be living in another country under another name

You may be a construction worker working on a home
You may be living in a mansion or you might live in a dome
You might own guns and you might even own tanks
You might be somebody's landlord, you might even own banks

You may be a preacher with your spiritual pride
You may be a city councilman taking bribes on the side
You may be workin' in a barbershop, you may know how to cut hair
You may be somebody's mistress, may be somebody's heir

Might like to wear cotton, might like to wear silk
Might like to drink whiskey, might like to drink milk
You might like to eat caviar, you might like to eat bread
You may be sleeping on the floor, sleeping in a king-sized bed

You may call me Terry, you may call me Timmy
You may call me Bobby, you may call me Zimmy
You may call me R.J., you may call me Ray
You may call me anything but no matter what you say

— w & m: Bob Dylan

© 1979 Special Rider Music. Reprinted by permission of Music Sales Corporation. On his *Slow Train*, Eric Burdon on *Chimes of Freedom* (S of Bob Dylan Honoring Amnesty Int'l) & recs by Etta James ꜰ, Mavis Staples ꜰ, Pop Staples Willie Nelson ꜰ.

Hashivenu

1. Hashivenu (x2) adonai elecha   2. Venashuva, venashuva
3. Chadesh (x2) yamenu k'kedem

AmDm AmDm AmE7 Am

— m: trad. (Israeli folk song)

Alleluia

1. Alleluia (x3)   2. Alleluia (x2)   3. Amen (x3)

— m: trad. (round)

Both arr © 2015 Hal Leonard Corporation. "Alleluia" is in *Rounds Galore*.

HEAL MY HEART

Jesus my brother, come heal my heart
There's a piece missing, I need help to find
'Cos my life's leaking out thru the hole left behind
Leaving me empty, helpless & blind
While I am empty, Lord fill me
While I am blind, teach me to see
And while I am helpless, come take my part
Jesus my brother / Heal my heart

C - Am - / Dm - F - / Am G F - / Dm - - G - - - C↓ /
F C Dm G / C↓ - - / F C G - / Am G F - Am G F -

There's a sea of emotion & I'm caught in a storm
Churning with feelings, tangled & torn
My love built a ship, it was swept off & lost
Now it lies broken, twisted & tossed
Oh I am an ocean, Lord, walk on the sea
Calm all the waves pounding in me
And as the sun rises, take me back to the start...

Jesus, my brother, come heal my heart
The bandages hide it, then fall apart
The covering's gone, the wound opens again
Illusions will tear before feelings can mend
Oh but breathe on me Jesus, the fresh air will heal it
Pain is my teacher, just let me feel it
And make of my pieces a work of your art...

— w & m: Linda Worster

HERE I AM, LORD

I, the Lord of sea & sky, I have heard my people cry
All who dwell in dark & sin, my hand will save
I who made the stars of night, I will make their darkness bright
Who will bear my light to them, whom shall I send?

G CG G GD / GEm C Am D :‖

Here I am, Lord, is it I, Lord?
I have heard you calling in the night
I will go, Lord, if you lead me
I will hold your people in my heart

G - GC G / - C Am D / 1st / GEm AmD G(C G)

I, the Lord of snow & rain, I have borne my people's pain
I have wept for love of them, they turn away
I will break their hearts of stone, give them hearts for love alone
I will speak my word to them, whom...

I, the Lord of wind & flame, I will tend the poor & lame
I will set a feast for them, my hand will save
Finest bread I will provide til their hearts be satisfied
I will give my life to them, whom...

— Text based on Isaiah 6, m: Daniel L. Schutte

HOLY NOW

When I was a boy, each week_on Sun. we would go to church_
And pay attention to the priest_& he would read the holy word
And consecrate the holy bread_& everyone would kneel & bow_
Today the only difference is_everything is holy now_
Everything, everything, everything is holy now _

D - A - / G - D - :‖ Bm A G (GA D -)

When I was in Sun. school, we would learn about the time
Moses split the sea in two, Jesus made the water wine
And I remember feeling sad that miracles don't happen still
Now I can't keep track, 'cos everything's a miracle
Everything (2x), everything's a miracle
    Wine from water is not so small
    But an even better magic trick is that anything is here at all
    So the challenging thing becomes
    Not to look for miracles, but finding where there isn't one

    A D G - / Em C D - / 1st / Em C A -

When holy water was rare at best, it barely wet my fingertips
But now I have to hold my breath like I'm swimming in a sea of it
It used to be a world half there, heaven's 2nd-rate hand-me-down
But I walk it with a reverent air 'cos everything is holy now

D - A - / G - D - :‖

    Read a questioning child's face
    And say it's not a testament, that'd be very hard to say
    See another new morning come
    And say it's not a sacrament, I tell you that it can't be done

This morning outside I stood & saw a little red-winged bird
Shining like a burning bush, singing like a scripture verse
It made me want to bow my head, I remember when church let out
How things have changed since then, everything is holy now
It used to be a world half there, heaven's 2nd-rate hand-me-down
But I walk it with a reverent air 'cos everything is holy now

D - A - / G - D - :‖ (3x)

— w & m: Peter Mayer

HOLY SPIRIT COME

_Holy Spirit come, _Living Christ now come
_Inward Teacher be my guide _ (repeat)

Em - Am7 - / Bm7 - Em - :‖

_Let me walk by faith not sight _
Turned from darkness toward the Light
Seeking always to be faithful to my God
In your presence I will stay / **In your presence every day**

C D Em - (5x)

To this world I'll reach my hand
It is there I'll take your stand
I will listen to the drumbeat in my soul / **In your...**

— w & m: Aaron Fowler

HOW GREAT THOU ART

O Lord my God, when I in awesome wonder
Consider all the worlds thy hands have made
I see the stars, I hear the rolling thunder
Thy pow'r throughout the universe displayed
Then sings my soul, my saviour God, to thee
How great thou art, how great thou art (repeat)

G - C - / G D G - :‖: G C G - / D - G - :‖

When thru the woods & forest glades I wander
And hear the birds sing sweetly in the trees
When I look down, from lofty mtn grandeur
And hear the brook & feel the gentle breeze

And when I think, that God, his son not sparing
Sent him to die, I scarce can take it in
That on the cross, my burden gladly bearing
He bled & died to take away my sin

When Christ shall come, with shout of acclamation
And take me home, what joy shall fill my heart
Then I shall bow, in humble adoration
And there proclaim "My God, how great thou art!"

— w: Stuart K. Hine

I BELIEVE

I believe there are some debts that we never can repay_
I believe there are some words that we never can unsay_
I don't know a single soul who didn't get lost along the way

C F C F / / F C G C (F - G -)

I believe in socks & gloves knit out of soft grey wool_, and that
There's a place in heaven for those who teach in public schools
And I know I get some things right, but mostly I'm a fool

_I believe in a good strong cup of _ginger tea
And that_all these shoots & roots will become a tree
All I know, is I can't help but see all of this as
So very holy _ _

Am F C G / / / F - G -

I believe in jars of jelly put up by careful hands
I believe most folks are doing just about the best they can
And I know there are some things that I will never understand

(as cho) _I believe there's healing in the sound of your voice
And that_a summer tomato is a cause to rejoice
_And that following a song was never really a choice
Never really _ _ _

(bridge) I believe in a good long letter written on real paper &
   with real pen
I believe in the ones I love & know I'll never see again
I believe in the kindness of strangers & the comfort of old friends
And when I close my eyes to sleep at night, it's good to say_
"Amen"_ _ _

F C Dm C (4x)   F - G -

I believe that life's comprised of smiles & sniffles & tears_
And in an old coat that still has another good year_
And I know that I get scared sometimes but all I need is here

— w & m: Carrie Newcomer

I DON'T KNOW HOW TO LOVE HIM

I don't know how to love him
What to do, how to move him
I've been changed, yes really changed
In these past few days when I've seen myself
I seem like someone else

C F - C / F - C G / Em G C G / Em Am Em Am / F↓ G -

I don't know how to take this
I don't see why he moves me
He's a man, he's just a man
And I've had so many men before
In very many ways he's just one more

/ " / " / " / " / F↓ G F C -

(bridge) _Should I bring him down
Should I scream & shout, should I speak of love
Let my feelings out? I never thought I'd come to this
_What's it all about?

F - E7 - / Am - F - / C Bb F C / F C Dm - (G -)

Don't you think it's rather funny / I should be in this position?
I'm the one who's always been / So calm so cool, no lover's fool
Running every show, he scares me so

(2nd half bridge) I never thought... / What's it all about?

Yet if he said he loved me / I'd be lost, I'd be frightened
I couldn't cope, just couldn't cope / I'd turn my head, I'd back away
I wouldn't want to know, he scares me so
(tag) I want him so, I love him so

F C F C

— w: Tim Rice, m: Andrew Lloyd Webber

KYRIE

Ky-rie, ky-rie, eleison _ (3x)

Dm - A Dm

— w: trad. (Latin Mass), m: trad. (Surinam)

L'CHI LACH

L'chi lach, to a land that I will show you
Lech l'cha to a place you do not know
L'chi lach, on your journey I will bless you, and
You shall be a blessing **(x3)** l'chi lach

(↑2) C G F FG / C G F G / Em Am F FG / C FG (x3) C -

L'chi lach, & I shall make your name great
Lech l'cha & all shall praise your name
L'chi lach, to the place that I will show you
L'sim-chat cha-yim **(3x)** l'chi lach

— w & m: Debbie Friedman & Savina Teubal

© 1989 the Deborah Lynn Friedman Trust. On her *And You Shall Be A Blessing*. In her *Sing Unto God* & *The Jewish Fake Bk*.

LADY OF THE SEASON'S LAUGHTER

Lady of the season's laughter in the summer's warmth be near
When the winter follows after teach our spirits not to fear
Hold us in your steady mercy, Lady of the turning year **(in 3/4 ↑2)**

Dm7 - Am7 D7 / Fadd9 G7 Dm7 E / Dm7 G Dm7 C

Sister of the evening starlight in the falling shadows stay
Here among us til the far light of tomorrow's dawning ray
Hold us in your... turning day.

Mother of the generations in whose love all life is worth
Everlasting celebrations bring our labors safe to birth... earth

Goddess of all times' progression, stand with us when we engage
Hands & hearts to end oppression, writing history's fairer page
Hold... turning age

— w: Kendryl Gibbons, m: David Hurd ("Julion")

© 1990 Unitarian Universalist Association. In *Singing the Living Tradition* & *Worship in Song*. Hurd wrote Julion for "Ye Who Claim the Faith of Jesus." Also used as "Praise the Spirit in Creation."

LAUDATE OMNES GENTES

Laudate omnes gentes / Laudate Dominum **(repeat)**

(in 3/4) CCG GAmAm / Am G / 1st / DmDmG C

(Eng:) Sing praises, all you peoples / Sing praises to the Lord
(Span:) Alabe todo_el mundo / Alabe al Señor
(Portuguese:) Cantai todos os povos / Louvai nosso Senhor

— w: the Taizé Community, m: Jacques Berthier

© 1978 Les Presses de Taizé, Taizé Community, France. GIA publications, Inc., exclusive North American agent. www.giamusic.com. On YT 13.

LET THE MYSTERY BE

Everybody is wonderin' what & where they all came from
Everybody is worried 'bout where they're gonna go when the
    whole thing's done
But no one knows for certain & so it's all the same to me
I think I'll just let the mystery be

D G A D / / D G D G / D A D -

Some say once you're gone you're gone forever & some say you're
    gonna come back
Some say you rest in the arms of the Saviour if in sinful ways
    you lack
Some say that they're comin' back in a garden, bunch of carrots &
    little sweet peas
I think I'll just let the mystery be

Some say they're goin' to a place called "Glory" & I ain't saying it
    ain't a fact
But I've heard that I'm on the road to Purgatory & I don't like the
    sound of that
'Cos I believe in love & I live my life accordingly
But I choose to let the mystery be

— w & m: Iris DeMent

© 1992 Universal Music Corp. and Songs of Iris. On her *Infamous Angel* 13, Greg Brown *Freak Flag*, 10,000 Maniacs *Campfire Songs*. In *SO!* 38:3.

LIVE UP TO THE LIGHT

The first gleam of light, the cold light of morning
Held a promise of day with its noontide glories
It dawned on me as I mused on my state / In great sadness_
The words that came to my spirit
How true & how clearly they rang

(↑5) Am Em / Am DmE / C BbG / Am E / C F / C DmG

Live up to the Light, the Light that thou hast
Live up to the Truth & remember, my child
You are never alone, no never
Oh live up to the Light that thou hast
And more will be granted thee, will be granted thee
Oh live up to the Light thou hast

C↓ DmG / DmG C / FG C / CF C / G EmAm / FG C

I do not regret the troubles & doubts
Which I have journeyed thru
They keep teaching me patience & humble / Devotion_
Forget not in darkness what_in the light
Ye knew to be the Truth

Dear God, we pray, increase our faith
And keep us in your Love & Light
Faith is but a gift from thee / Oh hear our prayer_
O thou, who art closer than breath_to us
Hold us secure lest we fall

— w & m: Susan Stark

© 1977 (renewed) Susan Stark Music. On her *Child of the Nuclear Age* & *Canción de la Loba*. The lyrics are adap from a journal entry by Caroline Fox.

THE LORD IS MY LIGHT

The Lord is my light, my light & salvation
In him *[God]* I trust **(x2)**

Am D Am D / /

— w: the Taizé Community, m: Jacques Berthier.

© 1982 Les Presses de Taizé, Taizé Community, France. GIA publications, Inc., exclusive North American agent. www.giamusic.com. On & in *Songs & Prayers from Taizé*. On YT 15. Lyrics are adap from Psalm 27.

THE MASTER OF THE SHEEPFOLD

**Oh the master guards the sheepfold bin, he wants to know
    "Is my sheep brung in?"
And he's callin', he's callin', callin' softly, softly callin'
For them all to come gatherin' in**

CG C CEm DmG / C F Em Dm / CG C

Oh the master of the sheepfold who guards the sheepfold bin
Went out on the wind & the rain path where the long night's rain
    begins
And he said to his hireling shepherd "Is my sheep, is they all
    brung in?" **(2x)**
And the hireling shepherd answered "O there's some that's wan & thin
And some that's got all weathered & they won't come gatherin' in
They is lost & good for nothing, but the rest they is all brung in" **(2x)**

CG C x2 / F - C G / Am Em Am Dm / C F CG C :‖

And the master of the sheepfold who guards the sheepfold bin
Went out on the wind & the rain path where the long night's rain
    begins
And he let down the bars to the sheepfold, callin' soft "Come in,
    come in" **(2x)**
Then up from the gloom in the meadow thru the long night's
    rain & wind
Up thru the wind & the rain path where the long night's rain begins
Come the long lost sheep of the sheepfold, they all come
    a- gatherin' in **(2x)**
    — trad. (US)

© 2015 by Hal Leonard Corporation. In *Heart Throbs: in Prose & Verse* (Grosset & Dunlap, NY, 1906). On Art Thieme *On the Wilderness Road*, Hills & Mangsen *Never Grow Up* 17, Adam Miller *Buttercup Joe*.

MIRIAM HA-NEVIAH (Miriam the Prophet)

Miriam ha-neviah, oz v'zimra b'yadah
Miriam tirkod itanu l'hagdil zimrat olam
Miriam tirkod itanu l'taken et ha-olam
Bimherah v'yameynu hi tevi-eynu el
Mey ha-yeshua, el mey ha-yeshua

(in 3/4)   EmEmB7 Em EmEmD G /

Em Am EmB7B7 Em /   / D - B7 Em /   /

    — w & m: Leila Gal Berne (tune: "Eliyahu Ha-navi")

© 1987 Leila Gal Berner. Miriam was Moses' sister & is referred to in Exodus as a prophet. "Strength & song are in her hands. Miriam will dance with us to strengthen the world's song. She will dance with us to heal the world..."

NEARER, MY GOD, TO THEE

Nearer, my God to thee, nearer to thee
E'en tho' it be a cross that raiseth me
Still, all my song shall be nearer, my God to thee
Nearer, my God to thee, nearer to thee

D G D A / D G DA D / DG D DG BmA / D G DA D

Tho' like the wanderer the sun gone down
Darkness be over me, my rest a stone
Yet in my dreams I'd be **nearer...**
    There let the way appear, steps unto Heaven
    All that thou sendest me in mercy given!
    Angels to beckon me nearer...
Then with my waking thoughts bright with thy praise
Out of my stony griefs Bethel I'll raise
So by my woes to be **nearer...**
    Or if on joyful wing, cleaving the sky
    Sun, moon and stars forgot, upward I fly
    Still all my song shall be **nearer...**
    — w: Sarah F. Adams (1841), m: Lowell Mason ("Bethany" 1856)

Arr. © 2015 by Hal Leonard Corporation. Based On Genesis 28:10-22.

OH, LET THE LIGHT

Oh, let the Light_light up your way _
It will not lead, _lead you astray
In the midnight hour it's bright as day
Oh let the Light light up your way

C - - - / F - C - / 1st / C G C -

This Light of Love shines in the day
And it keeps shinin' when skies are grey
In the midnight hour it's bright as day! / **Oh let the...**

(bridge) I am an instrument of hope, I am a messenger of peace
I am a singer in the storm, I can give my best, at least that's what
I hope to be about, so my soul can sing & shout!
Let it out, let it out, we're flying free!

C - F C / - - D G / 1st / D G C -

Well you can try _ & keep Love out _
Insist that darkness is all about
When your resistance has had its day / **Oh let...**
    And when you think you're all alone
    Beamed down & left here all on your own
    I'm here to tell you that it ain't true
    Oh, let that Love Light_come light up you!
There are some bright lights_in the midst of strife
Angels along the path of life
They could be me & they could be you
So let that Love that come light up you!
    — w & m: Susan Stark

© 1995 Susan Stark Music. On her *Connected at the Heart*.

ON EAGLE'S WINGS

You who dwell in the shelter of the Lord
Who abide in his shadow for life
Say to the Lord "My refuge
My rock in whom I trust!"

(in D)   G - D - / / F - Dm - / F Gm Asus A

And he will raise you up on eagle's wings
Bear you on the breath of dawn
Make you to shine like the sun
And hold you in the palm of his hand

D - - - / Em - A - / D D7 G Em / Bm D Em A D - - -

The snare of the fowler will never capture you
And famine will bring you no fear
Under his wings your refuge
His faithfulness your shield

You need not fear the terror of the night
Nor the arrow that flies by day
Though thousands fall about you
Near you it shall not come

For to his angels he's given a command
To guard you in all of your ways
Upon their hands they will bear you up
Lest you dash your foot against a stone
    — w & m: Michael Joncas

© 1979 Jan Michael Joncas. Published by OCP, 5536 Ne Hassalo, Portland, OR 97213. Based on Psalm 91.

ONE LOVE

_One love!_one heart! / Let's get together & feel all right
(Hear the children cryin') one love! (hear...) one heart!
(Sayin') give thanks & praise to the Lord & I will feel all right
Let's get together & feel all right

G - D - / C G D G :‖ 2nd

_Let them all pass all their_dirty remarks
(One love!) There is one question I'd really love to ask:
(One heart!) Is there a place for the_hopeless sinner
Who has_hurt all mankind just to save his own beliefs?

G Em C G / / / G Em CD G

(What about a)_one love? (what about a) one heart? / Let's...
(As it was in the beginning) one love! (so shall it be in the end)
   one heart! / Let's...

_Let's get together to fight this Holy Armageddon
(One love!) So when the man comes there will be no, no doom
(One song!) Have pity on those whose chances grows thinner
There ain't no hiding place from the Father of Creation

One love! (what about the...) one heart (what...) / Let's...
(I'm pleadin' to mankind!) one love (Oh Lord!) (one heart)

— w & m: Bob Marley

OZI V'ZIMRAT YAH

Ozi v'Zimrat Yah / Vayahi li lishuah (repeat)

C CF C CF / C CG C C(F) :‖

— Words from Exodus 15:2 & Psalm 118:14, m: Rabbi Shefa Gold

PARTING FRIENDS

Farewell, my friends, I'm bound for Canaan
I'm trav'ling thru the wilderness
Your company has been delightful
You, who doth [do not] leave my mind distressed
I go away, behind to leave you
Perhaps never to meet again
But if we never have the pleasure
I hope we'll meet on Canaan's land

[Em D Em -   D Em - / Em - Am Em   Bm Em - :‖

D Em - -   - D - / D - Em -   D B7 - / 1st 2 above]

— trad. (shape note hymn)

PSALM 91

Whoever dwells in the home of the most high
Will rest in the shadow of the Lord
And I will say of the Lord he is my refuge
The Lord is my God in whom I always trust

C Am F G / C Am Dm G / 1st / C Am FG C

   Surely he will save you from the fowler's snare
   And from all deadly disease
   Your safety is found underneath his wings
   His faithfulness will be your shield

Am F C G / Am F G - / 1st / Am F Dm G

If you will make the Lord God your refuge
And make the Most High your home
No harm will come to you or near your tent
His angels will guard you in all ways

   Says the Lord who loves me "I will save
   And protect he who worships my name
   He will call on me & I will answer him
   I'll deliver him & honor him — and honor him"

(last line:) Am F Dm G C (Am Dm G C -)

— w & m: Carol A. Baraff

ROOTED & GROUNDED IN LOVE

Apostle Paul so long ago
Bent down his knees to pray
For the saints in the community
And you & me today: may you be

C G Am F / AmG FEm Am - / 1st / B7 - E -

Rooted & grounded in love
Strengthened in the Spirit thru faith
To know the height & depth & length & breadth
Of God's understanding and grace

Am F Am - / C Am E - / Am F Am F / Am E Am -

He said we're all one body / Tho' each has different gifts
Given for the common good
Together we are lifted up &...

Let all you do be done in love
And open your heart wide
If you live by the Spirit
Let the Spirit be your guide & keep you...

If you are feeling anger / Don't let that sun go down
You won't be tested past your strength
There's always a way out when you are...

So when you feel like worrying
Turn everything to prayer
And God will search your heart & soul
And hope will find you there, you will be...

— w & m: Lisa Hubbell

SANCTUARY (Gilkyson)

Yeah tho' I walk thru the valley of the shadow
Thou art with me
Tho' my heart's been torn on fields of battle / **Thou art…**
Tho' my trust is gone & my faith not near
In love's sanctuary, thou art with me

G - D G / Em DG C - / G - D Em / DG DG C -
C G Em C - / GD AmEm DG C - - -

Thru desolation's fire & fear's dark thunder / **Thou art…**
Thru the sea of desires that drag me under / **Thou art…**
Tho' I've been traded in like a souvenir / **In love's sanctuary…**

Thru the doubter's gloom & the cynic's sneer / **Thou…**
In the crowded rooms of a mind unclear…
Tho' I'll walk for a while down a trail of tears / **In love's…**

— w & m: Eliza Gilkyson

© 2000 Gilkysongs (BMI). All rights administered by Bluewater Music Services Corp. On her *Hard Times in Babylon*.

SANCTUARY (Thompson)

Lord prepare me to be a sanctuary
Pure & holy, tried & true
With thanksgiving, I'll be a living
Sanctuary for you

C - G - / F - C G / 1st / F G CF C

— w & m: John Thompson & Randy Scruggs

© 1983 Whole Armor Publishing Company & Full Armor Publishing Company. All rights in the US administered by Peermusic III, Ltd.

SHALOM ALEICHEM

Shalom aleichem, mal'achei hasharet
Mal'achei elyon
Mimelech mal'achei ham'lachim
Hakadosh baruch Hu
Bo'achem leshalom, mal'achei hashalom
Mal'achei elyon
Mimelech mal'achei ham'lachim
Hakadosh baruch Hu

I: Dm - A - / - Dm A - / 1st / Gm - A -
F - C - / Dm - A - / Gm - A Dm / Dm A Dm -

Bar'chuni leshalom, mal'achei hashalom
Mal'achei elyon…
Tzetchem leshalom, mal'achei hashalom / **Mal'achei…**

II: (↑3) Em Bm C G / Am Em F# B7
C G Am Em / Am Em B7 Em
Am - Em - / Am D Em - / Am D Em C / Am6 - B7 -

— w: trad. (Hebrew prayer), m: Israel Goldfarb & Samuel E. Goldfarb

Arr. © 2015 by Hal Leonard Corporation: I: Godfarbs, II: Debbie Friedman

SHALOM RAV

Shalom rav al yisrael am'cha tasim l'olam (2x)

D C G A / D C G D

Ki ata hu melech adon, l'chol hashalom **(2x)**

A G A G / A G Em A

(bridge) V'tov be'einecha levarech, et am'cha yisrael
B'chol eit uv'chol sha'ah, bishlomecha

EmC DBm EmA D / EmF# Bm EmA BmA

— w: trad. (Hebrew scripture), m: Jeff Klepper & Daniel Freelander

© 1974 Jeffrey Klepper & Daniel Freelander. Klepper (a cantor) & Freelander (a leading reform rabbi) perform together as Kol B'Seder. "Grant abundant peace over Israel, your people, forever."

SIM SHALOM (Give Peace)

1 & 2. Sim shalom tovah uv'rachah, sim shalom
3. Sim shalom, sim shalom

Bm EmD AsusA Bm

— w & m: Linda Hirschhorn

© 1992 Linda Hirschhorn. Lyrics are from Hebrew liturgy."Give peace, kindness & blessing," the last blessing of the Shemoneh Esrei, which is considered perhaps the most impt prayer of the synagogue. *LS

SIMPLE FAITH

Ours is a simple faith, life is a short embrace
Heaven is in this place, every day
Hope is the ground we till, make each day what you will
Thankful for dreams fulfilled, every day

GC G D Em / CD G D - / 1st / C D G(C G)

There is no Hell to fear *[No room in this heart for fear]*,
   no judgment day drawing near
Trust that inner voice you hear, every day
Life's not a goal or race, it's about heart & faith
And living a life of grace, every day

Trust is an open hand, making an honest stand
Rooted here in the land, every day
Live in mystery, seeking the harmony
Here between you & me, every day

— w & m: David Tamulevich

© 2004 Mustard's Retreat Music (BMI). On Yellow Room Gang *Life at Big Sky* & on Mustard's Retreat *MR7*, Lost Cuzzins *It's All Relative*, Walkabout Clearwater Chorus *We Have a S*, Jamcrackers, YMCA Deep River Choir *Praise & Promise*, Marilyn Driggs *Green*, rec by Small Potatoes. In *SO!* 50:2. *LS

STILL SMALL VOICE

In a still small voice in the middle of the night
Brother Martin heard the simple truth
And he followed its pleading tho' it led to a crossroads
Parting in the days of my youth
From the heart of my city came a single scream
And I heard it thru all the white noise
And the papers told me that they'd killed the dream
But they never killed the still small voice

C ↓ - - / F - C - / 1st / F - G - /

Am - C7 - / F - D - / C ↓ - - / F G C -

All the lies come at you in a million ways
Some you hear & some you tell yourself
And they say that virtue is a pile of gold
And that weapons are a nation's wealth
But when kings stand naked in their ugly schemes
Will the poor of this world rejoice
Will they sell their children down a bloody stream
Or will they listen to a still small voice?

Now the one-eyed bandit in your living room
Will convince you that you have no time
It will swear to take you on your one free ride
While it's looking for your last dime
But the light of heaven is a simple gift
You can see it when you make that choice
It will shine like riches in your inmost heart
But it will speak in a still small voice?

Oh the sky will open when the trumpet sounds
And the thunder will shake these walls
And these stones so silent as they ring us 'round
They will shatter when they hear that call
And these chains will clatter when they hit the ground
And the people make a joyful noise
But when my Lover comes to call me home / It will be in a still...

— w & m: Bob Franke

© 1987 Telephone Pole Music Publishing Co. On his *Brief Histories* 13, Charlie King *Food Phone Gas Lodging*. In his *SB & SO!* 34.1

SWIMMING TO THE OTHER SIDE

**We are living 'neath the great Big Dipper
We are washed by the very same rain
We are swimming in this stream together
Some in power & some in pain
We can worship this ground we walk on
Cherishing the beings that we live beside
Loving spirits will live forever
We're all swimming to the other side**

C - G - / Am - Em - / F - C - / 1. Dm - G - :‖ 2. Dm G C -

I am alone & I am searching
Hungering for answers in my time
I am balanced at the brink of wisdom
I'm impatient to receive a sign
I move forward with my senses open
Imperfection it be my crime
In humility I will listen / **We're all swimming to the other side**

On this journey thru thoughts & feelings
Binding intuition, my head, my heart
I am gathering the tools together / I'm preparing to do my part
All of those who have come before me / Band together & be my guide
Loving lessons that I will follow / **We're all swimming to...**

When we get there we'll discover
All the gifts we've been given to share
Have been with us since life's beginning
And we never noticed they were there
We can balance at the brink of wisdom
Never recognizing that we've arrived
Loving spirits will live together / **We're all...**

— w & m: Pat Humphries

© 1990, 1992 Pat Humphries. Pat Humphries *Hands*, emma's revolution *Roots Rock & Revolution*, Magpie *Seed on the Prairie*, Holly Near *We Came To Sing* & recs by Elaine Silver & Lui Collins. In *For the Beauty of the Earth* & *SO!* 40.3

THANKSGIVING

Give thanks that we are gathered here, **give thanks, be thankful**
On this night free from want & fear, **give thanks, be...**
Give thanks that we are not alone, **give...**
Give thanks for peace within this home, **give...**

(↑3) G CG G D / G CG G DG :‖

**Give thanks for beauty in the world
Give thanks for all things living
Give thanks for hearts that join here in
Thanksgiving, thanksgiving**

That there is food upon your plate, **give thanks...**
That homelessness is not your fate...
That you are someplace safe & warm...
That you've found shelter in the storm...

For those who answer friendship's call...
For those who work for food for all...
For those who struggle from their birth...
For those who work for peace on earth...

— w & m: Si Kahn

© 2007 Joe Hill Music LLC (ASCAP). All rights administered by Conexion Media Group, Inc. On his *Thanksgiving*.

THEY'LL KNOW WE ARE CHRISTIANS BY OUR LOVE

We are one in the Spirit, we are one in the Lord **(2x)**
And we pray that all *[our]* unity may one day be restored
**And they'll know we are Christians by our love, by our love
Yes they'll know we are Christians by our love**

Em - - - / Am - Em - / / C - Em Am / Em Am Em -

We will walk with each other, we will walk hand in hand **(2x)**
And together we'll spread the news that God is in our land
　　We will work with each other, we will work side by side **(2x)**
　　And we'll guard each one's dignity & save each one's pride
All praise to the Father from whom all things come
And all praise to Christ Jesus his only son
And all praise to the Spirit who makes us one

Justice x Love

We are one in the Spirit we are one in our words **(2x)**
We raise one voice together so the voiceless will be heard
And they'll know we work for justice by our love...

We will walk… /…spread the news that <u>hope</u> is in this land…

We will stand for each other, we will stand side by side **(2x)**
And we'll guard each one's dignity & save each others' lives…

We are Christians & Muslims, we are Hindus & Jews
We are Pagans & Buddhists & some Atheists too
We are grey-haired & students & we all work for Truth…

— w & m: Peter Scholtes, new w ("Justice x Love"): Mary Shapiro

© 1966 (renewed), 2001 Lorenz Publishing Co. On her *The Time Is Now*, Jars of Clay *Redemption S,* & recs by Lynda Randle & Carolyn Arends.

TREE OF LIFE

There are things that we <u>know</u> that we don't know we know,
  come to the tree of life
There are things that we know…know, **come to the tree of life**
Come to… **(2x)** / There are things that we know… come…

(↑2) A - - E / - - - A :‖

insert: say, feel, do

— w & m: Matt Jones

© 1977 (renewed) Matt Jones (ASCAP). On Kim & Reggie Harris *Resurrection Day* 12.

THE TREES OF THE FIELD

You shall go out with joy & be led forth with peace
The mountains & the hills will break forth before you
There'll be shouts of joy & all the trees of the field
Will clap, will clap their hands & all
  The trees of the field will clap their hands **(3x)**
  While you go out with joy!

Em - / G DB7 / 1st / B7 Em // G D / - G / - D / B7 Em

— w: Steffi Geiser Rubin, based on Isaiah 55:12, m: Stuart Dauermann

© 1975 (renewed) Lillenas Publishing Company. All rights administered by Music Services. In *Worship in Song & Celebration Hymnal.*

Faith songs are also in **Dreams, Earthcare, Gospel, Healing,** and **Hope.** See Cultures Index under Hebrew, Yiddish & Holidays. Also see **Dignity:** Christians & Pagans, **Family:** Bring Him Home, Let the Little Children, **Freedom:** A Million Nightingales, Missionaries, **Millenial:** I Will Wait, **Outdoors:** Lord is Good to Me, Trees of the Wild, **Rich:** Dives & Lazarus, **Peace:** Blessed Are the Peacemakers, How Beautiful Are the Feet, **Struggle:** God's Counting on Me, O God of Earth & Altar, **Work:** Ballad of the Carpenter.

Family

BANANA PANCAKES

(intro) Can't you see that it's just <u>rain</u>ing?
There ain't no need to go out<u>side</u>

(in G) Am - - - / G - - (D)

But, baby, you hardly even notice when I try to show you this
Song is meant to keep you from doing what you're supposed to
Waking up too early, maybe we can sleep in
Make you banana pancakes, pretend like it's the weekend now

G D Am C7 (4x)

Now **- and we could pretend it all the / Time - can't you see…**

Am - - - / G - - - :‖

But just maybe, like a ukulele, momma made a baby
Really don't mind the practice 'cos you're my little lady
Lady lady, love me 'cos I love to lay here lazy
We could close the curtains, pretend like there's no world
Outside **and we could…**

Ain't no need, ain't no need / Mmm, mmm
Can't you see, can't you see? / Rain all day & I don't mind

Am - - - / G - - - :‖

(bridge) But the telephone is singing
Ringing, it's too early, don't pick it up
We don't need to, we got everything we need right here
And everything we need is enough, just so easy
When the whole world fits inside of your arms
Do we really need to pay attention to the alarm?
Wake up slow, mmm mm, wake up slow

Am - - - / D - - - :‖ Bm - - - / Em - C - / G D G -

— w & m: Jack Johnson

© 2005 by Bubble Toes Publishing (ASCAP). All rights administered by Universal Music Corp. On his *In Betw Dreams, En Concert.*

BIRTHDAY ROUND

1. We wish you a <u>hap</u>py <u>birth</u>day 2. A <u>joy</u>ous & <u>cel</u>ebrated <u>birth</u>day
3. For our friend _____ 4. May she (he, you) have a long, long <u>life</u>

— w trad, m: William Shield (1748-1829)

Arr. © 2015 by Hal Leonard Corporation. On *Rounds Galore & More V.I.* Lyrics have been attributed to Dorothy Dushkin of Kinhaven Music School.

BLESS THIS HOUSE

Oh bless this house & those who dwell here
Peace & joy & harmony
May everything be ever well here
Oh bless this house

D - G D / G D A - / 1st / D A D - /

Bless this house & those who hold
That good companions, tales oft told
Are worth far more than any gold / Oh bless…

G - - A (- - -) / D - - A / D - G - / D A D -

Bless the sky that brings us light / **Peace…**
Sun & Moon & Stars so bright / **Oh…**
   Bless the water flowing clear…
   That brings us nourishment & cheer…
Bless the hearth & bless the fire…
Warmth & food & heart's desire…
   Bless the earth on which we stand…
   May we live gently on the land…
So here's a health to all good friends…
Who gather as an old way *[year]* ends…
   And here's a health unto the new…
   May all good blessings flow to you…

   — w & m: Eileen McGann

BRING HIM HOME

God on high hear my prayer
In my need you have always been there
He is young, he's afraid
Let him rest heaven blessed
Bring him home **(x3)**

CF GF x2 / Em Dm G - / 1st / E - Am - / F C Dm G C -

(bridge) He's like the son I might have known
   if God had granted me a son
The summers die one by one, how soon they fly on & on
And I am old & will be gone

Em Dm Am G / F C F C / Dm - E G

Bring him peace, bring him joy
He is young, he is only a boy
You can take, you can give
Let him be, let him live
If I die, let me die / Let him live, bring him home
Bring him home, bring him home

CF GF x2 / Em D G - / 1st / E - Am -

F C Dm G / CF GF x2 / CF GF x3 C -

(reprise, later in musical) God on high, hear my prayer
Take me now to thy care
Where you are, let me be
Take me now, take me there / Bring me home, bring him home

   — m: Claude-Michel Schonberg w: Herbert Kretzmer & Alain Boublil

CAT'S IN THE CRADLE

My child arrived just the other day
He came to the world in the usual way
But there were planes to catch & bills to pay
He learned to walk while I was away
And he was talkin' 'fore I knew it & as he grew
He'd say "I'm gonna be like you, Dad
You know I'm gonna be like you"

D - F - / G - D - :‖ C ↓ - - / F Am D - / /

And the cat's in the cradle & the silver spoon
Little Boy Blue & the Man in the Moon
When you comin' home, Dad? I don't know when
But we'll get together then, Son
You know we'll have a good time then

D - C - / F - G - / 1st / F Am D - / /

My son turned 10 just the other day
He said, "Thanks for the ball, Dad, come on let's play
Can you teach me to throw?" I said "Not today
I got a lot to do." He said "That's ok"
And he walked away but his smile never dimmed
And said "I'm gonna be like him, yeah
You know I'm gonna be like him"

Well, he came home from college just the other day
So much like a man I just had to say
"Son, I'm proud of you, can you sit for a while?"
He shook his head & said with a smile
"What I'd really like, Dad, is to borrow the car keys
See you later, can I have them please?" **(this v. only: skip last chd grp)**

I've long since retired, my son's moved away
I called him up just the other day
I said "I'd like to see you if you don't mind"
He said "I'd love to, Dad, if I can find the time
You see my new job's a hassle & the kids have the flu
But it's sure nice talking to you, Dad
It's been sure nice talking to you"

(bridge) And as I hung up the phone it occurred to me
He'd grown up just like me / My boy was just like me

C G Am C / F Am D - / /

   — w & m: Harry Chapin & Sandy Chapin

CHILD OF MINE

Child of mine, you are the wildest wind
And the dearest dream **I will ever know**
Love's lasting light shines out from deep within
This father's heart **as I watch you grow**

(↑2) G - C D / C CD G (D) :‖

Child of mine, you are the break of dawn
And the brightest star **I will ever…**
Love's lasting light comes shining on & on
From this mother's heart **as I watch you…**

There is a road & that road is all your own
But we are here, you need not walk alone
To face not fear, each coming new unknown
Is the way to lift your wings

D - C G /   / Em - C G / Am Em D -

Child of mine, you are the sweetest song
And the greatest gift I will ever know **(short verse)**

Child of mine, where spirits fly above
There is but one that belongs to you
So let it grow & it will thrive on love
For it is love that sees us thru

> You have the hands that will open up the doors
> You have the hopes this world is waiting for
> You are my own, but you are so much more
> You are tomorrow on the wing / Child of mine

D - C G /   / Em - C G / Am Em D - / G -

— w & m: Bill Staines

COLORING OUTSIDE THE LINES

She sat down to color at her coloring book
And was carefully staying inside the lines
All of a sudden she grinned & said
I'm gonna color outside of the lines this time!

D - G D / - - E A / D - G D /   /

Coloring outside the lines
I'm gonna color outside of the lines this time (repeat)
I'm gonna color outside of the lines this time

D - G D / - - E A / D - G D /   /   /

It was a group that was learning how to dance & move
With particular steps they were supposed to find
All of a sudden someone jumped up & said
I'm gonna dance outside of the lines this time!
Dancing outside the lines / **I'm gonna** dance outside...

She was a 1st-year teacher trying things out
And was told it was best if you'd toe the line
Then her principal said "You're getting thru to your kids
So you can teach outside of the lines this time" / Teaching...

She was too tired to go to the back of the bus
So she took the first seat that she could find
She didn't say much but what she did spoke loud
I'm gonna sit outside of the lines this time! / Sitting...

There was a man beat up in a ditch by the road
Who was helped out by someone that he despised
So to love God & love your neighbor as yourself
You've got to love outside of the lines sometimes / Loving...

— w & m: Tom Hunter

FAMILY TREE

Before the days of Jello lived a prehistoric fellow
Who loved a maid & courted her beneath the banyan tree
And they had lots of children & their children all had children
And they kept on having children until one of them had me!

(↑2) C - G - / - - - C / 1st / G - F G C

We're a family & we're a tree
Our roots go deep down in history
From my great-great-granddaddy reaching up to me
We're a green & growing family tree

C AmG F C / - Am D G / F G C Em / C F C G C

My grandpa came from Russia, my grandma came from Prussia
They met in Nova Scotia, had my dad in Tennessee
Then they moved to Yokohama where Daddy met my Mama
Her dad's from Alabama & her mom's part Cherokee

Well one fine day I may go to Tierra Del Fuego
Perhaps I'll meet my wife there & we'll move to Timbuktu
And our kid will be bilingual & tho' she may stay single
She could, of course, commingle with the King of Kathmandu 'cos:

The folks in Madagascar aren't the same as in Alaskar, they got
Different foods, different moods & different colored skin
You may have a different name but underneath we're much the same
You're probably my cousin & the whole world is our kin

— w & m: John Forster & Tom Chapin

FATHER & SON

(father:) It's not time to make a change, just relax, take it easy
You're still young, that's your fault, there's so much you have to know
Find a girl, settle down, if you want you can marry
Look at me, I am old, but I'm happy

C Em F Dm / C Am Dm G :‖

I was once like you are now & I know that it's not easy
To be calm when you've found something going on, but
Take your time, think a lot, why think of everything you've got
For you will still be here tomorrow, but your dreams may not

C G F Dm / C Am Dm G / 1st / C Am G C

(son:) How can I try to explain, when I do he turns away again
It's always been the same, same old story
From the moment I could talk I was ordered to listen
Now there's a way & I know that I have to go away
I know I have to go G F C -

(father:) It's not time to make a change, just sit down, take it slowly
You're still young, that's your fault, there's so much you have to
   go thru / **Find a girl...**

(son:) All the times that I've cried, keeping all the things I knew inside
It's hard, but it's harder to ignore it
If they were right, I'd agree, but it's them they know not me
Now there's a way...

— w & m: Cat Stevens

FOUR HANDS

Four hands working at the table
Two are young & two are older
Four hands strong & able
Hands that work & hands that love

C - F - / C - G - / 1st / C - G C

Now, me & my grandma, we're building a house
Building it from pebbles & toothpicks
Grandma builds the roof & I build the walls
We're gonna fill it with **the people we love**

F C G C / / / F G C -

Now, me & my grandpa, we're baking a pie
Baking it from apples & raisins
Grandpa cuts the apples & I roll the dough
We're gonna feed it to **the...**

Now, me & my grandma, we're fixing our skates
Fixing 'em to fit us this year
Grandma makes mine longer & I make hers tight
We're gonna skate with...

Now, me & my grandpa, we're writing a song
We're gonna sing it for the family tomorrow
Grandpa writes the music & I write the words
We're gonna sing it for...

— w & m: Ruth Pelham

© 1984 Ruth Pelham Music. On Two of a Kind *Going on an Adventure*, Tom Hunter *I'll Sing for You*. In *SO!* 35:4.

GATHER THE FAMILY

Gather the family here we belong
And welcome good stranger come in
Our voices together all singing one song
And it's here that the future begins

C - F C / - - G - / C - G Am / - G F -

Our ancestors came from away far away
From a thousand traditions & kin
What we all share together as we stand here today
With a chance to start over again

C - G C / - - F - / " / " /

Our measure of worth's not in power or gold
The greatest truth comes from the heart
It's how we take care of the weak & the old
And this is a place we can start

And so like a forest our roots hold the past
While our branches reach into the sky
Let our gift to our children be family that lasts
And a future to which they can fly

— w & m: Michael Hough & David Tamulevich

© 1997 Mustard's Retreat Music (BMI). On Mustard's Retreat *Winds & The Crickets* †2, Yellow Rm Gang *Live at the Big Sky*, Skip Jones *Life Is Delicious*, Ken Gallipeau *Collection*, David HB Drake *Potluck*. In *SO!* 44:2. *LS

GOD DANCED (The Day You Were Born)

1. God danced the day you were born, _ the
Angels did the bump to Gabriel's horn _
God danced... / So grateful for the gift of you_ _

Am C D E / D E D E / 1st / D E Am -

2. _I saw _ God do _the Funky Chicken
_Steppin' & kickin' in blue suede shoes
_I saw _ God do _the Boogaloo too
Faced with the gift of you, _ I have heard

3. Some folks say that _ long ago _ God
Could not dance to _ save his soul, _ but people
I've seen him shake that _ jelly roll _
Thinkin' 'bout the gift of you _ _

— w & m: Andrew Lawrence

© 1999 Andrew Lawrence. On Hot Soup *The Way You Like It*, Charlie King & Karen Brandow *I Struck Gold*. *LS

HALLELUJAH

He'll be whistlin' while he works **(2x)**
He'll be whistlin', he'll be whistlin'
Whistlin' while he works
She'll be tending their garden green **(2x)**
She'll be tending, she'll be tending
Tending their garden green

Hallelu-jah / Hallelu-jah_ / Hallelu-jah (2x)

G - / Em - / G Em / D G :‖ C G / C G G / C G / D G

She'll be holding their little lamb
She'll be holding that little lamb
She'll be holding, she'll be holding / Holding that little lamb
He'll be singing lullabyes **(2x)**
He'll be singing, he'll be singing / Singing lullabyes

She'll be making sugar pie **(2x)**
She'll be making, she'll be making / Making him a sugar pie
He'll be kissing her each night **(2x)**
He'll be kissing, he'll be kissing / Kissing her each night

— w & m: Katherine Wheatley

© 2003, 2009 Katherine Wheatley. On her *Landed*.

HAPPY ADOPTION DAY

Oh who would have guessed, who could have seen
Who could have possibly known
All these roads we have traveled, the places we've been
Would have finally taken us home?

D A D G / Bm - A - / 1st / D A D -

And it's here's to you, & 3 cheers to you
Let's shout it: "Hip hip hip, hooray!"
For out of a world so tattered & torn
You came to our house on that wonderful morn
And all of a sudden this family was born
Oh happy Adoption Day!

G - D - / - E A - / D A D G / D A D A /
D A D G / D A D -

There are those who think families happen by chance
A mystery their whole life thru
But we had a voice & we had a choice
We were working & waiting for you

So no matter the name, no matter the age
No matter how you came to be
And no matter the skin, we are all of us kin
We are all of us one family

— w & m: John McCutcheon

© 1992 John McCutcheon/Appalsongs (ASCAP). On his *Family Garden* 13.

HI FI STEREO COLOR TV

There was a town in this country
And none of the children there could read, with a
Hi-fi stereo color TV / Stereo color TV

D G / D A / D DG / DA D

For the printed page they had no use
And they treated newspapers with abuse, with their **Hi-fi...**

The School Board was surprised indeed
To find out none of the kids could read, 'cos of...

To make sure all of the kids would pass
They replaced the teachers in every class, with a...

The children all soon learned to read
And then they found they had no need, for a...

So a plan was made by these clever creatures
To record the lessons for their teachers, on a...

With a video recorder in every chair
The children were free to roam everywhere from the...

Now up in the hills they roam like elves
While the TV sets just watch themselves, on a...

— w & m: Jay Ungar

© 1972 (renewed) Swinging Door Music (BMI). On Rosalie Sorrels *What Does It Mean to Love?* & Bob Reid *Marz Barz*. Tune is "Hi fie, diddle i diddle i fie" version of Devil & the Farmer's Wife.

I CRIED

Today was real tough, I got out of bed
I brushed my teeth & then I held my head
And then I cried, cried, cried, cried

Dm - G - / A - - - / Dm A Dm -

I said "I won't wear those shoes & I won't wear those socks
And I won't go to school if I can't bring my new rocks!"...

Breakfast was a scene, I wouldn't eat my eggs
I got jelly in my hair, spilled juice on my legs...

School was no better, my best friend was sick
I got a gumball on my homework, in gym I got kicked...

I went home & the house smelled great, fresh muffins out to cool
Daddy poured me a cup of milk & then he hugged & he held me full...

My dad said "What is wrong?" & here's what I said
I said "I wish that you & my mom would live together again"...

"Your mom & I are friends, no longer husband & wife
But we will love you always, we'll love you all our lives"
And then we cried, cried, cried, cried

Today was real tough, I got into bed
I cuddled with my teddy bear & then laid down my head
And then I cried, cried, cried, cried

— w & m: Ruth Pelham

© 1982 Ruth Pelham Music. On her *Under One Sky* & *Look to the People* (in Bm), Peter Alsop *Stayin' Over* & *S on Loss & Grief* 11, Holly Near & Ronnie Gilbert *Lifeline Extended*, Denver Women's Chorus (YT).

IT'S A LONG WAY

I been thinking 'bout the people that came before
It's a long, long way
Mothers & fathers from a distant shore
It's a long, long way
Some came for freedom some came for land / **It's a long...**
Some came bound & shackled hand in hand / **It's a...**

(↑2) C Am F C / - G C - (repeat 4x)

It's a long way with many miles behind us
It's a long way with many more to go
It's a long way til tomorrow finds us
It's a long, long way (2x)

F - C - / / F - C Am / F G C Am / F G C -

Some came with dreams of power, some came with dreams of gold...
Some came with whatever their 2 hands would hold...
No matter when you got here, no matter how...
We're all in the same boat now!...

If you want to go, you can't get there all by yourself...
If you want to go, you got to bring somebody else...
It's a long hard road, it's a long steep climb...
Reach back your hand, don't leave anyone behind...

When I was a boy, once I heard a man...
He said he had a dream about the promised land...
He said I may not get there & neither may you...
But our children's children may see it come true...

— w & m: Bill Harley

© 2001 Round River Music/Bill Harley. www.billharley.com. On his *Down In The Backpack* 15, Two of a Kind *Sing Me Your Story*.

KINDERGARTEN WALL

When I was a little kid not so long ago
I had to learn a lot of stuff I didn't even know
How to dress myself, tie my shoes, how to jump a rope
How to smile for a picture without looking like a dope
But of all the things I learned, my favorite of them all was
A little poem hanging on the kindergarten wall

C - F C / F C Dm G / C - F - / **2nd** / F C F C / **2nd**

"Of all you learn here remember this the best:
Don't hurt each other & clean up your mess
Take a nap every day, wash before you eat
Hold hands, stick together, look before you cross the street
Remember the seed in the little paper cup:
First the root goes down & then the plant grows up!"

/ " / " / " / " / " / F C G C

Well, it was 1st, 2nd, 3rd grade, 4th grade, too
Where I had to learn the big things the big kids do
To add, subtract & multiply, read & write & play
How to sit in a little uncomfortable desk for nearly half a day
But of all the things they taught me, of all the great & small
Still my favorite was the **poem...**

But lately I've been worried as I look around & see
An awful lot of grown-ups acting foolish as can be
I know there's lots of things to know I haven't mastered yet
Still it seems there's real impt stuff that grownups soon forget
I'm sure we'd all be better off if we would just recall that **little poem...**

— w & m: John McCutcheon

© 1988 John McCutcheon/Appalsongs (ASCAP). On his *Water from Another Time*, *Mail Myself to You*, Priscilla Herdman *Daydreamer*, Holly Brook *Dream Maker*, Fran Friedman *Songs for a Smile*, Aaron Fowler *When We Gather*. In SO! 37:3.

LET THE LITTLE CHILDREN

Let the little children come unto me
For of such is the kingdom of God

C - - - / F G C -

— w & m: Beverly Shepard

© 2000 Beverly Shepard www.beverlyshepard.ca. Lyrics are based on Luke 18:16. Sing over & over like a Taizé chant. *LS

MY DOG SAM

My dog Sam was a good old dog
He was my best friend
Now he's gone & he won't be back
And I'll never see him again / I'll never see him again

(in C) F C F C / F C G - / F G C Am / F G C - / /

My mom brought him from the pound / When I was only 3
She gave him baths, my dad gave him bones
But he mostly belonged to me / He mostly...

C - - G / C - G - / F G C Am / F G C - / /

Sam chased rabbits, Sam chased squirrels
One time he caught a skunk
We washed him in tomato juice
But you know that dog still stunk / You know...

The first night that I slept outside
I was so scared I thought I'd die
The sky was big & the night was dark but
Sam stayed right by my side / He slept...

The other night I woke from sleep
I knew something was wrong
I'd seen Sam in my dreams
& I knew that old Sam was gone

I've still got Sam's tennis ball
I keep it in my penny can
I'm gonna get me another dog
But I'll never get another Sam

— w & m: Bill Harley

© 1986 Round River Music/Bill Harley. www.billharley.com. On his *50 Ways to Fool Your Mother*.

ON CHILDREN

Your children_are not your children_
They are the sons & the daughters of life's_longing for itself
They come thru you_but they are not from you_
And tho they are with you they belong not to you_

G - - - / D - G - / C - G - / D - G -

You can give them your love_but not your thoughts_
They have their own thoughts _(x2)
You can house their bodies_but not their souls
For their souls dwell in a place of tomorrow which you cannot
Visit not even in your dreams
You can strive to be like them, but you cannot make them just
like you (2x)

G - - - / / G - - / C - G - / C - G / G D - G / /

— w: adap from the poem by Kahlil Gibran, m: Ysaye M. Barnwell

© 1981 Barnwell's Notes Inc. On Sweet Honey & the Rock *Good News* 11 & *Breaths*, *The Flirtations*, Betsy Rose *Heart of a Child*. In *SO!* 36:3.

ON THE DAY YOU WERE BORN

On the day that _____ (insert names) was born (3x)
The angels sang & they blew on their horns
And they danced, they danced
They smiled & raised up their hands
On the day, on the day that _____ was born

G - / D G / G C / G C / G D / G C / G D G -

Right now, somewhere, someone's being born
Somewhere, right now, someone's being born
Right now, somewhere, someone's being born
And the angels are singing & they're blowin' on their horns
And they're dancin', they're dancin'
They're smilin' & raisin' up their hands
'Cos right now, somewhere, someone's being born

(tag) Raisin' up their hands on the day, on the day each one of us
was born   G D C G

— w & m: Red & Kathy Grammer

© 1996 Smilin' Atcha Music. On his *Hello World*.

OYFN PRIPETSHIK

Oyfn pripetshik brent a fayerl, un in shtub iz heys
Un der rebe lernt kleyne kinderlekh dem alef-beys **(2x)**

(in 3/4) AmAmE Am FG* CCA   *2 beat measure
Dm AmAmE AmG* CCA / Dm AmAmE AmE* Am

**Zet zhe kinderlekh, gedenkt zhe, tayere vos ir lernt do
Zogt zhe nokh a mol un take nokh a mol: komets alef o! (2x)**

E Am FG* CCA / lines 2 & 3 as verse

Lernt, kinder, mit groys kheyshek, azoy zog ikh aykh on
Ver s'vet gikher fun aykh kenen ivre, der bakumt a fon **(2x)**

Lernt, kinder, hot nit moyre, yeder onheyb iz shver
Gliklekh der vos hot gelernt toyre, tsi darf der mentsh nokh mer?...

Az ir vet, kinder, elter vern, vet ir aleyn farshteyn
Vifl in di oysyes lign trern, un vi fil geveyn...

Az ir vet, kinder, dem goles shlepn, oysgemutshet zayn
Zolt ir fun di oysyes koyekh shepn, kukt in zey arayn!...

— w & m: Mark Warshawsky (1848–1907)

Arr. © 2015 by Hal Leonard Corporation. A rabbi teaches the Hebrew alphabet
to young children, telling them that learning to read & study Torah will give them
strength to cope with the oppression they will face as they grow up. Often sung
as a lullaby. v.4 & 5 say "As you grow older you will learn how many tears lie in
these letters, but the letters will give you strength." Warshavsky was a friend of
the great Yiddish writer, Sholem Aleychem. In *Coll Reprints fr SO!* V1-6

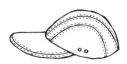

RIGHT FIELD

Saturday summers, when I was a kid
We'd run to the schoolyard & here's what we did
We'd pick out the captains & we'd choose up the teams
It was always a measure of my self esteem
 'Cos the fastest, the strongest, played shortstop & 1st
 The last ones they picked were the worst
 I never needed to ask, it was sealed
 I just took up my place in right field, playing

G Em / C AmD / CD CD / G Em /
C Am / C D / F -/ Am D

**Right field, it's easy, you know
You can be awkward & you can be slow
That's why I'm here in right field just watching the
  dandelions grow**

G Em / C AmD / CD CD G(C G)

Playing right field can be lonely & dull
Little Leagues never have lefties that pull
I'd dream of the day they'd hit one my way
They never did, but still I would pray
 That I'd make a fantastic catch on the run
 And not lose the ball in the sun
 And then I'd awake from this long reverie
 And pray that the ball never came out to me, here in...

Off in the distance, the game's dragging on
There's strikes on the batter, some runners are on
I don't know the inning, I've forgotten the score
The whole team is yelling & I don't know what for

Then suddenly everyone's looking at me
My mind has been wandering, what could it be?
They point at the sky & I look up above
And a baseball falls into my glove!

(last cho) Here in **right field**, it's important you know
You gotta know how to catch, you gotta know how to throw
That's why I'm here in right field, just...

— w & m: Willy Welch

© 1986 Playing Right Music. On Peter Paul & Mary *Peter Paul & Mommy Too*
(video), their *Around the Campfire* & Aaron Fowler *When We Gather.*

SO MANY WAYS TO BE SMART

**So many ways to be smart (2x)
With your hands, your feet, your head, your heart
So many ways to be smart**

D - A - / - D / D G D A / G A D -

Some folks are good at numbers & math
Some folks are good at making you laugh
Some folks are good at building a go-cart
So many ways to be smart — ay ay ay!

D - A - / - - D / - - G - / A - - -

Some folks are good at reading deep books
Some folks are good at reading people's looks
Some folks are good at drawing [music] & art / **So many...**

Some folks are good at getting along
Some folks are good at making up songs
Some folks are good at stopping a Wal-Mart...

Some folks are good at doing their best
Tho' it's hard to measure on a standardized test
Some folks have lots of common sense
It's all intelligence — **ay ay ay!**

— w & m: Stuart Stotts

© 1999 Stuart Stotts (BMI). On his *Everyone Started Out Small.* Two of a Kind
(title cut), Fran Friedman *Dreams for Tomorrow*, Dr. Rhythm *Dr. Rhythm II.* *LS

TURN OFF THE TV

Turn off the TV (turn off...) **you won't regret it
Turn off the TV** (turn...) **& just forget it
There must be 36 million things we all can do & see
And all you've got to do is turn off the TV**

G D / - G / - C / D G

We could go swimming or to a party with some friends
I could ride my skateboard or play a game that never ends
We could play baseball or go on a shoppin' spree
All you gotta do is turn off the TV

C G / D G :‖

We could go to the zoo & watch the animals play
Build a castle, be king & queen for the day
Put on our rollerblades & around the block we'll zoom
Ah, just don't make me clean up my room!

C G / D G / 1st / A D

— w & m: Lisa Atkinson

© 1999 George Kincheloe. On her *The Elephant in Aisle 4.* Inspired by the 4th
grade at Linda Vista Sch, San Jose CA.

WE WILL BUILD THIS HOUSE

We will build this house with the strength of our arms
With the love of our neighbors, we will build this house
We will build this house as a shelter from all harm
With the open door of justice, we will build this house

GD G Bm - / C G D - / 1st / C G D G

A house of warmth, a house just right
A house to keep away the darkest night
A house of hope, a house of peace
A house where all within may safely sleep

C G C G / C G D - :|

A house that's built to remind us all
Of how we are connected whether great or small
A house of dignity, a house without shame
A house with walls bearing all our names

It seems so simple, it seems so sweet
A roof above you, enough food to eat
In this richest nation on this world of care
How much do we need to have enough to share

— w & m: Sally Rogers

YOU GET A LITTLE EXTRA WHEN YOU WATCH TV

You get a little extra when you watch TV
Ain't that ducky! Well you're lucky if you see that
You get a little extra when you watch TV!

C - / G - / C CG C -

You sit too close & you get a big surprise
Lots of radiation in your body & your eyes
Your eardrums hum when someone turns it up too high
When you watch TV!
We learn lots about our bodies & our aches & pains
Headaches, hemorrhoids, heartburn, diarrhea, denture stains
You gotta buy more drugs t'stop your stresses & your strains...

C - / G - / C - / CG C :|

When someone in an advertisement tells me lies
I jump up & switch the channels & I get some exercise
So my body's getting healthy & my mind is getting wise
When I...

Daddies only love the Mommies when the dirt's all gone
From their shirts & shiny floors, the coffee has t'be right on
I'm so glad my Dad's not fussy, 'cos he'd leave my Mom
If he watched TV!

In real life it never works when people go &
Hit & kick & punch & smash each other's heads & toes, but
It always solves the problems on the cartoon shows
When you...

Last night on the highway when our car got stalled
We saw a bloody accident w bodies that were mauled
Tho my folks got sick, it didn't bother me at all
'cos I watched TV!

Now if you think that I am lazy, don't you call me names
I have learned impt skills from playing video games
If a spaceship should attack us I could shoot 'em down in flames
'cos I watched TV
And a big TV can really give you quite a rest
If you get one near your bed, you've got no reason to get dressed, you
Never have to talk to anyone, your life is a success
When you...!

— w & m: Peter Alsop

YOUR HOUSE IS STRONG

What if all the moments that felt like failure
Were really the ones that made me strong?
What if all the time when you thought you'd ruined me
There actually was nothing wrong?
I know there are times when you think our house
Will crumble & fall on our heads
Believe me when I say:

C Em / Dm FG / 1st / Dm Em / Dm Am / Dm G

Your **house is strong** & so are you
The broken spots are where the light shines thru
Your **house is strong** & so are we
It's the forgiving of **each other that sets us, sets us / Free**

C Em / Dm FG :| C (Em Dm FG)

I know it wasn't easy to watch me struggle
To finally get to my feet
I know it wasn't easy to work to feed us
When we kept interrupting your sleep
You always had time to hold me close
To listen & believe when I heard a ghost
I believed you when you said:

Our... / The haunted rooms are where the truth comes thru
Our... / It's the believing in each other that sets us...

(bridge) And there were those yrs when we couldn't
Speak without it ending in a fight
You had the wisdom to let me go
Crashing thru with no headlights
I don't know how you did it **(2x)**

C Em / Am FG / 1st / Dm FG / C Am Em FG / /

One day in the summer we made the time
To gather like the women we'd grown to be
Gathered like the harvest, we heard the news
And everything vanished from the screen
The mother we get is the mother we need
Even when we're all alone
I hear you sing to your own mama: / Your **house...**

C Em / Dm FG / 1st / Dm Em / Dm Am / Dm FG

— w & m: Nerissa Nields

The **Family Chapter** contains songs about children, parenting, life at home & school. See also: **Dignity**, **Healing**, **Home & Roots** (songs about specific locales & immigration), **Lullabies**, **Play**, **Time & Changes**

Other songs include Ballads: Safe from Harm (after Fear a bhata), Wind & the rain, Blues: It's nobody's fault but mine (on literacy), Papa's on the housetop, **Brit**: Julia, Ob-la-di ob-la-da, Wild World,

Earth: Habitat, Lambeth children, My granddaughter's wedding day, Where do the chilren play?, **Farm:** Homegrown tomatoes, **Funny:** Sandwiches, Scalloped potatoes, **Hope:** For real, **Musicals:** Matchmaker, **Peace:** In the name of all of our children, **Sea:** Old Zeb, Sonny's dream, **Sing:** Leader of the band, **Struggle:** I'm gonna say it now (on college), **Surfing:** In my room, You're my home.

Farm & Prairie

ALONG THE COLORADO TRAIL

Eyes like the morning star, cheeks like a rose
Laura was a pretty girl, God almighty knows
Weep all ye little rains, wail winds wail
All along, along, along the Colorado trail

C - F C / - - F G // 1st / C CAm FG C

Ride thru the lonely night, ride thru the day
Keep the herd a-movin' on, movin' on its way
   Ride thru the stormy night, dark is the sky
   Wish I'd stayed in Abilene where it's warm & dry
Face like a prairie flower laughing all the day
Laura was pretty girl, now she's gone away
   My aching heart is broke full sore, pinto never fail
   Laura was a pretty girl cut down in the gale
— Traditional Cowboy Song

(aka The Colorado Trail) Arr. © 2015 by Hal Leonard Corporation. In Carl Sandburg's *Amer Songbag*, *SO!* 31:4. Rec by Jo Stafford, Weavers, Kingston Trio.

BACK IN THE SADDLE AGAIN

I'm back in the saddle again
Out where a friend is a friend
Where the longhorn cattle feed on the lowly jimson weed
Back in the saddle again

C G C C₇ / F - C - / F - C A / 1. D - G - :‖ 2. D G C -

Ridin' the range once more / Totin' my old .44
Where you sleep out every night & the only law is right...

(bridge) Whoopie-ti-yi-yo, rockin' to & fro...
Whoopie-ti-yi-yay, I go my way...

F - C - / - - G - / 1st / Am G C -

— w & m: Gene Autry & Ray Whitley

© 1939 (renewed) Gene Autry's Western Music Publishing Co. & Katielu Music. Autry's signature song.

BRACERO

Wade into the river thru the rippling shallow water
Steal across the thirsty border, **Bracero**
Come bring your hungry body to the golden fields of plenty
From a peso to a penny, **Bracero**
Oh, welcome to California
Where the friendly farmers will take care of you

Em - D - / C - B₇ - :‖ C D G Em / Am D Em -

Come labor for your mother, for your father & your brother
For your sisters & your lover, **Bracero**
Come pick the fruits of yellow, break the flowers from the berries
Purple grapes will fill your bellies...

And the sun will bite your body as the dust will draw you thirsty
While your muscles beg for mercy...
In the shade of your sombrero drop your sweat upon the soil
Like the fruit your youth can spoil...

When the weary night embraces sleep in shacks that could be cages
They will take it from your wages...
Come sing about tomorrow with a jingle of the dollars
And forget your crooked collar...

And the local men are lazy & they make too much of trouble
Besides we'd have to pay them double...
Ah but if you feel you're falling, if you find the pace is killing
There are others who are willing...

Now they're putting laws in order meant for closing down the
   border / As if your life could get much harder...
'Cos if you don't have proper papers they can send you back
   forever / Leave behind your son & daughter...
And the raging politicians will sacrifice you for ambition
Fear & bigotry their weapons...
Oh welcome to *Arizona*
Where the *local sheriff swears he* will take care of you

— w & m: Phil Ochs

© 1966 Barricade Music, Inc. Copyright renewed. All rights controlled & administered by Almo Music Corp. On his *There But for Fortune* 12 & *In Conc*, Joe Jencks *Links in a Chain,*, John Gorka *What's That I Hear?* New v. by Amy Carol Webb.

CANNED GOODS

(intro) Let those December winds bellow & blow
I'm as warm as a July to-ma-to

(in G) C G / Em G C D G

Peaches on the shelf, potatoes in the bin
Supper's ready, everybody come on in
Taste a little of the summer (3x)
My grandma put it all in jars

C G / D G (4x) C D G

Well, there's a root cellar, fruit cellar down below
Watch your head now & down you go / **Peaches...**

D G / Em G

Maybe you're weary & you don't give a damn
I bet you never tasted her blackberry jam...

Ah, she's got magic in her, you know what I mean
She puts the sun & rain in with her green beans...

What with the snow & the economy & everything
I think I'll just stay down here & eat until spring...

(bridge) When I go to see my grandma I gain a lot of weight
With her dear hands she gives me plate after plate
She cans the pickles, sweet & dill
She cans the songs of the whippoorwill
And the morning dew & the evening moon
And I really got to go see her pretty soon
'Cos these canned goods I buy at the store
Ain't got the summer in them anymore
You bet, grandma, as sure as you're born
I'll take some more potatoes & a thunderstorm / **Peaches on...**

D G / Em G / C G / D G (7x)

— w & m: Greg Brown

DON'T FENCE ME IN

Oh give me land, lots of land under starry skies above,
   don't fence me in
Let me ride thru the wide-open country that I love,
   don't fence me in
Let me be by myself in the evening breeze, listen to the murmur
   of the cottonwood trees
Send me off forever but I ask you please, **don't fence me in**
Just turn me loose, let me straddle my old saddle
   underneath the Western skies
On my cayuse, let me wander over yonder
   til I see the mountains rise
I want to ride to the ridge where the West commences,
   gaze at the moon til I lose my senses
Can't look at hobbles & I can't stand fences, **don't fence me in**

C - - G / - - - C / C C7 F - / C A7 F CG C
F - C - / F - C G / " / " /

— w & m: Cole Porter

EARLY

Early one morning I walked out alone
I looked down the street, no one was around
The sun was just comin' up over my home
On Hickory St. in a little farm town &

(in 3/4, G) C G / D G :|

Oooo-ee, ain't the mornin' light pretty
When the dew is still heavy, so bright & early
My home on the range, it's a one-horse town
And it's all right with me

The plow broke the prairie, the prairie gave plenty
The little towns blossomed & soon there were many
Scattered like fireflies across the dark night
And one was called Early & they sure named it right 'cos

Many dry summers parched all the fields
They burnt the fine colors & cut down the yield
But the rain has returned to wash away our tears
It's the fullest green summer that we've seen for yrs. &

— w & m: Greg Brown

GHOST RIDERS IN THE SKY
(A Cowboy Legend)

An old cowpoke went ridin' out one dark & windy day
Upon a ridge he rested as he went along his way
When all at once a mighty herd of red-eyed cows he saw
A ploughin' thru the ragged skies & up a cloudy draw
Yippie-i-ay, yippie-i-oh
Ghost Riders in the sky

Am C - / / Am - / F - Am - // C - Am - / F Dm Am -

Their brands were still on fire & their hooves were made of steel
Their horns were black & shiny & their hot breath he could feel
A bolt of fear went thru him as they thundered thru the sky
For he saw the riders coming hard & he heard their mournful cry

Their faces gaunt, their eyes were blurred, their shirts all soaked
   with sweat
They're ridin' hard to catch that herd but they ain't caught 'em yet
'Cos they've got to ride forever on that range up in the sky
On horses snorting fire, as they ride on, hear their cry

As the riders loped on by him, he heard one call his name
If you want to save your soul from Hell a-riding on our range
Then cowboy change your ways today or with us you will ride
Tryin' to catch the Devil's herd, across these endless skies

— w & m: Stan Jones

HOMEGROWN TOMATOES

Ain't nothin' in the world that I like better
Than bacon & lettuce & homegrown tomatoes
Up in the mornin' out in the garden
Get you a ripe one, don't get a hard one
Plant 'em in the spring, eat 'em in the summer
All winter without 'em's a culinary bummer
I forget all about the sweatin' & diggin'
Every time I go out & pick me a big one
> **Homegrown tomatoes, homegrown tomatoes**
> **What'd life be without homegrown tomatoes?**
> **Only 2 things that money can't buy**
> **That's true love & homegrown tomatoes**

A - / D - / E7 - / A E7 :‖ (3x)

Well you can go out to eat & that's for sure
But it's nothin' a homegrown tomato won't cure
Put 'em in a salad, put 'em in a stew
You can make your very own tomato juice
You can eat 'em with eggs, eat 'em with gravy
Eat 'em with beans, pinto or navy
Put 'em on the side, put 'em in the middle
Put a homegrown tomato on a hotcake griddle

If I's to change this life I lead
I'd be Johnny Tomato Seed
'Cos I know what this country needs
It's homegrown tomatoes in every yard you see
When I die don't bury me
In a box in a cemetery
Out in the garden would be much better
I could be pushin' up homegrown tomatoes

— w & m: Guy Clark

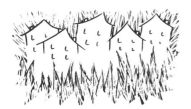

HOUSES IN THE FIELDS

They're growing houses in the fields betw the towns
And the Starlight drive-in movie's closing down
The road is gone to the way it was before
And the spaces won't be spaces anymore
> Two more farms were broken by the drought
> First the Wagners, now the Fullers pulling out
> Developers paid better than the corn
> But this was not the place where they were born

G D C - / Em D C - :‖ (4x)

There's houses in the fields, no prayers for steady rain this year
Houses in the fields, there's houses in the fields
And the last few farms are growing out of here___

C D - C / / Am D G - (C -)

At first he wouldn't sell & then he would
Now there'll be children playing where the silo stood
The word came from the marrow of his bones
It was the last sure way to pay off all the loans
> The new streets will be named for kings & queens
> And a ransom will be paid for every castle's dream
> The model sign is crested with a lion
> And the farmers they will have enough to die on

Oh I guess no one should be afraid of change
But tell me why is there a fence for every open range
It's a sign I'm getting on in years
When nothing new is welcome to these eyes & ears

Just **houses in the fields…**

— w & m: John Gorka

I'M AN OLD COWHAND
(From the Rio Grande)

I'm an old cowhand from the Rio Grande
But my legs ain't bowed & my cheeks ain't tanned
I'm a cowboy who never saw a cow
Never roped a steer 'cos I don't know how
And I sure ain't fixin' to startin' now
Oh yippy-i-o-ki-ay, yippy-i-o-ki-ay

(in C) Dm G C - / / Am Em / / / DmG C DmG C

I'm an old cowhand from the Rio Grande
And I learned to ride before I learned to stand
I'm a ridin' fool who is up to date
I know every trail in the Lone Star State
'Cos I ride the range in a Ford V8
Oh yippy-i-o-ki-ay…

I'm an old cowhand from the Rio Grande
And I come to town just to hear the band
I know all the songs that the cowboys know
'Bout the big corral where the dogies go
'Cos I learned them all on the radio
Oh yippy-i-o-ki-ay…

I'm an old cowhand from the Rio Grande
Where the West is wild round the Border land
Where the buffalo roam around the zoo
And the Indians make you a rug or 2
And the old Bar-X is a Bar-B-Q
Oh yippy-i-o-ki-ay…

— w & m: Johnny Mercer

NIGHT RIDER'S LAMENT

Last night as I was out a ridin'
Graveyard shift, midnight til dawn
The moon was as bright as a readin' light
For a letter from an old friend back home

(in 3/4) G - C - / G - D - / C - G - / C D G -

He asked me **why do** you **ride for** your **money**
Why do you **rope for short pay**
You **ain't getting' nowhere &** you're **losin'** your **share**
Boy, you **must have gone crazy out there**

G A D - / / G A D G Bm Em - / A - D -

He tells me "Last night I run onto Jenny
She's married & has a good life
Ah, you sure missed the track when you never come back
She's a perfect professional's wife"

She asked him **"Why does** he **ride for** his **money?**
Why does he **rope for short pay?**
He **ain't getting' nowhere &** he's **losin'** his **share**
He **must have gone crazy out there**
(as cho) **But they've never seen the Northern Lights**
Never seen a hawk on the wing
Never seen spring hit the Great Divide
And never heard Ol' Camp Cookie sing

Well I read up the last of that letter
And tore off the stamp for Black Jim
When Billy rode up to relieve me
He just looked at the letter & grinned

He sang "Now, why do <u>they</u> ride for their money?...
Son, they all must be crazy **out there"**

— w & m: Michael Burton

© 1975 (renewed), 1994 Michael Burton Music. On his *Pull Up Some Dust & Sit Down*, Jerry Jeff Walker *Ridin' High*, Nanci Griffith *Other Voices Other Rooms* 13, Garth Brooks *The Chase*.

OKLAHOMA HILLS

Many a month has come & gone since I wandered from my home
In those Oklahoma hills where I was born
Many a page of life has turned, many a lesson I have learned
Well I feel like in those hills I still belong

D - G E / A - D A / 1st / A - D -

Way down yonder in the Indian nation, a-ridin' my pony
  on the reservation / In those Oklahoma hills where I...
Now way downyonder in the Indian nationa cowboy's life
  is my occupation / In those Oklahoma hills where I...

But as I sit here today many miles I am away
From the place I rode my pony thru the draw
Where the Oak & Blackjack trees kiss the playful prairie breeze
In those Oklahoma hills where I was born

Now as I turn life a page to the land of the great Osage / **In the...**
Where the black oil rolls & flows & the snow-white cotton grow
In those Oklahoma hills...

— w & m: Woody Guthrie & Jack Guthrie

© 1945 (renewed) Unichappell Music Inc., Michael H. Goldsen, Inc. & Woody Guthrie Publications, Inc. All rights for Woody Guthrie Publications, Inc. administered by BMG Rights Management (US) LLC. Rec by Hank Thompson in 1961. Okla. declared it the state folk song in 2001.

OUR LITTLE TOWN

Now the RR came generations ago
And the town grew up as the crops did grow
The crops grew well & the town did too
They say it's dyin' now & there ain't a thing we can do
    I don't have to read the news or hear it on the radio
    I see it in the faces of everyone I know
    The cost goes up, what we made comes down
    What's gonna happen to our little town?

(in G) C G / D G :‖ (4x)

The summer is full of thunder, the kids run & play
Momma got a new wrinkle, poppa ain't got much to say
Rust grows along the RR track
The young folks leave, they don't come back
I don't... / The boards go up, the signs come down / And **what's...**

Tom lost his farm & we lost Tom
He left in the night, I don't know where he's gone
What he'd lost, he just couldn't face
What we're losin' can't be replaced
I don't... / The reason we're here is the farms around / So **what's...**

We've seen hard times many times before
Maybe this whole thing is just one more
It never was perfect, maybe no one's to blame
To see it die like this, it's a god damned shame
I don't... / The sun comes up, the sun goes down but...

— w & m: Greg Brown

© 1988 Hacklebarney Music (ASCAP). On his *One More Goodnight Kiss.*

RAGTIME COWBOY JOE

He always sings raggedy music to the cattle
As he swings back & forward in the saddle
On a horse (a pretty good horse) that is syncopated gaited
There is such a funny meter to the roar of his repeater
How they run, when they hear that fellow's gun
Because the Western folks all know
He's a high-faluting rootin' tootin' son of a gun from Arizona
Ragtime Cowboy Joe

G - / A - / D - / G E A D / 1st 2 / Em - / A D G

Out in Arizona where the bad men are
The only friend *[thing]* to guide you is an Evening Star
The roughest, toughest man by far is / Ragtime Cowboy Joe
He got his name from singin' to the cows & sheep
Every night they say he sings the herd to sleep
In a bass voice rich & deep / Croonin' soft & low

G C x2 / G C A D / 1st / A D G / D G x2 / D G A D /
G C x2 / F♯ Bm D

Dressed up ev'ry Sunday in his Sunday clothes
He beats it for the village where he always goes
And ev'ry girl in town is Joe's / 'Cos he's a ragtime bear
When he starts a-spieling on the dance hall floor
No one but a lunatic would start a war
Wise men know his .44 / Makes men dance for fair

— w & m: Lewis F. Muir, Grant Clarke & Maurice Abrahams

Arr. © 2015 by Hal Leonard Corporation. Orig rec Bob Roberts 14. Also by Jo Stafford (Eb), Chipmunks '59, Sons of the Pioneers 11. In *SO!* 40:3.

RIVERS OF TEXAS

We crossed the broad Pecos, we forded the Nueces
Swum the Guadalupe, we followed the Brazos
Red River runs rusty, the Wichita clear
But down by the Brazos I courted my dear

(in 3/4) C - F C / - - G - / 1st / C - G C

Li li li lee lee lee, give me your hand (3x)
There's many a river that waters the land

C F C G / C F G C / 1st / G - - C

The sweet Angelina runs glossy & gliding
The crooked Colorado runs weaving & winding
The slow San Antonio courses the plain
But I never will walk by the Brazos again
    The girls on Little River, they're plump & they're pretty
    The Sabine & Sulphur have many a beauty
    And down by the Natchez there's girls by the score
    But I never will walk by the Brazos no more
She hugged me & kissed me & called me her dandy
The Trinity is muddy, the Brazos quicksandy
I hugged her & kissed her & called her my own
But down by the Brazos she left me alone

    — trad. (US)

Arr. © 2015 by Hal Leonard Corporation. On Bill Staines *The Whistle of the Jay*, Faith Petric *Faith's Favorites*. In *Revels Garland of S*, *SO!* 54:2.

SWEET BETSY FROM PIKE

Oh don't you remember sweet Betsy from Pike
Who crossed the wide prairies with her lover Ike
With 2 yoke of cattle, a large yellow dog
A tall shanghai rooster & one spotted hog
Hoodle dang fol-dee-di-do, hoodle dang fol-dee-day

G - D G / - Em D - / G - C G / - - D G // /

One evening quite early they camped on the Platte
'Twas near by the road on a green shady flat
Where Betsy, sore-footed, lay down to repose
With wonder Ike gazed on that Pike County rose
    The shanghai ran off & their cattle all died
    That morning the last piece of bacon was fried
    Poor Ike was discouraged & Betsy got mad
    The dog drooped his tail & looked wondrously sad
They soon reached the desert, where Betsy gave out
And down in the sand she lay rollin' about
While Ike in great wonder looked on in surprise
Sayin' "Betsy, get up! You'll get sand in your eyes"
    Sweet Betsy got up in a great deal of pain
    Declared she'd go back to Pike Co. again
    But Ike gave a sigh & they fondly embraced
    And they traveled along with his arm round her waist
Long Ike & sweet Betsy attended a dance
Ike wore a pair of his Pike Co. pants
Sweet Betsy was covered with ribbons & rings
Says Ike "You're an angel, but where are your wings?"
    They swam the wide rivers & crossed the tall peaks
    And camped on the prairie for weeks upon weeks
    Starvation & cholera & hard work & slaughter
    They reached California spite of hell & high water

This Pike Co. couple got married of course
And Ike became jealous, obtained a divorce
Sweet Betsy, well satisfied, said with a shout
"Goodbye, you big lummux, I'm glad you've backed out"

    — w: John A Stone, m: trad. (US)

Arr. © 2015 by Hal Leonard Corporation. Orig pub in his *Put's Golden Songster* (1858). Rec by Burl Ives '41 & by Cisco Huston, Bob Gibson, Pete Seeger, Rosemary Clooney, Johnny Cash, etc. In *Fireside Bk of Folk S, SO!* 40:3.

TAKE ME BACK TO TULSA

Where's that gal with the red dress on? Some folks calls her Dinah
Stole my heart away from me, way down in Louisiana
Take me back to Tulsa, I'm too young to marry (2x)

G - - D / - - - G :‖

Little bee sucks the blossom, big bee gets the honey
Dark bee *[man]* raise the cotton, White man gets the money
    Oh walk & talk Suzy, walk & talk Suzy / Walk & talk…
She went down to the RR track, I went there to meet her
She pulled up her petticoat, I pulled out my…
    We always wear a great big smile, never do look sour
    Travel all over the country, playing *[music]* by the hour

    — w: Tommy Duncan, m: Bob Wills

© 1941 by Peer International Corporation & Red River Songs, Inc. Copyright renewed. All rights on behalf of Red River Songs, Inc. administered by Warner-Tamerlane Publishing Corp. Performed by Bob Wills & the Texas Playboys in the 1940 film *Take Me Back to Oklahoma*.

TELLING TAKES ME HOME

Let me sing to you all the old songs I know
Of wild, windy places locked in timeless snow
And wide, crimson deserts where the muddy rivers flow
It's sad, but the telling takes me home

G Am / A D / G Bm [or GC F#m] / C D

Come along with me to some places that I've been
Where people all look back & still remember when
And the quicksilver legends, like sunlight turn & blend / **It's…**

We'll walk along some wagon roads, or down the iron rails
Past lines of rusty Cadillacs that mark the boomtown trail
Where dreamers never win & doers never fail…

I could tell you all some lies that were just made up for fun
Where the loudest, meanest braggin' could beat the fastest gun
And I'll show you nameless graves that tell the way the West
    was won…

I'll sing of my amigos who come from down below
And whisper in their loving tongue the songs of Mexico
They work their stolen Eden, lost so long ago…

I'll sing about an emptiness the East has never known
Where coyotes don't pay taxes & a man can be alone
And you'd have to walk forever just to find a telephone…

Let me sing to you all the old songs I know
Of wild, windy places locked in timeless snow
And wide, crimson deserts where the muddy rivers flow…

    — w & m: Utah Phillips

© 1975 (renewed) On Strike Music. All rights administered by Music Management, PO Box 174, Pleasantville, NY 10570. On & in his *Starlight on the Rails*, On Ed Trickett *Telling…*, Rosalie Sorrels *My Last Go Round & Singing Thru the Hard Times* (tribute CD). In *SO!* 26:6.

THIS OLD TOWN

This old town should've burned down in 1929
That's when we stood in line
Waiting for our soup, swallowing our pride
> This old town should've burned down in 1931
> When the rain refused to come
> Air filled up our bellies, dust filled up our lungs
> And we thought our time had come

(↑2) G - D C / D C / Am G C D :‖ Am G C D

This old town was built by hand
In the dust bowl of the mother land
There must be rock beneath this sand
I'll be damned: this town still stands

C D G - / C D G D - / Em D C - /

Am - D (tacet) G - - -

This old town should've burned down in 1944
When the last men went to war
They came back different, if they came back at all
> This old town should've burned down in 1956
> That's when the twister hit
> All our hopes were buried beneath the boards & bricks
> And we almost called it quits

(bridge) Somewhere in the distance the city lights do shine
The sidewalks gleam with neon dreams that call from time to time
When my children's children ask me why didn't I go
I'll say the heart of any town is the people that you've know
They'll always call you home

Em - Bm C / - G Am D / 1st / Am D Am D / C G Am D

— w & m: Jonathan Vezner & Janis Ian

TROUBLE IN THE FIELDS

_Baby, I know that we got trouble in the fields
When the bankers swarm like locusts out there turning
   away our yield
The trains roll by our silos, silver in the rain
They leave our pockets full of nothing but our dreams & the
   golden grain

G C Bm C / G C D G :‖

Have you seen the folks in line downtown at the station?
They're all buying their tickets out & they're talking the Great
   Depression
Our parents had their hard times 50 years ago
When they stood out in these empty fields in dust as deep as snow

And all this trouble in our fields, if this rain can fall, these
   wounds can heal / _They'll never take our native soil_
But if we sell that new John Deere & then we'll work these crops
   with sweat & tears
_You'll be the mule, _I'll be the plow, _come harvest
   time, _we'll work it out_
There's still a lotta love here in these troubled fields_

C D G C / - D G Gsus / 1st / (C) G Am Bm C / Am D G -

There's a book up on the shelf about the dust bowl days, and
There's a little bit of you & a little bit of me in the photos on every page
Now our children live in the city & they rest upon our shoulders
They never want the rain to fall or the weather to get colder

— w & m: Nanci Griffith & Rick West

TUMBLING TUMBLEWEEDS

See them tumbling down
Pledging their love to the ground
Lonely but free I'll be found
Drifting along with the tumbling tumbleweeds

F - / E - / F C / G C

Cares of the past are behind
Nowhere to go but I'll find
Just where the trail will wind / **Drifting...**

(bridge) I know when night has gone
That a new world's born at dawn

G C / D G

I'll keep rolling along
Deep in my heart is a song
Here on the range I belong / **Drifting...**

— w & m: Bob Nolan

WAHOO

Oh gimme a horse, a great big horse & gimme a buckaroo
And let me wahoo wahoo wahoo!
Oh gimme a ranch, a big pair of pants & gimme a Stetson too...
Give me those wide open spaces
For I'm just like a prairie flower growing wilder every hour
Oh gimme a moon, a prairie moon & gimme a gal that's true...

(↑3)   G C7 G / D G :‖ B F♯ B / F♯ A D / 1st 2

Oh what did Miss Cleopatra say to Antony when they met?
She hollered...
Oh what did roaming Romeo yell to little Miss Juliet?
He hollered...
It started way back in Eden
Eve was the cause & it's no fib, she wahooed Adam for a rib
Oh what did Pocahontas yell the minute she saw John Smith?...

Oh, you open your mouth 2 ft. wide & take a big breath or 2
   then you can...
Oh, you wiggle your toes & grit your teeth like Dangerous Dan
   McGrew & then you...
Be careful not to sing soprano
I never could "Hi-de-hi-de-ho" 'cos that don't go up in Idaho
Buckle your belt & fix your hat & spit her out "kachew!"
   & then you...

— w & m: Cliff Friend

WINDMILLS

In days gone by, when the world was much younger
Men harnessed the wind to work for mankind
Seamen built [tall] ships to sail o'er the oceans
Landsmen built windmills, the corn for to grind

E B7 A E (4x)

It's around & around & around went the big sails
Turning the shafts & the great wooden wheels
Creaking & groaning, the mill stones kept turning
Grinding to flour the good corn from the fields

Thru Flanders & Spain & the lowlands of Holland
Thru the kingdoms of England & Scotland & Wales
Windmills grew up all along the wild coastlines
Ships of the land with their high canvas sails

The Lancashire lads worked hard with the good earth
Ploughing & sowing as the seasons declare
Waiting to reap the rich, golden harvest
While the miller, he idled, his mill to repair

Windmills so old, of wood blacked by weather
Windmills of stone flaring white in the sun
Windmills like giants ready for tilting
Windmills that died in the gales & are gone
— w & m: Alan A. Bell

© 1970 (renewed) Tamlyn Music Ltd. Rec by Alan Bell, Fred Holstein, Tommy Makem & Liam Clancy.

Farm & Prairie chap songs are about Western USA/Canada. See also: **Country, Earthcare, Freedom** (Native Amer songs), **Home & Roots.** Others include **Ballads:** One man shall mow my meadow **Jazz:** San Antonio Rose, **Love:** Shenandoah **Outdoors:** Lord is good to me **Peace:** Plant me a garden **Play:** Fiddle-i-fee, Grandpa's farm **Rich:** Leaving Eden, Tom Joad **Sing:** I want to sing to that rock & roll.

Freedom

1492

In 14 hundred & 92 Columbus sailed the ocean blue
It was a courageous thing to do, but **someone was already here**

Am DmAm Dm Am / G Am AmE Am

Columbus knew the world was round, so he looked for the East
  while westward bound
But he didn't find what he thought he found 'cos **someone...**

The Innuit & Cherokee, the Aztec & Menominee
The Onondaga & the Cree (2 claps)
Columbus sailed across the sea, but someone...

C F G C / F CAm (tacet) / G Am AmE Am

It isn't like it was empty space, Caribs met him face to face
Could anyone discover the place when **someone...?**
When someone was already here?

So tell me, who discovered what? He thought he was in a different spot
Columbus was lost, the Caribs were not, they were **already...**
— w & m: Nancy Schimmel

© 1991 Nancy Schimmel. On her & Candy Forest *Head 1st & Belly Down.* Sally Rogers *What Can One Little Person Do.* In *SO!* 36:2. Tune is based on "Tarantella Napoletana" inspired by Columbus' Italian birth.

ANOTHER BLACK MAN GONE

Another black man gone **(2x)**
Another black man gone to the county jail
Another black man gone

Am - / / Dm Em / Am -

Another mother's son **(3x)** doin' time / Another mother's son
Another innocent man **(3x)** on death row...
Another brown man gone **(3x)** for just being here...
Another poor man **(3x)** trying to get by...
Another prison wall **(3x)** that's got to fall...

Another black man gone **(2x)**
Another brown man, another poor man / Another black man gone
— w & m: Jon Fromer

© 2008 West Umbrella Music. On his *Gonna Take Us All.*

BOUND FOR FREEDOM

In Montgomery & in Selma & the streets of Birmingham
The people sent a message to the leaders of the land
We have fought & we have suffered but we know the wrong from right
We are family, we are neighbors, we are black & we are white

C - G - / Em - F G / 1st / Dm Em F G

Here I go bound for freedom, may my truth take the lead
Not the preacher, not the congress, not the millionaire
   but me
I will organize for justice, I will raise my voice in song
And our children will be free to lead the world & carry on

C - G - / Dm Em F G / 1st / Dm Em FG C

From a cell in Pennsylvania, from an inmate on death row
Mumia had the courage to expose the evil show
From the courtroom to the board room in the television's glare
How the greedy live off poor & hungry people everywhere

(bridge) Here I go tho' I'm standing on my own
I remember those before me & I know I'm not alone
I will organize for justice, I will raise my voice in song
And our children will be free to lead the world & carry on

C - F G / Em Am F G / C - G - / Dm Em FG C

From the streets of NY City 'cross the ocean & beyond
People from all nations create a common bond
With our conscience as our weapon, we are witness to the fall
We are simple, we are brilliant, we are one & we are all

— w & m: Pat Humphries

© 1997 Pat Humphries. On her *Hands*, emma's revolution *One*, King & Brandow
Sparks & Tears. Magpie *Give Light*. Mumia (Mu-MEE-ah) Abu-Jamal was convicted
& sentenced to death in 1982 for the murder of Phila. police officer Daniel Faulkner.

BRING HIM BACK HOME

Bring back Nelson Mandela, bring him back home to Soweto
I want to see him walking down the streets of South Africa
   tomorrow
Bring back Nelson Mandela... walking hand in hand with Winnie
   Mandela (now, now!) / Oo ya Mandela!

GC (x4) (repeat many times)

— w & m: Hugh Masekela, Tim Daly & Michael Timothy

© 1987 Kalahari Music, Universal/Anxious Music Ltd. & Michael Timothy Publishing.
All rights for Kalahari Music in the US & Canada administered by Warner-
Tamerlane Publishing Corp. All rights for Universal/Anxious Music Ltd. in the US
& Canada administered by Universal-Songs of PolyGram International, Inc. On his
Grazing in the Grass, Paul Simon *Graceland Anniversary Tour*. In '92 film *Sarafina!*
about the Soweto uprising. aka: "Bring Back Nelson Mandela."

CALYPSO FREEDOM (Freedom's Coming)

Freedom, give us freedom
Freedom's coming & it won't be long (repeat)

G D C G / - - D G :‖

Well I took a trip on a Greyhound bus
Freedom's coming & it won't be long
I got to fight segregation now this we must / Freedom's...

G - - - / - - D G :‖

Well I took a trip down to Alabama way / Freedom's...
We met a lot of violence on Mother's Day...

Well on to Mississippi with speed we go...
Blue-shirted policemen they meet us at the door...

Well you can hinder me here, you can hinder me there...
But I go right down on my knees in prayer...

— w: Bernice Johnson Reagon & Evelyn Marie Harris.

© 2015 Songtalk Publishing Company, Washington, D.C. and Hazel Eyes Music,
Amherst, MA. Authors were part of of Sweet Honey & the Rock. On their *All for
Freedom & S of Freedom 20th Anniversary*. On *Voices of the Civil Rights Movemt*
(Folkways). Sung to the tune of "Day-o".

CINCO SIGLOS IGUAL

Soledad sobre ruinas, sangre en el trigo / Rojo y amarillo
Manantial del veneno, escudo heridas / **Cinco siglos igual**

(↑2) C G Am F / C - G - / Am F C G / F E Am -

Libertad sin galope, banderas rotas / Soberbia y mentiras,
Medallas de oro y plata contra esperanza / **Cinco...**

En esta parte de la tierra la historia se cayó
Como se caen las piedras aun las que tocan el cielo
O están cerca del sol, o están cerca del sol

Dm DmG CF CA7 / Dm DmG CF CE7 / Am E Am -

Desamor, desencuentro, perdón y olvido
Cuerpo con mineral, pueblos trabajadores
Infancias pobres / **Cinco...**

Lealtad sobre tumbas, piedra sagrada
Dios no alcanzó a llorar, sueño largo del mal
Hijos de nadie...

Muerte contra la vida, gloria de un pueblo desaparecido
Es comienzo, es final
Leyenda perdida... / **En esta parte...**

Es tinieblas con flores, revoluciones
Y aunque muchos no están, nunca nadie pensó
Besarte los pies...

— w & m: Luis Gurevich & León Gieco

© 1991 SADAIC Latin Copyrights, Inc.

ELLA'S SONG

We who believe in freedom cannot rest
We who believe in freedom cannot rest until it comes

(↑2) A - - E / - - - A

Until the killing of black men, black mothers' sons
Is as important as the killing of white men, white mothers' sons

That which touches me most is that I had a chance to work with people
Passing on to others that which was passed on to me

To me young people come first, they have the courage where we fail
And if I can but shed some light as they carry us thru the gale

The older I get the better I know that the secret of my going on
Is when the reins are in the hands of the young, who dare to run
   against the storm

Not needing to clutch for power, not needing the light just to
   shine on me
I need to be one in the number as we stand against tyranny

Struggling myself don't mean a whole lot, I've come to realize
That teaching others to stand up & fight is the only way my
    struggle survives

I'm a woman who speaks in a voice & I must be heard
At times I can be quite difficult, I'll bow to no man's word

— w & m: Bernice Johnson Reagon

THE FOGGY DEW

As down the glen one Easter morn to a city fair rode I
There armed lines of marching men in squadrons passed me by
No pipe did hum, no battle drum did sound its dread tattoo
But the Angelus bell o'er the Liffey swell rang out in **the foggy dew**

Am GEm AmEm Am /   / C GC AmEm Am / 1st

Right proudly high over Dublin Town they hung out the flag of war
'Twas better to die 'neath an Irish sky than at Suvla or Sud-El-Bar
And from the plains of Royal Meath strong men came hurrying thru
While Britannia's sons with their great big guns sailed in thru...

But the bravest fell & the requiem bell rang mournfully & clear
For those who died that Eastertide in the springing of the year
And the world did gaze with deep amaze on those fearless men,
    but few
Who bore the fight that freedom's light might shine thru...

'Twas England bade our Wild Geese go that small nations might
    be free
But their lonely graves are by Suvla's waves & the fringe of the
    grey North Sea
Oh had they died by Pearse's side or fought with Cathal Brugha
Their graves we would keep where the Fenians sleep 'neath the
    hills of...

Back to the glen I rode again & my heart with grief was sore
For I parted then with valiant men I never would see more
But to & fro in my dreams I go & I kneel & pray for you
For slavery fled, O rebel dead, when you fell in...

— trad. (Irish "The Moorlough Shore")

FOUR GREEN FIELDS

"What did I have?" said the fine old woman
"What did I have?" this proud old woman did say
"I had 4 green fields, each one was a jewel
But strangers came & tried to take them from me
I had fine strong sons, they fought to save my jewels
They fought & died & that was my grief" said she

(in 3/4) GD G C G / GD G C D / GD G GC D
GD Em C D / BmAm G GC D / C G GD G

"Long time ago" said the fine old woman
"Long time ago" this proud old woman did say
"There was war & death, plundering & pillage
My children starved — by mtn, valley, & sea
And their wailing cries, they shook the very heavens
My 4 green fields ran red with their blood" said she

"What have I now?" said the fine old woman
"What have I now?" this proud old woman did say
"I have 4 green fields, one of them's in bondage
In strangers' hands that tried to take it from me
But my sons have sons as brave as were their fathers
My 4th green field will bloom once again" said she

— w & m: Thomas Makem

GET BACK (Black, Brown & White)

This little song that I'm singin' about, people you know it's true
If you're black & gotta work for a living, now this is what they
    will say to you
They says "If you was white, should be all right,
    if you was brown, stick around
But as you's black, oh brother: get back **(x3)**!"

D - /   / G D / A D

I was in a place one night, they was all having fun
They was all buyin' beer & wine, but they would not sell me none
    I went to an employment office, got a number 'n' I got in line
    They called everybody's number but they never did call mine
Me & a man was workin' side by side, this is what it meant
They was paying him a dollar an hour & they was paying me 50 cents
    I helped build this country & I fought for it too
    Now I guess that you can see what a black man have to do
I helped win sweet victories with my little plough & hoe
Now I want you to tell me brother, what you gonna do 'bout the
    old Jim Crow?

— w & m: William Lee Conley ("Big Bill") Broonzy

GET ON BOARD LITTLE CHILDREN (Gospel Train)

The Gospel train's a-comin', I hear her close at hand
I hear those car wheels rumblin' & rollin' thru the land

Get on board, children children (2x)
Get on...children: there's room for many-a-more

G - - CD / G C GD G / C - G - / C - GD G

I hear that train a comin', she's comin' 'round the curve
She's loosened all her stream & brakes & straining every nerve

The fare is cheap & all can go, the rich & poor are there
No second class upon this train, no difference in the fare

I hear that mob a-howling, they're headed for the square
Sayin' "Catch those freedom fighters" but we're gonna
    meet 'em there

Get on board, children children (2x)
Get on...children: let's fight for human rights

As freedom fighters we're aware that we may go to jail
But if you fight for freedom, the Lord will go your bail

As fighters we go hungry, sometimes don't sleep or eat
But when you fight for freedom, in the end you will be free!

— trad. (Afr-Amer spiritual), adap by SNCC workers

GET UP STAND UP

Get up, stand up, stand up for your rights! (3x)
Get up, stand up, don't give up the fight!

Am - - - (4x)

Preacher man, don't tell me heaven is under the earth
I know you don't know what life is really worth
It's not all that glitters is gold, half the story has never been told:
So now you see the light, eh! **stand up for your rights**

Get up, stand up, stand up for your rights!
Get up, stand up, don't give up the fight! (repeat)

Most people think great god will come from the skies
Take away everything & make everybody feel high
But if you know what life is worth you will look for yours on earth:
And now you see the light , you **stand up...** jah!

We sick an' tired of-a your ism-skism game
Dyin' 'n' goin' to heaven in-a Jesus' name, lord
We know when we understand: almighty god is a living man
You can fool some people sometimes, but you can't fool all the
    people all the time
So now we see the light we gonna **stand up...!**

— w & m: Bob Marley & Peter Tosh

© 1974 Fifty-Six Hope Road Music Ltd., Odnil Music Ltd., State One Music America LLC & Embassy Music Corporation. Copyright renewed. All rights in North America administered by Blue Mountain Music Ltd./Irish Town Songs (ASCAP) & throughout the rest of the world by Blue Mountain Music Ltd. (PRS). On his *Legend, Burnin'* & Peter Tosh *Equal Rights*

HONEY IN THE ROCK

There's honey in the rock for all God's children
Honey in the rock, oh honey in the rock
Honey in the rock for all God's children
Feed every child of God

Em - - - / B7 - Em - / 1st / Em B7 Em -

(as cho) There's **joy** in the rock... / Joy in the rock, oh joy...
It's honey in the rock... / **Feed...**

Some say Peter & some say Paul / **Feed every child of God**
Ain't but the one God made us all / **Feed...**

Am - Em - / / / - B7 Em -

If religion was a thing that your money could buy / **Feed...**
The rich would live & the poor would die / **Feed...**

There's **peace** in the rock... / Love in the rock, oh love...
Peace **in the rock for all God's children / Feed...**

One of these mornings, bright & fair / **Feed...**
I'm gonna put on my wings & feel the air / **Feed...**

I'll climb & climb & I'll never stop / **Feed...**
Until I reach that mtn top / **Feed...**

— w & m: Guy Carawan

© 1986 (renewed) by Sanga Music, Inc. All rights administered by Figs. D Music c/o The Bicycle Music Company. Carawan says "I heard the beautiful chorus to [this] from my neighbor Alice Wine when I lived on Johns Island, South Carolina. I added the verses, words & music, to make it a song I could sing." On his *The Land Knows You're Three* & YT by Nick Page.

I HAVE A MILLION NIGHTINGALES

1. & 2. I have a million / nightin-_gales on the /
branches of my / heart _
3. Singing free-_dom / freedom / free-_ / dom _
4. Singing free-_dom / freedom _/ free-_ / dom _

Am - / Em Asus / F G Am -

— w & m: Linda Hirschhorn

© 1989 Linda Hirschhorn. On Linda Hirschhorn *Gather Round*. Lyrics are inspired by Mahmoud Darwish (1948-2001), who was regarded as the Palestine national poet. In his work Palestine is a metaphor for lost Eden, birth & resurrection, dispossession & exile. *LS

I'M GONNA SIT AT THE WELCOME TABLE

I'm gonna sit at the welcome table
    I'm gonna sit... table **one of these days — hallelujah!**
    I'm gonna sit... / Gonna sit... table **one of these days!**

G - - - / C - - GD / G - E Am / C D G(C G)
C - - - / F - - FC / C - E7 F / C CG CF C

I'm gonna walk & talk with Jesus...
I'm gonna walk the streets of glory...
I'm gonna feast on milk & honey...
I'm gonna tell God how you treat me...
All God's children gonna sit together...
I'm gonna get my civil rights...
I'm gonna sit at the Woolworth's counter...

— African-American Spiritual [new v. SNCC]

Arr. © 2015 by Hal Leonard Corporation. In *Coll Reprints fr SO!* V1-6 & *Sing for Freedom*

THE INDIAN PRAYER (Indanee)

As long as the sun shall glow, **as...** the wind shall blow
As... the stream shall flow... the grass shall grow
This land, this land shall be / Indanee, Indanee

D G D G / A G A G / A - G - / D - G - (D - G -)

Weyheyya h**e**yho_weyheyya heyh**o** _ (3x)
Weyheyya h**e**yho_wheyy**a** (x2) heyheyh**o** _ hohohoh**o**

D - A G / / / D - G A D - G -

As... a deer shall spring ...a bird shall sing
...a whale is king *[whale's swimming]* ...their life shall bring

As...a baby's small ...as a boy [child] grows tall
...we all shall crawl ...this earth's a ball
[...the elders recall ...this earth shall call]

— w & m: Roland Vargas Mousaa & Tom Pacheco

© 1974 (renewed) Frank Music Corp. On Mousaa *In the Eye of the Great Spirit*, Pacheco *There Was a Time* (in C), Richie Havens *Mixed Bag II* 11 & Pat Humphries *Hands* 17. In *SO!* 46:4.

THE LAST BATTLE

An east wind blew in the storms of time
Where the Métis lived on the winding river
For on a steel rail the settlers came
To the South Saskatchewan & the land they claimed

G CD G - / Em Am D - / BmEm AmD G Em / Am - D -

Then three Métis & Gabriel
Rode like the wind to wild Montana
And on the Sweet Grass in a church of stone
They found their savior & they took him home, saying…

"Come Riel, we'll make a stand
Here at Batoche, beside the river
Oh never mind their Gatling guns
If we lose this time we've lost forever"

G - D G / Em Am D - / G CD G / C D G - /

Then the bullets flew & the cannons roared
And the Métis blood flowed like a river
Into the coulees where they ran to hide
It washed their dreams away & their spirit died - oh…

   Then a silence stole across the land
   The drums of war were gone forever
   But in the starlight on the barren plains
   The cry of Gabriel flies on the wind…

— w & m: Bill Gallaher

© 1988 Bill Gallaher. On his *Last…* (w/ Jake Galbraith), Gordon Bok *In the Kind Land*.

MINSTREL BOY

The Minstrel Boy to the war is gone
In the ranks of death you will find him
His father's sword he hath girded on
And his wild harp slung behind him
"Land of Song!" said the warrior bard
"Tho all the world betrays thee
One sword, at least, thy rights shall guard
One faithful harp shall praise thee!"

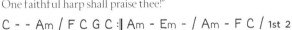

C - - Am / F C G C :‖ Am - Em - / Am - F C / 1st 2

The Minstrel fell! But the foeman's chain
Could not bring that proud soul under
The harp he lov'd ne'er spoke again
For he tore its chords asunder
And said "No chains shall sully thee
Thou soul of love & brav'ry!
Thy songs were made for the pure & free
They shall never sound in slavery!"

The Minstrel Boy will return we pray
When we hear the news we all will cheer it
The minstrel boy will return one day
Torn perhaps in body, not in spirit
Then may he play on his harp in peace
In a world such as Heaven intended
For all the bitterness of man must cease
And ev'ry battle must be ended

— w: Thomas Moore (1779–1852) m: trad. (Irish "The Moreen")

Arr. © 2015 by Hal Leonard Corporation. Written for friends killed in 1798 Irish Rebellion. v. 3 is from US Civil War. On Clancy Bros rec & In *Fireside Bk of Folk S*.

NICARAGUA, NICARAGÜITA

Ay, Nicaragua, Nicaragüita, la flor más linda de mi querer
Abonada con la bendita, Nicaragüita, Sangre de Diriangén
Ay, Nicaragua sos más dulcita que la mielita de Tamagás
Pero ahora que ya sos libre, Nicaragüita, yo te quiero mucho más **(2x)**

C - - G / F C G C / - - C7 D / 2nd / C - G C

— w & m: Carlos Mejía Godoy

© 1977 (renewed 2005) EMI Songs Espana Srl. All rights in the US & Canada controlled & administered by EMI Blackwood Music Inc. On his *Aromas de Libertad* & Billy Bragg *The Internationale*, Banda Bassotti *Asi Es Mi Vida & Chraeckpt Kreuzberg*, Frank Fernandez *Musica de mi Tierra*, Damba *Y Si Rompo Mi Camino*.

NKOSI SIKELELI AFRIKA (God Bless Africa)

Nkosi Sikelel' iAfrika
Malup'hakanyisw' up'hondo lwayo
Yiswa imithandazo yethu
Nkosi Sikelela / Thina lusap'ho lwayo

C - G C / - Dm C G / Am C G C / F C G C / /

Woza moya (3x)
Oyingcwele / Usisikelele / Thina lusap'ho lwayo

CBb C - - / / C G F / Dm C G C / / /

Morena boloka setjaba sa heso
O fedise dintwa le matshwe ne ho **(repeat)**
O se boloke, o _se boloke **(2x)**
Setjhaba sa heso / Setjhaba sa Afrika

Am C - G / Am CF CG C :‖ C G - C / / F C G C / /

— w & m: E. M. Sontonga.

Arr. © 2015 by Hal Leonard Corporation. On Ladysmith Black Mambazo *Long Walk to Freedom*, *In Harmony*, & *Ultimate Collection*. In *SO!* 31:4 & '87 film *Cry for Freedom*. This hymn became the pan-African liberation anthem & was often sung by the anti-apartheid movement. It became one of 2 national anthems of South Africa in 1994 & then the two were combined in 1997.

PRETTY BROWN

Pretty Brown, you're a song that I can't keep from singing
Pretty Brown, as you move, you don't know that you're winning
And your eyes say you're lost like an autumn leaf spinning
Turn around, dry your eyes, Pretty Brown

G - - D / Am - - G / 1st / C D G -

In the city did you find the good times you had in mind?
Reservation child, the city's not your home
Put it behind, turn round your mind
And you will find you'll smile, Pretty Brown

C - G - / C Am D - / C - G - / Am D G -

You're a stranger in the town & your world has tumbled down
But there's a million wishing they were young as you
So let it go, just let it go
Before you know, you'll laugh, Pretty Brown
   Let your black hair hang down low, dance like we did long ago
   And the beating of the drum will set you free
   Just give it time soon you'll do fine
   Your sun will shine once more, Pretty Brown

— w & m: David Campbell

© 1975 David Campbell. On his *Pretty…* Born in Guyana of Arawak Indian & Portuguese ancestry, resident of Vancouver BC.

QUÉ BONITA BANDERA

Qué bonita bandera (3x) / Es la bandera Puertorriqueña

I: Am - E - / - - Am - / Am - Dm - / Am E Am -

Azul, blanca colorada / En el medio tiene una_estrella
Qué bonita bandera / Es mi bandera puertorriqueña
  Dijo José de Diego / Bentances y Muñoz Rivera
   Qué bonita bandera / Es la bandera puertorriqueña
Quisiera verla flotando / Sobre mi Borinquen bella
Qué bonita bandera / Dime qué bonita bandera

II: Am - E - /   / Am E Am Dm / Am E Am -

  — w & m: Florencio Morales Ramos ["Ramito"]

© 1973 by Peer International Corporation. Copyright renewed. I: On Ramito Ramito *Raíces Borincanas*, Plena Libre *Corazón*. II: On Weavers *Wasn't That a Time*, Pete Seeger *Sing Out w/Pete* & in his *Amer Fav Ballads*. In v. 2 Ramito names 3 of Puerto Rico's early nationalist political leaders.

REDEMPTION SONG

Old pirates, yes, they rob I, sold I to the merchant ships
Minutes after they took I_from the bottomless pit
But my hand was made strong_by the 'and of the Almighty
We forward in this generation_triumphantly

G Em C Am /   /   / G Em C D

Won't you help to sing _these songs of freedom?
'Cos all I ever have: / Redemption songs (x2)

D G CD G / CD Em / CD G CD G

Emancipate yourselves from mental slavery,
  none but ourselves can free our minds
Have no fear for atomic energy, 'cos none of them can stop the time
How long shall they kill our prophets, while we stand aside & look
Some say it's just a part of it: we've got to fulfill the book

  — w & m: Bob Marley

© 1980 Fifty-Six Hope Road Music Ltd. & Odnil Music Ltd. All rights in North America administered by Blue Mountain Music Ltd./Irish Town Songs (ASCAP) & throughout the rest of the world by Blue Mountain Music Ltd. (PRS). On his *Uprising*.

SECORD'S WARNING

Come all you brave young soldier lads with your strong & manly bearing
I'll tell you a tale of a woman bold & her deed of honest daring
Laura Secord was American-born in the state of Massachusetts
But she made her home in Canada & proved so faithful to us

C G C FC / C G C - / FC G - /   /

There's American guns & 500 men so the warning must be given
And Laura Ingersoll Secord was the stalwart heart who
** braved the heat**
And the flies & the swamp to warn Colonel Fitzgibbon

C G C FC / FC (x4) / FC G C

There's soldiers pounding at the door & they come from across
  the border
American officers march inside, it's food & drink they've ordered
In comfort they have dined & drunk, their own success they've toasted
But they pay no heed to the woman who hears their plan so idly boasted

O James, I've overheard it all, a surprise attack they're making
Fitzgibbon they intend to smash, his men for prisoners taking
And James, a warning never you'll take with your wounded knee
  and shoulder
I myself must carry it past the sentries & the soldiers

It's an all-day tramp to the British camp by way of Shipman's Corners
There're snakes & flies & sweat in her eyes, there is no respite for her
She's lost her shoes in the muck of the bog, her feet are torn &
  blistered
But there's many a soldier lad to be spared if the message be
  delivered

So all you Yankee soldier lads who dare to cross our border
Thinking to save us from ourselves, usurping British order
There's women & men Canadians all of every rank & station
To stand on guard & keep us free from Yankee domination

  — w & m: Joe Grant & Steve Ritchie

© 1990 Joe Grant & Steve Ritchie. On Tanglefoot *Captured Alive* 14. In *SO!* 43:1.

SENZENINA

Senzenina (senzenina x2) (4x)
Sono sethu (Sono sethu ubumnyama)
Sono sethu (...yinyaniso)
Sibulawayo (sibulawayo x2)
Mayibuye (...i Afrika)

C - - C7 / Dm - CG C / - - CG Am / 2nd /

What have we done? (What have... x2)
Our only sin (Our only sin is we are black)
Our only sin (...is to tell the truth)
They're killing us (They're... x2)
Let Africa (Let Africa return again)

  — trad. (South African Zulu freedom song)

Arr © 2015 by Hal Leonard Corporation. In '92 film *The Power of One*.

SHTIL DI NAKHT

Shtil, di nakht iz oysgeshte-rnt / Un der frost - er hot gebrent_
Tsi gedenkstu vi ikh hob dikh gele-rnt
Haltn a shpayer in di hent_ (2x)

Am Dm G Am / C F C E / /: 1st / Dm Em Am - :|

A moyd, a peltsl un a be-ret / Un halt in hant fest a nagan_
A moyd mit a sametenem pon-im / Hit op dem soynes karavan
  Getsilt, geshosn un getro-fn / Hot ir kleyninke pistoyl
  An oyto, a fulinkn mit vo-fn / Farhaltn hot zi mit eyn koyl
Far tog, fun vald aroysgekro-khn / Mit shney girlandn af di hor
Gemutikt fun kleyninkn nitso-khn / Far undzer nayem, frayen dor

  — w & m: Hirsch Glik

Arr © 2015 by Hal Leonard Corporation. About Vitke Kempner, a female resistance fighter, who helped blow up a German military transport near Vilna in 1942. Glik escaped from the concentration camp in 1944 w/ 40 others but was killed in combat with Nazi forces soon afterwards.

SIYAHAMBA

Siyahamb' ekukhanyen' kwenkhos' (2x) (repeat)
Siyahamba, hamba (x2)
Siyahamb' ekukhanyen' kwenkhos' (repeat last 2 lines)

D - - - / A - D - :|: G - D - / A - D - :|

We are marching in the light of God (2x) (repeat)
We are marching, marching (x2)
We are marching **in the light of God** (repeat last 2 lines)
Substitute: praying, dancing, etc.

  — trad. (South African Zulu freedom song)

Arr © 2015 by Hal Leonard Corporation. In *Freedom is Coming: Songs of Protest & Praise from South Africa* & hymnals incl *Gather Comprehensive, New Century Hymnal* (UCC), *Singing the Journey* (UUA).

(Something Inside) So Strong

The higher you build your barriers /_The taller I become_ _
The farther you take my rights away /_The faster I will run_ _
You can deny me, you can decide
To turn your face away_ no matter 'cos there's

D - - DA / G - - GA :‖ Bm - C - / Em - A - (tacet)

_Something inside so strong
I know that I can make it, _tho' you're doing me wrong, so wrong
_You thought that my pride was gone, oh no
  Something inside so strong,   oh / Something inside…

D DA G GBm / G GA G A / 1st / G GA Bm - / G GA D -

The more you refuse to hear my voice / The louder I will sing
You hide behind walls of Jericho / Your lies will come tumbling
Deny my place in time, you squander wealth that's mine
_My light will shine so brightly, it will blind you because there's

(bridge) _Brothers & sisters when they insist we're just not
  good enough
_When we know better _just look 'em in the eyes & say
"We're gonna do it anyway, we're… anyway!" (2x)

C - G - / D - - - / 1st / Em - A - /   /

— w & m: Labi Siffre

That Kind of Grace

Sunday morning, Birmingham, quiet in the church
Bombs were planted, House of God, children's blood on the cross
And your daughter, she was one, angel without wings
How could anyone forgive those who do such things?

(in 3/4) Am G Am E / Am G AmAmE Am :‖

And when I sing Amazing Grace / Your face is what I see
I hope someday that kind of grace / Will find its way thru me

C C7 F C / C Am G E / Am G F C / E - Am -

Friday evening in Mobile, klansmen killing time
Saw young Michael walking by, he would do just fine
Quiet student, mother's best, pleading for his life
They strung him up to make a point, sharper than a knife

  Beulah Mae, his mother stood, people all around
  In the courtroom listening as the truth was found
  From her mouth no curses fell, no profanity
  "I would do to others what I'd have them do to me"

  C G Am E /   / Am G Am E / Am G AmAmE Am

And when I sing Amazing Grace / Her face is what I see…

Thursday afternoon in the car, turned the radio on
The verdict in Los Angeles, oh what have we done
Images of violence, yellow, black & white
Fifty-two dead, millions lost, who can win this fight

  And on the screen a face of tears, trembling thru & thru
  One we've seen so many times beaten on the news
  I could barely hear his words, full of fear & doubt
  "People, we can't live like this, we've got to work this out

And when I sing Amazing Grace / That face is what I see…

— w & m: Anne Hills & David Roth

Walk Proud, My Son

Use it up, wear it out, make it do or do without
We can't pay for the things you want to buy
Wear your old faded jeans, they are patched but they are clean
Walk proud my son & hold your head up high

C G C F / - - G - / 1st / C G C -

We lived a way back in the hills with the bears & the whippoorwills
The nearest store was 35 miles away
Tho' I'm now a full grown man if I close my eyes I can
Hear the words my mother used to say

Now I have a son of my own, he's even got his own telephone
Seems I have to buy him smth every day
He's got everything that money can buy & it makes me want to cry
'Cos I know he'll never hear his mother say

— w & m: Don Grooms

We Shall Not Give Up the Fight

We shall not give up the fight, we have only started
We have only started, we have only started (repeat)

D G / A D :‖

We shall not give up on peace, we have only started…
We'll put an end to bigotry, we have only started…
Together we'll have victory, hand holding hand…
Never ever put to flight, we are bound to win…

— South African Folk Song

We Still Have a Dream

We still have a dream (echo) we still have a dream (echo)
Every step of the way (echo) brings on a better day! (echo)
And the Spirit is willin' (echo) & the journey is long (echo)
We've got to be strong (echo) 'cos we still have a dream (echo)

(↑2) CF x4 /   / CF CE Am F / CAm FG CF C(F)

_Hey, brother, can your feet still walk?
_Hey, sister are you ready to talk?
_Hey, children, won't you lead the way?
It's time to march again
And these streets have seen a lot of feet over the years
Wars of liberation far away & right here
_They've seen our hopes, Lord, they've seen our tears
And it's time to march again

CF CF x2 /   / CE AmC7 / F Gsus G :‖

(bridge) Believe me when I tell you we shall not be moved
_We haven't come this far to bargain
_The bottom line is underneath our feet
And if you listen, you can hear an earthquake startin'

Am↓ FE /   / AmD CAm / Bb FG [DmEmFG]

— w & m: Betsy Rose

THE WEARING OF THE GREEN

O Paddy dear & did ye hear the news that's goin' round?
The shamrock is by law forbid to grow on Irish ground!
St Patrick's Day no more we'll keep, his colors can't be seen
For there's a cruel law ag'in **the Wearin' o' the Green"**
The wearin' o' the Green (x2) / For there's a cruel law ag'in...

D - A - / G D G D :| G - D - / G D A D

I met with Napper Tandy & he took me by the hand
And he said "How's poor old Ireland & how does she stand?"
"She's the most distressful country that ever yet was seen
For they're hanging men & women there for **the Wearin'**..."

"So if the color we must wear be England's cruel red
Let it remind us of the blood that Irishmen have shed
And pull the shamrock from your hat & throw it on the sod
But never fear, 'twill take root there, tho underfoot 'tis trod

When laws can stop the blades of grass from growin' as they grow
When the leaves in summertime their color dare not show
Then I will change the color too I wear in my caubeen,
'Til that day, please God, I'll stick to **the Wearin'**...

— trad. (18th c. Irish)

WHAT CAN ONE LITTLE PERSON DO

What can 1 little person do? What can 1 little me or you do?
What can 1 little person do to help this world go round?
One can help another 1 & together we can get the job done
What can 1 little person do to help this world?

D - G D / D - E A / D D7 G D / D E A D -

Harriet Tubman was alone on the darkened road to freedom
But she couldn't leave her people far behind
Moses stretched out her hand, she led them to the promised land
'Cos she knew she had justice on her side

When Sojourner Truth was free, she got down on her knees
Prayed to God to help her on her way
With her voice & with her might, she fought for what was right
'Cos she knew she had justice on her side

Rosa Parks sat on the bus & the driver said you must
Move to the back of the bus or else be thrown in jail
But she stayed & stood her ground, and she brought that old law
  down / 'Cos she knew she had justice on her side

Bro. Martin Luther King told the world "I have a dream"
He led this country's fight for human rights
We must fight for liberty until all of us are free
To know we have justice on our side

When Barack was a young man in Chicago's streets he planned
To help the least of us to find the meaning of hope
From Hawaii to DC, he fought for you & me
For he knew that he had justice on his side

— w & m: Sally Rogers

YOU'VE GOT TO BE CAREFULLY TAUGHT

You've got to be taught to hate & fear
You've got to be taught from year to year
It's got to be drummed in your dear little ear
You've got to be carefully taught

(↑7, in 3/4) C - Dm - / / / C Dm C -

You've got to be taught to be afraid
Of people whose eyes are oddly made &
People whose skin is a different shade / **You've...**

(tag) You've got to be taught before it's too late
Before you are 6 or 7 or 8
To hate all the people your relatives hate
You've... (2x)

Fmaj7 Caug Fmaj7 Caug / Fmaj7 Caug Fmaj7 D7
C - Dm - / C Em Dm D7 / C Dm C -

— w: Oscar Hammerstein II, m: Richard Rodgers

ZOG NIT KEYN MOL (Partisan Song)

Zog nit keyn mol az du geyst dem letstn veg
Khotsh himlen blayene farshteln bloye teg
Kumen vet nokh undzer oysgebenkte sho
S'vet a poyk ton undzer trot - mir zaynen do! (repeat lines 3 & 4)

(in Am) E7 Am / G C //: A7 Dm / AmE Am :|

Fun grinem palmenland biz vaysn land fun shney
Mir kumen on mit undzer payn, mit undzer vey
Un vu gefaln s'iz a shprits fun undzer blut
Shprotsn vet dort undzer gvure, undzer mut...

S'vet di morgnzun bagildn undz dem haynt
Un der nekhtn vet farshvindn mitn faynd
Nor oyb farzamen vet di zun in dem kayor
Vi a parol zol geyn dos lid fun dor tsu dor...

Dos lid geshribn iz mit blut un nit mit blay
S'iz not keyn lidl fun a foygl af der fray
Dos hot a folk tsvishn falndike vent
Dos lid gezungen mit naganes in di hent!...

To zog nit keyn mol az du geyst dem letstn veg
Khotsh kimlen blayene farshteln bloye teg
Kumen vet nokh undzer oysgebenkte sho
S'vet a poyk ton undzer trot - mir zaynen do!...

— w & m: Hirsch Glick (music adap from "Pokras")

The **Freedom** chapter contains songs of civil rights & liberation movements for African Americans, South Africa, Native Americans, Ireland. See also: **Home & Roots**, **Struggle**. Related songs incl **Dignity**: Colors of earth **Earthcare**: One drum **Faith**: Still small voice **Gospel**: People get ready, Soon & very soon, There'll be no distinction there, We are soldiers **Peace**: Is there anybody here.

Friendship & Community

ALL I REALLY WANT TO DO

I ain't lookin' to compete with you, beat or cheat or mistreat you
Simplify you, classify you, deny, defy or crucify you
All I really want to do is baby be friends with you   **(in A)**

D A E A D A E A /   / A - D - A D A E - A - - -

No & I ain't lookin' to fight with you, frighten you or uptighten you
Drag you down or drain you down, chain you down or bring
    you down
All I really want to do...

I ain't lookin' to block you up, shock or knock or lock you up
Analyze you, categorize you, finalize you or advertise you...

I don't want to straight-face you, race or chase you, track or trace you
Or disgrace you or displace you or define you or confine you

I don't want to meet your kin, make you spin or do you in
Or select you or dissect you or inspect you or reject you

I don't want to fake you out, take or shake or forsake you out
I ain't lookin' for you to feel like me, see like me or be like me

— w & m: Bob Dylan

© 1964 Warner Bros. Copyright renewed 1992 by Special Rider Music. Reprinted by permission of Music Sales Corporation. On his *Another Side of...*, Byrds *Mr Tamourine Man*. In *SO!* 14:6.

CLOSER TO FINE

I'm trying to tell you something about my life
Maybe give me insight btw black & white
And the best thing you've ever done for me
Is to help me take my life less seriously
It's only life after all

(↑2) G Am7 C D /   / D - C - /   / 1st /

Well darkness has a hunger that's insatiable
And lightness has a call that's hard to hear
I wrap my fear around me like a blanket
I sailed my ship of safety 'til I sank it
I'm crawling on your shores C - G -

I went to the doctor, I went to the mountains
I looked to the children, I drank from the fountain
There's more than one answer to these questions
Pointing me in a crooked line
And the less I seek my source for some definitive
The closer I am to fine **(2x)**

D - C G /   / D - C - / G - / 3rd / G Am7 C D /   /

I went to see the doctor of philosophy
With a poster of Rasputin & a beard down to his knee
He never did marry or see a B-grade movie
He graded my performance, he said he could see thru me
I spent 4 yrs prostrate to the higher mind, got my paper & I was
    free G D C D G -

I stopped by the bar at 3am
To seek solace in a bottle or possibly a friend
And I woke up with a headache like my head against a board
Twice as cloudy as I'd been the night before
And I went in seeking clarity C - G -

(last cho) We go **to the doctor,** we go **to the mtns**
We look **to the children,** we drink **from the fountain**
(as 1st 2 lines) We go to the bible, we go thru the workout
We read up on revival & we stand up for the lookout
There's more than one answer...

— w & m: Emily Saliers & Amy Ray

© 1989 Godhap Music. All rights controlled & administered by Songs of Universal, Inc. On *Indigo Girls*.

COME JOIN THE CIRCLE

Come join the circle, come join the circle, children
Come join the circle, come & join us in the circle

(↑2) Am - Em AmE / Am - Em EAm

(counter melody) In a circle we're equal, no one is left out
We all can see each other's eyes
A circle is powerful, it's unbroken
It helps to strengthen all our ties

— w & counter-melody: Paulette Meier, m: trad. (African American
    spiritual)

© 1997 Paulette Meier. Lessonsongs Music. On her *Come Join...* The orig. spiritual "Wade in the Water" was often used by Southern Black slaves to signal plans to escape. Arr Ginny Frazier.

83

COMMON GROUND

Come in the door is open, you are welcome here
Come in the door is open, leave out all doubt & fear
We'll plant a seed together & together watch it grow
And learn once more what we already know

(↑2) C - FG C / - - D G / FG C FG Am / C - G -

Lift up your v**o**ice, rejoice in what we've found
Let every he**a**rt take refuge in the sound
Feel the w**a**lls around us tremble, we will surely bring them
    down / And f**in**d ourselves on Common Ground (**2x**)

C FG C - / F G C - / F G Am F / Dm FG F - / Dm FG C -

This is how we celebrate our song & dance & art
This is how we touch the future, how we touch a heart
Tell your story to a child & they'll take it as their own
This is how we learn we're not alone

In our time together I begin to understand
There are bridges we can only cross together hand in hand
Soon we'll head on homeward & go our separate ways
But these echoes will be dancing down our days
    — w & m: Scott Ainslie & Tom Chapin

© 2001 Cattail Music, Ltd. & the Last Music Co. (ASCAP). On Chapin's *Common...*

DEEP IN THE DARKEST NIGHT

Deep in the darkest night / Under a midnight moon
Standing alone with the sea & the moon
You said that you'd come back soon
Deep in the darkest night

(↑2) CG Am /   / FC GAm / FC G / - C

Deep in a memory / A fugitive on the run
Looking for somewhere to make a bed
Somewhere to lie a restless head
Deep in a memory

**I'll be your harbour when there's a storm
I'll be your sunshine, I'll keep you warm
I'll be your shelter in the rain & snow
Remember wherever you go / Deep in the darkest night**

FC GC / FC G / FC GAm / 2nd / G C

Dans un noir de nuit / Je n'avais rien dit
Souvenir d'un été chaud / Souvenir de soleil et d'eau
Dans un noir de nuit

Deep in your heart you know
You're running against the wind
Taking your loneliness in your case
The same old sadness from place to place
Deep in your heart you know

(tag) Dans un noir de nuit (**2x**) / Deep in the darkest night

CG Am (**3x**)

    — w & m: Rick Kemp

© 1999 by Peermusic (UK) Ltd. On his *Escape*, Maddy Prior *Year, Going for Glory* & *Memento*, Backroom Boys & Girls *Brief Encounters*.

DON'T LET ME COME HOME A STRANGER

As I walked out one evening
To breathe the air & soothe my mind
I thought of friends & the home I had
And all the things I left behind, oh

C G C - / F - G Am / F - C - / F Em Dm G (C F C -)

A silent star shone on me
My eyes saw the far horizon
As if to pierce this veil of time
And escape this earthly prison, oh

**Will there come a time when the memories fade
And pass on with the long, long yrs?
When the ties no longer bind
Lord save me from this darkest fear
Don't let me come home a stranger
I couldn't stand to be a stranger**

C F C - / F C G Am / F - C - /

F Em Dm G - - / 1st / Am G C -

In this place so far from home
They know my name but they don't know me
They hear my voice, they see my face
But they can't lay no claim on me, oh

And as I walk this universe
I free my mind of time & space
I wander thru the galaxies
But never do I find my place, oh
    — w & m: Robin Williams & Jerome Clark

© 1983 Universal-Songs of PolyGram International, Inc. & Brantford Music. All rights controlled & administered by Universal-Songs of Polygram International, Inc. On Robin & Linda Williams *Stonewall Country* 14 , *Live in Holland* & *Fast Folk* 1:10. On Tim & Molly O'Brien *Away Out on the Mtn* 14, In *SO!* 39:4.

THE GATHERING OF SPIRITS

Let it g**o** my love, my tr**u**est, let it sail on silver w**in**gs
Life's a tw**in**kling, that's for c**e**rtain, but it's s**u**ch a fine th**in**g
**There's a gathering of spirits, there's a festival of friends
And we'll take up where we left off when we all meet again**

(↑2) G CG D - / C G D - / 1st / C G D G

I can't explain it, I couldn't if I tried
How the only things we carry are the things we hold inside
Like a day in the open, like the love we won't forget
Like the laughter that we started & it hasn't died down yet

C - G - / C G D - :‖

Oh yeah, now didn't we & don't we make it shine
Aren't we standing in the center of something rare & fine
Some glow like embers, like a light thru colored glass
Some give it all in 1 great flame, throwing kisses as they pass

Just east of Eden, but there's heaven in our midst
And we're never really all that far from those we love & miss
Wade out in the water, there's a glory all around &
The wisest say there's a 1000 ways to kneel & kiss the ground
    — w & m: Carrie Newcomer

© 2002 Carrie Newcomer Music. All rights administered by BMG Rights Management (US) LLC. On her *The Gathering of Spirits*, *Kindred Spirits*.

GLAD TO HAVE A FRIEND LIKE YOU

Jill told Bill that it was lots of fun to cook
Bill told Jill that she could bait a real fishhook
    So they made ooey gooey chocolate cake sticky-licky
    Sugar top & they gobbled it & giggled
    And they sat by the river & they fished in the water
    And they talked as the squirmy wormies wiggled

(↑2) G - Bm - C - D - /   / |: G D G D / G D G - :|

Singin' glad to have a friend like you
Fair & fun & skippin' free
Glad to have a friend like you
And glad to just be me

C D Bm Em / C D G - :|

Pearl told Earl that they could do a secret code
Earl told Pearl there was free ice cream when it snowed
    So they sent funny letters which contained mystery messages
    And nobody knew just how they made it & they
    Raised up the window & they scooped all the snow together,
    Put milk & sugar in & ate it

Peg told Greg she liked to make things out of chairs
Greg told Peg sometimes he still hugged teddy bears
    So they sneaked in the living room & piled all the pillows up &
    Made it a rocket ship to fly in & the
    Bears were their girls & boys & they were the astronauts who
    Lived on the moon with one pet lion

— w & m: Carol Hall

GOD BLESS US EVERY ONE

When the world is feeling cold & the sky more grey than blue
And the snow it seems to <u>fall</u> heavy-heartedly on you
Time to count your blessings tho seemingly but few
Time to take a look at what's within & without you
For health is more than walking & wealth much more than gold
But kindness overwhelming as a gentle hand to hold
So God bless us every one with the riches of the soul
And may hopelessness ne'er be the demon darkening our
   door

(in 6/8) D G D A / D G A D :|

G - D A / 2nd / G D - A / 2nd

When... / And the snow it seems to <u>lie</u>... on you
Remember when you see us, the hungry, lame, the meek
Who would feed us, heal us, keep us is the same one that you seek
For joy is more than dancing, good cheer much more than wine
But love is all enfolding as beholding hearts entwined...

When... (as v. 2) / To the counting house of blessings may we
    often chance to stray
And in company together spend many's the night & day...

— w & m: Maria Dunn

HOW COULD ANYONE

How could anyone ever tell you you were anything less than
    beautiful?
How could anyone ever tell you you were less than whole?
How could anyone fail to notice that your loving is a miracle?
How deeply you're connected to my soul

(in G)   Am7 D G Em / Am7 D G G7 / 1st / Am7 D G -

— w & m: Libby Roderick

HOWDI DO

I stick out my little hand to ev'ry woman, kid & man
And I shake it up & down **"Howjido, howjido"**
Yes, I shake it up & down **"Howjido**

Howdy doozle doodle doozie, howji hijie heejie hojie
Howji hojie heejie hijie, howjido, howjido, howjido, sir
Doodle doosie, howjido"

And when you walk in my door, I will run across my floor,
And I'll shake you by the hand **"Howjido, howjido"**
Yes, I'll shake it up & down **"Howjido**

On my sidewalk, on my street, any place that we do meet
Then I'll shake you by your hand **"Howjido, howjido"**
Yes, I'll shake it up & down **"Howjido**

When I first jump out of bed, out my window goes my head
And I shake it up & down... I shake at all my windows...

I feel glad when you feel good, you brighten up
   my neighborhood
Shakin' hands with ev'rybody... Shakin' hands with ev'rybody...

When I meet a dog or cat, I will rubby rub his back
Shakey, shakey, shakey paw... Shaking hands with everybody...

From right here in our town to the whole wide world around
We say "Hojee heejee hijee..."

— w & m: Woody Guthrie

I WILL BE YOUR FRIEND

If you got troubles & you need a helping hand **(3x)**
Come to me, I will be your friend
I will be your friend (2x)
If you got troubles & you need a helping hand / **Come...**

C - - - / F - - C / Am G C F / C F G C -
G - C - / F - C - /   "   /   "   /

If you are hungry & you got no place to stay **(3x)** / **Come...**
I will be your friend (2x) / If you are hungry...

If you are lonely & you got nobody to love **(3x)** / **Come...**

— w & m: Guy Davis

IF I NEEDED YOU

If I needed you would you come to me
Would you come to me & ease my pain?
If you needed me I would come to you
I would swim the seas for to ease your pain

C - - - / - F G C :‖

In the night forlorn, the morning's born
And the morning shines with the lights of love
You will miss sunrise if you close your eyes
That would break my heart in 2

The lady's with me now since I showed her how
To lay her lily hand in mine
Loop & Lil agree she's a sight to see
A treasure for the poor to find

— w & m: Townes Van Zandt

© 1972 JTVZ Music (ASCAP), Katie Bell Music (ASCAP) & Will Van Zandt Publishing (ASCAP). Copyright renewed. All rights administered by Wixen Music Publishing, Inc. On his *Legend* & *Live at the Old Quarter*, Emmylou Harris & Don Williams *Cimarron* & recs by Lyle Lovett, Andrew Bird, Guy Clark, Bobby Vee, Seldom Scene. In films *Crazy Heart* & *Broken Circle Breakdown*.

IT DON'T COST VERY MUCH

To smile when you're happy, to smile when you're sad
To look pleasing when mistreated, to be calm when you're mad
Oh be forgiving if someone abuse you for the good Lord looks
   for such
Live right each day & smile on your way & **it don't cost very much**

(in G) C - G - / Am Em A D / G - C G / CA7 GE AD G

**Yes it don't cost very much just to place a gentle touch
And to give a glass of water to a pilgrim in need of such
Well you may not be an angel & you may not go to church
But the good that you do will come on back to you & it...**

/   "   / G E A D /   "   /   "   /

Help the cripple by the wayside, help the blind man cross the street
Be careful but kind to strangers, speak politely to those you meet
To the blind man give him glasses, to the cripple man,
   give him a crutch
As you do for yourself, you can do for somebody else, **it don't...**

— w & m: Thomas A. Dorsey

© 1954 (renewed) Unichappell Music Inc. Rec by Mahalia Jackson 11.

IT'S A PLEASURE TO KNOW YOU

**It's a pleasure to know you, a pleasure to see you smile
A comfort to know we'll share the road awhile
Pleasure is fleeting & comforts are far between
It's a pleasure to know you & the comfort you bring**

(in 3/4) D - GBm Em / A - DBb A / 1st / A - D(G DA)

I came to your city after I left my home
And I was a stranger, dressed up in stranger's clothes
Favors I needed, but charity's out of style
And rare as the beauty in the face of a trusting child / And...

They say life's a journey, a hwy from birth to death
Mapped in despair & traveled in hopelessness
Well they may believe it, but just between you & me
The trick to the traveling is all in the company

Lovers may leave you, lovers may turn away
And children may scorn you, you know they will someday
The seasons are fickle & fate is not known as kind
But friendship's a diamond & trouble's the diamond mine

— w & m: Karl Williams

© 1983 Canny Lark Music. On his *Living at the End of Time*, Sally Rogers & Howie Bursen *When Howie Met Sally*, Ben Tousley *Take My Hand*. In *SO!* 33:2.

LEMA'AN ACHAI VERIAI (PSALM 122)

Lema'an achai v'ray-ai **(x2)**
Adabra na **(x2)** shalom bach **(repeat)**

Em - / Am Em / - Am / B7 Em

Lema'an bait Hashem Elokainu / Avaksha tov lach **(repeat)**

Because of my brothers & friends
Because of my sisters & friends
Please let me ask, please let me sing / Peace to you

This is the house, the house of the Lord
I wish the best for you **(repeat)**

— w & m: Shlomo Carlebach

© 1986 Rabbi Shlomo Carlebach (BMI). Used by permission of the estate of Rabbi Shlomo Carlebach. On his *Holy Brothers & Sisters*. Based on Psalm 122:8-9.

LOVE CALL ME HOME

When the waters are deep, **friends carry me over**
When I cry in my sleep, **love call me home**
**Time, ferry me down the river, friends carry me safely over
Life, tend me on my journey, love...**

C Am F G /   / C - F G /   /

When the waters are cold, **friends...**
When I'm losing my hold, **love...**

When I'm weary & cannot swim...
Open your arms & take me in...

Take the gift I bring...
Deep within me life is singing...

Life offers a chance for friends to carry us over
Time can stop or dance forever, **love...**

— w & m: Peggy Seeger

© 2000 Peggy Seeger/Harmony Music Ltd. On her *Love... & 3 Score & 10* 13. "Made for my friend, Christine Lassiter, who showed many how to live but also how to die graciously." On & in Peter & Alice Amidon *25 Anthems for Interfaith & Comty Choirs*.

OLD FRIENDS

I saw an old friend the other day
In San Francisco by the Bay
It took me back to only yesterday
The yrs somehow let slip away
   We laughed & talked about the days gone by
   And brushed a tear away with a sigh
   We promised not to let it be this long
   Like the old refrain from an old, old song

C F C Am / F - C - :‖ (4x)

**Remember old friends we've made along the way
The gifts they've given stay with us every day**

F Am F C /   /

Rise Again

Looking back it makes me wonder
Where we're going & how long we'll stay
I know the road brings rain & thunder
But for the journey, what will we pay?
  I often think the times get crazier
  As this old world goes round & round
  But just the memory makes it easier
  As the hwy goes up & down
Lately word's been coming back to me
There's a few I will no longer see
Their faces will be seen no more along the road
There'll be a few less hands to hold
  But for the ones whose journeys ended
  Tho they started so much the same
  In the hearts of those befriended
  Burns a candle with a silver flame

— w & m: Mary McCaslin

© 1977 (renewed) Folklore Productions, Inc. (ASCAP). All rights administered by Budde Music, Inc. (ASCAP) & Downtown DLJ Songs (ASCAP). On her *Old...* In *SO!* 37:1.

ONE KIND WORD

One kind word will warm the coldest winter
One kind word will start the seeds of spring
One...will make a summer garden / ...what a harvest it will bring

G Em C D / / C G C D / G Em C G

— w & m: Sarah Pirtle

© 2011 Discovery Center Music (BMI). On & in her *Better Together: Caring & Including Instead of Bullying.* *LS

OUTSIDE OF A SMALL CIRCLE OF FRIENDS

Look outside the window, there's a woman being grabbed
They've dragged her to the bushes & now she's being stabbed
Maybe we should call the cops & try to stop the pain
But Monopoly is so much fun, I'd hate to blow the game
And I'm sure it wouldn't interest anybody
Outside of a small circle of friends

G A G A / G Bm C D / B7 - Em - / C Am C D /
G Em Bb - / Gm - C -

Riding down the highway, yes my back is getting stiff
13 cars are piled up, they're hanging on a cliff
Maybe we should pull them back with our towing chain
But we gotta move & we might get sued & it looks like it's gonna rain...
  Sweating in the ghetto with the colored *[Panthers]* & the poor
  The rats have joined the babies who are sleeping on the floor
  Now wouldn't it be a riot if they really blew their tops?
  But they got too much already & besides we got the cops...
Oh there's a dirty paper using sex to make a sale
The Supreme Court was so upset, they sent him off to jail
Maybe we should help the fiend & take away his fine
But we're busy reading *Playboy* & the Sunday *NY Times*...
  Smoking marijuana is more fun than drinking beer
  But a friend of ours was captured & they gave him 30 yrs
  Maybe we should raise our voices, ask somebody why
  But demonstrations are a drag, besides we're much too high...

— w & m: Phil Ochs

© 1967 Almo Music Corp. Copyright renewed. On his *Pleasures of the Harbor*. v1 is about the murder of Kitty Genovese on 3/14/64 in NYC. 38 citizens were awakened not once but 3 times by her cries for help over a half hr period w/ no one calling the police for help. At the trial the neighbors stated "We didn't want to get involved."

PARTING SONG

Soon the morning sun will rise & dawn will bathe the sky
There's time for just this parting song before we say goodbye
So sing together one & all & raise a glass of wine
Here's hoping we shall meet again along the road of time

D AD GA D / / G D - A / 1st

We've shared our stories, yours & mine, we've shared our hopes & fears
In memories of distant youth we've both rolled back the yrs

The ever-turning, fateful wheel must cause our ways to part
And bringing untold mysteries, another day will start

For from endings come beginnings, from the old shall come the new / With hopes for tomorrow we'll see our parting thru

— w & m: Dave Webber

© 1993 Dave Webber. On his *Together — Solo*, Beggar's Velvet *Lady of Autumn* & Johnny Collins *Now & Then*.

SIDE BY SIDE

Oh we ain't got a barrel of money
Maybe we're ragged & funny
But we'll travel along, singin' a song / **Side by side**

G - C G / / C - G E / A D G -

Don't know what's comin' tomorrow
Maybe it's trouble & sorrow
But we'll travel the road, sharin' our load / **Side...**

(bridge) Thru all kinds of weather / What if the sky should fall?
Just as long as we're together / It doesn't matter at all

B7 - - - / E - - - / A - - - / D - - -

When they've all had their quarrels & parted
We'll be the same as we started
Just travelin' along, singin' a song...

— w & m: Harry Woods

© 1927 Shapiro, Bernstein & Co., Inc., New York. Copyright renewed. Rec by Nick Lucas ('27) & Kay Starr ('53).

STAND BY ME

When the night has come & the land is dark
And the moon is the only light we'll see _
No I won't be afraid, oh I won't be afraid
Just as long as you stand, stand by me _
So darling, darling, stand by me, oh stand by me
Oh stand, _stand by me

C - Am - / F G C - :|| (3x)

If the sky that we look upon, should tumble & fall
Or the mtn should crumble to the sea
I won't cry, I won't cry, no I won't shed a tear / **Just...**
Whenever you're in trouble won't you **stand...**

— w & m: Jerry Leiber, Mike Stoller & Ben E. King

© 1961 Sony/ATV Music Publishing LLC. Copyright renewed. All rights administered by Sony/ATV Music Publishing LLC, 424 Church Street, Suite 1200, Nashville, TN 37219. Orig rec by King (in A). On John Lennon *Rock 'n' Roll* (1975). Based on the gospel song "Lord, Stand by Me." Also draws on Psalm 46:2-3.

TO EVERYONE IN ALL THE WORLD

To everyone in all the world I reach my hand, I shake their hand
To everyone in all the world, I shake their hands like this
All, all together the whole wide world around
I may not know your lingo but I can say "By jingo!"
No matter where you live we can shake hands

C - G C / / F C G C / F C F C / F C G C -

A tous et chacun dans le monde, je tends la main, j'leur donne
   la main / A tous… je donne la main comme ça
Tous, tous ensemble, au monde entier je chante
C'est très facile entre humaine avec une poignée de main
N'importe où dans le monde on peut s'en tendre

— w & m: Pete Seeger, French w: Raffi

YOU'VE GOT A FRIEND IN ME

You've got a friend in me (2x)
When the road looks rough ahead
And you're miles & miles from your nice warm bed
You just remember what your old pal said
Boy **you've got a…** / Yeah **you've…**   (↑3)

C G C - / F - C - / F C E Am / / / D G C A / D G C -

You've… (2x) / You got troubles & I got 'em too
There isn't anything I wouldn't do for you
We stick together, we can see it thru / 'Cos **you've…**

(bridge) Some other folks might be a little bit smarter than I am
Bigger & stronger too, maybe
But none of them will ever love you
The way I do, it's me & you boy

F - B7 - / C B7 C - / B7 C D B7 / Em A Dm G

And as the years go by
Our friendship will never die
You're gonna see it's our destiny / **You've got a…** (3x)

C G C - / F - C - / F C E Am / D G C A / / D G C -

— w & m: Randy Newman

The **Friendship & Community** chapter has songs about relying on each other in good times & bad. See also: **Family, Home & Roots, Hope & Strength, Sing People Sing.**

Other songs include **Ballads**: Sae will we yet, **Dignity**: Power of loving you, **Faith**: Tree of life, **Healing**: Welcome to the circle, **Pub**: Parting glass, **Rich**: All in this together, **Trav**: I'm on my way, Me & Bobbie McGee.

ABDUL ABULBUL AMIR

The sons of the Prophet are brave men & bold
And quite unaccustomed to fear
But the bravest by far in the ranks of the Shah
Was **Abdul Abulbul Ameer.**

C G C C7 / F - C - / G - C F / C G C -

   Now the heroes were plenty and well-known to fame
   In the troops that were led by the Czar
   And the bravest of these was a man by the name
   Of **Ivan Skivinsky Skivar.**
One day this bold Russian had shouldered his gun
And donned his most truculent sneer
Downtown he did go, where he trod on the toe
Of **Abdul…**
   "Young Man" quoth Abdul "Has life grown so dull
   That you wish to end your career?
   Vile infidel know, you have trod on the toe / Of **Abdul…**

Said Ivan: "My friend, your remarks in the end
Will avail you but little, I fear,
For you ne'er will survive to repeat them alive / Mr. **Abdul…**
   "So take your last look at sunshine & brook,
   And send your regrets to the Czar
   For by this I imply, you are going to die / Count **Ivan…**
They fought all that night 'neath the pale yellow moon
The din it was heard from afar
And huge multitudes came, so great was the fame
Of Abdul & Ivan Skivar.
   As Abdul's long knife was extracting the life
   (In fact he was shouting "Huzza")
   He felt himself struck by that wily Calmuck / Count **Ivan…**
The Sultan drove by in his red-crested fly
Expecting the victor to cheer
But he only drew nigh to hear the last sigh / Of **Abdul…**
   Czar Petrovitch, too, in his spectacles blue
   Rode up in his new-crested car,
   He arrived just in time to exchange a last line / With **Ivan…**

There's a tomb rises up where the Blue Danube flows
Engraved there in characters clear
"Ah, Stranger, when passing, oh, pray for the soul / Of **Abdul…**
   A Muscovite maiden her lone vigil keeps
   'Neath the light of the pale polar star
   And the name that she murmurs, so oft as she weeps / Is
   Ivan…
— w & m: Percy French

Arr. © 2015 by Hal Leonard Corporation. Written in 1877, at one of many times of conflict betw Russia & Turkey. In *SO!* 32:2. On Brendan O'Dowda *The Complete Percy French Collection*, Charlie King *Brilliant S of Ireland*, Frank Crumit *Vintage Recs.*

ADDAMS FAMILY THEME

They're creepy & they're kooky, mysterious & spooky
They're all together ooky, **the Addams Family**

G Am D G / /

Their house is a museum where people come to see 'em
They really are a scream, **the…**

(bridge) Neat, sweet, petite

G - A - D - G -

So get a witch's shawl on, a broomstick you can crawl on
We're gonna pay a call on **the…**
— w & m: Vic Mizzy

© 1964, renewed 1992 by Unison Music Company, administered by Next Decade Entertainment, Inc. Theme song for TV series ↑3.

ALVIN

Did you ever step in a water pipe, pipe
Fall to the bottom of the water system?
And there did you meet a little alligator
Who answered to the name of Alvin? If you did
He's mine, I lost him

D G D A **(5x)**

I threw him *[my Alvin]* down the water pipe, pipe
Down to the bottom of the water system
Because he was getting too big for his britches
But now I'm getting lonely since
He's gone, I miss him
— w & m: Nick Thorkelson

© 1967 (renewed) Nick Thorkelson. aka: "Alfred the Alligator." Rec by Thorkelson's brother Peter Tork for the '68 Monkees *The Birds, the Bees & the Monkees*. Cut fr orig pressing but released on later reissues. Can have new parts enter either at * or **.

ALWAYS LOOK ON THE BRIGHT SIDE OF LIFE

Some things in life are bad, they can really make you mad
Other things just make you swear & curse
When you're chewing on life's gristle, don't grumble, give a whistle!
And this'll help things turn out for the best

Am - G - / / Am - G E / A7 - D -

And always look on the bright side of life
Always look on the light side of life

G E7 Am D G (E7 A D) / /

If life seems jolly rotten, there's smth you've forgotten
And that's to laugh & smile & dance & sing
When you're feeling in the dumps, don't be silly chumps
Just purse your lips & whistle: that's the thing! / **Always…**

For life is quite absurd & death's the final word
You must always face the curtain with a bow
Forget about your sin, give the audience a grin
Enjoy it, it's your last chance anyhow

So always look on the bright side of death
Just before you draw your terminal breath

Life's a piece of shit when you look at it
Life's a laugh & death's a joke, it's true
You'll see it's all a show, keep 'em laughing as you go
Just remember that the last laugh is on you

And always look on the bright side of life
Always look on the right **side of life (repeat)**
— w & m: Eric Idle

© 1979 Kay-Gee-Bee Music Ltd. All rights administered by BMG Rights Management (US) LLC. In Monty Python *Life of Brian*.

BEST DAY EVER

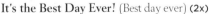

Mr. Sun came up & he smiled at me
Said it's gonna be a good one, just wait & see!
Jumped out of bed & I ran outside
Feeling so extra ecstatified!
It's the Best Day Ever! (Best day ever) **(2x)**

G - (C CD) / / B7 - Em / A D // GD G (CG CD) / /

I'm so busy, got nothing to do
Spent the last 2 hrs just tying my shoe
Every flower, every grain of sand
Is reaching out to shake my hand

(bridge) Sometimes the little things start closing in on me
When I'm feeling down I wanna lose that frown, I stick my head
   out the window & I look around

B7 Em B7 Em / FC FC GD GD

Those clouds don't scare me they can't disguise
This magic that's happening right before my eyes
Soon Mr. Moon will be shining bright
So the best day ever can last all night
(Yes the best day ever's gonna last all night now A D)
— w & m: Thomas Kenny & Andy Paley

© 2004 Music by Nickelodeon Inc. & Nickelodeon Notes Inc. All rights administered by Sony/ATV Music Publishing LLC, 424 Church Street, Suite 1200, Nashville, TN 37219. In episode "Best…" & *SpongeBob* movie ↑4.

THE CAMPFIRE SONG SONG

Let's gather around the campfire & sing our campfire song
Our C-A-M-P-F-I-R-E S-O-N-G song, & if
You don't think that we can sing it faster, then you're wrong
But it'll help if you just sing along

(↑3)   G - C G /   /   / A - D -

C-A-M-P... song / C-A-M-P...song & if
You don't think that we can sing it faster, then you're wrong
But it'll help if you just sing along

(tag) It'll help, it'll help if you just sing along!

A - D - G (C G -)

    — w & m: Carl Williams, Dan Povenmire, Jay Lender, Michael Culross &
    Michael Walker

© 2002 Music by Nickelodeon Inc. All rights administered by Sony/ATV Music
Publishing LLC, 424 Church Street, Suite 1200, Nashville, TN 37219. Featured in
"The Camping Episode" of SpongeBob Squarepants.

THE COURT OF KING CARACTACUS

Now the ladies of the harem of the court of King Caractacus
   were / Just passing by (repeat 4x)   (↑3)

C - - - / G - C - :‖ F - - - / C - / G - - - / C - - -

Now the noses on the faces of the / **Ladies of the harem of**
   the court of King Caractacus were...(repeat 4x)

C - / - - - - / G - C - :‖ F - / - - - - / C - - - /
G - / - - - - / C - - -

Now the boys who put the powder on the / Noses on the faces
   of the / **Ladies of the harem of the...**

Now the fascinating witches who put the scintillating stitches in
   the britches of the
Boys who put the powder on the / Noses of the faces of...

Now if you want to take some pictures of the
Fascinating witches who put the scintillating stitches in the
   britches of the... **Caractacus**
You're too late! because they've just - passed - by!

C - / - - - - - / - - / - - / - - - - / (tacet) F G C - - -

    — w & m: Rolf Harris & Charles Stanislaw Rich

© 1964 Ardmore & Beechwood T/AS Black Swan. Copyright renewed. All rights
administered by Sony/ATV Music Publishing LLC, 424 Church Street, Suite 1200,
Nashville, TN 37219. On Rolf Harris *Court of ...* King Caractacus was a 1st c. British
chieftain who led the British resistance to the Roman conquest.

DEAR ABBY

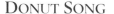

Dear Abby, Dear Abby, my feet are too long
My hair's falling out & my rights are all wrong
My friends they all tell me that I've no friends at all
Won't you write me a letter, won't you give me a call?
Signed, "Bewildered"

G - C G / - - A D / 1st / G - D G / C D G -

Bewildered, Bewildered, **you have no complaint**
You are what you are, & you ain't what you ain't
So listen up buster & listen up good
Stop wishing for bad luck & knocking on wood
(last cho only add) Signed, "Dear Abby"

Dear Abby, Dear Abby, my fountain pen leaks
My wife hollers at me & my kids are all freaks
Every side I get up on is the wrong side of bed
If it weren't so expensive I'd wish I were dead
Signed, "Unhappy" / Unhappy, Unhappy, **you have...**

Dear Abby... you won't believe this
But my stomach makes noises whenever I kiss
My girlfriend tells me it's all in my head
But my stomach tells me to write you instead
Signed, "Noisemaker" / Noisemaker...

Dear Abby... well I never thought
That me & my girlfriend would ever get caught
We were sitting in the back seat just shooting the breeze
With her hair up in curlers & her pants to her knees
Signed, "Just Married"...

    — w & m: John Prine

© 1973 (renewed) Walden Music, Inc. & Sour Grapes Music, Inc. All rights
administered by Walden Music, Inc. On his *Sweet Revenge* and *Prime Prine*.
(Melody is very similar to "Sweet Betsy from Pike")

DEM DEER

Hope you don't mind when an old man sings
Helps me to keep my mind on t'ings
So when I go where the animals thrive
I sing dis song on the treacherous drive

A - - - / - - E A :‖

Dem deer dey're here, den dey're dere
Dey're here, dey're dere, dey're everywhere (repeat)

At dawn in fields & coniferous groves
Bucks & does come alive in droves
Just when you think that the coast is clear
There in the road is a whitetail deer

In venison-land as the day goes by
Deer lay low when the sun is high
Sun goes down & de night draws near
Twilight brings out the whitetail deer

Bucks bed down where de tall grass grows
Fawns dey doze where de doe does doze
Dose does doze dere, dose does doze here
And dose are de habits of de whitetail deer

    — w & m: Lou & Peter Berryman

© 2005 Lou & Peter Berryman (SESAC). On their *Some Days*. Stay Tuned String
Band *Loony Tuned* & YT by Bryan Bowers.

DONUT SONG

Well I walked around the corner & I walked around the block
I walked right into a donut shop
And I picked up a donut & I licked off the grease
I handed the lady my 5 cent piece
Well she looked at my nickel & she looked at me
She said "This nickel is no good for me
There's a hole in the middle & it goes right thru"
I said "Lady, there's a hole in the donut too!
But thanks for the donut - toodle-oo *[goodbye!]*"

D - / - A / D - / D AD :‖ D AD

    — trad. (US - m: "Turkey in the Straw")

Arr. © 2015 by Hal Leonard Corporation. On recs by Randy Kaplan & Sarah Sharp.

ESPN

The bedroom is dark now except for the screen
Some guys wearing red shirts, some guys wearing green
There's a break in the action but I wait here for more
I've gotta go to the bathroom but someone might score! On:

ESPN (x2) / It's the principal reason that I'm single again
Love is for losers, only sports is your friend
And **who's got more sports on than ESPN?**

It's 3 in the morning & I'm still watching sports
I've skipped all the news & the weather reports
I've got celebrity hockey, cricket & skeet
And African pygmies shooting craps with their feet, on…

…I can quit anytime but I couldn't say when / **Who's…**

A lonely sports widow, my wife traded me
For the house & the car & the alimony.
The things I've got left I hold equally dear:
The sofa, the cable TV & the beer! I've got…

…If I could do it all over, hell, I'd do it again / 'Cos **who's…**

ESPN (x2) / *Vous êtes pourquois je suis single again*
La vie is for losers, le sport is your friend &
Who's got more sports on? You can watch with your shorts on
If a field or a court's on, it's ESPN!

G C / D G / G C / D - / - D G

— w & m: Mitchell Burnside Clapp

© 1986 Mitchell Burnside Clapp. On Bill Florian *Just for You*, Modern Man *The Wide Album*, David Buskin *Wealthy Man*.

FISH HEADS

Fish heads, fish heads, roly poly fish heads
Fish heads, fish heads, eat them up — yum!

(in G) Em G C G / Em G D G

In the morning laughing happy fish heads
In the evening floating in the soup
   Ask a fish head anything you want to
   They won't answer, they can't talk
I took a fish head out to see a movie
Didn't have to pay to get it in
   They can't play baseball, they don't wear sweaters
   They're not good dancers, they don't play drums
Roly poly fish heads are never seen drinking cappuccino
At Italian restaurants with oriental women — yeah!

— w & m: Robert Haimer & Bill Mumy ("Barnes & Barnes")

© 1978 Music Spazchow Publishing. On their *Voobaha* 14. Also rec by Wild Eyed Fischer, Buck 65, Eagle-Eye Cherry. On *Dr. Demento* & *Simpsons* ("Treehouse of Horrors VII" '96).

FROM A DOG'S STANCE

From a dog's stance the world's a bowl of food & no dog
   is in need
From a dog's stance no dog is ever rude, there's just one hungry
   mouth to feed
From… there is harmony & it rests upon your plate
It's the drool of hope, it's the look of guilt, **that's the stance of**
   every dog

G C DEm CD G /   / CD GEm CG D / CG (x2)   CD G

From a dog's stance we all have enough so why not
   give dogs more?
From… dogs cannot comprehend what all these cats are for
From… we are waitresses marching to the kitchen now
Bringing bowls of food, make that "people" food, **that's…**
(bridge) **Dogs are watching us (x3) from a dog's stance**

CD GEm CD G -

From… the world's a bowl of food & no dog is in need
There are no cats, no postmen, baths or fleas, just one hungry
   mouth to feed
From… there is harmony & it rests upon your plate
It's the drool of hope, it's the look of guilt, **that's…**

— w: Jay Mankita

© 1992 Jay Mankita. On his *Dog's Are Watching Us* & *Sing Down Trouble*. Parody of "From a Distance" by Julie Gold.

HELLO MUDDUH, HELLO FADDUH!
(A Letter From Camp)

Hello Mudduh, hello Fadduh
Here I am at Camp Granada
Camp is very entertaining
And they say we'll have some fun if it stops raining

G - D - / - - G - / B7 - C - / G D G -

I went hiking with Joe Spivy
He developed poison ivy
You remember Leonard Skinner
He got ptomaine poisoning last night after dinner
   All the counselors hate the waiters
   And the lake has alligators
   And the head coach wants no sissies
   So he reads to us from something called "Ulysses"
Now I don't want this should scare ya
But my bunkmate has malaria
You remember Jeffrey Hardy?
They're about to organize a searching party

(bridge) Take me home, oh Mudduh Fadduh
Take me home, I hate Granada
Don't leave me out in the forest
Where I might get eaten by a bear
Take me home, I promise I will not make noise
Or mess the house with other boys
Oh please don't make me stay
I've been here one whole day

Gm - Cm - /   / Gm - F - / Cm - D - :|

Dearest Fadduh, darling Mudduh
How's my precious little bruddah?
Let me come home if you miss me
I would even let Aunt Bertha hug & kiss me
   Wait a minute, it stopped hailing
   Guys are swimming, guys are sailing
   Playing baseball, gee that's better
   Mudduh, Fadduh, kindly disregard this letter

— w: Allan Sherman, m: Lou Busch

© 1963 (renewed) WB Music Corp. & Burning Bush Music. On his *Hello…*, *My Son the Nut*, *Rhino Hi-Five*. In *The New Novelty Fakebk*. Sherman wrote a "sequel" titled "Return to Camp Granada." Tune is "Dance of the Hours" from opera *La Gioconda*.

I Was Born About 10,000 Years Ago

I was born about 10,000 yrs ago
There ain't nothing in this world that I don't know
I saw Peter, Paul & Moses playing Ring Around the Roses
And I'll whup the guy who says it isn't so

I: D - A - / - - D - / G - D - / A - D -

I'm just a lonesome traveler, a great historical bum
Highly educated, from history I have come
I built the Rock of Ages, 'twas in the year of one
And that's about the biggest thing that man has ever done
    I saw Satan when he looked the Garden o'er
    I saw Eve & Adam driven from the door
    From behind the bushes peeping, seen the apple they was
    eating / & I swear that I'm the guy what ate the core
Well I built the Garden of Eden, it was in the year of 2
Joined the Apple Pickers Union & I always paid my dues
I'm the man who signed the contract to raise the rising sun
And that's about the biggest thing that man has ever done
    I taught Samson how to use his mighty hands
    Showed Columbus to this mighty land
    And for Phaoroh's little kiddies I built all the pyramiddies
    And to Sahara carried all the sand
I was straw boss on the pyramids, the Tower of Babel too
I opened up the ocean, let the migrant children thru
Well, I fought a million battles & I never lost a one
And that's about the biggest thing that man has ever done
    I taught Solomon his little ABC's
    I was the 1st one what ate Limburger cheese
    And while sailing down the bay with Methuselah one day
    I saved his flowing whiskers from the breeze
Well I was in the Revolution when we set this country free
It was me & a couple of Indians that dumped the Boston tea
Well I won the battle of Valley Forge & the Battle of Bully Run
And that's about the biggest thing that man has ever done
    Queen Elizabeth fell dead in love with me
    We were married in Milwaukee secretly
    But I snuck around & shook her, to go with General Hooker
    To fight mosquiters down in Tennessee

II: C - G C (4x)

III: G - - - / - - D - / G - C - / G D G -

    — trad. (US)

Arr. © 2015 by Hal Leonard Corporation. I. Odetta (in B), Chad Mitchell Trio, Matt McGinn, the Song Swappers. II. Woody Guthrie. III. Elvis 11, Seekers 12. In Carl Sandburg *Amer Songbag*. Some versions date to 1890's aka "Biggest Thing that Man Has Ever Done". Not to be confused with "Great Amer Bum" (in Rich & Poor).

Little Jack Horner

1. Little Jack Horner sat in a corner eating his Christmas pie
2. He stuck in his thumb & pulled out a plum & said "yum **x3**
3. Mmm what a good boy **x2** - what a good boy am I!"

1. Little Jack Horner was an informer for the F.B.I.
2. He turned in his mother, sister & brother, aunts & uncles
3. And everyday so proudly he'd say "Oh what a good snitch am I!"
    — trad. (nursery rhyme) w/ new lyrics by Sol Weber
© 1994 Sol Weber. In Rounds Galore.

Lydia, the Tattooed Lady

Oh Lydia, oh Lydia, say have you met Lydia?
Lydia, the Tattooed Lady
She has eyes that folks adore so
And a torso even more so
Lydia, oh Lydia, that encyclopedia
Oh Lydia, the Queen of Tattoo
    On her back is the Battle of Waterloo
    Beside it the "Wreck of the Hesperus" too
    And proudly above waves the red, white & blue
    You can learn a lot from Lydia! (in 3/4, ↓3)

G - / - D / CG CG / A D / G - / - C /
C - / G - / - C / GD G

    — w: E.Y. "Yip" Harburg, m: Harold Arlen

© 1939 (renewed) EMI Feist Catalog Inc. All rights administered by EMI Feist Catalog Inc. (Publishing) & Alfred Music (Print). In '39 Marx Bros film *At the Circus* 15 & orig '40 *Philadelphia Story*. Rec by Burl Ives 12, Kermit the Frog 15.

National Brotherhood Week

O the white folks hate the black folks & the black folks hate the
    white folks
To hate all but the right folks is an old established rule

D A - D / D G A D

But during National Brotherhood Week, National...
Lena Horne & Sheriff Clark are dancing cheek to cheek
It's fun to eulogize the people you despise
As long as you don't let 'em in your school

G - D - / A - D - :|

O the poor folks hate the rich folks & the rich folks hate the
    poor folks
All of my folks hate all of your folks, it's Amer. as apple pie!

But during National...
NYers love the Puerto Ricans 'cos it's very chic
Step up & shake the hand of someone you can't stand
You can tolerate him if you try

O the Protestants hate the Catholics & the Catholics hate the
    Protestants
And the Hindus hate the Muslims & everybody hates the Jews
But during...
It's natl everyone-smile-at-one-another-hood wk
Be nice to people who are inferior to you
It's only for a week, so have no fear
Be grateful that it doesn't last all year!

G - D - / A - D - :| E A D -

    — w & m: Tom Lehrer

© 1964 (renewed) Tom Lehrer. On his *That Was The Year That Was* 11 & Peter Gill *Presents Politically Incorrect (S of Lehrer)*. In Tomfoolery.

O HOW HE LIED

She sat 'neath the lilacs & played her guitar
Played her guitar, played her guitar
She sat 'neath the lilacs & played her guitar
Played her guita-a-a-ar

(in 3/4) G - - - / D - G - :‖

He sat down beside her & smoked his cigar / Smoked his cigar...
He told her he loved her, but oh how he lied / Oh how he lied...
She told him she loved him, but she did not lie...
They were to be married, but she up & died...
He went to the funeral, but just for the ride...
He sat on the tombstone & laughed til he cried...
The tombstone fell on him a squish-squash he died...
She went up to heaven & fluttered & *[or flip-flop she]* flied...
He went down below her & frizzled & fried...
The moral of this tale is never to lie *[or never trust guys]*...
Or you too may perish & sizzle & fry...

— trad. (US 19th c.)

PHAROAH, PHAROAH

Pharaoh, Pharoah, ooh baby (won't you) **let my people go**
   (a-huh!)
Yeah, Yeah, Yeah! (2x)

D G A G (4x)

Well-a burnin' bush told me just the other day
That I should come over here & say
That I gotta get my people out of Pharaoh's hand
And lead them all to the Promised Land (I said)...

Well-a me & God's people comin' to the Red Sea
And Pharaoh's army comin' after me
I raised my rod & stuck it in the sand
And all of God's people walked across dry land (I said)...

Well-a Pharaoh's army is comin' too
So what did you think that I did do
I raised my rod & I cleared my throat
And all of Pharaoh's army did the dead man's float (I said)...

— w: Tony Sbrana

POLITICAL SCIENCE

No one likes us, I don't know why
We may not be perfect, but heaven knows we try
But all around, even our old friends put us down
Let's drop the big one & see what happens

C - Caug [E7] - / C [Am] - A7 - / Fmaj - Fm - / C - Ab G

We give them money but are they grateful?
No, they're spiteful & they're hateful
They don't respect us, so let's surprise them
We'll drop the big one & pulverize them

Asia's crowded & Europe's too old
Africa is far too hot & Canada's too cold
And South America stole our name
Let's drop the big one, there'll be no one left to blame us

(bridge) We'll save Australia
Don't wanna hurt no kangaroo
We'll build an all-American amusement park there
They got surfin', too

F - C - / / / G7 - - -

Boom goes London & boom Paree
More room for you & more room for me
And every city the whole world round
Will just be another American town C - A7 -

(tag) Oh how peaceful it will be, we'll set everybody free
You'll wear a Japanese kimono, baby, there'll be Italian shoes for me
They all hate us anyhow
So let's drop the big one now **(2x)**

D7 - G7 - / E7 - A7 - / F C / D7 F C - / /

— w & m: Randy Newman

REUBEN & RACHEL

Reuben, Reuben, I've been thinking
What a fine world this would be
If the men were all transported
Far beyond the northern sea

C Am F G / / C G F C / - - G C

Oh my goodness, gracious, Rachel
What a strange world this would be
If the men were all transported
Far beyond the northern sea

Reuben, Reuben, I've been thinking
What a great life girls would lead
If they had no men about them
None to tease them, none to heed

Rachel, Rachel, I've been thinking
Life would be so easy then
What a lovely world this would be
If you'd leave it to the men

Reuben, Reuben, stop your teasing
If you've any love for me
I was only just a-fooling
As I thought, of course, you'd see

Rachel, if you'll not transport me
I will take you for my wife
And I'll split with you my money
Every payday of my life!

(parody) *Reuben Reuben I've been thinking*
What the heck have you been drinking?
Looks like water, tastes like wine
Oh my gosh, it's turpentine!

— w: Harry Birch, m: William Gooch (1871)

THE SAGA BEGINS

(intro) A long, long time ago in a galaxy far away
Naboo was under an attack
And I thought me & Qui-Gon Jinn could talk the federation
Into maybe cutting them a little slack
But their response, it didn't thrill us,
   they locked the doors & tried to kill us
We escaped from that gas, then met Jar Jar & Boss Nass
We took a bongo from the scene & we went to Theed to see the Queen
We all wound up on Tatooine, that's where we found this boy, oh...

GD Em Am C / Em - D - :‖

Em Am x2 / C↓ Am C D / G Em Am D / G Em C D G -

**My my this here Anakin guy
May be Vader someday later – now he's just a small fry
And he left his home & kissed his mommy goodbye, sayin'
"Soon I'm gonna be a Jedi" (2x)**

G C G D / / / Em - A7 - / Em - D7 -

Did you know this junkyard slave isn't even old enough to shave
But he can use the Force, they say
Ah do you see him hitting on the queen, tho' he's just 9 & she's 14
Yeah, he's probably gonna marry her someday
Well I know he built C3PO & I've heard how fast his pod can go
And we were broke it's true, so we made a wager or 2!
He was a prepubescent flyin' ace
   And the minute Jabba started off that race
Well I knew who would win 1st place, oh yes, it was our boy
We started **singin'**...

G Am C Am / Em D - / GD Em Am C / Em A7 D -

Em D Em D / C↓ Am C D /   "   / GD Em C D G -

Now we finally got to Coruscant, the Jedi Council we knew
   would want / To see how good the boy could be,
So we took him there & we told the tale how his midi-chlorians
   were off the scale
And he might fulfill that prophecy
Oh the Council was impressed, of course,
   could he bring balance to the Force?
They interviewed the kid — oh training they forbid!
Because Yoda sensed in him much fear & Qui-Gon said "Now listen here
Just stick it in your pointy ear, I still will teach this boy"
He was **singin'**...

(as intro) We caught a ride back to Naboo 'cos Queen Amidala
   wanted to / I frankly would've liked to stay
We all fought in that epic war & it wasn't long at all before
Little Hotshot flew his plane & saved the day
And in the end some Gungans died, some ships blew up & some
   pilots fried
A lot of folks were croakin', the battle droids were broken &
The Jedi I admire most met up with Darth Maul & now he's toast, well
I'm still here & he's a ghost, I guess I'll train this boy
And I was **singin...**

We were **singin'**...

   — w & m: Don McLean, new w: Al Yankovic (Parody of "American Pie")

SANDWICHES ARE BEAUTIFUL

**Sandwiches are beautiful, sandwiches are fine
I like sandwiches, I eat them all the time
I eat them for my supper, I eat them for my lunch
And if I had a hundred sandwiches, I'd eat them all at once**

Dm - - - / C - - - / Dm - - - / A - - Dm

A-roaming & a-traveling & wandering along
And if you care to listen to me, I will sing a happy song
I will not ask a favor, I will not ask a fee
But if you have yourself a sandwich, won't you give a bite to me?

Oh, once I went to England and visited the Queen
I swear she was the grandest lady that I've ever seen
I told her she was beautiful & could not ask for more
She handed me a sandwich & she threw me out the door

Oh, once I knew a pretty girl, the fairest in the land
All the young men in the county was askin' for her hand
They'd offer her the moon & they would offer her the sea
But I offered her a sandwich & she said she'd marry me

Now a sandwich may be egg or cheese or even peanut butter
But they all taste so good to me, it really doesn't matter
Jam or ham or cucumber, just any kind will do
But I like sandwiches, how about you?

   — w & m: Bob King

SCALLOPED POTATOES

1. You haven't been eating
2. Scalloped potatoes for
3. Three days _ like
4. We have _

   — w & m: Emily Fox

SECRET AGENT MAN

There's a man who leads a life of danger
To everyone he meets he stays a stranger
With every move he makes another chance he takes
Odds are he won't live to see tomorrow

Em Am Em - / Em - B7 - / Em - Am - / 1st

Secret Agent Man (2x)
They've given you a number & taken away your name

Bm Em Bm Em / C B7 - Em

Beware of pretty faces that you find
A pretty face can hide an evil mind
Oh be careful what you say or you'll give yourself away
Odds are you...

Swinging on the Riviera one day
And then laying in a Bombay alley next day
Oh don't you let the wrong words slip while kissing persuasive lips
Odds are you...

— w & m: P. F. Sloan & Steve Barri

© 1965 Universal Music Corp. Copyright renewed. Rec by Johnny Rivers for the TV series.

SHOPPING IS THERAPY

Bargains at Macy's, a sale on at Marshalls
Delicate tchotchkes and neatly wrapped parcels
Hand painted T-shirts that spread into wings
I feel so high when I'm out buying things

Em - - - / Cmaj7 - - - / Am D G C / G C Am B7

Colorful cookbooks, adorable note cards
Bette Midler albums & kitschy hip postcards
Stick 'em up stars that will glow in the night
Purchasing endlessly makes me feel right

Why deal with troubles when you can go shopping?
Billions of items to buy, so get hopping
Wouldn't that DVD fit in just right?
Here, buy an iPod, buy 2, they're so light!

E - - - / A - - - / Am D G C / G C Am B7

Homeless people, unemployment
Tend to make me sad
But then I go shopping & buy myself things
And then I don't feel so bad

Em - Am B7 / Em - C - / - - A - / G C Am D G - - -

— w: Abby Smith

© 1986 Abby Smith. Sung to tune "My Favorite Things" by Rodgers & Hammerstein.

STAR TREKKIN' ACROSS THE UNIVERSE

Star Trekkin' across the universe
On the Starship Enterprise under Captain Kirk
Star Trekkin' across the universe
Only going forward 'cos we can't find reverse

D - CD / - C - A / 1st / D C A D

("Lt. Uhura, report") There's Klingons on the starboard bow, starboard bow, starboard bow
There's Klingons on the starboard bow, starboard bow, Jim
(last time:) There's... the starboard bow, better calm down!

A - E A / /

("Analysis, Mr. Spock") It's life, Jim, but not as we know it, not... **(x3)**
It's life, Jim, but not as we know it, not as we know it, Captain

("Medical update, Dr. McCoy") It's worse than that, he's dead, Jim, dead... **(x3)** / It's... dead, Jim, dead

("Starship Capt. James T. Kirk") Ah! We come in peace, shoot to kill... **(x3)** / We... shoot to kill, men
(last time:) We... in peace, shoot to kill, Scotty, beam me up!

Star Trek... Only going fwd & things are getting worse!

("Engineer, Mr. Scott") Ye canna change the laws of physics... Jim

Star... Only going fwd, still can't find reverse

— w & m: Rory Kehoe, Grahame Lister & John O'Connor

© 1987 Bark Publishing & Bushranger Publishing. All rights administered by Bark Publishing. Rec by The Firm (1987). This is a cumulative song: every time you sing a new 2-line v., sing all the previous v. in reverse order.

VATICAN RAG

First you get down on your knees, fiddle with your rosaries
Bow your head with great respect & genuflect (x3)!
Do whatever steps you want if
    you have cleared them with the Pontiff
Everybody say his own Kyrie eleison doin' the Vatican Rag

(in C) G - C - / / G - C A / F C A D G C

Get in line in that processional, step into that small confessional
There the guy who's got religion'll tell you if your sin's original
If it is, try playin' it safer, drink the wine & chew the wafer
2, 4, 6, 8, time to transubstantiate!

G - C - / / F - Fm - / Ab - G -

So get down upon your knees, fiddle... / ...genuflect
Make a cross on your abdomen when in Rome do like a Roman
Ave Maria "Gee it's good to see ya"
Gettin' ecstatic an' sorta dramatic an' doin' the Vatican Rag!

G - C - / / / F C A / D G D G / D G C

— w & m: Tom Lehrer

© 1965 (renewed) Tom Lehrer. On his *That Was the Yr That Was, Best of Blasphemy*, Courtney Kenny *Amer Cabaret S*, Fred Wedlock *The Folker/Frolics*. In *Tomfoolery*.

WAL I SWAN

I run the old mill over here to *[in]* Reubensville
My name's Joshua Ebenezer Frye
I know a thing or 2, you bet your neck I do
They don't ketch me for I'm too darn sly
I've seen Bunco men, always got the best of them
Once I met a couple on the Boston train
They says "How be you?" I says "That'll do!
Travel right along with your darn skin game!"

D - A - / D - E A / 1st / D - A D :||

Wal I swan! I must be getting on
Giddup [giddy up], **Napoleon, it looks like rain**
Wal I'll be durned, the butter ain't churned
[Wal I'll be switched, the hay ain't pitched]
Come in when you're over to the farm again

I drove the old mare over to the County Fair
Took 1st prize on a load of summer squash
Stopped at the cider mill coming over by the hill
Come home tighter than a drum, by gosh!
I was so durn full I give away the old bull
Dropped both my reins clean out on the fill
Got home so darn late couldn't find the barn gate
Ma says "Joshua, 'tain't possible!"

We had a big show here about a week ago
Pitched up a tent by the old mill dam
Ma says "Let's go in to see the sideshow
Just take a look at the tattooed man"
I seen a cuss look sharp at my pockethook
Says, "Gimme 2 tens for a 5?"
I says "You durn fool, I be the constable
Now you're arrested sure as you're alive"

I drove the old bay into town yesterday
Hitched her up to the RR fence
Tied her good & strong, but a train came along
I ain't seen the "hoss" or the wagon since
Had to foot it home, so I started off alone
When a fella says "Hurry, your barn's on fire!"
But I had the key in my pocket, you see
So I knew that the cuss was a fool or a liar

— w & m: Benjamin Hapgood Burt

Arr. © 2015 by Hal Leonard Corporation. From the 1907 play *Yankee Tourist*. Rec by Al Bernard in '28 13. In *Read 'Em & Weep*.

WHAT I WANT IS A PROPER CUP OF COFFEE

A Sultan sat on his oriental mat, in his harem in High Street, Persia
He took one sip of coffee, just a drip, & he said to his servant,
  "Curse ya!" *[Kersia]*
"Ah, curse ya, curse ya, curse ya! That's the worst cup of coffee in
  Persia!"

I: Am - - E / Am CD C GC / F C - GC

'Cos all I want is a proper cup of coffee, made in a proper
  copper coffee pot
I may be off my dot, but I want a cup of coffee from a
  proper copper pot
Iron coffee pots & tin coffee pots, they are no use to me!
If I can't have a proper cup of coffee from a proper copper
  coffee pot, I'll have a cup of tea!

C - - GC / Dm FG G GC / C - - F / CG CF CG C

In days of old when knights & men were bold & whiskey was
  much cheaper
Dick Turpin rode to a coffee shop & showed his pistols to the
  keeper
He said "Stand & deliver! Can't you see that I'm all a-quiver?"

When Bonaparte found that he was in the cart & he lost that
  Waterloo fight
He gave his sword to Wellington, the lord & he said "You British,
  you do fight!
Now you've had your Waterloo, sir, tell me what am I having
  with you, sir?"

Now King Solomon & his queen would carry on, so we heard in
  the ancient scandals
He gave her lots of silver coffee pots with diamond spouts &
  handles
And said the Queen of Sheba "I'd rather have any old tea-bag"

II: Am CD C GC /   / E7 Am D7 G
C - - G / Dm - D7 G / F C F G / CG CF CG C

— w & m: R.P. Weston & Bert Lee (1926)

WHY AM I PAINTING THE LIVING ROOM?

Holes in the ozone the size of Brazil
Barges of trash in the chewable breeze
Pools of industrial wasteland paté
Sulfur dioxide dissolving the trees
Pretty soon it will all end with a boom
Why am I painting the living room?

(in 3/4) C - / / F - / C - / G - / - C

I have the whole day off / 'Cos it's a Saturday
There is a bluegrass band / Somewhere along the bay
Look at the lilacs bloom / **Why am I painting...**

A pinhead evangelist pays for his sin
With a $5 fine for a black collar crime
Kingpins of industry knowingly nod
Just like Lake Erie they're 12% slime
They wink at the president too I assume / And **here I am...**

I hear the bluebird sing / Don't let the day go by
Look at the blossoms blow / Over the blue blue sky
All with a wild perfume / And **here I am painting...**

Why am I painting the living room? (6x)

Ah yes I can see how my tombstone will read
Here lies someone of exceptional worth
Tho' she did not do a lot for her kind
Or help hold together this crumbling earth
Here lies a woman they're saying of whom
Sure had a good-looking living room

— w & m: Lou & Peter Berryman

© 1988 Lou & Peter Berryman (SESAC). In *New Berryman Berryman SB*. On their *Love Is the Weirdest of All*, Brian J. Kenny *It's a Mean Season*, Sally Rogers & Claudia Schmidt *Evidence of Happiness*.

THE WORMS CRAWL IN (The Hearse Song)

Do you ever think as a hearse goes by
That you may be the next to die?
They wrap you up in a big white sheet
From your head down to your feet
[And throw you down about 6 ft deep]

`Dm - / - A :‖`

They put you in a big black box
And cover you up w dirt & rocks
All goes well for about a week
Then your coffin begins to leak

The worms crawl in, the worms crawl out
The worms play pinochle on your snout
They eat your eyes, they eat your nose
They eat the jelly between your toes

A big green worm with rolling eyes
Crawls in your stomach & out your eyes
Your stomach turns a slimy green
And pus pours out like whipping cream
You spread it on a slice of bread
And that's what you eat when you are dead

— trad. (US)

Arr. © 2015 by Hal Leonard Corporation. In *Amer Songbag*.

YOU WENT THE WRONG WAY, OLD KING LOUIE

(intro) Louis the 16th was the King of France
In 1789 / He was worse than Louis the 15th
He was worse than Louis the 14th
He was worse than Louis the 13th
He was the worst since Louis the 1st

`E♭7 E / A♭7 E / E B7 / C#m B7 / E A / E♭7 E`

King Louis was living like a king, but the people were
    living rotten
So the people they started an uprising which they called the
    French Revolution
And of course you remember their battle cry which will
    never be forgotten:

`A Dm / C - / B♭ Dm7 G`

You went the wrong way, Old King Louie
You made the population cry
'Cos all you did was sit & pet with Marie Antoinette
In your place at Versailles

`C - /    / - A♭ / - C`

And now the country's gone kablooie
So we are giving you the air
That oughta teach you not to spend
All your time fooling 'round at the Folies Bergere

(bridge) If you had been a nicer king, we wouldn't do a thing
But you were bad, you must admit
We're gonna take you & the Queen down to the guillotine
And shorten you a little bit

`F Fm / C - / 1st / C G`

You came the wrong way, Old King Louie
And now you ain't got far to go
Too bad you won't be here to see that great big Eiffel Tower
Or Brigitte Bardot

To you King Louie we say phooey
You disappointed all of France
But then what else else could we expect from a king in silk stockings
And pink satin pants?

You filled your stomach with chop suey
And also crêpe suzettes & steak
And when they told your wife Marie that nobody had bread,
She said "Let 'em eat cake"

(bridge) We're gonna take you & the Queen down to the guillotine
It's somewhere in the heart of town
And when that fella there is thru with what he's gonna do
You'll have no place to wear your crown

You came the wrong way Old King Louie
Now we must put you on the shelf
That's why the people are revolting, 'cos Louie
You're pretty revolting yourself

— w & m: Allan Sherman

© 1963 (renewed) Curtain Call Productions (ASCAP). Admin by TuneCore. On his *My Son The Nut* 13. Tune is derived from "La Marseillaise," "You Came A Long Way From St. Louis" & the Peter Gunn theme.

The **Funny Songs** chapter contains humorous & camp songs for adults & older kids. See also: **Play** (for younger kids), **Pub Songs**.

Others include **Ballads**: Get up & bar the door, There was a pig went out to dig **Brit**: I'm Henry the 8th **Country**: Jackson, Okie from Muskogee **Dignity**: Sensitive new age guys **Farm**: Wahoo **Golden**: Swinging on a star **Good**: Tie me kangaroo down **Home**: Your state's name here **Jazz**: Istanbul **Rich**: One meatball **Rock**: Monster mash **Sea**: Paddy West **Sing**: Folk song army **Struggle**: Love me I'm a liberal **Surfing**: These boots are made for walkin' **Work**: Dump the bosses off your back.

Golden Oldies

ALOHA OE

Ha'aheo e ka ua i nā pali
Ke nihi a'ela i ka nahele
E hahai (uhai) ana paha i ka liko
Pua 'āhihi lehua o uka

G - C G / D(7) - - - / 1st / C D G G7

Aloha 'oe (x2) / E ke onaona noho i ka lipo
One fond embrace, a ho'i a'e au / **Until we meet again**

C - G - / D(7) - G G7 / 1st / D(7) - G -

Farewell to thee (2x)
Thou charming one who dwells among the bowers
One fond embrace before we part / Until…

— w & m: Queen Lili'uokalani (1878)

Arr © 2015 Hal Leonard Corporation. Rec by Burl Ives. In films *Blue Hawaii* and *Lilo & Stitch*. In *Daily Ukulele*.

AS TIME GOES BY

You must remember this, a kiss is still a kiss
A sigh is just a sigh
The fundamental things apply
As time goes by

(in G) Am7 D Dm D7 / G Am7 G - / A - D AmD / 2nd

And when 2 lovers woo, they still say "I love you"
On that you can rely
No matter what the future brings / **As…**

(bridge) Moonlight & love songs, never out of date
Hearts full of passion, jealousy & hate
Woman needs man & man must have his mate
That no one can deny

C - E7 - / Am - Edim - / Em C7 A7 - / D7 Ddim D7 -

It's still the same old story, a fight for love & glory
A case of do or die
The world will always welcome lovers / **As…**

— w & m: Herman Hupfeld

© 1931 (renewed) WB Music Corp. Wilson Dooley sang in *Casablanca* ('42 16). Rec by Rudy Vallee in '31, Billie Holiday, Jimmy Durante, Tony Bennett.

BEYOND THE SEA

Somewhere _ beyond the sea, somewhere
Waiting for me, _ my lover stands on golden sands
_And watches the ships that go sailin'

CAm Dm7G x2 / CE AmG CAm FA / DmG CAm Dm7 G

Somewhere _ beyond the sea, she's there
Watching for me, _ if I could fly like birds on high
_Then straight to her arms I'd go sailin'

/   "   /   "   / DmG AmF G C(B7)

(bridge) It's far _ beyond the stars, it's near
Beyond the moon, _ I know _
Beyond a doubt my heart will lead me there soon _

E AB7 E AB7 / E ED7 GEm AmD / GEm AmD G G7

We'll meet _ beyond the shore, we'll kiss
Just as before _ happy we'll be beyond the sea
_ And never again I'll go sailin'

La Mer (orig lyrics)

La mer_ qu'on voit danser le long
Des golfes clairs_a des reflets d'argent, la mer
_Des reflets changeants sous la plui-e

La mer_ au ciel de l'été confond
Ses blancs moutons_ avec les anges si purs, la mer
_Bergère d'azur infini-e

(bridge) Voyez, _ près des étangs, ces grands
Roseaux mouillés, _ voyez_
Ces oiseaux blancs et ces maisons rouillées_

La mer, _ les a bercés le long
Des golfes clairs, _et d'une chanson d'amour, la mer
_A bercé mon cœur pour la vi-e

— w: Jack Lawrence, m: Charles Trenet & Albert Lasry

Original French lyric To "La Mer" by Charles Trenet. © 1945, 1946, 1947 (renewed) by France Music Corp. & Range Road Music Inc. Rec by Charles Trenet ('46), Bobby Darin ('59), Kevin Spacey in '04 film *Beyond the Sea* 15.

BUTTON UP YOUR OVERCOAT

Button up your overcoat when the wind is free
Take good care of yourself, you belong to me
Eat an apple every day, get to bed by 3 / **Take…**
Be careful crossing streets (ooh), don't eat meats (ooh)
Cut out sweets (ooh), you'll get a pain & ruin your tum-tum
Keep away from bootleg hooch when you're on a spree / **Take…**

C - D7 - / G7 - C (G) :‖ F - C - / Am D7 G7 - / 1st 2

Button up your overcoat when the wind is free / **Take…**
Wear your flannel underwear when you climb a tree / **Take…**
Don't step on hornet's tails (ooh) or on nails (ooh)
Or 3rd rails (ooh) you'll get a pain & ruin your tum-tum
Don't go out with college boys when you're on a spree
Take good…

— w & m: B. G. DeSylva, Lew Brown & Ray Henderson

© 1928 by Chappell & Co., Stephen Ballentine Music Publishing Co. & Ray Henderson Music Co. Copyright renewed. In '29 musical *Follow Through*. Recs by Ruth Etting (orig), Helen Kane 15, Bing Crosby, Sarah Vaughan (Ab) etc.

BY THE BEAUTIFUL SEA

By the sea, by the sea, by the beautiful sea
You & I, you & I, oh how happy we'll be
When each wave comes a-rolling in, we will duck or swim
And we'll float & fool around the water
Over & under & then up for air
Pa is rich, ma is rich, so now what do we care?
I love to be beside your side, beside the sea
Beside the seaside, by the beautiful sea

D7 - / G - / GD D7 / G - / 1st 2 / C BmE / AD G

— w: Harold R. Atteridge, m: Harry Carroll

Arr. © 2015 by Hal Leonard Corporation. In *Daily Ukulele*. Rec by Bill Murray 11 & in the '59 Marilyn Monroe film *Some Like It Hot*.

BYE BYE BLACKBIRD

Pack up all my cares & woe, here I go, singing low
Bye bye, blackbird
Where somebody waits for me, sugar's sweet, so is she…
No one here can love & understand me
Oh what hard luck stories they all hand me
Make my bed & light the light, I'll arrive late tonight
Blackbird, bye bye

G CG BmD AmG / G Adim Am D / Am Caug Am D /
- - G - // - - Dm Ddim / AmCm GA Cm D /
G CG BmD DmE / Am - D G

— w: Mort Dixon, m: Ray Henderson

© 1926 (renewed 1953) Olde Clover Leaf Music (ASCAP)/administered by BMG Rights Management (US) LLC & Ray Henderson (ASCAP)/administered by Ray Henderson Music. Rec by Gene Austin ('26 11), Joe Cocker ('69), Peggy Lee ('95 12). In *Daily Ukulele*.

CATCH A FALLING STAR

Catch a falling star & put it in your pocket
Never let it fade away
Catch a falling star & put it in your pocket
Save it for a rainy day

G GC G GC (4x)

For love may come & tap you on the shoulder / Some starless night
And just in case you feel you want to hold her
You'll have a pocketful of starlight

C - - - / G - - G7 / 1st / G - D7 -

For when your troubles start multiplyin' / And they just might
It's easy to forget them without tryin'
With just a pocketful of starlight

— w & m: Paul Vance & Lee Pockriss

© 1957 (renewed) by Music Sales Corporation (ASCAP) & Emily Music. Perry Como's last #1 hit ('57). Tune is based on Brahms' Academic Festival Overture. In films *Princess Diaries, Love Actually* & *Never Been Kissed*. In *Daily Ukulele Leap Yr.*

FIVE FOOT TWO, EYES OF BLUE
(Has Anybody Seen My Gal?)

Five feet two, eyes of blue, but oh what those Five feet could do
Has anybody seen my gal?
Turned up nose, turned down hose, never had no other beaus
  [flapper, yes sir, one of those] / **Has…**
Now if you run into a five feet two, covered with fur
Diamond rings & all those things, bet your life it isn't her
But could she love — could she woo? could she could she could
  she coo? / **Has…**

G B7 E7 - / A7 D7 G (D) :‖ B7 - E7 - / A7 - D7 - / 1st 2

— w: Joe Young & Sam Lewis, m: Ray Henderson

© 1925 Leo Feist, Inc. copyright renewed 1953 Warock Corp., EMI Feist Catalog Inc. & Ray Henderson Music Co. in the United States. All rights for EMI Feist Catalog Inc. administered by EMI Feist Catalog Inc. (Publishing) & Alfred Music (Print). All rights for the Sam Lewis & Ray Henderson Shares in the British Reversionary territories administered by Redwood Music Ltd. Some sources credit w: Jack Mahoney, m: Percy Wenrich in 1914 as orig. version. Rec by Calif Ramblers in 1925, Dean Martin 15. In *Daily Ukulele*.

THE GLORY OF LOVE

You've got to give a little, take a little
And let your poor heart break a little
That's the story of, that's the glory of love

C G / C FFm / C G C (G v2: C7)

You've got to laugh a little, cry a little
And let the clouds roll by a little / **That's…**

(bridge) As long as there's the 2 of us
We've got the world & all its charms
And when the world is thru with us
We've got each other's arms

F - / C - / F Fm / D7 G7   II: F Fm / C C7 / 1st / CAm DmG

You've got to win a little, lose a little
Always have the blues a little / **That's…**

— w & m: Billy Hill

© 1936 Shapiro, Bernstein & Co., Inc., New York. Copyright renewed. #1 hit for Benny Goodman ('36) & R&B vocal gp The Five Keys (II: '51 13). Also Patti Page 15, in '67 film *Guess Who's Coming to Dinner* & by Midler in *Beaches*. In *Daily Ukulele*.

I DON'T KNOW WHY (I Just Do)

I don't know why I love you like I do
I don't know why, I just do
I don't know why you thrill me like you do
I don't know why you just do
You never seem to want my romancing
The only time you hold me is when we're dancing
I don't know why I love… (as lines 1 & 2)

C - Am - / Em Adim Dm G / - - Dm7 - / G - C -
C A Dm G / Am Dm - G / C - Am A / Dm G C -

— w: Roy Turk, m: Fred E. Ahlert

TRO - © 1931 (renewed) Cromwell Music, Inc., New York, NY, Pencil Mark Music, Azure Pearl Music, David Ahlert Music & Beeping Good Music. All rights for Pencil Mark Music administered by BMG Rights Management (US) LLC. All rights for Azure Pearl Music, David Ahlert Music & Beeping Good Music administered by Bluewater Music Services Corp. Recs by Frances Day, Kate Smith, Sinatra, etc. In *Daily Ukulele*.

IT HAD TO BE YOU

It had to be you, it had to be you
I wandered around & finally found the somebody who
Could make me be true, could make me be blue
And even be glad, just to be sad, thinking of you

Cmaj7 - A7 - / D7 - - - / G - Am - / D7 - G -

Some others I've seen, might never be mean
Might never be cross or try to be boss, but they wouldn't do
For nobody else gave me a thrill, with all your faults I love you
    still / It had to be you, wonderful you, it had to be you

/   "   /   "   / Dm Ddim CE AmDdim / G - C -

— m: Isham Jones, w: Gus Kahn

© 1924 (renewed) Gilbert Keyes Music & the Bantam Music Publishing Co. All
rights administered by WB Music Corp. Sung by Ruth Ettig in the '36 film *Melody
in May*, Priscilla Lane in *Roaring 20's* ('39), Dooley Wilson in *Casablanca* ('42),
Betty Hutton in *Incendiary Blonde* ('45), Danny Thomas in *I'll See You in my
Dreams* ('51), Diane Keaton in *Annie Hall* ('77), Megan Cavanaugh in *A League of
Their Own.*

ME & MY SHADOW

Me & my shadow, strolling down the avenue
Me & my shadow, not a soul to tell our troubles to
And when it's 12 o'clock, we climb the stair, we never knock for
    nobody's there
Just me & my shadow, all alone & feeling blue

C DdimF DmG C / C B7 AmD G / C Am A DmG / 1st

— w: Billy Rose, m: Al Jolson & Dave Dreyer

© 1927 by Bourne Co. (ASCAP) & Larry Spier, Inc. Copyright renewed. Orig rec
by Jolson. Also Helen Morgan, Judy Garland 18, Frank Sinatra & Sammy Davis Jr,
Mills Bros 13, Robbie Wms, etc.

MISS THE MISSISSIPPI & YOU

(intro) I'm growing tired of the big city lights
Tired of the glamor & tired of the sights
In all my dreams, I am roaming once more
Back to my home on the old river shore

(in 3/4) G - Am - / D - A7 D / C - Em Am / A7 - D7

I am sad & weary, far away from home
Miss the Mississippi & you
Days are dark & dreary, everywhere I roam
Miss the Mississippi & you
Rolling [*roaming*] **the wide world over**
Always alone & blue
Nothing seems to cheer me under heaven's dome…

G G7 C Cm / G AAD G - :‖ C - G - / Em A7 D7 - / 1st 2

Memories are bringing happy days of yore…
Mockingbirds are singing 'round the cabin door…
Rolling… / **…blue**
Longing for my homeland, muddy water shore…

— w & m: Bill Halley

© 1932 by Peer International Corporation. Copyright renewed. Rec by Jimmie
Rodgers ('32 18). Emmylou Harris ('80 13). In *Daily Ukulele.*

MISTER SANDMAN

Mr. Sandman, bring me a dream
Make him the cutest that I've ever seen
Give him 2 lips like roses & clover
Then tell him that his lonesome nights are over
Sandman, I'm so alone / Don't have nobody to call my own
Please turn on your magic beam / Mr. Sandman…

F E7 / A7 D / G C / F DdimC / 1st 2 / Gm - / FC F

Mr Sandman…. / Make him the cutest that I've ever seen
Give him the word that I'm not a rover
Then tell him that his lonesome nights are over
Sandman, I'm so alone…

Mr Sandman… / Give him a pair of eyes with a come-hither gleam
Give him a lonely heart like Pagliacci
And lots of wavy hair like Liberace
Mr. Sandman, someone to hold
Would be so peachy before we're too old
So please turn on your magic beam
(tag) Mr. Sandman, bring us, please, please bring us
Mr Sandman, bring us a dream

— w & m: Pat Ballard

© 1954 (renewed) Edwin H. Morris & Company, A division of MPL Music
Publishing, Inc. Rec by The Chordettes 14.

MOONLIGHT BAY

We were sailing along on Moonlight Bay
We could hear the voices ringing, they seemed to say:
"You have stolen her heart, now don't go 'way"
As we sang "Love's Old Sweet Song" on Moonlight Bay

D DG D - / A7 - D - :‖

— w: Edward Madden, m: Percy Wenrich (1912)

Arr. © 2015 by Hal Leonard Corporation. Doris Day & Gordon McRae sang in '51
film *On Moonlight…* Rec by Bing Crosby 11, Doris Day. In *Daily Ukulele.* Beatles
sang on Morecambe & Wise TV show in '63.

OLD CAPE COD

If you're fond of sand dunes & salty air
Quaint little villages here & there
You're sure to fall in love with Old Cape Cod
If you like the taste of a lobster stew
Served by a window with an ocean view / **You're sure…**

D AmD / G C7 / 1. DB7 E7 A7 - :‖ 2. DB7 E7A7 D -

(bridge) Winding roads that seem to beckon you
Miles of green beneath the skies of blue
Church bells chimin' on a Sun. morn
Remind you of the town where you were born

GA DEdim / EmA D / GDdim GB7 / EmE7 A7

(w/ 2nd ending:) If you spend an evening you'll want to stay
Watching the moonlight on Cape Cod Bay / **You're…**

— w & m: Claire Rothrock, Milton Yakus & Allan Jeffrey (1957)

© 1956 George Pincus & Sons Music Corp., 1650 Broadway, New York, NY 10019.
Copyright renewed.Rec by Patti Page. Four Freshmen, Bette Midler, Anne Murray,
Puppini Sisters. In *Daily Ukulele Leap Yr.*

QUE SERA, SERA (Whatever Will Be, Will Be)

When I was just a little girl
I asked my mother what will I be
Will I be pretty, will I be rich
Here's what she said to me

A - / - E - / - - / - A

Que sera, sera, whatever will be, will be
The future's not ours to see
Que sera, sera; what will be, will be

D - / A - / E - / A -

When I grew up & fell in love
I asked my sweetheart what lies ahead
Will we have rainbows day after day
Here's what my sweetheart said

Now I have children of my own
They ask their mother, what will I be
Will I be handsome, will I be rich
I tell them tenderly

— w & m: Jay Livingston & Ray B. Evans

© 1955 by Jay Livingston Music & St. Angelo Music. Copyright renewed. Sung by Doris Day in '56 Hitchcock film *The Man Who Knew Too Much.*

SENTIMENTAL JOURNEY

Gonna take a **sentimental journey**
Gonna set my heart at ease
Gonna make a **sentimental...** / To renew old memories

(↑2) G - - - / - - - D / G - C7 - / G - D G

Got my bag, got my reservation
Spent each dime I could afford
Like a child in wild anticipation
Long to hear that "All aboard!"

(bridge) 7, that's the time we leave at / 7, I'll be waitin' up for
Heaven, countin' every mile of / RR track that takes me back

C - - - / G - - - / A7 - - - / D7 Am7 G D7

Never thought my heart could be so yearn-y
Why did I decide to roam?
Gotta take that **sentimental...** / **Sentimental...** home

— w & m: Bud Green, Les Brown & Ben Homer

© 1944 (renewed) Morley Music Co. & Holliday Publishing. 1st #1 hit for Doris Day, rec in '45 w/ Les Brown & his Band of Renown. Unofficial homecoming song for many returning WWII vets.

SWEET ADELINE

Sweet Adeline, my Adeline
At night, dear heart, for you I pine
In all my dreams your fair face beams
You're the flower of my heart, Sweet Adeline

GC GB7 CE7 A7 / D7 - G D / 1st / GC AD G(C G)

— w: Richard H. Gerard (1903), m: Harry Armstrong (1898)

Arr. © 2015 by Hal Leonard Corporation. 1st performed by the Quaker City 4 in 1904. Inspired by a girl who worked at music counter in a NYC dept store. Theme song of John Fitzgerald, Boston mayor, congressman & grandfather of JFK.

SWEET SUE, JUST YOU

Every star above knows the one I love
Sweet Sue, just you
And the moon up high knows the reason why
Sweet Sue, it's you
No one else, it seems, ever shares my dreams
And without you, dear, I don't know what I'd do
In this heart of mine you live all the time / **Sweet...**

(in D) Em7 A7 x2 / D - - - :‖ D7 - - - / G - Gm - / 1st 2

— w: Will J. Harris, m: Victor Young

© 1928 Shapiro, Bernstein & Co., Inc., New York. Copyright renewed. Recs by Mills Bros 14, Fats Waller 15, Bing Crosby 14, Gene Austin, Django Reinhardt, Miles Davis, Benny Goodman, etc.

SWINGING ON A STAR

Would you like to swing on a star
Carry moonbeams home in a jar
And be better off than you are
Or would you rather be a <u>mule</u>?

(in G) E7 - A7 - / D7 - G - :‖

A mule is an animal with long funny ears
Kicks up at anything he hears
His back is brawny but his brain is weak
He's just plain stupid with a stubborn streak
And by the way, if you hate to go to school
You may grow up to be a mule

G C G C / G C G Em / A - D - / Em A D - /
G C G E / Am D G -

Would you like to swing on a star...
Or would you rather be a pig?

A pig is an animal with dirt on his face
His shoes are a terrible disgrace
He's got no manners when he eats his food
He's fat & lazy & extremely rude
But if you don't care a feather or a fig
You may grow up to be a pig

Would you like to swing... / Or would you rather be a fish?

A fish won't do anything but swim in a brook
He can't write his name or read a book
To fool the people is his only thought
And tho' he's slippery, he still gets caught
But then if that sort of life is what you wish
You may grow up to be a fish

(tag) And all the monkeys aren't in the zoo
Every day you meet quite a few
So you see it's all up to you
You can be better than you are
You could be swingin' on a star

E7 - A7 - / D7 - G - / 1st / D7 - Em - / A D G -

— w: Johnny Burke, m: Jimmy Van Heusen

© 1944 by Bourne Co. (ASCAP) & Dorsey Bros. Music. A division of Music Sales Corporation (ASCAP). Copyright renewed. Sung by Bing Crosby in the '44 film *Going My Way* (in F). Frank Sinatra 11, Bruce Willis & Danny Aiello in '91 film *Hudson Hawk* 11.

TIP-TOE THRU THE TULIPS WITH ME

Tiptoe to the window
By the window, that is where I'll be
Come **tiptoe thru the tulips / With me**

C A7 Dm G / C E7 F Fm / 1st / C - - (G)

Tiptoe from your pillow
To the shadow of a willow tree
And **tiptoe thru...**

(bridge) Knee deep in flowers we'll stray
We'll keep the showers away

Dm7 Cdim Em7 A7 / B7 - Em G7

And if I kiss you in the garden
In the moonlight, will you pardon me?
Come **tiptoe...**

— w: Al Dubin, m: Joe Burke

WALKIN MY BABY BACK HOME

Gee *[but]* it's great after being out late
Walkin' my baby back home
Arm & arm over meadow & farm
Walkin' my baby back home

C Gaug   x2 / C Gaug Em A / Dm A Dm - / Dm G C (Gaug)

We go along harmonizing a song
Or I'm reciting a poem
Owls go by & they give me the eye
Walkin' my baby back home

> **(bridge)** We stop for a while, she gives me a smile
> And snuggles her head to my chest
> We start in to pet & that's when I get
> Her talcum *[powder]* all over my vest

Em - - A7 / C - Em B7 / Em - - - / A7 - D7 G7

After I kinda straighten my tie / She has to borrow my comb
One kiss, then I continue again / **Walkin'...**

> **(bridge)** She's afraid of the dark so I have to park
> Outside of her door til it's light
> She says if I try to kiss her, she'll cry
> I dry her tears all thru the night

Hand in hand to a barbecue stand / Right from her doorway we roam
Eats! *[We kiss]* & then it's a pleasure again / **Walkin'...**

— w: Roy Turk, m: Fred E. Ahlert (1930)

WHEN THE RED, RED ROBIN COMES BOB, BOB BOBBIN' ALONG

When the red, red robin comes bob bob bobbin' along, along
There'll be no more sobbin' when he starts throbbin' his old
　sweet song
Wake up **(x2)** you sleepy head, get up **(x2)** get out of bed
Cheer up **(x2)** the sun is red, live love laugh & be happy
What if I've been blue? Now I'm walking thru the fields of flowers
Rain may glisten but still I listen for hrs & hrs
I'm just a kid again doing what I did again, singing a song
When the red, red robin...

C G C - / C G C C7 / F - C - / D - G - / 1st 2 /
F Fm C A / 1st

— w & m: Harry Woods

YES SIR THAT'S MY BABY

Yes sir, that's my baby, no sir, I don't mean maybe
Yes sir, that's my baby now
Yes ma'am, we've decided, no ma'am, we won't hide it
Yes ma'am, you're invited now / By the way, by the way
When we meet the preacher I'll say / **Yes sir... now**

C - G - / G7 - C - :‖ C7 - F - / D7 - G7 - / 1st 2

— w: Gus Kahn, m: Walter Donaldson

YOU BELONG TO ME

See the pyramids along the Nile
Watch the sun rise on a tropic isle
Just remember, darling, all the while
You belong to me

(↑) C - Em - / F - Em A7 / F Fm C Am / Dm - G -

See the marketplace in old Algiers
Send me photographs & souvenirs
Just remember when a dream appears / **You...** Dm G C -

(bridge) I'll be so alone / Without you
Maybe you'll be lonesome / Too & blue

C - - - / F - - - / D7 - - - / G - G7 -

Fly the ocean in a silver plane
See the jungle when it's wet with rain
Just remember til you're home again / **You...**

— w & m: Pee Wee King, Redd Stewart & Chilton Price

The **Golden Oldies** Chapter contains popular songs up into 1950's.
See also **Jazz & Swing, Musicals, Rock Around the Clock**.
Other songs include **Farm:** Ragtime Cowboy Joe, **Friendship:**
Side by side, **Funny:** Lydia the tatooed lady, Reuben & Rachel, Wal
I Swan, **Good:** Hernando's Hideaway, Hot time in the old town,
Home: Beautiful Ohio, **Outdoors:** Blue skies, **Sing:** Ukelele lady.

Good Times

THE 59TH STREET BRIDGE SONG
(Feelin' Groovy)

_Slow down, you move too fast
You got to make the mornin' last
Just kicking down the cobble stones
Looking for fun & feelin' groovy

(in G) C G D G (4x)

Hello lamppost, whatcha knowing?
I've come to watch your flowers growing
Ain'tcha got no rhymes for me?
Doot-in' doo doo, feelin' groovy

I've got no deeds to do, no promises to keep
I'm dappled & drowsy & ready to sleep
Let the morning time drop all its petals on me
Life I love you, all is groovy

— w & m: Paul Simon

© 1966, 1967 Paul Simon (BMI). On Simon & Garfunkel *Parsley, Sage, Rosemary & Thyme* 13.

BIG MAMOU

**Oh s'en allez à Grand Mamou
Jolis mondes, mais jolie fille, moi j'connais j'mérite pas ça
Hey ha-ha, hey Mignonne
Oh mais moi j'm'en va, moi tout seul à Grand Mamou**

(↑2) G - / - D / - - / - G

Why'd you go & leave me in Big Mamou?
You left me for another alone & so blue
Please come back, oh come back
I know what I say & I did not say that

How come you run from Big Mamou?
Can't you hear me aloud clearly calling for you?
Hey, ha ha, ooh la la!
Hurry, hurry home to your lonely papa

Why'd you go & leave me in Big Mamou?
You left me for another alone & so blue
I know what I say — I did not say that
Come back & love me in Big Mamou

Why did you go away & leave me in Big Mamou?
You left me for another alone & so blue
Oh la la, ooh, ha ha !
Come on home to lonely Papa!

(tag) I know what I say, I know what I do
I didn't say or do that in Big Mamou

— w & m: Link Davis & Macy Lela Henry

© 1953 by Peer International Corporation. Copyright renewed. Rec by Hank Williams Jr.

LA CUCARACHA

**La Cucaracha, la Cucaracha ya no puede caminar
Porque no tiene, porque le falta una pata para_andar**
[orig. *"dinero para gustar"* - alt. *"marijuana que fumar"*]

(in 3/4) D - - A / - - - D

Pobre la Cucaracha se queja de corazón
Por no_usar ropa planchada por la_escasez del carbón.

La ropa sin almidón, se pone todos los dias
Y sin ésas boberias se me figura melón

Ya murió la cucaracha, ya la llevan a_enterrar
Entre cuatro zopilotes y_un ratón de sacristán

— trad. (Mexican, ca. 1915)

Arr. © 2015 by Hal Leonard Corporation. Originates from time of the Mexican revolution. There are many versions of this song, many of which are unprintable in a family SB. In *Fireside Bk of Amer S*, Sandburg *Amer Songbag*.

DANCE FOR THE NATIONS

1. Round & round we turn, we hold each others' hands &
2. Weave ourselves in a cir-cle, the
3. Time is gone, the dance goes on

Em Am B7 Em (3x)

— w & m: John Krumm

© 1985 John Krumm. On *Rounds Galore & More V2*.

DANCING QUEEN

(intro = lines 3 & 4 of chorus)

Friday night & the lights are low
Looking out for the place to go
Where they play the right music, getting in the swing
You come to look for a king
  Anybody could be that guy
  Night is young & the music's high
  With a bit of rock music, everything is fine
  You're in the mood for a dance
And when you get the chance

(in G) G C / G Em / DDsus x2 / DEm x2 :‖ Am D

You are the dancing queen, young & sweet, only 17
Dancing queen, feel the beat from the tambourine
You can dance, you can jive having the time of your life
See that girl, watch that scene, diggin' the dancing queen

G C (x2) / G C G - / D B7 Em A / C Am G (C G (x2) C)

You're a teaser, you turn 'em on
Leave them burning & then you're gone
Looking out for another, anyone will do
You're in the mood for a dance / And when you get the chance

— w & m: Benny Andersson, Bjorn Ulvaeus & Stig Anderson

© 1977 Universal/Union Songs Musikforlag AB. Copyright renewed. All rights in the United States & Canada controlled & administered by Universal-Songs of PolyGram International, Inc. & EMI Grove Park Music, Inc. On Abba Arrival 12.

DIGGY LIGGY LO

Diggy Liggy Li & Diggy Liggy Lo
Fell in love at the fais-do-do
The pop was cold & the coffee chaud
For Diggy Liggy Li & Diggy Liggy Lo

A - / - E / - - / - A

Diggy Liggy Li loved Diggy Liggy Lo
Everyone knew he was her beau
No one else could ever show
So much love for Diggy Liggy Lo

D - / A - / E - / - A

There's a place they find romance
Where they do the Cajun dance
Steal a kiss with ev'ry chance
Show their love with ev'ry glance

Finally went to see her Pa
Now he's got a Papa-in-law
Moved out where the Bayou's low
Now he's got a little Diggy Liggy Lo

— w & m: J.D. Miller

© 1954 Sony/ATV Music Publishing LLC. Copyright renewed. All rights administered by Sony/ATV Music Publishing LLC, 424 Church Street, Suite 1200, Nashville, TN 37219. Recs by Doug Kershaw, John Fogerty, Nitty Gritty Dirt Band, Santiano, Lavallee Tradition, Buck Owens.

DON'T WORRY BE HAPPY

Here's a little song I wrote, you might want to sing it note for note
Don't worry, be happy
In every life we have some trouble, but when you worry you
  make it double / **Don't worry, be happy x2 now**

(↑4) G - Am - / C - G - :‖

(Woo woo...) **don't worry**
(Woo...) **be happy** (woo...) **don't worry, be happy** (repeat)

Ain't got no place to lay your head, somebody came & took your bed
Don't worry...
The landlord say your rent is late, he may have to litigate...

Ain't got no cash, ain't got no style, ain't got no girl to make you
  smile, but...
'Cos when you worry your face will frown & that will bring
  everybody down, so...

— w & m: Bobbi McFerrin

© 1988 by Probnoblem Music. All rights in the US & Canada administered by Universal Music-Careers. On his Simple Pleasures.

DOWN AT THE TWIST & SHOUT

Sat. night & the moon is out
I wanna head on over to the Twist & Shout
Find a 2-step partner & a Cajun beat
When it lifts me up, I'm gonna find my feet
Out in the middle of a big dance floor
When I hear that fiddle, wanna beg for more
Wanna dance to a band from a Lousian' / Tonight

(↑2, in G) C - / G - / D - / G - :‖

And I never have wandered down to New Orleans
Never have drifted down a bayou stream
But I heard that music on the radio
And I swore someday I was gonna go
Down Highway 10 past Lafayette
There's a Baton Rouge & I won't forget
To send you a card with my regrets
'Cos I'm never gonna come back home

D - / G - :‖ Em - / A - / D - / - G

They got a alligator stew & a crawfish pie
A gulf storm blowin' into town tonight
Livin' on the delta it's quite a show
They got hurricane parties ev'ry time it blows
But here up north it's a cold, cold rain
And there ain't no cure for my blues today
Except when the paper says Beausoleil
Is a comin' into town, baby let's go down

Bring your mama, bring your papa, bring your sister too
They got lots of music & lots of room
When they play you a waltz from a 1910
You're gonna feel a little bit young again
Well you learn to dance with your rock 'n' roll
You learn to swing with a do-si-do
But you learn to love at the fais-so-do
Do when you hear a little *Jolie Blonde*

— w & m: Mary Chapin Carpenter

© 1990 EMI April Music Inc. & Getarealjob Music. All rights controlled & administered by EMI April Music Inc. On her Shooting Straight in the Dark.

HERNANDO'S HIDEAWAY

I know a dark secluded place
A place where no one knows your face
A glass of wine, a fast embrace
It's called **Hernando's Hideaway, olé!**

A7 - - - / Dm - - - / 1st / Dm A DmA Dm

All you see are silhouettes
And all you hear are castanets
And no one cares how late it gets / Not at **Hernando's...**

(bridge) At the golden fingerbowl or any place you go
You will meet your uncle Max & everyone you know
But if you go to the spot that I am thinking of
You will be free, to gaze at me & talk of love

A7 - - - / Dm D7 Gm - / 1st / E7 - A7 -

Just knock 3 times & whisper low
That you & I were sent by Joe
Then strike a match & you will know
You're in **Hernando's Hideaway, olé**!

— w & m: Richard Adler & Jerry Ross

I'LL TELL ME MA

I'll tell me ma when I go home
The boys won't leave the girls alone
They pull my hair, they stole my comb
Well that's alright 'til I go home
She is handsome, she is pretty
She is the belle of Belfast City
She is courtin' 1, 2, 3
Please won't you tell me, who is she?

G CG / D7 G :‖ G C / G D7 / G C / GD7 G

Albert Mooney says he loves her
All the boys are fighting for her
They knock at the door & they ring at the bell
Sayin' "Oh my true love, are you well?"
Out she comes as white as snow
Rings on her fingers & bells on her toes
Old Jenny Murray says she'll die
If she doesn't get the fella with the roving eye

Let the wind & the rain & the hail blow high
And the snow come tumbling from the sky
She's as nice as apple pie
She'll get her own lad by & by
When she gets a lad of her own
She won't tell her Ma when she gets home
Let them all come as they will
For it's Albert Mooney she loves still

— trad. (orig. 19th c. English children's song)

IKO IKO

My grandma & your grandma were sittin' by the fire
My grandma told your grandma "I'm gonna set your flag on fire"
**Talk-in' 'bout, Hey now! Hey now! I-ko, i-ko, un-day
Jock-a-mo fee-no ai na-ne, jock-a-mo fee na-ne**

D - - A / - - - D :‖

Look at my king all dressed in red, **I-ko i-ko, un-day**
I betcha 5 dollars he'll kill you dead, **jock-a-mo fee na-ne**

My flag boy & your flag boy were sittin' by the fire
My flag boy told your flag boy, "I'm gonna set your flag on fire"

See that guy all dressed in green? **I-ko...**
He's not a man, he's a lov-in' machine, **jock-a-mo...**

— w & m: Rosa Lee Hawkins, Barbara Ann Hawkins, Joan Marie Johnson, Joe Jones, Maralyn Jones, Sharon Jones & Jessie Thomas

IT'S RAINING MEN

Humidity is rising, barometer's getting low
According to all sources, the street's the place to go
'Cos tonight for the 1st time just about half-past 10
For the 1st time in history it's gonna start raining men!

Em - - - / - - B7 - / Em - Am - / B7 - - -

**It's raining men! Hallelujah! It's raining men! Amen!
I'm gonna go out to run & let myself get absolutely
  soaking wet!
It's raining... Hallelujah! It's raining... every specimen
Tall, blonde, dark & lean, rough & tough & strong & mean**

C D B7 Em / Am - B7 - :‖

God bless Mother Nature, she's a single woman too
She took off to heaven & she did what she had to do
She taught every angel & rearranged the sky
So that each & every woman could find her perfect guy

C D B7 Em / / / C - B7 -

It's raining men, hallelujah, it's raining men, amen! (2x)

C D B7 Em / /

(bridge) I feel stormy weather moving / in, about to begin
Hear the thunder, don't you lose your / head, rip off the roof &
  stay in bed!

Em - G - / C - B7 - :‖

— w & m: Paul Jabara & Paul Shaffer

JAMBALAYA (On the Bayou)

Goodbye Joe, me gotta go, me-oh my-oh
Me gotta go pole the pirogue down the bayou
My Yvonne, the sweetest one, me-oh my-oh
Son of a gun we'll have big fun on the bayou

C - G - / - - C - :||

Jambalaya & a crawfish pie & filé gumbo
'Cos tonight I'm gonna see my ma chère amie-o
Pick guitar, fill fruit jar & be gay-oh / Son of a gun...

Thibodaux, Fontaineaux, the place is buzzin'
Kinfolk come to see Yvonne by the dozen
Dress in style & go hog wild, me-oh my-oh / **Son of...**

Settle down far from town get me a pirogue
And I'll catch all the fish in the bayou
Swap my mon' to buy Yvonne what she need-oh / **Son...**

"Goodbye Joe" j'ai pour allez, mi-o-ma-yo
J'ai pour allez moi tout seul sur le bayou
Ma Yvonne, la plus jolie sur le bayou
Tonnerre m'écrase un va avoir un bon temp sur le bayou

Jambalaya des tartes d'écrevisse, filé gombo
Par a soir moi j'valez voir ma chère ami-o
Jouer l'guitar, boire de la jogue et fair de la musique
Tonnerre m'écrase…

Thibodaux, Fontenaux, la place après sonner
Ça vien "en tas" pour voir Yvonne par les douzaines
*Faire bien l'amour et faire le fou, faire la musique / **Tonn…***

— w & m: Hank Williams

JOLIE BLONDE

Jolie Blonde, 'gardez donc, quoi t'as fait!
Tu m'as quitté pour t'en aller
Pour t'en aller avec un autre, oui, que moi
Quel espoir et quel av'nir mais moi je peux avoir?

(in C, 3/4) C G / D G :||

Jolie blonde, tu m'as laissé moi tout seul
Pour t'en aller chez ta famille
Si t'aurais pas écouté tous les conseils de les autres
Tu serais ici avec moi aujourd'hui
   Jolie blonde, tu croyais il y avait juste toi
    Il y a pas juste toi dans le pays pour moi aimer
    Je vas trouver juste une autre jolie blonde
    Bon Dieu sait, moi, j'aime tant!
Jolie blonde, mourir, ça serait pas rien
C'est de rester dans la terre aussi longtemps
Moi j' vois pas quoi faire si tu reviens pas, bébé
T'en revenir avec moi dans la Louisiane

(newer varient) Jolie Blonde (ay) où toi, t'es chère bébé?
Tu m'as dit, tu peux m'aimer
Mais quoi t'après faire, jolie fille? Tu connais mieux ouais puissant
Quel avenir et quel espoir que moi j'avoir?

Jolie Blonde petite malheureuse bébé
Quoi tu fais, mais aujourd'hui?
Moi tu m' connais j'aime pas juste toi dans le pays
Laissez autres qui moi aimer

— trad. (Cajun)

THE JOLLY TINKER

As I went down a shady lane, at a door I chanced to knock
The servant she came to the door & axed me could I stop
Or could I mend a rusty hole that never had a drop?
Well indeed I could, **don't you know I** can?
To me right-fol-looral-laddy, well indeed I can

G - F G / G - - F / || G - C - / G F G -   (v. 1 only)

She brought me thru the kitchen & she brought me thru the hall
And the servants cried "The Devil! Are you going to block us all?"
Well indeed I'm not, **don't you know** I'm not? / **To me...**

G - F G / G - - F // G - C - / G F G -

She brought me up the stairs for to show me what to do
She fell on the feather bed & I fell on it too
Well indeed I did, **don't you know I** did? / **To me...**

She took up the frying pan & she began to knock
O then for to let the servants know that I was at me work
Well indeed I was, **don't you know I** was?...

She put her hand into her pocket & she pulled out 50 pound,
Sayin' "Take this, me jolly tinker & we'll have another round"
Well, indeed, I will, don't you know I will?...

She put her hand into her pocket & she pulled out her gold watch
Sayin' "Take this, me jolly tinker, for I know you are no botch"
Well indeed I'm not, **don't you know** I'm not?...

Now I'm a jolly tinker this 40 yrs or more
And such a rusty hole as that I never blocked before
Well indeed I didn't, **don't you know I** didn't?...

— trad. (Irish)

MY HUSBAND'S GOT NO COURAGE IN HIM

As I went out one May morning
To view the fields & leaves a-springing
I saw 2 maidens standing by
And one of them her hands was wringing

Am G - Am (4x)

Oh dear-o ! (x2)
My husband's got no courage in him / Oh dear-o!

Am GAm Am GAm / Am G - Am / Am GAm

All sorts of vittles I did provide
All sorts of meats that's fitting for him
With oyster pie & rhubarb too
But nothing will put **courage in him**
    Me husband can dance & caper & sing
    And do anything that's fitting for him
    But he cannot do the thing I want / Because **he has no...**

Me husband's admired wherever he goes
And everyone looks well upon him
With his handsome features & well-shaped leg
But still **he's got no...**
    Every night when I goes to bed
    I lie & throw me leg right o'er him
    And me hand I clamp betw his thighs / But I can't put **any...**

For 7 long yrs I've made his bed
And every night I've lain beside him
And this morning I rose with me maidenhead
For nothing will **put...**
    I wish me husband he was dead
    And in his grave I'd quickly lay him
    And then I'd try another one / That's got a bit of **courage...**

So all ye maids take heed by me me
Don't marry a man before you try him
Or else you'll sing this song like me
When you find he's **got no…**
    — trad. (English)

Arr. © 2015 by Hal Leonard Corporation. On Maddy Prior & June Tabor *Silly Sisters*, Maddy Prior *Ballads & Candles*, The Once *Row Upon Row of the People*, Trembling Bells & Bonnie Prince Billy *The Marble Downs*, Roots Quartet *Prehistory*, Jon Boden *A Folk S a Day*, AL Lloyd *Turtle Dove*.

NINE TIMES A NIGHT

A rambling young sailor to London came down
He'd been paid off his ship in old Liverpool town
They asked him his name & he answered them quite:
"I belong to a family called **Nine Times a Night**"

Am G E Am / - G Am E / Am G Am Dm / Am G E Am

Well a handsome young widow who still wore her weeds
Her husband had left her his money & deeds
Resolved she was on her conjugal rights
And to soften her sorrow with **9 times...**

So she's called to her serving maids Ann & Amelia
To keep a watch out for this wonderful sailor
And if ever he happened to chance in their sight
To bring her fond tidings of **9...**

She was favored by fortune the very next day
These 2 giggling girls saw him coming their way
They've rushed up the stairs full of amorous delight
Crying "Here comes that sailor with his **9...**"

She's jumped out of bed & she's pulled on her clothes
And straight to the hall door like lightning she goes
She's looked him once over & gave him a smack
And the bargain was struck, no more sailing for Jack

The wedding was over, the bride tolled the bell
Jack trimmed her sails 5 times & that pleased her well
She vowed to herself she was satisfied quite
But she still gives sly hints about **9...**

Says Jack "My dear bride, you mistook me quite wrong
I said to that family I did belong
9 times a night's a bit hard for a man
I couldn't do it myself, but my sister she can"
    — trad. (English)

Arr. © 2015 by Hal Leonard Corporation. On AL Lloyd *An Evening w/* Frankie Armstrong *Out of Love Hope & Suffering*, Harry Boardman *Lancashire Mon.*

LA PORTE EN ARRIERE (The Back Door)

Moi et la belle on avait été au bal
On a passé dans tout les honky-tonk
On a revenu le lendemain matin
Le jour était après s'casser
J'ai **passé dedans la porte d'en arrière**

G - / - - / C - / G - / D - G -

L'après-midi moi j'étais au village
Je m'ai saoulé que j'pouvais pus marcher
Ils m'ont ramené back à la maison
Y'avait la compagnie, c'était du monde étranger
J'ai **passé dedans la porte d'en arrière**

Mon vieux père, une fois quand j'arrivé
Il assayait de changer mon idée
J'ai pas écouté, moi j'avais trop la tête dure
Un jour va v'nir mon neg' tu va 'voir du r'gret
T'as **passé...**

J'ai eu un tas d'amis quand j'avais d'l'argent
Asteur j'ai pus d'argent, ben y venons pus me voir
J'étais dans l'village et moi j'm'ai mis dans l'tracas
La lois ma ramasser, moi j'sus parti dans la prison
On va...
    — w & m: D. L. Menard

© 1962, 1975 (renewed) Flat Town Music Co. On his *Le Trio Cadien*, *Cajun Memories*, *Happy Go Lucky* & Kate & Anna McGarrigle *McGarrigle Hour*. In *Cajun & Creole Song Makers*.

QUINN, THE ESKIMO (Mighty Quinn)

Everybody's building the big ships & the boats
Some are building monuments, others jotting down notes
Everybody's in despair, every girl & boy
But when Quinn the Eskimo gets here
    everybody's gonna jump for joy
Come all without, come all within
You'll not see nothing like the mighty Quinn (repeat)

(↑2) G C G C / / / G Bm C G ‖: G - D G / G Bm C G :‖

I like to do just like the rest, I like my sugar sweet
But guarding fumes & making haste, it ain't my cup of meat
Everybody's 'neath the trees feeding pigeons on a limb
But when Quinn... all the pigeons gonna run to him / **Come...**

A cat's meow & a cow's moo, I can recite 'em all
Just tell me where it hurts ya honey & I'll tell you who to call
Nobody can get no sleep, there's someone on everyone's toes
But when... everybody's gonna wanna doze / **Come...**
    — w & m: Bob Dylan

© 1968 by Dwarf Music, renewed 1996 by Dwarf Music. Reprinted by permission of Music Sales Corporation. On his *Self-Portrait* 12 & *Biograph*. Orig rec by Manfred Mann 14. Also Hollies 12. Earth Band, Persuasions, Kristofferson (on *Chimes of Freedom* Amnesty coll of Dylan S).

STAINES MORRIS

Come ye young men, come along
With your music, dance & song
Bring your lasses in your hands
For 'tis that which love commands
Then to the Maypole haste away
For 'tis now our holiday (repeat refrain)   (↑2)

Am DE F Am / C - E Am / | / ||: C G F C / - - E Am :||

It is the choice time of the year
For the violets now appear
Now the rose receives its birth
And the pretty primrose decks the earth

Here each bachelor may choose
One that will not faith abuse
Nor repay with coy disdain
Love that should be loved again

And when you well reckoned have
What kisses you your sweetheart gave
Take them all again & more
It will never make them poor

When you thus have spent your time
'Til the day be past its prime
To your beds repair at night
And dream there of your day's delight

— trad. (English Morris dance)

For centuries in remote English villages Morris dancers have welcomed spring in early May. There are now women's & mixed as well as the trad. men's "sides" of 6 dancers. This tune is danced by Morris men in the village of Longborough in the Cottswalds & dates back to at least the time of Queen Elizabeth I. On Morris On, Carthy & Swarbrick *Prince Heathen*, Revels *Wild Mountain Thyme*, Robts & Barrand *Mellow w Ale fr the Horn*, Fairport Convention *House Full*, Maddy Prior *7 for Old England*. In Revels Garland of Song.

TAKE IT EASY

Well I'm a-running down the road trying to loosen my load
I've got 7 women on my mind
4 that want to own me, 2 that want to stone me
One says she's a friend of mine

G - - - / G D C - / G - D - / C - G -

Take it easy (x2)
Don't let the sound of your own wheels drive you crazy
Lighten up while you still can, don't even try to understand
Just find a place to make your stand & **take...**

Em - C G / Am C Em - / C G C G / Am C G -

Now I'm a-standin' on the corner in Winslow, Arizona
With such a fine sight to see
It's a girl, my Lord, in a flatbed Ford
Slowin' down to have a look at me
Come on baby, don't say maybe
I gotta know if your sweet love is gonna save me
We may lose & we may win, but we will never be here again
Open up I'm climbin' in to **take...**

Well I'm a-running down the road trying to loosen my load
Got a world of trouble on my mind
I'm lookin' for a lover who won't blow my cover
She's just a little hard to find
Take... (x2) / Don't let the sound...
Come on baby, don't say...
I gotta know if your...

— w & m: Jackson Browne & Glenn Frey

© 1972 (renewed) Swallow Turn Music. On & in his *For Everyman*.

TIE ME KANGAROO DOWN SPORT

Watch me wallabies feed, mate, watch me wallabies feed
They're a dangerous breed, mate, so watch me wallabies feed
  (Altogether now!)
Tie me kangaroo down, sport , tie me...down (2x)

D G A D (4x)

Keep me cockatoo cool, Curl, keep me... cool
Don't go acting the fool, Curl, just keep...
    Take me koala back, Jack, take... back
    He lives somewhere out on the track, Mac, so take...
Mind me platypus duck, Bill, mind me...
Don't let him go running amok, Bill, just mind...
    Play your didgeridoo, Blue, play...
    Keep playing til I shoot thru, Blue, play...
Tan me hide when I'm dead, Fred, tan me...
So we tanned his hide when he died, Clyde & that's it hanging on
  the shed

— w & m: Rolf Harris

© 1960, 1961 (renewed 1988, 1989) Castle Music Pty. Ltd. All rights for the U.S. & Canada controlled & administered by Beechwood Music Corp. On his recs 12.

UNDER THE SEA

The seaweed is always greener in somebody else's lake
You dream about going up there, but that is a big mistake
Just look at the world around you right here on the ocean floor
Such wonderful things surround you — what more is you lookin' for?

G DG G DG / | / C G D G / | /

Under the sea (x2)
Darling it's better down where it's wetter, take it from me
Up on the shore they work all day, out in the sun they slave
  away / While we devotin' full time to floatin' under...

C D G - / | / C D Em A / C D G (DG G DG)

Down here all the fish is happy as off thru the waves they roll
The fish on the land ain't happy, they sad 'cos they in their bowl
But fish in the bowl is lucky, they in for a worser fate
One day when the boss get hungry, guess who's gon' be on the plate?

Under... / Nobody beat us, fry us & eat us in fricassee
We what the land folks loves to cook, **under...** we off the hook
We got no troubles, life is the bubbles **under...**

...Since life is sweet here, we got the beat here naturally
Even the sturgeon & the ray, they get the urge & start to play
We got the spirit, you got to hear it **under...**

...When the sardine begin the beguine, it's music to me
What do they got? a lot of sand — we got a hot crustacean band
Each little clam here know how to jam here **under...**

(tag) Each little slug here cuttin' a rug here **under...**
Each little snail here know how to wail here,
   that's why it's hotter under the water
Yeah we in luck here, down in the muck here **under...**

C D G - / C D Em A / C D G (DG G DG)

  — m: Alan Menken, w: Howard Ashman

© 1988 Wonderland Music Company, Inc. & Walt Disney Music Company. In *The Little Mermaid* ♩4.

UP AMONG THE HEATHER

It's up among the heather on the hill o' Bennachie
'Twas there I met a bonnie lassie kilted tae the knee
When a bum'bee stung me richt below *[weel above]* the knee
And we both gaed haem a-mournin' for the hill o' Bennachie

Am - - - / G - - - / Am - - - / - G Am -

Said I tae my lassie "Where are ye gaun tae spend the day?"
"Oh I'm gaun tae spend the day on the hill o' Bennachie
Where the lads & the lassies they a' sit sae free
Amongst the bloomin' heather on the hill o' Bennachie"

As I was a-walkin' on the hill o' Bennachie
'Twas there I set a bonnie lassie sitting on ma knee
I took her & whirled her & aye she said tae me
"O Jock we'll gang a-wanderin' on the hill o' Bennachie"

Said I tae my lassie "Will you take my advice?
Never let a soldier laddie kiss ye mair than twice
For a' the time he's kissin' ye he's makin' up a plan
For tae ha'e another rattle at yer old tin can"

  — w: Walter Watson, m: trad Scottish

Arr © 2015 Hal Leonard Corporation. This variant rec by Elizabeth Stewart in 1960. Also by Irish Rovers, Clancy Tradition, Carlyle Fraser, The Galliards. Bennachie ("Hill of the Breast") is a range of hills in Aberdeenshire, Scotland.

WANG DANG DOODLE

Tell Automatic Slim, tell Razor Totin' Jim
Tell Butcher Knife Totin' Annie, tell Fast Talking Fanny
We gonna pitch a ball, down to that union hall
We gonna romp & tromp til midnight,
   we gonna fuss & fight til daylight

E7 - - - (4x)

We gonna pitch a wang dang doodle all night long
All night long, all night long (2x)
We gonna pitch a wang dang doodle all night long

Tell Kudu-Crawlin' Red, tell Abyssinian Ned
Tell ol' Pistol Pete, everybody gonna meet
Tonight we need no rest, we really gonna throw a mess
We gonna break out all the windows, we gonna kick down
   all the doors

Tell Fats & Washboard Sam, that everybody gonna jam
Tell Shaky & Boxcar Joe, we got sawdust on the floor
Tell Peg & Caroline Dye, we gonna have a time
When the fish scent fill the air, there'll be snuff juice everywhere

  — w & m: Willie Dixon

© 1962 (renewed 1990) Hoochie Coochie Music (BMI). All rights controlled & administered by Bug Music, Inc., a BMG Chrysalis company. Rec by Howlin' Wolf, Koko Taylor, Grateful Dead, Booker T, Pointer Sisters. In *Real Blues Bk.*

WHISTLE WHILE YOU WORK

Just whistle while you work (whistle)
And cheerfully together we can tidy up the place
So hum a merry tune (hum)
It won't take long when there's a song to help you set the pace

C - - - / G - - - / 1st / G - - C

And as you sweep the room, imagine that the broom
Is someone that you love & soon you'll find you're dancing to the tune
When hearts are high the time will fly so whistle while you work

F - - - / F Fm C - [instr: C - - -] G - - C

Just whistle while you work (whistle)
Put on that grin & start right in to whistle loud & long
Just hum a merry tune (hum)
Just do your best & take a rest & sing yourself a song

When there's too much to do, don't let it bother you
Forget your troubles, try to be just like a cheerful chick-a-dee
And whistle while you work (whistle)
Come on get smart, tune up & start to whistle while you work

  — w: Larry Morey, m: Frank Churchill

© 1937 by Bourne Co. (ASCAP). Copyright renewed. Sung by Adriana Caselotti in '37 film *Snow White*.

WRAP THAT RASCAL

Wanna get frisky, don't wanna pay the price?
Modern love is risky, follow this advice
Wrap that rascal! Wrap that rascal!
You gotta wrap that rascal if you wanna get along with me

D - / - - / G7 - D - / A7 G7 D -

Two young lovers, lying in bed
One snuggled up to the other & said / "Why don't we **wrap that...**

If you have affection, share with someone else
If you have infections, keep them to yourself / **Wrap that...**

(bridge) You can be creative, you can be amused
You can look for places that ain't never been used
You can stick it here, ooo & you can stick it there
But if you ain't gonna wrap it you can stick it in your ear
You gotta **wrap...**

D - (4x) / G7 - D - / A7 G7 D -

Papa make a baby, Mama bound to fall
If you don't want to bring 'em up don't bring it up at all
Unless you **wrap...**

You can buy 'em bumpy, you can buy 'em smooth
Lubricated, decorated! red white & blue! / Why don't you...

(bridge) Who appointed Thomas? Who carpet bombed Iraq?
Who gave us the S&L's to carry on our back?
Epidemic AIDS? Economic stress?
If Bush's daddy used one we would not be in this mess
He shoulda wrapped **that rascal! Wrap that rascal!**
He shoulda wrapped... 'stead of going down in history

  — w: Charlie King

© 1992 Pied Asp Music (BMI). On his *Inside Out*. Sung to tune of "Keep It Clean," trad. song adap. by Dave Van Ronk on his *No Dirty Names.*

YMCA

Young man, there's no need to feel down
I said, young man, pick yourself off the ground
I said, young man, 'cos you're in a new town
There's no need to be unhappy
    Young man, there's a place you can go
    I said... when you're short on your dough
    You can stay there & I'm sure you will find
    Many ways to have a good time

G - - - / Em - - - / C - - - / D C G D :‖

It's fun to stay at the YMCA (2x)
They have everything for young men to enjoy
You can hang out with all the boys
It's fun to stay at the... (2x)
You can get yourself clean, you can have a good meal
You can do whatever you feel

G - - - / Em - - - / Am - - - / D - - - :‖

Young man, are you listening to me?
I said... what do you want to be
I said... you can make real your dreams
But you've got to know this one thing
    No man does it all by himself
    I said, young man, put your pride on the shelf
    And just go there, to the YMCA
    I'm sure they can help you today

Young man, I was once in your shoes
I said I was down & out with the blues
I felt no man cared if I were alive
I felt the whole world was so jive
    That's when someone came up to me
    And said young man take a walk up the street
    There's a place there called the YMCA
    They can start you back on your way

— w & m: Jacques Morali, Henri Belolo & Victor Willis

YOU GOT TO KNOW HOW

You can make me do what you wanna do,
    but you got to **know how**
You can make me sigh, you can make me cry, but you got...
You can make me do like this, you can make me do like that
Oh! baby, but you got to **know...**

C - G - / - Ab G C - / - C7 E7 Am / D7 - G -

Once a pal of mine stole a guy of mine but I got him back now
It was the the same old song, she couldn't keep him long
    'cos she didn't **know how**
Well I love my man, I make him holler, oh my!
Yes sir, I really **know...**

C - G - / - Ab G C - / - C7 E7 Am / D7 G C -

Technique ain't tough if you care enough, you can learn to...
I might drop a hint how to strike my flint if you yearn to...
Well, don't tell me about the life you led,
    don't try to drink me into bed
No, baby, no, that ain't the way how

(bridge) You got to take your time, you know it ain't no crime
    if it lasts all night
I think you'll be ideal when you begin to feel that you're doin' right
When you love me right, you hear me holler "oh my!"
Yes sir, I really **know how**

C C7 E7 Am / D7 - G - / 1st / D7 G C -

And if you stay with me who knows how it will be when we finally...
We'll get a house in town, no need to move around when we really...
Well there's tricks that I don't even know,
    ones we'll make up as we go
Oh Mister, when we really know how
Yes Mister, when you really...

    — w & m: Sippie Wallace

YOUR DISCO NEEDS YOU

Your disco, your disco, your disco needs you! (4x)

Em C G B (4x)

Desperately seeking someone willing to travel
You're lost in conversation & useless at Scrabble
Happiness will never last, darkness comes to kick your ass
So let's dance thru all our fears, war is over for a bit
The whole world should be moving to your heart,
    your lonely heart

Em C Em C / / Am C Am C / - - G - / Am - B

We're sold on vanity but that's so see-thru
Take your body to the floor, your disco needs you
From Soho to Singapore, from the mainland to the shore
So let's dance thru all our fears, war is over for a bit
You're a slave to the rhythm, do your part, cure a lonely heart

— w & m: Kylie Minogue, Robert Peter Williams & Guy Chambers

The **Good Times** chapter has songs about partying, dancing & ribald songs. See also: **Blues, Pub Songs, Sing People Sing!**

Other songs include **Ballads**: Blow away the morning dew, **Country**: Help me make it thru the night, **Dream**: Blackberry pie, **Farm**: Wahoo, **Healing**: Onawa's waltz, **Jazz**: Let's do it, **Surfing**: Your mama don't dance, **Old-timey**: Ya'll come, **Outdoors**: Hal-an-tow, **Play**: Mango walk, **Pub**: Pace egging, **Sea**: Can't you dance the polka?

Gospel & Spirituals

AIN'T THAT GOOD NEWS

I've got a <u>robe</u> in that Kingdom, ain't that good news? (2x)
I'm going to lay down this world, I'm going to
   shoulder up my cross
Goin' to take it home to my Jesus, ain't that...
My Lord, ain't...

G C - G / - - - D / G - C - / 1st / C - G -

(Substitute: shoes, crown, harp, robe, Savior, **etc.)**

   — trad. (African-Amer. Spiritual)

Arr. © 2015 by Hal Leonard Corporation. On Sweet Honey in the Rock *Good News* 11.

AMEN

Amen, amen / Amen, amen, amen

G - - - / GC GC GD G

Sing it over (<u>am</u>e<u>n</u>) (x2)
Sing it over (<u>am</u>e<u>n</u>, am<u>e</u>n, am<u>e</u>n)

See the little baby (**amen**), wrapped in a manger (**amen**)
On Christmas morning (**amen x3**)

See him in the temple... talking with the elders...
Who marvelled at his wisdom (**amen x3**)

Down at the Jordan... where John was baptizing...
And saving all sinners...

See him at the seaside... talking with the fishermen...
And makin' them disciples...

Marchin' in Jerusalem... over palm branches...
In pomp & splendor...

See him in the garden... prayin' to his father...
He's deep in sorrow...

Led before Pilate... then they crucified him...
But he rose on Easter!...

Hallelujah... He died to save us...
And he lives forever!...

   — w & m: Jester Hairston

© 1957, 1966 by Bourne Co. (ASCAP). Copyright renewed. Sung by Sidney Poitier in '63 film *Lilies of the Field*. Rec by Curtis Mayfield ('64) & Otis Redding. In *Worship in Song*.

CUP OF SORROW

I want to drink from your cup of sorrow
I want to bathe in your holy blood
I want to sleep with the promise of tomorrow
Altho' tomorrow may never come

D G D - / A - D - :‖

I'll send a prayer out across the ocean
To a man that's forced out of his home
I'll send a prayer out across the ocean
So that he may not suffer there alone

I want to sit at your table of wisdom
So that not one crumb shall go to waste
For if we keep down this pathway to destruction
Ah well our children will suffer for our haste

   — w & m: Amos Lee

© 2011 Soma Eel Songs, LLC (BMI). On his *Mission Bell* (in A 17).

DON'T TRY SO HARD

Another Monday comes & I just wanna breathe
'Cos it's a <u>long</u>, long week for someone wired to please
I keep taking my aim, pushing it higher, wanna shine bright, even
   brighter / now — wish I could tell myself:

G ↓ Em C /   / D Em D G / C - D -

**Don't try so hard / God gives you grace & you can't earn
   it, don't think that you're not worth it
Because you are / He gave you his love & he's not leaving,
   gave you his son so you'd believe it
You're lovely even with your scars / Don't try so hard**

G ↓ Em - / C D Em D :‖ Am - D - / G - - -

Do you remember how the summers felt when we were kids
Oh we didn't think much about it, we just lived
Taking our time, beautiful leisure — when did we start trying to
   measure up?
And all this time love has been trying to tell us:

   — w & m: Ben Glover & Amy Grant

© 2013 9T One Songs (ASCAP), Ariose Music (ASCAP) & Grant Girls Music LLC (ASCAP). 9T One Songs & Ariose Music Admin. at CapitolCMGPublishing.com. Grant Girls Music LLC Admin. by the Loving Company. On her *How Mercy Looks from Here* 14.

DON'T YOU HEAR JERUSALEM MOAN?

Don't you hear Jerusalem moan? (2x)
Thank God there's a heaven & a ringing in my soul & my
    soul got free / Don't you hear Jerusalem moan?

G - - - / - D G - / G - - - - - / G D G -

Now the Methodist preacher, you can tell him where to go
Don't you hear Jerusalem mourn?
Don't never let a chicken get big enough to crow / **Don't...**

Well a hard-shell preacher you can tell him how he do / **Don't...**
Well he chews his own tobacco & he drinks his own brew...

Well a Baptist preacher you can tell him by his coat...
Has a bottle in his pocket & he can't hardly talk...

Well a Campbellite preacher his soul is saved...
Well he has to be baptized every other day...

Well the Holy Roller preacher he sure am a sight...
Well he gets 'em all a-rolling & he kicks out the light...

Well the Presbyterian preacher he lives in town...
His neck's so stiff he can't hardly look around...

— trad. gospel

Arr. © 2015 by Hal Leonard Corporation. Made popular in '20s by Gid Tanner & the Skillet Lickers. Other recs Hot Rize, Nitty Gritty Dirt Band, Rani Arbo, etc.

DONE MADE MY VOW

Done made my vow to the Lord / And I never will turn back
I will go, I shall go / To see what the end will be

Em - - - / C B7 Em - / - - C - / Em B7 Em -

When I was moaner just like you / **To see...**
O I moaned & moaned til I came thru / **To...**

Em - C Em / - B7 Em - :/

When every star refused to shine... / I know King Jesus will be mine...

(sung with cho) Done made my vow to the Lord **(3x)** / **To...**

— trad. (African-Amer. Spiritual)

Arr. © 2015 by Hal Leonard Corporation. Rec by Black gospel choirs. In *Amer Negro Spirituals*.

DOWN TO THE VALLEY TO PRAY

As I went down to the valley *[river]* to pray
Studying about that good ol' way
And who shall wear the starry crown?
Good Lord, show me the way
    O sisters, let's go down
    Let's go down, come on down
    O sisters, let's... / Down to the valley to pray

D - A D / D - A G D // A D G G D / A D G D

(substitute: brothers, fathers, mothers, sinners, **etc.)**

— trad. (gospel)

Arr. © 2015 by Hal Leonard Corporation. Alison Krauss sang (as "Down to the River to Pray") in '00 film *O Brother Where Art Thou?*

DRIFTING TOO FAR FROM SHORE

Out on the perilous deep / Where dangers silently creep
And storms so violently sweep
You're drifting too far from the shore

(in 3/4) C G C - / G - C - / - - F Dm / C G C -

You're drifting too far from the shore (2x) (peaceful shore)
Come to Jesus today, let him show you the way / You're...

F - C - / G - C - / - - - F / C G C -

Today the tempest rolls high / And clouds overshadow the sky
Sure death is hovering nigh / **You're...**

Why meet a terrible fate / Mercies abundantly waits
Turn back before it's too late / **You're...**

— w & m: Charles E. Moody

Arr. © 2015 by Hal Leonard Corporation. 1923, published by Stamps-Baxter. Hank Williams Sr, Bill Monroe, Emmy Lou Harris, Seldom Scene, etc.

DRY BONES

Ezekiel cried them dry bones **(3x)**
Now hear the word of the Lord
Ezekiel connected them dry bones **(3x)**
Now hear the word of the Lord

D - / A D / 1st / D A D :|

Well your toe bone connected to your foot bone
Your foot bone connected to your heel bone
Your heel bone connected to your ankle bone
Your ankle bone connected...leg bone
leg /knee, knee/thigh, thigh/hip, hip/back
back/shoulder, shoulder/neck, neck/head
Now hear the word of the Lord

D - **(4x)** Eb - / E - / F - / F# - / G - / Ab - / A - / A E A

Them bones, them bones gonna walk around **(3x)** Now...

A - / E A / 1st / A E A :|

Disconnect them bones, them dry bones **(3x)** Now...

Head/neck, neck/shoulder, shoulder/back, back/hip
Hip/thigh, thigh/knee, knee/leg, leg/ankle
Ankle/heel, heel/foot, foot/toe / **Now...**

A - **(4x)** / Ab - / G - / F# - / F - / E - / Eb - / D - / D A D

Them bones, them bones, them dry bones **(3x)** Now...

D - / A D / 1st / D A D

— trad. (African-American spiritual)

Arr. © 2015 by Hal Leonard Corporation. Inspired by Chap 37 of Ezekiel.

GLORY BOUND

When I hear that trumpet sound
I will lay my burdens down
I will lay them deep into the ground
Then I'll know that I am glory bound

D - G - / / A A G D - / /

I'll be travelling far from home
But I won't be looking for to roam
I'll be crossing o'er the great divide
In a better home soon I will reside

Hallelujah (4x)

G D D* - / G D A G G* / 1st / G D A D D - (*extra beat)

When I'm in my resting place
I'll look on my mother's face
Never more will I have to know
All the loneliness that plagues me so

So I'm waiting for that train to come
And I know where she's coming from
Listen can you hear her on the track
When I board I won't be looking back

— w & m: Ruth Moody

© 2006 Ruth Moody. On Wailin' Jennys *Firecracker*.

GOING UP HOME (to Live in Green Pasture)

Troubles & trials often betray those
On in [*Causing*] the weary body to stray
But we shall walk beside the still waters
With the Good Shepherd leading the way   **(in 3/4)**

(D) G D G C - - / G - - D - - / 1st / G - D G (C G)

Those who have strayed were sought by the master
He who once gave his life for the sheep
Out on the mtn still he is searching
Bringing them in forever to keep

Going up home to live in green pastures
Where we shall live & die never more
Even the Lord will be in that number
When we have reached that heavenly shore

We will not heed the voice of the stranger
For he would lead us all to despair
Following on with Jesus our savior
We shall all reach that country so fair

— w & m: Ralph Stanley && & Avril Gearheart

© 1968 by Fort Knox Music, Inc. & Trio Music Company. Copyright renewed. All rights for Trio Music Company administered by BMG Rights Management (US) LLC. On Ralph Stanley *Man of Constant Sorrow*, *Over the Sunset Hill* 12, Emmy Lou Harris *Roses in the Snow* 14.

HE LOOKED BEYOND MY FAULT & SAW MY NEED

Amazing Grace shall always be my song of praise
For it was grace that bought my liberty
I do not know just why he ever came to love me so
He looked beyond my fault[s] **& saw my need**[s]

C↓ Am F Dm / C Am D G / C C7 F Fm / CAm DmG C (G)

II: C - F - / C - Dm G / 1st / C G C -

I shall forever lift mine eyes to Calvary
To view the cross where Jesus died for me
How marvelous the grace that caught my falling soul / **He...**

CE FG C CG / Am FC D G / CE F CAm Fm /
CAm DmG C -

II: C F C - / Am FC G - / C G C Am / C DmG C -

— w & m: Dottie Rambo

© 1968 (renewed) New Spring Publishing Inc. (ASCAP). Admin. at CapitolCMGPublishing.com. I: Dottie Rambo 15. II: trad. "Danny Boy".

HE'LL UNDERSTAND & SAY WELL DONE

If when you give the best of your service
Telling the world that the Savior has come
Be not dismayed when men don't believe you
He'll understand & say well done

C - F C / G - - C / - - F C / F CF CG C

Misunderstood, yes, the savior of sinners
Hung on the cross, he was God's only son
O hear him call his Father in heaven
It's not my will, God almighty but thine be done

O when I come to the end of my journey
Weary of life & the battle is won
Carrying the staff & the cross of redemption / He'll...

F - C - / " / " / " /

If when you've tried and failed in your trying
Hands sore & scarred from the work you've begun
Take up your cross & run quickly to meet him / **He'll...**

— w & m: Lucie Campbell

© 1950 (renewed 1978) Screen Gems-EMI Music Inc. Copyright renewed. Rec by Davis Sisters, Johnny Cash.

HOLD TO GOD'S UNCHANGING HAND

Time is filled with swift transition
Naught of earth unmoved can stand
Build your hopes on things eternal
Hold to God's unchanging hand   (↑2)

C - - - / - - - G / C - CE Am / CAm FG C -

Trust in him who will not leave you
Whatsoever yrs may bring
If by earthly friends forsaken
Still more closely to him cling

Hold to his hand, God's unchanging hand (2x)
Build your hopes on things eternal / Hold to God's...

Covet not this world's vain riches
That so rapidly decay
Seek to gain the heavenly treasures
They will never pass away

When your journey is completed
If to God you have been true
Fair & bright the home in glory
Your enraptured soul will view

— w: Jennie Wilson, m: F.L. Eiland & Clyde Williams

Arr. © 2015 by Hal Leonard Corporation

I Am a Pilgrim

I am a pilgrim & a stranger
Traveling thru this wearisome land
I got a home in that yonder city, good Lord
And it's not, not made by hand

(in D) A - D - / G - D - / - - G - / D A D -

I got a mother, a sister & a brother
Who have gone this way before
I'm determined to go & see them, good Lord
Over on that distant shore

I'm going down to that river Jordan
Just to bathe my weary soul
If I could touch but the hem of his garment, good Lord
Well, I know [*believe*] it would make me whole

— trad. (bluegrass)

I Don't Feel No Ways Tired

I don't feel no ways tired
I've come too far from where I started from
Nobody told me that the road would be easy
I don't believe He brought me this far to leave me

C - F G C / F Am D G / Am Em F C / Am F F C C

— w & m: Curtis Burrell

I Hear a Call

I hear a call, now will I answer
Forsake my all to serve another
Tho darkness falls, stay a believer
I hear a call, now will I answer

G C G - / C - G - / C - Em C / G C D G

I see a light, now will I follow
Fill up this life that grows more hollow
Make joy reside where there lives sorrow
I see a light, now will I follow

**I hear a call from out of nowhere
And from everywhere I go
I hear a call, now will I answer**

C - G - / C ↓ D - / G C D G (C G D G)

I feel a touch, now will I hold on
Be there with love for those with no one
With a kindness such it lives tho' I'm gone
I feel a touch, now will I follow

**(final cho) I hear a call from out of nowhere
And from everywhere I go**
I see a light, now will I follow
I feel a touch, now will I hold on / I hear a call, now will I answer

C - G - / C ↓ D - / G C G C /   / G C D G

— w & m: Tony Arata

I Saw the Light

I wandered so aimless, life filled with sin
I wouldn't let my dear savior in
Then Jesus came like a stranger in the night
Praise the Lord, I saw the light

G - - - / C - G - / 1st / G - D G

**I saw the light I saw the light
No more darkness, no more night
Now I'm so happy, no sorrow in sight / Praise…**

Just like a blind man I wandered along
Worries & fears I claimed for my own,
Then like the blind man that God gave back his sight / **Praise…**

I was a fool to wander & stray
Straight is the gate & narrow the way
Now I have traded the wrong for the right…

— w & m: Hank Williams

I Want to Die Easy

I want to die easy **when I die (2x)**
I want to die easy **when I die, shout salvation as I fly**
I want to die easy when I die

C G C - / - - - (G) / C - F C / 1st

I want to see my <u>mother</u> **when I die (2x)**
I want to see my mother **when I die, shout salvation as I fly**
I want to die easy when I die
(insert father, sister, brother **ending with** meet Jesus**)**

— trad. (African-Amer. spiritual)

I'm Going to Live the Life I Sing About

**I'm gonna live the life I sing about in my song
I'm gonna stand for right, always shun the wrong
If I'm in the crowd, if I'm alone, on the streets or in my home
I'm gonna live the life I sing about in my song**

Em Em B7 Em Am Em / - - B7 - / Em - Am Em / 1st

Everyday, everywhere, on a busy thoroughfare
Folks may watch me, some may spot me, say I'm foolish but I
    don't care
I can't sing one thing & then live another, be a saint by day & a
    devil undercover
I've got to **live the life I sing about…**

Em - - - / - - F# B7 / Em - Am Em / Em Em B7

Em Am Em -

If at day, if at night, I must always walk in the light
Some mistake me, underrate me because I want to do what's right
I can't go to church & shout all day Sunday, go out & get drunk &
    raise hell all day Monday
I've got to **live the life…**

— w & m: Thomas A. Dorsey

I'VE GOT A HOME IN THAT ROCK

I've got a home in-a that rock, **don't you see? (2x)**

Betw the earth & sky I thought I heard my Savior cry
You got a home in-a that rock, **don't you see?**

C G C(F C) / C - G - / C C7 F - / 1st

A poor man Lazarus poor as I, **don't you see? (2x)**
Poor man Lazarus... when he died he had a home on high
He had him a **home in-a that rock...**

Now the rich man Dives lived so well, **don't you see? (2x)**
Rich man Dives lived so well, when he died he found a home in
   hell / He had no **home...**

God gave Noah the rainbow sign... **(2x)**
God gave Noah the rainbow sign, no more water but fire next
   time / Better get a **home...**

> — trad. (African-Amer. spiritual)

Arr. © 2015 by Hal Leonard Corporation. Rec by Paul Robeson (in Bb), Josh White
15. Weavers. In *Josh White SB & Coll Reprints fr SO! V1-6.*

IN MY TIME OF DYING

Well, in my time of dyin' / I don't want nobody to mourn
All I want my friends to do / Is to take my body home
Well well well, so I can die easy (3x)
   Jesus gonna make up my dyin' bed

C - / - G / C F / C G C // - - / F - / C F / C GC

Meet me Jesus meet me / Meet me in the middle of the air
If these wings should fail me, Lord
Won't you meet me with another pair
Well, well well, won't you meet me, Jesus? **(3x)**
   Jesus gonna make up my dyin' bed

Goin' down to the river / Stick my sword up in the sand
Gonna shout "My trouble's over / I've done made it to the
   promised land" / **Well...** I've done crossed over **(3x) Jesus...**

Ever since I been acquainted with Jesus
We haven't been a minute apart
He placed a receiver in my hand / True religion in my heart
Well... I can ring up my Jesus **(3x) Jesus...**

> — trad. blues

Arr. © 2015 by Hal Leonard Corporation. Recs by Josh White, Bob Dylan, Be Good
Tanyas & John Mellencamp.

JOY COMES BACK

I wanna be ready (3x)
When joy comes back to me

C - - CF / 1st / C - G - / C - - -

'Cos I've been downhearted **(3x)** But I won't be down for long
I've been too long cryin' **(3x)** I ain't gonna cry no more
I've been tied to the ground Lord **(3x)** I'm gettin' lighter every day
I've been surrounded by midnight **(3x)** The sun's gonna shine again

> — w & m: Sean Staples

© 2003 Wesley Park Music (BMI). On Rani Arbo *Big Old Life* (in A), Heather
Waters *Propeller*, Alistair Moock *Singing Our Way Thru*, Harmony Mtn Singers (YT).

KEEP YOUR LAMPS TRIMMED & BURNING

Troubles & trials are almost over
Almost over, almost over
Troubles & trials are almost over
For this old world is almost done
[or See what the Lord has done or For our race is almost run]

Am - - - / Em - - - / 1st / Am Em Am -

Keep your lamp trimmed & burnin' **(3x)**
For this old world...
Heaven's journey is almost over...
Brother, don't you worry...
2000 yrs have come & gone...
Sister, don't stop prayin'...
Many are gone but not forgotten...

> — trad. (blues)

Rec by Hot Tuna, Miss. Fred McDowell, PP&M. On Tim O'Brien & Darrell Scott *Real
Time*, Rev Gary Davis *Amer Street S.* In *Coll Reprints fr SO V7-12.*

LET THE SUN SHINE DOWN ON ME

Roll on, clouds in the mornin' (3x)
Let the sun shine down on me

Am - - - / - - G Am / 1st / Am G Am -

I looked out this mornin'
Deep down **trouble I see**
Yes I looked out this mornin' / **Let the sun shine down...**

Am - - - / - G Am - :|

Saw that big cloud a-risin'
Hard **trouble I see**
Heard my mother cryin' / **Let the sun...**

There was water, but I couldn't drink it
Deep down **trouble...**
Bread, but I couldn't eat it... / **Let...**

I know there's a great day comin'
When no more **trouble...**
When we'll all shout together... / **Let...**

> — w & m: Jean Ritchie

© 1963, 1971 (renewed) Geordie Music Publishing. On her *Mtn Hearth & Home* (13),
Peter Pickow *Singin' the Moon Up* (15) & Maria Larson *Open the Door Softly*. In
her *Celeb of Life & For the Beauty of the Earth.*

THE MEETING IS OVER

Brothers, **now our meeting is over,** brothers, **we must part**
And if I never see you any more, I will love you in my heart

Dm Am C Dm / / - - C Dm / Dm - Am Dm

Yes we'll land on the shore (3x) & be saved forever more
(insert: sisters, fathers, mothers)

> — trad. (19th c. shape note hymn)

Arr. © 2015 by Hal Leonard Corporation. On Dillard Chandler *The End of S.* Jean
Ritchie *Sweet Rivers, Trad. Music of Beech Mtn. NC.* In *Amer Ballads & FolkS.*

O HAPPY DAY

O happy day **(x2)**
When Jesus washed, O when he washed, when Jesus washed
He washed my sins away, O happy...

G C G E7 / C D C D C D / G C G D

He taught me how to watch / Fight & pray, fight & pray
And live rejoicing / Every day, every day!

G - C - / G GC G D :|

— w & m: Edwin R. Hawkins

ON THE ROCK WHERE MOSES STOOD
(Crying Holy Unto the Lord)

Cryin' holy unto the Lord (2x)
Oh, if I could I surely would
Stand on that rock (Lord Lord) **where Moses stood**

(↑2) G - - - / C - G - / 1st / G D G -

Sinner run & hide your face **(2x)**
Go run to the rocks & hide your face
The rocks cried out "No hiding place"
 Lord I ain't no sinner now **(2x)**
 I've been to the river & I've been baptized
 And I ain't no sinner now
Lord I ain't no stranger now **(2x)**
I've been introduced to the Father & the Son
And I ain't no stranger now

— w & m: A.P. Carter

PEOPLE GET READY

People get ready, there's a train a comin'
You don't need no baggage, you just get on board
All you need is faith to hear the diesels hummin'
You don't need no ticket, you just thank the Lord

C Am F C / / / Em Dm F C

People get ready for the train to Jordan
It's picking up passengers from coast to coast
Faith is the key, open the doors & board 'em
There's hope for all among those loved the most

There ain't no room for the hopeless sinner
Who would hurt all mankind just to save his own
Have pity on those whose chances grow thinner
For there's no hiding place against the Kingdom's throne

— w & m: Curtis Mayfield

SOFTLY & TENDERLY

Softly & tenderly Jesus is calling
Calling for you & for me
See on the portals he's waiting & watching
Watching for you & for me

(in 6/8) D - G D / - E A - / 1st / DDG DDA D -

Come home, come home
Ye who are weary, come home
Earnestly, tenderly, Jesus is calling
Calling "O sinner, come home!"

O for the wonderful love he has promised
Promised for you & for me
Tho' we have sinned, he has mercy & pardon
Pardon for you & for me

— w & m: Will L. Thompson (1880)

SOME HAVE FATHERS

Some have <u>fathers</u> **gone to glory (3x)**
On the other bright shore

(a capella) Dm - / | / | / DmC Dm

(**substitute:** mothers, sisters, brothers)

We all have loved ones gone **(3x)**
On the other bright shore

Some glad day we'll go & see them / **On...**
Won't that be a happy meeting...

— trad. (gospel)

SOON & VERY SOON

Soon & very soon, **we are going to see the King (3x)**
Hallelujah, Hallelujah, we are going...

D - - - / A - D - / 1st / D Gm A D

No more cryin' there, **we are... (3x)** / **Hallelujah...**

(bridge) Should there be any rivers we must cross
Should there be any mtns we must climb
God will supply all the strength that we need
Give us grace til we reach the other side
We have come from every nation, God knows each of us by name
Jesus took his blood & he washed our sins, he washed them all away
Yes there are those of us who have laid down our lives
But we all shall meet again on the other side

G A D Bm / Em A D D7 :| (3x) 1st / Em A G -

— w & m: Andrae Crouch

SOWING ON THE MOUNTAIN

Sowing on the mountain, reaping in the valley (3x)
You're gonna reap just what you sow

D - / A D / - G / D A D

God gave Noah the rainbow sign **(3x)**
It won't be water, but fire next time

Won't be water...**(3x)** / God gave...

— w & m: Woody Guthrie

© 1997 Woody Guthrie Publications, Inc. All rights administered by BMG Rights Management (US) LLC. On his *Muleskinner Blues* 14, his & Cisco Houston *Lonesome Valley*, Ramblin' Jack Elliot *Best of Vanguard*, *Essential* 11, Flatlanders *Hills & Valleys*, Coon Creek Girls. In *Coll Reprints fr SO!* V1-6.

THE STORM IS PASSING OVER

Take courage my soul & let us journey on
Tho' the night is dark & I am far from home
Thanks be to God, the morning light appears
The storm is passing over (x3) hallelujah (2x)

D G D - / G - D - / A G D - / - - EmD G D DA D - / /

Hallelujah x4 / **The storm…**

D A G D / - - EmD G DA D -

— w & m: Charles Albert Tindley

Arr. © 2015 by Hal Leonard Corporation. Per choral arr (in G) on YT.

TALK ABOUT SUFFERING

Talk about suffering here below
And let's keep loving Jesus
Talk about... / **And let's keep a-followin' Jesus**

(a capela) Em - / EmBm Em :‖

The gospel train is comin'
Now don't you want to go
And leave this world of sorrow [trials]
And troubles here below?

G GAm / Em - / 1st / EmB7 Em

O can't you hear it <u>father</u> / And don't...
(insert: mother, brothers, etc.)

— trad. (gospel)

Arranged by Ricky Skaggs. © 1980 Universal - PolyGram International Publishing, Inc. Rec by Ricky Skaggs & Tony Rice, Doc Watson, John Renbourn, Greg Graffin.

THEM BONES GONNA RISE AGAIN

Lord he thought he'd make a man — **them bones gonna rise**
again / Took a little water, took a little sand — **them...**
I knows it, knows it, indeed I knows it, children
I knowed it (whee!) them bones...

C - - G C / / C - F - / 1st

Put him in that garden fair, **them...** / Saw him mighty lonely there...
Took a rib from Adam's side / Made Miss Eve to be his bride
Put them in that garden fair / Saw them mighty happy there
Apples, peaches, pears & such / But 1 fruit you must not touch
'Round that tree old Satan slunk / At Miss Eve his eye he wunk
My that fruit looks mighty fine / Take a bite, the Lord won't mind

So she took a pick & she took a pull / Then she filled her apron full
Next day when the Lord came round / Saw those cores all over
the ground
Adam, Adam, where art thou? / Here I am Lord, coming now!
Adam who these cores did leave? / Wasn't me Lord, must a been Eve
Adam you must leave this place / Earn your bread by the sweat
of your face
So he took a pick & he took a plow / And that's why we're all
singing now
This is the end, there ain't no more / Eve got the apple, Adam got
the core
Moral of the story be / Don't leave your cores for the Lord to see

— trad. (African-Amer. spiritual)

Arr. © 2015 by Hal Leonard Corporation. In *Songfest*.

THERE'LL BE NO DISTINCTION THERE

There will be no more sorrow on that heavenly shore
There'll be no wolves at the cabin door
We'll all be wealthy & the poor will all be there
We'll all be rich & happy in that land bright & fair
There'll be no distinction there

D - - - / - - A - / 1st / | Bm - - - / D A D -

There'll be... (2x) For the Lord is just & the Lord is right
And we'll all shine bright in the heavenly light / There'll...

In the same kind of raiment in the same kind of shoes
We will all sit together in the same kind of pews
The white folks & the colored folks, the gentiles & the Jews
We'll praise the Lord together & there'll be no drinkin' booze

Oh when we get to heaven we will know & understand
No woman will be flirting with another woman's man
There'll be no trouble in that holy, happy land
We'll play on golden instruments & shout to beat the band

We're never blue in heaven, nothing there to wreck the mind
Everybody is our neighbor, all the folks are good & kind
No aggravating women there to boss the men around
When we enter into heaven, we will wear a golden crown

— w & m: A.P. Carter

1st rec in 1922. Blind Alfred Reed *Completed Rec Works*, Carter Fam recs, New Lost City Ramblers *S fr the Depression*, Tim O'Brien *Oh Brother Can You Spare a Dime?* 12, Bare Bones *Put Your Loving Arms*. "We'll all shine bright..." in cho was orig. "We'll all be white..."

TROUBLES OF THE WORLD

Soon I will be done with the troubles of the world
Troubles of the world, troubles of...
Soon I will be done with the troubles of the world
I'm going home to live with God

Em EmC Em - / Am B7 - Em / 1st / Em B7 Em(Am EmB7)

No more weepin' & wailin' **(3x)** / I'm going home to live...

Em - - - / B7 - Em - /1st/ Em B7 Em - - -

I want to see my mother **(3x)**
I'm going home to live...
I want to meet my Jesus **(3x)** /
I'm going home to live...

— trad. (African-Amer. spiritual)

Arr. © 2015 by Hal Leonard Corporation. Recs by Mahalia Jackson 11, Ollabelle Reed, Little Richard, Bro Samuel Cheatham.

We Are Soldiers in the Army

We are Soldiers in the army
We have [got] to fight, altho' we have to cry
We have to hold up the bloodstained [freedom] banner
We have to hold it up until we die!

D - A - / - - D - / - - G - / D - A D

My mother was a Soldier
She had her hand on the Gospel [freedom] plow
But one day she got old, she couldn't fight anymore
She said "I'll stand here & fight anyhow!"

D - - - / - E A - / D - G - / A - D

My father was a Soldier / He had... (as v.1)

I'm so glad that I'm a Soldier / I've got my hand...
One day I'll get old & can't fight anymore / & I'll...

Well Mandela, he is a Soldier / He's got his hands…
He spent half of his life in prison
But he kept on fighting anyhow

I'm glad that we are Soldiers / We've got our hands…
We've spent half of our lives fighting for freedom
But we'll stand here fighting anyhow

— trad. (gospel), new lyrics by Freedom Singers

We've Come This Far By Faith

We've come this far by faith / Leaning on the Lord
Trusting in His Holy Word / He's never failed me yet
Oh oh, oh, can't turn around / We've come this far...

D - - - / G DA AD D / Bb - - - / D A AD D
D A D GEm / DA AD D

_I will trust in the Lord (3x) til I die (repeat)

D - - - / G - D - / - F# Bm - / E - A -
D - - - / G F# Bm C / G Ddim D A / D G D -

I'm gonna stay on the battlefield (3x) til I die (repeat)
I'm gonna treat everybody right (3x) til I die (repeat)

— w & m: Albert Goodson

When I Lay My Burdens Down

Glory, glory, hallelujah, when I lay my burdens down
Glory glory... when I lay my heavy burdens down

D - G D / - - DA D

I'm going home to be with Jesus [meet my Savior] when I...
All my troubles will be over...
I will be leaving all my troubles...
I'll be resting from my labors...
I'm gonna be crossing over Jordan...
I'll be marching in the Kingdom...
I'm gonna see my friends & loved ones...
I'm gonna eat at that welcome table...

— trad. (African-Amer. spiritual)

Where the Soul of Man Never Dies

To Canaan's land, I'm on my way
Where the soul of man never dies
My darkest night will turn to day / Where the soul...

D - - - / - - A - / 1st / D DA D -

Dear friends, there'll be no sad farewells (No sad farewells)
There'll be no tear-dimmed eyes (No tear-dimmed eyes)
Where all is peace & joy & love (Where all is love)
And the soul of man never dies (And the soul never dies)

A rose is blooming there for me.../ And I will spend eternity...
A love light beams across the foam.../ It shines to light the way to home
My life will end in deathless sleep.../ And everlasting joys I'll reap...
I'm on my way to that fair land_./ Where there will be no parting hand_.

— w & m: William A. Golden (1914)

Working On a Building

If I was a sinner, I tell you what I'd do
I'd quit my sinning & I'd work on the bldg too

A - - - / - - E A

I'm working on a building (x2)
I'm working on a building for my Lord, for my Lord
It's a holy ghost building (2x) / It's a holy... for my Lord...

A - - - / A* E A :‖   (*extra beat)

(insert: liar/lying, gambler/gambling, drunkard/drinking)
If I was a preacher I tell you... I would keep on preaching...

— trad. (gospel)

You Raise Me Up

When I am down & oh my soul, so weary
When troubles come & my heart burdened be
Then I am still & wait here in the silence
Until you come & sit awhile with me

C F C - / - - G - / F - C F / C G C -

You raise me up, so I can stand on mountains
You raise me up to walk on stormy seas
I am strong when I am on your shoulders
You raise me up to more than I can be

Am F C G /   / C F C F / C G C -

There is no life, no life without its hunger
Each restless heart beats so imperfectly
But when you come & I am filled with wonder
Sometimes I think I glimpse eternity

— w & m: Brendan Graham & Rolf Løvland

See also: **Country.** Other songs include **Blues:** You've got to move, **Freedom:** Honey in the rock, I'm gonna sit at the welcome table, **Friendship** It don't cost much, **Lullabies:** Watch the stars, **Old-timey:** Who will sing for me?

Healing & Letting Go

BIRD ON THE WIRE (Bird on a Wire)

Like a bird on the wire, like a drunk in a midnight choir
I have tried in my way to be free
Like a worm on a hook, like a knight from some old fashioned
  book / I have saved all my ribbons for thee

(↑2) G D G C / G D G - :‖

   If I, if I have been unkind
   I hope that you can just let it go by
   If I, if I have been untrue
   I hope you know it was never to you

C - G - / Am - G - / 1st / Am - D -

Oh like a baby, stillborn, like a beast with his horn
I have torn everyone who reached out for me
But I swear by this song & by all that I have done wrong
I will make it all up to thee
   I saw a beggar leaning on his wooden crutch
   He said to me, "You must not ask for so much"
   And a pretty woman leaning in her darkened door
   She cried to me, "Hey, why not ask for more?"

— w & m: Leonard Cohen

BOUNTIFUL RIVER

Deep love like a Bountiful River / **Fills the soul, renews the heart**
My love is always & ever / **We will never part**
Sailing, sailing together / **Fills the soul, renews...**
Flowing, flowing forever / **We will...**
O Bountiful River (3x) We...

C Dm / G C :‖ (6x)

Reviving, reviving this river / **Fills the soul...**
Embarked on an endless endeavor / **We will never...**
Blending one voice with another / **Fills...**
Weaving our lives with these waters / **We...**

An eagle circling in heaven / **Fills...**
The eagle & river repeating / **We...**
Life giver, this Bountiful River / **Fills...**
Our spirits are mingled forever / **We...**

Our love for our sons & our daughters / **Fills...**
Time now to care for these waters / **We...**

— w & m: Pete Seeger & Lorre Wyatt

BY WAY OF SORROW

You've been taken by the wind
You have known the kiss of sorrow
Doors that would not take you in
Outcast & a stranger

(in C) Am - G C - - - / F C G F - :‖

You have come by way of sorrow
You have come by way of tears
But you'll reach your destiny
Meant to find you all these yrs (2x)

Am G C F / / / F - G F / Am - G C

You have drunk a bitter wine
With none to be your comfort
You who once were left behind
Will be welcome at love's tables

All the nights that joy has slept
Will awake to days of laughter
Gone the tears that you have wept
You'll dance in freedom ever after

— w & m: Julie Miller

CAN I STAND HERE FOR YOU?

Can I stand here for you?_ / May I use my heart as a gate?
We may not need words, we may not need songs
We may only need our 2 hearts beating _

G Am D - / Am - G / - Am - G / C D Am D G G

— w & m: Kate Munger

CROSSING THE BAR

Sunset & evening star
And one clear call for me
And may there be no moaning of the bar
When I put out to sea
　　When I put out to sea **(2x)**
　　And may there be no moaning of the bar
　　When I put out to sea

(↑3)　G C D G / - D G - :// ∥
G C G – / Em D G – / - C D Em / C D G -

But such a tide as moving seems asleep
Too full for sound & foam
When that which drew from out the boundless deep
Turns again home
　　Turns again home **(2x)**
　　When that which drew from out the boundless deep
　　Turns again home

Twilight and evening bell
And after that the dark!
And may there be no sadness of farewell
When I embark...

For tho' from out our bourne of time & place
The flood may bear me far
I hope to see my Pilot face to face
When I have crossed the bar...

— w: Alfred Lord Tennyson (1889), m: Rani Arbo

FALL DOWN AS THE RAIN

When my life is over & I have gone away
I'm gonna leave this big ol' world & the trouble & the pain
And if I get to heaven, I will not stay
I'll turn myself around again & fall down as the rain
Fall down as the rain **(x2)**
I'll turn myself...& fall down...

D - C - / G - - D :∥ **(3x)**

And when I finally reach the ground, I'll soak into the sod
I'll turn...come up as goldenrod
Come up...

And then when I turn dry & brown, I'll lay me down to rest
I'll...as part of an eagle's nest
As part...

And when that eagle learns to fly, I'll flutter from that tree
I'll...as part of the mystery
As part...

— w & m: Joe Crookston

GO ON AHEAD AND GO HOME

Go on ahead & go home **(x2)** / Boy, you've done your best, time you took your rest in the sheltering loam
Go on ahead & go home **(x2)** / The spirits of the dead will meet you up ahead, & you won't be alone

GD GC GC G / - A7 Am D / 1st / G AD G(C GD)

Go let your mama see you smile **(x2)** / Mama's gonna wait however long it takes, but it's sure been awhile
Go let your mama see you smile **(x2)**/ She's standing in the sun sayin' "Boy, your work's been done by a long, long mile"

Down where the cotton grows tall **(x2)** / Where the bramble & rose & blue hydrangea grows beside the old mare's stall
Down where the cotton grows tall**(x2)**/ And a fragrant delta breeze shakes the cypress trees down deep in the Fall

In the deep of the night **(x2)** / By the river so still where sorrows come to heal & wrongs are made right
Down in the deep of the night **(x2)** / On a creaking porch swing, the ancient ones they sing "Everything is all right"

　　— w & m: Iris Dement

HE WILL HEAL THE BROKEN-HEARTED

I He will heal the broken-hearted
He will bind their wounds, my Lord
He will heal the broken-hearted
He will bind their wounds

DG DG D G / D G D A / 1st / D GA D -

　　— w & m: Beverly Shepard

HERE IS MY HOME

Good friends from whom we now must part
Where are we bound?
Your singing *[hands &]* voices lift my heart
Here is my home

C FC F G / C CF G - / 1st / C CG C -

Come darkness, come light / Where are we bound
Come morning, come night / Here is my home

G - C F / C - F - / C FC F G / C CG C -

For those who sing *[work]* in harmony / **Where are...**
Can learn to live in unity / **Here is my...**

If we can join ourselves in song / **Where...**
Our hearts will live when we are gone / **Here...**

The spirit that finds music here / **Where...**
Will sing forever in the air / **Here...**

　　— w & m: Si Kahn

HOLD ON STRONG

Hard times are coming, you can feel it in the air
You can read it in the paper, you can see it everywhere
Gonna be trials & tribulation, astonishment & shock
You're gonna need a strong foundation, need a solid rock

We gotta hold on to each other, hold on strong
We gotta... until the danger's gone
We... all night long / We... got to hold on

D - - G / A - - D :‖

It's easy to get lonely, yeah, it's easy to get lost
And it's easy to get crumpled up, towed away & tossed
Don't let yourself get isolated, don't get caught up in despair
Don't run & hide, just come inside, you know you'll find us there

Even the tallest tree in the forest can't make it on its own
You're gonna need some friends around you when that wind
   begins a-blowin'
It's gonna shake up all our branches, it's gonna tug on all our roots
Til the only thing left standing is the love that's great & true

    — w & m: Ben Bochner

© 2007 Ben Bochner. *songsforthegreatturning.net/building-community/* 15. *LS

I BID YOU GOODNIGHT
(Lay Down Brother)

Lay down, dear <u>brother</u>, lay down & take your rest
Lay your head upon the Savior's breast
I love you, but Jesus loves you best
And I bid you goodnight (x3) (may repeat)

(↑2) G - C G / - - - D / G C - G / C D G - / (etc.)

(insert: sister, mother, father, **etc.**)

(over refrain) One of these mornings bright & early in the sun
All the pilgrims of the spirit on the shores beyond
Go walking in the valley of the shadow of death
His rod & his staff start to comfort me
Lord send fire not a flood next time
I remember right well (x2)
I'll be walking in Jerusalem just like John

    — w & m: Ira D. Sankey

Arr. © 2015 by Hal Leonard Corporation. Rec by Joseph Spence ↑4, Aaron Neville ↑3, Soweto Gospel Choir 15, Grateful Dead, Incredible String Band, Bill Staines, Waterson-Carthy. In Peter Amidon *55 Anthems for the Small Church Choir.*

I HAVE HEARD THY PRAYER

I have heard thy prayer, I have seen thy tears
Behold, I will heal thee

(in 3/4) Am Dm G Am / F Dm Dm G Am -

    — w & m: Beverly Shepard

© 2000 Beverly Shepard, www.beverlyshepard.ca. *LS. From II Kings 20:5.

I WILL STAND FAST

The echoes of childhood whisper violence
Cold wind beating out of the past
Rage in your throat, muffled silence
Hold on, I will stand fast
In the darkness your guardians had left you
Cold wind beating out of the past
None to hear your cries, none to defend you
Hold on, I will stand fast

D A D - / G Bm A - / G A D G Bm / G A D - :‖

I will stand fast (x2)
You are safe in the daylight at last
Nightmare & fear, they have no power here
I will stand fast

G A D - / G D A - / G A D Em / G A D -

I will listen to the terrors that tried you / **Cold wind...**
I will cradle the child that breathes inside you / **Hold on...**
Tho' you take the shape of a hundred ancient horrors / **Cold...**
Tho' you strike at me & flee into your sorrow / **Hold on...**

Birds flash upon a branch in winter / **Cold wind...**
Ice in the sun begins to splinter / **Hold on...**
You will walk with no fetters to bind you / **Cold...**
All the love you have wanted will find you / **Hold on...**

    — w & m: Fred Small

© 1988 Pine Barrens Music (BMI). On his *I Will...* & in his *Promises Worth Keeping.* On Troubadour *From Celtic Renaissance.*

IN THIS LIFE

In this life tho' the sounds be strained & thin
Let the voice inside me rise & the strength be beckoned in
For these words within ring more clearly on the outside
They resound beyond the hillside: **I am worthy, I am safe**

(↑2) G C G - C / F - - D / 1st / Em C D G

In this life tho' my fingers try & fail
Let me breathe thru hollow wood, living reed let sound prevail
For this whistler's tune shatters emptiness with sweetness
Filling in the gap betw us: **I am worthy...**

In this life I am but one of a million starving others
Robbed of everything but hunger, we are prisoners together
I am one, but one of many single voices in the silence
That refuse the lies that bind us: we are worthy, we are safe

Em C - G / Em C - D / Em C G D / Em C D G

In this life tho' my body's stiff & heavy
Let the grace inside my limbs stay the stillness that defends me
For each move I make brings me closer to the dancer
I am healing from my terror: **I am...**

    — w & m: Pat Humphries

© 1993 Pat Humphries. On her *Hands.*

Knockin' On Heaven's Door

Mama, take this badge off of me
I can't use it anymore
It's gettin' dark, too dark to see
I feel like I'm knockin' on heaven's door

G D Am7 - / G D C - :‖

Knock, knock, knockin' on heaven's door (3x)
Just like so many times before

I'm gonna wipe the blood from off my face
I just can't see thru it anymore *[I'm sick & tired of the war]*
Got a long black feeling & it's hard to trace / & **I feel...**
[I need someone to talk to & new hiding place / I...]

Mama, I can't hear that thunder roar
Echoing from God's distant shore
I feel him calling for my soul / **I feel...**

Mama, put my guns in the ground
I can't shoot them anymore
That long black cloud *[train]* is comin' down / **I feel...**

Lord, these guns have caused too much pain
This town will never be the same
So for the bairns of Dunblane
We ask "Please never again!"

The Lord is my shepherd, I shall not want
He makes me down to lie
In pastures green, he leadeth me
The quiet waters by

Lord, put all these guns in the ground
We just can't shoot them anymore
It's time that we spread some love around
Before we're knockin' on heaven's door

— w & m: Bob Dylan (3 addl v. by Ted Christopher)

In films *Pat Garrett & Billy the Kid*, *Rush* & *Treasure Planet*. On recs by Eric
Clapton, Grateful Dead, Guns 'N' Roses, Roger Mcguinn, Ladysmith Black
Mambazo, Jean Wyclef, Warren Zevon. In March '96 a gunman entered a
schoolhouse in the village of Dunblane in Scotland and killed 16 children & one
teacher. Ted Christopher, who lives in Dunblane created a video tribute to the
children based (w/ Dylan's permission) on the above song that included siblings
of the victims singing on choruses. The song reached #1 on UK charts & raised
funds for children's charities. Video included the Christopher song below along
w/ the new verses to "Knockin'" above.

Throw These Guns Away

When evening comes & light is fading
And your heart is heavy from the tears
Lift up your eyes & look to heaven
For 17 new stars have appeared

G - C - / | | / Am - D - (later v: Am D G -)

They shine their light down upon us
And the message of their love is clear
Lost familiar voices softly whispering in the wind
Pleading that this time we will hear

> **Throw these guns away (x2)**
> **They've caused this world too much pain**
> Let our old friends play in a safer day
> Say the bairns of Dunblane

G - Bm - / C - G - / 1st / C D G -

We twa hae paidled in the burn
Frae morning sun til dine *[=dinner time]*
Tho' seas between us braid *[=broad]* hae roared
Sin *[=since]* Auld Lang Syne

> **Throw these guns away (x2) / They've caused...**
> **Let the children play (x2)**
> **For the bairns of Dunblane**

We're building the roads that the future travels
We can ensure that no other town must bear
More **lost familiar voices... wind / Pleading...**

— w: Ted Christopher, v3 is Robt Burns
© 1996 Roadshow Music

Let Me Make Peace

I'm not afraid of dying of old age or disease
Or in some tragic accident that I could not foresee
I'm not afraid that death might mean my life would be cut short
But I am afraid of dying with hatred in my heart (↑2)

CDm Am F C / AmG C Bb G / F E Am G / AmG CF CG C

So let me make peace with all that I've come to resent &
remember that everyone I meet is heaven sent
Hate is the poison we drink when we sit down at anger's
feast / Let me get up from that table, let me make peace

FC x3 FG / AmGC F / AmD F C -

I'm not afraid of dying in mighty hurricane
Or to leave before my purpose on this earth has been made plain
I'm not afraid that I'll outlive my family & all my friends
But I am afraid of dying before I make amends

I'm not afraid of dying before all the world's at peace
Tho' my anger at injustice will always need release
Let me speak truth to power with courage & with grace
And let me die knowing that I've made the world a better place

"It's gonna take us all" our friend Jon Fromer would oft intone
For if you're looking for freedom you won't find it alone
And tho' our feet our tired, we do the work & carry on
Jon you are our hero, you are lighting the road we're on

— w: Steve Deasy, Lester Dor, & Lisa Sinnett, m: Steve Deasy
© 2010 Steve Deasy Music. On his *People Were Once Welcome Here*.

May You Walk

May you walk in your life as a <u>warrior</u>
Clear & loving & strong
May you walk in your life as a <u>warrior</u>
Trusting the path you are on

C FG C - / F C G - / C FG Am Em / F G C -

(insert: healer, lover, woman**)**

— w & m: Betsy Rose
© 1998 Betsy Rose. On her *Welcome to the Circle*.

Mercy Now

My father **could use a little mercy now**
The fruits of his labor fall & rot slowly on the ground
His work is almost over, it won't be long & he won't be around / I
love my father, he **could use some mercy now**

G - C - / D - G - :‖

My brother **could use a little mercy now**
He's a stranger to freedom, he's shackled to his fears & doubts
The pain that he lives in is almost more than living will allow
I love my brother, he **could use some...**

My church & my country **could use a little...**
As they sink into a poisoned pit that's going to take forever to
    climb out
They carry the weight of the faithful who follow them down
I love my church & country, they **could use some...**

Every living thing **could use a little...**
Only the hand of grace can end the race towards another mushroom
    cloud
People in power, well they'll do anything to keep their crown
I love life & life itself **could use some...**

Yeah, we all **could use a little...**
I know we don't deserve it, but we need it anyhow
We hang in the balance, dangle 'tween hell & hallowed ground
Every single one of us **could use some...**

— w & m: Mary Gauthier

MI SHEBEIRACH

Mi shebeirach avoteinu / M'kor hab'racha l'imoteinu
May the source of strength who blessed the ones before us
Help us find the courage to make our lives a blessing
And let us say amen

G Em Bm CD /   / Em Bm C G / C Bm Am G / C D G -

Mi shebeirach imoteinu / M'kor hab'racha l'avoteinu
Bless those in need of healing with r'fuah sh'leimah
The renewal of body, the renewal of spirit / **And let us say...**

— w & m: Debbie Friedman & Drorah Setel

MY GRATEFUL HEART

_My grateful heart, so filled with years of living
Memories flow by me like petals on a stream
_My grateful heart forgives so many sorrows
Brings peace that lasts forever, illuminates the dream

G Am D G /   / G C D G / Em Am D G

Mi corazón es tan agradecido
Pasan los recuerdos, arroyo_abajo van
Mi corazón perdona los dolores
Ofrece paz eterna, y_al sueño da su luz

Our grateful hearts recall your gentle spirit
Blessings of your being surround us like a prayer
Our grateful hearts now feel your spirit soaring
Wherever love is shining, we'll know that you are there
(tag) Our grateful... / ...we'll always find you there

— w & m: Laura Fannon

THE OCEAN REFUSES NO RIVER

The ocean refuses no river, no river **(2x)**
Alleluia, allelu allelu **(2x)**

Am G Am **(4x)**

— w & m: Lila Flood

ONAWA'S WALTZ

1. I've been waiting all the day long
To see the stars in your eyes _
My **2.** love come dance with me now
See how the evening flies _
And **3.** as you sleep, my dear, know that I'll be near
To hold you when you arise _

[F A7 Bb F / Gm C F -]

— w & m: John Krumm

ONE HEART AT A TIME

The way we're going to heal this world is **one heart at a time**
Man & woman, boy and girl, **one heart...**
Heart to heart our lives entwine, heart to heart our hopes combine
It starts with your heart hearing mine, **one...**
One heart at a time, one heart at a time
Listening, laughing, crying, one heart at a time

G - CD G /   ‖: C - G - / - Em CD G :‖

Lessons that the lost heart learns **one...**
It works out if we just take turns **one...**
Brothers, sisters, can't you see: it's as simple as can be
I hear you and you hear me...

Look at what contempt has cost / Every chance for closeness lost
Find the courage that we need to face each other's rage & greed
Listening is the future's seed...

People of all different kinds / Linking lives & hands & minds
Links of caring we create can pull this world away from hate
Listening like it's not too late...

— w & m: Fl!p Breskin

PRAYER

The curtain of daybreak, it is hanging
The wind whispers a morning grace
Before the sky you will find me standing
Let me live in this holy place

G - C G / - Em C D / 1st / G Em D G

All before me, peaceful / All behind me, peaceful
Under me, peaceful / Over me, peaceful
All around me peaceful (2x)

G - C - / Am - D - / G - Em - / Am - D - / 1st / Am - D G

In the house of freedom, there I wander
In the house of life shall I pass my days
In old age traveling, with you I'll wander
Walk with me in this holy place

Homeward now down this road I wander
Where my soul's long lines are deeply traced
Homeward now shall I make my journey
Lo, yonder this holy place

— w: Josh Bogin/Traditional Native American, m: Josh Bogin

© 1990 Josh Bogin. Anne Dodson *In Its Own Sweet Time*.

PURE GRACE

Lay down your body, let go **(2x)**
You are pure love now, you are pure grace / Lay down...

A Em A - / / - G Em D / 1st

— w & m: Marti Mariette

© 2011 Marti Mariette. On Threshold Choir *Walking Each Other Home*. http://thresholdchoir.org *LS.

SENDING YOU LIGHT

I am sending you light to heal you, to hold you
I am sending you light to hold you in love
No matter where you go, no matter where you've been
You'll never walk alone, I feel you deep within **(in 3/4)**

G - Am G / Em G CCD G // G - - - / /

No matter what you feel or what you choose to show
I'm always there for you & so I want you to know

I walk the path with you, go slow, dear one, don't hurry
I'll go just like you need to go, there is no need to worry

— w & m: Melanie DeMore

© 1993 Melanie Demore. In her *In the Mother House* 13.

SHINE ON

Knocked me off of my feet, but I think it's time for me
To start walking again, stop running away from it
Next time you see me I will be singing
A new song, I am learning to / Shine on

C - G - / Am - F G :‖ C -

Shine on, shine on / There'll be time enough for darkness
   when everything's gone
Shine on, shine on
There is work to be done in the dark before dawn

C - G - / Am G C - :‖

It's been hard not to give in & it ain't easy living
In hard times, I know it's weighing on your mind
Next time you see me I'll be uplifting
Yes, I will give you hope! I am learning as I go to / Shine on

I know how dark it seems, feel it coming up
Inside of me & I feel it in you too, in everything you do
Next time you see me, we'll both be laughing
O just to be alive! we are learning to shine / Shine on

(tag) There is work to be done so you you've got to shine on

Am G C -

— w & m: May Erlewine

© 2005 May Erlewine. On *Seth Bernard & Daisy May*. *LS

SO MANY ANGELS

So many angels all around me / **So many**... it's you I see
So... gathered around / **So**... it's you I found

(in 3/4) D - G D / - - Em A / D - G - / - D A D

— w & m: Karen Drucker & Kate Munger

© 2012 Karen Drucker & Kate Munger. http://thresholdchoir.org *LS.

STAY WITH ME

Stay with me, remain here with me / Watch & pray **(2x)**

Am Dm6 Am Dm6 / Am G C G / Am Dm E -

Bleibet hier und wachet mit mir / Wachet und betet **(2x)**

— w: Taizé Community, m: Jacques Berthier

© 1984 Les Presses de Taizé, Taizé Community, France. GIA Publications, Inc., exclusive North American agent. www.giamusic.com. On Taizé rec *Wait for the Lord* 15 & in *S & Prayers from Taizé*.

TROUBLE IN THIS WORLD

Trouble in this world will catch you off your guard
It'll be all right, it'll be all right
Comes so easy, but it leaves so hard / **It'll be...**

C - Am - / F - G - / 1st / F - G C

Yes, trouble in this world will find you on your knees...
Crying, Lord have mercy on me if you please...
   Well you kneel to the Lord & you will bless yourself...
   Ain't no need to kneel to no one else...
Yes, trouble in this world is like a newborn child...
Looks so sweet, but then it acts so wild...
   Well you think you've left your trouble far behind...
   All of a sudden, you've got trouble in mind...
Well it might be outside, or it might be in...
Might be sorrow, or it might be sin...
   Well you just wrap your trouble in a big brown sack...
   Turn it over and it won't come back...
Well it sounds so simple, but it's hard to do...
Just tell me your trouble & I'll tell mine to you...
   Well the rain keeps falling on the fool & the wise...
   God loves a sinner when a sinner cries...
But you can't see mercy when you're blinded by this world...
So many swine before so great a pearl...
   Yes trouble will find you as you're on your way...
   But take my hand & we'll be home someday...
Yes trouble will find us as we're makin' our way...
But keep on walkin' we'll be home someday...

— w & m: Bob Franke

© 1993 Telephone Pole Music Publishing Co. On his *Heart of the Flower* 11.

WALLS

Some walls are made of stone / Sometimes we build our own
Some walls stand for yrs / And some wash away with tears

(↑2) C F G C / / Am F G C / Am - G - C (F G C)

Some walls are lined with gold
Where some hearts stay safe & cold
Some walls are made of doubt / Holding in & keeping out

Some walls / If there's any hope for love at all
Some walls must fall

C F G C / Am - G C / Am F G C

Some walls are built on pride / Some keep the child inside
Some walls are made in fear / That love let go will disappear

(bridge) How will we ever know what might be found
Until we let the walls come tumbling down

Am D G Em / G Bm Am D

— w & m: Mary Ann Kennedy, Pam Rose & Randy L. Sharp

© 1994 EMI April Music Inc., EMI Longitude Music & My Pug Music. All rights on behalf of EMI April Music Inc. & EMI Longitude Music administered by Sony/ATV Music Publishing LLC, 424 Church Street, Suite 1200, Nashville, TN 37219. aka "Some Walls." On Kennedy Rose (YT ↑2), Randy Sharp *The Connection*, Peter Paul & Mary *In These Times* (both ↑7), Aaron Fowler & Laura Dungan *Awaken*, Ernie Garland *Edge of the World*, Hank & Claire *Heart of the Matter*.

WELCOME TO THE CIRCLE

Welcome to the circle — how far have you come?
Do you need some company, a candle & a song
Are you feeling weary, tired of being strong?
Welcome to the circle, it's a place where you belong

G - - D / G CG CG AmD / G GC G C / C GC AmD G

Do you have a burden that feels too much to bear
Do you have a bitterness you don't know how to share
Do you get too angry to breathe, to laugh, or pray?
Well there's no one in this circle who has never felt this way
No one in this circle who has never felt this way

G - - D / G CG CG AmD / G GC G C / C GC AmD G / /

So welcome to this circle, whatever brought you here
The valleys & the mountain tops, the muddy & the clear
And know your work is worthy & know your heart is true
And know that all you give away will come circling back to you
You've got to know that all... to you

— w & m: Betsy Rose

© 1991 Betsy Rose. On her *Welcome...* ↑3. *LS

WHEN YOU WALK ON

There's a long & winding river from the darkness to the dawn
It will carry and deliver you **when you walk on**

G F G F / G F CF C

No one here can say for certain what lies in the great beyond
You'll pass through that parted curtain **when you...**

You may grasp at the illusion, the confusion of your mind
Ah but soon you will remember to surrender one more time

Am Em F C / Am Em F G

You may fade out the doorway, fly away above the throne
Those who stay carry your story, a little glory lingers on

Tho' the world you leave behind you will become a distant song
Every soul you loved will find you **when...**

— w & m: Eliza Gilkyson

© 2005 Gilkysongs (BMI). All rights administered by Bluewater Music Services Corp. On *Paradise Hotel*.

WIDE RIVER TO CROSS

There's a sorrow in the wind blowin' down the road I've been
I can hear it cry while shadows steal the sun
But I can not look back now, I've come too far to turn around
And there's still a race ahead that I must run

(in 3/4) C - - - / Am F C - :‖

I'm only halfway home, I gotta journey on
To where I'll find the things I have lost
I've come a long long road, still I've got miles to go
I've got a wide wide river to cross

Am C Am C / Dm F C - /

I have stumbled, I have strayed, you can trace the tracks I made
All along the memories my heart recalls
But I'm just a refugee, won't you say a prayer for me?
'Cos sometimes even the strongest soldier falls

— w & m: Buddy Miller & Julie Miller

© 2005 Bughouse, West Bay Music Inc., Julie's Freakin' Out Music, 29 Cove Road Music & Blind Driver Music. All rights administered by Bug Music, Inc., A BMG Chrysalis Company. On his *Yes We Can* ↑2, Rec by Diana Krall & Levon Helm

WISDOM GUIDE ME

On the road to freedom there's a blackbird singing
Wisdom guide me thru my fear
It's a song of joy sets my whole soul ringing, so
Wisdom be my guide

D - G D / G D G A / 1st / G A D -

When the map is lost & the way's confusing
Wisdom guide me thru my fear
When the path's divided & there's no clear choosing, then **wisdom...**
    Oh a time of trouble is a time of turning...
    It's a sharp, hard focus on your deepest yearning, so...

Oh blackbird fly / Seeing far, seeing wide
Oh lift me high / And wisdom be my guide

G D A D / G - D - / - A D G / - A D -

When the day is dark & the storm cloud's looming...
When the lightning's flashing & the thunder's booming, then...
    Remember every heart has a silver lining...
    It knows beyond the storm there's a bright joy shining, so...

— w & m: Eileen McGann

© 2001 Eileen Mcgann/Dragonwing Music (SOCAN). www.eileenmcgann.com. On her *Beyond the Storm*. In *SO!* 46:2.

WITHIN OUR DARKEST NIGHT

Within our darkest night you kindle the fire that never
Dies away, that never dies away **(repeat)**

B7 Em - - / EmD G CG D / GEm C - B7 / EmAm B7 **(2x)**

Dans nos obscurités, allume le feu qui ne
S'éteint jamais, qui ne s'éteint jamais **(repeat)**

En nuestra oscuridad, enciende la llama
De tu_amor Señor, de tu_amor Señor **(repeat)**

— w: the Taizé Community, m: Jacques Berthier

Many families & small choirs are finding that it is a source of ease & comfort to sing simple, quiet songs with & for those who are in the process of passing from living into dying. There are over a hundred groups doing this wonderful work called Threshold Choirs across the US & Canada (thresholdchoir.org). In New England another group of similar bedside choirs called Hallowell can be found at hallowell-singers.org.

For more songs on this subject see: **Faith, Hope & Strength**, **Time & Changes** (incl many songs about death & dying). Other songs include **Love:** Speed of the sound of loneliness, **Rich:** Imagine healthcare. Online leadsheets for most of the chants in this chapter can be found at our website, www.riseupandsing.org. Chants elsewhere include **Faith:** Laudata omnes gentes, Lord is my light, **Family:** Let the little children, **Peace:** Blessed are the peacemakers

Home & Roots

ACROSS THE BORDERLINE

There's a place where I've been told, every street is paved with gold
And it's just **across the borderline**
And when it's time to take your turn, here's a lesson that you
    must learn
You could lose more than you ever hope to find

(↑2) C GC F GC / C Am G - / C GC C F / C G C -

When when you reach the broken promised land
    & every dream slips thru your hand
Then you'll know that it's too late to change your mind
'Cos you've paid the price to come so far just to wind up
    where you are / And you're still just across...

FG C F C / - Am G - / FG C FG AmF / C G C -

Up & down the Rio Grande, a thousand footprints in the sand
Reveal a secret no one can define
The river flows on like a breath in betw our life & death
Tell me who's the next to **cross...**

En la triste oscuridad hoy tenemos que cruzar
Este río que nos llama màs allá
But hope remains when pride is gone & it keeps you moving on
Calling you **across...**

— w: John Hiatt & James Dickinson, m: Ry Cooder

ARE YOU FROM DIXIE?

Hello there stranger, how do you do
There's smth I'd like to say to you
You seem surprised I recognize
I'm no detective, but I just surmise
    You're from the place I'm longing to be
    Your smiling face seems to say to me
    You're from my homeland, my sunny homeland
    Tell me can it be?

G - / 　 / D - / A D :‖

Are you from Dixie, I say from Dixie
Where the fields of cotton beckon to me?
I'm glad to see you, tell me "How be you?"
And the friends I'm longing to see
    Are you from Alabama, Tennessee or Caroline
    Any place below the Mason-Dixon Line?
    Are you from Dixie, I say from Dixie?
    'Cos I'm from Dixie too!

G C / G - / 1st / A D // G - / C G / - C / GD G

It was a way back in old '89
When first I crossed that Mason-Dixon Line
Gee but again I long to return
To those good old folks I left behind
    My home was way down in old Alabam'
    On the plantation near Birmingham
    And there's one thing certain I'm surely flirtin'
    With those southbound trains

— w: Jack Yellen, m: George L. Cobb (1915)

BEAUTIFUL OHIO

Drifting with the current down a moon-lit stream
While above the heavens in their glory gleam
And the stars on high
Twinkle in the sky
Seeming in a paradise of love divine
Dreaming of a pair of eyes that looked in mine
Beautiful Ohio, in dreams again I see
Visions of what used to be

C G / - C / - Dm / G C / 1st 2 / CA Dm / G C

— w: Ballard MacDonald (1918), m: Mary Earl

Arr. © 2015 by Hal Leonard Corporation. Mary Earl was a pen name used by Robt ("Bobo") King. The tune is based on Rimsky-Korsakov's "Song of India" & Stephen Foster's "Beautiful Dreamer". Became official state song in 1969. Lyrics were later updated by Wilbert McBride.

CALEDONIA

I don't know if you can see the changes that have come over me
In these last few days I've been afraid that I might drift away
So I've been telling old stories, singing songs that make me think
    about where I came from
And that's the reason why I seem so far away today

(↑4) C Dm Em F (4x)

Let me tell you that I love you & I think about you all the time
Caledonia you're calling me & now I'm going home
But if I should become a stranger you know that it would
    make me more than sad
Caledonia's been everything I've ever had

C G C F / - C G C / 1st / F G C -

I have moved & I've kept on moving, proved the points that I
    needed proving
Lost the friends that I needed losing, found others on the way
I have tried & I've kept on trying, stolen dreams, yes there's no
    denying
I have traveled hard, sometimes with conscience flying some-
    where with the wind

Now I'm sitting here before the fire, the empty room, the forest choir
The flames that couldn't get any higher, they've withered, now
    they've gone
But I'm steady thinking, my way is clear & I know what I will do
    tomorrow
When the hands have shaken & the kisses flow, well I will disappear

— w & m: Douglas Menzies MacLean

© 1977 (Renewed), 1983 Limetree Arts and Music. Sub-published by Fintage Publishing B.V. On his *Craig Dhu, Sounds of Caledonia*. In *SO!* 34:4. Orig. line 3 of v. 2: "I have kissed the ladies & left them crying..."

CANCIÓN MIXTECA

¡Qué lejos estoy del suelo donde he nacido
Inmensa nostalgia invade mi pensamiento
Y al verme tan solo y triste cual hoja al viento
Quisiera llorar, quisiera morir de sentimiento

(in 3/4) A - E - / - - A - / - A7 D - / A E A -

¡Oh Tierra del Sol! Suspiro por verte
Ahora que lejos yo vivo sin luz, sin amor
Y al verme tan solo y triste cual hoja al viento
Quisiera llorar, quisiera morir de sentimiento

E - A - /   / - A7 D - / A E A - (rhythm varies)

— w & m: Jose Lopez Alaves (m:1912, w:1915)

© 1929 by Edward B. Marks Music Company. Copyright renewed. Originally about Alavez's feelings of homesickness for his home region of Oaxaca after moving to Mexico City. In modern times, the song has become an anthem both for the region of Oaxaca & Mexican citizens living abroad who miss their homeland. Sung by Harry Dean Stanton in '84 film *Paris, Texas*.

CHITLIN COOKIN' TIME
IN CHEATHAM COUNTY

There's a quiet & peaceful county in the state of Tennessee
You will find it in the book they call "Geography"
Not famous for its farming, its minin' or its stills, but
They know they're chitlin cookin' in them Cheatham Co. hills
When it's chitlin cookin' time in Cheatham Co., I'll be
    courtin' in them Cheatham Co. hills
And I'll pick a Cheatham Co. chitlin cooker, I've a longin'
    that a mess of chitlin fills

Am - - E [Dm] / Am - - AmE Am :|

There's an art in chitlin cookin' & all good chitlin cooks
They must master it by practice 'cos it ain't wrote down in bks
In the hills of Cheatham Co. in sunny Tennessee
When chitlins are in season is where I long to be
Of all good things put before me, I think chitlins are the best
And when I press my dying pillow, let chitlins be my last request

— w & m: Arthur Smith

© 1944 (renewed) Berwick Music Corp. Recs by Ralph Blizard, Pokey LaFarge, Malcolm Price & Holy Modal Rounders. In *SO!* 39:2. Tune is derive fr "St. James Infirmary Blues".

DOWN IN THE MILLTOWN

When my shift is over & I'm headed home
I don't listen to the radio, I like to be alone / I like to be alone

C - - - / F - C - / - - (G F C - - -)

I've had my fill of people & all that factory noise
I listen to the engine, it's a sound that I enjoy / It's a sound...
    So I drive on past the drive-in, on past the movie lights
    Past the fenced-in fantasies that slip into the night / I slip...

Down in the milltown, the milltown so low
Hang your head over, feel the wind blow

F Em - F / C F G C (F C F C)

I wonder what's for dinner, if she'll be waiting there
She has to wake up early, she has to do her hair / She...
    And if I need a cold one, there's a tavern up the street
    The company of loners is still company to me / Yes they're...
And if my dreams treat me badly & I cry out at night
Shake me to my senses & I will be all right / Yes I will be...

— w & m: John Gorka

© 1987 Blues Palace Music (ASCAP). On his *I Know* 12, *Live at Caffe Lena* & *Fast Folk* 2:1. In *SO!* 33:1.

DOWN UNDER

Traveling in a fried-out combie
On a hippie trail, head full of zombie
I met a strange lady, she made me nervous
She took me in & gave me breakfast & she said:

Am G Am FG (4x)

"Do you come from a land down under
Where women glow & men plunder?
Can't you hear, can't you hear the thunder?
You better run, you better take cover"

C G Am FG (4x)

Buying bread from a man in Brussels / He was 6 ft 4 & full of muscle
I said "Do you speak-a my language?"
He just smiled & gave me a Vegemite sandwich & he said:
"I come... / Where beer does flow & men chunder / Can't..."

Dying in a den in Bombay / With a slack jaw & nothin' much to say
I said to the man "Are you trying to tempt me
Because I come from the land of plenty?"
And he said: "O you come..."

— w & m: Colin Hay & Ron Strykert

FERRY ME OVER

I was forced to wander because that I was poor / And to leave the
    hills of Caledonia seemed more than I could endure
And when that I was travelin' oh what thought came to my mind
That I had never seen her beauty 'til she was far behind
Ferry me over, ferry me there / To leave the hills of Cale-
    donia, is more than the heart can bear

CEm F AmC F / CEm Dm DmF G (repeat 3x)

When lost in distant days gone by where the simple joys I'd know
The foreign winds cried "Caledonia it's time you were goin' home"
So I will find the tallest ship that's ever faced the foam &
I will sail to Caledonia for Caledonia's my home / Ferry...

By some friend or neighbor's side where the fires of love burn bright
With songs & stories I'll share my adventurin' until the mornin' light
And should some young man ask of me "Is it brave or wise to roam?"
I'd bid him range the wide world all over, the better to know his
    own home...

— w & m: Andy M. Stewart

HOME (Bonoff)

Traveling at night, the headlights were bright
And we'd been up many an hour
And all thru my brain came the refrain
Of home & its warming fire

D Em G D / - - A - / 1st / D A D -

And home sings me of sweet things
My life there has its own wings
To fly over the mountains / Tho' I'm standing still

D - G D / - - Em A - / 1st / F Em A -

The people I've seen, they come in between
The cities of tiring life
The trains come & go, but inside you know
The struggle will soon be a fight

Traveling at night, the headlights were bright
But soon the sun came thru the trees
Around the next bend the flowers will send
The sweet scent of home in the breeze

— w & m: Karla Bonoff

HOME (Phillips)

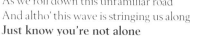

Hold on to me as we go
As we roll down this unfamiliar road
And altho' this wave is stringing us along
Just know you're not alone
'Cos I'm going to make this place your home

C F C F / / Am F C F / C↓ Am - / FG C -

Settle down, it'll all be clear
Don't pay no mind to the demons, they fill you with fear
The trouble it might drag you down, if you get lost you can
    always be found / Just know...

C F C F / / Am F C G / C↓ Am - / FG C -

— w & m: Drew Pearson & Greg Holden

I AM A PATRIOT

And the river opens for the righteous (x2)
And the river opens for the righteous someday

G C G C / /

I was walking with my brother
And he wondered_what's on my mind, I said:
"What I believe in my soul ain't what I see with my eyes
And we can't turn our backs this time

G C G C / G C D C / 1st / Em - D C

I am a patriot & I love my country
Because my country is all I know
I want to be with my family, the people who understand me
I've got nowhere else to go"

And I was talking with my sister, she looked
So fine, I said "Baby, what's on your mind?" she said_
"I want to run like the lion released from the cages
Released from the rages burning in my heart tonight"

I am a patriot & I love my country / Because...all I know
And I ain't no communist & I ain't no capitalist
And I ain't no socialist & I ain't no imperialist
And I ain't no Democrat & I ain't no Republican
I only know one party & it is freedom / I am (x3)

G C G C / G C D C / Em C Em C (4x) G C D -

— w & m: Steve Van Zandt

LEAVING THE LAND

It's time to go, Jenny, no need to close the door
What if the dust gets in the house, it doesn't matter any more
You & that dust have been at war for far too many yrs
Now the war is over, Jenny dear

(↑2) C↓ F (x2) /   / Dm G C F [Bogle: G] / Dm – G –

Leaving the land (2x)
Leaving all I've ever been & everything I am / Leaving...

/   "   /   / F G C F G / C↓ (x2)

Remember when I brought you here, those long bright yrs ago
For all that time you've been my heart but this land has been my soul
The long bright days are over now tho' still the heart beats on
But Jenny dear, the soul has gone

And all I see around me sings to me of the past
4 generations loved this land, never thought I'd be the last
All that toiling, all that dreaming, birth & death & joy & pain
It was all for nothing, all in vain

It's time to go, Jenny, drive quickly down the track
We'll never see what lies ahead if we keep on looking back
Behind is just an empty house, old memories & ghosts
And our small dreams gathering dust

   — w & m: Eric Bogle

© 1986 Larrikin Music Publishing Pty. Ltd. Trading As Happy As Larry Music Publishing. Reprinted by permission of Music Sales Corporation. On his *Singing the Spirit Home*, Mary Black *By the Time It Gets Dark* (in B), Jean Redpath *Leaving...*, Mary Forde *Next*, Quintessence *S for a Winter's Night*, Seoirse Ó Dochartaigh *Péire Stróicthe!*, Mahones *TAFKAHIM*. In *Eric Bogle Songs Bk 1*.

MY TENNESSEE MOUNTAIN HOME

Sittin' on the front porch on a summer afternoon
In a straightback chair on 2 legs leaned against the wall
Watch the kids a-playin' with June bugs on a string
And chase the glowin' fireflies when evening shadows fall

G – C G / – – D G :‖

In my Tennessee mountain home
Life is as peaceful as a baby's sigh
In my Tennessee mountain home
Crickets sing in the field nearby

G – C – / G – DC G :‖

Honeysuckle vine clings to the fence along the lane
Their fragrance makes the summer wind so sweet
And on a distant hilltop an eagle spreads its wings
And a songbird on a fencepost sings a melody

G – C G / G D G – / 1st / G – D G

Walking home from church on Sun. with the one you love
Just laughing, talking, making future plans
And when the folks ain't lookin' you might steal a kiss or 2
Sittin' in the porch swing holding hands

G – C G / G DC G – :‖

   — w & m: Dolly Parton

© 1972 (renewed 2000) Velvet Apple Music. On her *My Tennessee Mountain Home & Heartsongs*, Maria Muldaur & Elisabeth Andreassen *Short Stories*. Lyrics are about her rural childhood upbringing in a one-room cabin in Locust Ridge, TN. Parton has composed over 3,000 songs & was inducted into the Country Music Hall of Fame in 1999.

OLD HOME PLACE

It's been 10 long yrs since I left my home
In the hollow where I was born
Where the cool fall nights make the wood smoke rise
And a fox hunter blows his horn

G B7 C G / – – D – / 1st / G D G –

I fell in love with a girl from the town
I thought that she would be true
I ran away to Charlottesville / And worked in a sawmill or 2

What have they done to the old home place
Why did they tear it down?
And why did I leave the plow in the field
And look for a job in the town?

D – G – / A – D – / G B7 C G / – D G –

Well, the girl ran off with somebody else / The taverns took all my pay
And here I stand where the old home stood / Before they took it away

Now the geese fly south & the cold wind moans
As I stand here & hang my head
I've lost my love, I've lost my home / And now I wish that I was dead

   — w: Mitchell F. Jayne, m: Rodney Dillard

© 1963 (renewed) by Lansdowne-Winston Music Publishers. On The Dillards *Back Porch Bluegrass*, J.D. Crowe.

OUR TOWN

And you know **the sun's settin' fast**
And just like they say, nothing good ever lasts
Well, go on now & kiss it goodbye
But hold on to your lover 'cos your heart's bound to die
Go on now & say goodbye
To our **town, to** our **town**
Can't you see the sun's settin' down
On our **town, on** our **town**
Goodnight (last cho 7th & 8th lines: "I can **see the sun** has
   gone **down on** my **town, on** my **town...**")

G C / G D / etc.

Up the street beside that red neon light
That's where I met my baby on one hot summer night
He was the tender & I ordered a beer
It's been 40 yrs & I'm still sitting here
But you know **the sun's settin' fast / And just like they say...**
   It's here I had my babies & I had my 1st kiss
   I've walked down Main Street in the cold morning mist
   Over there is where I bought my 1st car
   It turned over once but then it never went far
   And I can see **the sun's settin' fast / And just...**
I buried my Mama & I buried my Pa
They sleep up the street beside the pretty brick wall
I bring them flowers about every day
But I just gotta cry when I think what they'd say
If they could see how **the sun's settin' fast / And j...**
   Now I sit on the porch & watch the lightning-bugs fly
   But I can't see too good, I got tears in my eyes
   I'm leaving tomorrow but I don't wanna go
   I love you, my town, you'll always live in my soul / But I can see...

   — w & m: Iris DeMent

© 1992 Songs of Iris. On her *Infamous Angel* 13, Kate Rusby *Storytellers* 13.

129

The River that Flows Both Ways

Once the Sachems told a story
'Bout a land the Great Spirit blessed
And the people followed the legend
From the great waters in the west
And they stopped where they found that the fishing was good
The earth it was fertile & game ran in the woods

G - D - / - - G - ‖ C G C G / C D C G

And now I could be happy, just spending my days
On the river that flows both ways (repeat)

C G C G / C D C G ‖

1st came the trappers, then the traders
Their own fortunes for to find
And the valley treated them kindly
So the farmers, they followed close behind
Then the sloops sailed well-laden 'round the battery
With flour from Yonkers, furs from Albany

Writers & painters have shown its beauty
In its waters & on the shores
While musicians sing its praises
And keep alive the river's lore
With the sun setting golden o'er the Palisades
Afternoon ends & then the daylight fades

Maybe it's the moonshine, maybe it's the starlight
Reflected in Haverstraw Bay
Maybe it's the fog that rolls off the Highlands
At the break of a brand new day
But apple cider & pumpkins, strawberries & corn
Make the people of the river, glad they were born

— w & m: Rick Nestler

Sacred Ground

All the places I have been, I treasure in my mind
Orbiting my restless wind, they were never left behind
Friends have taken different roads & scattered from this place
But no matter where they go, I cherish every face
Until there comes a time when we **will turn around**
And meet **again on sacred ground**

(↑5) C ↓ F C / F C F G ‖ C Em Am F / Dm G C -

Joseph left his father's land never to return
Driven by the white man's hand & by his brothers spurned
But roots still reach thru ancient loam where singing is long gone
Spirits call the children home to hear the welcome song
Until there comes a time when they **will turn around**
And gather **again on sacred ground**

(bridge) All that passed before us, all that lies ahead
Forms the fabric of our lives, woven thread to thread
Tales told, songs of old, the ringing of a bell
Bring us back to what we know & what is left to tell

G - C F / F C G C Dm G / C ↓ F G / Am G F Dm G

Tonight beneath the starry bowl, the wind is whispering warm
To comfort all those southern souls evicted by the storms
In my heart the table's set for Thanksgiving Day
And every wanderer wandering yet will have a place to stay
Until there comes a time when we **will turn around**
And stand **again on sacred ground**

— w & m: Heidi Muller

The Streets Of Old Quebec

A little man with a violin outside the window plays &
People pass him by there, dressed in leather & berets
"Bonjour madame **(x2)** may I play a song for you?
Bonjour madame **(x2)**, j'ai une petite chanson pour vous"

(↑2) G - C Bm / C - G D / 1st / C G D G

On the hour cathedral bells peal out across the square &
Artists in the alley ways, they hang all their pictures there
And men in high-wheeled carriages with bear rug robes of brown
Whistle softly to their horses while showing riders around the town

Along the streets of old Quebec the flowers bloom
In the boxes on the windows underneath our room
O'er the streets of old Quebec, the white birds fly
From the rooftops to the river where the boats go by

G C G Am Bm C / Am D - G ‖

With a flashing smile, a little brown-eyed child dashes down
    along the street
And the cobblestones, like old rolling bones, they click & clatter
    'neath her feet
Thru memory's eyes, an old man sighs as he sips his sidewalk wine
Where goes the child? Where goes the dream?
    Where goes the flying time?

The little man with his violin moves off along the way
From high stone walls, the shadows fall & evening lights begin to play
Their dancing diamonds, their flaming fires
    from tiny windows stream
Then 'round about, each one flickers out
    & night dissolves back into dreams

— w & m: Bill Staines

Sweet Home Alabama

Big wheels keep on turning
Carry me home to see my kin
Singing songs about the Southland
I miss Alabamy once again & I think it's a sin, yes

D C G - (4x)

Well I heard Mr. Young sing about her
Well I heard ole Neil put her down
Well I hope Neil Young will remember
A Southern man don't need him around anyhow

Sweet home Alabama / Where the skies are so blue
Sweet home Alabama / Lord, I'm coming home to you

In Birmingham they love the gov'nor (boo, boo, boo)
Now we all did what we could do
Now Watergate does not bother me
Does your conscience bother you? Tell the truth

Ah, ah, ah, Alabama…**(4x)**

Now Muscle Shoals has got the Swampers
And they've been known to pick a song or 2
Lord they get me off so much
They pick me up when I'm feeling blue (& the governor's true),
   now how about you?

— w & m: Ronnie Van Zant, Ed King & Gary Rossington

© 1974 Songs of Universal, Inc., EMI Longitude Music, Universal Music Corp. & Full
Keel Music. Copyright renewed. All rights controlled & administered by Songs of
Universal, Inc. & Universal Music Corp. On Lynard Skynyrd *2nd Helping*.

WELCOME, WELCOME, EMIGRANTE

So welcome, welcome, emigrante
To my country, welcome home / Welcome, welcome…
To the country that I love

(in G) C - G E7 / Am D G - :‖

I am proud **(x3)** of my forefathers
And I say "They built this country"
And they came from far away to a land they didn't know
The same way you do, my friends

G D GC G / - E7 Am D / C Am G - / D A D -

I am proud **(x3)** of my forefathers
And I sing about their courage
For they spoke a foreign language & they labored with their hands
The same way you do, my friends

I am proud…forefathers / And I sing about their patience
For the work they did was lowly & they dirtied up their clothes
They spoke a foreign language & they labored with their hands
And they came from far away… / The same way…

G D GC G / - E7 Am D / C Am G - / / / D A D -

— w & m: Buffy Sainte-Marie

© 1964 Gypsy-Boy Music, Inc. Copyright renewed. All rights administered by
Kobalt Songs Music Publishing. On her *Many a Mile* 13, *Best of V2* & on *Broadside
Ballads V3*. In *Carry It On*.

WEST VIRGINIA MY HOME

West Virginia, o my home
West Virginia's where I belong
In the dead of the night, in the still & the quiet,
  I slip away like a bird in flight
Back to those hills, the place that I call home

D - G - / D - A - / 1st / D A D -

It's been yrs now since I left there
And this city life's about got the best of me
I can't remember why I left so free,
   what I wanted to do, what I wanted to see
But I can sure remember where I come from

Well, I paid the price for the leaving
And this life I have's not one I thought I'd find
Well, let me live, love, let me cry, when I go, just let me die
Among the friends who'll remember when I'm gone

(bridge) Home **(x3)** / Oh I can see it so clear in my mind
Home **(x3)** / I can almost smell the honeysuckle vine
In the dead of the night, in the still & the quiet…

G - D - / - - A - :‖ D - G - / D A D -

— w & m: Hazel Dickens

© 1975 Happy Valley Music. Copyright renewed. On her *A Few Old Memories*,
Trapezoid *3 Forks of Cheat* & *Sister Where Art Thou?*

YERUSHALAIM SHEL-ZAHAV
(Jerusalem, Jerusalem)

Avir harim tsalul kayayin vere'akh oranim
Nisah beru'akh ha'arbayim im kol pa'amonim
U'vtardemat ilan va'even shvuyah bakhalomah
Ha'ir asher badad yoshevet uvelibah - khomah

(in 3/4) Am Dm DmAA A7 / - Dm AmAmE Am :‖

Yerushalayim shel zahav v'shel nekhoshet v'shel or
Halo lekhol shirayikh ani kinor (repeat)

DmDmG C F Am / F CCG AmAmE Am :‖

Khazarnu el borot hamayim lashuk velakikar
Shofar koreh behar habayit ba'ir ha'atikah
Uvame'arot asher baselah alfei shmashot zorkhot
Nashuv nered el Yam Hamelakh b'derech Yerikho

Akh bevo'i hayom lashir lakh velakh likshor k'tarim
Katonti mitze'ir banayikh ume'akharon ham'shorerim
Ki shmekh tsorev et hasfatayim keneshikat saraf
Im eshkakhech Yerushalayim asher kulah zahav

Jerusalem of Gold

The mountain air is clear as water, the scent of pines around
Is carried on the breeze of twilight & tinkling bells resound
The trees & stones there softly slumber, a dream enfolds them all
So solitary lies the city & at its heart, a wall

O Jerusalem of gold & of light & of bronze
I am the lute for all your songs (repeat)

The wells are filled again with water, the square with joyous
  crowd
On the Temple Mount within the City, the shofar rings out loud
Within the caverns in the mtns, a thousand suns will glow
We'll take the Dead Sea road together that runs thru Jericho

But as I sing to you, my city & you with crowns adorn
I am the least of all your children of all the poets born
Your name will scorch my lips for ever like a seraph's kiss, I'm told
If I forget thee, golden city, Jerusalem of gold

— w & m: Naomi Shemer-Sapir

© 1967 (renewed) Warner/Chappell Music Ltd. All rights in the U.S. & Canada
administered by WB Music Corp. Better known as "Jerusalem of Gold."

YOUR STATE'S NAME HERE

Sometimes when the grass is blown by the breeze
There's a faraway look in the leaves of the trees
A memory returns heartbreakingly clear
Of a place I call home, (your state's name here)
    No sky could be deeper, no water so clear
    As back in the meadows of (your state's name here)
    I'm gonna go back altho' I don't know when
    There's no other place like (your state's name again)

(in 3/4) C - F C / F C - G / 1st / F C G C :‖

O (your state's name here), **O** (again) **what a state
I have not been back since** (a reasonable date)
**Where the asphalt grows soft in July every year
In the warm summer mornings of** (your state's name here)

G - - - / / C - F C / F C G C

My grampa would come & turn on the game
And fall asleep drinking (your local beer's name)
While gramma would sing in the garden for hours
To all of (the names of indigenous flowers)
    The songs that she sang were somewhat obscure
    She learned from the local townspeople I'm sure
    The language they use is not very clear
    Like (place a colloquialism right here)

I'd love to wake up where (the state songbird) sings
Where they manufacture (the names of some things)
Like there on the bumper, a sticker so clear
An "I", then a heart, and then (your... name here)
    Whisper it soft, it's a song to my ear
    (Your state's name here, your state's name here)
    It's there I was born and it's there I'll grow old
    By the rivers of blue & the arches of gold

— w & m: Lou & Peter Berryman

© 1988 Lou & Peter Berryman (SESAC). Note: This is definitely a 2-person song: 2nd voice sings parts in parentheses. On their *Love Is The Weirdest of All*, Steve Gillette & Cindy Mangsen *Berrymania*, Chenille Sisters *May I Suggest*. In their *Big SB & SO!* 33.2.

Home & Roots contains songs about the places or countries where we live & songs about immigration & exile. See also **Family** (re home you live in), **Farm & Prairie**, **Freedom**, **Good Times** (Cajun areas of Louisiana), **Travelin'**.

Other songs include **Blues:** Kansas City, Sweet home Chicago, **Country:** Jackson, Okie from Muskogee, **Earth:** Mahogany tree (Mexican rainforest), **Friendship:** Howdi do, **Golden:** Aloha oe, Miss the Mississippi & you, **Jazz:** Georgia on my mind, Sweet Georgia Brown, **Love:** Sweet Thames flow softly, Wild rose of the mtn, **Old-timey:** Little cabin on the hill, Rocky Top, **Outdoors:** Follow that road, **Peace:** Jerusalem, We are one (Korea), **Rich:** Leaving Eden, Place called England, **Rock:** Memphis Tennessee, **Sea:** Santa Lucia, **Time:** Feel so near, **Trav:** Rusty old Amer dream, **Work:** No Irish need apply, Silken dreams (Allentown PA).

Hope & Strength

ANOTHER TRAIN

The beginning is now & will always be
You say you lost your chance & fate brought you defeat
But that means nothing, you look so sad
You've been listening to those who say you missed your chance

C G Am G/ F C F G :‖

There's another train, there always is
Maybe the next one is yours, get up & climb aboard
Another train

C G Am G / F C F G / C (F C G)

You may feel you're done, but there's no such thing
Altho' you're standing on your own, your own breath is king
The beginning is now, don't turn around
For regrets of bad mistakes will only drain you

We crawl in the dark sometimes, we can think too much
We can we fill our heads with the craziest things that only
    break our hearts
I know you've seen what this earth can do
When it's dragging down another load of us, us worrisome fools

I know it's hard, we can feel confused
We can crown ourselves with it all, 'til we feel we cannot move
Building worlds that don't exist
Imagination sometimes plays the worst tricks

— w & m: Pete Morton

© 1988 Harbourtown Music. On his *One Big Joke* 14, *Another... & Flying an Unknown Flag*, Poozies *Chantoozies & Raise Your Head*, Eileen McGann *Journeys*, Sally Barker *Another*. In *SO!* 41.1.

ARISE! ARISE! (National Anthem)

Atlantic & Pacific flow
The Great Lakes & the Gulf of Mexico
The land betw sustains us all
To cherish it, our tireless call

F - - C - - - / - - - G - - - / F - - C - / - - F C -

Arise! Arise!
I see the future in your eyes
To one more perfect union we aspire
And lift our voices from the fire

F - C - / - - - F - - - / Dm - F Am - / C - F C - -

We reached these shores from many lands
We came with hungry hearts & hands
Some came by force & some by will
At the auction block or the darkened mill

We died in your fields & your factories
Strange fruit hangin' from the poplar trees
With an old coat hanger in a room somewhere
A trail of tears, an electric chair

Our great responsibility
To be guardians of our liberty
Til tyrants bow to the people's dream
And justice flows like a mighty stream

— w & m: Jean Rohe

BIRD BY BIRD

Trouble isn't easy, trouble brings doubt
Fear comes in & the joy goes out
How we gonna make it? What are we gonna do?
How are we gonna make it when <u>trouble</u> **comes thru?**
    We'll take it bird by bird
    A little at a time, take it bird by bird
    And stone by stone
    A little at a time, take it stone / by stone

G D / Em C :‖ (4x) D G

Change isn't easy, change is hard
Fear comes in & it can tear you apart
How we gonna make it? What are we gonna do?
How are we gonna make it when change **comes thru?**

Dreams aren't easy, dreams can get lost
Fear comes in & the dream gets tossed
How we gonna make it? What are we gonna do?
How we gonna make this dream come true?

— w & m: Joe Crookston

BRANCHING OUT

When I grow up I want to be a tree
Want to make my home with the birds & the bees
And the squirrels, they can count on me
When I grow up to be a tree

C - / F - / C - / G -

I'll let my joints get stiff, put my feet in the ground
Take the winters off & settle down
Keep my clothes 'til they turn brown
When I grow up, I'm gonna settle down

I'm gonna reach (x2) / I'm gonna reach, reach for the sky
I'm gonna... (x2) / I'm...til I know why

C - / F - / C - / G - :‖

When the spring comes by I'm gonna get real green
If the dogs come by I'm gonna get real mean
On windy days, I'll bend & lean
When I grow up I'm gonna get real green

(bridge) If I should fall in storm or slumber
Please don't turn me into lumber
I'd rather be a Louisville Slugger
Swinging for the seats

F - F↓ / C ↓ - - / 1st / G - - -

— w & m: John Gorka

CREEK'S GONNA RISE

I'm not one who listens to the voices in my head
I put stock in what I've seen come true
And I don't believe in vengeance & I don't believe in magic
I believe in spending time with you
    I've been looking for you for a long, long time
    I've met many others on my way
    How was I to know that what I lost I'd find again?
    I just had to wait for a better day

C - F - / C Am G - / 1st / CF CG C - :‖

Well the creek's gonna rise & the creek's gonna fall
And the geese are gonna fly when they hear that call
But they'll come back home on the eve of the spring
And we will find what we were missing, find what we
    were missing / Find what we were missing once again

C - F - / C - G - / Am - F - / CF CG x2 / CF CG C -

I used to curse the darkness & I used to curse my luck
I used to weep & struggle & resist
But come the time when trouble is your own best friend
You might as well embrace it with a kiss
    The day I lost my baby was the day I turned towards you
    The day I lost control I found restraint
    The day I gave away my gold I learned to hear the bell
    That tolls as loud for sinners as for saints

The church where we were married went ablaze one night
The flames consumed the walls, the quilt, the bell
In the morning all was ashes, all our tears filled the creek
How could someone say, all will be well?
    We gathered at the house next door that January day
    We were the same but everything had changed
    A child stood up & said that love & music & our memories
    These cannot be destroyed, just rearranged

— w & m: Nerissa Nields

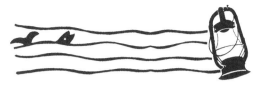

CROSSING THE WATER

We are crossing the water our whole life thru
We are making a passage that is straight & true
Every heart is a vessel, every dream is a light
Shining thru the darkness of the blackest night

C - FG C / F C Dm G / 1st / F C G C

For there is no shallow water & naught but love to keep
Us safely from the dangers & the devils of the deep
Yet with every breath within us, we search forevermore,
To find some peaceful harbor on that far off shore

G - C - / F C Dm G :‖

For some it is a glory, for some it is a game
For some it is a story filled with emptiness & pain
But as rising winds in chorus, we search for steady ground
There is only that before us, there can be no turning 'round

Oh there is no other journey that will ever be the same
No second chance horizon that will call you by your name
When the welling waves wash o'er you, and the stormy winds
    they drive
Give your heart a song, sing it loud & long, keep your dreams alive!

— w & m: Bill Staines

FAST CAR

You got a fast car / I want a ticket to anywhere
Maybe we make a deal
Maybe together we can get somewhere
Any place is better / Starting from zero got nothing to lose
Maybe we'll make smth / Me myself I got nothing to prove

Cmaj7 G / Em D / (4x) :‖

You got a... / I got a plan to get us out of here
I been working at the convenience store
Managed to save just a little bit of money
Won't have to drive too far
Just 'cross the border & into the city
You & I can both get jobs
And finally see what it means to be living

You see my old man's got a problem
He live with the bottle that's the way it is
He says his body's too old for working
His body's too young to look like his
My mama went off & left him
She wanted more from life than he could give
I said somebody's got to take care of him
So I quit school & that's what I did

You got... / Is it fast enough so we can fly away?
We gotta make a decision
Leave tonight or live & die this way

(bridge) So I remember when we were driving, driving in your car
The speed so fast I felt like I was drunk
City lights lay out before us
And your arm felt nice wrapped 'round my shoulder
I _ had a feeling that I belonged
I _ had a feeling I could be someone
Be someone, be someone

Cmaj7 - / G - / C G / Em C / C Em D - /   / C Em

You got... / We go cruising to entertain ourselves
You still ain't got a job
I work in a mkt as a checkout girl
I know things will get better
You'll find work & I'll get promoted
We'll move out of the shelter
Buy a bigger house & live in the suburbs **(to bridge)**

You got... / I got a job that pays all our bills
You stay out drinking late at the bar
See more of your friends than you do of your kids
I'd always hoped for better
Thought maybe together you & me would find it
I got no plans I ain't going nowhere
So take your fast car & keep on driving

— w & m: Tracy Chapman

FOR REAL

Death took the husband of a neighbor of mine
On a highway with a drunk at the wheel
She told me keep your clean hands off the laundry he left
And don't tell me you know how I feel
She had a tape that he'd sent her from a Holiday Inn
And she never played it much in the day
But when I heard him say he loved her thru the window at night
I just stayed the hell away

C ↓ / F C / 1st / F - / Bb Am / F C / Bb Am / G -

There's a hole in the middle of the prettiest life
So the lawyers & the prophets say
Not your father nor your mother nor your lover's
Gonna ever make it go away
And there's too much darkness in an endless night
To be afraid of the way we feel
Let's be kind to each other
Not forever but for real

/ " / " / " / " / Bb Am / F D9 / F Bb / Am -

My father never put his parachute on
In the Pacific back in World War II
He said he'd rather go down in familiar flames
Than get lost in that endless blue
And some of that blue got into my eyes
And we never stopped fighting that war
Until I first understood about endlessness
And I loved him like never before

It's lucky that my daughter got her mother's nose
And just a little of her father's eyes
And we've got just enough love that when the longing takes me
Well it takes me by surprise
And I remember that longing from my highway days
Tho' I never could give it a name
It's lucky I discovered in the nick of time
That the woman & the child aren't to blame

For the **hole in the middle of a pretty good life**
I only face it 'cos it's here to stay
Not my father... lover / Nor the highway made it go away
And there's... night / To be <u>ashamed</u> **of the way** I **feel**
I'll be kind to my loved ones / **Not forever but for real**

Some say that God is a lover / Some say it's an endless void
And some say both & some say she's angry
And some say just annoyed
But if God felt a hammer in the palm of his hand
Then God knows the way we feel
And love lasts forever / Forever & for real / Love lasts forever

C ↓ / F C / 1st / F -

Bb Am / F D9 / F Bb / Am - / F Bb Am -

— w & m: Bob Franke

© 1983 Telephone Pole Music Publishing Co. In his *S of.* On his *For...*13 & *Fast Folk 2:4*,
David Wilcox *E. Asheville Hardware* 13, Lui Collins *There's a Light* 11, Magpie *Give Light.*

GIVE LIGHT

<u>Give light</u> **& people will find the way (3x)**
People will find the way I do believe

G Em AmD G / Am D AmD G / 1st / Am D C G

(**insert** Teach peace, Stand together, Give love)
     — w & m: Greg Artzner & Terry Leonino (Magpie)

© 1996 Greg Artzner & Terry Leonino. On their *Give Light* (w/ Kim & Reggie
Harris), *In This World & Long Walk to Freedom Reunion Conc.* In *SO!* 42:3.

HOPE FOR ONE & ALL

If the morning star still disappears behind a sky of blue
If people rise & go to work like they always do
As long as young folks fall in love & kids keep growing tall
With the earth below & the sky above **there's hope for one & all**

CF CG C G / CF GAm F G / F C F G / CF GAm FG C

If the moon still moves the deep blue sea & rules the hearts of men
If the world keeps turning quietly, here we go again
If the winter grass turns April-green when the rain begins to fall
If there's water flowing from the stream **there's...**

There's hope for you & me my friend with our backs
    against the wall / If there's water flowing from the stream...

F Em F G / CF GAm FG C

If a man still does the best he can, tho no one cares
If mothers rock their babes to sleep & say a little prayer
If the old car starts when the wind blows cold, way down in the fall
If there's one good spark in the falling dark **there's...**

There's hope for you...wall / If there's one good spark, **there's ...**
     — w & m: David Mallett

© 2010 BMG Ruby Songs (ASCAP). All rights administered by BMG Rights
Management (US) LLC. On his *In the Falling Dark* & Tom May *Blue Roads, Red Wine.* *LS

I AM WILLING

I am open & I am willing
For to be hopeless would seem so strange
It dishonors those who go before us
So lift me up to the light of change

C - - - / G - C - / - - Am F / G - C -

There is hurting in my family
And there is sorrow in my town
There is a panic all across the nation
And there is wailing the whole world round

May the children see more clearly
And may the elders be more wise
May the winds of change caress us
Even tho' they burn our eyes

Give me a mighty oak to hold my confusion
And give me a desert to hold my fears
Give me a sunset to hold my wonder
And give me an ocean to hold my tears
     — w & m: Holly Near

© 2003 Hereford Music. On her *Show Up* & Chris & Holly "Show Me."

I STAND FOR LOVE

<u>I</u> stand for love, <u>I</u> stand for peace
<u>I</u> stand for joy & for release
For what is beautiful & true
<u>I</u> stand for hope, <u>I</u> stand for you **(repeat)** (↑3)

G Bm / CD G / CD Em / 1. BmC AmD :‖ 2. AmD G

You know our world is in great pain
She needs our loving care again
But there are those who fail to see
What we have done & what we need
    There is a cost for every act
    And now there is no turning back
    We burn a bridge, we bang a drum
    It's time to rise, the time has come / **To stand for...**

(**bridge**) If you're thinking it's not urgent
That we've got more time to kill
If I'm not the one who'll change things
Then for Heaven's sake, who will?

EmD C / / / Am D

So I will move & I will climb
That mtn one step at a time
I won't be swayed, I will not stop
Until we've made it to the top

Where we will stand for love & peace
<u>We'll</u> **stand for joy &... / For what is beautiful...**
We'll **stand for hope, we'll stand for you**
     — w & m: David Roth

© 2007 David Roth. On his *Rhubarb Trees* (w/ Anne Hills).

I Will Survive

At first I was afraid, I was petrified
Kept thinking I could never live without you by my side
But then I spent so many nights thinking how you did me wrong
And I grew strong & I learned how to get along

Am Dm / G Cmaj7 / Fmaj7 Dm / Esus E

And so you're back from outer space
I just walked in to find you here with that sad look upon your face
I should have changed that stupid lock, I should have made you
  leave your key
If I had known for just one second you'd be back to bother me

Go on now go, walk out the door, just turn around now
'Cos you're not welcome anymore
Weren't you the one who tried to hurt me with goodbye
Did you think I'd crumble, did you think I'd lay down & die

Oh no, not I – I will survive
Oh as long as I know how to love, I know I'll stay alive
I've got all my life to live, I've got all my love to give
And I'll survive – I will survive

It took all the strength I had not to fall apart
Kept trying hard to mend the pieces of my broken heart
And I spent oh so many nights just feeling sorry for myself
I used to cry, but now I hold my head up high

And you see me, somebody new
I'm not that chained up little person still in love with you
And so you felt like dropping in & just expect me to be free
But now I'm saving all my loving for someone who's loving me

Go on now go, walk out the door, just turn around now
'Cos you're not welcome anymore
Weren't you the one who tried to break me with goodbye
Did you think I'd crumble? Did you think I'd lay down & die?

— w & m: Dino Fekaris & Frederick J. Perren

If Not Now

If not n**o**w,_tell me wh**e**n _ **(2x)**
We may n**e**ver see this m**o**ment or pl**a**ce in time ag**ai**n
If not n**o**w, if not n**o**w, tell me wh**e**n _

(↑2) G C G - /   / G↓ Em C D G / C D G -

I see sorrow & trouble in this land **(2x)**
Altho' there will be struggle we'll make the change we can
If not now, tell me when

I may never see the promised *[healed]* land **(2x)**
And yet we'll take the journey & we'll walk it hand in hand / **If...**

(bridge) We'll w**o**rk until it's d**o**ne, every d**au**ghter, every s**o**n
Every s**ou**l that ever l**o**nged for smth b**e**tter_/ Smth br**i**ghter_ _

C↓ G C D G / C D G D - / C - - -

It will take a change of heart for this to mend **(2x)**
But miracles do happen every shining now & then / **If...**

— w & m: Carrie Newcomer

Lay Down Your Weary Tune

Lay down your weary tune, lay down
Lay down the song you strum
And rest yourself 'neath the strength of strings
No voice can hope to hum

G - C G - - / Em D - (C) / G - C - - - / G D G - (D)

Struck by the sounds before the sun
I knew the night had gone
The morning breeze like a bugle blew
Against the drums of dawn

The ocean wild like an organ played
The seaweeds wove its strands
The crashin' waves like cymbals clashed
Against the rocks & sands

I stood unwound beneath the skies
And clouds unbound by laws
The cryin' rain like a trumpet sang
And asked for no applause

The last of leaves fell from the trees
And clung to a new love's breast
The branches bare like a banjo played *[moaned]*
To the winds that listened best

I gazed down in the river's mirror
And watched its winding strum
The water smooth ran like a hymn
And like a harp did hum

— w & m: Bob Dylan

Many Rivers to Cross

Many rivers to cross but I can't seem to
Find my way over
Wandering I am lost as I travel
Along the white cliffs of Dover

(↑5) C E F E / F G F C :‖

Many rivers to cross & it's only / my will that keeps me alive
I've been licked, washed up for yrs & I merely
Survive because of my pride

(bridge) And this loneliness won't leave me alone
It's such a drag to be on your own
My woman left & she didn't say why
Well I guess, I have to try

F - C - /   / F - C Am / F - G -

Many rivers... but where to / begin, I'm playing for time
There'll be times when I find myself thinking of committing
Some dreadful crime

— w & m: Jimmy Cliff

MAY I SUGGEST

May I suggest, may I suggest to you
May I suggest this is the best part of your life
May I suggest this time is blessed for you
This time is blessed & shining, almost blinding bright
Just turn your head & you'll begin to see
The thousand reasons that were just beyond your sight
The reasons why, why I suggest to you
Why I suggest this is the best part of your life

C - G - / F G C - :‖ F - C - / FC FC G - / **1st 2**

There is a world that's been addressed to you
Addressed to you, intended only for your eyes
A secret world like a treasure chest to you
Of private scenes & brilliant dreams that mesmerise
A lover's trusting smile, a tiny baby's hands
The million stars that fill the turning sky at night
Oh I suggest, oh I suggest to you / Oh **I suggest this...**

There is a hope that's been expressed in you
The hope of 7 generations, maybe more
And this is the faith that they invest in you
It's that you'll do one better than was done before
Inside you know, inside you understand
Inside you know what's yours to finally set right
And I suggest, & I suggest to you / **I suggest...**

This is a song comes from the west to you
Comes from the west, comes from the slowly setting sun
With a request, with a request of you
To see how very short these endless days will run
And when they're gone & when the dark descends
Oh we'd give anything for one more hour of light
(instrum) And **I suggest...**

— w & m: Susan Werner

OLD TIN CUP

Caught a little rain in an old tin cup
You know it don't take a lot
I sat on my porch & I watched it fill up
And here is what it brought:

(in G) C G D Em / C G D - / C D C G / - D G -

You can catch a dream in the middle of the night
You know it don't take a lot
And find it's gone with the morning light
Hold on to what you've got

Hold on to what you've got, it may not be a lot
Hold on to what you've got
Or you'll find it's gone with the morning light **(3rd line of v.)**
Hold on to what you've got

Life fills up in the twinkle of an eye
You know it don't take a lot
And you can't stop time from slipping by
Hold on to what you've got

(bridge) A little bit of love, to see us thru
A place to sleep, a friend or 2
A song & a story & something true
Hold on to what you've got

Bm - C G / C G - D / C D C G / - D G

You can make a lot out of something plain
You know it don't take a lot
Like an old tin cup left out in the rain
Hold on to what you got

— w & m: Eve Goldberg

QUIET HILLS

There is darkness in these hills, but I am not afraid **(2x)**
There is darkness in these hills, tho' some may tremble, I am still
Hope lives in these quiet hills

I: C Am FG C / C↓ D G / C↓ Bb G / C F C -

There is darkness in the land, I seek the taste of hope **(2x)**
There is darkness in the land with sorrows more than we can stand
Hope lives in these quiet hills

There is darkness in my heart, but the taste of hope is sweet **(2x)**
There is darkness in my heart yet I can feel the healing start...

II: G - C G / - - - D / G - - - / - - C G

— w & m: Claudia Schmidt

READY FOR THE STORM

Oh the waves crash in & the tide pulls out, it's an angry sea but there is no doubt
That the lighthouse will keep shining out to warn the lonely sailor
And the lightning strikes and the wind cuts cold thru the sailor's bones to the sailor's soul
Til there's nothing left that he can hold except the rolling ocean

(↑5) Am - G - / F - Em - :‖

But I am ready for the storm, yes sir ready
I am ready for the storm, I'm ready for the storm _

Am F G - / Am F G - Am - - -

Oh give me mercy for my dreams 'cos every confrontation
Seems to tell me what it really means to be this lonely sailor
And when you take me by your side, you love me warm, you love me
And I should have realized, I had no reason to be frightened

Oh & distance it is no real friend & time will take its time
And you will find that in the end it brings you me, the lonely sailor
But when the sky begins to clear the sun it melts away my fear
I'll cry a silent, weary tear for those that need to love me

— w & m: Douglas Menzies MacLean

RIGHT HERE

We traveled long, we traveled far
To be right here, where we are
Reach out a hand, no need to fear
'Cos all we need is right here
All we need, all we need / All we need is right here (repeat)

D - G - / D - A - / D - G - / D A D(G D) :‖

The night was dark but the day is bright
Together we can lift our eyes
To all we love & we hold dear / **'Cos all...**

— w & m: Sam Turton

© 2005 Sam Turton (SOCAN). On his *At Home* 14.

ROCK ME ON THE WATER

O people, look around you, the signs are everywhere
You've left it for somebody other than you to be the one to care
You're lost inside your houses, there's no time to find you now
For your walls are burning & your towers are turning, I'm going
    to leave you here & try to get down to the sea somehow _

G Em C G(C) / GF CD Em - / G Em C A / G D Em C G* -

The road is filled with homeless souls, every woman, child & man
Who have no idea where they will go but they'll help you if they can
Now everyone must have some thought that's going to pull them
    thru somehow
Well the fires are raging hotter & hotter but the sisters of the sun
    are going to rock me on the water now **(*omit G)**

Rock me on the water, sister will you soothe my fevered brow
Rock me on the water, I'll get down to the sea somehow

GD C GD C / GD Em A C (G Em CG A G D EmG C)

O people, look among you, it's there your hope must lie
There's a seabird above you gliding in one place like Jesus in the sky
We all must do the best we can & then hang on to that gospel plow
When my life is over, I'm going to stand before the father, but the
    sisters of the sun are going to rock me... now

— w & m: Jackson Browne

©1971 (renewed) Swallow Turn Music (ASCAP). On his debut album, Johnny Rivers *Home Grown*, Brown & Shipley *Shake off the Dream* & Linda Ronstadt (her 3rd alb)

SHELTER FROM THE STORM

'Twas in another lifetime, one of toil & blood
When blackness was a virtue & the road was full of mud
I came in from the wilderness, a creature void of form
"Come in" she said "I'll give you shelter from the storm"

C Em F C / C Em F - / / 1st

And if I pass this way again, you can rest assured
I'll always do my best for her, on that I give my word
In a world of steel-eyed death, and men who are fighting to be warm
"Come in" she said...

Not a word was spoke between us, there was little risk involved
Everything up to that point had been left unresolved
Try imagining a place where it's always safe & warm...

I was burned out from exhaustion, buried in the hail
Poisoned in the bushes & blown out on the trail
Hunted like a crocodile, ravaged in the corn...

Suddenly I turned around & she was standin' there
With silver bracelets on her wrists & flowers in her hair
She walked up to me so gracefully & took my crown of thorns...

Now there's a wall between us, smth there's been lost
I took too much for granted, got my signals crossed
Just to think that it all began on a long-forgotten morn...

Well, the deputy walks on hard nails & the preacher rides a mount
But nothing really matters much, it's doom alone that counts
And the one-eyed undertaker, he blows a futile horn...

I've heard newborn babies wailin' like a mourning dove
And old men with broken teeth stranded without love
Do I understand your question, man, is it hopeless & forlorn?...

In a little hilltop village, they gambled for my clothes
I bargained for salvation & they gave me a lethal dose
I offered up my innocence & got repaid with scorn...

Well I'm livin' in a foreign country but I'm bound to cross the line
Beauty walks a razor's edge, someday I'll make it mine
If I could only turn back the clock to when God & her were born...

— w & m: Bob Dylan

© 1974, 1976 Ram's Horn Music. On his *Blood on the Tracks* 14, Jimmy LaFave *Austin Skyline*, Rodney Crowell *The Outsider.*

SHOW THE WAY

You say you see no hope, you say you see no reason we should dream
That the world would ever change, you're saying love is
    foolish to believe
'Cos there'll always be some crazy with an army or a knife
To wake you from your daydream, put the fear back in your life

C Am / Dm G :‖

Look, if someone wrote a play just to glorify what's stronger than hate
Would they not arrange the stage to look as if the hero came too late?
He's almost in defeat, it's looking like the evil side will win
So on the edge of every seat from the moment that the whole
    thing begins, it is:

Love who mixed the mortar & it's love who stacked
    these stones
And it's love who made the stage here altho' it looks like
    we're alone
In this scene set in shadows like the night is here to stay
There is evil cast around us but it's love that wrote the play
For in this darkness love can show the way

F G C Am / F - G - / 1st / F - G F / Dm G C -

So now the stage is set, feel your own heart beating in your chest
This life's not over yet so we get up on our feet & do our best
We play against the fear, we play against the reasons not to try
We're playing for the tears burning in the happy angel's eyes, for it's:

— w & m: David Wilcox

© 1994 Irving Music, Inc. & Midnight Ocean Bonfire Music. All rights administered by Irving Music, Inc. On his *Big Horizon* 15 & *Live S & Stories.* Also rec by Peter Paul and Mary *Discovered: Live in Conc.*

SHOWER THE PEOPLE

You can play the game & you can act out the part
Tho' you know it wasn't written for you
Tell me, how can you stand there with your broken heart
Ashamed of playing the fool?
One thing can lead to another / It doesn't take any sacrifice
Oh father & mother, sister & brother
If it feels nice, don't think twice, just:

C G / Am F :|| (4x)

**Shower the people you love with love
Show them the way that you feel
Things are gonna be much better / If we only will**

Dm7 G /   / Dm7 GE / Am

You can run but you cannot hide / This is widely known
And what you plan to do with your foolish pride
When you're all by yourself alone
Once you tell somebody the way that you feel
You can feel it beginning to ease
I think it's true what they say about the squeaky wheel
Always getting the grease, better to...

— w & m: James Taylor

SINGING THROUGH THE HARD TIMES

Sometimes our living gets so dark & lonesome
It seems like there's nothing we can do
So we reach out to each other & raise a song together
And let our voices carry us thru

E - A - / E - B7 - / 1st / E B7 E -

**We are singing thru the hard times (x2)
Working for the good times to come (repeat)**

And when the war clouds gather, it's so easy to get angry
And just as hard not to be afraid
But you know in your own heart, no matter what happens
You just can't turn your back & walk away

So hand in hand together, we help each other carry
The light of peace within us every day
If we can learn to live it, to walk & talk & give it
That world of peace won't be so far away

— w & m: Utah Phillips

SOMEWHERE TO BEGIN

**People say to me, you gotta be crazy
How can you <u>sing</u> in times like these?
Don't you read the news, don't you know the score?
How can you <u>sing</u> when so many others grieve?**

(↑2)   G D Em C / G Em D - :||

People say to me, what kind of fool believes
That <u>songs</u> will make a difference in the end?
By way of a reply, I say a fool such as I
Who sees a <u>song</u> as somewhere to begin

G D Em C / G Em D - / 1st / G D G -

A <u>song</u> is somewhere to begin
A search for something worth believing in
If changes are to come, there are things that must be done
And a <u>song</u> is somewhere to begin

G D C - / G Em D - / G D Em C / G D G -

(insert: dream / a dream, love / love**)**

— w & m: T.R. Ritchie

THREE LITTLE BIRDS

**Don't w<u>o</u>rry about a thing
'Cos <u>e</u>very little thing gonna be all <u>r</u>ight
Singin', don't w<u>o</u>rry... / ...all right!**

A - / D A :||

Rise up this m<u>o</u>rnin' smiled with the <u>ri</u>sin' sun
3 little b<u>i</u>rds sit by my d<u>oo</u>rstep
Singin' sw<u>ee</u>t songs of melodies p<u>u</u>re & true
Singin'_this is my message to y<u>ou</u>:

A E / A D / A E / D A

— w & m: Bob Marley

TURN THE WORLD AROUND

We come from the <u>fire</u>, living in the <u>fire</u>
Go back to the <u>fire</u>, turn the world around **(repeat)**

G C D G **(etc. - repeat as needed)**

We come from the water, living in the... **(repeat)**
We come from the mountain, living <u>on</u>... **(repeat)**
Whoa oh so is life / ah ha so is life **(repeat)**

**Do you know who I am? Do I know who you are?
See we one another clearly - do we know who we are?
Do you know who I am? Do I know who you are?
See we one another clearly - do we know who we are?
Whoa oh so is life a ba tee / wah ha ah so is life (repeat 4x)**

Water make the river, river wash the mountain
Fire make the sunlight, **turn...**
Heart is of the river, body is the mountain
Spirit is the sunlight, **turn...**
We are of the spirit, truly of the spirit
Only can the spirit, **turn... (repeat)**

— w & m: Harry Belafonte & Robert Freedman

UNKNOWN BLESSINGS

O the stars above us twinkle, yeah they put on quite a show
They say the light that meets our eyes today
   was born a million years ago
And it spells out quite a story in strands of DNA
The same spark that birthed the universe is born in us today

(↑2)   C ↓ F C / C ↓ ↓ F G / 1st / C ↓ F -

And they're already on their way (x2)
Give thanks for unknown blessings already… (repeat)

C↓ F CG / C ↓ FG C :|

O this world is a funhouse mirror, sometimes you feel just like a clown
Everything's distorted, everything seems upside down
And the truth it just gets twisted like a rope gets torn & frayed
Till you feel like you can't hold on no more
   till you just might slip away

Well now history's a spiral, sometimes it's hard to see
Thru the smoke & the blood & the tear-gas that it's the path of victory
It's a crooked road we walk upon strung with miracles on the way
But like raindrops to the ocean we'll make it there someday
And we're already on our way…

— w & m: Ben Bochner

© 2012 Ben Bochner. On his *Heartland*. •LS

WHAT A WONDERFUL WORLD

I see trees of green, red roses too
I see them bloom for me & for you
And I think to myself, what a wonderful world

C Em F Em / Dm C E7 Am / Ab - Dm G C (- Fmaj7 G)

I see skies of blue, clouds of white
Bright blessed days, dark sacred nights
And I think…

(bridge) The colors of a rainbow so pretty in the sky
Are also on the faces of people going by
I see friends shaking hands saying "How do you do?"
They're really saying "I love you"

Dm G C - /   / Am G Am G / Am Edim Dm G7

I hear babies cry, I watch them grow
They'll learn much more than I'll ever know…

II: C Em F C / F C E Am / F - G - Am - F -
/   "   /   "   / F - G - C F C -
(bridge) G - C - /   / F C F C / F C Dm - G -

— w & m: George David Weiss & Bob Thiele

© 1967 by Range Road Music Inc., Quartet Music & Abilene Music, Inc. Copyright renewed. All rights for Quartet Music administered by BMG Rights Management (US) LLC. All rights for Abilene Music, Inc. administered worldwide by Imagem Music LLC. Louis Armstrong 15, Israel "IZ" Kamakawiwo'ole (II). Playing for Change. In Peter Amidon *25 Anthems for Interfaith & Comty Choirs*.

WHY WALK WHEN YOU CAN FLY

In this world there's a whole lot of trouble, baby
In this world there's a whole lot of pain
In this world there's a whole lot of trouble but
A whole lot of ground to gain
   Why take when you could be giving?
   Why watch as the world goes by?
   It's a hard enough life to be living
   Why walk when you can fly?   (in G)

DG C / / / Em C // C G / AmG C / DG C / Em C

In this world… sorrow / **In this world**… shame
In this world… sorrow / And a whole lot of ground to gain
   When you spend your whole life wishing
   Wanting & wondering why
   It's a long enough life to be living
   Why walk when you can fly?

In this world… golden / **In this world**… plain
In this world you've a soul for a compass
And a heart for a pair of wings
   There's a star on the far horizon
   Rising bright in an azure sky
   For the rest of the time that you're given / **Why walk…**

— w & m: Mary Chapin Carpenter

© 1994 Why Walk Music. On her *Stones in the Road*.

WITCH HAZEL

I am looking at a witch hazel blooming in a garden
Bright yellow flowers in the middle of wintertime
And I tell my heart be strong like the witch hazel flower
And you will not be injured by this dark & troubled time

C C7 F C / - Am D G / 1st / C Am DG C

D D7 G D / D Bm E A / 1st / D Bm EA D

Oh, I take myself along to a place I know in winter
And I look at that south sloping bank all covered with ice
And I tell my heart it all will melt & run down to the ocean
And you will not be injured…

We must say goodbye to the one we love, we must say
   goodbye to many
And we must say goodbye in way too short a time
And I tell my heart be strong like the witch hazel flower…

— w & m: Tom Gala

© 1989 Tom Gala. On his *Story After Story* 15, Kitty Kelly & the Phila. Ceili Band, Herdman Hills & Mangsen *Voices of Winter* and on YT 12.

The **Hope & Strength** chapter contains songs to inspire & honor our journey of keeping hope alive & our capacity to carry on. See also: **Dignity & Diversity, Dreams, Earthcare, Faith, Friendship & Community, Gospel, Healing, Lullabies, Peace, Sing People Sing, Struggle.**

Other songs include: **Blues**: Don't ever let nobody drag your spirit down, **Country**: The river, **Good**: Don't worry be happy, **Family**: Bring him home, We will build this house, **Farm**: Tumbling tumbleweed, **Home**: Sacred ground, **Millennial**: I won't give up, **Musicals**: I dreamed a dream, **Outdoors**: Redbird's wing, Wings to fly, **Sea**: Down by the river, **Trav**: Rusty old Amer dream.

Jazz & Swing

AIN'T MISBEHAVIN'

No one to talk with, all by myself
No one to walk with but I'm happy on the shelf
Ain't misbehavin', I'm savin' my love for you

G E7 Am D7 / G G7 C Cm / G E7 Am D7 G - - -

I know for certain the one I love
I'm thru with flirtin', it's just you I'm thinkin' of / **Ain't...**

(bridge) Like Jack Horner in the corner
Don't go nowhere, what do I care?
Your kisses are worth waitin' for, believe me

Em - C7 - / A7 - E7 - / D B7 Em A7   D E7 A7 D7

I don't stay out late, don't care to go
I'm home about 8, just me & my radio / **Ain't...**

— w: Andy Razaf, m: Thomas "Fats" Waller & Harry Brooks

AIN'T SHE SWEET

Ain't she sweet, see her walking down that street
Now I ask you very confidentially, ain't she sweet?
Ain't she <u>nice</u>, look her over once or twice
Now I ask you... ain't she nice?
    Just cast an eye in her direction
    O me o my, ain't that perfection?
I repeat: don't you think that's kind of neat?
And I ask... ain't she sweet?

(in c) C Ab G7 C Ab G7 / C E7 A7 D7 G7 C :‖

F7 - C - / F7 - C Dm G7 / as above

— w: Jack Yellen, m: Milton Ager

BEI MIR BIST DU SCHÖN
(Means That You're Grand)

(intro) Of all the boys I've known & I've known some
Until I first met you, I was lonesome
And when you came in sight, dear, my heart grew light
And this whole world seemed new to me
You're really swell, I have to admit you
Deserve expressions that really fit you
And so I've racked my brain hoping to explain
All the things that you do to me

Am Dm E7 / Am Dm E7 / Am Dm / Adim E :‖

Bei mir bist du schön, please let me explain
Bei mir... means you're grand / **Bei...** again I'll explain
It means you're the fairest in the land
I could say bella bella, even say wunderbar
Each language only helps me tell you how grand you are
I've tried to explain, **bei mir... schön**
So kiss me & say you understand

Am - - - / E7 - Am - :‖ Dm - Am - / Dm - E7 - / 1st 2

The bear missed the train **(x2)** / *The bear... & now he's walking*
He's walking here & there, he's walking everywhere
He's walking up & down, he's walking thru the town!

The chicken caught a cold **(x2)** / *The... & now he's sneezing*
He aches from head to toe, his little head does droop
His mother cooked herself to make him chicken soup!

— Original w: Jacob Jacobs, m: Sholom Secunda

BEWITCHED

He's a fool & don't I know it, but a fool can have his charms
I'm in love & don't I show it? Like a babe in arms
Love's the same old sad sensation, lately I've not slept a wink
But this half-pint imitation put me on the blink

Dm G Em A7 Dm G Em Edim / Dm G Em Am Dm7 Cmaj7
/   "   / Dm G Em Am Dm7 G

I'm wild again, beguiled again / A simpering, whimpering
    child again / **Bewitched, bothered & bewildered am I**
Couldn't sleep & wouldn't sleep / When love came & told me I
    shouldn't sleep / **Bewitched...**

C Dm7 / C E F Ddim / C D G A Dm7 G7
/ " /   "   / C D G C7 F A7

Lost my heart, but what of it? / My mistake *[he is cold]* I agree
He's such a laugh, but I love it / Altho' the laugh's on me

Dm - / Am - / Dm G / Em7 Am Dm G

I'll sing to him each spring to him / And long for the day when
    I'll cling to him / **Bewitched...**

C Dm7 / C E F Ddim / C D Dm G C -

— w: Lorenz Hart, m: Richard Rodgers

CHATTANOOGA CHOO-CHOO

Pardon me, boy, is that the Chattanooga choo-choo?
Track 29, boy, you can gimme a shine
I can afford to board a Chattanooga choo-choo
I've got my fare, & just a trifle to spare

G - - - / AmD AmD G - :‖

(bridge) You leave the Pennsylvania Station 'bout a quarter to 4,
    read a magazine & then you're in Baltimore
Dinner in the diner, nothing could be finer than to have your
    ham 'n' eggs in Carolina
When you hear the whistle blowin' 8 to the bar, then you know
    that Tennessee is not very far
Shovel all the coal in, gotta keep it rollin', woo woo, Chattanooga,
    there you are

CG (x3) CC7 / FAdim CA D7 AbG7

/   "   / FAdim CA D7 GC

There's gonna be a certain party at the station
Satin & lace, I used to call "funny face"
She's gonna cry, until I tell her that I'll never roam
So Chattanooga choo-choo, won't you choo-choo me home?

G - - - / AmD AmD G - / - - C EbA7 / GEm AD G -

— w: Mack Gordon, m: Harry Warren

© 1941 (renewed) Twentieth Century Music Corp. All rights administered by EMI
Feist Catalog Inc. (Publishing) & Alfred Music (Print). Rec by Glenn Miller w/ Tex
Beneke. In film *Sun Valley Serenade*.

CHEEK TO CHEEK

Heaven, I'm in heaven
And my heart beats so that I can hardly speak
And I seem to find the happiness I seek
When we're out together **dancing cheek to cheek**   (↑2)

GEm AmD x2 / GBm EmA B7 E / Am D B7 E / Am D G -

Heaven, I'm in heaven
And the cares that hung around me thru the week
Seem to vanish like a gambler's lucky streak
When we're out together **dancing cheek to cheek**

(bridge) O I love to climb a mountain & to reach the highest peak
But it doesn't thrill me half as much as **dancing cheek to...**
O I love to go out fishing in a river or a creek
But I don't enjoy it half as much as **dancing cheek to cheek**
    Dance with me, I want my arm about you
    The charm about you will carry me thru to **heaven, I'm in...**

D GDG / DG Am7D G :‖ Gm - Eb - / D - Em7 AD

— w & m: Irving Berlin

© 1935 by Irving Berlin. Copyright renewed. In '35 Fred Astaire film *Top Hat* 15.
Rec by Fitzgerald & Armstrong 11, Sinatra 13, Bennett & Gaga

DINAH

Dinah, is there anyone finer in the state of Carolina?
If there is & you know her, show her to me!
Dinah, with her Dixie eyes blazin'
How I love to sit & gaze into the eyes of Dinah Lee!
    Every night, why do I shake with fright?
    Because my Dinah might change her mind about me!
Dinah — If she wandered to China
I would hop an ocean liner, just to be with Dinah Lee!

D - - - / A7 - D(Ddim EmA) :‖

Bm Daug Bm - / E - A - / 1st 2 above

— w: Sam M. Lewis & Joe Young, m: Harry Akst

© 1925 Mills Music, Inc. Copyright renewed Morley Music Co., B & G Akst
Publishing Co. & Mills Music, Inc. Harry Akst Reversionary Interest controlled by
Bourne Co. (ASCAP). Introduced by Eddie Cantor in the '23 musical *Kid Boots*.
Rec by Chet Baker, Louis Armstrong, Fats Waller, Bing Crosby 13.

DON'T GET AROUND MUCH ANYMORE

Missed the Saturday dance, heard they crowded the floor
Couldn't bear it without you, **don't get around much anymore**
Thought I'd visit the club, got as far as the door
They'd have asked me about you, **don't get around...**
    Darling, I guess my mind's more at ease
    But nevertheless, why stir up memories?
Been invited on dates, might have gone but what for?
Awfully different without you, **don't get around...**

(↑2) G - E7 - / A7 D7 G (D7) :‖

C - G - / A7 C BmE AmD7 / 1st 2 above

— w & m: Duke Ellington & Bob Russell

© 1942 Sony/ATV Music Publishing LLC & Music Sales Corporation. Copyright
renewed. All rights on behalf of Sony/ATV Music Publishing LLC administered
by Sony/ATV Music Publishing LLC, 424 Church Street, Suite 1200, Nashville, TN
37219. Orig recs by Ellington 16 & by The Ink Spots 14. Also Ella (F), Etta James,
Nat King Cole, Tony Bennett 13, Willie Nelson, Harry Connick Jr.

DON'T SIT UNDER THE APPLE TREE
(With Anyone Else But Me)

(intro) I wrote my mother, I wrote my father
And now I'm writing you too
I'm sure of mother, I'm sure of father
And now I want to be sure, very very sure of you

C A Dm G / C A D G / 1st / D7 - G -

Don't sit under the apple tree with anyone else but me
Anyone else but me, anyone else but me (no, no, no)
Don't sit under the apple tree
Til I come marching home

C - - - / G - C CG / C - - A / D7 G C (G)

Don't go walking down lovers' lane with **anyone else...**
Anyone else but me...
Don't go showing off all your charms in somebody else's arms
You must be true to me

(bridge) I just got word from a guy who heard from the
    guy next door to me
The girl he met just loves to pet & it fits you to a "T"
So don't sit under the apple tree / **Til I come marching home**

F D7 CG7 C / Am D7 G7 - / C - - A7 / D7 G7 C -

Don't give out with those lips of yours to **anyone else...**
Watch the girls on the foreign shores, you have to report to me
When you **come marchin' home**

Don't hold anyone on your knee, you'd better be true to me,
You better be true to me **(2x)**
Don't hold anyone on your knee, you're gettin' the 3rd degree
When you **come marchin' home**

(bridge) When you're on your own where there is no phone &
    I can't keep tab on you
Be fair to me, I'll guarantee this is one thing that I'll do
I won't sit under the apple tree with anyone else but you / **Til...**

Don't sit under the apple tree with **anyone... / Anyone...**
I know the apple tree is reserved for you & me / **Til you...**

    — w & m: Lew Brown, Sam H. Stept & Charlie Tobias

GEORGIA ON MY MIND

Georgia, Georgia, the whole day thru
Just an old sweet song keeps Georgia on my mind
Georgia, Georgia, a song of you
Comes as sweet & clear as moonlight thru the pines

C E7 Am FFm / CA7 DmG E(A D7G)

C E7 Am FFm / CA7 DmG C(F CE)

    Other arms reach out to me, other eyes smile tenderly
    Still in peaceful dreams I see, the road leads back to you

AmDm AmF AmDm AmD / AmDm CB7 EmA DmG

Georgia, Georgia, no peace I find
Just an old sweet song keeps Georgia on my mind **(2x)**

C E7 Am FFm / CA7 DmG E7 A7 / D7 G CF C

    — w: Stuart Gorrell, m: Hoagy Carmichael

I CAN'T GIVE YOU ANYTHING BUT LOVE

I can't give you anything but love, baby
That's the only thing I've plenty of, baby
Dream awhile, scheme awhile, we're sure to find
Happiness & I guess all those things you've always pined for
Gee I'd like to see you looking swell, baby
Diamond bracelets Woolworth doesn't sell, baby
Til that lucky day you know darned well, baby / I can't...

C - Dm7 G / 1st / C7 - F - / D7 - G - /
    "   / C7 - F - / - Adim C A7 / Dm G C -

    — w & m: Jimmy McHugh & Dorothy Fields

I GOT RHYTHM

I got rhythm, I got music
I got my gal *[man]*, **who could ask for anything more?**
I got daisies in green pastures
I got my gal *[man]*, **who...**
Old man trouble I don't mind him
You won't find him 'round my door
I got starlight, I got sweet dreams
I got my gal *[man]*, **who...**

CA DmG CA DmG / CA DmG DmG C :‖

E7 - A7 - / D7 - G7 - / 1st 2 above

    — w & m: George Gershwin & Ira Gershwin

I'M GONNA SIT RIGHT DOWN & WRITE MYSELF A LETTER

I'm gonna sit right down & write myself a letter
And make believe it came from you
I'm gonna write words, oh so sweet, they're gonna knock me
    off my feet
A lot of kisses on the bottom, I'll be glad I got 'em
I'm gonna smile & say "I hope you're feeling better"
And close "with love" the way you do
I'm gonna sit right down...

G Em Gmaj7 Em / G B7 CE7 Am / - D7 G E7 / A7 - D7 -
/   "   /   "   / C A7 G E7 / A7 D7 G -

    — w: Joe Young, m: Fred E. Ahlert

IS YOU IS, OR IS YOU AIN'T (Ma' Baby)

I got a gal who's always late any time we have a date
But I love her, yes I love her
I'm gonna walk up to her gate & see if I can get it straight
'Cos I want her, I'm gonna ask her

EmD CB7 EmD CB7 / C7 - B7 - :‖

Is you is or is you ain't my baby
The way you're acting lately makes me doubt
You is still my baby, baby
Seems my flame in your heart's done gone out

EmD CB7 Em - /A7 D7 G B7 / 1st / A7 D7 G -

(bridge) A woman is a creature that has always been strange
Just when you're sure of one you'll find she's gone & made a change

C Cm G G7 / C F E7 AmB7

Is you... / Maybe baby's found somebody new
Or is my baby still my baby true?

EmD CB7 Em - /A7 D7 B7 E7 / A7 D7 G (B7)

    — w & m: Billy Austin & Louis Jordan

ISTANBUL (Not Constantinople)

Istanbul was **Constantinople**
Now it's Istanbul, not Constantinople
Been a long time gone, old Constantinople
Still it's Turkish delight on a moonlit night

Em - / - - / B7 - / Em -

Every gal in **Constantinople** / Lives in Istanbul, not...
So if you've a date in... / She'll be waiting in Istanbul

(bridge) Even old New York / Was once New Amsterdam
Why they changed it I can't say / People just liked it better that way

Em - / 　 / C B7 / Em B7 /

Take me back to... / No, you can't go back to...
Now it's Istanbul, not... [*Been a long time gone…*]
Why did Constantinople get the works?
That's nobody's business but the Turks

Em - / 　 / B7 - / Em B7 / - Em

— w: Jimmy Kennedy, m: Nat Simon

© 1953 by Chappell & Co. Copyright renewed. Rec by The Four Lads ♪, They
Might Be Giants ♪.

IT'S A SIN TO TELL A LIE

Be sure it's true when you say "I love you"
It's a sin to tell a lie
Millions of hearts have been broken
Just because these words were spoken
I love you, yes, I do, I love you
If you break my heart I'll die, so
Be sure it's true...

C B7 C - / C E7 FA Dm / G7 - B7 C / D7 - Ab G7 /
/ 　 " 　 / 　 " 　 / F Fm C A7 / D7 G C - /

— w & m: Billy Mayhew

© 1936 (renewed) WB Music Corp. Orig rec by Fats Waller. Also Ink Spots '41,
Holliday '42 ♪, Something Smith & the Redheads '55 in Bb, Bennett '64. In DULY.

IT'S ONLY A PAPER MOON

Say it's only a paper moon sailing over a cardboard sea
But it wouldn't be make-believe if you believed in me
Yes, it's only a canvas sky hanging over a muslin tree
But it wouldn't be make-believe if...
　　Without your love, it's a honky-tonk parade
　　Without your love, it's a melody played in a penny arcade
It's a Barnum & Bailey world, just as phony as it can be / **But...**

C A7 Dm G Dm7 G C - / C A7 F D7 Dm7 G C - :‖
F Gaug C - Dm G C - / F Gaug C A7 Em A Dm G
/ 1st 2 above /

— w: Billy Rose & E.Y. "Yip" Harburg, m: Harold Arlen

© 1933 (renewed) Chappell & Co., Inc., Glocca Morra Music & S.A. Music Co. All
rights for Glocca Morra Music administered by Shapiro, Bernstein & Co., Inc. Orig
in Broadway play The Great Magoo set in Coney Island. In '33 film Take a Chance.
Rec by Paul Whiteman orch w/ Peggy Healey (used in '73 film Paper Moon) ♪,
Ella '45 in Bb, Nat King Cole, Sinatra ♪. McCartney ♪.

LET'S DO IT (Let's Fall In Love)

Birds do it, bees do it,_even educated fleas do it
Let's do it, let's fall in love
In Spain, the best upper sets do it, _Lithuanians & Letts do it
Let's do it, let's fall in love
The Dutch in old Amsterdam do it,_not to mention the Finns
Folks in Siam do it, _think of Siamese twins
Some Argentines without means do it, people say in Boston
　　even beans do it
Let's do it, let's fall in love

(↑2) C G C FFm / C G CAm FG / 1st / C G CF C
Am D7 G C7 / F Fm Eb G / C G C FFm / C G CF C

Romantic sponges (they say) do it, oysters down in Oyster Bay do it
Let's do it, let's fall in love
Cold Cape Cod clams ('gainst their wish) do it, even lazy jellyfish
　　do it / **Let's do it, let's...**
Electric eels, I might add, do it, tho' it shocks 'em I know
Why ask if shad do it? Waiter bring me shad roe!
In shallow shoals English soles do it, goldfish in the privacy of bowls
　　do it / **Let's do it ...**

The dragonflies in the reeds do it, sentimental centipedes do it...
Mosquitos (heaven forbid!) do it, so does every katydid do it...
The most refined ladybugs do it when a gentleman calls
Moths in your rugs do it, what's the use of moth balls?
Locusts in trees do it, bees do it, even over-educated fleas do it...

The chimpanzees in the zoo do it, some courageous kangaroos do it
Let's do it, let's fall in love
I'm sure giraffes on the sly do it, heavy hippopotami do it / **Let's...**
Old sloths who hang down from the twigs do it,
　　tho' the effort is great
Sweet guinea pigs do it, buy a couple & wait
The world admits bears in pits do it, even pekineses in the Ritz do it
Let's do it, let's fall in love

— w & m: Cole Porter

© 1928 (renewed) WB Music Corp. Written for Irène Bordoni to sing in musical
Paris. In films Grand Slam '33, Can-Can '60 & Midnight in Paris '11. Rec by Billie ♪,
Ella ♪, Frank (in A). Orig 1st line contains ethnic slurs.

LET'S GET AWAY FROM IT ALL

Let's take a boat to Bermuda, let's take a plane to St. Paul
Let's take a kayak to Quincy or Nyack, **let's get away from it all**
Let's take a trip in a trailer, no need to come back at all
Let's take a powder to Boston for chowder, **let's get away...**
　　We'll travel 'round from town to town, we'll visit ev'ry state
　　And I'll repeat "I love you, Sweet!" in all the 48
Let's go again to Niag'ra, this time we'll look at the Fall
Let's leave our hut, dear, get out of our rut, dear, **let's get...**

CDm CC7 FD EmA7 / DmG EmA D G
/ 　　 " 　　 / DmG EmA DG C
FD EmA DmG C / GE Am D G / as lines 3 & 4

— w & m: Tom Adair & Matt Dennis

© 1941 (renewed) by Music Sales Corporation (ASCAP). Rec by Jo Stafford ♪,
Sinatra, Rosemary Clooney ♪.

MY BABY JUST CARES FOR ME

My baby don't care for shows, my baby don't care for clothes

My baby just cares for me

My baby don't care for furs & laces [cars & races]

My baby don't care for high-toned places

My baby don't care for rings or other expensive things

She's sensible as can be

[Liz Taylor is not his style & even Lana Turner's smile

Is somethinga he can't see]

My baby don't care who knows it / **My baby just...**

G - - - / - BmE Am - / - B7 Em - / A7 - D7 -
G - - - / Dm DmE Am - / C F#7 G E7 / Am D G -

— w: Gus Kahn, m: Walter Donaldson

ON A SLOW BOAT TO CHINA

I'd love to get you on a slow boat to China

All to myself alone

Get you & keep you in my arms evermore

Leave all your lovers weeping on a faraway shore

Out on the briny with the moon big & shiny

Melting your heart of stone

I'd like to get you on a slow boat to China

All to myself alone

G E C Edim / G B7 C E / C Edim G E / A7 - Am D
/   "   /   "   / C Cm G E / A D G -

— w & m: Frank Loesser

ON THE SUNNY SIDE OF THE STREET

Grab your coat & get your hat, leave your worry on the doorstep

Just direct your feet **to the sunny side of the street**

Can't you hear a pitter-pat & that happy tune is your step?

Life can be so sweet **on the sunny side...**

    I used to walk in the shade, with those blues on parade

    But I'm not afraid this rover crossed over

If I never have a cent, I'll be rich as Rockefeller

Gold dust at my feet **on the sunny...**

G B7 C D / Em A7 Am D /   1st   / Em A7 AmD G
G7 - C - / A7 - D7 - / G B7 C D /   "   /

— w: Dorothy Fields, m: Jimmy McHugh

(OUR) LOVE IS HERE TO STAY

It's very clear _our love is here to stay_

Not for a year, _but ever & a day _

The radio & the telephone & the movies that we know

May just be passing fancies _ & in time may go _ (in C - starts G,A)

(G7) D7 Dm7G C - / D7 Dm7G Gm7 A /
GA7 Dm7G CF BmE / Am D7 Dm7 G

But oh my dear, our love is here to stay

Together we're going a long, long way

In time the Rockies may crumble, Gibraltar may tumble: they're

    only made of clay / But our love is here to stay

1st 2 above / G A7 Dm7G EA7 DmAdim / CAm Dm7G C -

— w & m: George Gershwin & Ira Gershwin

PENNIES FROM HEAVEN

Every time it rains, it rains **pennies from heaven**

Don't you know each cloud contains **pennies...?**

You'll find your fortune falling all over the town

Be sure that your umbrella is upside down

Trade them for a package of sunshine & flowers

If you want the things you love, you must have showers

So, when you hear it thunder, don't run under a tree

There'll be **pennies...** for you & me

(↑2) C D7 F G /   / C7 - F A7 / D7 - G -
/   "   / C C7 F - / - Fm Em A7 / D7 G C -

— w: John Burke, m: Arthur Johnston

SAN ANTONIO ROSE

Deep within my heart lies a melody

A song of old San Antone

Where in dreams I live with a memory

Beneath the stars all alone

G - C A / D - G - :‖

It was there I found beside the Alamo

Enchantment strange as the blue up above

A moonlit path that only she would know

Still hears my broken song of love

(bridge) Moon in all your splendor know only my heart

Call back my Rose, Rose of San Antone

Lips so sweet & tender like petals falling apart

Speak once again of my love, my own

D - A - / - - D (D7) :‖

Broken song, empty words I know

Still live in my heart all alone

For that moonlit path by the Alamo

And Rose, my Rose of San Antone

— w & m: Bob Wills

STRAIGHTEN UP & FLY RIGHT

(intro) A buzzard took a monkey for a ride in the air,
  the monkey thought that everything was on the square
The buzzard tried to throw the monkey off of his back,
  but the monkey grabbed his neck & said "Now listen, Jack:

G G7 C EmD /   /

Straighten up & fly right, straighten up & stay right
Straighten up & fly right - cool down papa, don't you blow
  your top
Ain't no use in divin', what's the use of jivin'
Straighten up & fly right - cool down papa..."

G Dm C AmD / G Dm C EmD / 1st / G Dm C DG

The buzzard told the monkey "You are chokin' me, release your
  hold & I will set you free"
The monkey looked the buzzard right dead in the eye & said
  "Your story's kind of touching but it sounds just like a lie
Straighten up & fly right, straighten up & stay right
Straighten up & fly right - cool down papa, don't you blow
  your top"

B7 - E7 - / A7 - D7 - / G Dm C EmD / G Dm C DG

— w & m: Nat King Cole & Irving Mills

SWEET GEORGIA BROWN

No gal made has got a shade on **Sweet Georgia Brown**
Two left feet, but oh so neat, has Sweet...
They all sigh & want to die for...
I'll tell you just why, you know I don't lie, not much

(in C starts on A,B,C#) A7 - - - / D7 - - - / G7 - - - /
C G C E7

It's been said she knocks 'em dead when she lands in town
Since she came, why it's a shame, how she cools them down
Fellers she can't get are fellers she ain't met
Georgia claimed her, Georgia named her, **Sweet...**

/   "   /   "   /Am E7 Am E7 / C A7 D7G7 C

All those tips the porter slips to **Sweet...**
They buy clothes at fashion shows with one dollar down
Oh boy! tip your hats! Oh joy! she's the "cat's"!
Who's that, Mister? 'Tain't her sister! **Sweet...**

— w & m: Ben Bernie, Maceo Pinkard & Kenneth Casey

THEY CAN'T TAKE THAT AWAY FROM ME

The way you wear your hat, the way you sip your tea
The memory of all that, **no no, they can't take that away...**
The way your smile just beams, the way you sing off key
The way you haunt my dreams, **no...**

C - Dm7 G7 / C Gm FA Dm7 / 1st / Gm - FG C(B7)

We may never, never meet again on the bumpy road to love
Still I'll always, always keep the memory of

EmA7 (x3) Em / EmA EmA7 Dm7 G

The way you hold your knife, the way we danced 'til 3
The way you've changed my life, oh **no, they... / No they...**

C - Dm7 G7 / Gm7 - FE7 Am7Fm / C Dm7G C -

— w & m: George Gershwin & Ira Gershwin

WHEN YOU'RE SMILING
(The Whole World Smiles with You)

When you're smiling **(x2)** / The whole world smiles with you
When you're laughing **(x2)** / The sun comes shinin' thru
But when you're crying you bring on the rain
So stop your sighing, be happy again
Keep on smiling 'cos when you're smiling
The whole world smiles with you

G Bm / E Am / - Am7 / D G /
G7 C / A D / G E7 /AmD G

— w & m: Mark Fisher, Joe Goodwin & Larry Shay

YOU'RE NOBODY 'TIL SOMEBODY LOVES YOU

You're nobody til somebody loves you
You're nobody til somebody cares
You may be king, you may possess the world & its gold
But gold won't bring you happiness when you're growing old
The world still is the same, you never change it
As sure as the stars shine above
You're nobody til somebody loves you
So find yourself somebody to love!

(↑3) C E A - / Dm G C - / C D7 F G / Dm D7 F G /
/   "   / F A Dm - / F D7 C A / Dm G C -

— w & m: Russ Morgan, Larry Stock & James Cavanaugh

Jazz & swing standards can also be found in **Golden Oldies** and
Musicals. See also in **Farm**: I'm an old cowhand **Hope**: What a
wonderful world **Trav**: Route 66.

Love

ALL I WANT IS YOU

If I were a flower growing wild & free
All I'd want is you to be my sweet honey bee
And if I were a tree growing tall & green
All I'd want is you to shade me & be my leaves

G - C G / - - D G :‖

All I want is you, will you be my bride
Take me by the hand & stand by my side
All I want is you, will you stay with me?
Hold me in your arms & sway me like the sea

If you were a river in the mtns tall
The rumble of your water would be my call
If you were the winter, I know I'd be the snow
As as long as you were with me, let the cold wind blow

If you were a wink, I'd be a nod
If you were a seed, I'd be a pod
If you were the floor, I'd wanna be the rug
And if you were a kiss, I know I'd be a hug

If you were the wood, I'd be the fire
If you were the love, I'd be the desire
If you were a castle, I'd be your moat
And if you were an ocean, I'd learn to float

— w & m: Barry Polisar

ALMOST EVERY CIRCUMSTANCE

7 days are in the week in almost every circumstance
And there's 4 seasons in the year or so we learned at school
Ah but never count your chickens when you're dealing
with the women
For many's the wise man fell asleep & wakened up a fool

G - - C - / G - - D - / 1st / G - D G

The 1st time I met my love was on a Mon. morning
And the 2nd time I saw her was a Tues. afternoon
When she kissed me on a Wed. I couldn't wait for Thurs.
But I can tell you now my boys that Thurs. never came

My love, she took the wintertime & turned it into springtime
I never thought that love could change the world so much before
I gave my heart & in return she promised me the summertime
But I can tell you now my boys that summer never came

— w & m: Colum Sands

BEESWING

I was 19 when I came to town, they called it the Summer of Love
They were burning babies, burning flags, the Hawks against the
  Doves / I took a job in the steamie down on Cauldrum St.
And I fell in love with a laundry girl who was working next to me

(↑2) C - - - / - - - F - :‖ **(v. 3 & 5 repeat 3x)**

Oh she was a rare thing, fine as a bee's wing
So fine, a breath of wind might blow her away
She was a lost child, oh she was running wild
She said "As long as there's no price on love I'll stay
And you wouldn't want me any other way"

Am - C - / Am C F - :‖ Am G C -

Brown hair zigzag around her face & a look of half-surprise
Like a fox caught in the headlights there was animal in her eyes
She said "Young man, oh can't you see I'm not the factory kind?
If you don't take me out of here, I'll surely lose my mind"

(2nd cho) ...Oh she was a rare thing, fine as a bee's wing
So fine that I might crush her where she lay / **She was a lost...**

We busked around the mkt towns & picked fruit down in Kent
And we could tinker lamps & pots & knives wherever we went
And I said that we might settle down, get a few acres dug
Fire burning in the hearth & babies on the rug
She said "Oh man, you foolish man, it surely sounds like hell
You might be lord of half the world, you'll not own me as well"

We was camping down the Gower one time, the work was
  pretty good
She thought we shouldn't wait for the frost & I thought maybe
  we should
We was drinking more in those days & tempers reached a pitch
And like a fool I let her run with her rambling itch

Oh the last I heard she's sleeping rough back on Derby beat
White Horse in her hip pocket & a wolfhound at her feet
And they say she even married once a man named Romany Brown
But even a Gypsy caravan was too much settling down
And they say her flower is faded now, hard weather & hard booze
But maybe that's just the price you pay for the chains you refuse

(last cho) Oh she was a rare thing, fine as a bee's wing
And I miss her more than ever words could say
If I could just taste all of her wildness now
If I could hold her in my arms today
Well I wouldn't want her any other way

— w & m: Richard Thompson

BÉSAME MUCHO

Bésame, bésame mucho
Como si fuera esta_noche la última vez
Bésame, bésame mucho
Que tengo miedo_a perderte, perderte después

Am - Dm - / - E Am - / A7 - Dm - / Am B7E7 Am -

Quiero tenerte muy cerca / Mirarme_en tus ojos verte junto_a mí
Piensa que tal vez mañana / Yo ya_estaré lejos, muy lejos de ti

Dm - Am - / E7 - Am A7 / 1st / B7 - E7 -

— w & m: Consuelo Velázquez

© 1941 by Promotora Hispano Americana de Musica, S.A. Copyright renewed. All
rights administered by Peer International Corporation. Rec by Andrea Bocelli &
great YT rec by Cesaria Evora 17.

BRING ME A BOAT

Bring me a boat to cross to my dear
I stand here alone, with my sweetheart so near
Bring me a boat to cross o'er the Tyne
For its deep murky waters part his heart & mine   (in C, 3/4)

And the Tyne it flows on & out to the sea
If a boat I am granted then safe let me be
And gently I'll go, for gently I'll row
As gently you breathe as you ebb & you flow

F C G C / F C F - / - C G C / F C G C
F - G C /   "   /   "   /   "   /

Does he know I stand each day on the shore?
Does he know I'd give all to see him once more?
Does he know I've wept 10,000 times o'er
And is he still waiting as he was before?

The boatman he wants the gold I can't give
My parents are poor so I've nothing to give
Only my heart & that will not float
So please don't deny me & bring me a boat

— w: Kate Rusby, m: Phil Cunningham

© 2003 Kate Rusby & Philip Cunningham. On Kate Rusby Underneath the Stars
(in G 13), Lucy Bunce Penny on the Water & on Goitse.

BUCKETS OF RAIN

Buckets of rain, buckets of tears
Got all them buckets comin' out of my ears
Buckets of moonbeams in my hand
You got all the love, honey baby, I can stand

D - /   / G - D - / AG DA D -

I been meek & hard like an oak
I seen pretty people disappear like smoke
Friends will arrive, friends will disappear
If you want me, honey baby, I'll be here

I like your smile & your fingertips
I like the way that you move your hips
I like the cool way you look at me
Everything about you is bringin' me misery

Little red wagon, little red bike
I ain't no monkey, but I know what I like
I like the way you love me strong & slow
I'm takin' you with me, honey baby, when I go

Life is sad, life is a bust
All ya can do is do what you must
You do what you must do & ya do it well
I'll do it for you, honey baby, can't you tell?

— w & m: Bob Dylan

© 1974, 1976 Ram's Horn Music. Reprinted by Permission of Music Sales
Corporation. On his Blood on the Tracks 13, Bette Midler S for a New Depression,
John Renbourn So Early in the Spring, Neko Case Live fr Austin TX, Beth Orton
Heart of Soul, Van Ronk Down in Wash Sq.

A CASE OF YOU

_Just before our love got lost you said
_"I am as constant as a northern star" & I said
"Constantly in the darkness, where's that at?
If you want me I'll be in the bar"_

C - G - / Am - - - / Dm - C - / G Am Gsus G - -

On the back of a cartoon coaster
In the blue TV screen light
_I drew a map of Canada
O Canada
With your face sketched on it twice

C - G - / Am - - - / Dm - C - / C Am - - / F C G -

Oh you're in my blood like holy wine
You taste so bitter & so sweet
Oh I could drink a case of you, darling
And I would still be on my feet, oh I would still be on my feet

F - Em - / Dm G C - / C - CG Am - - - / F C G - C - - -

Oh_I am a lonely painter
_I live in a box of paints
_I'm frightened by the devil
And I'm drawn to the ones that ain't

I remember that time you told me, you said
"Love is touching _ souls,"_ surely you touched mine
'Cos part of you pours out of me
_In these lines from time to time

I met a woman, she had a mouth like yours
She knew your life, she knew your devils & your deeds
And she said_"Go to him, _stay with him if you can
_But be prepared to bleed"

— w & m: Joni Mitchell

© 1971 (renewed) Crazy Crow Music. All rights administered by Sony/ATV Music
Publishing LLC, 424 Church Street, Suite 1200, Nashville, TN 37219. On her Blue 11.

CECILIA

Celia, you're breaking my heart
You're shaking my confidence daily
Oh Cecilia, I'm down on my knees
I'm begging you please to come home / Come on home

C - FC / FCG - / FCFC / FCG - / C - - -

Making love in the afternoon with Cecilia
Up in my bedroom (making love)
I got up to wash my face
When I come back to bed someone's taken my place

C - F - / C F G C / 1st / C - G C

(tag) Jubilation, she loves me again
I fall on the floor & I laughing (repeat)

F C F C / F C G - :‖

— w & m: Paul Simon

© 1969 Paul Simon (BMI). On *Bridge Over Troubled Waters, Old Friends*.

CLOSE THE DOOR LIGHTLY (When You Go)

Turn around, _ don't whisper out my name
For like a breeze _ it'd stir a dying flame
I'll miss someone, _ if it eases you to know
But close the door lightly when you go _

(in D)   A - - D / A - G D / 1st / G A D -

Who was the one that stole my mind? _
Who was the one that robbed my time? _
Who was the one that made me feel unkind?
So fare thee well, sweet love of mine _

G A D - / / G A - D / G A D -

Take your tears to someone else's eyes
They're made of glass & they cut like wounding lies
Memories are drifting like the snow
So, close the door lightly when you go

Don't look back to where you once had been
Look straight ahead when you're walking thru the rain
And find a light, if the path gets dark & cold
But close the door lightly when you go

— w & m: Eric Andersen

© 1966 (renewed) EMI U Catalog Inc. All rights administered by EMI U Catalog Inc. (Publishing) & Alfred Music (Print). On his *'Bout Changes & Things* & Anne Hills *Bittersweet Street*.

CUCURRUCUCÚ PALOMA

Dicen que por las noches no más se le iba en puro llorar
Dicen que no dormía *[comía]* no más se le iba en puro tomar
Juran que_el mismo cielo se_estremecía_al oír su llanto
Cómo sufrió por ella, que_hasta_en su muerte la fue llamando

G - - - / C - - - / D₇ - - G / - - D₇ G

Ay (x5) cantaba / Ay... gemía / Ay... lloraba *[cantaba]*
De pasión mortal, moría

G - - D₇ / - - - G :‖

Que una paloma triste muy de mañana le va~a cantar
A la casita sola con sus puertitas de par en par
Juran que_esa paloma no_es otra cosa más que su alma
Que todavía la_espera a que regrese la desdichada

Cucurrucucú paloma / Cucurrucucú no llores
Las piedras jamás, paloma / ¡Qué van a saber de_amores!
Cucurrucucú (x2) Cucurrucucú paloma, ya no llores

G - - D₇ / - - - G :‖ G - C - / D₇ - G -

— w & m: Thomas Mendez Sosa

© 1954 by Editorial Mexicana de Musica Internacional, S.A. Copyright renewed. All rights administered by Peer International Corporation. Rec by Lola Betran, Joan Baez, Harry Belafonte.

DARCY FARROW

Where the Walker runs down into the Carson Valley plain
There lived a maiden, Darcy Farrow was her name
The daughter of old Dundee & fair was she
And the sweetest flower that bloomed o'er the range

D - G D / - - G Em A / 1st / G A D A G A D

Her voice was sweet as the sugar candy
Her touch was as soft as a bed of goose down
Her eyes shone bright like the pretty lights
That shine in the night out of Yerington town

She was courted by young Van der Meer
And quite handsome was he, I am to hear
He brought her silver rings & lacy things
And she promised to wed before the snows came that year

But her pony did stumble & she did fall
Her dyin' touched on the hearts of us all
Young Vandy in his pain put a bullet to his brain
And we buried them together as the snows began to fall

They sing of Darcy Farrow where the Truckee runs thru
They sing of her beauty in Virginia City, too
At dusty sundown to her name they drink a round
And to young Vandy whose love was true

— w & m: Steve Gillette & Tom Campbell

© 1965 (renewed) Compass Rose Music (BMI) & Rumpole Dumple Music (ASCAP). On *Steve Gillete*, his *Alone... Direct* & Fourtold (w/ Cindy Mangsen), John Denver *Rocky Mtn High*, Nanci Griffith *Other Voices Too*, Ian & Sylvia *Early Morning Rain*, Jim Rice *I've Got 'Em Covered*. In *SO!* 30:4.

DARK-EYED MOLLY

Deep & dark are my true love's eyes
Blacker still is the winter turning
As the sadness of parting proves
And brighter now is the lantern burning
That lightens my path to love

(in 3/4 ↑3) D - - - ‖: G Em A D - - - / A₇ - D - - - :‖

No fiddle tune will take the air
But I'll see her swift feet a-dancing
And the swirl of her long brown hair
Her smiling face & her dark eyes glancing
As we stepped out Blinkbonny Fair

And if my waiting prove in vain
Then I will pack & track ever take me
And the long road will ease my pain
No gem of womankind will make me
E'er whisper love's words again

For in drink I'll seek good company
My ears will ring with the tavern's laughter
And I'll hear not her last sweet sighs
Then who's to know in the morning after
That I long for her dear dark eyes?

— w & m: Archie Fisher

© 1976 (renewed) Archie Fisher. On his *Man w/ a Rhyme*, Stan Rogers *Turnaround*, Sheena Wellington *Strong Women Rule* & Tannahill Weavers *Live*. Fisher says tune is an old Basque lullaby & lyrics are partly fr Gaelic poetry. In *SO!* 38:3.

DARKEST HOUR

It's the 10th of January & I still ain't had no sleep
She comes waltzing in the nighttime made of wings
She is dressed up like a bandit with a hundred sparkling rings
Looking for my company to keep
Coming closer to me, she doesn't say a word
In the shadow of the carved rock tower
Where the sounds of the night were the only things we heard

In my darkest hour (↑2)

C - FG Am / C F G - :‖ F G C F / - Dm G - / 1st / F G C -

She don't want to hear no secrets, she would guarantee me that
She knows there ain't no words that can describe her
With her white silk scarves & her black Spanish hat
She knows there ain't no way I can deny her
Yes her blue velvet perfume filling up the night
The guards are all asleep that watch the tower
The moonlight held her breast as she easily undressed

In my darkest hour

Her father's in his chambers with his friends all gathered 'round
They are plotting their enemy's demise
With their last detail done they await the coming sun
While I am staring in my lover's eyes
Her brothers & her sisters are all thru for tonight
Pretending that they've just come into power
But she far most of all knows that they can only fall

In my...

Hungry wings, their melodies while my love awakens me
In the midst of the sunburst first light
Her hands are holding up the skies as I hid my opened eyes
Every move just for herself & that's all right
Soon I went along my way with no words that could explain
As she began descending to the tower
Her safety now concerns me, her circumstance to blame...

— w & m: Arlo Guthrie

DIAMONDS & RUST

Well I'll be damned, here comes your ghost again
But that's not unusual, it's just that the moon is full
And you happened to call
And here I sit, hand on the telephone
Hearing a voice I'd known, a couple of light years ago
Heading straight for a fall

Em C / G D / Em / 1st 2 / Em -

As I remember, your eyes were bluer than robin's eggs
My poetry was lousy you said, where are you calling from?
A booth in the Midwest
10 yrs ago I bought you some cuff-links
You brought me something, we both know what
    memories can bring
They bring diamonds & rust

Well you burst on the scene already a legend
The unwashed phenomenon, the original vagabond
You strayed into my arms
And there you stayed, temporarily lost at sea
The Madonna was yours for free, yes the girl on the half-shell
Would keep you unharmed

(bridge) Now I see you standing with brown leaves falling
    around & snow in your hair
Now you're smiling out the window of that crummy hotel
    over Washington Square
Our breath comes out white clouds, mingles & hangs in the air
Speaking strictly for me we both could have died then & there

Bm Am / | / C G / Fmaj7 GB7 Em

Now you're telling me you're not nostalgic
Then give me another word for it, you who are so good
    with words
And at keeping things vague
Because I need some of that vagueness now, it's all come
    back too clearly
Yes I loved you dearly & if you're offering me diamonds & rust
I've already paid

— w & m: Joan Baez

DIMMING OF THE DAY

This old house is falling down around my ears
I'm drowning in a river of my tears
When all my will is gone, you hold me sway
I need you at the dimming of the day

G - D - / C G D - / 1st / C GD G -

(bridge) You pulled me like the moon pulls on the tide
You know just where I keep my better side...

D - A - / D - A DG C -

What days have come to keep us far apart?
A broken promise or a broken heart
Now all the bonny birds have wheeled away
I need you at the dimming...

(bridge) Come the night you're only what I want
Come the night you could be my confidant...

I see you on the streets in company
Why don't you come and ease your mind with me?
I'm living for the night we steal away
I need you at the dimming...

— w & m: Richard Thompson

DON'T THINK TWICE, IT'S ALL RIGHT

It ain't no use to sit and wonder why, babe
It don't matter, anyhow
An' it ain't no use to sit and wonder why, babe
If you don't know by now
When the rooster crows at the break of dawn
Look out your window and I'll be gone
You're the reason I'm a-travelin' on
But don't think twice, it's all right

(⬆5) C G Am -/ F - C G / 1st / D7 - G G7
C - C7 - / F - D7 - / C G Am F / C G C -

It ain't no use in turnin' on your light, babe
The light I never knowed
It ain't no use in turnin' on your light, babe
I'm on the dark side of the road
Still I wish there was somethin' you would do or say
To try and make me change my mind and stay
We never did too much talkin' anyway / **But...**

It ain't no use in callin' out my name, gal
Like you never did before
It ain't no use in callin' out my name, gal
I can't hear you anymore
I'm a-thinkin' and a-wond'rin' all the way down the road
I once loved a woman, a child I'm told
I'd give her my heart but she wanted my soul...

I'm walkin' down that long, lonesome road, babe
Where I'm bound, I can't tell
But goodbye is too good a word, gal
So I'll just say "fare thee well"
I ain't sayin' you treated me unkind
You could have done better but I don't mind
You just kinda wasted my precious time...

— w & m: Bob Dylan

FALLING

You hear me shout when no one's about
You find me where I can't be seen
I feel the air flowing, for life's in full swing
So tell me why I cannot breathe **(in 3/4 ⬆2)**

C G Am F / Am G F G / C G Am F / Am F G -

And here I am falling, oh why am I falling
Take me to where I belong
I'm standing here falling, before you falling
If it weren't for your wings I'd be gone

C F C G / Am F G - / C F Am G / F G C -

Time moves on and time won't be long
In time I will fear not the day
I'm endlessly knowing that you'll never know
What I might want you to say
    My back it aches, my body it breaks
To grow my own wings I have tried
And painless I came no aim must remain
Alone and adrift on the tide

— w & m: Kate Rusby

FALLING SLOWLY

I don't know you but I want you all the more for that
Words fall thru me & always fool me & I can't react
And games that never amount to more than they're meant will
    play themselves out _

C F C F /   / AmG FG Am7G F -

Take this sinking boat & point it home, we've still got time
Raise your hopeful voice, you have a choice, you'll make it now

C F Am7 F /   /

Falling slowly, eyes that know me & I can't go back
And moods that take me & erase me & I'm painted black
You have suffered enough & warred with yourself, it's time that
    you won

Take this sinking boat & point it home, we've still got time
Raise your hopeful voice, you've made it now
Falling slowly, sing your melody, I'll sing along

C F Am7 F /   /   /

— w & m: Glen Hansard & Marketa Irglova

GENTLE ANNIE

Thou wilt come no more, gentle Annie
Like a flow'r thy spirit did depart
Thou art gone, alas! like the many
That have bloomed in the summer of my heart

(⬆2) G D G C / G Em Am D / 1st / G D G -

Shall we never more behold thee
Never hear thy winning voice again
When the springtime comes, gentle Annie
When the wild flow'rs are scattered o'er the plain?

C - G - / Em A Am D - / G D G C / G D G -

We have roamed & loved mid the bowers
When thy downy cheeks were in their bloom
Now I stand alone mid the flowers
While they mingle their perfumes o'er thy tomb

Ah! the hrs grow sad while I ponder
Near the silent spot where thou art laid
And my heart bows down when I wander
By the streams & the meadows where we stray'd

— w & m: Stephen C. Foster (1856)

GENTLE ON MY MIND

It's knowing that your door is always open & your path
Is free to walk _
That makes me tend to leave my sleeping bag rolled up
And stashed behind your couch _
And it's knowing I'm not shackled by forgotten words & bonds
And the ink stains that have dried upon some line
That keeps you in the backroads by the rivers of my mem'ry
That keeps you ever **gentle on my mind**

```
C ↓ / Dm - / G - / C - / C ↓ / C Dm - / G - / - C -
```

It's not clinging to the rocks & ivy planted on their columns
Now that binds me
Or smth that somebody said because they thought
We fit together walking
It's just knowing that the world will not be cursing or forgiving
When I walk along some RR track & find
That you're waving from the backroads of my mem'ry
And for hrs you're just **gentle on...**

Tho' the wheat fields & the clotheslines & the junkyards
And the highways come betw us
And some other woman crying to her mother
'Cos she turned & I was gone
I still might run in silence, tears of joy might stain my face
And the summer sun might burn me 'til I'm blind
But not to where I cannot see you walking on the backroads
By the rivers, flowing **gentle...**

I dip my cup of soup back from the gurgling, crackling
Cauldron in some train yard
My beard a roughening coal pile & a dirty hat
Pulled low across my face
Thru cupped hands round a tin can I pretend to hold you to my
    breast & find
That you're wavin' from the backroads of my mem'ry
Ever smiling, ever **gentle...**

— w & m: John Hartford

I REMEMBER LOVING YOU

I look at my brown suitcase
And think of all the places that I've been
RR yards & prison guards
All the dumpy little towns along the stem
And the whispering of the people
As they watch every move that I go thru
I remember all these things
Mostly I remember loving you

```
A - / - - E - / - - / - - A - :‖
```

I remember loving you, back when the world was new
And I think you loved me too, I remember loving you

```
D - - A - - / E - - A - -
```

The buckskin smells so the people tell
As we huddled in the boxcar from the rain
Flashing lights that cut the night
The RR bulls that pulled us off the train
When the winter's cold & the Norther blows
I'm huddled in the corner til I'm blue
I remember all these things
Mostly I remember loving you

Winter streets where the frozen sleet
Comes soaking thru the cardboard in my shoes
Where the promised land might be a place
Where a man could find free cigarettes & booze
And the alleyways full of ragged strays
The doorway wine I tell my troubles to / **I remember all...**

— w & m: Utah Phillips

IF YOU COULD READ MY MIND LOVE

If you could read my mind love, what a tale my thoughts
    could tell
Just like an old-time movie 'bout a ghost from a wishin' well
In a castle dark or a fortress strong
With chains upon my feet, you know that ghost is me
And I will never be set free as long as I'm a ghost
That you can't see

```
G - Dm6 - /    / G - C / D Em C G /
C Em Am D / G - - -
```

If I could read your mind love, what a tale your...
Just like a paperback novel, the kind that drugstores sell
When you reach the part where the heartaches come
The hero would be me, but heroes often fail
And you won't read that book again because the ending's
Just too hard to take

(starts as line 3) I'd walk away like a movie star
Who gets burned in a 3-way script, enter "No. 2"
A movie queen to play the scene of bringing all the good
    things out / In me, but for now love, let's be real

```
G - C / D Em C G / C Em Am D / Em C G -
```

I never thought I could act this way & I've got to say that I
    just don't get it
I don't know where we went wrong, but the feelin's gone
    & I just can't get it / Back

```
C Em Am D /    / G - - -
```

(v.1 lines 1-3) If you could read my... ...fortress strong
With chains upon my feet, but stories always end
If you read betw the lines, you'll know that I'm just tryin' to
Understand the feelings that you [we] lack

```
G - Dm6 - /    / G - C / D Em C G /
C Em Am D / Em C G -
```

I never thought I could feel this way...

— w & m: Gordon Lightfoot

IN SPITE OF OURSELVES

She don't like her eggs all runny,
   she thinks crossin' her legs is funny
She looks down her nose at money,
   she gets it on like the Easter bunny
She's my baby I'm her honey, **I'm never gonna let** her go

C - - - / F - C - / G - C -

He ain't got laid in a month of Sundays,
   I caught him once & he was sniffin' my undies
He ain't too sharp but he gets things done,
   drinks his beer like it's oxygen
He's my baby & I'm his honey, **never... let** him **go**

In spite of ourselves we'll end up a-sittin' on a rainbow _
Against all odds, honey, we're the big door prize _
We're gonna spite our noses right off of our faces _
There won't be nothin' but big old hearts dancin'
   in our eyes _

F - C - / G - C - / 1st / C G C -

She thinks all my jokes are corny,
   convict movies make her horny
She likes ketchup on her scrambled eggs,
   swears like a sailor when she shaves her legs
She takes a lickin' & keeps on tickin', **I'm...** her **go**

He's got more balls than a big brass monkey,
   he's a wacked-out weirdo & a lovebug junkie
Sly as a fox & crazy as a loon,
   payday comes & he's a-howlin' at the moon
He's my baby I don't mean maybe, **never...** him **go**

— w & m: John Prine

IT AIN'T ME BABE

Go 'way from my window, leave at your own chosen speed
I'm not the one you want, babe, I'm not the one you need
You say you're lookin' for someone who's never weak but
   always strong
To protect you an' defend you, whether you are right or wrong
Someone to open each & every door
But it ain't me babe, no no no
It ain't me babe, it ain't me you're lookin' for babe

G C BmD G / Bm C BmD G / Bm Am Bm Am /   /
C - D - / G - CD / G - CDG - - -

Go lightly from the ledge babe, go lightly on the ground
I'm not the one you want babe, I will only let you down
You say you're lookin' for someone who will promise never to part
Someone to close his eyes for you, someone to close his heart
Someone who will die for you & more / **But it ain't me...**

Go melt back into the night, babe,
   everything inside is made of stone
There's nothing in here moving & anyway I'm not alone
You say you're lookin' for someone
   who'll pick you up each time you fall
To gather flowers constantly & to come each time you call
A lover for your life & nothing more...

— w & m: Bob Dylan

KILLING THE BLUES

Leaves were falling just like embers in colors red & gold
They set us on fire _ burning just like a moonbeam in our eyes
Somebody said they saw me _ swinging the world by the tail
Bouncing over a white cloud _ killing the blues _

A - - - / D - A - / E - AD / A E A -

I am guilty of something, I hope you never do
Because there is nothing _ sadder than losing yourself in love

Now you ask me just to leave you _ to go out on my own
And get what I need to, _ you want me to find what I've already had

— w & m: Rowland J. Salley

LOVE AT THE FIVE & DIME

Rita was 16 yrs, hazel eyes & chestnut hair
She made the Woolworth counter shine
And Eddie was a sweet romancer & a darn good dancer
And they'd waltz the aisles of the 5 & dime

(↑3) G - Am7 - / C - G - :|

Eddie played the steel guitar & his mama cried 'cos he played in
   the bars / And he kept young Rita out late at night
So they married up in Abilene, lost a child in Tennessee
But still that love survived 'cos they'd sing:

Dance a little closer to me
Dance a little closer now, dance a little closer tonight
Dance a little closer to me, 'cos it's closing time
And love's on sale tonight at this 5 & dime

Bm - Am7 - /   /   / C D G -

One of the boys in Eddie's band took a shine to Rita's hand
So Eddie ran off with the bass man's wife
Oh but he was back by June, singin' a different tune
Sporting Miss Rita back by his side & he sang...

Eddie traveled with the barroom bands 'til arthritis took his
   hands / Now he sells insurance on the side
And Rita's got her house to keep, she writes dime store novels
   with a love so sweet
And they dance to the radio late at night & still sing...

— w & m: Nanci Griffith

LOVE CHOOSES YOU

Love comes unbidden, it can't be forbidden
It takes you & shakes you right down to your shoes
It knows heartache & trial, but accepts no denial
You can't choose who you love, love chooses you

(in 3/4 ↑2) G - Dsus Em / C - D G :‖

In the wink of an eye love looses an arrow
We control it no more than the flight of the sparrow
The swell of the tide, or the light of the moon
You can't choose who you love, love chooses you

Tell me now if I'm wrong, are you feeling the same?
Are your feet on the ground? Are you calling my name?
Do you lie awake nights? Please say you do
'Cos you can't choose who you love, love chooses you

C - - D G - - - / C - D - G - - - :‖

Love cuts like a torch to a heart behind steel
And tho' you may hide it, love knows how you feel
And tho' you may trespass on the laws of the land
Your heart has to follow when love takes your hand

And it seems we're 2 people within the same circle
It's drawn tighter & tighter til you're all that I see
I'm full & I'm empty & you're pouring thru me
Like a warm rain fallin' thru the leaves on a tree

— w & m: Laurie Lewis

LOVE MINUS ZERO / NO LIMIT

My love she speaks like silence without ideals or violence
She doesn't have to say she's faithful yet she's true like ice, like fire
People carry roses & make promises by the hours
My love she laughs like the flowers, valentines can't buy her

G - - GD C - G GD / C - G - Am - D - / 1st /
C - G - / C D G -

In the dime stores & bus stations, people talk of situations
Read books, repeat quotations, draw conclusions on the wall
Some speak of the future, my love she speaks softly
She knows there's no success like failure & that failure's no success at all

The cloak & dagger dangles, madams light the candles
In ceremonies of the horsemen even the pawn must hold a grudge
Statues made of matchsticks crumble into one another
My love winks, she does not bother, she knows too much to argue
   or to judge

The bridge at midnight trembles, the country doctor rambles
Bankers' nieces seek perfection expecting all the gifts that wise
   men bring
The wind howls like a hammer, the night blows cold & rainy
My love she's like some raven at my window with a broken wing

— w & m: Bob Dylan

OCHI CHYORNYE (Dark Eyes)

Ochi chyornye, ochi strastnye
Ochi zhguchye i prekrasnye
Kak lyublyu ya vas, kak boyus' ya vas
Znat', uvidyel vas ya v nyedobryi chas

(B7) Em - / B7 Em / Am Em / B7 Em

Ochi chyonye, ochi plamenny
I manyat oni v strany dal'niye
Gdye tsarit lyubov', gdye tsarit pokoi
Gdye stradan'ya nyet, gdye vrazhdye zapryet

Ne vstrechal by vas, ne stradal by tak
Ya prozhil by zhizn' ulybayuchis'
Vy zgubili menya, ochi chyornye
Unyesli navek moyo schastiye

— w: Yevhen Hrebinka (Yevgenii Grebyonka),
   m: Florian Hermann ("Valse Hommage")

ONCE IN A VERY BLUE MOON

I found your letter in my mailbox today
You were just checking if I was okay
And do I still miss you, well, you know what they say
Just once in a very blue moon (3x)
And I feel one coming on soon

G D C - / G D C D / 1st / C D G Em / C D G - /
C D B7 Em / C D G -

No need to tell me you'd like to be friends
And help me get back on my feet again
'Cos if I still miss you, it's just now & then / **Just once...**

(bridge) There's a blue moon shining
When I'm reminded of all we've been thru
Such a blue moon shining
Does it ever shine down on you?

Fmaj7 - Em Am / F G FG C / 1st / Dm - G -

'Cos you act like it never even hurt you at all
And I'm the only one getting up from the fall
Tell me, don't you feel, can't you recall / **Just...**

— w & m: Patrick Alger & Eugene Levine

REASON TO BELIEVE

If I listen long enough to you
I'd find a way to believe that it's all true
Knowing that you lied, straight-faced while I cried
But still I'd look to find a reason to believe

C G C - / F G C - / D - G F C - / Am F G -

(bridge) Someone like you makes it hard to live without somebody else
Someone like you makes it easy to give, never think of myself
F G Am* G* /   /   *6 beats

If I gave you time to change my mind
I'd find a way to leave the past behind / **Knowing...**

— w & m: Tim Hardin

SPEED OF THE SOUND OF LONELINESS

_You come home late & you come home early _
_You come on big when you're feeling small _
You come home straight & you come home curly
Sometimes you don't come home at all

G - C - / D - G - :‖

So what in the world's come over you
And what in heaven's name have you done
You've broken the speed of the sound of loneliness
_ You're out there running just to be on the run _

Well I got a heart that burns with a fever
And I got a worried & a jealous mind
How can a love that'll last forever
Get left so far behind

It's a mighty mean & a dreadful sorrow
It's crossed the evil line today
Well, how can you ask about tomorrow
We ain't got one word to say

— w & m: John Prine

SWEET PEA

Sweet pea, apple of my eye
Don't know when & I don't know why
You're the only reason I keep on coming home

C E7 / Am D / CAm FG C(Am FG)

Sweet pea, what's all of this about?
Don't get your way, all you do is fuss & pout / **You're...**

(bridge) I'm like the Rock of Gibraltar, I always seem to falter
And the words just get in the way
Oh I know I'm gonna crumble, I'm trying to stay humble
But I never think before I say

E7 - / Am - / D - / G -

Sweet pea, keeper of my soul
I know sometimes I'm out of control / **You're...**

— w & m: Amos Lee

SWEET SPOT

Nothing fancy, nothing fake
Nothing wasted & no deal to make
What you need is what you want to take
And what you take you use

(↑3) G - Em - / / / C - G -

I'm just looking for that sweet spot
Where I can <u>live</u> the way that I want
I'll be waiting for you out front
If you want me to / Are you comin' too?

C - GD / / / C - G - / /

The fire is steady & the beat is strong
Give is good & wide & long
You don't even have to hold on / 'Cos it's got ahold of you
I'm just looking for that sweet spot
Where I can <u>love</u> the way...

(bridge) And when I find that sweet spot
Gonna give it everything I've got
Turn up the radio a whole lot / For the afternoon

D Am / / / C D

Soft as a woman, strong as a man
Throws your head back in a full-mouth laugh
It's like knowing you can sleep at night / But you don't want to
I'm just looking for that sweet spot
Where I can love...

— w & m: Tift Catherine Merritt

SWEET THAMES FLOW SOFTLY

I met my girl at Woolwich Pier beneath a big crane standing
And oh the love I felt for her, it passed all understanding
Took her sailing on the river, **flow sweet river flow**
London town was mine to give her, **sweet Thames, flow softly**
Made the Thames into a crown, **flow sweet river flow**
Made a brooch of Silvertown, **sweet Thames, flow softly**

C G CF G / C G CG C /
C F C G / C F CG FC / G - FC G / - - FC GC

At London Yard I held her hand, at Blackwall Point I faced her
At the Isle of Dogs I kissed her mouth & tenderly embraced her
Heard the bells of Greenwich ringing, **flow sweet river flow**
All the time, my heart was singing, **sweet Thames, flow softly**
Limehouse Reach I gave her there, **flow sweet...**
As a ribbon for her hair, **sweet Thames...**

From Shadwell Dock to 9 Elms Reach, we cheek-to-cheek
   were dancing
Her necklace made of London Bridge, her beauty was enhancing
Kissed her once again at Wapping, **flow...**
After that there was no stopping, **sweet...**
Richmond Park, it was her ring, **flow...**
I'd have given her anything, **sweet...**

From Rotherhithe to Putney Bridge, my love I was declaring
And she, from Kew to Isleworth, her love for me was swearing
Love had set my heart a-burning, **flow...**
Never saw the tide was turning, **sweet...**
Gave her Hampton Court to twist, **flow...**
Into a bracelet for her wrist, **sweet...**

But now, alas, the tide has changed, my love she has gone from me
And winter's frost has touched my heart & put a blight upon me
Creeping fog is on the river, **flow...**
Sun & moon & stars gone with her, **sweet...**
Swift the Thames runs to the sea, **flow...**
Bearing ships & part of me, **sweet...**

— w & m: Ewan MacColl

TE RECUERDO AMANDA

Te recuerdo_Amanda, la calle mojada
Corriendo_a la fábrica donde trabajaba / Manuel
La sonrisa ancha, la lluvia en el pelo
No importaba nada ibas a_encontrarte / Con él (x4)

(in 3/4) G - Bm - / C - F - / G - - - :‖

Con él, son cinco minutos
La vida_es eterna en cinco minutos
Suena la sirena "De vuelta_al trabajo"
Y tú caminando, lo_iluminas todo
Los cinco minutos te hacen florecer

Em - D / Dmaj7 - C - / Dmaj7 C x2 / Bm - C - / A C A -

Con él, que partió a la sierra
Que nunca hizo daño, que partió a la sierra
Y en cinco minutos quedó destrozado
Suena la sirena "De vuelta_al trabajo"
Muchos no volvieron, tampoco Manuel
Te recuerdo Amanda, la calle mojada
Corriendo_a la fábrica donde trabajaba / Manuel

— w & m: Victor Jara

LA VIE EN ROSE

Quand il me prend dans ses bras
Il me parle tout bas, je vois la vie en rose
Il me dit des mots d'amour
Des mots de tous les jours, et ça me fait quelque chose

G - Bm - / Em - Am D / Am - D7 - / Am - C D

Il est entré dans mon cœur
Une part de bonheur dont je connais la cause
C'est lui [toi] pour moi, moi pour lui [toi] dans la vie
Il me l'a dit, l'a juré pour la vie / Et dès que je l'aperçois
Alors je sens en moi, mon cœur qui bat

G - Bm - / Em - C - / Am [Cm] - G - / A7 - Am D̂
/ " / Am D G -

Hold me close & hold me fast
The magic spell you cast, this is **La Vie En Rose**
When you kiss me Heaven sighs
And tho' I close my eyes, I see **La Vie...**

When you press me to your heart
I'm in a world apart, a world where roses bloom
And when you speak angels sing from above
Everyday words seem[s] to turn into love songs
Give your heart & soul to me / And life will always be **La...**

— Orig Fr. w: Edith Piaf, m: Luis Guglielmi, Eng. w: Mack David

WHERE ARE YOU TONIGHT?

Where are you tonight I wonder?
And where will you be tonight when I cry?
Will sleep for you come easy, tho' I alone can't slumber?
Will you welcome in the morning at another man's side?

I: (↑2) C Em G F / C Em Dm F / Am Em F - / 1st

How easy for you the years slipped under
And left me a shadow the sun can't dispel
I built for you a tower of love and admiration,
I set you so high I could not reach myself
And **where are you...**

I look through my window at a world filled with strangers
The face in my mirror is the one face I know
You have taken all that's in me, so my heart is in no danger
My heart is in no danger, but I'd still like to know

If there is a silence that can't be broken
If there beats a pure heart, to her I will go
And time will work its healing and the spirit will grow stronger
But in the meantime I'd still like to know

II: (↑7) C - G F / C - Dm F / - G C Am / 1st

— w & m: Andy M. Stewart

WITH A GIGGLE & A HUG & A TICKLE & A KISS

I never thought I'd fall again, least not like this
With a giggle & a hug & a tickle & a kiss
It's hard to think I'd let myself be captured by your charms
In the middle of a snowstorm I'm melting in your arms

(in G) C G D G :‖ (4x)

Your brown eyes burn with a glistenin' fire
That spells my name in embers that sparkle with desire
I could see myself with you just sittin' in a chair
The dreams in your eyes light the curls in your hair

The days I spend with you seem to slide right by
You're my sweet honey bee & the apple of my eye
Tho' I thought it would lessen & I'd soon tire
Instead of letting go, I'm climbing higher & higher

Tho' the world's too crazy, it might never come true
But before I give up, I'm gonna fight for you
My heart beats fast & my face is all flushed
I'll marry you tomorrow, I don't wanna seem rushed

— w & m: Barry Louis Polisar

YOLANDA

Esta no puede ser no más que una canción
Quisiera fuera una declaración de amor
Románticas, sin reparar en formas tales
Que pongan freno a lo que siento ahora a raudales
Te amo (x2) / Eternamente, te amo

G C / D7 G :‖ (3x)

Si me faltaras no voy a morirme
Si he de morir quiero que sea contigo
Mi soledad, se siente acompañada
Por eso a veces sé que necesito
Tu mano (x2) / Eternamente tu mano

Cuando te vi, sabía que era cierto
Ese temor de hallarme descubierto
Tú me desnudas con siete razones
Me abres el pecho siempre que me colmas
De amores **(x2)** / Eternamente de amores

Si alguna vez me siento derrotado
Renuncio a ver el sol cada mañana
Rezando el credo que me has enseñado
Miro tu cara y digo en la ventana:
Yolanda **(x2)** / Eternamente, Yolanda

— w & m: Silvio Rodrigues

© 1984 Sociedad General de Autores de Espana Sgae. Rec by Pablo Milanes & w/ Rodrigues. Mercedes Sosa.

Find more love songs in other genre chapters throughout the book (Ballads, Blues, Country, Jazz, etc.) and also in **Faith**: One love, **Home**: Leaving the land, **Hope**: For real, **Lullabies**: Who will sing me lullabies?, **Outdoors**: Peaceful easy feeling, Shenandoah, Some sweet country, Underneath the stars, Wild rose of the mtn, **Sing**: Last call, **Time**: Good luck John, These Times, **Travelin**: Girl from the North Country, Me & Bobby McGee, Wooden heart (after Muss i denn).

Lullabies

A La Nanita Nana

A la nanita nana, nanita ea, nanita ea
Mi niño*[a]* *[Jesus]* tiene sueño - bendito sea **(x2) (repeat)**

Am - - - / Dm Am E Am :‖

Fuentecilla que corre clara y sonora
Ruiseñor que_en la selva, cantando llora
Callen mientras la cuna se balancea / **A la nanita nana, nanita ea**

A E - A /   / Dm Am E Am /   /

— w: Juan Francisco Muñoz y Pabón, m: José María Ramón Gomis (1904)

Arr. © 2015 by Hal Leonard Corporation. In '06 film *Cheetah Girls 2*.

Alright For Now

Goodnight baby, sleep tight my love
May God watch over you from above
Tomorrow I'm workin' — what would I do
I'd be lost & lonely if not for you

(↑2) C G C G / C Am F C :‖

(bridge) So close your eyes / We're alright / For now

Em - Dm - /   / G - G7 -

I've spent my life travelin', I've spent my life free
I could not repay all you've done for me
So sleep tight baby, unfurrow your brow
And know I love you, we're alright for now

— w & m: Tom Petty

© 1989 Gone Gator Music. On his *Full Moon Fever*.

And We Shall Want No More

Hush my darling don't you know?
Into your dreams we both shall go
Into a land where no one's poor
And you shall want no more (2x)

D - A D / G↓ - A / 1st / G D Asus A / G A D -

The merchant's store is full of shoes
And things to eat & all things new
And you shall have whate'er you please / **And you shall...**
Come_with me _ **(2x)**
Into a <u>land</u> where no <u>one</u> is poor / And <u>we</u> shall...

Bm D A Bm / G A Bm - / G A D Bm / 2nd /   /

The schools are full of children
Who can't wait to learn of all things new
With books to read for everyone / **And** <u>they</u> shall...

The world is full of people who
All live & work for something new
And peace is found on every shore / **And** we...

(final v.) The world is full...who / All live & work...new
<u>When</u> peace is found on every shore / <u>Then</u> we... **(3x)**

D - A D / G↓ - A / 1st / G D Asus A /
G A Bm - / G A D -

— w & m: Joanna Katzen

© 1991 Joanna Katzen. On her YT rec & Joann & Ray Scudero *Poor Working Slob*. *LS & at www.sweetheartsongs.org. *LS

BABY MINE

Baby mine, don't you cry / Baby mine, dry your eyes
Rest your head close to my heart never to part / **Baby of mine**

G - Am - /   / C - Am D / G - - -

Little one when you play / Don't you mind what they say
Let those eyes sparkle & shine never a tear / **Baby...**

If they knew sweet little you
They'd end up loving you too
All those same people who scold you
What they'd give just for the right to hold you

Em G A B7 /   / Em - Bm - / Em A D AmD

From your head down to your toes / You're not much, goodness knows
But you're so precious to me, sweet as can be / **Baby...**

— w: Ned Washington, m: Frank Churchill

© 1941 by Walt Disney Productions. Copyright renewed. world rights controlled by Bourne Co. (ASCAP). On recs by Alison Krauss, Art Garfunkel & *in '41 film Dumbo.*

BLUEGRASS BOY

Hush-a-bye, my bluegrass boy, put away your little toys
All the stars in the heavens, we will count them
Hush the fiddle, hush the bow, mandolin, guitar, banjo
All is sleepy from the schoolhouse to the mountain

(in 3/4) G Am D G / F C G - :‖

Hush-a-bye, now don't you cry while I sing this lullaby
All is peaceful now where darkness spreads her mantle
Stars are blinking one by one, now your busy day is done
Close your eyes in the light of this candle

Soon the night will pass away & the dawning of the day
Will awaken you with joy, my bluegrass boy
And the birdies on the wing, melodies upon the wind
Will be songs for you to sing, my bluegrass boy

— w & m: Peter Rowan

© 1996 Sea Lion Music. On his *Bluegrass Boy*. Priscilla Herdman *Moondreamer.*

DREAM ANGUS

Can ye no hush your weepin'-o
All the wee lambs are sleepin'-o
Birdies are nestlin', nestlin' together
Dream Angus is hurtlin' thru the heather

D Em G D / D - - G /   / 1st

Dreams to sell, fine dreams to sell
Angus is here wi' dreams to sell
Hush now, wee bairnie, & sleep without fear
Dream Angus will bring you a dream, my dear

List' to the curlew cryin'-o / Faint are the echoes dyin'-o
Even the birdies & beasties are sleepin'
But my bonny bairn lies weepin', weepin'

Sweet the lavrock (=skylark) sings at morn
Heraldin' in a bright new dawn
Wee lambs they coorie (=huddle) doon together
Along with the ewies (=sheep) in the heather

— trad. (Scottish)

Arr. © 2015 by Hal Leonard Corporation. Recs by Barbara Dickson, Annie Lennox, The Corries, Jackie Oates, Orealis etc.

DREAMLAND

Sun goes down & says goodnight
Pull your covers up real tight
By your bed we'll leave a light
To guide you off to dreamland

(in C) F G C - / F C G - / C F G Am / F Am G C

Your pillow's soft, your bed is warm
Your eyes are tired when day is done
One more kiss & you'll be gone / On your way to dreamland

(bridge) Every sleepy boy & girl
In every bed around the world
Can hear the stars up in the sky
Whispering a lullaby

G - F C /   /   / F C F G

Who knows where you'll fly away
Winging past the light of day
The Man in the Moon & the Milky Way
Welcome you to dreamland

— w & m: Mary Chapin Carpenter

© 1990 EMI April Music Inc. & Getarealjob Music. All rights controlled & administered by EMI April Music Inc. On her *Til Their Eyes Shine*, Priscilla Herdman & Art Garfunkel.

DREAMS OF HARMONY

To end the round:
    *From * (on final time thru) go to Coda*
    *At ** both voices sing Part 1 once in unison*
    *Then at end of Part 1 go from *** to "Ending".*

1. Goodnight - Bonne nuit / Oyasuminasai
Buenas noches - Lala / salama - Wan an
Spokoinyu noche _ / Gute nacht - Lila / tov _ / _ _

G Bm / C D / Em Bm / C G / Am - / D - / 1st 2 :‖
ending: G -

2. Wherever you rest your / head tonight
We are all one family / let's hold tight &
Fill the world with dreams of / harmony / tonight! _ / _ _
last time, instead of 2nd "tonight" go to:
harmony, no / matter what words we / use to say _
then all sing Part 1 ending: Goodnight

— w & m: Joanne Hammil

© 1988 JHO Music. Pt. 1 is "Goodnight" in English, French, Japanese, Spanish, Swahili, Chinese, Russian, German & Hebrew. On her *Pizza Boogie, Rounds & Partner S, V. 1* & recs by Roger Tincknell, Amidons, Freyda Epstein, Kathy Reid-Naiman, Tom Hunter & *Rounds Galore & More, V. 3.* In *SO!* 37:1, *Rounds Galore* *LS

DUERME NEGRITO

Duerme duerme, negrito [*Movila*]_que tu mamá
Está_en el campo _ negrito _ (repeat)

C - G - / C - - - :‖

_ Te va_a traer cordonices para ti / Te va... rica fruta para ti
Te... carne de cerdo para ti / Te... muchas cosas para ti
Y si el negro no se duerme viene_el diablo blanco y
¡Zas! le come la patita! chacapumba
Chacapum a pumba chacapum

C G (4x) C - / - G / - C

_ Trabajando / Trabajando duramente, **trabajando sí**
Trabajando y va de luto, **trabajando sí**
Trabajando y no le pagan... / Trabajando y va tosiendo...
Pa el negrito chiquitito, pa_el negrito sí
Trabajando si x2

C - / C Am (4x) C - / /

— trad. (Latin Amer. folksong)

FAIS DODO

Fais dodo, Colas, mon p'tit frère
Fais dodo, t'auras du lolo
Maman est en haut, qui fait des gâteaux [*du gâteau*]
Papa est en bas, fait du chocolat

C - G C / - Am G C / F C F C / /

Ta sœur est en haut qui fait des chapeaux
Ton frère est en bas qui fait des nougats

Ton cousin Gaston fait des gros bonbons
Ta cousine Charlotte fait de la compote

— trad. (French nursery rhyme)

GO TO SLEEPY, LITTLE BABY

Go to sleepy, little baby, 'fore the booger man catch you
All of them horses in that lot, **go to sleepy little baby,** (a capella)

Go to sleep (x2), go to sleepy, little baby
Mama went away & she told me to stay & take good care of
this baby

Go to sleep (x2), go... / All them horses in that lot, **go...**

Can't you hear them horses trot? **go...** / **Go to sleep (x2), go...**

— trad. (Georgia Sea Islands)

Didn't Leave Nobody but the Baby

Go to sleep, you little baby (2x)
Your mama's gone away & your daddy's gonna stay
Didn't leave nobody but the baby

(a capella) [D G D - / / D - - - / 1st]

Go to sleep, you little baby (2x)
Everybody's gone in the cotton & the corn
Didn't leave nobody but the baby

Don't you weep, pretty baby (2x)
She's long gone with her red shoes on
Gonna need another lovin' baby
  Don't you weep, pretty baby (2x)
  You & me & the devil makes 3
  Don't need no other lovin' baby
Go to sleepy, little baby (2x)
Come lay your bones on the alabaster stones
And be my everlovin' baby

   — w & m: Gillian Welch, T-Bone Burnett, Alan Lomax & Sidney Carter

GOOD NIGHT, MY SOMEONE

Goodnight, my someone, goodnight, my love
Sleep tight, my someone, sleep tight, my love
Our star is shining its brightest light
For goodnight, my love, for goodnight

G - D - / - - G - / - G7 C A7 / D A7 D -

Sweet dreams be yours, dear, if dreams there be
Sweet dreams to carry you close to me
I wish they may & I wish they might
Now goodnight, my someone, goodnight

/ " / " / " / C D G -

(bridge) True love can be whispered from heart to heart
When lovers are parted they say
But I must depend on a wish & a star
As long as my heart doesn't know who you are

C - Dm - / - G C - / - - G - / D A7 D D7

  — w & m: Meredith Willson

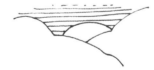

HAND UPON YOUR HEART

Place your hand upon your heart
Set your heart upon your deepest wish
Send your wish to the place where the sun begins
And you will find peace of mind

D A / - D / Bm Em / A D

Place your hand upon your heart
Let your heart feel all the love there is
Send your love to the place where the moon begins
And you will find peace of mind

Place your hand... / Make your heart as still as still can be
Send your calm to the place where the stars begin / **And you...**

Place... In your heart, say thanks for all you have
Send your thanks to the place where it all begins / **And...**

  — w & m: Patricia McKernon Runkle

I Don't Want To Live on the Moon

Well I'd like to visit the moon
On a rocket ship high in the air
Yes I'd like to visit the moon
But I don't think I'd like to live there
Tho' I'd like to look down at the earth from above
I would miss all the places & people I love
So altho' I might like it for one afternoon
I don't want to live on the moon

C G Am / F G C - :‖ F C Dm C / / F C G Am / F G C -

I'd like to travel under the sea
I could meet all the fish everywhere
Yes I'd travel under the sea
But I don't think I'd I'd like to live there
I might stay for a day there if I had my wish
But there's not much to do when your friends are all fish, and
An oyster & clam aren't real family
So **I don't want to live** in the sea

(bridge) I'd like to visit the jungle, hear the lions roar
Go back in time & meet a dinosaur
There's so many strange places I'd like to be
But none of them permanently

F C G C / / F C G Am / F G C -

So if I should visit the moon
Well I'll dance on a moonbeam & then
I will make a wish on a star
And I'll wish I was home once again
Tho' I'd like to look down at the earth from above
 I would miss all the places & people I love
So altho' I may go I'll be coming home soon
'Cos **I don't want to live on the moon**
    — w & m: Jeff Moss

© 1978 Festival Attractions, Inc. Sung by Aaron Neville w/ Ernie (Jim Henson) on *Sesame Street*.

Kitty Alone

Saw a crow a-flying low, **kitty alone, kitty alone**
Saw a crow a-flying low, **kitty alone a-lye**
Saw a crow a-flying low & a cat a-spinning tow
Kitty alone a-lye, rockum a-rye-ree

I: G - - D G / - - C G / - - C - / G - D G

In came a little bat, **kitty alone, kitty alone**
In came a little bat, **kitty alone a-lye**
In came a little bat with some butter & some fat
Kitty alone a-lye, rockum a-rye-ree   (continue pattern)

Next come in was a honeybee / with his fiddle across his knee
Next come in was 2 little ants / fixing around to have a dance
Next come in was little Jon / one shoe off & one shoe on
Next come in was little Pete / fixing around to go to sleep
Bee-o bye-o, baby-o / bye-o bee-o, baby-o

II: G - - - / - Bm Am D / G Bm CD GD C / Bm AmD G -
    — trad. (Appalach.)

Arr. © 2015 by Hal Leonard Corporation. On Jean Ritchie *Children's S & Games fr So. Mtns I*, Sally Rogers *At Quiet O'Clock*, Kevin Roth *Lullabies for Little Dreamers* II: A. Linda Schrade *Sleepytime Serenade*. Jean Ritchie said she made up v. for her sons, Peter & Jon.

Let It Be Your Lullabye

When you <u>sing</u> you've got to <u>sing</u> with the strength of a
   lullabye / You'll never know til you try
When you sing you've got to <u>sing</u> with the patience of a
   lullabye / You'll never know til you try
Your <u>song</u>'s inside you, let your <u>song</u> guide you
Let it be your lullabye

C - - - / - F G - / 1st / C Am G - / F G C Am / F G C -

When you <u>work</u> you've got to work with the strength...
Your <u>work</u>'s inside you, let your <u>work</u> guide you...
(insert: dream, love, etc.)
    — w & m: Lorre Wyatt

© 1984 Roots & Branches Music (BMI) www.lorrewyatt.com. On Bright Morning Star *Sweet & Sour* & Lorre Wyatt *Braving the Storm*.

Love Makes a Family

Here I am lying alone in my bed
Listening to voices below
I hear people laughing & hearing what's said
Listening now & I know, that
Love, love makes a family / Oh love, love makes...

(in G)   C G D G / C G D - / C G D Em / C - D - //
G D G - / /

Some of us live in this house here with me
Some of us live far away
All of us knowing that love is the key
They're all in my heart here to stay / **Love...**

Some came as babies & some came as friends
Some of us young & some old
Some for a while, some here til the end
They welcome us in from the cold...
    — w & m: Marcy Marxer

© 1996 2 Spoons Music (ASCAP). On her *Blanket Full of Dreams* (w/ Cathy Fink ↑2).

Lullaby For Teddy-o

Sleep my Teddy-o, let all your worries go
I'm here with you, near with you, sleep my Teddy-o

(↑2)   C G C FC G / C Em FG C

The day has come to an end, the moon he is my friend
The darkness creeps, the mountain sleeps **& so does Teddy-o**

The orange sun has set, the grass is cool & wet
There's peace for miles, the river smiles **& so does...**

The birds are in their nest, the flowers bend & rest
The stars are yours, the grizzly snores **& so...**
    — w & m: Eileen Packard

© 1980 Eileen Packard. On her *Incredible Spreadable* (Peanutbutterjam w/ Paul Recker), The Packards & Priscilla Herdman *Stardreamer* ↑2.

Moon & Me

Everybody else has closed their eyes
It's as quiet as can be
Everyone will sleep until sunrise
Everyone but moon & me

(↑3)   G - C G / - Em Am D / G - B7 Em / Am D G -

Rise Again

I can see her shining in the sky
Thru the branches of the willow tree
Me here in my bed & her so high / Just us 2, **the moon & me**

Moon & me (x2) / No one but the moon & me
I can see her shining, shining down on me / Just us 2, the...

C G D G / B7 - Em - / C D G Em / Am D G -

If there was a wish that I might try
I think I know what it would be
One night I'd have wings & then we'd fly
Together just **the moon...**

(bridge) Floating high above the world
Like a boat in a starry sea
While the earth was lost in sleep
We would sail **the moon...**

C - D - / G B7 Em - / Bm - E7 - / Cm - D -

But I'm only down here in my bed / Not sailing in some starry sea
Still I have these pictures in my head
Just dreaming 'bout **the moon...**
— w & m: Bill Harley

© 1988 Round River Music/Bill Harley, www.billharley.com. On his *Play It Again* &
You're In Trouble & Priscilla Herdman *Moondreamer.*

Owl Moon

You gotta be quiet **under a shining owl moon (2x)**
You gotta be quiet, yes you gotta be quiet
Under a shining (x3) owl moon

C - FC GC / C - FC G - / C - (as needed) /
FC FC FG C

You gotta make your own heat **under a shining owl... (2x)**
You gotta make your own heat & **you gotta** be quiet
Under a... (x3) owl moon

You gotta be brave **under... (2x)**
...be brave ...make your own heat & ...be quiet / **Under...**

You gotta have hope... / Yes **you gotta** have hope...
— w & m: Bruce O'Brien

Inspired by the book *Owl Moon* by Jane Yolen. ©1995 Bruce O'Brien. On his *Love
Is In The Middle.* *LS

Pocket Full of Stardust

Got a pocket full of stardust, gonna sprinkle it around
Gonna look at the moon, shining on the ground
Got a wish & a dream & a magic word
Gonna whisper it to you so it's barely heard

C G C G / C G C C7 / F - C - / - G C -

Got a handful of seeds, gonna sprinkle them around
Gonna grow a little garden from the fertile ground
I got a rainbow of flowers to share with you
And they're still sleeping in the morning dew

Got a heart full of love, gonna sprinkle it around
Gonna make you smile like a merry-go-round
I've got friends & family like the leaves of a tree
And the best part is they all love me
— w & m: Cathy Fink

© 2002 2 Spoons Music (ASCAP). On her *Pocket Full of Stardust* (w/ Marcy Marxer).

Rozhinkes Mit Mandlen (Raisins & Almonds)

In dem beys hamikdesh, in a vinkl kheyder
Zitst di almone, Bas Tsiyoyn aleyn
Ir ben-yokhidl, Yidelen, vigt zi keseyder
Un zingt im tsum shlofn a lidele sheyn / **Ay-lyu-lyu-lyu-lyu**

Am - Em Am / Em - B7 Em / C - - - / C Am E Am
Dm - Am -

Unter Yideles vigele _
Shteyt a klor-vays tsigele _
Dos tsigele iz geforn handlen_/ Dos vet zayn dayn baruf_
"Rozhinkes mit mandlen"_/ Shlof-zhe, Yidele, shlof_

Am Dm Am - / / E - Am - / Dm - Am - / E - Am - / /

In dem lidl, mayn kind, lign fil nevies
Az du vest amol zayn tsezeyt oyf der velt
A soykher vestu zayn fun ale tvues
Un vest in dem oykh fardinen fil gelt / **Ay-lyu-lyu-lyu-lyu**

Un az du vest vern raykh, Yidele
Zolst zikh dermonen in dem lidele
"Rozhinkes mit mandlen" / Dos vet zayn dayn baruf_
Yidele vet alts handlen / Shlof-zhe, Yidele, shlof _

Es vet kumen a tsayt fun vertpapirn
Kantorn veln zayn in der gantser velt
Der grester vestu zayn fun ale bankirn
Un vest in dem oykh fardinen fil gelt / **Ay-lyu-lyu...**

Un az du vest vern raykh, Yidele / Zolst...

Es vet kumen a tsayt fun ayznbanen,
Zey veln farfleytsn di gantse velt,
Ayzerne vegn vestu oysshpanen
Un vest in dem oykh fardinen fil gelt / **Ay-lyu...**

Un az du vest...
— w & m: Abraham Goldfaden (1840-1906)

Arr. © 2015 by Hal Leonard Corporation. Orig written for operetta, *Shulamith,
Daughter of Jerusalem.* Traditionally women sat apart fr men behind a screen in
synagogues. When boys 1st sat w/ the men, women showered them w/ raisins & almonds.
Teachers also put these on study tables as rewards. In Fran Minkoff *New Jewish SB.*

Sea of Dreams

In the morning comes the sun
And it shines on everyone
Whether great or small it warms us all
Until the day is done

G D G - / G ↓ Em - / C G D Em / C D G -

And when that light has passed
The stars can shine at last
With their lights so small they guide us all
Across the sea so vast

(bridge) And on that sea of dreams tonight
We wander far from shore
And we, the dreamers of the dream
Will find our peace once more

C ↓ - G / C D G - / 1st / C Em Am D
— w & m: Joel Mabus

© 1994 Joel Mabus/Fingerboard Music (BMI). On his *Promised Land 12* & *Retold.*

161

SLEEP MY BABY (Suo Gân)

Sleep my baby on my bosom
Warm and cozy will it prove
Round thee mother's arms are folding
In her heart a mother's love
There shall no one come to harm thee
Naught shall ever break thy rest
Sleep my darling babe in quiet
Sleep on mother's gentle breast

G - C D / G - CD G : | G - C G /   / 1st 2

Sleep serenely, baby, slumber
Lovely baby, gently sleep
Tell me wherefore art thou smiling
Smiling sweetly in thy sleep?
Do the angels smile in heaven
When thy happy smile they see?
Dost thou on them smile while slumb'ring
On my bosom peacefully

Do not fear the sound of a breeze
Brushing leaves against the door
Do not dread the murmuring seas
Lonely waves washing the shore
Sleep child mine, there's nothing here
While in slumber at my breast
Angels smiling, have no fear
Holy angels guard your rest

Huna blentyn yn fy mynwes
Clyd a chynnes ydyw hon
Breichiau mam sy'n dyn amdanat
Cariad mam sy dan fy mron
Ni cha dim amharu'th gyntun
Ni wna undyn â thi gam
Huna'n dawel, anwyl blentyn
Huna'n fwyn ar fron dy fam

— trad. (Welsh), Eng w: Robert Bryan

Arr © 2015 Hal Leonard Corporation. 1st pub. ca. 1800. Bryan (1858-1920) was a Welsh folklorist & poet. Welsh lullabye. On Mormon Tabernacle Choir's *Love is Spoken Here*, Charlotte Chuch's *Voice of an Angel* & in Steven Spielberg's 1987 film, *Empire of the Sun*.

SULIRAM

Suliram, suliram ram ram
Suliram yang manis _
Adu hai indung suhoorang _
Bidjakla sana dipandang manis (la suli-)

A D E - / A D A - / D E A - / E - A -

(bridge) Tingi la, tingi, si matahari (suliram)
Anakla koorbau mati toortambat (suliram)
Sudala lama saiya menchari _
Baruse klarung sa ya mendabat (**la suli-...**)

A E7 A (E7 A) / - D A (E7 A) / D E A - / E - A -

— trad. (Surinam)

Arr. © 2015 by Hal Leonard Corporation. On Weavers Goodnight Irene 12 & Miriam Makeba The Unforgettable... In Jerry Silverman's FS Encyclopedia.

THE SUN SETTLES DOWN

The sun _ settles down_
The moon_rises high_
Night_calms the earth_
The stars_fill the sky_
Good night,_good night sleep tight
And wake in the morning light _

(↑2) C F C - / - - F - / C F C - / - Am Gm - /
Fmaj7 Fm CEm Am / F G C -

Today has now gone / Tomorrow is drawing nigh
Soon comes the dawn / Then up we'll rise, you & I

Too soon you must go / So much to say, much to do
Sleep, sleep tonight / The angels will wait for you

— w & m: Jonathan Lutz

© 1978 Jonathan Lutz. On his YT video. *LS.

TIME IS NOW FOR SLEEPING

Day is over, the sky is gold & red / **Time is now for sleeping**
Shadows lengthen round about your bed / **Time...**
Oh see how the night sets the stars alight / **Time...**

Am Em Dm Em / Dm Em Am - / Am G F Em / Dm G Am -
F Em Dm Em /   "   /

Listen closely, far-off night birds cry / **Time...**
High above us, tall winds kiss the sky...
Oh hear how the trees whisper in the breeze...

The sun is sinking, the moon is on the rise...
Stars are twinkling & sleep is in your eyes...
Oh see how the moon tiptoes past your room...

— w & m: Patricia McKernon Runkle

© 1985 Patricia Mckernon. On her Midnight Minstrel 13.

TWINKLE, TWINKLE, LITTLE STAR

Twinkle twinkle, little star, how I wonder what you are!
Up above the world so high like a diamond in the sky
Twinkle twinkle, little star, how I wonder what you are!

C - FC GC / CF CG CF CG / 1st

When the blazing sun is gone, when he nothing shines upon
Then you show your little light, twinkle twinkle all the night...

Then the traveller in the dark, thanks you for your tiny spark
He could not see which way to go if you did not twinkle so...

In the dark blue sky you keep & often thru my curtains peep
For you never shut your eye til the sun is in the sky...

As your bright & tiny spark, lights the traveller in the dark
Tho' I know not what you are, twinkle twinkle, little star...

Twinkle twinkle little bat, how I wonder what you're at
Up above the world you fly like a tea tray in the sky...

— w: Jane Taylor ("The Star"), m: trad. (French)

© 2015 Hal Leonard Corporation. Taylor's poem was orig pub in 1806 in *Rhymes for the Nursery*. The tune "Ah! vous dirai-je, Maman", 1st pub in 1761, was used by Mozart for his *12 Variations on...* Parody is by Lewis Carroll (1865).

WATCH THE STARS

Watch the stars, see how they run **(2x)**
You know the stars run down **at the setting of that sun**
Watch the stars, **see how** they run

(↑2) G D G - / C - G - / C G D Em / 1st

Watch the moon, **see how** she shines *[it glows]* **(2x)**
You know the moon comes out **at the setting of the sun**
Watch the moon...

Watch the wind, **see how** it blows **(2x)**
You know the wind it blows **at the setting of that sun**
Watch the wind...

> — trad. (Afr-Amer. spiritual)

WATER, SUN, EARTH & SKY

1. Water, sun, earth & sky / Round the world a butterfly
Rests its wings in hush-a-bye / Water, sun, earth & sky
Rocka- **2.** bye, little butterfly. Wings of / gold, sky of blue
_None so beautiful as you, Oh / you are my little_butterfly

(in D) A D **(4x)**

> — w & m: Cathy Fink & Marcy Marxer

WHEREVER YOU GO (I Love You)

Wherever you go, whatever you do
Thru all the changes you go thru
I'll be there right next to you / I love you _

C G / C F / C G / GC C

When you're too small to reach the sink
So all you do is sit & think
About how clean you would have been
Know that I will love you then

F G / C F / C G / F G

When you can button up your shirt
And brush off your own dust & dirt
When you can spell & write your name
I will love you just the same

When you lose your 2 front teeth
And miss the things you used to eat
And try to reach things up above
I will give you all my love

When you crawl into your bed
And on a pillow lay your head
When you're drifting off to sleep
I will love you while you dream

> — w & m: Cathy Fink & Marcy Marxer

WHO CAN SAIL? (Vem Kan Segla)

Vem kan segla förutan vind?
Vem kan ro utan åror?
Vem kan skiljas från vännen sin
Utan att fälla tårar?

(in 6/8 ↑3) Am - / Dm G7 C E / Dm E Am - / B7 E Am -

Jag kan segla förutan vind
Jag kan ro utan åror
Men ej skiljas från vännen min
Utan att fälla tårar

Who can sail without the wind? / Who can row without oars?
Who can separate from a friend / Without shedding tears?

I can sail without the wind / I can row without oars
But I can't leave a friend behind / Without shedding tears

> — trad. (Swedish)

WHO WILL SING ME LULLABIES

Lay me down gently, lay me down low
I fear I am broken & won't mend, I know
There's one thing I ask when the stars light the skies
Who now will **sing me lullabies?** / O who now... **(in 3/4 ↑4)**

G C G D / G C D - / C D G C / Em D G D / Em D G (C G D)

In this big world I'm lonely, for I am but small
Oh angels in heaven, don't you care for me at all?
You've heard my heart breaking for it rang thru the skies
So why won't you... **(2x)**

I lay here, I'm weeping for the stars they have come
I lay here not sleeping, now the long night has begun
The man in the moon, oh he can't help but cry
For there's no one to... **(2x)**

(tag) Who will sing me to sleep **(4x)** Who will sing

G C G D **(4x)** G (C G D G -)

> — w & m: Kate Rusby

See also: **Family, Play** and in **Ballads**: Safe from harm (after Fear a Bhata), **Dreams:** When you wish upon a star, **Earthcare:** Rockin' in a weary land, **Golden:** Mr. Sandman, **Healing:** I bid you goodnight.

Millennial Songs

1, 2, 3, 4

1, 2, 3, 4, tell me that you love me more
Sleepless long nights, that is what my youth was for
Old teenage hopes are alive at your door
Left you with nothing but they want some more

C ↓ Am F (4x)

Oh uh oh, you're changing your heart
Oh uh oh, you know who you are

G - F - / /

Sweetheart, bitter heart, now I can tell you apart
Cozy & cold, put the horse before the cart
Those teenage hopes who have tears in their eyes
Too scared to own up to one little lie

1, 2, 3, 4, 5, 6, 9 or 10
Money can't buy you back the love that you had then (repeat)

(tag) For the teenage boys
They're breaking your heart (repeat)

1, 2, 3, 4 (Sesame Street version)

1, 2, 3, 4, monsters walking across the floor
I love counting, counting to the number 4
Oh you're counting, counting with me
To 1 less than 5 & 1 more than 3

Oh uh oh, we're counting to 4
Oh... let's count some more

1, 2, 3, 4, penguins that went by the door
I love counting, counting to the number 4
I see 4 here, I see 4 there
My favorite number, nothing can compare

...chickens just back from the shore / I love...
...penguins that went by the door
...monsters walking across the floor

(tag) Oh! / Counting to 4 (repeat) / Counting to 4 (2x)

— w & m: Feist & Sally Seltmann

A TEAM

White lips, pale face, breathing in snowflakes
Burnt lungs, sour taste
Light's gone, day's end, struggling to pay rent
Long nights, strange men

(↑2) G - G ↓ / Em C G - :‖

And they say she's in the Class A Team
Stuck in her daydream been this way since 18
But lately her face seems slowly sinking, wasting,
    crumbling like
Pastries & they scream, the worst things in life come free to us

Am - C - / G - D - :‖

'Cos we're [she's] just under the upper hand & go[es] mad
    for a couple grams
And she don't want to go outside tonight
And in a pipe she flies to the Motherland or sells love to
    another man
It's too cold outside for angels to fly / For angels to fly
(2nd v.:) An angel will die

Em C G - :‖ (5x)

Ripped gloves, rain coat, tried to swim & stay afloat
Dry house, wet clothes
Loose change, bank notes, weary-eyed, dry throat
Call girl, no phone

(bridge) Covered in white, with closed eyes & hoping for a better life
This time, we'll fade out tonight straight down the line

G Em C G / Am C G -

— w & m: Ed Sheeran

AIN'T NO REST FOR THE WICKED

I was walkin' down the street when out the corner of my eye
I saw a pretty little thing approaching me
She said "I never seen a man who looked so all alone
Oh could you use a little company?
And if you pay the right price, your evening will be nice
And you can go & send me on my way"
I said "You're such a sweet young thing why do you do this to
    yourself?" / She looked at me & this is what she said:

D F / G FC :‖ (4x)

"Oh, there ain't no rest for the wicked
Money don't grow on trees
I got bills to pay, I got mouths to feed
There ain't nothing in this world for free
But no I can't slow down, I can't hold back
Tho' you know I wish I could
But no there ain't no rest for the wicked
Until we close our eyes for good"

D FC :‖ (8x)

Not even 15 mins. later I'm still walkin' down the street
When I saw the shadow of a man creep out of sight & then
He swept up from behind, he put a gun up to my head
He made it clear he wasn't lookin' for a fight, he said
"Give me all you got, I want your money not your life
But if you try to make a move I won't think twice" I told him
"You can have my cash but 1st you know I gotta ask
What made you want to live this kind of life?" he said…

Well now a couple hrs passed & I was sitting in my house
The day was winding down & coming to an end
So I turned to the TV & flipped it over to the news
And what I saw I almost couldn't comprehend
I saw a preacher man in cuffs, he'd taken money fr the church
He'd stuffed his bank account with righteous dollar bills,
But even still I can't say much because I know we're all the same
Oh yes we all seek out to satisfy those thrills, you know

(last cho: substitute "We" for "I")

— w & m: Jared Champion, Lincoln Parish, Donald Schultz,
Matthew Schultz & Daniel Tichenor

AMERICAN IDIOT

Don't wanna be an American idiot
Don't want a nation under the new media
And can you hear the sound of hysteria?
The subliminal mindf*** America

(in G) (tacet) - - - (G C FC GF) (4x)

Welcome to a new kind of tension
All across the alienation
Where everything isn't meant to be okay
Television dreams of tomorrow
We're not the ones who're meant to follow
For that's enough to argue

C - - - / G - - - / D - - - G - - - / 1st 2 / D - - -(tacet)

Well maybe I'm the faggot America
I'm not a part of a redneck agenda
Now everybody do the propaganda
And sing along to the age of paranoia

Don't want to be an American Idiot
One nation controlled by the media
Information age of hysteria
It's calling out to idiot America

— w: Billie Joe, m: Green Day

ANYONE ELSE BUT YOU

You're a part-time lover & a full-time friend
The monkey on your back is the latest trend
I don't see what anyone can see in anyone else _ but you
I kiss you on the brain in the shadow of the train
Kiss you all starry-eyed, my body swingin' from side to side
I don't…
Here is the church & here is the steeple
We sure are cute for 2 ugly people…
Pebbles forgive me, the trees forgive me
So why can't you forgive me?…
I will find my niche in your car
With my MP3, DVD, rumple-packed guitar…

G - / Cmaj7 - / G - Cmaj7 - :‖ (repeat 5x)

Du dudu du dudu du dudu dudu (3x) / Du

G - / Cmaj7 - :‖

Up up, down down, left right, left right, "b" "a", start
Just because we use cheats doesn't mean we're not smart / **I don't…**
You are always tryin' to keep it real
I'm in love with how you feel / **I don't …**
We both have shiny, happy fits of rage
You want more fans, I want more stage…
Don Quixote was a steel-driving man
My name is Adam, I'm your biggest fan!…
Scrunched [squinched] up your face & did a dance
Shook a little turd out of the bottom of your pants…

— w & m: Kimya Dawson & Adam Green

BIRDHOUSE IN YOUR SOUL

(intro) I'm your only friend, I'm not your only friend but I'm a little
Glowing friend but really I'm not actually your friend, but I am

A G C D / G Am Bb E

Blue canary in the outlet by the light switch
  who watches over you
Make a little birdhouse in your soul, not to put too fine a
  point on it, say I'm the only bee in your bonnet
Make a little birdhouse in your soul

A D A D / AE F#mD C F C F / CAm FE A (D A D)

I have a secret to tell from my electrical well
It's a simple message & I'm leaving out the whistles & bells
So the room must listen to me, filibuster vigilantly
My name is blue canary one note spelled l-i-t-e
_My story's infinite_like the Longines Symphonette it doesn't rest

A D A D / AE A D E :‖ F#m D B7 D E

There's a picture opposite me of my primitive ancestry which
Stood on rocky shores & kept the beaches shipwreck free
Tho' I respect that a lot, I'd be fired if that were my job
After killing Jason off & countless screaming Argonauts
Bluebird of friendliness like guardian angels it's always near

— w & m: John Linnell & John Flansburgh

BLACK HORSE & THE CHERRY TREE

Woo hoo, woo hoo (2x)

Em - B7 Em / /

Well my heart knows me better than I know myself
So I'm gonna let it do all the talking / **Woo, hoo...**
I came across a place in the middle of nowhere
With a big black horse & a cherry tree / **Woo, hoo...**

Em - / - - / - - B7 Em :‖

I fell in fear upon my back
I said don't look back, just keep on walking / **Woo, hoo...**
And the big black horse said look this way
He said, hey lady, will you marry me?...

But I **said no-no, no, no-no-no**
I said, no, no, you're not the one for me
No-no, no, no-no-no
I said, no, no, you're not the one for me

Em D C Em / - D C7 Em :‖

And my heart had a problem in the early hrs
So I stopped it dead for a beat or 2...
But I cut some cord & I shouldn't have done that
And it won't forgive me after all these yrs...

So I sent it to a place in the middle of nowhere
With a big black horse & a cherry tree...
Now it won't come back 'cos it's oh-so-happy
And now I've got a hole for the world to see, and it **said...**

Big black horse & a cherry tree
Big black horse, my heart's forsaken me (repeat)

Em D C Em / - D C7 Em :‖

— w & m: Katie ("KT") Tunstall

BOULEVARD OF BROKEN DREAMS

I walk a lonely road, the only one that I have ever known
I don't know where it goes but it's home to me & I walk alone
I walk this empty street on the Blvd. of Broken Dreams
Where the city sleeps & I'm the only one & I walk alone
I walk alone **(x2)** / I walk alone, I walk a-

Em G D A :‖ **(6x)**

(bridge) My shadow's the only one that walks beside me
My shallow heart's the only thing that's beating
Sometimes I wish someone out there will find me
Til then I walk alone

C G D Em / / / C G B7 -

I'm walking down the line that divides me somewhere in my mind
On the border line of the edge & where I walk alone
Read betw the lines what's f-ed up & everything's all right
Check my vital signs & know I'm still alive & I walk alone

— w: Billie Joe, m: Green Day

F***IN' PERFECT

Made a wrong turn once or twice
Dug my way out, blood & fire
Bad decision, that's all right
Welcome to my silly life
Mistreated, misplaced, misunderstood
Mis- no way it's all good, it didn't slow me down
Mistaken always 2nd guessing
Underestimated, look, I'm still around

G D / Em C :‖ **(4x)**

Pretty, pretty please, don't you ever, ever feel
Like you're less than f-ing *[less than]* **perfect**
Pretty, pretty please, if you ever, ever feel
Like you're nothing, you're f-ing perfect to me

G D / Em C :‖

You're so mean when you talk
About yourself, you are wrong
Change the voices in your head
Make them like you instead
So complicated, look how big you'll make it
Filled with so much hatred, such a tired game
It's enough, I've done all I can think of
Chased down all my demons, see you do the same

The whole world's scared so I swallow the fear
The only thing I should be drinking is an ice cold beer
So cool in lying & we try, try, try
But we try too hard, it's a waste of my time
Done looking for the critics, 'cos they're everywhere
They don't like my jeans, they don't get my hair
Strange ourselves & we do it all the time
Why do we do that? Why do I do that?

— w & m: Alecia Moore, Max Martin & Johan Schuster

GOOD RIDDANCE (Time Of Your Life)

Another turning point, a fork stuck in the road
Time grabs you by the wrist, directs you where to go
So make the best of this test & don't ask why
It's not a question but a lesson learned in time

G - C D / / Em D C G / /

It's something unpredictable, but in the end is right
I hope you had the time of your life

Em G Em G / Em D G -

So take the photographs & still frames in your mind
Hang it on a shelf in good health & good time
Tattoos of memories & dead skin on trial
For what it's worth, it was worth all the while

— w: Billie Joe, m: Green Day

HEY, SOUL SISTER

Your lipstick stains on the front lobe of my left side brains
I knew I wouldn't forget you & so I went & let you blow my mind
Your sweet moonbeam, the smell of you in every single
    dream I dream
I knew when we collided, you're the one I have decided who's
    one of my kind

`C G Am F / C G Am FG :‖`

Hey soul sister, ain't that Mr. Mr. on the radio, stereo,
    the way you move ain't fair, you know
Hey soul sister, I don't want to miss a single thing you do
Tonight

`F GC F GC / F GC F G / C (G Am FG)`

Just in time, I'm so glad you have a one-track mind like me
You gave my life direction, a game show love connection we
    can't deny
I'm so obsessed, my heart is bound to beat right out my un-
    trimmed chest
I believe in you, like a virgin, you're Madonna & I'm always gonna
    wanna blow your mind

The way you can cut a rug, watching you's the only drug I need
So gangsta, I'm so thug, you're the only one I'm dreaming of
You see, I can be myself now finally, in fact there's nothing I
    can't be
I want the world to see you'll be, with me

    — w & m: Pat Monahan, Espen Lind & Amund Bjørkland

HEY THERE DELILAH

_Hey there Delilah, what's it like in New York City?
I'm a thousand miles away but girl, tonight you look so pretty,
Yes you do, Times Square can't shine as bright
As you, I swear it's true

`(↑2) C - Em - / / Am - F G / Am - G -`

_Hey there Delilah, don't you worry about the distance
I'm right there if you get lonely give this song another listen,
Close your eyes, listen to my voice,
It's my disguise, I'm by your side

Oh it's what you do to me (4x)
What you do to me (omit before bridge)

`C - Am - (4x) C -`

_Hey there Delilah, I know times are getting hard
But just believe me, girl, someday I'll pay the bills with this guitar
We'll have it good, we'll have the life
We knew we would, my word is good

_Hey there Delilah, I've got so much left to say
If every simple song I wrote to you would take your breath away
I'd write it all, even more in love with me
You'd fall, we'd have it all / **Oh it's what...**

(bridge) A thousand miles seems pretty far, but they've got
    planes & trains & cars
I'd walk to you if I had no other way
Our friends would all make fun of us, and we'll just laugh along
    because
We know that none of them have felt this way
Delilah I can promise you that by the time we get thru
The world will never ever be the same / And you're to blame

`F - G - / C - Am -:‖ F - G - / Am - - - / G - - -`

_Hey there Delilah you be good & don't you miss me
2 more yrs & you'll be done with sch & I'll be making history
Like I do, you'll know it's all because of you
We can do whatever we want to
Hey there Delilah here's to you / This one's for you

`C - Em - / / Am - F G Am - / F G Am - / G - - -`

    — w & m: Tom Higgenson (of Plain White T's)

I & LOVE & YOU

Load the car & write the note
Grab your bag & grab your coat
Tell the ones that need to know
We are headed north

`(↑2) C - F C - - - / / / Am G F - - -`

One foot in & one foot back
But it don't pay, to live like that
So I cut the ties & I jumped the tracks
For never to return

Ah Brooklyn, Brooklyn, take me in
Are you aware the shape I'm in?
My hands they shake, my head it spins
Ah Brooklyn, Brooklyn, take me in

`C - F C - - - (4x)`

When at first I learned to speak / I used all my words to fight
With him & her & you & me / Oh but it's just a waste of time
    (Yeah it's such a waste of time)

That woman, she's got eyes that shine
Like a pair of stolen polished dimes
She asked to dance, I said it's fine
I'll see you in the morning time / **Ah, Brooklyn...**

(bridge) 3 words that became hard to say / I & love & you
What you were then, I am today / Look at the things I do
Ah, Brooklyn...

`C - F C - - - / Am G F - - - :‖`

Dumbed down & numbed by time & age
Your dreams to catch the world, the cage
The highway sets the traveler's stage / All exits look the same

3 words that became hard to say / I & love & you **(3x)**

`C - F C - - - / Am G F - - - / / /`

    — w & m: Scott Avett, Seth Avett & Robert Crawford

I WILL WAIT

Well I came home like a stone
And I fell heavy into your arms
These days of dust, which we've known
Will blow away with this new sun

C - F - / C - G - :‖

But I'll kneel down, wait for now
And I'll kneel down, know my ground

Am G CF CG G - / / /

And I will wait, I will wait for you (2x)

C - Em G / / /

So break my step & relent
Well you forgave & I won't forget
Know what we've seen & him with less
Now in some way shake the excess

But I will wait, I will... / And I will wait...

Now I'll be bold as well as strong
And use my head alongside my heart
So tame my flesh & fix my eyes
A tethered mind freed from the lies

But I'll kneel down, wait for now / And I'll kneel down...

(bridge) Raise my hands / Paint my spirit gold
Bow my head / Keep my heart slow

C CG Am - / F CG G :‖

'Cos I will wait, I... / And I will wait...

— w & m: Mumford & Sons

I WON'T GIVE UP

When I look into your eyes,_it's like watching the night sky_
Or a beautiful sunrise,_for there's so much they hold_

(↑2) GD D GD D / GD D A -

And just like them old stars, I see that you've come so far
To be right where you are, how old is your soul?

I won't give up on us, even if the skies get rough
I'm giving you all my love, I'm still looking up

G D Bm A / G D A -

And when you're needing your space, to do some navigating
I'll be here patiently waiting to see what you find

'Cos even the stars they burn, some even fall to the earth
We got a lot to learn, God knows we're worth it
No I won't give up

G D Bm A / G D A - / G -

(bridge) I don't wanna be someone who walks away so easily
I'm here to stay & make the difference that I can make_
Our differences they do a lot to teach us how to use
The tools & gifts we've got yeah we got a lot at stake_
And in the end you're still my friend, at least we did intend for us
    to work, we didn't break, we didn't burn
_We had to learn how to bend_without the world caving in
_I had to learn what I got _& what I'm not / And who I am_

Em - / A - :‖ C - / A - / C A / D -

I won't give up...

— w & m: Jason Mraz & Michael Natter

I'M YOURS

Well, you done done me & you bet I felt it, I tried to be chill but
    you're so hot that I melted
I fell right thru the cracks , now I'm trying to get back
Before the cool done run out I'll be giving it my bestest
    and nothing's gonna stop me but divine intervention
I reckon, it's again my turn to win some or learn some

(in G ↑4) G - D - / Em - C - :‖ (as needed)

But I won't hesitate, no more
No more, it cannot wait, I'm yours

Well, open up your mind & see like me,
    open up your plans & damn
You're free, look into your heart & you'll find love (x4)

Listen to the music of the moment, people dance & sing,
    we're just one big
Family & it's our God-forsaken right to be loved, loved, loved, loved
Loved (last line: A7 -)

So I won't hesitate, no more
No more, it cannot wait I'm sure
There's no need to complicate, our time
Is short, this is our fate, I'm yours

(bridge) Do-do-do... do you want to come on, scootch on over
Closer dear & I will nibble your ear

G Em D - / C - A7 -

I've been spending way too long checking my tongue in the mir-
    ror & bending over bkwds just to try to see it clearer
But my breath fogged up the glass & so I drew a new face
    and I laughed
I guess what I'll be saying is there ain't no better reason to rid
    yourself of vanities & just go with the seasons
It's what we aim to do, our name is our virtue

But I won't hesitate, no more
No more, it cannot wait I'm yours
Well open up your mind & see open up your plans & damn
You're free, look into... & you'll find the sky is yours

(tag) So please don't (x3) there's no need to complicate
'Cos our time is short, this oh (x2) this is our fate, I'm yours
(end on G)

— w & m: Jason Mraz

IF I HAD $1,000,000

If I had a million dollars (if I had a million dollars)
Well, I'd buy you a house (I would buy you a house)
And if I had... / I'd buy you furniture for your house (maybe a
    nice chesterfield or an ottoman)
And if... / Well I'd buy you a K-Car (a nice Reliant automobile)
And... dollars, I'd buy your love

(↑2) G D C - (6x) / G D C D

> **If I had a... (**I'd build a tree fort in our yard)
> **If I...** (you could help, it wouldn't be that hard)
> **If:** (maybe we could put a little tiny fridge in there somewhere)

> **C D G Em (3x)**

(spoken) We could just go up there & hang out
Like open the fridge & stuff & there'd be foods laid out for us
With little pre-wrapped sausages & things—mmm
They have pre-wrapped sausages but they don't have
Pre-wrapped bacon (well can you blame them?) Yeah!

C D / G D / C - / G D / C D

If I had... (if I had...)
Well, I'd buy you a fur coat (but not a real fur coat that's cruel)
And if... / I'd buy you an exotic pet (like a llama or an emu)
And... / I'd buy you John Merrick's remains (all them crazy ele-
    phant bones) / **And if I had..., I'd buy your love**

If I had..., we wouldn't have to walk to the store
If..., we'd take a limousine 'cos it costs more
If..., we wouldn't have to eat Kraft Dinner

(spoken) But we would eat Kraft Dinner
Of course we would, we'd just eat more
And buy really expensive ketchups with it
That's right, all the fanciest dijon ketchup—mmmmmm.

C D / G D / C - / G D

If I had... / I'd buy you a green dress (but not a real green dress,
    that's cruel)
... I'd buy you some art (a Picasso or a Garfunkel)
... I'd buy you a monkey (haven't you always wanted a monkey?)
If I had a million dollars I'd buy your love

    — w & m: Steven Page & Ed Robertson

LIVE & DIE

All it will take is just one moment and
You can say goodbye to how we had it planned
Fear like a habit, run like a rabbit out & away
Thru the screen door to the unknown

C Em F C / - Am F G :‖

And I want to love you & more, I want to find you & more
Where do you reside when you hide? How can I find you?
'Cos I want to send you & more, I want to tempt you & more
Can you tell that I am alive? let me prove it
You and I, we're the same, live & die, we're the same
Hear my voice, know my name, you & I, we're the same

Am - Dm - / F C Em F - :‖ C Am F G /   /

Left like a pharaoh, sing like a sparrow anyway
Even if there is no land or love in sight
We bloom like roses, leave like Moses, out & away
Thru the bitter crowd to the daylight

    — w & m: Scott Avett, Seth Avett & Robert Crawford

NAKED AS WE CAME

_She says "Wake up, it's no use pretending"
I'll keep stealing, breathing her
_Birds are leaving over autumn's ending
    One of us will die inside these arms _

D Em* /   /   / D Em* A9 (*bass run E,F#,B,A)

Eyes wide open_ _ / Naked as we came _
One will spread our_ / Ashes 'round the yard _

Em* A9 /   /   / Em* D (Em* D Em*)

She says "If I leave before you, darling / Don't you waste me in the ground"
I lay smiling like our sleeping children / **One...**

    — w & m: Sam Beam

OLD BEFORE YOUR TIME

When I was a younger man lookin' for a pot of gold
Everywhere I turned the doors were closin'
It took every ounce of faith I had to keep on keepin' on
And still I felt like I was only losin'
I refused then like I do now to let anybody tie me down
And I lost a few good friends along the way
I was raised up poor & I wanted more & maybe I'm a little too proud
Lookin' back I see a kid who was just afraid
Hungry & old before his time

G C G C / G C D7 - :‖ C G - C / G - D - :‖ C - D G

Thru the yrs I've known my share of broken hearted fools
And those who couldn't choose a path worth taking
There's nothin' in the world so sad as talking to a man
Who never knew his life was his for making
Ain't it about time you realize? It's not worth keepin' score
You win some, you lose some & you let it go
What's the use of stacking on every failure, another stone
Till you find you've spent your whole life building walls
Lonely & old before...

(bridge) It took so long to see / That truth was all around me

C - Em - / C - Em D

Now the wren has gone to roost, the sky is turnin' gold
Like the sky my soul is also turnin'
Turnin' from the past, at last & all I've left behind
Could it be that I am finally learnin'?
Learnin' that I'm deserving of love & the peaceful heart
I won't tear myself apart no more for tryin'
I'm tired of lyin' to myself, tryin' to buy what can't be bought
It's not livin' that you're doin' if it feels like dyin' / It's cryin', growin' **old...**

    — w & m: Ray LaMontagne

ROLLING IN THE DEEP

There's a fire starting in my heart
Reaching a fever pitch, it's bringing me out the dark
Finally I can see you crystal clear
Go ahead & sell me out & I'll lay your ship *[s**t]* bare

(↑3) Am - Em - / G - Em G / 1st / G - Em G

See how I leave with every piece of you
Don't underestimate the things that I will do
There's a fire starting in my heart
Reaching a fever pitch & it's bringing me out the dark

The scars of your love remind me of us
They keep me thinking that we almost had it all
The scars of your love, they leave me breathless
I can't help feeling

F - G - / Em - F - / 1st / Em - E -

We could have had it all (you're gonna wish you never had met me)
Rolling in the deep (tears are gonna fall, rolling in the deep)
You had my heart inside of your hand (you're gonna...)
And you played it, to the beat (tears...)

Am - G - / F - - G :‖

Baby, I have no story to be told
But I've heard one on you & I'm gonna make your head burn
Think of me in the depths of your despair
Make a home down there as mine sure won't be shared
The scars...

Throw your soul thru every open door
Count your blessings to find what you look for
Turn my sorrow into treasured gold
You'll pay me back in kind & reap just what you sow

We could have had...

— w & m: Adele Adkins & Paul Epworth

THE SCIENTIST

_Come up to meet you, tell you I'm sorry
You don't know how lovely you are
_I had to find you, tell you I need you
Tell you I set you apart
_Tell me your secrets & ask me your questions
Oh let's go back to the start
_Running in circles, coming in tails
Heads on a science apart

(in C ↑5) Am7 - F - C / - Cadd9 - :‖ (4x)

_Nobody said it was easy
_It's such a shame for us to part
_Nobody said it was easy
_No one ever said it would be this hard _
_Oh take me back to the start _

F - - - / C - Cadd9 - / 1st / C - Cmaj7 Am G - / - - C -

I was just guessing at numbers & figures
Pulling your puzzles apart
Questions of science, science & progress
Do not speak as loud as my heart
Tell me you love me, come back & haunt me
Oh & I rush to the start
Running in circles, chasing our tails
Coming back as we are

— w & m: Guy Berryman, Jon Buckland, Will Champion & Chris Martin

SOMEONE LIKE YOU

I heard that you're settled down
That you found a girl & you're married now
I heard that your dreams came true
Guess she gave you things I didn't give to you
Old friend, why are you so shy?
Ain't like you to hold back or hide from the light
I hate to turn up out of the blue uninvited but I couldn't
stay away, I couldn't fight it
I had hoped you'd see my face & that you'd be reminded
that for me it isn't over

C - Em - / Am - F - :‖ (3x, v.2 = 2x) G Am F - /   /

Never mind, I'll find someone like you
I wish nothing but the best for you too
Don't forget me, I beg, I remember you said
"Sometimes it lasts in love but sometimes it hurts instead" (2x)

C G Am F (5x)

You know how the time flies
Only yesterday was the time of our lives
We were born & raised in a summer haze
Bound by the surprise of our glory days / **I hate to turn up...**

(bridge) Nothing compares, no worries or cares
Regrets & mistakes, they are memories made
Who would have known how
Bittersweet this would taste?

G - / Am - / F - / Dm Em F -

— w & m: Adele Adkins & Dan Wilson

SONS & DAUGHTERS

_When we arrive, sons & daughters
_We'll make our homes on the water
We'll build our walls aluminum
We'll fill our mouths with cinnamon / Now

D G (4x) / D (G D G)

These currents pull us 'cross the border
Steady your boats, arms to shoulder
Til tides will pull our hull aground
Making this cold harbor now / Home

Take up your arms, sons & daughters
We will arise from the bunkers
By land, by sea, by dirigible
We'll leave our tracks untraceable / Now
(tag) Here all the bombs fade away (D G repeating)

— w & m: Colin Meloy

UNDER THE BRIDGE

Sometimes I feel like I don't have a partner
Sometimes I feel like my only friend
Is the city I live in, the City of Angels
Lonely as I am together we cry

(↑2) D A Bm G (4x)

I drive on her streets 'cos she's my companion
I walk thru her hills 'cos she knows who I am
She sees my good deeds & she kisses me windy
I never worry, now that is a lie

I don't ever want to feel like I did that day
Take me to the place I love, take me all the way
I don't ever want to feel like I did that day
Take me to the place I love, take me all the way (yeah x3)

Em D A Bm (4x)

It's hard to believe that there's nobody out there
It's hard to believe that I'm all alone
At least I have her love, the city she loves me
Lonely as I am, together we cry

(tag) **Under the bridge downtown** is where I drew some blood
Under the bridge... I could not get enough
Under... forgot about my love
Under... I gave my life away (yeah x2)
Here I stay (yeah x2) here I stay

G Bb F Eb (5x)

— w & m: Anthony Kiedis, Flea, John Frusciante & Chad Smith

VIVA LA VIDA

I used to rule the world
Seas would rise when I gave the word
Now in the morning I sleep alone
Sweep the streets I used to own

(↑2) C D / G Em :‖

I used to roll the dice
Feel the fear in my enemy's eyes
Listen as the crowd would sing
"Now the old king is dead! Long live the king!"

One minute I held the key / Next the walls were closed on me
And I discovered that my castles stand
Upon pillars of salt & pillars of sand

I hear Jerusalem bells are ringing
Roman Cavalry choirs are singing
Be my mirror, my sword & shield
My missionaries in a foreign field

For some reason I can't explain
Once you go there was never
Never an honest word
And that was when I ruled the world

C D / G Em / C D / Bm Em

It was the wicked & wild wind
Blew down the doors to let me in
Shattered windows & the sound of drums
People couldn't believe what I'd become

Revolutionaries wait / For my head on a silver plate
Just a puppet on a lonely string / Oh who would ever wanna be king?

I hear Jerusalem bells are ringing... (repeat v. 4)

For some reason I can't explain
I know St. Peter won't call my name
Never an honest word
And that was when I ruled the world

— w & m: Guy Berryman, Jon Buckland, Will Champion & Chris Martin

WE ARE YOUNG

Give me a second, I, I need to get my story straight
My friends are in the bathroom getting higher than the Empire State
My lover she is waiting for me just across the bar
My seat's been taken by some sunglasses asking 'bout a scar

(↑3) G - - - / Em - - - / C - - - / Am - D -

I know I gave it to you months ago
I know you're trying to forget
But betw the drinks & subtle things & the holes in my apologies
You know I'm trying hard to take it back

So if by the time the bar closes & you feel like falling down
I'll carry you home

Am Bm EmD C / C D

Tonight
We are young
So let's set the world on fire,_we can burn brighter
Than the sun (repeat)

G - - - / Em - - - / C - - - / G - D - :‖

Now I know that I'm not all that you got
I guess that I, I just thought, maybe we could find new ways
To fall apart, but our friends are back, so let's raise the cup
'Cos I found someone to carry me home / **Tonight...** (cho)

Carry me home tonight_(4x - then repeat with below)
The world *[moon]* is on my side, I have no reason to run
_So will someone come & carry me home tonight?
_The angels never arrived _but I can hear the choir
_So will someone come & carry me home?

G - C - / G - D - :‖ (4x)

— w & m: Jeff Bhasker, Andrew Dost, Jack Antonoff & Nate Ruess

YOU & I

Don't you worry there, my honey
We might not have any money
But we've got our love to pay the bills
Maybe I think you're cute & funny
Maybe I wanna do what bunnies
Do, with you, if you know what I mean

C - / F - / Am - F - :‖

Oh let's get rich & buy our parents
Homes in the south of France
Let's get rich & give everybody nice sweaters &
Teach them how to dance
Let's get rich & build a house
On a mountain making everybody look like ants
From way up there, you & I, you & I _

C E7 / F C / 1st / F G / 1st / F D7 / C G C -

Well, you might be a bit confused
And you might be a little bit bruised
But baby how we spoon like no one else
So I will help you read those books
If you will soothe my worried looks
And we will put the lonesome on the shelf

— w & m: Ingrid Michaelson

The **Millenial** chapter contains alterative, indie rock & singer songwriter songs after 1995. In the last 20 years the boundary lines between genres has become increasingly blurred. Although "alternative" and "indie" used to have a narrower meaning (e.g. growing out of punk and grunge), the songs in this chapter represent a wide range of approach by newer, younger singer songwriters and bands that often cross the boundary lines of rock, pop, and folk. See also: **British Invasion, Surfing USA.** And in **Earthcare**: Panning for gold, **Home**: Home (Phillips), **Time**: 100 Years, Carry on, Casmir Pulaski Day, I will follow you into the night.

AIN'T NO SUNSHINE

Ain't no sunshine when she's gone
It's not warm when she's away
Ain't no sunshine when she's gone & she's always gone too long
Any time she goes away

Am EmG Am - /   / Em7 - Dm7 - / 1st

Wonder this time where she's gone
Wonder if she's gone to stay
Ain't no sunshine... & this house just ain't no home
Anytime she...

(bridge) And, I know **(x5)** I know **(x5)** **(repeat)**
I know **(x5)**
I know **(x2)** hey I oughta leave a young thing alone
But **ain't no sunshine when she's gone**

(a capella) [Am - - -   3x] Am EmG Am -

Ain't no sunshine...
Only darkness every day _
Ain't no sunshine... & this house just ain't no home
Anytime she...

— w & m: Bill Withers

BABY LOVE

Ooh baby love, my baby love, I need you, oh how I need you_
But all you do is treat me bad,_break my heart & leave me sad_
Tell me what did I do wrong to make you stay away so long?

C C7 AmA7 Dm - / C Dm C Dm / C FEm DmG

'Cos baby love, my... been missing ya, miss kissing ya_
Instead of breaking up **(don't throw our love away)**, let's do some kissing & making up **(don't throw...)**
Don't throw our love away, in my arms why_don't you stay?

Need ya, I need ya, baby love, ooh baby love **(to instr.)**

Need to hold you once again, my love, feel your warm embrace, my love
Don't throw our love away **(don't...)**, please don't do me this way **(don't...)**
Not happy like I used to be, loneliness has got the best of me my love

My baby love **(x2)** I need you, oh how I need you
Why you do me like you do **(don't...)** after I've been true to you? **(don't...)**
So deep in love with you, baby baby baby ooh

— w & m: Brian Holland, Edward Holland & Lamont Dozier

Bring It On Home To Me

If you ever change your mind / About leaving, leaving me behind
Oh-oh bring it to me, bring your sweet loving
Bring it on home to me (yeah, yeah x3)

C - G - / C - F - / C - F G / C F C G

I know I laughed when you left
But now I know I only hurt myself / **Oh-oh bring...**

I'll give you jewelry & money too
That ain't all, that ain't all I'll do for you...

You know I'll always be your slave / Til I'm buried, buried in my grave...

I tried to treat you right / But you stayed out, stayed out at night
   but I forgive you / **Bring it to me...**

— w & m: Sam Cooke

© 1962 (renewed) ABKCO Music, Inc., 85 Fifth Avenue, New York, NY 10003.

Chapel of Love

Going to the chapel & we're gonna get married (2x)
Gee I really love you & we're gonna get married
Going to the chapel of love

(↑2) C - - - / Dm G Dm G / 1st / Dm G C -

Spring is here, the sky is blue, whoa oh oh
Birds all sing as if they knew / Today's the day we'll say "I do"
And we'll never be lonely anymore / because we're **going...**

C - - - / Dm G Dm G / C - C↓A / Dm G C -

Bells will ring, the sun will shine, whoa oh oh
I'll be his & he'll be mine / We'll love until the end of time
And we'll never be lonely anymore...

— w & m: Phil Spector, Ellie Greenwich & Jeff Barry

© 1964 Universal-Songs of PolyGram International, Inc., Trio Music Company & Mother Bertha Music, Inc. Copyright renewed. All rights for Trio Music Company controlled & administered by Bug Music, Inc., a BMG Chrysalis Company. All rights for Mother Bertha Music, Inc. controlled & administered by EMI April Music Inc. Orig rec by Darlene Love & by The Ronettes. Also rec by Dixie Cups, Bette Midler, & Beach Boys.

Cupid

Cupid, draw back your bow & let your arrow go
Straight to my lover's heart for me, for [nobody but] me
Cupid, please hear my cry & let your arrow fly
Straight to my lover's heart for me

G Em G C / G D G C / 1st / G D C G

Now I don't mean to bother you, but I'm in distress
There's danger of me losing all of my happiness
For I love a girl who doesn't know I exist
And this you can fix, so

G - D - / - - G - / - - C - / D - G -

Now, Cupid, if your arrow make her love strong for me
I promise I will love her until eternity
I know betw the 2 of us her heart we can steal
Help me if you will, so

(tag) Now Cupid, don't you hear me calling you? I need you
Cupid, help me, I need you, Cupid / Don't fail me

G Em G Em (3x)

— w & m: Sam Cooke

© 1961 (renewed) ABKCO Music, Inc., 85 Fifth Avenue, New York, NY 10003.

Dark End of the Street

At the dark end of the street
That's where we always meet
Hiding in shadows where we don't belong
Living in darkness, to hide our wrong, **you & me**
At **the dark end of the street, you & me**   (↑2)

C G Am - /   / C F G C - / F G C F C - / F G C F C (G)

I know time is gonna take its toll
We have to pay for the love we stole
It's a sin & we know it's wrong
Oh but our love keeps coming on strong, steal away / To **the...**

(bridge) They're gonna find us, they're gonna find us
They're gonna find us, love, someday, **you & me / At the...**

C - G - / Am - C F C - / F G C F C -

And when the daylight hour rolls around
And by chance we're both downtown
If we should meet, just walk on by
Oh darling, please don't cry, / Tonight we'll meet **at the...**

— w & m: Dan Penn & Chips Moman

© 1967 (renewed 1995) Screen Gems-EMI Music Inc. Rec by James Carr 17.

Do You Know the Way to San Jose

Wo wo wowo, wo wo wowo wo wo (2x)
Do you know the way to San Jose?
I've been away so long I may go wrong & lose my way
Do you know the way to San Jose?
I'm going back to find some peace of mind in San Jose

C F / C G - :‖

   L.A. is a great big freeway
   Put a hundred down & buy a car
   In a week, maybe 2, they'll make you a star
   Weeks turn into yrs, how quick they pass
   And all the stars that never were
   Are parking cars & pumping gas

Em Am / Em Am Em / Em6 Cmaj7 G / Dm7 G / G - /   /

You can really breathe in San Jose
They've got a lot of space, there'll be a place where I can stay
I was born & raised in San Jose
I'm going back to find some peace of mind in San Jose
   Fame & fortune is a magnet
   It can pull you far away from home
   With a dream in your heart you're never alone
   Dreams turn into dust & blow away
   And there you are without a friend
   You pack your car & ride away

(tag) I've got lots of friends in San Jose (**wo wo...**)
Do you know... (**wo wo...**) / Can't wait to get back to...

C F C - :‖ (to fade)

— w: Hal David, m: Burt Bacharach

© 1967 (renewed) Casa David & New Hidden Valley Music. Rec by Dionne Warwick

173

GOODNIGHT, SWEETHEART, GOODNIGHT
(Goodnight, It's Time To Go)

Goodnight sweetheart, well, it's time to go (2x)
I hate to leave you but I really must say
Goodnight, sweetheart, goodnight

C Am Dm G7 / | / C C7 F Fm / C DmG7 C -

Well, it's 3 o'clock in the morning
And baby, I just can't get right
Well I hate to leave you baby, don't mean maybe
Because I love you so

F Fm C C7 / | / F Fm C A / Dm7 - G7 -

Mother & your father / Won't like it if I stay here too long
One kiss in the dark / And I'll be going, you know I hate to go

— w & m: James Hudson & Calvin Carter

© 1953, 1954 (renewed) by Arc Music Corporation (BMI). Worldwide rights owned by Arc/Conrad Music LLC. All rights administered by BMG Rights Management (US) LLC. Orig rec by The Spaniels (in G ↑7).

HOW SWEET IT IS (To Be Loved by You)

How sweet it is to be loved by you (2x)

Dm - C - (2x)

I needed the shelter of someone's arms & there you were
I needed someone to understand my ups & downs & there you were
With sweet love & devotion, deeply touching my emotion
I want to stop & thank you baby (x2)

C Am G F / | / C F C F / |

I close my eyes at night and wonder what would I be without
    you in my life
Everything was just a bore, all the things I did seems I'd done 'em
    before
But you brightened up all my days with a love so sweet in so
    many ways / **I want to stop...**

(2 lines instr.) You were better to me than I've been to myself, for
    me there's you & nobody else / **I want to...**

— w & m: Edward Holland, Lamont Dozier & Brian Holland

© 1964 (renewed 1992) Jobete Music Co., Inc. All rights controlled & administered by EMI Blackwood Music Inc. on behalf of Stone Agate Music (A division of Jobete Music Co., Inc.). On Marvin Gaye 15 & James Taylor Gorilla 17.

I HEARD IT THROUGH THE GRAPEVINE

Ooh, I bet you're wondering how I knew
'Bout your plans to make me blue
With some other guy that you knew before
Betw the 2 of us guys, you know I love you more
It took me by surprise, I must say
When I found out yesterday, don't you know that...

Dm7 - - - / A7 - G7 - / 1st 2 / Bm - G / Dm - G

I heard it thru the grapevine
Not much longer would you be mine
Oh I heard it thru the grapevine
Oh & I'm just about to lose my mind, honey, honey yeah

Dm7 - - - / G - - - :‖

I know that a man ain't supposed to cry
But these tears I can't hold inside
Losin' you would end my life you see
'Cause you mean that much to me
You could have told me yourself
That you love someone else, instead I...

People say believe half of what you see
Son & none of what you hear
I can't help bein' confused
If it's true please tell me dear
Do you plan to let me go
For the other guy you loved before? Don't you know...

— w & m: Norman J. Whitfield & Barrett Strong

© 1966 (renewed 1994) Jobete Music Co., Inc. All rights controlled & administered by EMI Blackwood Music Inc. on behalf of Stone Agate Music (A division of Jobete Music Co., Inc.). Rec by Marvin Gaye ↑1, Gladys Knights & the Pips (in Cm).

I TRY

_ Games, changes & fears
When will they go from here? When will they stop?
I believe that fate has brought us here
And we should be together, babe, but we're not

D A / Em Em7 :‖

_I play it off, but I'm dreaming of you
_And I'll keep my cool, but I'm feelin'
I try to say goodbye & I choke, try to walk away & I stumble
Tho' I try to hide it, it's clear, my world crumbles when
    you are not here (repeat last 2 lines)

G F#m / Em7 A ‖: D A / Em7 G :‖

_I may appear to be free / But I'm just a prisoner of your love
And I may seem all right & smile when you leave
But my smiles are just a front, just a front, hey

(bridge) _ Here is my confession / May I be your possession?
Boy, I need your touch, your love, kisses & such
With all my might I try, but this I can't deny, deny

Fmaj7 Am7 / Fmaj7 Em7 / C7 Bm / Em -

— w: Macy Gray, m: Macy Gray, Jeremy Ruzumna, Jinsoo Lim & David Wilder

© 1999 Music of Stage Three (BMI), Mel-Boopie Music (BMI), Ooky Spinalton Music (ASCAP), Jinsoo Lim Music (ASCAP) & Roastitoasti Music (ASCAP). Worldwide rights for Music of Stage Three & Mel-Boopie Music administered by Stage Three Music (US) Inc., a BMG Chrysalis company. Worldwide rights for Ooky Spinalton Music, Jinsoo Lim Music & Roastitoasti Music administered by Wixen Music Publishing, Inc. On Macy Gray Oh How Life Is.

I WANT YOU BACK

When I had you to myself, I didn't want you around
Those pretty faces always made you stand out in a crowd
But someone picked you from the bunch, one glance was all it
    took / Now it's much too late for me to take a 2nd look

G - C - / EmG CG AmD G :‖

Oh baby, give me one more chance (to show you that I love
    you) / **Won't you please let me back in your heart**
Oh darlin', I was blind to let you go (let you go baby)
But now since I see you in his arms (I want you back)
Yes I do now (I want you...), **ooh ooh baby** (I want...)
Yeah yeah yeah yeah (I...) **Na na na na**

G Em C AmD / EmG CG AmD G :‖ G - - - / - - -

Trying to live without your love is one long sleepless night
Let me show you, girl, that I know wrong from right
Every street you walk on, I leave tear stains on the ground
Following the girl I didn't even want around

 — w & m: Freddie Perren, Alphonso Mizell, Berry Gordy & Deke Richards

THE LOCO-MOTION

Everybody's doin' a brand new dance now, **come on baby,**
 do the locomotion
I know you'll get to like it if you give it a chance now...
My little baby sister can do it with ease
It's easier than learning your ABC's
So come on, come on, do the locomotion with me

(↑3) C Am C Am /   / F Dm / F D / C G C

You gotta swing your hips now, come on, baby
Jump up, jump back, oh well, I think you've got the knack

C F - / C - G -

Now that you can do it let's make a chain now, **come...**
Chug-a chug-a motion like a RR train now...
Do it nice & easy now & don't lose control
A little bit of rhythm & a lot of soul
Come on, come on...

Move around the floor in a locomotion...
Do it holdin' hands if you get the notion...
There's never been a dance that's so easy to do
It even makes you happy when you're feeling blue
Come on, come on...

 — w & m: Gerry Goffin & Carole King

MUSTANG SALLY

Mustang Sally, guess you better slow your Mustang down
Mustang Sally now baby, guess you better slow your Mustang
 down
You been running all over the town now, oh I guess I'll have to
 put your flat feet on the ground

C - - - / F - C - / G F C -

All you want to do is ride around Sally, ride Sally ride **(x2)**
All you want to do... / One of these early mornings,
 oh you gonna be wiping your weeping eyes

I bought you a brand new Mustang 'bout 1965, now you come
 around signifying woman, you don't wanna let me ride
Mustang Sally baby, guess you better slow that Mustang down
You been running all over the town, got to
 put your flat feet on the ground

 — w & m: Bonny Rice

MY GUY

Nothing you could say can tear me away from **my guy**
Nothing you could do 'cos I'm stuck like glue to **my...**
I'm stickin' to my guy like a stamp to a letter, like birds of a feather
 we stick together
I'm tellin' you from the start I can't be torn apart from...

(↑3) GEm x4 / GEm x2 B7 - / AmD x4 / GEm AD G -

Nothing you can do could make **me** untrue to **my...**
Nothing you could buy could make **me** tell a lie to...
I gave my guy my word of honor to be faithful & I'm gonna
You best be believing I won't be deceiving...

(bridge) As a matter of opinion I think he's tops, my opinion is
 he's the cream of the crop
As a matter of taste to be exact he's my ideal as a matter of fact

AmD x3 G / EmBm x2 A7 D7

No muscle-bound man could take my hand from...
No handsome face could ever take the place of...
He may not be a movie star, but when it comes to being happy
 we are
There's not a man today who could take me away from...

 — w & m: William "Smokey" Robinson

(You Make Me Feel Like) A NATURAL WOMAN

Looking out on the morning rain
I used to feel so uninspired
And when I knew I had to face another day
Lord, it made me feel so tired
Before the day I met you, life was so unkind
But you're the key to my peace of mind   **(in 3/4 x2)**

G - D - / F - C - :‖ Am Bm x2 / Am Bm C

**'Cos you make me feel, you make me feel
You make me feel like a natural woman**

D G C G / C G - Am -

When my soul was in the lost & found
You came along, to claim it
I didn't know just what was wrong with me
'Til your kiss helped me name it
Now I'm no longer doubtful of what I'm living for
And if I make you happy I don't need to do more

 (bridge) Oh baby, what you done to me
 You make me feel so good inside
 And I just wanna be close to you
 You make me feel so alive

G - F - /   / C - Bb - / C Em Am D

 — w & m: Gerry Goffin, Carole King & Jerry Wexler

ON BROADWAY

They say the neon lights are bright **on Broadway** (**on Broadway**)
They say there's always magic in the air (**on...**)
But when you're walkin' down that street &
    you ain't had enough to eat
The glitter rubs right off & you're nowhere **on Broadway**

DC x4 / | GF x3 GA / 1st

They say the girls are something else **on Broadway...**
But looking at them just gives me the blues (**on...**)
'Cos how ya gonna make some time when all you have is
    one thin dime?
And one thin dime won't even shine your shoes **on...**

They say that I won't last too long **on Broadway...**
I'll catch a Greyhound bus for home, they all say...
But oh! they're dead wrong, I know they are, I can play
    this here guitar
And I won't quit til I'm a star on Broadway...

— w & m: Barry Mann, Cynthia Weil, Mike Stoller & Jerry Leiber

© 1962, 1963 (renewed 1990, 1991) Screen Gems-EMI Music Inc. Orig rec by The Drifters 14.

PLEASE MR. POSTMAN

(Wait!) Oh yes, waita minute Mr. Postman
(Wait!) Wait Mr. Postman

C - / Am -

Please Mr. Postman, look & see
Is there a letter in your bag for me?
Cos it's been a mighty long time *[You know it's been so long]*
Since I heard fom this boyfriend of mine

C - / Am - / F - / G -

There must be some word today
From my boyfriend so far away
Please Mr. Postman look & see
Is there a letter, a letter for me?
I've been standing here waiting Mr. Postman
So, so patiently
For just a card or just a letter
Saying he's returning home to me

So many days you passed me by
You saw the tears standing in my eye
You wouldn't stop to make me feel better
By leaving me a card or a letter

You better wait a minute, wait a minute
Oh you better wait a minute
Please please, Mr. Postman
Please check & see, just one more time for me
[Don' pass me by, you see the tears in my eye]
[Deliver de letter, de sooner de better]

— w & m: Robert Bateman, Georgia Dobbins, William Garrett, Freddie Gorman & Brian Holland

© 1961 renewed 1989) Jobete Music Co., Inc. All rights controlled & administered by EMI April Music Inc & EMI Blackwood Music Inc. on behalf of Jobete Music Co., Inc. & Stone Agate Music (a division of Jobete Music Co., Inc.). Orig rec by Marvelettes 12 (1st#1 hit for Motown label). On also rec by Beatles (in A) & Carpenters.

SUNNY

Sunny, yesterday my life was filled with rain
Sunny, you smiled at me & really eased the pain
Now the dark days are gone & the bright days are here, my Sunny
    one shines so sincere / **Sunny, one so true, I love you**

(↑7) Am C F E / | Am C F Bb / Bm E Am -

Sunny, thank you for the sunshine bouquet
Sunny, thank... the love you brought my way
You gave to me your all & all, and now I feel 10 ft tall
Sunny, one so true...

Sunny, thank you for the truth you let me see
Sunny, thank you for the facts from A to Z
My life was torn like wind-blown sand & a rock was formed
    when we held hands / **Sunny, one so true, I love you**

Sunny...that smile upon your face /...that gleam that glows with grace
You're my spark of nature's fire, you're my sweet complete desire...

— w & m: Bobby Hebb

© 1966 Portable Music Company, Inc. Copyright renewed. Administered by Downtown DMP Songs. On his orig rec in '66 on Imperial Recs 17. Written after JFK assassination & stabbing death of Hebb's older brother near a Nashville nightclub.

THE TIDE IS HIGH

The tide is high but I'm holding on
I'm gonna be your "Number 1"
I'm not the kinda man *[girl]* **who gives up**
Just like that, oh no

C - F G (4x)

It's not the things you do, that really hurts me bad
But it's the way you do the things, you do to me / **I'm not...**

The tide is high but I'm holding on
I'm gonna be Number 1 / **Number 1** (x2)

C - F G / | F - G -

Every man *[girl]* wants you to be his girl *[her man]*
But I'll wait my dear 'til it's my turn / **I'm not...**

— w & m: John Holt, Tyrone Evans & Howard Barrett

© 1968 (renewed) by Embassy Music Corporation (BMI). On their '67 rec 17. Blondie Autoamerican ('80 in B), Atomic Kitten Feels So Good ('02 11) & in '03 Lizzie McGuire Movie.

UNDER THE BOARDWALK

Oh when the sun beats down & burns the tar up on the roof
And your shoes get so hot, you wish your tired feet were fireproof
Under the boardwalk down by the sea
On a blanket with my baby is where I'll be

C - G - / - - C C7 / F - C - / - G C -

(Under...) out of the sun, (...) we'll be havin' some fun
(...) people walking above, (...) we'll be falling in love
Under the boardwalk, boardwalk

Am - G - / | Am -

From the park you hear the happy sound of a carousel
You can almost taste the hot dogs & French fries they sell...

— w & m: Artie Resnick & Kenny Young

© 1964 by Alley Music Corp. & Trio Music Company. Copyright renewed. All rights for Trio Music Company administered by Bug Music, Inc., a BMG Chrysalis company. Orig rec by The Drifters 11.

WAY YOU DO THE THINGS YOU DO

You got a smile so <u>b</u>right
You know you could have been a <u>c</u>andle
I'm holding you so <u>t</u>ight
You know you could have been a <u>h</u>andle
The way you swept me off my <u>f</u>eet
You know you could've been a <u>b</u>room
The way you smell so <u>s</u>weet
You know you could've been some <u>p</u>erfume

DG x4 /   /   / DG x3 D / GC x4 / 1st /   /
DG DG DA A

Well you could have been anything that you wanted to
And I can tell, the way you do the things you do

A - G - /   /

As pretty as you are / You know you could've been a flower
If good looks was a minute / You know you could be an hour
The way you stole my heart
You know you could have been a cool crook
And baby you're so smart
You know you could have been a school book

You make my life so rich
You know you could've been some money
And baby you're so sweet
You know you could have been some honey

DG x4 (4x)

  — w & m: William "Smokey" Robinson & Robert Rogers

YOU ARE NOT ALONE

You're not alone, I'm with y<u>o</u>u, I'm lonely t<u>oo</u>_
What's that s<u>o</u>ng_can't be s<u>u</u>ng by <u>2</u>?
_A broken home,_a broken heart,_isolated & afr<u>ai</u>d
Open up, this is a r<u>ai</u>d, I wanna get it thru to y<u>o</u>u,
  you're not al<u>o</u>ne _

Am - C - / Am - Dm CF C / F C Dm AmC / Dm F C -

You're not alone, every night I stand in your place
Every tear on every face tastes the same
A broken dream, a broken heart, isolated & afraid
Open up this is a raid, I'm gonna get it thru to you...

An open hand, an open heart, there's no need to be afraid
Open up this is a raid, I wanna get it thru…

F C Dm AmC / Dm F C -

  — w & m: Jeff Tweedy

YOU'RE NO GOOD

Feeling better now that we're thru
Feeling better cos I'm over you
I learned my lesson, it left a scar
Now I see how you really are

Am D Am D /   / F G C - / Am D E -

You're no good (x3), baby you're no
Good — I'm gonna say it again! (repeat)

Am D Am D (4x)

I broke a heart that's gentle & true
Well I broke a heart over someone like you
I'll beg his forgiveness on bended knee
I wouldn't blame him if he said to me:

I'm telling you now baby & I'm going my way
Forget about you baby 'cos I'm leaving to stay / **You're...**

Am D Am D (6x)

  — w & m: Clint Ballard, Jr.

YOU'VE REALLY GOT A HOLD ON ME

I don't like you, but I love you
Seems that I'm always thinkin' of you
Tho-oh-oh you treat me badly, I love you madly
You really got a hold on me (you really...) (2x)

C - - - / Am - - - / C - F - D7 G / C - - - / Am - - -

I don't want you, but I need you
Don't wanna kiss you, but I need to
Tho-oh-oh you do me wrong now, my love is strong now
You really...

(bridge) Baby, I love you & all I want you to do
Is just — hold me (x4) / _ _ _ _ Tighter (2x)

C - F - / C - - G - / C - AmG C /   /

I wanna leave you, don't wanna stay here
Don't wanna spend another day here
Tho-oh-oh I wanna split now, I can't quit now / **You...**

  — w & m: William "Smokey" Robinson

The **Motown** chapter contains African American popular music from 50's to 80's. See also: **Blues, Rock around the Clock, Surfing USA.** See also **Dignity:** Sisters are doin' it for themselves, We are family, **Friendship:** Stand by me, **Good:** Iko iko, **Gospel:** People get ready.

Musicals

ALMOST LIKE BEING IN LOVE

What a day this has been, what a rare mood I'm in
Why it's almost like being in love
There's a smile on my face for the whole human race / **Why...**

(↑3) Fmaj7 G7 Em7 A7 / Dm7 G7 C - :‖

All the music of life seems to be
Like a bell that is ringing for me

Bm E7 Amaj7 - / Dm7 - Bm E

And from the way that I feel when that bell starts to peal
I would **swear I was falling**, I could **swear...** / **It's almost...**

Fmaj7 G7 Em7 A7 / Dm7 Adim C Adim / Dm7 G7 C -

When we walked up the brae, not a word did we say / **It was...**
But your arm linked in mine made the world kinda fine / **It...**
All the music of life... **(as above)**

— w: Alan Jay Lerner, m: Frederick Loewe

©1947 (renewed 1975) the Lerner Heirs Publishing Designee & the Loewe Foundation Publishing Designee. All rights controlled & administered by EMI April Music Inc. In *Brigadoon* (Gene Kelly sings in film). Rec by Sinatra, Mildred Bailey, Mary Martin, Ella & Nat King Cole (used as closing song in '93 *Groundhog Day*).

AQUARIUS

When the moon is in the 7th house
And Jupiter aligns with Mars
Then peace will guide the planets
And love will steer the stars

Cmaj7 D Em - / / / C D G -

This is the dawning of the Age of Aquarius, Age of...
Aquarius (2x)

F - - - Am - / D - - - / Am - - -

(bridge) Harmony & understanding, sympathy & trust abounding
No more falsehoods or derisions, golden living dreams of visions
Mystic crystal revelations & the mind's true liberation
Aquarius (2x)

G C G C / / GE Am GDm Em // Dm - - - / Am - - -

(tag) Let the sunshine **(2x)** The sunshine in **(repeating)**

Am E7 / - Am / F C :‖ **(repeating)**

— w: James Rado & Gerome Ragni, m: Galt MacDermot

©1966, 1967, 1968, 1970 (renewed) James Rado, Gerome Ragni, Galt Macdermot, Nat Shapiro & EMI U Catalog Inc. All rights administered by EMI U Catalog Inc. (Publishing) & Alfred Music (Print). In *Hair* (as medley w/ "Let the Sunshine In"). On Grammy-winning alb by The 5th Dimension *Age of...*. Refers to astrological belief that forthcoming age replacing current Age of Pisces would be characterized by love, light & humanity.

AS LONG AS HE NEEDS ME

As long as he needs me, oh yes, he does need me
In spite of what you see, I'm sure that he needs me
Who else would love him still when they've been used so ill?
He knows I always will **as long as he needs me**
    I miss him so much when he is gone
    But when he's near me I don't let on
The way I feel inside, the love, I have to hide
The hell! I've got my pride **as long as...**

Cmaj7Am7 x2 Cmaj7Edim DmG / DmBb G FmG Cmaj7 :‖

F G C - / Am D7 Dm G / 1st above / Dm D7 DmG C

As long as he needs me I know where I must be
I'll cling on steadfastly **as long...**
As long as life is long, I'll love him right or wrong
And somehow, I'll be strong **as...**
    If you are lonely, then you will know
    When someone needs you, you love them so
I won't betray his trust tho' people say I must
I've got to stay true, just **as...**

— w & m: Lionel Bart

© 1960 (renewed) Lakeview Music Co., Ltd., London, England. TRO-Hollis Music, Inc., New York, controls all publication rights for the US & Canada. In Oliver 16.

BEAUTY & THE BEAST

Tale as old as time, true as it can be
Barely even friends, then somebody bends unexpectedly
Just a little change, small to say the least
Both a little scared, neither one prepared, beauty & the beast_

(↑5) C F C G / C Em F G / 1st / Am FG C -

(bridge) Ever just the same, ever a surprise
Ever as before, ever just as sure as the sun will rise

Em F Em F / G Am Bb(G)

Tale as old as time, tune as old as song
Bittersweet & strange, finding you can change, learning
    you were wrong
Certain as the sun rising in the east
Tale as old as time, song as old as rhyme, beauty... **(2x)**

C F C G / C Em F G / 1st / Am FG C Am / F DmG C -

— m: Alan Menken, w: Howard Ashman

© 1991 Walt Disney Music Company & Wonderland Music Company, Inc. Won academy award for best song in '91 film *Beauty & the Beast*. Sung 1st by Angela Lansbury†1 with & reprise by Céline Dion & Peabo Bryson during titles. Based on the trad. fairy tale written by French novelist Jeanne-Marie Leprince de Beaumont in 1756.

BUTTERCUP

I'm called Little Buttercup, dear Little Buttercup
Tho' I could never tell why
But still I'm called Buttercup, poor little Buttercup
Sweet Little Buttercup I!

C G C G / C F C - / A Dm G C / - G C -

I've snuff & tobaccy & excellent jacky
I've scissors & watches & knives
I've ribbons & laces to set off the faces
Of pretty young sweethearts & wives

Am E7 Am E7 / Am - E7 - / 1st / Am D7 G -

I've treacle & toffee, I've tea & I've coffee
Soft tommy & succulent chops
I've chickens & conies & pretty polonies
And excellent peppermint drops

G C G C / F C F - / D G D Em / G D G -

(as v.1) Then buy of your Buttercup, dear Little Buttercup
Sailors should never be shy
So, buy of your Buttercup, poor little. Buttercup
Come, of your Buttercup buy!

— w: William S. Gilbert, m: Sir Arthur Sullivan

Arr © 2015 by Hal Leonard Corporation. In their 4th opera, *HMS Pinafore*. Opened in 1871 at Opera Comique in London to 571 performances, the 2nd longest-running musical theatre piece ever at that time.

CONSIDER YOURSELF

Consider yourself at home / Consider... one of the family
We've taken to you so strong
It's clear we're going to get along
Consider... well in / Consider... part of the furniture
There isn't a lot to spare
Who cares? What ever we've got, we share!

G - - - / - - Am - / G - Em - / C Adim A7 D :|

If it should chance to be we should see some harder days
Empty larder days, why grouse?
Always a chance we'll meet somebody to foot the bill
Then the drinks are on the house!

G7 - - - / C - - - / A7 - - - / D A D -

Nobody tries to be lah-di-dah or uppity / There's a cup-o'-tea for all
Only it's wise to be handy with a rolling pin
When the landlord comes to call!

(Last cho) Consider... our mate / We don't want to have no fuss
For after some consideration, we can state / ...one of us!

G - - - / Am - F - / G - - E7 / Am D G -

— w & m: Lionel Bart

© 1960 (renewed) Lakeview Music Co. Ltd., London, England. TRO - Hollis Music, Inc., New York, controls all publication rights for the USA & Canada. In *Oliver*.

DEFYING GRAVITY

Smth has changed within me, smth is not the same
I'm thru with playing by the rules of someone else's game
Too late for 2nd-guessing, too late to go back to sleep
It's time to trust my instincts, close my eyes & leap

C F C F / C F Am Bb / Bb C x2 / Bb C F G

It's time to try **defying gravity** / I think I'll try...
Kiss me goodbye, I'm...
And you won't pull me down

Am F Gsus G / / / C (F C F)

I'm thru accepting limits 'cos someone says they're so
Some things I cannot change but til I try I'll never know
Too long I've been afraid of losing love, I guess I've lost
Well if that's love, it comes at much too high a cost

I'd sooner buy **defying gravity**
Kiss me goodbye, I'm... / I think I'll try...
And you won't bring me down / (tag) Bring me down!

— w & m: Stephen Schwartz

© 2003 Grey Dog Music. In *Wicked*, a reworking of the Wizard of Oz story told primarily from the standpoint of Elphaba, the Wicked Witch of the West. Featured on *Glee*.

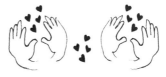

HEART

You've gotta have **heart,_all you really need is heart** _
When the odds are sayin' you'll never win, that's when the grin should start _
You've gotta have **hope, _mustn't sit around & mope** _
Nothin's half as bad as it may appear, wait'll next yr & hope
When your luck is battin' zero, get your chin up off the floor_
Mister, you can be a hero,_you can open any door
  (there's nothin' to it but to do it)
You've gotta **have heart, miles 'n miles n' miles of heart**
Oh it's fine to be a genius of course but keep that old horse before the cart, _first you've gotta have heart_

(in C - starts on E) Dm7 G C A7 / F Fm C (G) :| GmC x2 FC F

AmD x2 G - / 1st above / F Fm CA / DmG C -

(bridge)_A great slugger **we haven't got,**_a great pitcher **we...**
_A great ballclub **we...** what've we got? _

C FG x2 / C FG G -

We've got **heart,_all you really need is...** / When the odds
  are sayin' **you'll never win, that's when the grin... start**
We've got **hope, _we don't sit around & mope** _
Not a solitary sob do we heave, mister, 'cos we've got hope
We're so happy that we're hummin',_that's the hearty thing to do
'Cos we know our ship will come in_so it's 10 yrs overdue_
We've got **heart, _miles 'n miles n' miles of heart_**
Oh it's fine to be a genius of course but keep that old horse before the cart_   (last time: F Fm C A7)

(tag) So what the heck's the use of cryin'? why should we curse?
  we gotta get better 'cos we can't get worse!
And to add to it:_we've got heart!_ / We've got... (x2)

F Fm C A7 / D7 G7 CAm DmG / CAm DmG CG C

(reprise tag) Who minds them pop bottles flyin', the hisses & boos? the team has been consistent - yeah we always lose!
But we're laughin' cuz: _we've got... / We've... (x2)

— w & m: Richard Adler & Jerry Ross

© 1955 (renewed) Lakshmi Puja Music Ltd. & J & J Ross Music Co. All rights administered by the Songwriters Guild of America. In *Damn Yankees*! 18.

HELLO YOUNG LOVERS

Hello, young lovers, whoever you are
I hope your troubles are few
All my good wishes go with you tonight
I've been in love like you

(in 3/4) Dadd9 D Dmaj7 D6 / Dmaj7 D6 Em A /
Gm A F A / Em A D -

Be brave, young lovers, & follow your star
Be brave & faithful & true
Cling very close to each other tonight
I've been in love like you

(bridge) I know how it feels to have wings on your heels
And to fly down the street in a trance
You fly down a street on the chance that you'll meet
And you meet — not really by chance

G Am G Am / G Am G - / F# - Bm - / Em7 - Em A

Don't cry, young lovers, whatever you do
Don't cry because I'm alone
All of my memories are happy tonight
I've had a love of my own

(tag) I've had a love of my own, like yours / I've had a... own

G Gm F# Bm / Em FFA7 D -

— w: Oscar Hammerstein II, m: Richard Rodgers

© 1951 by Richard Rodgers & Oscar Hammerstein II. Copyright renewed.
Williamson Music, a division of Rodgers & Hammerstein: an Imagem Company,
owner of publication & allied rights throughout the world. In their 5th musical,
King & I. Based on the novel *Anna & the King of Siam* by Margaret Landon, which
was in turn derived from the memoirs of Anna Leonowens, governess to the
children of King Mongkut of Siam (=Thailand) in the 1860s. Sung by Anna to the
wives of the king about her late husband.

I CAIN'T SAY NO

(intro) It ain't so much a question of not knowin' what to do
I've know'd what's right & wrong since I've been 10!
I heared a lot of stories & I reckon they are true
About how girls are put upon by men
I know I mustn't fall into the pit
But when I'm with a feller, I fergit!

D - A - D A D - / Em A D - :‖ A E A - / - - D -

I'm jist a girl who cain't say no / I'm in a turrible fix
I always say "Come on, let's go" / Jist when I oughta say "Nix!"

D EmA D EmA / / / D EmA D -

> When a person tries to kiss a girl
> I know she oughta give his face a smack
> But as soon as someone kisses me
> I somehow, sorta, wanta kiss him back!

A7 Adim Em A / - - D - / 1st / A7 - - -

I'm jist a fool when lights are low / I cain't be prissy & quaint
I ain't the type that can faint / How can I be what I ain't?
I cain't say no!

D EmA D EmA / D EmA Am Edim / G - Bb - /
D - Bb - / D6 - A D

(bridge) What you gonna do when a feller gits flirty
And starts to talk purty? What you gonna do?
S'posin' that he says that yer lips're like cherries
Or roses or berries? What you gonna do?
S'posin' that he says that you're sweeter 'n cream
And he's gotta have cream or die?
What you gonna do when he talks that way? / Spit in his eye?

A - Bm E / / / A - B7 E /
A - D - / Em - D - / A E A E / A E Em A

I'm jist a girl... / Cain't seem to say it at all
I hate to disappoint a beau / When he is payin' a call
> For a while I act refined & cool
> A-settin' on the velveteen settee
> Then I think of that old golden rule
> And do for him what he would do for me!
I cain't resist a Romeo / In a sombrero & chaps
Soon as I sit on their laps / Smth inside of me snaps / **I...no!**

— w: Oscar Hammerstein II, m: Richard Rodgers

© 1943 by Williamson Music, A division of Rodgers & Hammerstein: an Imagem
Company. Copyright renewed. In Oklahoma (stage ↑3, film ↑1).

I DREAMED A DREAM

I dreamed a dream in time gone by
When hope was high & life worth living
I dreamed that love would never die
I dreamed that God would be forgiving

C↓ (C, B, A, G) / F↓ (F, E, D) DmG :‖

Then I was young & unafraid
When dreams were made & used & wasted
There was no ransom to be paid / No song unsung, no wine untasted

(bridge) But the tigers come at night
With their voices soft as thunder
As they tear your hope apart / As they turn your dream to shame

A7 - Dm - / A7 - D - / G - Cm - / G - D (G)

He slept a summer by my side
He filled my days with endless wonder
He took my childhood in his stride
But he was gone when autumn came
> And still I dream he'll come to me
> That we will live the yrs together
> But there are dreams that cannot be
> And there are storms we cannot weather
I had a dream my life would be
So different from this hell I'm living
So different now from what it seemed
Now life has killed the dream I dreamed

— w: Alain Boublil, Jean-Marc Natel & Herbert Kretzmer m: Claude-Michel
Schonberg.

© 1986 by Alain Boublil Music Ltd. (ASCAP). Mechanical & publication rights for the
USA administered by Alain Boublil Music Ltd (ASCAP) c/o Joel Faden & Co., Inc. MLM
250 West 57th St., 26th Floor, New York, NY 10107 tel (212) 246-7203, fax (212)
246-7217. jfaden@joelfaden.com. In Les Miserables From Les Misérables. On Glee

I WHISTLE A HAPPY TUNE

Whenever I feel afraid, I hold my head erect
And whistle a happy tune so no one will suspect I'm afraid

G - C - / D - G D G -

While shivering in my shoes, I strike a careless pose
And whistle a happy tune & no one ever knows I'm afraid

The result of this deception is very strange to tell
For when I fool the people I fear, I fool myself as well!

Eb - G - / D - A A7 D7

I whistle a happy tune & ev'ry single time
The happiness in the tune convinces me that I'm not afraid

Make believe you're brave & the trick will take you far
You may be as brave as you make believe you are / **(whistle)**
You may be as brave as you make believe you are!

C - G - / / / Em - - EmD G - - -

— w: Oscar Hammerstein II, m: Richard Rodgers

© 1951 by Richard Rodgers & Oscar Hammerstein II. Copyright renewed. Williamson Music, a division of Rodgers & Hammerstein: an Imagem Company, owner of publication & allied rights throughout the world. The opening song of King & I. Sung by the governess Anna to her son to persuade him not to be afraid as they arrive in Siam.

I'D DO ANYTHING

I'd do anything for you dear, anything
For you mean everything to me, I know that
I'd go anywhere for your smile, anywhere
For your smile, everywhere I'd see
Would you climb a hill? (anything!) wear a daffodil? (...)
Leave me all your will?... Even fight my Bill? What, fisticuffs?
I'd risk everything for one kiss, everything
Yes I'd do anything (anything?) **anything for you**

G↓ Em Am D **(4x)** GEm AmD AmD G / C GEm D D7
G↓ Em Am D / GD Em7 A7D7 G

I'd do... everywhere I'd see
Would you lace my shoe?... paint your face bright blue?...
Catch a kangaroo?... go to Timbuctu? (& back again!)
I'd risk everything... anything for you

Would you rob a shop?... would you risk the drop?...
Tho' your eyes go pop... when you come down plop? hang everything!
We'd risk life & limb to keep you in the swim
Yes <u>we'd</u> do anything (anything?) **anything for you!**

— w & m: Lionel Bart

© 1960 (renewed) Lakeview Music Co., Ltd., London, England. TRO-Hollis Music, Inc., New York, controls all publication rights for the US & Canada. In Oliver 13. Sung by Oliver, Fagin, Bette & others in Fagin's Lair.

IF I LOVED YOU

If I loved you, time & again I would try to say
All I'd want you to know
If I loved you, words wouldn't come in an easy way
Round in circles I'd go!
Longin' to tell you but afraid & shy
I'd let my golden chances pass me by!
Soon you'd leave me, off you would go in the mist of day
Never, never to know / How I loved you – if I loved you

(↑2) G Edim G Gaug [B7] / C Edim G D [2nd v. B7] :‖
Em Am B7 - / Em Am FA D /
G Edim G Gaug / C F# G DmG / AmG C AmD G

— w: Oscar Hammerstein II, m: Richard Rodgers

© 1945 by Williamson Music, a division of Rodgers & Hammerstein: an Imagem Company. Copyright renewed. From Carousel 16. Rec by Streisand 11, Sinatra 12.

IT AIN'T NECESSARILY SO

It ain't necessarily so (2x)
The things that you're liable to read in the Bible
It ain't necessarily so

Dm G Dm - / / Dm Ddim G7 Ddim/ G7 A7 Dm -

Little David was small, but oh my! **(2x)**
He fought Big Goliath who lay down & dieth
Little David was small, but oh my!

Oh Jonah, he lived in the whale **(2x)**
For he made his home in that fish's abdomen
Yes Jonah he lived...

Li'l Moses was found in a stream **(2x)**
He floated on water til old Pharaoh's daughter
She fished him, she says, from that stream

It ain't necessarily so (2x)
They tell all you children the devil's a villain
But **it...**

Methus'lah lived 900 years **(2x)**
But who calls that livin' when no gal will give in
To no man what's 900 years?

(tag) I'm preachin' this sermon to show
It ain't necessarily, ain't necessarily
Ain't necessarily so!

Gm - D - / G Edim D Gm / D Em7 D6 -

— w & m: George Gershwin, DuBose & Dorothy Heyward & Ira Gershwin

© 1935 (renewed) Nokawi Music, Frankie G. Songs, Dubose & Dorothy Heyward Memorial Fund & Ira Gershwin Music. All rights for Nokawi Music administered by Imagem Sounds. All rights for Ira Gershwin Music administered by WB Music Corp. In Porgy & Bess. Rec by Ella Fitzgerald & Louis Armstrong, Peggy Lee.

LIDA ROSE / WILL I EVER TELL YOU

Lida Rose, I'm home again Rose, to get the sun back in the sky
Lida... I'm home again Rose, about a thousand kisses shy
Ding dong ding, I can the chapel bell chime
Ding dong ding, at the least suggestion I'll pop the question

...I'm home again Rose, without a sweetheart to my name
...now everyone knows that I am hoping you're the same
So here is my love song, not fancy or fine
...O won't you be mine?

(↑2) C Edim G - / - B7 C C7 / F Fm C Am / D7 - G7 -
        "   / - B7 C EdimA /   "   / Dm G C

(same chords as above) Dream of now, dream of then
Dream of a love song that might have been
Do I love you? Oh, yes, I love you
And I'll bravely tell you / But only when we dream again
Sweet & low, sweet & low
How sweet that mem'ry, how long ago
Forever? Oh, yes forever / Will I ever tell you? Ah no

— w & m: Meredith Willson

© 1957 (renewed) Frank Music Corp. & Meredith Willson Music. In The Music Man 15. Marian (the librarian) sings "Will I Ever Tell You" while a barbershop quarter sings "Lida Rose."

MATCHMAKER

Matchmaker, Matchmaker make me a match
Find me a find, catch me a catch
Matchmaker... look thru your book
And make me a perfect match

D Daug D6 Daug / D6 - Daug D6 / 1st / Em A D -

...I'll bring the veil / You bring the groom slender & pale
Bring me a ring for I'm longing to be / The envy of all I see
    For Papa, make him a scholar
    For Mama, make him rich as a king
    For me? well, I wouldn't holler
    If he were as handsome as anything!

Gm - C - / Fmaj7 - Dm7 - / Em7 - A7 - / Dm D7 Gm A

...make me a match / Find me a find, catch me a catch
Night after night in the dark I'm alone
So find me a match of my own

...you know that I'm / Still very young, please take your time
Up to this minute I misunderstood
That I could be stuck for good
    Dear Yente, see that he's gentle
    Remember, you were also a bride
    It's not that I'm sentimental
    It's just that I'm terrified!

...plan me no plans / I'm in no rush, maybe I've learned
Playing with matches a girl can get burned
So bring me no ring, groom me no groom
Find me no find, catch me no catch
Unless he's a matchless match!

D Daug D6 Daug / D6 Daug D Ddim / D D7 G Gm
G - - - / D - E7 - / - - Em A D - - -

    — w: Sheldon Harnick, m: Jerry Bock

© 1964 Bock IP LLC & Mayerling Productions, Ltd. Copyright renewed 1992. All rights for Mayerling Productions, Ltd. administered by R&H Music, a division of Rodgers & Hammerstein: an Imagem Company. In Fiddler on the Roof 13. Based on Tevye & his 3 Daughters & other tales by Sholom Aleichem. Set in Russia in 1905.

OH, LADY BE GOOD!

Oh sweet & lovely, lady be good / Oh **lady be good to me**
I am so awf'ly misunderstood / So **lady...**
Oh please have some pity / I'm all alone in this big city
I tell you I'm just a lonesome babe in the wood / So...

G C7 G E7/ Am D7 G (D7) :‖C - G -/ Em A7 D D7 /1st 2

    — w & m: George Gershwin & Ira Gershwin

© 1924 (renewed) WB Music Corp. In Lady Be Good ('24 Broadway show w/ Fred & Astelle Astaire & unrelated '41 film). '47 hit for Ella Fitzgerald 13.

OL' MAN RIVER

There's an old man called the Mississippi
That's the old man I would like to be
What does he care if the world's got troubles?
What does he care if the land ain't free?

C - - F / C - F G / Am - - Dm / Am - FG C

Old man river, that old man river
He must know smth, but don't say nothin'
He just keeps rollin', he keeps on rollin' along

C F C F / C Am C Am / G - - - C (F C G7)

(as cho) He don't plant taters, he don't plant cotton
And them that plants 'em is soon forgotten
But old man river he just keeps rollin' along.
    (bridge) You & me, we sweat & strain
    Body all achin' & racked with pain
    Tote that barge! Lift that bale!
    You get a little drunk & you lands in jail

    Em Am Em Am /   /   / Em B7 Em G7

(as cho) I gets weary & sick of tryin'
I'm tired of livin' & scared of dyin' / **But old man...**

Black folks work on the Mississippi
Black folks work while the White folks play
Pullin' those boats from the dawn to sunset
Gettin' no rest til the Judgement Day
    (bridge) Don't look up & don't look down
    You don't dare make the White boss frown
    Bend your knees & bow your head
    And pull that rope until you're dead

Let me go 'way from the Mississippi
Let me go 'way from the White man boss
Show me that stream called the River Jordan
That's the old stream that I long to cross

    — w: Oscar Hammerstein II, m: Jerome Kern

© 1927 Universal-PolyGram International Publishing, Inc. Copyright renewed. In *Showboat*. Sung by Paul Robeson in '36 film (in A).

ON THE STREET WHERE YOU LIVE

I have often walked down this street before
But the pavement always stayed beneath my feet before
All at once am I several stories high
Knowing I'm on the street where you live

G6 [Em] - G - / Bm Edim Am D / Am Adim G - / A7 D G

Are there lilac trees in the heart of town?
Can you hear a lark in any other part of town?
Does enchantment pour out of ev'ry door?
No, it's just on the street where you live!
    (bridge) And oh! the towering feeling
    Just to know somehow you are near
    The overpowering feeling
    That any second you may suddenly appear!

B7 - C - / Cm - G - / Edim - F# - / B7 F# D D7

People stop & stare, they don't bother me
For there's nowhere else on earth that I would rather be
Let the time go by, I won't care if I
Can be here on the street where you live

    — w: Alan Jay Lerner, m: Frederick Loewe

© 1956 (renewed) Chappell & Co., Inc. In My Fair Lady 16. Sung by Eliza's suitor Freddy near the end of the 1st act after she refuses to see him. Many recs.

PEOPLE WILL SAY WE'RE IN LOVE

(intro) Why do they think up stories that link my name with yours?
Why do the neighbors gossip all day, behind their doors?
I have a way to prove what they say is quite untrue
Here is the gist, a practical list of "don'ts" for you

G Edim Am D / G Edim D Edim - / G B7 Em C /
G Edim D AmD7

Don't throw bouquets at me / Don't please my folks too much
Don't laugh at my jokes too much **/ People will say we're...!**
Don't sigh & gaze at me / Your sighs are so like mine
Your eyes mustn't glow like mine **/ People...**
Don't start collecting things / Give me my rose & my glove
Sweetheart they're suspecting things **/ People...**

C - - - / - - G - / C - D7 - / Dm Ddim C G /
/   "   /   "   /   "   / Dm G C - /
F - Bb - / E7 A7 D7 G / C - AmD D7 / C DmG7 C -

(as intro) Some people claim that you are to blame as much as I
Why do you take the trouble to bake my favorite pie?
Grantin' your wish, I carved our initials on that tree
Just keep a slice of all the advice you give so free

Don't praise my charm too much / Don't look so vain with me
Don't stand in the rain with me **/ People...**
Don't take my arm too much / Don't keep your hand in mine
Your hand feels so grand in mine **/ People...**
Don't dance all night with me / Til the stars fade from above
They'll see it's all right with me **/ People will say we're in love!**

— w: Oscar Hammerstein II, m: Richard Rodgers

© 1943 by Williamson Music, a division of Rodgers & Hammerstein: an Imagem
Company. Copyright renewed. In Oklahoma 11.Others realize that Laurey & Curly
are in love but neither wants to admit it. Many recs incl Crosby, Sinatra & the Ink Spots.

SOMEONE TO WATCH OVER ME

_There's a somebody I'm longing to see
_I hope that he turns out to be
Someone who'll watch over me _

G - Am D7 / G Ddim Am E / C - Am - G (E Am D)

_I'm a little lamb who's lost in the wood
_I know I could always be good / _To one **who'll watch...**

(bridge) _Altho' he may not be the man some girls think of as
    handsome / To my heart he carries the key

G C - - G / Edim - B7E7 A7D7

Won't you tell him please to put on some speed
Follow my lead, oh how I need / **Someone…**

— w & m: George Gershwin & Ira Gershwin

© 1926 (renewed) WB Music Corp. In O Kay! Rec by Ella. In film: Sinatra in Young at
Heart ('54 12), Julie Andrews in Star! ('68 13), Roberta Flack & Sting in Someone...
('87), Mr Holland's Opus ('95). '09 remake of Fame. Musical is based on the play
La Presidente & is about 2 English bootleggers in Prohibition era America.

STRANGER IN PARADISE

Take my hand, I'm a **stranger in paradise**
All lost in a wonderland, a **stranger...**
If I stand starry-eyed, that's a danger in paradise
For mortals who stand beside an angel like you

(↑2) Em A Dmaj7 - / Em Gm D - :‖

I saw your face & I ascended
Out of the commonplace into the rare
Somewhere in space I hang suspended
Until I know there's a chance that you care

Abm - Eb - / D - Gm - / F# - E6 - / Em A Dmaj7 -

Won't you answer the fervent prayer of a **stranger...**
Don't send me in dark despair from all that I hunger for
But open your angel's arms to the **stranger...**
And tell him that he need be a stranger no more

— w & m: Robert Wright & George Forrest

© 1953 Frank Music Corp. Copyright renewed & assigned to Scheffel Music Corp.,
New York, NY. All rights controlled by Scheffel Music Corp. In Kismet. Musical
is based on music of Alexander Borodin (1833-87), "The Gliding Dance of the
Maidens". Sung by the young Caliph pretending to be a gardener to Marsinah in a
garden of a house her father wishes to buy. Rec by Tony Bennett in '55.

THERE'S NO BUSINESS LIKE SHOW BUSINESS

The butcher, the baker, the grocer, the clerk
Are secretly unhappy men because
The butcher... / Get paid for what they do but no applause
They'd gladly bid their dreary jobs goodbye
For anything theatrical — and why?

G F# F E7 / Am D G - / G7 Am F7 G / 2nd /
B G#m (=Abm) F# - / G - [Gadd9 G] Am7 D7

**There's no business like show business
Like no business I know**
Everything about it is appealing
Everything the traffic will allow
Nowhere could you get that happy feeling
When you are stealing that extra bow

G - Em - / G - - - / D - G - / / / A7 - D7 -

    There's no people like show people
    They smile when they are low
    Yesterday they told you you would not go far
    That night you open & there you are
    Next day on your dressing room they've hung a star
    Let's go on with the show

G - Em - / G7 - C - ‖: Am - B7 E7 / A7 D7 G (E7) :‖

The costumes, the scenery, the makeup, the props
The audience that lifts you when you're down
The headaches, the heartaches, the backaches, the flops
The sheriff who escorts you out of town
The opening when your heart beats like a drum
The closing when the customers won't come

There no business... / ...I know
You get word before the show has started
That your favorite uncle died at dawn
On top of that your pa & ma have parted
You're broken-hearted, but you go on

    There's no people like show people
    They smile when they are low
    Even with a turkey that you know will fold
    You may be stranded out in the cold
    Still you wouldn't change it for a sack of gold
    Let's go on with the show! **(2x)**

G - Em - / G7 - C - / Am - B7 E7 / A7 D7 G E7 / 2nd
A7 D7 B7 E7 / A7 D7 G -

— w & m: Irving Berlin

© 1946 by Irving Berlin. Copyright renewed. In Annie Get Your Gun. Recs:
Andrews Sisters w/ Bing Crosby 12, Ethel Merman in '54 film Annie...11, Judy
Garland, Ethel Merman & Barbra Streisand on Garland's TV show in '63, Nathan
Lane in the '00 film Love's Labour's Lost 15.

TILL THERE WAS YOU

There were bells on the hill, but I never heard them ringing
No I never heard them at all **till there was you**
There were birds in the sky, but I never saw them winging
No I never saw them at all **till...**
   And there was music & there were wonderful roses they
   tell me / In sweet fragrant meadows of dawn & dew
There was love all around, but I never heard it singing
No I never heard it at all **till...**

C Em7 Dm7 Fm / CEm DmG C (DmG) :|

F Fm C A7 / Dm D7 G Gaug / 1st 2 above

— w & m: Meredith Willson

TIT-WILLOW

On a tree by a river a little tom-tit
Sang **"Willow, titwillow, titwillow"**
And I said to him, "Dicky-bird, why do you sit / Singing...
"Is it weakness of intellect, birdie?" I cried
"Or a rather tough worm in your little inside?"
With a shake of his poor little head, he replied / Oh... **(in 3/4)**

G CG / GD G / 1st / DA D / DmE EAm / / D7C ED / 2nd

He slapped at his chest, as he sat on that bough / Singing...
And a cold perspiration bespangled his brow / Oh...
He sobbed & he sighed & a gurgle he gave
Then he plunged himself into the billowy wave
And an echo arose fr the suicide's grave / "Oh..."

Now I feel just as sure as I'm sure that my name / Isn't...
That 'twas blighted affection that made him exclaim / "Oh...
And if you remain callous & obdurate, I
Shall perish as he did & you will know why
Tho' I probably shall not exclaim as I die / "Oh..."

— w: William S. Gilbert, m: Sir Arthur Sullivan

TOMORROW

The sun'll come out tomorrow, bet your bottom dollar
That tomorrow there'll be sun!
Just thinkin' about tomorrow clears away the cobwebs
And the sorrow til there's none!
When I'm stuck with a day that's gray & lonely
I just stick out my chin & grin & say "Oh!"   (↑2)

D F#m G EmF#m / Bm - G A :| Dm F Bb C / F Am Asus A

The sun'll come out tomorrow, so ya gotta hang on
Til tomorrow come what may
Tomorrow! Tomorrow! I love ya tomorrow!
You're always a day away! **(last time: repeat last 2 lines)**

/ " / " |: D F#m D Gm / D GA D (A):|

— w: Martin Charnin, m: Charles Strouse

A WHOLE NEW WORLD

I can show you the world - shining, shimmering, splendid
Tell me, princess, now when did you last let your heart decide?
I can open your eyes, take you wonder by wonder
Over, sideways & under on a magic carpet ride

C - - AmG / DmE Am F C :|

A whole new world, a new fantastic point of view
No one to tell us no, or where to go, or say we're only dreaming
A whole new world, a dazzling place I never knew
But when I'm way up here, it's crystal clear that now I'm in a
   whole new world with you

G - FE AmC / FC FC AmD GF / 1st / FC FC AmDBbG C

Unbelievable sights, indescribable feeling
Soaring, tumbling, freewheeling thru an endless diamond sky
A whole... (don't you dare close your eyes) a hundred thousand
   things to see (hold your breath, it gets better)
I'm like a shooting star, I've come so far, I can't go back to where I
   used to be

C - - AmG / DmE Am F C /   "   /   "   /

A whole... (every turn a surprise) with new horizons to pursue
   (every moment red-letter)
I'll chase them anywhere, there's time to spare, let me share this
   whole new world with you
A whole… (echo) that's where we'll be **(echo)**
A thrilling chase, a wondrous place for you & me

G - FE AmC/ FC FC AmD BbG C / FG G x2 / FG FG F C

— m: Alan Menken, w: Tim Rice

YOU'LL NEVER WALK ALONE

When you walk thru a storm, hold your head up high
And don't be afraid of the dark
At the end of the storm is a golden sky
And the sweet, silver song of a lark
   Walk on thru the wind, walk on thru the rain
   Tho' your dreams be tossed & blown
   Walk on, walk on with hope in your heart
   And you'll never walk alone / You'll never...

(↑2) G - D - / C G D F / Am F C Am / FC DmC B7 G
C B7 Em A / G Bm C D / G Gaug C A / GB7 EmB7 G D
G Em C D G -

— w: Oscar Hammerstein II, m: Richard Rodgers

The **Musicals** chapter contains songs from Broadway songs, musical theater, film musicals, G&S. See also: **Golden Oldies**, **Jazz & Swing**. And in **Dignity**: Seasons of love, **Faith**: I don't know how to love her, **Family**: Bring him home, Consider yourself, **Freedom**: You've got to be carefully taught, **Good**: Hernando's Hideaway, **Lullabies**: Goodnight my someone, **Outdoors**: June is busting out all over.

Old-Timey & Bluegrass

ARE YOU TIRED OF ME, MY DARLING?

Are you tired of me, my darling?
Did you mean those words you said
That made me yours forever
Since the day that we were wed?

D G / A D :‖

Tell me, would you live life over?
Could you make it otherwise?
Are you tired of me, my darling?
Answer only with your eyes

A D / E A / D G / A D

Do you ever rue the springtime
When we 1st each other met?
How we spoke in warm affection
Words my heart can ne'er forget

Do you think of blooms departed
From the cheeks you thought so fair?
Do you think I've grown cold-hearted
Beneath the load of woman's cares *[With the passing of the yrs]*

— w & m: A.P. Carter, Maybelle Carter & Sara Carter

THE BLACKEST CROW

As time draws near, my dearest dear, when you & I must part
How little you know of the grief & woe in my poor aching heart
Tis but I'd suffer for your sake, believe me dear it's true
I wish that you were staying here or I was going with you

(in 3/4, Em) D G - Em / / G - EmD Em / 1st

I wish my breast were made of glass wherein you might behold
Upon my heart your name lies wrote in letters made of gold
In letters made of gold my love, believe me when I say
You are the one that I will adore until my dying day

The blackest crow that ever flew would surely turn to white
If ever I prove false to you, bright day will turn to night
Bright day will turn to night my love, the elements will mourn
If ever I prove false to you the seas will rage & burn

— trad. (US)

BLUE MOON OF KENTUCKY

Blue moon of Kentucky, keep on shining
Shine on the one that's gone & proved untrue
Blue moon of Kentucky, keep on shining
Shine on the one that's gone & left me blue

(in 3/4) C - F - / C - G - / C - F - / C G C (C7)

It was on a moonlight night, the stars were shining bright
And they whispered from on high, your love has said goodbye
Blue moon of Kentucky...
Shine on the one that's gone & said good-bye

F - C - / F - C G / C - F - / C G C -

— w & m: Bill Monroe

BURY ME BENEATH THE WILLOW

My heart is sad and I'm in sorrow
For the only one I love
When shall I see him, oh no, never
Til we meet in heaven above

O bury me beneath the willow
Under the weeping willow tree
So he may know where I am sleeping
And perhaps he'll weep for me

C - F - / C - G - / 1st / C G C -

They told me that he did not love me
I could not believe it was true
Until an angel softly whispered
He has proven untrue to you

Tomorrow was our wedding day
But, Lord, oh Lord, where is he?
He's gone to seek him another bride
And he cares no more for me

— trad. (Appach.)

CLUCK OLD HEN

My old hen's a good old hen / She lays eggs for the RR men
Sometimes 1, sometimes 2
Sometimes enough for the whole damn crew!

Am G Am G / Am G Em Am :‖

Cluck old hen, cluck & sing
Ain't laid an egg since way last spring
Cluck old hen, cluck & squall
Ain't laid an egg since way last fall

Am C Am G / Am C Em Am :‖

My old hen, she won't do / She lays eggs & 'taters too
Sometimes 9, sometimes 10
That's enough eggs for the RR men

My old hen, she's raised on a farm
Now she's in the new ground diggin' up corn
The first time she cackled, she cackled a lot
Next time she cackled, she cackled in the pot

Had a little hen, she had a wooden leg
The best darn hen that ever laid an egg
Laid more eggs than any hen around the barn
Another little drink wouldn't do me any harm

— trad. (Appalach.)

Arr © 2015 by Hal Leonard Corporation. Rec by New Lost City Ramblers, Bryan Bowers, Alison Krauss, Frank Proffitt, Doc Watson & Clarence Ashley

THE CUCKOO

Gonna build me a log cabin on a mtn so high
So I can see Willie *[my true love]* as *[s]*he goes walking by

Em - D Em / /

O the cuckoo, she's a pretty bird, she warbles as she flies
She never says cuckoo til the 4th day of July

I played cards in England & I played cards in Spain
And I bet you $10 that I'll beat you next game
    Jack o' diamonds **(x2)**, I know you from old
    You robbed my poor pockets of silver & gold
My horses ain't hungry, they won't eat your hay
I'll ride on a little further, I'll feed them on the way
    I'll eat when I'm hungry & I'll drink when I'm dry
    If some woman don't shoot me, well I'll live til I die.

— trad. (Appalach. - orig. English)

Arr © 2015 by Hal Leonard Corporation. Rec by Doc Watson, Elizabeth LaPrelle, Clarence Ashley. In '03 film *Cold Mountain*. Pentangle rec one variant of this v old English song

DON'T THIS ROAD LOOK ROUGH & ROCKY

Darling, I have come to tell you
Tho' it almost breaks my heart
But before the morning, darling
We'll be many miles apart

(↑3) G GC G - / - - D - / 1st / D - G -

Don't this road look rough & rocky
Don't that sea look wide & deep
Don't my baby look the sweetest
When she's in my arms asleep

C - G - / - - D - / G GC G - / D - G -

Can't you hear the night birds crying
Far across the deep blue sea
While of others you are thinking
Won't you sometimes think of me?

One more kiss before I leave you
One more kiss before we part
You have caused me lots of trouble
Darling you have broke my heart

— w & m: Lester Flatt & Earl Scruggs

© 1955 by Scruggs Music, Inc. & Peer International Corporation. Copyright renewed. All rights for Scruggs Music, Inc. in the US administered by Peermusic III, Ltd. All rights outside the US administered by Peer International Corporation. On their recs.

FLY AROUND MY PRETTY LITTLE MISS

Fly around my pretty little miss, fly around my daisy
Fly around my pretty... you almost drive me crazy

D - - - / - - A D **(instr:)** D G D A / D G DA D

The higher up the cherry tree, the riper grows the cherry
The more you hug & kiss the girls, the sooner you will marry

Coffee grows on white oak trees, the river flows with brandy
If I had my pretty little miss, I'd feed her sugar candy

Going to get some weevily wheat, I'm going to get some barley
Going to get some weevily wheat & bake a cake for Charlie

18 horses in my team, leader he is blind
Everywhere I drive that team, pretty girl on my mind

Possum up in a 'simmon tree, raccoon on the ground
Possum up in a 'simmon tree, shakin' 'simmons down

— trad. (Appalach.)

Arr © 2015 by Hal Leonard Corporation. Rec by Ola Belle Reed, New Lost City Ramblers. In *Old-Time String Band SB*

FOX ON THE RUN

She walks thru the corn leading down to the river
Her hair shone like gold in the hot morning sun
She took all the love that a poor boy could give her
And left me to die like a fox on the run
Like a fox (x3) / On the run

(↑5) G D Am C / Am D C G :‖ C - - - / G - - -

Now everybody knows the reason for the fall
When woman tempted man down in Paradise, his home
This woman tempted me & she took me for a ride
Like the weary fox, I need a place to hide

C G D G / C G A7 D / 1st /C G D G / /

Well, take a glass of wine to fortify your soul
We'll talk about the world & friends we used to know
I see a stream of girls who have put me on the floor
The game is nearly over, the hounds are at my door

— w & m: Tony Hazzard

© 1968 Mann Music Publishing Ltd. Copyright renewed. All rights for the US & Canada controlled & administered by Universal-Songs of PolyGram International, Inc. Rec by The Country Gentlemen 14, Tom T. Hall, Seldom Scene, Manfred Mann

GOLD WATCH & CHAIN

Darling, how can I stay here without you
I have nothing to cheer my poor heart
This old world would seem sad, love, without you
Tell me now that we're never to part

Oh I'll pawn you my gold watch & chain, love
And I'll pawn you my gold diamond ring
I will pawn you this heart in my bosom
Only say that you'll love me again

(in G)   C - G - / D - G - :‖

Darling, how could I stay here without you
I have nothing to ease my poor heart
This old world would seem sad, love, without you
Tell me now that we never will part

Take back all the gifts you have given
But a ring & a lock of your hair
And a card with your picture upon it
It's a face that is false but is fair

Tell me why that you do not love me,
Tell me why that your smile is not bright,
Tell me why you have grown so cold-hearted
Is there no kiss for me, love, tonight?

Oh the white rose that blooms in the garden
It grows with the love of my heart
It broke thru on the day that I met you
It will die on the day that we part

— w & m: A.P. Carter

GOOD-BYE MISS LIZA

Look-a-here, Liza, listen to me, you're not the gal that you
  promised to be / Didn't you say you'd always be true?
You went out driving with Mr. Brown, now I'm the laughing-
  stock of the town
People said to never trust you
Throw up your hands, babe, I'm a-gonna go, I was a good
  man while I had the dough

G - C - / G - - D / 1st / G - D G / A - - A D (D)

(So it's) goodbye Miss Liza, I'm going to leave you
You know when I go, I'm the fella with the dough-do-do
So sing a little song, travel along, yes travel along
Bid you good-day, babe, I'm on my way –
  Goodbye, Eliza [*sweet Liza*] Jane

G - C - / D - G - / C - - / D C G D G

Give me here my gold watch & chain, give me that umbrella,
  said it might rain
Give me the clothes that I paid for too
Dive in the trunk & hand me them things, give me here my
  diamond ring
And get Mr. Brown to dress you all up new / **Throw up your…**

— w: Andrew B. Sterling, m: Harry Von Tilzer, 1903

GREY CAT ON A TENNESSEE FARM

Just look to the man who can if he will
Prosper in the valley of the Tennessee hills
Oh the big cat spit in the little kitten's eye
The little cat, little cat, don't you cry
Do love liquor & I will take a dram
I'm gonna tell you, pretty Polly Ann

D - / - A D :‖ (3x)

Cattle in the pasture, hogs in the pen
Sheep on the ranch & a-wheat in the bin / **Oh the big cat…**
    Corn in the crib & porter in the yard
    Meat in the smokehouse & a big can of lard…
Fruit in the cellar & cheese on the board
A big sack of coffee & sugar in the gourd…
    Horses in the stable & money in his pocket
    A baby in the cradle & a pretty woman to rock it…

— trad. (old-timey)

HANDSOME MOLLY

Well I wish was in London or some other seaport town
I'd step my foot in a steamboat & I'd sail the ocean round

G - - D7 / - - C G

While sailing round the ocean, while sailing round the sea
I'd think of Handsome Molly wherever she may be

She rode to church on Sunday, she passed me on by
I saw her mind was changing by the roving of her eye

Her hair was black as a raven, her eyes were black as coal
Her cheeks were [*teeth shown*] like lilies out in the morning cold

Don't you remember Molly when you gave me your right hand?
You said if you ever married I would be your man

Now you've broke your promise, go marry whom you please
While my heart is broken, you're lying at your ease

— trad. (variant of an English broadside)

HELLO STRANGER

Hello stranger, put your loving hand in mine (2x)
You are a stranger & you're a pal of mine
D - - - / G - - D / A - - D -

Get up, rounder, let a working man [*girl*] lay down (2x)
You are a rounder, but you're all out & down

Every time I ride the 6th & 4th streetcar (2x)
I can see my baby peeping thru the bars

She bowed her head, she waved both hands at me (2x)
I'm prison bound, I'm longing to be free

Oh I'll see you when your troubles are like mine (2x)
Oh I'll see you when you haven't got a dime

Weeping like a willow, mourning like a dove (2x)
There's a girl up the country that I really love

— w & m: A.P. Carter

I'M THINKING TONIGHT OF MY BLUE EYES

It would've been better for us both had we never
In this wide & wicked world had never met
For the pleasures we've both seen together
I am sure, love, I'll never forget

A D / E A :‖

Oh I'm thinking tonight of my blue eyes
Who is sailing far over the sea
Oh I'm thinking tonight of my blue eyes
And I wonder if he ever thinks of me

Oh you told me once, dear, that you loved me
You said that we never would part
But a link in the chain has been broken
Leave me with a sad & aching heart

When the cold, cold grave shall enclose me
Will you come near & shed just one tear?
And say to the strangers around you
A poor heart you have broken lies here

— w & m: A.P. Carter

© 1929 by Peer International Corporation. Copyright renewed. On *Will the Circle Be Unbroken*.

JOHN HARDY

John Hardy, he was a desperate little man
He carried 2 guns every day
He killed him a man on the West Virginia line
You oughta seen John Hardy gettin' away (poor boy) / You...

(in D) G - D - / / / D - - - / - A D -

John Hardy, he got to that East Stone bridge
He thought he would be free
But up steps a deputy & took him by the arm
Says "Johnny come along with me" / Says...

He sent for his mama & his papa too
To come & go his bail
But there ain't no bail on a murderin' charge
So they threw John Hardy back in jail / They...

John Hardy had a pretty little girl
The dress that she wore was blue
She threw her arms around his neck *[came skipping thru that old jail hall]*
Sayin' "Daddy, I have always been true (to you)..."

John Hardy had another little girl
The dress that she wore was red
She followed John Hardy to his hangin' ground
Sayin' "Johnny, I had rather see you dead / Well Johnny..."

I've been to the East & I've been to the West
I've traveled this wide world around
I've been to that river & I've been baptized
And now I'm on my hanging ground / Now...

— trad. (US)

Arr. © 2015 by Hal Leonard Corporation. Rec by Leadbelly, Mike Seeger, Dock Boggs, Carter Family. In *Coll Reprints fr SO!* V7-12. The historical John Hardy killed a man during a craps game, was found guilty of murder & hanged in 1894.

LITTLE CABIN HOME ON THE HILL

Tonight I'm alone without you, my dear
It seems there's a longing for you still
All I have to do now is sit alone & cry
In our little cabin home on the hill

D - G D / - - A - / D - G D / - A D -

O someone has taken you from me
And left me here all alone
Just to listen to the rain beat on my window pane / In our...

G C G D - / " / " / " /

I hope you are happy tonight as you are
But in my heart's a longing for you still
I just keep it there so I won't be alone...

Now when you have come to the end of the way
And find there's no more happiness for you
Just let your thoughts turn back once more if you will
To our little cabin home on the hill

— w & m: Lester Flatt & Bill Monroe

© 1947 Peer International Corporation & Bill Monroe Music, Inc. Copyright renewed. All rights for Bill Monroe Music, Inc. administered by BMG Rights Management (US) LLC. On their *More Bona Fide Bluegrass*, *Million Dollar Quartet* & recs by David Grisman, Ricky Skaggs, Elvis, John Hartford & The Osborne Bros. (Usually played in G.)

LITTLE MAGGIE

Over yonder stands little Maggie with a dram glass in her hand
She's drinking away her troubles & a-courtin' some other man

D - C - / D A D -

Oh how can I ever stand it to see them 2 blue eyes
A-shining in the moonlight like 2 diamonds in the sky?

Pretty flowers were made for blooming, pretty stars were
    made to shine
Pretty women were made for lovin', Little Maggie was made for mine

Last time I saw little Maggie she was sitting on the banks of the sea

With a .44 strapped around her & a banjo on her knee

I'm going down to the station with my suitcase in my hand
I'm a-goin' to leave this country, I'm goin' to some far distant land

Go way, go way Little Maggie, go & do the best you can
I'll get me another woman, you can get you another man

— trad. (Appalach.)

Arr © 2015 by Hal Leonard Corporation. These w per orig Stanley Bros. Also by Doc Watson, Ricky Skaggs, Robt Plant. In *Old-time String Band SB & Coll Reprints fr SO!* V1-6.

LITTLE SATCHEL

Under my bed you can set your little satchel
And on my head come lay your little hand
If you will be my own true lover
And I will be your loving little man

(in D) G - D - / A D - :‖

Run to the house & ask your papa
A bride of mine you'll ever be
If he says no, come back & tell me
And I'll wait til you get free

If you get free, well then we'll get married
Look how happy we will be
Oh we'll go to California
Any place you want to go

I wish I was a little angel
And over these prison walls I would fly
Fly on back to the arms of my darling
Stay at home & there I will die

As you can see I'm no little angel
Neither have I wings to fly
I'll go back all broken-hearted
Weep & moan until I die

— trad. (Appalach.)

MY DIXIE DARLING (Dixie Darling)

My Dixie darling, listen to this song I sing
Beneath the silver moon, with my banjo right in tune
My heart is ever true, I love no one but you
My Dixie darling, my Dixie queen

G - / D G :‖

Way down below the Mason-Dixie line
Down where the honeysuckles are entwined
There's where the southern winds are blowing
There's where the daisies growing
The girls of the North in their gay finery
Whirling around in the society
Singing a song of Dixie darling
Where I long to be

G - / / D - / G - / 1st 3 / D G

Going down South to have a big time
To see my girl in old Caroline
I'll drink my booze & do as I please
For all those girls I long to squeeze
Singing songs of Dixie darling
There's where I long to be going
Down where the jellyroll's rolling
With my Dixie queen

— w & m: A.P. Carter

ORPHAN GIRL

I am an orphan, on God's highway
But I'll share my troubles, if you go my way
I have **no mother, no father / No sister, no brother**
I am an orphan girl

G - D - / G - C - :‖ G D G -

I have had friendships, pure & golden
But the ties of kinship, I have not known them
I know **no mother... / I am an...**

But when he calls me I will be able
To meet my family at God's table
I'll meet my **mother**, my **father... / No more an...**

Blessed Savior, make me willing
And walk beside me, until I'm with them
Be my **mother**, my **father... / I am an...**

— w & m: Gillian Welch

RED ROCKING CHAIR

Ain't got no use for your red rocking chair
I ain't got no sugar baby now / I ain't got no honey baby now

Am C - Am / C - Am - / /

Who'll rock the cradle, who'll sing the song?
Who'll rock cradle when I'm gone? **(2x)**
    It's I'll rock the cradle, I'll sing the song
    It's I'll rock the cradle when you're gone **(2x)**
It's all I can do, it's all I can say
Gonna send you to your momma next payday **(2x)**
    It's all I can do, it's all I can say
    I can't get along this a way **(2x)**

— trad. (Appalach.)

ROCKINGHAM CINDY

Where'd you get your whiskey, where'd you get your dram?
I got it from a little girl way down in Rockingham
Rocky Road Cindy, rocky road to town
Rocky Road Cindy, way down in Rockingham

D - - A / D G A D // G - D - / G - A G

I went down to Rockingham, I did not go to stay
I fell in love with a pretty girl and I could not get away

Lips as red as a red rose, her hair was huckleberry brown
The sweetest girl I ever saw, way down in Rockingham

First I kissed Cindy once & then I kissed her twice
I'll tell you where I kissed her, gonna kiss her there tonight

— trad. (Appalach.)

ROCKY TOP

Wish that I was on ole **Rocky Top** / Down in the Tennessee hills
Ain't no smoggy smoke on **Rocky...** / Ain't no telephone bills

G - C G / Em D G - :‖

Once I had a girl on... / Half bear the other half cat
Wild as a mink but sweet as soda pop / I still dream about that

Rocky Top, you'll always be / Home sweet home to me
Good ole Rocky Top / Rocky Top, Tennessee (2x)

Em - D - / F - C - / - - G - / G F G - / /

Once 2 strangers climbed on... Lookin' for a moonshine still
Strangers ain't come down from... Reckon they never will
Corn won't grow at all on... Dirt's too rocky by far
That's why all the folks on... Get their corn from a jar

I've had yrs of cramped-up city life / Trapped like a duck in a pen
All I know is it's a pity life / Can't be simple again

— w & m: Boudleaux Bryant & Felice Bryant

SAIL AWAY LADIES

Ain't no use sit 'n' cry / **Sail away, ladies, sail away**
You'll be an angel by & by / **Sail away, ladies...**
Don't you rock 'em, daddy-o (4x)

D AD / D - :‖ D G / - D / - A / - D

I got a home in Tennessee / **Sail away ladies, sail...**
That's the place I wanna be / **Sail ...**
Ever I get my new house done... / Give my old one to my son...
Come along girls & go with me... / We'll go down to Tennessee...
Hush little baby don't you cry... / You'll be an angel by & by...
Ain't no use to sit 'n' cry & ... / You'll be an angel by & by...

— trad. (US)

Arr © 2015 by Hal Leonard Corporation. Rec by Uncle Dave Macon, Elizabeth LaPrelle, Kingston Trio. In *Coll Reprints fr SO!* V1-6 & *Anthology of Amer Folk M.*

THE STORMS ARE ON THE OCEAN

I'm going away to leave you love, I'm going away for a while
But I'll return to you sometime if I go 10,000 miles
The storms are on the ocean, the heavens may cease to be
This world may lose its motion love, if I prove false to thee

(in 3/4) GC G GD G / ‖ C G CD G / C G GD G

Oh who will dress your pretty little feet, oh who will glove your hand?
Oh who will kiss your rosy red cheeks when I'm in a far-off land?

Oh, Papa will dress my pretty little feet & Mama will glove my hand
You can kiss my rosy red cheeks when you return again

Oh, have you seen those mournful doves flying from pine to pine?
A-mourning for their own true love just like I mourn for mine

I'll never go back on the ocean love, I'll never go back on the sea
I'll never go back on the blue-eyed girl til she goes back on me

— w & m: A.P. Carter, Maybelle Carter & Sara Carter

© 1927 by Peer International Corporation. Copyright renewed. Rec by Carter Family 14, Maybelle Carter, June Carter Cash, Jean Ritchie & Doc Watson, Alison Krauss & Bobby Osborne.

TRAIN ON THE ISLAND

Train on the island thought I heard it blow
Run & tell my true love I'm sick & I can't go
_ _ I can't hold the wheel

A - DA / - DAE / ADEA

Train on the island, heading for the west
Run & tell my true love, the one I love the best / **I can't hold...**

Train on the island, heading for the west
Me & my gal we fell out might be for the best / **I can't hold...**

Train on the island thought I heard it squeal
Go tell my true love, I can't hold the wheel / **I can't hold...**

— trad. (Appalach.)

Arr. © 2015 by Hal Leonard Corporation. Earliest recs by J.P. Nestor & Uncle Norman Edmonds of Galax VA, both in 1927. Also on recs by Tommy Jarrell, Bruce Molsky & Big Hoedown, Old Crow Medicine Show, Alice Gerrad & Hazel Dickens. In Harry Smith's *Anthology of American Folk Music.*

WATERBOUND (trad.)

Chickens crowing in the old plowed field **(3x)**
Down in North Carolina
Waterbound & I can't get home (3x) / **Down in...**

D - / A GD / - DG / DA D :‖ (instr) G - / D - / G - / DA D

Me & Tom & Dave goin' home **(3x)** / Before the water rises
The old man's mad & I don't care **(3x)** / I'm gonna get his daughter
If he don't give her up we're gonna run away **(3x)** / **Down in...**
I'm goin' home with the one I love **(3x)** / **Down...**

— trad. (Appalach. banjo tune)

Arr © 2015 by Hal Leonard Corporation. On *New Golden Ring.* Also rec by Michael Cooney, Kathy Kallick. Often played in A (these chords 17).

WATERBOUND (Powell)

I went out late one night
The moon & the stars were shining bright
A storm come up & the trees come down
I tell you boys I was waterbound

Am - - C / G C - F - / - - - C - / - G C Am - - -

Waterbound on a stranger's shore
River rising to my door
It carried my home to the field below
I'm waterbound, nowhere to go
 Carve my name on an old barn wall
 Or no one would know I was there at all
 The stable's dry on a winter's night
 Turn your head, you can see the light
A black cat crawling on an old boxcar
A rusty door & a fallen star
Ain't got a dime in my nation sack
I'm waterbound & I can't get back
 It's I'm gone & I won't be back
 You don't believe me, count my tracks
 The river's long & the river's wide
 I'll meet you boys on the other side
So say my name & don't forget
The water still ain't got me yet
Ain't nothing but I'm bound to roam
I'm waterbound & I can't get home

— w & m: Dirk Powell

© 2004 Crying Bayou Music & Folklore Productions Inc. All rights administered by Budde Songs/Downtown DMP Songs. On his *Time Again* 14.

WAVES ON THE SEA

Oh the waves on the sea how they roll
And the chilly winds how they do blow
My own true love got drownded in the deep
And the ship never got to the shore

G - - - / C - G - / ‖ G D7 G -

 Well I left my dear darling a-grieving **(2x)**
 I left my dear darling grieving after me
 And I never expect to see her anymore
The 1st on the deck was a porter of the ship
And a rough-looking fellow was he
Said I care no more for my wife & my child
Than I do for the fish in the sea
 Oh the next on the deck was the captain of the ship
 And a nice-looking fellow was he
 Said 10 poor soldiers got drownded in the deep
 And the ship's still out to the sea

One cold night as I lay on my bed
I fell so fast asleep
And thoughts of my true love come runnin' thru my head
And poor sailors that sail on the deep
    Oh the moon shines so bright & the stars give us light
    And my mother is waiting for me
    She may look, she may weep, she may look to the deep
    She may look to the bottom of the sea
Then 3 times around turned the gallant old ship
Yes 3 times around turned she
And as she turned the 3rd time around
She sank to the bottom of the sea

    — trad. (English ballad)

WAY DOWN THE OLD PLANK ROAD

I'd rather be in Richmond with all the hail & rain
Than for to be in Georgia, boys, wearing that ball & chain
Won't get drunk no more (2x)
Won't get… way down the old plank road

D - A D / - - - A / / D - - A / D - A D

I went down to Mobile but I get on the gravel train
Very next thing they heard of me, had on the ball & chain

Doney, oh dear Doney, what makes you treat me so?
Caused me to wear the ball & chain & now my ankle's sore

Knoxville is a pretty place, Memphis is a beauty
If you want to see them pretty girls, hop to Chattanoogie

I'm going to build me a scaffold on some mtn high
So I can see my Doney girl as she goes riding by

My wife died a Fri. night, Sat. she was buried
Sun. was my courting day & Mon. I got married

18 pounds of meat a week, whiskey here to sell
How can a young man stay at home, pretty girls look so well?

    — trad. (Tennessee)

WHO WILL SING FOR ME?

Oft I sing for my friends as death's cold form I see
When I reach my journey's end, who will **sing one song for me?**
I wonder (I wonder) **who will sing** (will…) **for me?**
When I come to cross that silent sea, who will sing for…

A - D A / - D A E A / / E A E A / A A D A E A

When friends shall gather round & look down on me
Will they turn & walk away or will they **sing one song…**

So I'll sing until the end, and cheerful try to be
Ever knowing there'll be some who will **sing…**

    — w & m: Ralph Stanley & Carter Stanley

WILDWOOD FLOWER

Oh I'll twine and will mingle my waving black hair
With the roses so red & the lilies so fair
And the myrtle so bright with the emerald dew
The pale emalita & eyes look like blue

A - E A /   / A - D A / 1st

I will dance, I will sing, & my laugh shall be gay
I will charm every heart, in his crown I will sway
When I woke from my dreaming, my idol was clay
All portion of love had all flown away

Oh he taught me to love him & promised to love
And to cherish me over all others above
How my heart is now wondering, no misery can tell
He left me no warning, no words of farewell

Oh, he taught me to love him & called me his flower
That was blooming to cheer him thru life's dreary hour
Oh I long to see him & regret the dark hour
He's gone and neglected this pale wildwood flower

    — w & m: A.P. Carter

Y'ALL COME

When you live in the country everybody is your neighbor
On this one thing you can rely
They'll all come to see you & they'll never, ever leave you
Sayin' you all come to see us by & by

A - D - / A - E - / 1st / A E A -

Y'all come! (Y'all come!) **(2x)**
Well you all come to see us when you can
Y'all come! (Y'all…) **(2x)**
Well you all come to see us now & then

Kinfolks a-comin', they're comin' by the dozen
Eatin' everything from soup to hay
And right after dinner they ain't looking any thinner
And here's what you hear them say:

Grandma's a-wishin' they'd come to the kitchen
And help do the dishes right away
But they all start a-leavin', but even tho' she's grievin'
You can still hear poor old Grandma say:

    — w & m: Arlie Duff

The **Old Timey & Bluegrass** chapter contains songs with roots in Appalachia, bluegrass & early country music such as the Carter Family. There are related songs in the **Country, Gospel & Spirituals, Home & Roots** and **Travelin'** chapters. See also in **Outdoors**: Winter's come & gone **Sing**: Oh mandolin, **Time**: Your long journey, Travelin': Roving Gambler, **Work**: Call the captain, Nine pound hammer.

Outdoors

BLACKBERRY PIE

Well I stopped all day to pick wildflowers
Down by the banks where the blackberry grows
All in the shadows of the late autumn hrs
All in the brambles & the late blooming rose
Well I picked all the white ones & picked all the blues
For those are the ones that would go with her dress
And I'll dance tonight, wear holes in my shoes
Til I am the one that she loves the best

G - - C / G - - D - - - / G - - C / G - D G - - - :‖

So dally down where the river runs
Where the forest bathes the senses clean
And dally down where the fiery sun
And the rhythm moon makes a faery dream
And you might think that my heart would lie
That many a girl has caught my eye
But my heart all along belongs to the girl
Who baked me a blackberry pie

C G C G / - - - D - - - / 1st / G - D G - - -
/ " / " / G - - C - - - / G D G - - -

And tho' I've stayed single all of these yrs
'Tween the twisting rope & the wounding wind
Never staying long enough to see the spring
Where I had seen the harvest in
And I don't give a tinker's damn for the road
Tho many they say I'm bound to roam
And I just might be the last one in
Tho' I will be coming home G D G -

And many a glass I'll drink tonight
Where the wine-red hand is from work or fight
There is no judge more fair than time
For there is no one to change his mind
And each time I look in the parting glass
Those yrs that look both ways to know
I'll sing the last song of my youth
But I'll sing it again tomorrow

— w & m: John Hardy

BLUE SKIES

Blue skies smiling at me
Nothing but blue skies do I see
Bluebirds singing a song
Nothing but bluebirds all day long

Am
maj 7

Am - Am(maj7) - Am7 - D - / C - G7 - C - (E7 -) :‖

(bridge) Never saw the sun shining so bright
Never saw things going so right
Noticing the days hurrying by
When you're in love, my how they fly

C - Fm C / Fm C G7 C / 1st / Fm C G7 C E7

Blue days all of them gone / Nothing but blue skies from now on

— w & m: Irving Berlin

CALIFORNIA STARS

I'd like to rest my heavy head tonight
On a bed of California stars
I'd like to lay my weary bones tonight / **On a bed...**

(12) G - / D - / C - / G -

I'd love to feel your hand touching mine
And tell me why I must keep working on
Yes I'd give my life, to lay my head tonight / **On...**

I'd like to dream my troubles all away / **On...**
Jump up from my star-bed, make another day
Underneath my California stars

They hang like grapes on vines that shine
And warm the lovers' glass like friendly wine
So I'd give this world just to dream a dream with you / **On** <u>our...</u>

— w & m: Jay Bennett, Woody Guthrie & Jeffrey Tweedy

CASSIOPEIA

Nighthawks glide in the darkness, the city lights far from their flight
A cloud silhouette hangs far to the west, above us the clear spring sky
Cassiopeia, dance with Orion tonight
Cassiopeia, with the silvery light in your eyes

G CG CG D(G) / // C G DAm D(G) / C GD G(C G)

Hardly a car on the hwy & hardly a light on the road
Just the ruby shine of coyote eyes & the midnight stars all aglow

Somewhere east of Othello I saw her black velvet gown
Strewn with thousands of rhinestones & the North Star there in
      her crown

Orion is the bold hunter, a sword of 3 stars he does bear
He beckons the lady to come to his side, your Majesty,
      rise from your chair

(last cho) Cassiopeia... / Cassiopeia, you'll be dancing tonight

— w & m: Heidi Muller

EREV SHEL SHOSHANIM (Evening Of Roses)

Erev shel shoshanim
Netzeh na el habustan
Mor besamim ulevona
Leraglech miftan

(↑5) Am D / Dm Am / Am G / - Am

Layla yored le'at
Veru'ach shoshan noshvah
Havah elchash lach shir balat
Zemer shel ahava

Am D / Dm Am / Dm Am / G Am

Shachar homa yonah
Roshech maleh t'lalim
Pich el haboker shoshana
Ektefenu li

— w & m: Moshe Dor

© 1958 (renewed) Moshe Dor. Rec by Miriam Makeba.

FULL MOON RISING

Full moon rising, circle 'round
Shine your light when the sun goes down
Give a little happiness, give a little shout
Give a little lovin' til the sun comes out
All night long sing your song **(2x)**

‖: C - - F / C - F C :‖ (C) Dm G C Am / Dm G C -

— w & m: Terry Garthwaite

© 2011 Terry Garthwaite. On Holly Near *Peace Becomes You.*

GUM TREE CANOE

On the Tombigbee River so bright I was born
In a hut made of husks of the tall yellow corn
And there I first met with my Julia so true
And I rowed her about in **my gum tree canoe**

(in 3/4 ↑5) D - G D / - - A - / 1st / - - A D

Singing row away, row o'er the waters so blue
Like a feather we'll float in my gum tree canoe (repeat)

‖: D - G - / A - - D :‖

All day in the fields the soft cotton I hoe
I think of my Julia & sing as I go
Oh I catch her a bird with a wing of true blue
And at night sail her round in **my...**

With my hands on the banjo & a toe on the oar
I sing to the sound of the river's soft roar
While the stars they look down at my Julia so true
And dance in her eye in **my...**

One day the stream bore us so far away
That we couldn't come back, so we thought we'd just stay
Then we spied a tall ship with a flag of true blue
And it took us in tow with our **gum tree canoe**

— w: S. S. Steele, m: A. F. Winnemore (1847)

Arr. © 2015 by Hal Leonard Corporation. Rec by John Hartford Ð2, Frank Crumit.

HAL-AN-TOW

Take no scorn to wear the horn, it was the crest when you was born
Your father's father wore it & your father wore it too

D Em G EmA / D Em DA D

Hal-an-tow, jolly rumbalow
We were up long before the day-o
To welcome in the summer, to welcome in the May-o
The summer is a-coming in & winter's gone away-o

DA D - A / DA D G GA / D Em G G͡A / D Em DA D

What happened to the Spaniards that made so great a boast-o?
Why they shall eat the feathered goose & we shall eat the roast-o

Robin Hood & Little John have both gone to the fair-o, and
We will to the merry green wood to hunt the buck & hare-o

God bless Aunt Mary Moses & all her power and might-o
And send us peace to England, send peace by day & night-o

— trad. (English)

Arr. © 2015 by Hal Leonard Corporation. Sung each May 8th in the Cornish town of Helston, the same day as the processional Furry Dance. On The Waterstons *Frost & Fire.* In Revels *Garland of Spring.*

I CAN SEE CLEARLY NOW

I can see clearly now, the rain is gone
I can see all obstacles in my way
Gone are the dark clouds that had me blind
It's gonna be a bright (bright),
  bright (bright) **sun-shiny day (2x)**

D G D - / - G A - / 1st / C G D - / |

I think I can make it now, the pain is gone
All of the bad feelings have disappeared
Here is the rainbow I've been prayin' for
It's gonna be a bright...

(bridge) Look all around, there's nothin' but blue skies
Look straight ahead, nothin' but blue skies...

F - C - / F - A (C#m G C#m G C D A -)

— w & m: Johnny Nash

© 1972 (renewed) Nashco Music. On his *I Can...* Jimmy Cliff *We All Are One,* Ray Charles *True to Life,* Richie Havens *His Last Songs,* Anne Murray *What a Wonderful World.*

June Is Bustin' Out All Over

June is bustin' out all over!
All over the meadow & the hill!
Buds are bustin' outa bushes & the rompin' river pushes…
Every little wheel that wheels beside the mill!
June is bustin'…!
The ocean is full of Jacks & Jills
With her little tail a-swishin', ev'ry lady fish is wishin'
That a male would come & grab her by the gills!
Because it's June! June, June, June
Just because it's June, June, June!

G - - - / - - D - / Em - - - / A - D - :‖

G - - - / C D G -

June… / The saplin's are bustin' out with sap!
Love has found my brother "Junior" & my sister's even loonier
And my ma is gettin' kittenish with Pap
June… / The sheep aren't sleepin' any more
All the rams that chase ewe sheep are determined there'll be new
 sheep
And the ewe sheep aren't even keepin' score! / **Because it's…**

June… / The ladies the men are payin' court
Lots of ships are dippin' anchor just because the captains hanker
For the comforts they can only get in port
June… / The moonlight is shining on the shore
And the girls who were contrary with the boys in January
Aren't nearly so contrary anymore!
Because…

— w: Oscar Hammerstein II, m: Richard Rodgers

Long Is Our Winter

1 & 2. Long is our winter, dark is our night
O come set us free, o saving light
3. Come set us free, o saving light,
O come dwell among us, o saving light

Em D C B7 / C G D G

— w & m: William Ferris & Eleanor Walker

The Lord Is Good To Me

The Lord is good to me & so I thank the Lord
For giving me the things I need, the sun & rain & an apple seed
Yes, he's been good to me

D - - - / GD GD G D / D A D -

I owe the Lord so much for everything I see
I'm certain if it weren't for him, there'd be no apples on this limb
He's been good to me

(bridge) Oh here am I 'neath the blue, blue sky a-doin' as I please!
Singin' with my feathered friends, hummin' with the bees

G - - - / D Bm E A E7 A7

I wake up every day as happy as can be
Because I know that with his care, my apple trees, they will still
 be there / Oh the Lord is…

And every seed I sow will grow into a tree
And someday there'll be apples there for everyone in the world
 to share / The Lord is…

— w & m: Kim Gannon & Walter Kent

Misty Morning

1. On a grey & misty morning 2. I looked out upon the sea
3. Seabirds cried, soft breezes sighed 4. As you sailed away_

Em G Am D

— w & m: John Krumm

Red Winged Blackbird

Thought I heard a red winged blackbird
Red winged blackbird down my road (repeat)

D - G D / G D A - / 1st / G D A D

He'll be there beside the river
When Winter finally breaks its bones
He'll be king among the rushes
He'll be master of his home

D - - - / - - - A / D - - Bm / G D A D

Safe as Moses in the rushes / Builds his home on the river wide
Every time I hear him singing
Makes me feel like Spring inside

He'll be in there singing his heart out / He'll be telling me stories too
Of where he went to winter last year
Of how he's going back there too

— w & m: David Francey

Redbird's Wing

I have left the ground behind, on windy whispers I am climbing
Past the spruce & spindly pine, where winding waters sing
Mama moose & grizzly bear, with finned & feathered, they do share
That wild country lying there **beneath this redbird's wing**

(↑2) C GC F G / Am↓ FC F G / 1st / Am↓ FC FG C

Floes of ice & fields of snow, great granite ledges far below
Oh I am a climber in my soul, in search of everything
I am moving, flying free, yet oh so small as I've come to see
That shining mtn over me & **beneath…**

Roll & tumble, dip & glide, tiny shadow on the mtnside
Here feelings have no place to hide, **beneath… (2x)**

FC GC F↓ G / Am↓ FC FG C /   /

— w & m: Bill Staines

© 1987 Mineral River Music (BMI). All rights controlled & administered by Bug Music, Inc., a BMG Chrysalis Company. On his *1st Million Miles* V2 14.

SHENANDOAH

Lord have mercy on my mind
Mercy on my memory_
I'm lying 'neath the same Virginia sky
Where she laid beside me biding time
Trying to abide me_
Every night when the night was long
She was clinging to me_
Told me twice that her love was strong
Stronger than the love in old love songs / She was singing to me

(in C ↑4)   (F* chord = 4 beats)

G C C↑ Am / C AmF* / 1st / C AmF C↑ Am / C AmF :‖

O _ Shenandoah / 'Cross the rolling water
O _ Shenandoah / Where's your restless **daughter?**_

Am G F - / C AmF / 1st / C AmF*

Don't know what I gave them for / All my little lessons
How you start the peas before the corn
How you start before the air is warm / She was never listenin'
I could see there in her sorry eyes / Hear it in her breathing
Didn't come to me like some surprise / Didn't even ask her why_
When she said "I'm leavin'"
O Shenandoah / Where's your willful **daughter?**

I brought in the winter squash / I brought in the melon
Cortland, Empire, Macintosh
On the afternoon before the frost / I could feel it comin'
I can see her now in the flowery clothes / All those things I
    bought her / Trailing her perfume wherever she goes

G C C↑ Am / C AmF* / 1st / C AmF C↑ Am / 2nd / 1st 3

(tag) 'Cross the rolling water, Shenandoah
Where's your reckless daughter, Shenandoah?
Mercy on your daughter

C AmF C↑ Am /   / C AmF* (Am G F C)

— w & m: Anais Mitchell

© 2007 Treleven Music (ASCAP)/Candid Music Pub. Ltd. On her *The Brightness*.

SOME SWEET COUNTRY

I'm goin' home to some sweet country
Home, to some sweet country **(2x)**
Hasten me home & away

C - - - / F - C - / - - - Am / C G C -

I'm gonna walk thru fields of clover
Walk, thru fields of clover **(2x)**
Hasten me…

(bridge) There lies a meadow so peaceful & quiet
But for the grass as it sways
Far from the smoke, oh your money won't buy it / **Hasten…**

F - C - / F G C - / F - Am F / C G C

I'm gonna drink cool clear water / Drink, cool…

— w & m: Susan Crowe, Cate Friesen & Katherine Wheatley

© 1999, 2006 Susan Crowe, Cate Friesen & Katherine Wheatley. On her rec w/ Betty & the Bobs.

SONG FOR A WINTER'S NIGHT

The lamp is burnin' low upon my table top
The snow is softly falling
The air is still in the silence of my room
I hear your voice softly calling

(↑2) G D Em C / G D G (D) :‖

If I could only have you near
To breathe a sigh or 2
I would be happy just to hold the hands I love
On this winter night with you

G D C D / Bm Em Am D / G D Em C / G D C - (G -)

The smoke is rising in the shadows overhead
My glass is almost empty
I read again between the lines upon each page
The words of love you sent me

If I could know within my heart
That you were lonely too / **I would be happy just…**

The fire is dying now, my lamp is growing dim
The shades of night are lifting
The morning light steals across my window pane
Where webs of snow are drifting

(last cho ends:) …And to be once again with you   C D G -

— w & m: Gordon Lightfoot

© 1965 (renewed) WB Music Corp. On his *Gord's Gold*, Sarah McLachlan *Wintersong*, *Sounds of the Season*, Tony Rice *Me & My Guitar*, John McDermott *A Day to Myself*, Sara Thomsen *Winter Wanderings* & Catie Curtis Xmas alb.

TREES OF THE WILD

1. & 2. You shall indeed go out with joy & be led forth in peace

3. Before you mtns & hills shall break into cries of joy_

4. And all the trees of the wild shall clap (clap-clap, clap) _ clap
    their hands!

C F G C(G) :‖ (4x)

— w & m: Nancy Schimmel

© 1989 Nancy Schimmel. On Linda Hirschhorn *Roots & Wings* & in *Rounds Galore.*LS. Lyrics derived from Isaiah 55:12.

UNDERNEATH THE STARS

Underneath the stars I'll meet you
Underneath the stars I'll greet you
And there beneath the stars I'll leave you
Before you go of your own free will, _ _ go gently

C F Am G /   /   / F - G C F Am G (C F Am G)

Underneath the stars you met me
Underneath the stars you left me
I wonder if the stars regret me
At least you'll go of your own free will, go gently

Here beneath the stars I'm landing
And here beneath the stars not ending
Why on earth am I pretending?
I'm here again, the stars befriending
They come & go of their own free will, go gently

C F Am G (4x) / F - G C F Am G (C F Am G)

Underneath the stars you met me
And underneath the stars you left me
I wonder if the stars regret me
I'm sure they'd like me if they only met me / They come & go...

— w & m: Kate Rusby

© 2003 Kate Rusby. On her *Underneath...* There is a great YT video of this song w/ deep space photos fr Hubble telescope.

WILD ROSE OF THE MOUNTAIN

If I had my life to live, I'd surely live it over
Only walk in brand new shoes & just lay down in clover
Only work on Christmas Day, all the rest go sportin'
Spend my days down at the creek & ev'ry night go courtin'
Honey from the honey comb, water from the fountain
Sugar from the sugar cane & my wild rose of the mountain

A E D A D A /   / D D A D E / 1st // A D A   x2 / A D A - D

When I think of home sweet home, it makes my eyes grow misty
Poppa singing gospel tunes & Momma sippin' whiskey
Whiskey from a white oak barrel sure do make good liquor
Makes the nights seem twice as bright & the days go by much quicker

If I had a pickup truck, I'd fill it up with water
Paint a catfish on the side & make believe I'd caught her
Drive it slowly down the road, try to keep from bumpin'
Park it down beside the creek & watch those fish come jumpin'

If I had a new-made quilt, I'd fill it all with feathers
Take my Rosie by the hand & lay down there together
Oh the days that I was young! Thoughts that keep returning
Drive the winter night away just like a log fire burning

— w & m: Si Kahn

© 1982 Joe Hill Music LLC (ASCAP). All rights administered by Conexion Media Group, Inc. On his *In My Heart, Doing My Job* & *Aragon Mill* & in his SB. On John McCutcheon *Water fr Another Time* & *Fine Time at Our Hse* & rec by Misty Mamas.

WINGS TO FLY (Crow)

Crow mobbing up a hawk on soar
Clouds soaring in the sky
Me working down here on this rocky old earth
Working on wings to fly, good Lord
I've been working... fly

(↑2) G Em /   /   / C D G /   /

New friend's catching up a fish tonight
He's gonna haul 'em til the stars come tumbling down
Me, I'm riding high tonight
Been dreaming of him coming around, good Lord / I'm dreaming...

Geese come rising out of the field
Headed to the eastern shore
Me, I'd fly on every wing
Just to find you something more, dear friend / Just to give you...

Shearwater swooping on an old gray wave
North wind scooping up the sea
These cold autumn days make me run with joy
Looking for a way to be free, good Lord / I'm... way to be me

This moon's gonna keep me walking tonight
This sky is gonna make me sing
All I want is to share with you
Smth of this feeling, dear man / You're smth of...

Crow mobbing **(as v.1 to)** ...in the sky
Hammering down here... / Working on wings...

— w & m: Cindy Kallet

© 1981 Cindy Kallet. On her *Working on Wings to Fly.* *LS.

WINTER'S COME & GONE

Oh little <u>red</u> bird, come to my window sill
Been so lonesome shaking that morning chill
Oh little <u>red</u> bird, open your mouth & say
Been so lonesome, just about flown away

(↑3)   G - - - / - - - Em :‖

So long now, I've been out in the rain & snow
But winter's come & gone, a little bird told me so

C G - - / G Em G G Em G

Oh little <u>blue</u> bird, pearly feather breast
5 cold nickels, all that I got left
Oh little blue... what am I gonna do?
5 cold nickels ain't gonna see me thru

Oh little <u>black</u> bird on my wire line
Dark as trouble in this heart of mine
Poor little <u>black</u> bird sings a worried song
Dark as trouble til winter's come & gone

— w & m: Gillian Welch & David Rawlings

© 1998 Irving Music, Inc., Say Uncle Music & Cracklin' Music. All rights for Say Uncle Music controlled & administered by Irving Music, Inc. All rights for Cracklin' Music controlled & administered by Bug Music Inc, a BMG Chrysalis Company. On her *Hell Among the Yearlings,* Herdman Hills & Mangsen *At the Turning of the Year,* Dailey & Vincent *Bros fr Different Mothers,* Eliz Mitchell *You Are My Little Bird,* Karen Taylor *Faith & Laundry.*

The **Outdoor** chapter contains songs that celebrate nature, seasons of the year (vs. **Time** for seasons of life), weather & wilderness. More outdoors songs in the **Earthcare, Farm & Prairie** and **Lullabies** (night) chapters.

Others include **Ballads:** Searching for lambs, Ye banks & braes, **Blues:** Fishin' blues, **British:** Fields of gold, **Faith:** Trees of the field, **Friendship:** God bless us every one, **Hope:** Quiet hills, Ready for the storm, **Jazz:** It's only a paper moon, **Love:** Song for a winter's night, Sweet Thames flow softly, **Time:** Who knows where the time goes?

AL KOL ELEH (For All These Things)

Al hadvash ve'al ha'okets, al hamar vehamatok
Al biteynu hatinoket shmor Eli hatov
Al ha'esh hamevo'eret, al hamayim hazakim
Al ha'ish hashav habayta, min hamerkhakim

`CG Am A7 Dm / - - G C :‖`

Al kol eleh, al kol eleh / Shmor nah li Eli hatov
Al hadvash ve'al ha'okets / Al hamar vehamatok
Al na ta'akor natu'a / Al tishkakh et hatikvah
Hashiveyni va'ashuva / El ha'arets hatovah

`C CF (2x) / C Dm C E / Am Dm Am - / C G C - :‖`

Shmor Eli al ze habayit, al hagan, al hakhoma
Miyagon, mipakhad peta, umimilkhama
Shmor al hame'at sheyesh li, al ha'or ve'al hataf
Al hapri shelo hivshil od, veshene'esaf

Merashresh ilan baru'akh, merakhok nosher kokhav
Mish'alot libi bakhoshekh , nirshamot achshav
Ana shmor li al kol eyle, ve'al ahuvey nafshi
Al hasheket al habékhi, ve'al ze hashir

— w & m: Naomi Shemer

THE BAND PLAYED WALTZING MATILDA

Now when I was a young man I carried my pack
And I lived the free life of a rover
From the Murray's green basin to the dusty outback
Well, I waltzed my Matilda all over
    Then in 1915, my country said, son
    It's time you stopped rambling, there's work to be done
    So they gave me a tin hat & they gave me a gun
    And they marched me away to the war
And the band played Waltzing Matilda
As the ship pulled away from the quay
And amidst all the cheers, the flag-waving & tears
We sailed off for Gallipoli

(in 3/4) `C F C Am / C G C - :‖ G - F C /    / 1st 2`
`C F C - / - - G - / F - C Am / C G C -`

And how well I remember that terrible day
How our blood stained the sand & the water
And of how in that hell that they called Suvla Bay
We were butchered like lambs at the slaughter
    Johnny Turk he was waiting, he'd primed himself well
    He shower'd us with bullets & he rained us with shell
    And in 5 minutes flat, he'd blown us all to hell
    Nearly blew us right back to Australia

But **the band played...** / When we stopped to bury our slain
We buried ours, & the Turks buried theirs
Then we started all over again

And those that were left, well we tried to survive
In that mad world of blood, death & fire
And for 10 weary wks I kept myself alive
Tho around me the corpses piled higher
    Then a big Turkish shell knocked me arse over head
    And when I woke up in my hospital bed
    And saw what it had done, well I wished I was dead
    Never knew there were worse things than dying
For I'll go no more **waltzing...**
All around the green bush far & free
To hump tent & pegs, a man needs both legs
No more waltzing Matilda for me

So they gathered the crippled, the wounded, the maimed
And they shipped us back home to Australia
The legless, the armless, the blind, the insane
Those proud wounded heroes of Suvla
    And as our ship pulled into Circular Quay
    I looked at the place where my legs used to be
    And thanked Christ there was nobody waiting for me
    To grieve, to mourn & to pity
But **the band...** / As they carried us down the gangway
But nobody cheered, they just stood & stared
Then they turned all their faces away

And so now every April, I sit on my porch
And I watch the parade pass before me
And I see my old comrades, how proudly they march
Reviving old dreams of past glory
    And the old men march slowly, old bones stiff & sore
    They're tired old heroes from a forgotten war
    And the young people ask, what are they marching for?
    And I ask myself the same question
But **the band** plays... / And the old men still answer the call
But as year follows year, more old men disappear
Someday no one will march there at all

(tag) Waltzing Matilda **(x2)**
Who'll come a-waltzing Matilda with me?
And their ghosts may be heard as they march by that billabong
Who'll come a-waltzing Matilda with me?

`C F / C G / CG AmF / C GC`

— w & m: Eric Bogle

BETWEEN THE WARS

I was a miner, I was a docker
I was a railwayman **between the wars**
I raised a family in times of austerity
With sweat at the foundry **between...**

D Em G D / A Bm G A / A Bm G D / A Bm GA D

    I paid the union & as times got harder
    I looked to the govt to help the working man
    But they brought prosperity down at the armoury
    We're arming for peace, me boys **between...**

    A Bm G D / A - - - / D Em G D /   "   /

I kept the faith & I kept voting
Not for the iron fist but for the helping hand
For theirs is a land with a wall around it
And mine is a faith in my fellow man
    Theirs is a land of hope & glory
    Mine is the green field & the factory floor
    Theirs are the skies all dark with bombers
    And mine is the peace we knew **between...**

Call up the craftsmen, bring me the draftsmen
Build me a path from cradle to grave
And I'll give my consent to any govt
That does not deny a man a living wage
    Go find the young men never to fight again
    Bring up the banners from the days gone by
    Sweet moderation, heart of this nation
    Desert us not, we are **between...**

— w & m: Billy Bragg

BLESSED ARE THE PEACEMAKERS

1. & 2. Blessed are the peacemakers **(2x)**
3. For they shall be callèd the **4.** children of God

— w & m: Beverly Shepard

BONNIE LIGHT HORSEMAN

When Boney commanded his armies to stand
He leveled his cannon right over the land
He leveled his cannon his victory to gain
And he slew my light horseman on the way comin' in

(in D, a capella) D A / G D / G Bm / Em G

Broken hearted I'll wander
Broken hearted I'll remain
Since my Bonnie Light Horseman
In the wars he was slain

If I was a small bird & had wings for to fly
I'd fly across the salt sea to where my love does lie
And with my fond wings, I'd beat over his grave
And kiss the pale lips, that lie cold in the clay

Now the dove she laments for her mate as she flies
"Oh where, tell me where, is my darling?" she cries
And where in this wide world is there one to compare
With my Bonnie Light Horseman who was slain in the war?

— trad. (Irish)

BRING 'EM HOME

If you love your Uncle Sam / **Bring 'em home (2x)**
Support our boys in Vietnam / **Bring 'em...**

(↑2) G - - - / Em - - - / C - G C / G D G -

It'll make our generals sad, I know / **Bring...**
They want to tangle with the foe...
    They want to test their weaponry...
    But here is their big fallacy
Our foe is hunger & ignorance
You can't beat that with bombs & guns
    I may be right, I may be wrong
    But I got a right to sing this song

— w & m: Pete Seeger

CHARIOTS

O shepherd, O shepherd, come leave off your piping
Come listen, come learn, come hear what I say
For now is the time that has long been forespoken
For now is the time there'll be new tunes to play
For soon there comes one who brings a new music
Of sweetness & clarity none can compare
So open your heart for heavenly harmony
Here on this hill will be filling the air

D G D G / D - - A / 1st / D - A D
G - D - / G - D A / D - - G / D - A D

With chariots of cherubim chanting
And seraphim singing "Hosanna!"
And a choir of archangels a-caroling come
Hallelujah Hallelu
All the angels a-trumpeting glory
In praise of the Prince of Peace!

D - G A / D - G D /   / G D G D / - - G - / D A D -

See on yon stable the starlight is shimmering
And glimmering & glistening & glowing with glee
In Bethlehem blest this baby of bliss will be
Born here before you as bold as can be
And you'll be the first to hear the new symphony
Songs full of gladness & glory & light
So learn your tunes well & play your pipes proudly
For the Prince of Paradise plays here tonight

Bring your sheep bleating to this happy meeting
To hear how the lamb with the lion shall lie
Midst mooing & braying you'll hear the song saying
The humble & lowly will be the most high
Let the horn of the herdsman be heard up in heaven
For the gates are flung open for all who come near
And the simplest of souls shall sing to infinity
Lift up & listen & you shall hear

The warmonger's charger will thunder for freedom
The gun-maker's furnace will dwindle & die
And muskets & sabers & swords shall be sundered
Surrendered to the sound that is sweeping the sky
And the shoes of the mighty shall dance to new measures
And the jackboots of generals shall jangle no more
As sister & brother & father & mother
Agree with each other the end to all war

As a candle can conquer the demons of darkness
As a flame can keep frost from the deepest of cold
So a song can give hope in the depths of all danger
And a line of pure melody soar in your soul
So sing your songs well & sing your songs sweetly
And swear that your singing it never shall cease
Til the clatter of battle & drums of disaster
Be drowned in the sound of the pipes of peace

    — w & m: John Kirkpatrick

© 1995 Squeezer Music. Author was commissioned to write a couple of new carols for a "Wassail" tour organized by Folkworks in the north of England in 1995. One was this new classic, through-composed for band, solo voices & a small choir. On his *Wassail!* & Nowell Sing We Clear *Just Say Noel* (both 13).

CHRISTMAS IN THE TRENCHES

My name is Francis Tolliver, I come from Liverpool
2 yrs ago the war was waiting for me after school
To Belgium & to Flanders, to Germany to here
I fought for King & country I love dear
It was Christmas in the trenches where the frost so bitter hung
The frozen fields of France were still, no Christmas song was sung
Our families back in England were toasting us that day
Their brave & glorious lads so far away

D Bm G Em / A - G D / D Bm G Em / A - D - /
A - G D / Bm - G A /   "   /   "   /

I was lyin' with my mess-mates on the cold & rocky ground
When across the lines of battle came a most peculiar sound
Says I "Now listen up me boys," each soldier strained to hear
As one young German voice sang out so clear
"He's singin' bloody well you know" my partner says to me
Soon one by one each German voice joined in harmony
The cannons rested silent. The gas clouds rolled no more
As Christmas brought us respite from the war

As soon as they were finished, a reverent pause was spent
"God rest ye merry, gentlemen" struck up some lads from Kent
The next they sang was Stille Nacht, "Tis Silent Night" says I
And in 2 tongues one song filled up that sky
"There's someone comin' towards us" the front-line sentry cried
All sights were fixed on one lone figure trudging from their side
His truce flag, like a Christmas star, shone on that plain so bright
As he bravely strode, unarmed, into the night

Then one by one on either side walked into no-man's-land
With neither gun nor bayonet we met there hand to hand
We shared some secret brandy & wished each other well
And in a flare-lit soccer game we gave 'em hell
We traded chocolates, cigarettes & photographs from home
These sons & fathers far away from families of their own
Young Sanders played his squeeze box & they had a violin
This curious & unlikely band of men

Soon daylight stole upon us & France was France once more
With sad farewells we each began to settle back to war
But the question haunted every heart that lived that wondrous night
"Whose family have I fixed within my sights?"
It was Christmas in the trenches where the frost so bitter hung
The frozen fields of France were warmed as songs of peace were sung
For the walls they'd kept betw us to exact the work of war
Had been crumbled & were gone forevermore

(as 1st 4 lines) My name is Francis Tolliver, in Liverpool I dwell
Each Christmas come since WWI I've learned its lessons well
That the ones who call the shots won't be among the dead & lame
And on each end of the rifle we're the same

    — w & m: John McCutcheon

© 1984 John McCutcheon/Appalsongs (ASCAP). In his SB & SO! 31:4. On his *Water From Another Time*, Live at Wolf Trap & Charlie King & Karen Brandow *Sparks & Tears*. also rec by Robbie O'Connell, John McDermott, Seamus Kennedy

CROW ON THE CRADLE

The sheep's in the meadow, the cow's in the corn
Now is the time for a child to be born
He'll cry for the moon & he'll laugh at the sun
If he's a boy, he'll carry a gun
Sang the crow on the cradle   **(in 3/4)**

Am - - - / F C E Am / - - - Em / 1st / DDE Am - -

If it should be that our baby's a girl
Never you mind if her hair doesn't curl
Rings on her fingers & bells on her toes
And a bomber above her wherever she goes / **Sang...**

Rockabye baby, the dark & the light!
Somebody's baby is born for a fight
Rockabye baby, the white & the black!
Somebody's baby is not coming back...

Your mammy & pappy, they'll scrape & they'll save
Build you a coffin & dig you a grave
Hushabye little one, why do you weep?
We've got a toy that will put you to sleep...

Bring me a gun & I'll shoot that bird dead
That's what your mammy & pappy once said
Crow on the cradle, oh what should I do?
That is a thing that I leave to you...

    — w & m: Sydney Carter

© 1962 (renewed) Warner-Tamerlane Publishing Corp. On Jackson Browne *Love Is Strange*, Pete Seeger *If I Had a Hammer*, Judy Collins *Maids & Golden Apples*, Show of Hands *As You Were*. In *Coll Reprints fr SO!* V1-6.

DAY AFTER TOMORROW

I got your letter today & I miss you all so much here
I can't wait to see you all & I'm counting the days here
I still believe that there's gold at the end of the world
And I'll come home to Illinois **on the day after tomorrow**

CF CF C G / Am C - G / F C - F / CF CF CG C

It is so hard & it's cold here & I'm tired of taking orders
And I miss old Rockford town up by the Wisconsin border
What I miss, you won't believe, shoveling snow & raking leaves
And my plane will touch down **on the day...**

I close my eyes every night & I dream that I can hold you
They fill us full of lies, everyone buys 'bout what it means to be a
    soldier
I still don't know how I'm supposed to feel 'bout all the blood
    that's been spilled
Will God on this throne get me back home **on...**

You can't deny the other side don't want to die any more than we do
What I'm trying to say is don't they pray to the same God that we do?
And tell me how does God choose, whose prayers does he refuse?
Who turns the wheel, who throws the dice **on...**

I am not fighting for justice, I am not fighting for freedom
I am fighting for my life & another day in the world here
I just do what I've been told, we're just the gravel on the rd
And only the lucky ones come home **on...**

And the summer, it too will fade & with it brings the winter's
    frost, dear
And I know we too are made of all the things that we have lost here
I'll be 21 today, I been saving all my pay
And my plane will touch down **on...**
    — w & m: Kathleen Brennan & Tom Waits

© 2004 Jalma Music (ASCAP). On his *Real Gone*, Joan Baez *Day after...*

LE DÉSERTEUR

Monsieur le Président, je vous fais une lettre
Que vous lirez peut-être si vous avez le temps
Je viens de recevoir mes papiers militaires
Pour partir à la guerre avant mercredi soir

C Em Edim Dm / G Am D G / 1st / FG Am DG C

    Monsieur le Président, je ne veux pas la faire
    Je ne suis pas sur terre pour tuer des pauvres gens
    C'est pas pour vous fâcher, il faut que je vous dise
    Ma décision est prise, je m'en vais déserter

F Am B7 Em / A7 Dm D G / 1st above / Fm C DG C

Depuis que je suis né j'ai vu mourir mon père
J'ai vu partir mes frères et pleurer mes enfants
Ma mère a tant souffert qu'elle est dedans sa tombe
Et se moque des bombes et se moque des vers
    Quand j'étais prisonnier, on m'a volé ma femme
    On m'a volé mon âme et tout mon cher passé
    Demain de bon matin je fermerai ma porte
    Au nez des années mortes j'irai sur les chemins

Je mendierai ma vie sur les routes de France
De Bretagne en Provence et je dirai aux gens
"Refusez d'obéir, refusez de la faire
N'allez pas à la guerre, refusez de partir"
    S'il faut donner son sang allez donner le vôtre
    Vous êtes bon apôtre, Monsieur le Président
    Si vous me poursuivez prévenez vos gendarmes
    Que je n'aurai pas d'armes et qu'ils pourront tirer
    — w: Boris Vian, m: Harold Berg

© 1964 (renewed) Editions Paul Beuscher SA. All rights in the US & Canada admin by WB Music Corp. Above are Vian lyrics exc final 2 lines are Mouloudji's. Written during the battle of Dien Bien Phu in '54. Orig recs by Vian & by Marcel Mouloudji (whose father was Algerian). Banned by French govt. An antiwar anthem during French colonial war in Algeria & US war in Vietnam. On Peter Paul & Mary *In Concert*, Joan Baez *European Tour* & rec by Serge Reggiani. In *Coll Reprints fr* SO! V7-12.

DOCTOR, MY EYES

Doctor, my eyes have seen the yrs & the slow parade of fears
Without crying, now I want to understand
I have done all that I could to see the evil & the good
Without hiding, you must help me if you can
    Doctor, my eyes tell me what is wrong
    Was I unwise to leave them open for so long?

C - Em - / Am F C - :‖ Am - C - / Am G F - (C - F -)

I have wandered thru this world, as each moment has unfurled
I've been waiting to awaken from these dreams
People go just where they will, I never noticed them until
I got this feeling that it's later than it seems
    Doctor, my eyes tell me what you see
    I hear their cries, just say if it's too late for me

    Doctor... I cannot see the sky
    Is this the prize for having learned how not to cry?
    — w & m: Jackson Browne

© 1970, 1972 Criterion Music Corp. & Open Window Music. On his *Los Angeles CA* 15 & rec by Jackson 5, Wilson Phillips. Written during Vietnam War.

DOVER

Elijah was a sergeant, 42 yrs old
From Mesa Arizona, Elijah won't grow old
Patrick was with C Troop, 2nd Armored Cav
His buddies all remember how Patrick loved to laugh
Seth was from East Brunswick, just a newlywed
Somewhere in New Jersey Seth's young widow bows her head
Daniel was from Boston, shipped out from Fort Bragg
His mother got back Daniel with a folded flag

(in 3/4) A - - G / - - D A :‖ (4x)
Oh big airplane, bring 'em down easy
Out of the Delaware sky
Oh big airplane, Dover is waiting
To welcome the fallen you fly

A - G - / D - A E / 1st / D - A E D - - -

William served in Anbar, combat engineer
1st Marine Division, William is not here
Alan rebuilt bridges for Battalion B
Next to cause of death, they wrote the letters I.E.D.
Gussie was a scrub nurse hailing from Fort Bliss
Gussie had a spirit this world's gonna miss
Jeremiah's son cries on his mamma's knee
There was no armor plating on his dad's humvee

(bridge) Scrubbed wooden pallets with white straps cinched over
Long boxes of flag-draped aluminum
The C-5 is crowded when it lands in Dover
The honor guard comes to make room again & again & again & again

`Em - C - / Em - A - :||`

Making straight for Nineveh, just like Jonah's whale
Holy truth you swallow, overseas you sail
Precious is your cargo, sacred was their gift
Offered in a sandstorm from which your wings lift
Those who should take notice can't watch you set down
Behind barbed wire fences miles from their town
No one breathes to question this silent parade
Except for the anguished loved ones left to say

Oh big airplane, bring 'em down easy
Out of the Delaware sky
Oh big airplane, Dover is waiting
To welcome the heroes **you fly** / Home

`A - G - / D - A E / 1st  / D - A E D - - - / A - - -`

— w & m: John Flynn

© 2003 Flying Stone Music (ASCAP). On his *Two Wolves*. Written to honor the fallen soldiers of the Iraq war, whose bodies were flown back to Dover Air Force Base in Delaware.

FIGHT NO MORE FOREVER

In 1877 / Winter coming again
The chief of the Nez Perce Nation
Chief Joseph surrendered & spoke of his pain
He spoke of his people's pain   **(in 3/4, ↑4)**

`C G Am - / F C G - / F - C - / F - C G / C G F C`

Warriors killed, children frozen / Families broken apart
Like promises from the white people
It leaves such a sadness & pain in my heart / A sadness...

I do not want war / & I'm weary of being betrayed
We will never be defeated
Tho' I surrender my gun & my blade / I surrender...

Hear me, all you people / From where the sun now stands
I will fight no more forever
I will never again hold a gun in these hands
I will not hold...

Just let me be a free person / Free to stay or roam
To have my own religion
To work & to speak, to return to my home
Be free to return...

It was 1877 / Winter coming again
The chief of the Nez Perce Nation
Chief Joseph surrendered, may his spirit remain
May the spirit of Joseph remain

— w & m: Michael Stern

© 1995, 2005 Michael Stern, www.mikesongs.net. On his *Fight No...& Strangest Dream*. *LS.

FOR WHAT IT'S WORTH

There's something happening here
But what it is ain't exactly clear
There's a man with a gun over there
Telling me I got to beware
I think **it's time we stop,** children, **what's that sound?**
Everybody look what's going down

`E A (4x) // E D / A C`

There's battle lines being drawn
Nobody's right if everybody's wrong
Young people speakin' their minds
Getting so much resistance from behind
It's time we stop, hey, what's...

What a field day for the heat
A thousand people in the street
Singing songs & carrying signs
Mostly say, "hooray for our side"

Paranoia strikes deep
Into your life it will creep
It starts when you're always afraid
Step out of line, the man come & take you away
We better **stop... (4x)**

— w & m: Stephen Stills

© 1966 (renewed) Cotillion Music Inc., Ten East Music, Springalo Toones & Richie Furay Music. All rights administered by Warner-Tamerlane Publishing Corp. On Buffalo Springfield, Tab Benoit *Legacy*, Crosby, Stills *CSNY/Deja Vu*, Keb' Mo' *Peace: Back by Popular Demand*, Lucinda Williams *Lu in '08*.

FROM A DISTANCE

From a distance the world looks blue & green
And the snow-capped mountains white
From a... the ocean meets the stream
And the eagle takes to flight
...there is harmony / And it echoes thru the land
It's the voice of hope, it's the voice of peace
It's the voice of every man

`G C D G / C D G -:|| C D Em - / C G D - /`
`C G C G / C D G -`

From... we all have enough / And no one is in need
There are no guns, no bombs, no disease
There's no hungry mouths to feed
...we are instruments marching in a common band
Playing songs of hope, playing songs of peace
They're the songs of every man

(bridge) God is watching us **(x2)** / God is... **from a...**

`C D G Em / C D G -`

From... you look like my friend / Even tho' we are at war
...I can't comprehend / What all this war is for
...there is harmony / And it echoes thru the land
It's the hope of hopes, it's the love of loves
It's the heart of every man

(repeat last 2 lines, ending:) It's the <u>song</u> of every man

— w & m: Julie Gold

© 1986, 1987 Julie Gold Music (BMI) & Wing & Wheel Music (BMI). Wing & Wheel Music administered worldwide by Irving Music, Inc. Bette Midler *Experience the Divine*, Nanci Griffith *From A Distance* (in F#), Kathy Mattea *Time Passes By* (in F). Ironically this song was popular among US soldiers during the First Gulf War.

GONNA TAKE US ALL

We need the Buddhists & the Baptists, Quakers & Catholics too
The atheists & agnostics, Muslims & Jews
We need people of all nations, all colors & all creeds
_ To put an end to war now, _put an end to greed
_ Gonna take us all to make a change
_ Take us all to win the peace
_ Gonna take us all in the streets
_ It's gonna take us all / _ _ _ It's gonna take us all_ _

C F C F (4x) ‖: Dm Em / F G :‖ (- C F) C F

We need the immigrants & the unions, the greens & the gays
Hip-hoppers & the beboppers & the women for equal pay
Farmworkers out in the sun, homeless out in the rain
The seniors & the soccer moms for a world that is humane

We need your friends & your neighbors, the poets & the painters
The socialists & the anarchists, the pacifists & the humanists
Every culture & community, takes black & white & brown
Times we won't see eye to eye, but we stand on common ground

— w & m: Jon Fromer

© 2009 West Umbrella Music (recorded 2008). On his *Gonna Take Us All* 15.

HAWKS

"Let's **1.** go" cried the bellicose / hawks. _ "It's
2. Off to the wars we / _ are! _ We'll
3. Maim & kill for peace & free- / _ dom." (Let's)

Elves

"Hey **1.** ho" cried Santa's / elves. _ "It's
2. Off to the shop we / _ are. _ We'd
3. Like to stay but time is / _ short." (Hey)

> — orig round ("The Merrie Dwarves") w & m: Pati Nagle, new w
> ("Elves"): Jan Maier, Evy Mayer & Randy Speigel, new w ("Hawks"):
> Martha Davey

© 1978 Pati Nagle. New words © 2015 Pati Nagle, Evy Mayer & Martha Davey. This
round (w/ 2 versions of lyrics) is adap fr an orig round by Pati Nagle. On *Rounds
Galore & More* V2. Both versions work as "catches." Listen carefully to how the
1st words of measures 2, 4 & 6 fall on different beats & combine to form a hidden
sentence sung by the 3 different parts! For "Elves" use broken slurs.

HOW BEAUTIFUL UPON THE MOUNTAIN

How beautiful upon the mountain
Are the steps of those who walk in peace (repeat)

D G D - / G - A - / 1st / G A D -

Across the bridge at Selma you came marching side by side
In your eyes, a new world on the way
Hope was in your heart & justice would not be denied
You sang "We shall overcome some day"
God knows the courage you possessed
And Isaiah said it best:

D - G D / - - A -:‖ G - D - / G - A -

Marching round the White House, marching round the Pentagon
Marching round the mighty missile plants
Speaking truth to power, singing peace in Babylon
Asking us "Why not give peace a chance?"
God knows the courage you possess / **And Isaiah...**

Now the generations who have joined you on this road
Look to you with power in their eyes
Now you know the torch has passed as they pick up the load
Now you see their eyes are on the prize! / **God knows...**

— w & m: Tom Paxton

© 2008 Pax Music (ASCAP). All rights administered by BMG Rights Management
(US) LLC. On his *Comedians & Angels*, Roy Bailey *Below the Radar*, Charlie King &
Karen Brandow *The Distance Remaining*. See Isaiah 52:7.

I BELIEVE PEACE WILL COME

_ I believe that peace will come (**3x**)
I believe that peace will come _

G - C G / Em - C D / 1st / Em D G -

I believe that hope survives...
I believe that love will rise...
I believe in humankind...

— w & m: Linda Allen

© 2005 Linda Allen (BMI). www.lindasongs.com. On her *Where I Stand.* *LS.

I'VE GOT PEACE IN MY FINGERS

I've got peace (**x3**) **in my fingers / Watch what I can do!**
I've got peace... / **I'm gonna** shake hands with you

D - - - / G A D - :‖

I've got words (**x3**) **in my head / Watch what...**
I've got words... / **I'm gonna** talk things over with you

I've got love (**x3**) **in my heart / Watch...**
I've... / I'm gonna give some to you (**repeat**)

I've got peace (**x3**) **in my fingers / Words** (**x3**) **in my head**
I've got love (**x3**) **in my heart / I'm gonna** give some to you!

D - - G / / / G A D -

— w & m: Susan Salidor

© 1995 Susan Salidor. On her *Little Voices in my Head. Songs in the Key of Cha.
Susan Salidor SB. Come & Make a Circle 2* 15. *LS.

IF NOT ME, THEN WHO

If not me, then who? / If not now, then when?
If not here, then where will peace begin?
I am where peace begins _

(in 3/4) G C G D / / G - B7 - C / D - G (C G D)

Oh it's me, that's who / And it's now, that's when
And it's here, that's where peace begins / **I am where...**

— w & m: Carol A. Johnson

© 1999 Noeldner Music (BMI). www.caroljohnsonmusic.com. On her *Circle of Peace* 11.

IF YOU WANT PEACE (Work For Justice)

If you want peace, work for justice (3x)
No justice, no peace

(↑2) G - - - / D - G - / - - C - / D - G -

You can't have peace in a world of <u>hunger</u>
With one dog over & one dog under
You... hunger **Not in this world**
Until the last chain falls
<u>Hunger</u> **will make slaves of us all**

C - G - / D - G - / 1st / A - D - /
CG AmG D - / CG D G -

You can't have peace in a world of <u>war</u>
Where the rich get richer & the poor stay poor**...**
You can't have peace... / War **will make slaves of us all**

You can't have peace... of <u>hatred</u>
Your way, evil – my way, sacred / **You can't...** / Hatred **will...**

You can't... <u>violence</u> / A world of terror, fear & silence**...**

  — w & m: Charlie King

IN THE NAME OF ALL OF OUR CHILDREN

We will sing with each other **as the world turns round**
We'll sing with each other **as the day grows long**
We will sing with each other **growing wise & strong**
In the name of all of our children

D - G D / A - D A / D D7 G - / D A - D

We'll remember the young ones **as the world turns...**
We'll remember the young ones **as the day...**
We'll remember**... growing...** / **In the name of all...**

We will cherish our elders**...**
We will care for the earth**...**
We will break bread together**...**
We will love one another**...** *[make up verses]*

  — w & m: Sally Rogers

IS THERE ANYBODY HERE?

Is there <u>anybody</u> here who'd like to change his clothes into a uniform?
Is there <u>anybody</u> here who thinks they're only serving on a <u>raging</u> storm?
Is there <u>anybody</u> here with <u>glory</u> in their eyes, <u>loyal</u> to the end, whose <u>duty</u> is to die?
I wanna see him, I wanna wish him luck, I wanna shake his hand, wanna call his name
Put a medal on the man _ _ _

C - Am - / F A7 Dm G7 / C Em C Em //
F G C F G / C - - -

Is there anybody here who'd like to wrap a flag around an early grave?
Is there anybody here who thinks they're standing taller on a battle wave?
Is there anybody here who'd like to do his part, soldier to the world & a hero to his heart? / **I wanna...**

(bridge) Is there <u>anybody</u> here, <u>pr</u>oud of the parade
Who'd <u>like</u> to give a cheer & show they're not afraid?
<u>I</u>'d like to ask him what he's trying to defend
<u>I</u>'d like to ask him what he thinks he's gonna win

Am G / Am DG / E Am / D G

Is there anybody here who thinks that following the orders takes away the blame?
Is there anybody here who wouldn't mind a murder by another name?
Is there anybody here whose pride is on the line, with the honor of the brave & the courage of the blind? / **I...**

  — w & m: Phil Ochs

JERUSALEM

I woke up this morning & none of the news was good
And death machines were rumbling 'cross the ground where Jesus stood
And the man on my TV told me it had always been that way
And there's nothin' anyone can do or say
And I almost listened to him, yeah I almost lost my mind
Then I regained my senses again, looked into my heart to find
That I believe that one fine day all the children of Abraham
Will lay down their swords forever in Jerusalem

(↑2) C - - F / C Am F G / 1st / C G C -
Am C F C - / Am C F G / C - - F / C Am G C

Well maybe I'm only dreaming & maybe I'm just a fool
But I don't remember learning how to hate in Sunday School
But somewhere along the way I strayed & I never looked back again
But I still find some comfort now & then
Then the storm comes rumbling in & I can't lay me down
And the drums are drumming again & I can't stand the sound
But I believe there'll come a day when the lion & the lamb
Will lie down in peace together in Jerusalem

And there'll be no barricades then, there'll be no wire or walls
And we can wash all this blood from our hands and all this hatred from our souls
And I believe that on that day all the children of Abraham
Will lay down their swords together in Jerusalem

  — w & m: Steve Earle

JOHNNY HAS GONE FOR A SOLDIER

(Shule Aroon)

Shule shule shule aroon
Me oh my, I love him so
But only time will heal my woe
Johnny has gone for a soldier

(↑5) Am E Am - / C - - Am / C - Am - / 1st

Here I sit on Buttermilk Hill
Who can blame me, cry my fill?
And every tear can turn a mill
Johnny has gone…

I sold my rack, I sold my reel / I even sold my spinning wheel
To buy my love a sword of steel / **Johnny…**

Me, oh my, I loved him so / Broke my heart to see him go
And only time will heal my woe…

With fife & drum he marched away / He would not heed what I
    did say / He'll not come back for many a day…

Oh my baby, oh my love / Gone the rainbow, gone the dove
Your father was my one true love…

I'll dye my dress, I'll dye it red / And thru the streets I'll beg for
    bread / For the lad that I love from me has fled…

Siúil, siúil, siúil a rún
Siúil go socair agus siúil go ciúin
Siúil go doras agus éalaigh liom
Is go dté tú mo mhúirnín slán
[pron: Shule, shule, shule aroon
Shule go succir agus, shule go kewn
Shule go dheen durrus oggus aylig lume
Iss go jay too mavoorneen slahn]

II, cho: Am G Am - / G Em Am - / C G F Am / Em E Am -

v: Am G F Am - / Em G Am - / C G Am F / Am Em Am -

— trad. (Irish "Siúil a Rún")

Arr. © 2015 by Hal Leonard Corporation. aka "Buttermilk Hill." On Seeger *Am
Fav Ballads* v4 12, Peter Paul & Mary *Moving* (II Ð1 as "Gone the Rainbow"), Judy
Collins *Golden Apples of the Sun*, Elane *The Fire of Glenvore* (II). In *Peoples SB*,
SO! 7:2, Fireside Bk of Folk S. There are many variants of this song, which was
popular in US Civil War.

LAMB & LION

1. May lamb & lion lie down together
2. Joy & wonder never cease
3. Halleluia **(2x)**   4. Grant us peace _

G - C D :‖ **(4x)**

— w & m: Lorraine Lee Hammond

© 1990 Lorraine Lee Hammond/Snowy Egret Music (BMI). On *Rounds Galore &
More V2*.

LAUGHLIN BOY

Have you heard many a story
Told by old & young with joy
About the faithful deed of daring
That was done by the Laughlin boy **(2x)**
Listen to me children, well I wouldn't tell a lie (2x)

D - / - DA / D - / D AD /   // D - / D AD

That Laughlin boy was a boy of honor
And he loved Virginia well
But he would not fire a rifle
So he sat in a cold jail cell **(2x)**
        He was pierced & he was beaten
        40 stripes he gladly bore
        But he would not serve the devil
        In that awful civil war **(2x)** / **Listen…**

12 grey soldiers stood before him
And they aimed their rifles true
He prayed Lord, oh please forgive them
For they know not what they do **(2x)**
        Those young soldiers would not fire
        They defied the general's plan
        So the army changed his sentence
        Who could murder such a man? **(2x)** / **Listen…**

They hauled him far away to Richmond
Far away from his kids & wife
There, pneumonia wracked his body
That good man soon lost his life **(2x)**
        Now his wife is sadly weeping
        Seven children wonder why
        Lord it seems that truth & honor
        Sure can come at an awful price **(2x)** / **Listen…**

— w & m: Bill Jolliff

© 1999 William Jolliff. On Tracy Grammer *Flower of Avalon*, Barry & Brooks *The
Old York Rd*, Beyond the Pale *Paleontology*. Tune adap from "Johnson Boys"
(trad).

LION & THE LAMB

Someday when the lion _ lies down with the lamb _
And the river of peace flows like diamonds,
    like dust thru our hands _
We will sing over _ the breadth of this land

(in 3/4) D G DDsus D / Bm - BmA AsusA / 1st

We'll take our part, give body & heart
Bathe in the fountain of freedom & art
Stand on the prairie with the wind blowing free
Take to the river, drift to the sea
Long for the hwy, & cherish the home
Ever the dreamer, never alone / Never alone _

GD GD **(6x)** / GD D

Come home to find a satisfied mind
A moment in darkness, a minute in time
A touch without thinking, & hope without fear
A valley that's boundless, a river that's clear
A sky full of lovers & brothers & friends
Old sister moon & nights without end / Nights without end

We'll take our rest, the finest & best
Of each living thing, each heart in each breast
We will give names to each thing that is new
Each promise, each whisper, each word that is true
Each time you reached out & someone was there
Each time you woke up in the cool morning air
The cool morning air

— w & m: Tom James

LOVE IS ALL AROUND

Love is all around (4x)

D A G D / - A D A / 1st / D A D -

The Earth is our treasure, how lucky are we
Love is all around
Home to billions of people just like you & me
Love is all around

D - G D / - A D A / 1st / D A D -

We're living here together as we spin thru space / **Love is all...**
Sisters & brothers of the human race...

When you look up at night & see the stars in the sky / **Love...**
Do you wonder who we are, how did we get here & why...

May the road we all travel be paved with peace...
Step by step love will grow & hatred will cease...

Come on, people, let's build a world that's caring & kind...
We need each & everyone, yes, now is the time...

— w & m: Ruth Pelham

NOT IN MY NAME

_You see the plane in the distance
_You see the flame in the sky
See the young ones running for cover
See the old ones wondering why
They tell us that the world is a dangerous place
We live in a terrible time
But in Hiroshima, NY, or in Baghdad
It's the innocent who die for the crime

Am F / G Am :‖ Dm Am / / / F E

Not in my name (8x)

Am - / F - / G - / Am - :‖

The witnesses watch thru the window
Their hearts locked in horror & pain
At the man lying strapped to a gurney
As the poison is pumped thru his veins
And I'm wondering who are the prisoners
Who holds the lock & the key
Who holds the power over life, over death
When will we finally be free?

(bridge) We stray & we stumble in seeking the truth
And wonder why it's so hard to find
But an eye for an eye & a tooth for a tooth
Leaves the whole world toothless & blind

Dm Am / G C / 1st / F E

Thru the ages I have watched all your holy wars
Your jihads, your Crusades
I have been used as inspiration, I've been used as an excuse
For the murder & the misery you've made
I thought I made it clear in the Bible
In the Torah & in the Koran
What is it in my teaching about loving your enemies
That you people don't understand?

— w & m: John McCutcheon

ONE CRANE

One crane, 2 cranes, 3 cranes, 4
We can make an end to war
5 cranes, 6 cranes, 7 cranes, 8
We can change, it's not too late

D - - G / G Em A D :‖

Circle of our cranes **around the world**
For every boy & every girl
Circle of our cranes **from hand to hand**
For every home in every land

D - - G / - D - A / 1st / G D A D

(substitute: song, friend, etc. for "crane")

— w & m: Stuart Stotts

ONE WORLD

One world in which we live together
One sun shining on you and me
One ocean flows into another
One day we all will be free (2x)

C G Am G / / F Em Dm C / F C G - / /

One moment can change a whole lifetime
One life can change eternity
One stranger befriended, one broken heart mended
One child loved, one captive set free (2x)

One day when the lamb and the lion
And our pride and our anger lie down
Weapons to plowshares, a joy born of love's tears
A sacrifice and a crown (2x)

One day we will all meet our Maker
Til that day we must do what we can
To stand by each other, to love one another
Every child, every woman and man (2x)

— w & m: Michael Stern

PAZ Y LIBERTAD (Peace & Liberty)

Paz, _ queremos paz _
Y libertad_en este mundo _ (repeat)

C CF C CF / C CG C - :‖

Para los niños de todo el mundo
Queremos paz y libertad (repeat)

C - / G C :‖

Ya no más hambre, ya no más guerra
Queremos paz en esta tierra (repeat)

Para los pobres y los viejitos
Queremos paz y libertad (repeat)

Ya no más bombas con radiación
No más ideas de exterminación (repeat)

Peace, we want peace & liberty in this world
For the children all over the world we want peace & liberty
No more hunger & no more war, we want peace on this earth
For the poor & the elderly we want peace & liberty
And no more bombs, no more radiation, no more ideas of extermination

— w & m: José-Luis Orozco

(What's So Funny 'Bout)
PEACE, LOVE & UNDERSTANDING

As I walk this wicked world
Searching for light in the darkness of insanity
I ask myself, is all hope gone?
Is there only pain, hatred, & misery?
And each time I feel like this inside, there's one thing I wanna know
What's so funny 'bout peace, love, & understanding? (2x)

(↑2) C F C F / Am D G - :‖
C G C F / C G Am D / C G C -

And as I walk on thru troubled times
My spirit gets so downhearted sometimes, sometimes
Where are the strong & who are the trusting?
And where is the harmony, sweet harmony?
'Cos each time I feel it slipping away, it just makes me wanna cry
What's so funny...

— w & m: Nick Lowe

PEACE TRAIN

Now I've been happy lately, thinking about the good things to come
And I believe it could be, something good has begun

CG C FC F / FG Am FG F

Oh I've been smiling lately, dreaming about the world as one
And I believe it could be, some day it's going to come

'Cos out on the edge of darkness, there rides a peace train
Oh peace train take this country, come take me home again

Now I've been smiling lately, thinking about the good things to come
And I believe it could be, smth good has begun

Oh peace train sounding louder, glide on the peace train
(Ooh-wah eee-yah ooh-wah) Come on the peace train

Yes, peace train holy roller, everyone jump upon the peace train
(Ooh-wah...) Come on now peace train

Get your bags together, go bring your good friends too
'Cos it's getting nearer, it soon will be with you

Now come & join the living, it's not so far from you
And it's getting nearer, soon it will all be true

Now I've been crying lately, thinking about the world as it is
Why must we go on hating, why can't we live in bliss?

— w & m: Cat Stevens

PEACE WILL COME

Peace, _ peace will _
Peace will come_ **& let it begin with me**
We, _ we need _
We need peace _ **& let it...**
Oh my own life_is all I can hope to control
Oh let my life_be lived for the good, good of my soul
Let it bring peace, _ sweet peace _
Peace will come_ **& let...**

G - C - / G - D G :‖ C - G - / C - G D / 1st 2

— w & m: Tom Paxton

PLANT ME A GARDEN

Gonna plant me a garden **(echo)**, gonna make it grow **(echo)**
Gonna water it well... gonna weed & hoe...
Gonna plant me a garden... neath the sun above...
And the seeds I'll plant... are the seeds of love...

(↑2) C - - - / - - G - / C - Am - / C G C -

Gonna plant 'em in the yard for my friends to see
Gonna plant 'em for you, gonna plant 'em for me
With a little bit of care, they'll grow to be
Flowering rainbows across the sea

And when they've grown from shore to shore
Our sisters & brothers all around the world
Will harvest fruits brought by the dove
And in those fruits are the seeds of love

— w & m: Sally Rogers

QUITE EARLY MORNING

Don't you know it's darkest before the dawn
And this thought keeps me moving on
If we could heed these early warnings
The time is now quite early morning **(repeat last 2 lines)**

(in G) D G / ‖: C G / D G :‖

Some say that humankind won't long endure
But what makes them so doggone sure?
I know that you who hear my singing
Could make those freedom bells go ringing / I know...

And so keep on while we live
Until we have no, no more to give
And when these fingers can strum no longer
Hand the old banjo to young ones stronger...

So tho' it's darkest before the dawn
These thoughts keep us moving on
Thru all this world of joy & sorrow
We still can have singing tomorrow...

— w & m: Pete Seeger

© 1969 (renewed) by Sanga Music, Inc. All rights administered by Figs. D Music c/o the Bicycle Music Company. On his *Banks of Marble* 14, *Essential, Together* (w/ Arlo) & in his *WHATFG*. On Holly Near on *WHATFG: S of Seeger* V1 & *Early Warnings*, Annie Patterson *Deep Roots*, Guy Carawan *Land Knows You're There* & Peggy Seeger on YT.

REUBEN JAMES

(The Sinking of the Reuben James)

Have you heard of a ship called the good Reuben James
Manned by hard fighting men, both of honor & fame?
She flew the Stars & Stripes of the land of the free
But tonight she's in her grave at the bottom of the sea

Tell me what were their names (x2)
Did you have a friend on the good Reuben James
(repeat)

A - E A / / A - D A / 1st ‖: A - D - / E - A - :‖

100 men were drowned in that dark, watery grave
When that good ship went down only 44 were saved
'Twas the last day of October, we saved the 44
From the cold icy waters off that cold Iceland shore...

It was there in the dark of that uncertain night
That we watched for the U-Boats and waited for a fight
Then a whine & a rock & a great explosion roared
And they laid the Reuben James on that cold ocean floor...

Now tonight there are lights in our country so bright
In the farms and in the cities they're telling of the fight.
And now our mighty battleships will steam the bounding main
And remember the name of that good Reuben James...

Many yrs have passed since those brave men are gone
Those cold ocean waters, they're still & they're calm
Many yrs have passed & still I wonder why
The worst of men must fight & the best of men must die...

— w & m: Woody Guthrie

© 1941, 1942 Universal Music Corp. Copyrights renewed. Orig rec by Almanac Singers 14. Also rec by Woody 11, Will Geer, Weavers, Kingston Trio. In Seeger *WHATFG*. Tune is based on "Wildwood Flower" which was in turn derived from Jos. Philbrick Webster's song "I'll Twine 'Mid the Ringlets" pub in 1860.

SALAAM (Od Yavo' Shalom Aleinu)

_Od yavo' shalom aleinu **(3x)**
Ve al kulam **(repeat)**

D - / G - / D - / GD AD :‖

Salaam / Aleinu ve al kol ha olam
Salaam / Salaam_ (repeat)

D - / G - / D - / A -

— w & m: Mosh Ben-Ari

© 1998 Globalev Productions. Peace=salaam in Arabic & shalom in Hebrew. (often sung 15 in G)

SEASON OF PEACE

Season of peace, ground snowy white
We are at peace with each other tonight
But in how many places, while we sit at ease
Does the firing of guns break the silence of peace

(↑2) D D(G) x2 / / D D(G) A A(G) / D D(G) x2

Season of peace — season of war
When will these battles divide us no more
Work for the day when all wars will cease
And each day that we live is a season of peace

D - - - / G D A A(G) / D - G - / D D(G) x2

But in how many places do people still fight
Slave against master, black against white
Catholic & Protestant, Muslim & Jew
Friend against neighbor, me against you

Now on this earth all shattered & torn
May our hopes be, like the season reborn
May we work together with all that we're worth
To bring a true season of peace on this earth

— w & m: Si Kahn

© 1991 Joe Hill Music LLC (ASCAP). All rights administered by Conexion Media Group, Inc. On his *I Have Seen Freedom* 12.

SEEDS OF WAR

1. & 2. May we look upon our / treasure _
Our furniture & our / garments _
3. And try to dis- / cover _ / whether the seeds of / war _
4. Are nourished by / these, our pos- / sessions _ / _ _

— w: John Woolman, m: Paulette Meier

Round arrangement by Diana Porter & Leonard Webb. © 2010 Paulette Meier, Lessonsongs Music. Lyrics paraphrased from *A Plea for the Poor* (1763) by Woolman, a Quaker abolitionist. He believed that an unnecessarily affluent lifestyle was a major cause of war, slavery, the suffering of overworked workers & environmental destruction. cf. James 4:1-3. On her *Timeless Quaker Wisdom in Plainsong*.

THESE HANDS

Some hands have held the world together
Some hands have fought in wars forever
Tell me what shall I do with these hands of mine

C CF C - / / F C G C

Some hands have blessed a million people
Some hands helped free the world from evil / **Tell me what...**

What shall I do with these hands of mine (2x)
The world could use a hero of the human kind / So tell…

F - G - / C - F - / - - - C / F C G C

Some hands can stop a life from dying
Some hands comfort a baby crying...

(bridge) I want to sing it fr my heart, I want to hear it in the wind
Til it blows around the world & comes back again
All that we can ask is for ours to be free
To use them when we want for whatever the need

Am - F C / Am - G C / Dm - Em - / F - G -

Some hands give voice to a nation
Some hands wrote "The Times They Are a-Changin'"...

— w & m: Dave Gunning & George Canyon

© 2011 Dave Gunning. On Dave Gunning *No More Pennies* ↑2.

TOGETHER WE CAN MOVE MOUNTAINS

Together We Can Move Mountains
Together we can move mountains
Alone we can't move at all **(repeat)**

(in 3/4) D - G - / Em A D - :∥

You know, people, sometimes we despair
When we think we're alone & nothin's gonna change
We get stepped on, abused, ignored & confused
Made to suffer & told we're to blame, but

D - G - / / / A G A -

The ones who get rich while we scrape to get by
Know our unity means their defeat
So they set us against one another, sister & brother, color 'gainst color
Keeping us weak, they're keeping us weak but

From the smallest seed, a mighty tree can grow
With its roots planted firmly in the ground
Reach for the sun. Only then will you know
All the love & the beauty & the life to be found, because

— w & m: Bev Grant

© 1976 (renewed) Beverly Grant. On Bev Grant & the Human Condition
Kulonyaka, The Whiteville Choir Union Power ↑2.

UNTIL

Until the swords turn into ploughshares
Until the children eat their fill
Until the mansions admit the lowly
We have no cause for standing still

A - - - / A - E - / A - - - / - E A -

When the voices of conscience calling
Lead not to prison but freedom's road
We'll see the false gods around us falling
It's then we'll harvest the seed we sowed

D - A - / " / " / " /

When the voices of women singing
Are heard in houses of might & power
We'll hear the rafters around us ringing
We'll see a glimpse of our finest hour

When the blood of Black brothers flowing
Makes us weep tears for every one
When the hatred's no longer glowing
We'll know the new world has just begun

So keep your eyes on the far horizon
The prize we're seeking is shining there
Oh it's a long haul but it's a strong call
That leads us onward to open air

— w & m: Judy Small

© 1993 Crafty Maid Music. On her *2nd Wind & Never Turning Back*

WAIST DEEP IN THE BIG MUDDY
(The Big Muddy)

It was back in 1942
I was a member of a good platoon
We were on maneuvers in-a Loozianna
One night by the light of the moon
The captain told us to ford a river
That's how it all begun
We were knee deep in the Big Muddy
But **the big fool said to push on**

(↑3) Am ↓ / AmE Am / 1st / Dm E / 1st / Dm E /
Am - / E Am

The Sgt. said "Sir, are you sure
This is the best way back to the base?"
"Sgt., go on! I forded this river
'Bout a mile above this place
It'll be a little soggy but just keep slogging
We'll soon be on dry ground"
We were waist deep in the Big… / And **the big fool…**

The Sgt. said "Sir, with all this equipment
No man will be able to swim"
"Sgt., don't be a Nervous Nellie"
The captain said to him
"All we need is a little determination
Men, follow me, I'll lead on"
We were neck deep in the Big…

All at once, the moon clouded over
We heard a gurgling cry
A few seconds later, the captain's helmet
Was all that floated by
The Sergeant said, "Turn around men
I'm in charge from now on"
And we just made it out of **the Big...**
With the captain dead & gone

We stripped & dived & found his body
Stuck in the old quicksand
I guess he didn't know that the water was deeper
Than the place he'd once before been
Another stream had joined the Big Muddy
'Bout a half mile from where we'd gone
We were lucky to escape from **the...** / When **the big...**

Well I'm not going to point any moral
I'll leave that for yourself
Maybe you're still walking, you're still talking
You'd like to keep your health
But every time I read the paper
Them old feelings come on / We're **waist deep...**
And **the big fool says to push on**

Waist deep in the... / And the big fool says... (repeat)
Waist deep! Neck deep!
Soon even a tall man'll be over his head, we're / **Waist...**

— w & m: Pete Seeger

TRO - © 1967 (renewed) Melody Trails, Inc., New York, NY. On his *Essential* & *At 89* & in his *WHATFG: A Singalong Memoir*. On WHATFG: *S of Pete Seeger* V1 (Richard Shindell), Dick Gaughan *Sail On* & Ani DiFranco *Sowing the Seeds*, Charlie King & Karen Brandow *Higher Ground*. CBS censored this song when Seeger sang it on the Smothers Bros Show in '68 (see YT).

WE ARE ONE

Smiling face, outstretched hand, thru disputes small & grand
We will lay down our guns, **we are one** *[urinin hana]*
In the rage, thru the war, we have shared pain before
In our grief when it's done, **we are one, we...**

(↑2) C - G Am / F C G - / 1st / F C GF C

Where the earth touches sky, we are born, we all die
Where the clear waters run, we are one, we…

F C G Am / F C GF C

When the light touches land over sea, over sand
When each day has begun, **we are one**
As the rock wears away & the tide rolls & sways
By the moon, by the sun, **we are one, we...**

In the soft of the night we are learning not to fight
In our hearts, in the drum, **we are one**
In the birth of a child, thru the fierce & the mild
In our daughters & sons, **we are one, we...**

— w & m: Pat Humphries

© 2000 Pat Humphries. On emma's revolution *One* (in B) & Charlie King & Karen Brandow *Puppet Town & Remembering Sacco & Vanzetti* 15. Written as an expression of hope for peace & reconciliation in Korean peninsula. Orig refrain is in Korean.

WHEN A SOLDIER MAKES IT HOME

Halfway around the world tonight in a strange & foreign land
A soldier packs his memories as he leaves Afghanistan
And back home they don't know too much, there's just no way to tell
I guess you had to be there for to know that war was hell

(↑2) C Em FG C / Am Em F G / / C Em F G

 And there won't be any victory parades for those that's
  coming back
 They'll fly them in at midnight & unload the body sacks
 And the living will be walking down a long & lonely rd
 Because nobody seems to care these days when a soldier makes
  it home

F AmF C F / Am Em F G / / C Em FG C

They'll say it wasn't easy, just another job well done
As the govt in Kabul falls to the sounds of rebel guns
And the faces of the comrades being blown out of the sky
Leaves you bitter with the feeling that they didn't have to die

Halfway around the world tonight in a strange & foreign land
A soldier unpacks memories that he saved from Vietnam
Back home they didn't know too much, there was just no way to tell
I guess you had to be there for to know that war is hell

 And there wasn't any big parades for those that made it back
 They flew them in at midnight & unloaded all the sacks
 And the living were left walking down a long & lonely rd
 Because nobody seemed to care back then when a soldier
  made it home

The night is coming quickly & the stars are on their way
As I stare into the evening looking for the words to say
That I saw the lonely soldier, just a boy that's far from home
And I saw that I was just like him while upon this earth I roam

 And there may not be any big parade if I ever make it back
 As I come home under cover thru a world that can't keep track
 Of the heroes who have fallen, let alone the ones who won't
 Which is why nobody seems to care when a soldier makes it home

— w & m: Arlo Guthrie

© 1996 Arloco Music Inc. All rights administered by BMG Rights Management (US) LLC. On his *Mystic Journey & More Together Again* (w/ Pete Seeger) & in *SO!* 35:1.

The **Peace** chapter includes songs about war & struggle to end wars. Others are in **Earthcare** and **Hope & Strength** chapters.

Others include **Ballads**: Safe from harm (new w: Fear a bhata), **Faith**: Sim shalom, **Freedom**: Minstrel boy, Secord's warning, **Friendship**: To everyone in all the world, **Good**: Dance for nations, **Healing**: Let me make peace, Prayer, Walls, **Jazz**: Don't sit under the appletree (WWII), **Lullabies**: And we shall want no more, Dreams of harmony, **Rich**: It's a hard life (N.Ireland), **Sea**: Adieu sweet lovely Nancy, **Sing**: Common ground, **Struggle**: Eve of destruction, Let justice roll down, Until.

Play

APPLES & BANANAS

I like to eat, eat, eat apples & bananas (2x)

D - A7 - / - - D -

I like to ate, ate, ate ayples & banaynays
...eat, eat, eat — eeples & beeneenees
...ite, ite, ite — ipples & bininis
...oat, oat, oat — oaples & bononos
...ute, ute, ute — upples & bununus
— trad.

THE BARE NECESSITIES

Look for the bare necessities, the simple bare necessities
Forget about your worries & your strife
I mean the bare necessities, old Mother Nature's recipes
That bring the bare necessities of life

C - F - / C A D G / 1st / C A D G C -

Wherever I wander, wherever I roam
I couldn't be fonder of my big home
The bees are buzzin' in the tree to make some honey just for me
When you look under the rocks & plants & take a glance at the
    fancy ants / Then maybe try a few
The bare necessities of life will come to you, they'll come…

G - C - / / F Fm C D / Am A Dm DG /
C A - / Dm G C G C

Look for… that's why a bear can rest at ease / With just **the bare…**

Now if you pick a pawpaw or a prickly pear
And if you prick a raw paw, next time beware
Don't pick the prickly pear by the paw, when you pick a pear, try
    to use the claw
But you don't need to use the claw when you pick a pear of the
    big pawpaw / Have I given you a clue? / **The bare…**

Just try and relax, yeah, in my backyard
'Cos let me tell you, boy, you're workin' too hard
Don't spend your time lookin' around for something you want
    that can't be found
When you find out you can live without it & go along not
    thinkin' about it / I'll tell you something true: / **The bare…**
— w & m: Terry Gilkyson

BLING BLANG

Bling, Blang, hammer with my hammer
Zingo, Zango, cutting with my saw (repeat)

D - - - / A - G D :://

You get a hammer & I'll get a nail
And you catch a bird & I'll catch a snail
You bring a board & I'll bring a saw
And we'll build a house for the baby-o

D - - - / / / D - G -

I'll grab some mud & you grab some clay
So when it rains it won't wash away
We'll build a house that'll be so strong
The winds will sing my baby a song

Run bring rocks & I'll bring bricks
A nice pretty house we'll build & fix
We'll jump inside when the cold wind blows
And kiss our pretty little baby-o

You bring a ladder & I'll get a box
We'll build our house out of bricks & blocks
When the snowbird flies & the honeybee comes
We'll feed our baby on honey in the comb
— w & m: Woody Guthrie

THE BLUE TAIL FLY (Jimmy Crack Corn)

When I was young I used to wait
On master & give him his plate
And pass the bottle when he got dry
And brush away **the blue-tail fly**
Jimmy crack corn & I don't care (3x)
My master's gone away

D G / D A / D G / A D // D A / - D / - G / A D

And when he'd ride in the afternoon
I'd follow after with a hickory broom
The pony being rather shy
When bitten by **the blue…**

One day he rode around the farm
The flies so numerous they did swarm
One chanced to bite him on the thigh
The devil take **the blue…**

The pony run, he jump, he pitch
He threw my master in the ditch
He died & the jury wondered why
The verdict was...

He lies beneath the 'simmon tree
His epitaph is there to see
"Beneath this stone I'm forced to lie
The victim of..."

> — w & m: Daniel Decatur Emmett (orig pub 1840s)

Down on Grandpa's Farm

We're on our way, we're on our way, on our way to Grandpa's farm **(2x)**
Down on Grandpa's farm there is a <u>little red hen</u> **(2x)**
The <u>hen</u>, she makes a sound like this: "<u>cluck cluck</u>" **(2x)**

D - - A / - - - D // D - DA D / / - - A - / - - D -

(insert:) big brown cow / "moo"
little white duck / "quackquack"

> — trad. (US)

Mi Chacra

V<u>e</u>ngan a ver mi ch<u>a</u>cra que_es herm<u>o</u>sa (2x)
1. El pollito hace_asi - pío pío **(2x)**
O va camarada, o va camarada, o va o va o va **(2x)**

D - DA D / // D - - A / - - - D // - - A - / - - D -

2. El chanchito hace asi "oinc oinc"
3. El perrito hace asi "guau guau"
4. Y la vaca hace asi "muu muu"
5. El patito hace así "cuac cuac"
6. El burrito hace asi "jii jaa"
7. El gatito hace asi "miau miau"
Come & see my farm that is so beautiful! **(2x)**

> — trad. (Argentina)

J'ai Perdu le Do de Ma Clarinette

J'ai perdu le <u>do</u> de ma clarinette (2x)
Ah! si papa il savait ça (tralala!) **(2x)**
(or 2nd time: *il me taperait sur les doigts (tralala!)*)
Au pas, camarade (x2) au pas (x3) (2x)
[*Marchons, camadarade (x2) marchons! (x3)*]
(insert: ré, mi, fa, so, la, ti - or add 2 notes to each subseq v.)

D - A D / / D - A - / - - D - / - - - A / - - - D

(can insert as 5th line:) Il dirait "ohé!" – il chanterait "ohé!"

A D A D

> — trad. (French)

Fiddle-I-Fee

Bought me a <u>cat</u>, the <u>cat</u> pleased me
Fed my <u>cat</u> under yonders tree
Cat went fiddle-i-fee, fiddle-i-fee

D - - - / - - A D / D A D -

I bought me a hen, **the hen pleased me**
Fed my hen under yonders tree
Hen **went** cluck *[chipsy chopsy]*, **cat went fiddle-i-fee**

D - - / - - A D |: D - - - (as needed) :| D A D -

(add to each v:) duck/quack *[slishy-sloshy]*,
goose/honk *[qua-qua!]*, hen/cluck, dog/woof *[boo]*, sheep/baa,
cow/moo, horse/neigh, pig/oink, baby/waa *[mammy]*

> — trad. (US)

Found a Peanut

Found a peanut **(x3) just now**
Just now I found a peanut, found a peanut **just now**

(in 3/4) D - - A7 / - D A7 D

Cracked it open **(x3) just now**
Just now I cracked it...

addl v.: It was rotten, Ate it anyway, Got a stomach ache
Called the doctor
Penicillin... / **Just now** <u>took</u> penicillin...
Didn't work, Operation, Died anyway, Went to heaven,
Wouldn't take me, Went the other way, Didn't want me,
Was a dream, Then I woke up, Found a peanut

> — w: trad. (US), m: trad. ("Clementine")

Hopalong Peter

Old Uncle Peter, he got tight
Started up to heaven one stormy night
The road being rough & him not well
He lost his way & he went to...

C - / - G / C F / G GC* *(1st v. only G -)

Hopalong Peter where you going? (2x)
Hopalong Peter won't you bear in mind
I ain't comin' back til the gooseberry time

Old Mother Hubbard & her dog were Dutch
A bow-legged rooster & he hobbled on a crutch
The hen chewed tobacco & the duck drank wine
The goose played the fiddle on the pumpkin vine

Down in the barnyard playin' 7-up
The old tomcat & the little yellow pup
The old Mother Hubbard she's a-pickin' out the fleas
The rooster in the cream jar up to his knees

I've got a sweet gal in this here town
If she weighs an ounce she weighs 700 pounds
Every time my sweet gal turns once around
The heel of her shoe makes a hole in the ground

> — trad. (Appalachian)

I HAD AN OLD COAT (The Recycling Song)

I had an old coat & the coat got torn
What'll I do? (what'll I do?) **(repeat)**
I had an old coat & the... / So I cut it down & a jacket was born
And I sing every day of my life

C - - - - / - - - - / **1st** / G - - -
C - F C - / Am - - F G / C - G - C - - -

In a couple of yrs those threads got thin / **What'll...**
In a couple... / **What'll...** / In a couple...
So I called it a shirt & I tucked it in / **And I sing...**

Then the sleeves wore out in the east & west **(3x)**
So I pulled them off & I had a vest / **And I sing...**
    (But) the vest got stained with cherry pie **(3x)**
    So I cut & I sewed til I had a tie / **And...**
And when that tie was looking lean **(3x)**
I made a patch for my old blue jeans...
    (And) when that patch was next to nuttin' **(3x)**
    I rolled it up into a button...
And when that button was almost gone **(3x)**
With what was left I made this song / **Which** I sing...

— w & m: Paul Kaplan

© 1985 Paul Kaplan Music (ASCAP). On his *The Folk Process*, Sally Rogers & Claudia Schmidt *While We Live, Kids Cars & Campfires*. In *SO!* 32:3. *For the Beauty of the Earth.* *LS.

IF YOU LOVE A HIPPOPOTAMUS

If you love a hippopotamus & you love her a lot-amus
She will be your friend (your friend) **& that can be mighty
    handy now & then**

G - Em - / D - - G

'Cos if you're stuck outside & you find that the door won't budge
Your friend the hippo can lean on it & give it that extra nudge
    (uggghhh!)

G - Em - / D - - -

And if you want a cookie, but it's too high on the shelf
You can climb on the back of a hippopotamus & get one for your-
    self (& one for her too)

(as v. 2) 'Cos if you're put to bed & you find that you just can't sleep
Your friend the hippopotamus into your room will creep
And she'll sing you a lullaby 'til you begin to snore
Then she'll tiptoe out_hippopotamusly & shut the door (wham!)

— w & m: Connie Kaldor

© 1980 Word of Mouth Music. On her *A Duck in NY City* (accompanies bk of same title) & on Heather Bishop *Belly Button*. *LS.

IT'S NO FUN WHEN YA GOTTA
EAT AN ONION

It's no fun when ya gotta eat an onion! **(2x)**

G - / /

(intro) When Dad cuts onions, he just cries
That smell brings tears into his eyes
It brings the tears to my eyes too
I know he'll make me eat his stew!

G - / / Em B7Em / A D

Sometimes when I take a bite
Of something that I think's all right
I find some onion in my mouth
And Mom won't let me spit it out, she says
"It's just a small piece, don't you fuss!"
But it will burn if it gets crushed
I chew around it, but I'm stuck
I guess I'll have to swallow, yucch!

Em - / G - / **1st** / G B7Em / G - / / Em B7Em / A D

Now onion lovers love to tell
How much they love that onion smell
How onions make your blood run thinner
If you eat them in your dinner
Well I don't care what someone thinks
If you eat onions, your breath stinks!
And you might cause your best friend's death
If you say "Hi!" with onion breath!

Onions raw or onions cooked, or
Onions tossed or sauced or gooked
With batter fried or onions plain
Or onions baked with fancy names, yeah
Like 'Au Gratin' or 'Fondue'
Or onions hidden in my stew
With eggs or cheese in a souffle
They're still just onions anyway!

(as intro) So kids remember when you eat
Check each mouthful, I repeat
Cause onions are a grown-up plot!
Some kids like onions, I do not!

— w & m: Peter Alsop

© 1986. Moose School Music (BMI) www.peteralsop.com. On his *Take Me with You!*

JENNY JENKINS

Will you wear white, oh my dear, oh my dear?
Will you wear white, Jenny Jenkins?
No I won't wear white, for the color's too bright
I'll buy me a foldy-roldy, tildy-toldy, seek-a-double
Use-a-cozza roll to find me / Roll, Jenny Jenkins, roll

D A / D A - / D G / D - / / D A D -

Will you wear green... / **No I won't**...it's a shame to be seen
blue... for the color's too true
yellow... for I'd never get a fellow
brown... for I'd never get around
beige... for it shows my age
orange... / No orange I won't wear & it rhymes, so there!
What will you wear?... / O what do you care if I just go bare

— trad. (US)

Arr. © 2015 by Hal Leonard Corporation. David Grisman & Jerry Garcia *Not For Kids Only*. Sharon Lois & Bram *School Days*, Two of a Kind *Friends*.

LET'S GO FLY A KITE

With tuppence for paper & strings
You can have your own set of wings
With your feet on the ground you're a bird in a flight
With your fist holding tight _
To the string of your kite – o, o, o!

(in 3/4, ↑3) G - / - D / GG₇ CA / G D / G G₇

Let's go fly a kite
Up to the highest height!
Let's go fly a kite & send it soaring
Up thru the atmosphere
Up where the air is clear
Oh let's go fly a kite!

C - / G - / D - G - :‖

When you send it flyin' up there
All at once you're lighter than air
You can dance on the breeze over 'ouses & trees / **With...**

— w & m: Richard M. Sherman & Robert B. Sherman

© 1963 Wonderland Music Company, Inc. Copyright renewed. In film *Mary Poppins*.

LITTLE BIRD, LITTLE BIRD

Little bird, little bird **fly thru my window (3x)**
And buy molasses candy
Fly thru my window my sugar lump (2x)
And buy molasses candy (*extra beat)

A - A* A / E - E* A / 1st / E - A - //
A - E - / A E A - / E - A -

insert: chickadee, jaybird, whippoorwill, robin, bluebird, crow,
bobwhite, hummingbird

— trad. (Amer. play party song)

Arr. © 2015 by Hal Leonard Corporation. Players join hands in a circle & raise their joined hands to form windows. One or more birds in the center go in & out the windows. At "buy molasses candy" bird stops at another player, who then goes to the center. In *Amer FS for Children*. On Pete Seeger *Birds, Beasts, Bugs, & Little Fishes* (as "Fly thru My Window") & Eliz Mitchell *You Are My Little Bird*.

LITTLE BLACK BULL

The little black bull came down the meadow
Hoosen Johnny, hoosen Johnny
The little black bull came down the meadow / **Long time ago**
Long time ago (2x)
The little black bull came down the meadow / **Long time ago**

G - / D G / - - / GD G / GC G / / G - / GD G

1st he'd paw & then he'd bellow...
He whet his horn on a white oak sapling...
He shake his tail, he jar the river...
He wink his eye at the little red heifer...
He paw his dirt in the heifer's faces...

— trad. (US)

Arr. © 2015 by Hal Leonard Corporation. Alt repeat line: **"Houston, Sam Houston."** aka "Hoosen Johnny." On Pete Seeger *Birds Beasts Bugs & Fishes*, Seegers *Folk Songs for Children*. In *Amer Songbag*, Sandburg says this is a song Abraham Lincoln would have heard often in Illinois.

LITTLE CABIN IN THE WOODS

In a cabin in the woods, little man by the window stood
Saw a rabbit hopping by, knocking at his door
"Help me **(x2)** help" he said "Ere the hunter shoot me dead!"
"Little rabbit, come inside, safely to abide"

D A - D / / D - - A / D A - D

— trad. (US)

Arr. © 2015 by Hal Leonard Corporation. aka "In a Cabin..." 2 different versions created by Henson Productions in 1988. Substitute hand motions for words in subseq v.

LITTLE JOHNNY BROWN

Little Johnny Brown
Spread your comfort *[blanket]* **down** (repeat)

D - / 1st / D G / - D

Fold one corner, **Johnny Brown**
Fold another corner, **Johnny... (3x)**

D - :‖ (4x)

Take it to your lover *[Give it to your friend now]*... **(4x)**
Show him *[her]* your motions *[Make a little motion]*... **(4x)**
Float *[look, hop]* like a buzzard... **(4x)**

— trad. (African-Amer party song)

Arr. © 2015 by Hal Leonard Corporation. Bessie Jones *Put Your Hand on Your Hip*, Ella Jenkins *Little*..., Linda Tillery & the Cultural Heritage Choir *Say Yo' Business*, Sandy & Carolyn Paton *I've Got a Song!* Circle singers, put blanket/towel on the floor, spread & fold it, & give it away. Next person floats like a buzzard into the circle & begins again.

LITTLE SALLY WALKER

Little Sally Walker, sitting in a saucer
Crying & a-weeping over all she has done
Rise, Sally, rise, wipe the tears from your eyes
Put your hands on your hips, let your backbone slip
Turn to the East, turn to the West
Turn to the very one that you love the best
Shake it to the East, shake it to the West
Shake it to the very one that you love the best

D - - - :‖ (8x)

— trad. (African-Amer party song)

Arr. © 2015 by Hal Leonard Corporation. In Bessie Jones & Bess Lomax Hawes *Step It Down*. On Pete Seeger *Song & Play Time*, Lead Belly *Sings for Children*. "Little Sally" sits in the center & acts out the parts of the song. On "turn to the very one," 'Sally' faces the one she chooses. On "shake it to the very one" that person becomes next "Sally." You can change name if boys are chosen.

A Manatee Sneezed on Me

When we were on vacation down in Florida last spring
My brother said go get your bathing suit
A family of manatees is swimming by the dock
They're gentle & the little ones are cute
My mom said it was OK so my dad said OK too
I paddled over to them on my raft
Suddenly my head was wet with something like shampoo
I yelled out as everybody laughed

(↑3) G C D G / G C D - / C D G C / Am - D - :‖

A manatee sneezed on me (2x)
You might think that it's funny / It's not! (2x)

C - G - / D - - - / G (C D G) /   /

You know that the manatees had come to drink fresh water
    from the hose
My brother Sean was holding in his hand
A little water must have gotten up the mama's nose
I'd like to laugh about it but I can't, 'cos

A manatee sneezed on me (2x)
Its nasal capacity's a lot / **A manatee sneezed...**
You might think that it's funny...

C - G - / D - G - / 1st / D - - - / G (C D G)

(bridge) It could've been worse, the sneeze was clear, there are
    worse sneezes I hear
There was a huff & then a snuff
    and then she sprayed me with her stuff
There was no clue, no big "ha-choo,"
    she simply snorted & it flew
She felt so bad for what she'd done,
    she tried to clean me with her tongue

C D G C / Am D G - / 1st / Am - D -

A manatee sneezed on me (2x)
Her nasal capacity I got! / **A manatee... / You might think...**

(tag) I did not know just what to do & so I hollered "God bless you!"

C D AmD G

   — w & m: John Flynn

© 1999 Flying Stone Music (ASCAP). On his *A Manatee...*

Mango Walk

Now tell me, Joe, do tell me for true
Do tell me for true, do tell me
That you **don't go to no mango walk**
And steal all the number 'leven
   My brother did a-tell me that you go mango walk
   You go mango walk (2x)
   My brother did a-tell me that you go mango walk
   And steal all the number…

(in D) A D (4x) ‖: D - / A D :‖

I tell you, Sue, I tell you for true
I tell you for true, I tell you
That **I don't go to no…**

   — trad. (Jamaica)

On John Langstaff *Songs for Singing Children*, Neilds *Rock All Day, Rock All Night*

214

Mi Cuerpo Hace Música

Mi cuerpo, mi cuerpo, hace música (2x)

G - C G / - - D G

Mis manos hacen cla cla cla *[pom pom pom]*
mis pies hacen ta ta ta *[bom bom bom]*
Mi boca hace la la la / Mi cintura hace cha, cha cha

G C D G :‖ (4x)

There's music, there's music, there's music inside me
My hands say clap clap clap / My feet say tap tap tap
My mouth says la la la / My waist & hips says cha cha...

   — trad. (South Amer.)

Arr. © 2015 by Hal Leonard Corporation. Sarah Pirtle *The Wind Is Telling Secrets*, Sol Y Canto *El Doble de Amigos*, Josh Levine *Josh Levine for Kids*, Mr. Eric & Mr. Michael *Bouncy Blue from the Learning Groove*, Peter Paul & George *Dance Around The World*, Tom Pease *Celebrate!*

Michael Finnegan

There was an old man named Michael Finnegan
He grew whiskers on his chinnegan
Shaved them off but they grew innegan
Poor old Michael Finnegan (Beginnegan!)

D - / A - / D - / A D

There was... / He got drunk from drinkin' ginnegan
Then he promised never to sinnegan / **Poor old...**

There... / He went fishing with a pinnegan
Caught a fish but he dropped it innegan / **Poor...**

There... / Climbed a tree & barked his shinnegan
Took off several yards of skinnegin...

There... / He grew fat & he grew thinnegan
Then he died & we had to beginnagin...

   — trad. (US)

Arr. © 2015 by Hal Leonard Corporation.

Miss Mary Mack

Miss Mary Mack, Mack, Mack
All dressed in black, black, black
With silver buttons... / All down her back...

(a capella) G - /   / D - / G -

She asked her mother... / For 50 cents...
To see the elephants... / Jump over the fence...

They jumped so high... / They touched the sky...
And they didn't come back... / Til the 4th of July...

   — trad. (African-American play party song)

Arr. © 2015 by Hal Leonard Corporation. In SO! 37:3.

Mister Rabbit

Mr. Rabbit (x2) your ears are mighty long
Yes my Lord, they were put on wrong
Every little soul's gonna shine, shine
Every little soul's gonna shine along

D - DA D / D - G D / D - A D /   /

Mr Rabbit (x2) your coat is mighty grey
Yes my Lord, 'twas made that way
Mr Rabbit (x2) Your feet are mighty red / **Yes...** I'm almost dead

Mr Rabbit...tail is mighty white / ...and I'm a-getting out of sight
...you look mighty thin / ...been cutting thru the wind

(Pete Seeger adap) **Mr. Rabbit (x2)** your ears are mighty long
Yes, don't you know they were put on wrong
Every little soul's gonna shine, shine
Every little soul's gonna shine along

Mr. Rabbit (x2) your nose always twitches
Yes, don't you know it always itches / **Every little soul...**

Mr....your tail's so tight / **Yes…** it was put on right
... where have you been? / Down to Mr. Angelo's garden
...what do you eat? / Carrots & cabbages from my head to my feet

— trad. (US)

Arr. © 2015 by Hal Leonard Corporation. In Animal *FS for Children*. On Pete Seeger *Birds Bugs Beasts & Fishes*, Peggy Seeger *Animal Folk S for Children*, Kathy Reid-Naiman *Sally Go Round The Sun*.

My Aunt Came Back

Oh my aunt came back (echo) from Timbuktu **(echo)**
She brought with her (echo) a wooden shoe **(echo)**

D - A - / - - D -

Oh my aunt came back (echo) from old Japan **(echo)**
She brought with her (echo) a waving fan **(echo)**

Oh my aunt came back... from old Algiers...
She brought with her... a pair of shears...

Oh my aunt...from Guadeloupe
She brought...a hula hoop

Oh my aunt...from the county fair / ...a rocking chair
Oh my aunt...from the city zoo / ...a nut like you!

— trad. (US play party song)

Arr. © 2015 by Hal Leonard Corporation. Add an approp motion when mentioning each new item for 1st time, e.g. tap foot for wooden shoe. In *S to Sing & Sing Again*. In & on New England Dancing Masters *I'm Growing Up*.

Pancake Hat

I went to a party & I wore my hat
Put it on a bed & along came a cat
The cat sat down & squished it flat
Now I call it my pancake hat
Pancake hat, pancake **hat (2x)**
It used to be fine with a feather and that
Now I call it my pancake hat

D - / - A / 1st / D AD // D - / G - / D DA / D AD

The sun was hot so I went for a swim
Put on my hat & I jumped right in
My hat swelled up & I said drat
Now I call it my muffin hat
Muffin **hat... now I call it my** muffin **hat**

I wore my hat out to play
The wind came along & blew it away
It rolled in a pasture under a cow
Cow took a bite: it's a donut now!
Donut **hat... now I call it my** donut **hat**
(tag as final line) And if that's not that, I'll eat my hat

— w & m: Sarah Pirtle

© 1988 Discovery Center Music (BMI). On her *The Wind is Telling Secrets*. Tune is derived fr "Turkey in the Straw." *LS.

Rubber Duckie

Rubber Duckie, you're the one, you make bath time lots of fun

Rubber... I'm awfully fond of you
...joy of joys, when I squeeze you, you make noise
...you're my very best friend, it's true **(↑3)**
Every day when I make my way to the tubby
I find a little fellow who's cute & yellow & chubby (rub a dub dubby)
...you're so fine & I'm lucky that you're mine *[I'd like a whole pond of]*
...I'm awfully fond of you

C DmG C FDdim / CAm DmG I. C(Em DmG) :‖ 2. C B7

Em B7 Em - / G Am Dm G / 1st 2 above

— w & m: Jeff Moss

© 1970 Festival Attractions, Inc. Copyright renewed. Sung by Ernie (voiced by Jim Henson). On *Sesame Street Bk & Record* ('71 Best Children's Grammy in Bb).

Silly, Silly Song

Sing me a silly, silly song, **my dear**
Sing me a silly, silly song
You can make it short or you can make it long
Just sing me a silly, silly song

G - - C / G C D - / G - C - / G D G -

Draw me a picture of a rose, **my...**
You can make it pretty & you can give it a nose / Just draw...

Bring me a fuzzy, fuzzy cat...
You can make it skinny or you can make it fat / Just bring...

Bring me a juicy, juicy pear...
And you can have some pear because I love to share / Just...

Let me give to you a great big hug
Let me give to you a hug
We can hug each other like 2 snuggly bugs / Just let me...

(bridge) Well, you gave me a song & you gave me a rose
You gave me a cat & a juicy, juicy pear
You gave me a hug & I gave you one, too
And that's because I love, love you

Em Bm C G / C G D G / A D A D / A - - D - - -

— w & m: Susan Stark

© 1987 Susan Stark Music. On her *Rainbow People*.

Sing a Song of Sixpence

Sing a song of sixpence, a pocket full of rye
4 & 20 blackbirds baked in a pie
When the pie was opened, the birds began to sing
Now wasn't that a dainty dish to set before the King?

C - G - / - - - C :‖

The King was in his counting house counting out his money
The Queen was in the parlor eating bread & honey
The maid was in the garden hanging out the clothes
Along came a blackbird & pecked off her nose!

— trad. (English nursery rhyme)

Arr. © 2015 by Hal Leonard Corporation.

SKIDAMARINK (Skinnamarink)

Skidamarink *[skinamarink]* a-dink a-dink,
  skidamarink a-doo / I love you (repeat)
I love you in the morning & in the afternoon
I love you in the evening & underneath the moon *[when the
  stars are shining bright]* / Skidamarink…

G C G C / G Am D7 - / Am D7 Am D7 / Am D7 G -

G G7 C - / A - D - / 1st / Am D7 G -

— w: Felix F. Feist, m: Al Piantidosi

Arr. © 2015 by Hal Leonard Corporation. Orig appeared in the 1910 musical *The Echo*. Sharon Lois & Bram created a show they called Skinnamarink TV. On Cathy Fink & Marcy Marxer *Jump Children*. Jimmy Durante adap as "Inky Do."

SOMEBODY COME & PLAY

Somebody come & play, somebody come & play today
Somebody come & smile the smiles
  & sing the songs, it won't take long
Somebody come & play today

G C (x4) / G - - - / G Em C D G(C GC)

Somebody… play, somebody come & play my way
Somebody come & rhyme the rhymes
  & laugh the laughs, it won't take time / Somebody…

(bridge) Somebody come with me & see the pleasure in the wind
Somebody come before it gets too *[see the time is getting]* late to begin

C - G - / C - Am D

Somebody… / Somebody come & play today
Somebody come & be my friend
  & watch the sun till it rains again / Somebody…

— w & m: Joe Raposo

© 1970 Jonico Music, Inc. Copyright renewed. Rights in the US administered by Green Fox Music, Inc. Rights outside the US administered by Jonico Music, Inc. On Sesame Street videos incl one by PS22 Chorus.

UPSIDE DOWN

Who's to say_what's impossible?
Well they forgot_this world keeps spinning
And with each new day_I can feel
A change in everything _ & as the surface breaks
Reflections fade_but in some ways
They remain the same_ & as my mind
Begins to spread its wings,_there's no stopping
Curiosity _ I want to turn the whole thing

D - - - / Em - - - :‖ (4x)

Upside down _I'll find the things they say
Just can't be found _I'll share this love I find
With everyone _we'll sing & dance
To Mother Nature's songs _I don't want this feeling
To go away___

D Em G A (4x) D - - - (Em - - - D - - - Em - - -)

Who's to say _I can't do everything?
Well I can try _& as I roll along
I begin to find _things aren't always
Just what they seem _I want to turn the whole thing

Upside down…
To Mother Nature's songs _this world keeps spinning &

D Em G A (4x)

(bridge) There's no _ time to waste _
Well it all _ keeps spinnin' spinnin' round & round &

F#m - Em - / F#m - G A

(tag) Upside down _who's to say what's impossible &
Can't be found?_I don't want this feeling
To go away___ please don't go
Away___ is this how it's supposed / To be?

D Em G A / / D - - - Em - - - / / D - - -

— w & m: Jack Johnson

© 2006 Bubble Toes Publishing & Universal Pictures Music. All rights controlled & administered by Universal Music Corp. In the film *Curious George* 12 & in *Daily Ukulele*.

WHAT I AM

If what I am is what's in me then I'll stay strong, that's who I'll be
And I will always be the best me that I can be
There's only one me I am it – have a dream, I'll follow it
It's up to me to try _ _

(↑2) G Em G D / G Em D - :‖

Oh I'm-a keep my head up high (high!), keep on reachin'
High (high!) never gonna quit, I'll keep gettin' stronger
_And nothing's gonna bring me *[us]* down (no!), never
  gonna stop *[give it up]*
Gotta go (go!) because I know, I'll keep gettin' stronger

G C Em D / G Em D - :‖

_And what I am is (thoughtful!) & what I am
Is (musical!) & what I am is (smart!) & what I am
Is (brave!) & what I am is (helpful!) & what I am
Is (special!) there's nothing I can't achieve because in
  myself I believe

G Em D G / / / G - - -

_What I am is (super!) & what I am is
Is (proud!) & what I am is (friendly) & what I am
Is (grouchy) & what you are is (magical!) & what you are
Is (special!) there's nothing I can't achieve because in
  myself I believe

— w & m: Christopher N. Jackson & Bill Sherman

© 2010 Sesame Street, Inc. & Easy Reader Music. All rights for Sesame Street, Inc. controlled & administered by Universal Music Corp. All rights for Easy Reader Music controlled & administered by Songs of Universal, Inc. Performed by Will. i. am on Sesame Street video.

The **Play** chapter contains playful / fun songs for younger ones. See also the **Earthcare, Family, Funny Songs, Lullabies** and **Peace** chapters. Others include **Dignity**: Colors of earth, **Friendship**: Glad to have a friend like you, I will be your friend, **Millenial**: 1,2,3,4 (Sesame St version), **Rich**: One meatball.

Pub Songs

ALL FOR ME GROG

And it's all for me grog, me jolly jolly grog
All gone for beer & tobacco
Oh I spent all me tin with the lassies drinking gin
Far across the western ocean I must wander

D - G D / - - A - / 1st / D A - D

Where are me boots, **me noggin' noggin'** boots?
All gone for beer & tobacco
For the leather's all wore out & the heels are knocked about
And me toes are **looking out for better weather**

Where is me shirt, **me noggin' noggin'** shirt? / **All gone...**
For the collar is all worn & the sleeves they are all torn
And the tail is **looking out...**

Where is me wench, **me noggin'... / All...**
Oh her lips is all wore out & her front is kicked about
And her tail is **looking out...**

O **where is me** bed... **/ All...**
For I lent it to a whore & now the sheets are tore
And the springs are **looking...**

I'm sick in the head for I haven't been to bed
Since first I came ashore with me plunder
I see centipedes & snakes & I'm full of pains & aches
And I think I'll take a trip out over yonder
 — trad. (English)

Arr. © 2015 by Hal Leonard Corporation. On *The Dubliners*, Clancy Bros *Irish Drinking S*, Irish Rovers *Drunken Sailor*, rec by Lou Killen.

Gone to the Dogs

Gone to the dogs, the grafters & the hogs
All gone for bombs & for bailouts (bailouts!)
For they've squandered all our wealth, now we cannot
 pay for health
And across the Western ocean jobs are wandering

Oh where are our schools, our decent public schools?
All gone for bombs &...
And where are our farms, our fruitful family farms?...
And where are our jobs, our decent paying jobs?...
Oh where's our security, our so-ci-al security?...
And where's our R&D for high technology?...

Oh gone to the dogs, the grafters & the hogs... **/ ...health**
And across the Western ocean & across the Southern border
And across the picket line our jobs are wandering
 — w: Sally Rogers & Howie Bursen, m: trad. (English "All for Me Grog")

© 1991 Sally Rogers, Thrushwood Press Publishing. On her *We'll Pass Them On*. *LS.

All for Me Job

Oh it's all for me job, me bloody, bloody job
Just to make the boss an extra dollar
Since the award's been done away, they've cut me leave & cut me pay
Now the family & me must live in squalor

Where is me wife, me lovely, lovely wife?
Just to make the boss an extra dollar
Working 7 days a week, you know we hardly ever meet
Maybe I'll catch up with her tomorrow

Where are me kids, me lovely, lovely kids?
Just to make the boss an extra dollar
Since the last I saw them play, they've grown up & moved away
If you come across them kindly will you holler?

I'm sick in the head & I haven't been to bed
The doctor says I ought to take more slumber
But if I say I won't work back, then I'll get the bloody sack
Then across the Western Deserts I must wander

This land we used to know as the land of the fair go
All gone to make the boss an extra dollar
But now in union we will fight til we've won back every right
Then we'll never need no more to live in squalor

Oh it's all for me job, me bloody, bloody job
Just to make the boss an extra dollar
But now in union we will fight til we've won back every right
Then we'll never need no more to live in squalor!
 — w: Geoff Francis & Peter Hicks, m: trad. (English "All for Me Grog")

© 2006 Geoff Francis & Peter Hicks. On *Stand Up & Shout: Hard-Hitting S for a New Aust...*

THE BARLEY MOW

Here's good luck to the pint pot, **good luck to the Barley Mow**
 (shout while drinking: Good Luck!)
Jolly good luck to the pint pot, **good luck to the Barley Mow**
Oh the pint pot, half a pint, gill,
 half a gill, quarter gill, nipperkin & a round bowl
Here's good luck, good luck to the barley mow

D - A D / - - A - / D - - - (etc.) / D A D -

Here's good luck to the quart pot, **good luck to the Barley Mow**
Jolly good luck to the quart pot, **good luck to the Barley Mow**
Oh the quart pot, pint pot, half a pint...

other v. add: half gallon, gallon, half barrel, barrel, landlord, his
 daughter, brewer, company
 — trad. (English)

Arr. © 2015 by Hal Leonard Corporation. In *Revels Garland of S*. On John Roberts & Tony Barrand *Live at Holstein's*.

Bully in the Alley

Help me, Bob, I'm bully in the alley
Way, hey, bully in the alley!
Help me, Bob, I'm bully in the alley
Bully down in Shinbone Al!

D - - - / G D A - / 1st / G A D -

Well, Sally is the girl that I love dearly / **Way, hey...**
Sally is the girl that I spliced nearly / **Bully down... – so**

For 7 long years I courted Sally / **Way...**
All she did was dilly-dally / **Bully...**

I'll leave my Sal & I'll become a sailor...
I'll leave my gal & ship aboard a whaler...

I'll come back & I'll marry Sally...
We'll have kids & count them by the tally...

I thought I heard the old man saying...
One more chorus [pull] then we're belaying...

— trad. (West Indies halyard chantey)

Arr. © 2015 by Hal Leonard Corporation. Many seaports have a Shinbone Alley, usually in a seedy part of town. On Finest Kind *For Honour & for Gain*, Blue Murder *No One Stands Alone*, Paddy & the Rats *Rats on Board*, Storm Weather Shanty Choir *Way Hey*, Musical Blades *High Sea's Drifter*, etc.

Calton Weaver (Nancy Whisky)

I am a weaver, a Calton weaver
I am a rash & a roving blade
I've got silver in my pockets
I'll go and follow the roving trade
Whisky, whisky, Nancy whisky
Whisky, whisky, Nancy O

(↑2) D - A - / D - G A / 1st / || / D - A D

As I walked into Glasgow city
Nancy Whisky I chanced to smell
I walked in, sat down beside her
It's 7 long yrs since I loved her well

The more I kissed her, the more I loved her
The more I kissed her, the more she smiled
I forgot my mother's bidding
And Nancy soon had me beguiled

'Twas very early the next morning
Finding myself in a strange bed
I went to rise but I was not able
For Nancy's charms, they held my head

I'll go back to the Calton weaving
I'll surely make those shuttles fly
I'll make more at the Calton weaving
Than ever I did at the roving trade

So come all ye weavers, ye Calton weavers
All ye weavers where e'er ye be
Beware of Whiskey, Nancy Whisky
She'll ruin you like she ruined me

‖: C - F G / / Am - F G / 1st ‖ / C - F G C

— trad. (Scottish)

Arr. © 2015 by Hal Leonard Corporation. Rec by Ewan MacColl, Clancy Bros 11, Poitín (11.15). In *Coll Reprints fr SO!* V1-6. Calton is a weaving village that became a district of Glasgow.

Du, Du Liegst Mir Im Herzen

Du, du liegst mir im Herzen
Du, du liegst mir im Sinn
Du, du machst mir viel Schmerzen
Weißt nicht wie gut ich dir bin
Ja, ja, ja, ja! / Weißt...   (in 3/4)

G - - D / - - - G / 1st / D - G - // C G B7 Em / Am D G -

So, so wie ich dich liebe / So, so liebe auch mich!
Die, die zärtlichsten Triebe / Fühle ich ewig für dich
Ja, ja... / Fühle ich...

Doch, doch darf ich dir trauen, / Dir, dir mit leichtem Sinn
Du, du kannst auf mich bauen, / Weißt ja, wie gut ich dir bin
Ja, ja... / Weißt ja...

Und, und wenn in der Ferne / Mir, mir dein Bild erscheint
Dann, dann wünsch' ich so gerne / Daß uns die Liebe vereint!
Ja, ja... / Daß uns...

— trad. (German ca. 1820)

Arr. © 2015 by Hal Leonard Corporation. In '61 film *Judgment at Nuremberg* & '74 film *Blazing Saddles*. In *Songfest*.

Fathom the Bowl

Come all ye bold heroes give an ear to my song
I'll sing in the praise of good brandy & rum
Let's lift up our glasses, good cheer is our goal
Give me the punch ladle, I'll fathom the bowl
I'll fathom the bowl (x2) / Give me...

(in 3/4) G - - - / D - C G / - - C D / G C D G //
G D G D / G C D G

From France we do get brandy, from Jamaica comes rum
Sweet oranges & lemons from Portugal come
But stout, beer, & cider are England's control / **Give...**

My wife she do disturb me, as I lie at my ease
She does as she likes, she says as she please
My wife, she's a devil, she's black as the coal...

My father he do lie in the depths of the sea
With no stone at his head, but what matters for he?
There's a clear crystal fountain near him it doth roll...

— trad. (English)

Arr. © 2015 by Hal Leonard Corporation. Rec by the Watersons. In *Revels Garland of S.* "Punch" (Hindi "paantsch") was orig made w/ 5 ingredients: alcohol, sugar, lemon, water & tea or spices.

Garnet's Home-Made Beer

Oh the year was 1978
How I wish I'd never tried it now!
When a score of men was turned quite green
By the scummiest ale you've ever seen

C - G C / - F C Ĝ - / C G C - / - - - F

God damn them all, I was told
This beer was worth its weight in gold
We'd feel no pain, shed no tears
But it's a foolish man who shows no fear
At a glass of Garnet's homemade beer

G C - F / C F C F / G C G F̂ - / C F C F / - - G C

O Garnet Rogers cried the town / **How I wish...**
For 20 brave men all masochists who
Would taste for him his homemade brew
    This motley crew was a sickening sight / **How...**
      There was caveman Dave with his eyes in bags
      He'd a hard-boiled liver & the staggers and jags
We hadn't been there but an hour or 2...
When a voice said "Give me some homemade brew"
And Steeleye Stan hove into view
    Now Steeleye Stan was a frightening man...
      He was 8 foot tall & 4 foot wide
      Said "Pass that jug or I'll tan your hide"
Stan took one sip & pitched on his side...
Garnet was smashed with a gut-full of dregs
And his breath set fire to both me legs
    So here I lie with me 23rd beer...
      It's been 10 yrs since I felt this way
      On the night before me wedding day

    — w: Ian Robb, m: Stan Rogers ("Barrett's Privateers")

© 1979 Ian Robb. On Ian Robb *From Different Angels*. Garnet is the brother of the late folksinger Stan Rogers.

GET UP JACK, JOHN SIT DOWN (Jolly Roving Tar)

O ships will come & ships will go as long as the waves do roll
Each sailor lad, likewise his dad, will love the flowing bowl
Afloat, ashore, they do adore a lass that's plump & round
When the money's gone it's the same old song: "Get up,
    Jack! John, sit down!"
Come along, come along, you jolly brave boys, there's lots
    of grog in the jar
We'll plough the briny ocean with the jolly roving tar

(a capela) D G D A D / ‖: D G D Â / D G D A D :‖

An old sheath-knife & sou'wester are staunch old friends at night
A glass o' grog in rain or fog will steer a sailor right
From old Brazil to Bunker Hill we scatter dollars roun'
When the money's gone...

Go take a cruise on men o'war to China or Japan
In Asia there the maidens fair all love a sailor man
While Tom & Joe palaver oh & buy the girls a gown / **When...**

When Jack's ashore, oh, then he steers to some old boarding house
He's welcomed in with rum & gin & fed on pork & souse
He'll spend & lend & ne'er offend & lay drunk on the groun'...

When Jack is old & weather beat, too weak to roust about
In some rum-shop they let him stop, at 8 bells he's turned out
He cries, he cries up to the skies, I'll soon be homeward bound
For my money's gone 'tis the same old song / **Get up...**

    — w: Ed Harrigan, m: Dave Braham (1885)

Arr. © 2015 by Hal Leonard Corporation. Pork souse is either head cheese or cold pork in a sauce. Orig cho: "Heigh laddie, ho laddie, swing the capstan 'roun' / When the money's gone..." Orig fr a NY music theater show *Old Lavender*. Coll by Frank Warner in NH & included in Loaxes *Amer FS & Ballads*. Neither Lomax nor Warner were aware of origin.

JOHNNY COME DOWN TO HILO

Never seen the like since I been born
An American sailor with his sea boots on, sayin'
Johnny come down to Hilo / Poor old man

D - - - / - - - A / D - G D D / D A D -

Wake her, shake her
Wake that gal with the blue dress on / Johnny come down...

I got a gal across the sea
She's a 'Badian beauty & she says to me / **Johnny...**
    Sally's in the garden picking peas
    The hair on her head hanging down to her knees...
My wife she died in Tennessee
And they sent her jawbone back to me...
    I put that jawbone on the fence
    And I ain't heard nothing but the jawbone since...
Hilo girls they dress so fine
They ain't got Sunday on their mind...
    She's a Down East gal with a Down East smile
    And a dollar a time is well worth-while...
So hand me down my riding cane
I'm off to see Miss Sarah Jane...

    — trad. (Barbados)

Arr. © 2015 by Hal Leonard Corporation. On Alan Mills *S of the Sea*, Salty Dick's *Uncensored Sailor S*, Bounding Main *Going Overbd*, Rambling Sailors *Ports of Call*.

LET UNION BE

Come, my lads let us be jolly, drive away dull melancholy
For to grieve it is a folly **when we're met together**

D DA A AD / D DĜ GD AD

Let union be in all our hearts
Let all our hearts be joined as one
We'll end the day as we begun, we'll end it all in pleasure
Right-folla-rolla-rolla, too-ra-lie-doe (2x)
Right-folla... when we're met together

D - GD Â / / D G A AD / **as verse**

Solomon, in all his glory, told each wife a different story / In our
    cups we'll sing him glory **when we're met...**

Courting & drinking are quite charming, piping & dancing there's
    no harm in / All these things we'll take delight in...

Grab the bottle as it passes, do not fail to fill your glasses / Water
    drinkers are dull asses...

Cease your quarreling & fighting, evil speaking & backbiting
All these things take no delight in...

    — trad. (English)

Arr. © 2015 by Hal Leonard Corporation. On Jon Boden *A Folk S a Day* & *In Harmony's Way* (self-titled). In *Revels Garland of S*.

O DU LIEBER AUGUSTIN (Ach du lieber Augustin)

O *[ach!]* du lieber Augustin, Augustin, Augustin,
O du lieber Augustin, alles ist hin!
Geld ist weg, Mädl ist weg, alles weg, alles weg *[Augustin]*!
O du lieber Augustin, alles ist hin!]

C - G C / / G C G C / 1st /

O du... / ...hin! / Stock ist weg, Rock ist weg, Augustin liegt im
Dreck / **O du...**

    — trad. (Viennese student song)

Arr. © 2015 by Hal Leonard Corporation. Presumed to be composed by the balladeer Marx Augustin in 1679 but in print only around 1800. A drunken Augustin was accidentally dumped in a pit of plague corpses & could not extricate himself when he awoke. He began playing his bagpipes to die as he had lived & was rescued when people heard his pipes. Same tune as "Did You Ever See a Lassie?"

PACE EGGING SONG

Here's 1, 2, 3 jolly lads all in one mind
We are come a pace-egging & I hope you'll prove kind
And I hope you'll prove kind with your eggs & strong beer
For we'll come no more nigh you until the next year

D - - - / - A D A / D G - D / - G A D

And the first that comes in is Lord Nelson you'll see
With a bunch of blue ribbons tied round by his knee
And a star on his breast that like silver doth shine
And I hope he remembers it's pace-egging time

And the next that comes in it is Lord Collingwood
And he fought with Lord Nelson till he shed his blood
And he's come from the sea old England to view
And he's come a-pace-egging with all of his crew

The next that comes in is our Jolly Jack Tar
He sailed with Lord Nelson all thru the last war
He's arrived from the sea, old England to view
And he's come a-pace-egging with our jovial crew

And the last that comes in is old Toss-Pot you'll see
He's a valiant old man & in every degree
He's a valiant old man & he wears a pigtail
And his only delight is in drinking mulled ale

Come ladies & gentlemen, sitting by the fire
Put your hands in your pockets & give us our desire
Put your hands in your pockets & treat us all right
If you give naught, we'll take naught, farewell & good night

— trad. (English)

Arr. © 2015 by Hal Leonard Corporation. On Watersons *Frost & Fire* & Jon Boden
A Folk S a Day. In *Revels Garland of S*. Easter (pace=pasch) processional &
begging song from 17th c. Shropshire.

PARLEZ-NOUS À BOIRE

O parlez-nous à boire, non pas de mariage
Toujours en regrettant, nos jolis temps passés

G - - - / - - D G

Si que tu te maries avec une jolie fille
T'es dans des grands dangers, on va la voler

G - C - / G - D G

Si que tu te maries aves une vilaine fille
T'es dans des grands dangers, faudra tu fais ta vie avec

Si que tu te maries avec une fille bien pauvre
T'es dans les des grands dangers, faudra travailler toute la vie

Si que tu te maries avec une fille qu'a de quoi
T'es dans des grands dangers, tu vas attraper des grandes re-
    proches

Fameux, toi, grand vaurien, t'as tout gaspillé mon bien (2x)

— trad. (Cajun)

Arr. © 2015 by Hal Leonard Corporation. Rec by Beausoleil, Balfa Bros, New Lost
City Ramblers, Steve Riley & Mamou Playboys.

THE PARTING GLASS

Of all the money that e'er I spent
I spent it in good company
And all the harm that e'er I've done
Alas it was to none but me
And all I've done for want of wit
To mem'ry now I can't recall
So fill to me the parting glass
Good night & joy be with you all

Bm G D A / D - - A / Bm G D A / D G D Bm - /

D G D D G D / G A D A / " / " /

If I had money enough to spend
And leisure time to sit a while,
There is a fair maid in this town
That sorely has my heart beguiled
Her rosy cheeks & ruby lips
I own she has my heart enthralled / So fill to me...

Of all the comrades that e'er I had
They're sorry for my going away
And all the sweethearts that e'er I had
Would wish me one more day to stay
But since it falls unto my lot
That I should rise & you should not
I gently rise & softly call / Good night...

— trad. (Scottish w: "Armstrong's Goodnight", m: "The Peacock")

Arr. © 2015 by Hal Leonard Corporation. Poem dates to 1605. On Clancy Bros
Come Fill Up Your Glass, Steeleye Span *Horkstow Grange*, Wailin' Jennys *40 Days*,
Loreena McKennitt *Wind That Shakes the Barley*. In '98 Irish film *Waking Ned
Devine* (sung by Shaun Davey). Dylan used the tune for his "Restless Farewell." In
Revels Garland of S & Amidons *25 Anthems for Interfaith & Comty Choirs*.

ROLL THE OLD CHARIOT ALONG

We'll roll the old chariot along (3x)
And we'll all hang on behind

Dm - - - / C - - - / 1st / C - Dm -

Well a plate of Irish stew wouldn't do us any harm (3x)
And we'll all hang on behind
(insert: night on the town, drop of Nelson's blood, etc)

O we'd be all right if the wind was in our sails... (3x) / And...
(insert: we make it 'round the Horn..., etc.)

— trad. (Af-Amer Spiritual adap as sailor song)

Arr. © 2015 by Hal Leonard Corporation. In *For the Beauty of the Earth*, SO! 27.6,
Sandburg *Amer Songbag*. There are 2 versions of this song: "We'd be all right if..."
& "...wouldn't do us any harm." The versions are rarely mixed. Make up your own verses!

SAM'S GONE AWAY

I wish I was a cabin boy aboard a man o'war!
Sam's gone away aboard a man o'war!
Pretty work, brave boys, pretty work, I say!
Sam's gone away aboard a man o'war!

C - G - / C - G C / - - F C / - - G C

(insert: cook, mate, first mate, captain)

(last v. You'll never be a hero aboard a man o'war!

— trad. (US chantey)

Arr. © 2015 by Hal Leonard Corporation. Jack Stanesco collected "Sam Gone
Away" fr fishermen on St. Vincent's Island while in the Peace Corps there. On *The
New Golden Ring: 5 Days Singing V2*.

THE SCOTSMAN

A Scotsman clad in kilt left a bar one evening fair
And one could tell by how he walked, he'd drunk more than his share
He stumbled on until he could no longer keep his feet
Then he staggered off into the grass to sleep beside the street
Ring ding deedle deedle di de oh, ring di deedle o dee
He stumbled off into the grass to sleep beside the street

`C F G C / - F C G ‖: F - C G / CG CF G C :‖`

Later on, 2 young & lovely girls just happened by
And one says to the other with a twinkle in her eye
See yon sleeping Scotsman, so strong & handsome built?
I wonder if it's true what they don't wear beneath the kilt
Ring ding…deedle dil / I wonder if it's true…

They creeped up to the sleeping Scotsman quiet as could be
Lifted up his kilt above the waist so they could see
And there, behold, for them to view, beneath his Scottish skirt
Was nothing but what God had graced him with upon his birth
Ring…dir / Was nothing…

They marveled for a moment, then one said we'd best be gone
But let's leave a present for our friend, before we move along
So as a gift they left a blue silk ribbon, tied into a bow
Around the bonny star of the Scot's kilt-lifting show
Ring…dow / Around…

The Scotsman woke to nature's call & stumbled toward the trees
Behind a bush, he lifts his kilt & he gawks at what he sees
Then in a startled voice he says to what's before his eyes
"My friend, I don't know where you've been but I see you won 1st
    prize!"
Ring ding…deedle di / "My friend…"

— w & m: Benjamin Michael Cross (aka Mike Cross)

© 1979 Vic-Ray Publishing (ASCAP), 203 SW 3rd Ave, Gainesville, FL 32601-6519.
On his *Live & Kickin'*, *Folk Sing Along S* & *Best of the Funny Stuff*. In *New Folk Favorites*.

SEVEN DRUNKEN NIGHTS

As I went home on a <u>Mon</u> night as drunk as drunk could be
I saw a <u>horse outside the door</u> where me old <u>horse</u> should be
I called me wife & I said to her "Will you kindly tell to me
Who owns that <u>horse outside the door</u> where me old <u>horse</u>
    should be?"
"O you're drunk, you're drunk, you silly old fool & still
    you cannot see
That's a <u>lovely milk cow</u> that me mother sent to me"
I've traveled this wide world over 10,000 miles or more
[Well it's many a day I've traveled, a hundred miles or more]
But a <u>saddle on a milk cow</u>, sure I never saw before

`A - AD A / D A - D / A - D - / A - DA ‖A - - - / - - EA :‖`

As I went home on a <u>Tues.</u> night as drunk as drunk could be
I saw a <u>coat behind the door</u> where me old <u>coat</u> should be
I called me wife & I said to her "Will you kindly tell to me
Who owns that <u>coat behind the door</u> where…"
"Oh, you're drunk… & still you cannot see
That's a <u>woolen blanket</u> that me mother sent to me"
Well, it's many a day I've traveled, a hundred miles or more
But buttons on a blanket, sure I never saw before

As I went home on a <u>Wed.</u> night. as drunk as drunk could be
 I saw a <u>hat on the hat rack</u> where me <u>chamberpot</u> used to be
I **called me wife & I said to her "Will you kindly tell to me
Who owns that** <u>J.B. Stetson</u> **where me** <u>chamberpot</u> **used to be**

Thurs. / 2 boots beneath the bed / geranium flowerpots
Laces on a flowerpot
Fri. / pair of trousers / apron / apron with a button up fly
Sat. / head upon the bed / cabbage / whiskers on a cabbage

Now when I came home on a Sun. night a little after 3
I saw a man running out the door with his pants about his knees
I called me wife & I said to her "Will you kindly tell to me
Who was that man running out the door with his pants… knees?"
**"O you're drunk… / 'Twas nothing but a tax collector the
    Queen sent to me" / I've traveled this wide world over…**
But an Englishman that could last 'til 3 I never saw before"
    — trad. (Eng. Child Ballad #274 "Our Goodman")

Arr. © 2015 by Hal Leonard Corporation. aka 4 Nights Drunk, The Cabbage Head,
You Old Fool. Rec by Steeleye Span, Dubliners, Weavers. Many versions are
unprintable here. In *Coll Reprints fr* SO! V1-6.

THE SOLDIER AND THE SAILOR'S PRAYER

A soldier & a sailor were walking one day
Said the soldier to the sailor "Come let us pray
And if we have one <u>prayer</u>, **we might as well have 10
Let's have a bloody** <u>litany</u>," **said the sailor "Amen!"**
"Let's have a bloody litany (x2) / Let's… said the…

(in 3/4) `G - GGD G / - D AD / G - - D /`

`G Ĉ GGD G / C D̂ G D̂ / G Ĉ GGD G`

"Now what shall we pray for? Let's pray for some beer
Some glorious, beautiful, wonderful beer
And if we have one pint, **we might as well have 10
Let's have a bloody** brewery," **said the sailor "Amen"**
"Let's have a bloody brewery…

"Now what… for a wench
Glory, O Glory, may she be French
And if we… wench, we… 10 / Let's have a bloody harem"…

"Now who **shall we pray for? Let's pray for the** <u>Queen</u>
Glory, O Glory, long may she reign
And if she has one child, may she also have 10
May she have a bloody regiment," **said…**

"Now who **shall we pray for? Let's pray for the** <u>Duke</u>
That wonderful handsome, great smiling plook
And if he loses one hair may he also lose 10
May the bastard go baldy," **said…**

"Now what shall we pray for, let's pray for <u>our peace</u>
From Cape Town to Belfast, from Glasgow to Greece
And if we have one year, may we also have 10
May there never, ever be another war," **said the sailor
    "Amen!"…**

— trad. (British Isles), adap by Hamish Imlach

aka "A Soldier's Prayer". Arr. © 2015 by Hal Leonard Corporation. Tune is same
as "Pleasant & Delightful." On Harry Cox *What Will Become of England?*, Mike
Seeger *Southern Banjo Sounds*, Susan Renaker *Live*, Menagerie *Return to the Ash
Grove*, Brigid Tunney *Flax in Bloom: The Voice of the People*, field recs made in N.
Ireland in 1952-3. You can listen online to an interview by Alan Lomax w/ Archie
Lennox in Aberdeen, Scotland.

WHISKEY IN THE JAR

As I was going over the Cork & Kerry Mountains
I met with Capt. Farrell & his money he was countin'
I first produced my pistol & then produced my rapier
Sayin' "Stand & deliver for I am a bold deceiver!"
Musha ring, dum a doo, dum a da
Whack fol the daddy-oh (2x) / There's whiskey in the jar

(↑2) G Em / C GEm / 1st / C G // D - / G - / C - / GD G

I counted out his money & it made a pretty penny
I put it in my pocket & I took it home to Jenny
She sighed & she swore that she never would deceive me
But the devil take the women for they never can be easy

I went into my chamber all for to take a slumber
I dreamt of gold & jewels and for sure it was no wonder
But Jenny drew my charges & she filled them up with water
Then sent for Capt. Farrell to be ready for the slaughter

'Twas early in the morning just before I rose to travel
Up comes a band of footmen & likewise Capt. Farrell
I first produced my pistol for she'd stolen away my rapier
But I couldn't shoot the water, so a prisoner I was taken

If anyone can aid me 'tis my brother in the army
If I can find his station in Cork or in Killarney
And if he'll come & join me we'll go roving in Kilkenny, and
I'm sure he'll treat me better than my darling sporting Jenny

Now there's some take delight in the hurling & the bowling
And others take delight in the carriage wheels a-rolling
But I take delight in the juice of the barley
And courting pretty fair maids in the morning bright & early

— trad. (Irish)

Arr. © 2015 by Hal Leonard Corporation. Rec by Clancy Bros, Dubliners, Irish Rovers

The **Pub Songs** chapter contains rousing songs that sing well in pub type settings, usually sung a capella with strong harmonies (not just drinking songs). See also **Ballads & Old Songs, Good Times, Sea & Sailors.**

Rich & Poor

ALL IN THIS TOGETHER

How can I even try to explain what I've seen?
Little kids helpless on the floor like in some bad dream
Some couldn't move their limbs at all, but one was trying to feed
The little boy lying next to her & it helped me to see, that:

(in 3/4) C Am F G / C Am F E7 / Am E C D7 / F C F G

We're all in this together, living right now
Let's try & make it better for each other somehow
No one should go hungry, everyone should feel loved
We're all in this together, every one of us

C Am F G /   / Am C FFE Am / F C FFG C

Since I walked away from the kids that day thru the bustling streets
I look a little deeper at every stranger I meet
I see much more in common than I used to do
You smile just like me, I hurt just like you / And **we're...**

C Am F G / C Am F E7 / Am C FFE Am / F C F G

(bridge) Somewhere a child newly born gazes in a mother's eyes
While the father of another will soon have to die
So the circle turns & I've come to learn only love can save the day
Like those little kids at the orphanage whose eyes seem to say that

E7 - Am - /   / F - E7 Am / F C F G

(3rd line cho) We all want to be happy, we all need to be loved

(tag) So I hope that you feel the way I do & will reach out a hand
'Cos we're all in this together: let's do what we can

Am E C D7 / F C FFG C

— w & m: Jimmy Scott

© 2009 English Channel Music. www.jimmyscottsongwriter.com. On Jana Stanfield *What Would You Do This Year If You Had No Fear.* *LS.

THE BELLS OF RHYMNEY

"Oh what will you give me?" say the sad bells of Rhymney
"Is there hope for the future?" cry the brown bells of Merthyr
"Who made the mine owner?" say the black bells of Rhondda
"And who robbed the miner?" cry the grim bells of Blaina

(↑2) G - CG A G / G - FAm D /   / 1st

"They will plunder willy-nilly" cry the bells of Caerphilly
"They have fangs, they have teeth!" shout the loud bells of Neath
"Even God is uneasy" say the moist bells of Swansea
"And **what will you give me?**" say the sad bells of Rhymney

"Throw the vandals in court!" say the bells of Newport
"All will be well if, if, if, if" cry the green bells of Cardiff
"Why so worried, sisters why?" sang the silver bells of Wye
"And **what will you give me?**" say the sad bells of Rhymney

G - CG A G / G Em FAm D / GF Em FEm D / 1st

— w: Idris Davies (1927), m: Pete Seeger

TRO - © 1959 (renewed), 1964 (renewed) Ludlow Music, Inc., New York, NY. In
Seeger *WHATFG*. On his *I Can See a New Day* 15 & *Essential*. On The Byrds, Judy
Collins *#3 & S* of Pete Seeger (V1 & V3). In *SO!* 8.2. Davies was a Welsh coal
miner, born in Rhymney. Later, he was a school teacher & a friend of the poet,
Dylan Thomas. Towns in v.1 were in impoverished areas of Wales. Those in v.2 & 3
are in wealthier areas. Cardiff is the capital. The lyrics follow pattern of the English
nursery rhyme *"Oranges & Lemons."*

THE CORPORATE WELFARE SONG
(End Welfare As We Know It)

It's time to end welfare as we know it
And get those greedy chiselers off the dole
It's time to end welfare as we know it
Teach them a little self-control
For far too long we've allowed these corporate hogs
To belly up to the public trough
No more welfare as we know it
No more hand-outs, cut them off!

(↑3) C - / - G / - - / - C / - - / - F / FAdim CA / DG C /

(as cho) Now we should all be irate at the huge welfare state
Right here in this mightiest of nations
AFDC is disgraceful to me
I'm talking Aid for Dependent Corporations
Free enterprise – hah! the cruelest of lies
It cost us 200 billion just last year
If they paid their fair share we'd have billions to spare
It's time to tell them the bucks stop here!

That Taco Bell chihuahua begs for bucks for Frito-Lay
And Poppin' Fresh from Pillsbury needs more dough every day
That thief Ronald McDonald & his side-kick Mayor McCheesy
Hamburglarize our treasury in ways that make me queasy
That nasty little mermaid took tax dollars overseas
To hire thugs to bring poor Haitian workers to their knees

Am E / - Am |: Dm Am / B7 E :|

They've been picking every pocket from sea to shining sea
We must intervene to break this cycle of dependency
ADM & Cargill, General Motors, Ford & Boeing
AIG & Lehman & that welfare line keeps growing, growing, growing
Now Congress says we can't afford to subsidize the needy
But before we slash the safety net, let's tell the truly greedy:

(tag) And we mean business! **No more handouts...**
It's for their own good! **No more...**

— w & m: Anne Feeney

© 1999 Anne Feeney. On her *Have You Been To Jail For Justice?*

DIVES & LAZARUS

As it fell out upon one day, rich Divers made a feast
And he invited all his friends & gentry of the best
Lazarus laid him down & down & down at Divers' door
"Some meat, some drink, Bro. Diverus, do bestow upon the poor"
"Thou art none of my brothers, Lazarus, that lies begging at my door
No meat nor drink will I give thee, nor bestow upon the poor"

Am AmG Am G / Am AmG AmG Am :|| C G Am Em / 2nd /

Then Lazarus laid him down & down & down at Divers' gate
"Some meat, some drink, Bro. Diverus, for Jesus Christ, his sake"
"Thou'rt none of my brothers, Lazarus, that lies begging at my gate
No meat nor drink will I give thee for Jesus Christ, his sake"

(subseq v.) Am AmG Am G / Am AmG AmG Am /

C G Am Em / 2nd /

Then Divers sent out his merry men to whip poor Lazarus away
They'd not the power to strike one stroke, but flung their whips away
Then Divers sent out his hungry dogs to bite him as he lay
They had no power to bite at all, but licked his sores away

As it fell out upon one day, poor Lazarus sickened & died
There came 2 angels out of Heaven, his soul therein to guide
"Rise up, rise up, Bro. Lazarus & come along with me
For there's a place prepared in Heaven to sit on an angel's knee"

As it fell out upon one day, rich Divers sickened & died
There came 2 serpents out of hell, his soul therein to guide
"Rise up, rise up, Bro. Diverus & come with us to see
A dismal place prepared in Hell, from which thou canst not flee"

Then Divers looked up with his eyes & saw poor Lazarus blessed
"Give me one drop of water, Bro. Lazarus, to quench my flaming thirst
O was I now but alive again the space of one half hour!
O that I had my peace again, then the devil should have no power"

— trad. (English, Child ballad #56)

Arr. © 2015 by Hal Leonard Corporation. Tune is the same as "Star of the County
Down." On Maddy Prior 7 for *Old England*, Martin Simpson *Bramble Briar*, June
Tabor *Freedom & Rain*. In *Oxford Bk of Carols*.

DOWN ON THE CORNER

Early in the evenin' just about supper time
Over by the courthouse they're starting to unwind
4 kids on the corner trying to bring you up
Willy picks a tune out & he blows it on the harp
Down on the corner, out in the street
Willy & the Poor Boys are playin', bring a nickel, tap your feet

C - GC /   / F - C - / 1st // F C G C /   /

Rooster hits the washboard & people just got to smile
Blinky thumps the gut bass & solos for a while
Poorboy twangs the rhythm out on his kalamazoo
And Willy goes into a dance & doubles on kazoo

You don't need a penny just to hang around
But if you've got a nickel, won't you lay your money down?
Over on the corner there's a happy noise
People come from all around to watch the magic boy

— w & m: John Fogerty

© 1969 Jondora Music. Copyright renewed. On Creedence Clearwater Revival
Willy & the Poor Boys, Kathy Mattea *Right Out of Nowhere.*

HOLE IN THE BUCKET

I went down to the city & I found myself a job
Working for the people who do need some helping out
But then in truth I found there was so little left to give
The govt might save their lives, might not help them to live

(↑3, in C) F C F C / Am C F - / / /

There's a hole in the bucket & the people fall out, there's
   money underground but you can't get it out
When you stand at the State House, smile & say "Please?"
There's a crack in the floor & the people fall thru & they
   wind up coming back to you
From a place it seems like they can never leave
There's a hole in the system for the people in need

C - G GC / F - C - :‖ G F C -

How do you tell a woman who is 82 yrs old
Poor & lying in her bed & needing help at home
That there is no more money, there is nothing you can do
Just hold on for a better year & we'll try to get to you

O beautiful for spacious skies & amber waves of grain
America, you're beautiful but you have got to change
You think of how to save your skin but you never mind the bones
Have we become a country where the hearts have turned to stones?

— w & m: Catie Curtis

I CANNOT SLEEP

I cannot sleep for thinking of the children
Who cannot sleep, gone supperless to bed
I cannot sleep for thinking of the young lads
Who roam the roads, no place to lay their head

C G C Am / Dm G C G / C G Am C / Dm G C -

If there were one, it would be cause to wonder
If there were one, it would be cause to weep
But they are numbered into many thousands
And for each one, I cannot sleep

Dm G C Am / Dm G C C7 / F G C Am / Dm G C -

The stores are full, the bins are overflowing
In sight of food, the hungry children wait
And on the roads, the boys begin to wander
Because at home, there's nothing on the plate

We will not sleep, my sister on the mill line
We will not sleep, my brother from the plow
Until we've stored the wealth we have created
Within the lives of those who hunger now

— w & m: Malvina Reynolds

IMAGINE HEALTHCARE

Imagine you have healthcare, it's easy if you try
Freedom to choose your doctor, coverage money can't buy
Imagine 1st class treatment when you're unemployed

G C G C /   / C Em Am C D -

Imagine no insurance, no greedy middleman
No premium, no co-pay, a single-payer plan
Imagine a long illness & you don't lose your home

You may say I'm a dreamer, I'm not dreaming by myself
I hope someday you'll join us **(2nd cho:** "we'll join them"**) &**
   the world can live in health

C D G B7 C D G B7 / C D G B7 C D G (C G C)

Can you say "Universal"? I wonder if you can?
Now try "Comprehensive," does this sound like a plan?
It's worked for years in Europe, Canada & Japan

— w: Charlie King

IN THE BLEAK MIDWINTER

In the bleak midwinter frosty wind made moan
Earth stood hard as iron, water like a stone
Snow had fallen, snow on snow, snow on snow
In the bleak... long ago

C G Am Dm G / C G Am DmG C / F Am CDm G / 2nd

Christ a homeless stranger, so the gospels say
Cradled in a manger & a bed of hay
In the... stable place sufficed
Mary & her baby, Jesus Christ

Once more child & mother weave their magic spell
Touching hearts with wonder, words can never tell
In... in this world of pain
Where our hearts are open love is born again

What can I give Him, poor as I am?
If I were a shepherd, I would bring a lamb
If I were a Wise Man, I would do my part
Yet what I can I give him: I can give my heart

— v.1 & 4: Christina Georgina Rossetti (1872), v.2 & 3:John Andrew
   Storey, m: Gustav Theodore Holst ("Cranham" 1906)

IT'S A HARD LIFE WHEREVER YOU GO

I am a backseat driver from America
They drive to the left on Falls Road
And the man at the wheel's name is Seamus
We pass a child on the corner he knows
And Seamus says, "Now, what chance has that kid got?"
And I say from the back, "I don't know"
He says, "There's barbed wire at all of these exits
And there ain't no place in Belfast for that kid to go"

(in C) G F C - (8x)

It's a hard life, it's a hard life, it's a very hard life
It's a hard life wherever you go
If we poison our children with hatred
Then, the hard life is all that they'll know
And there ain't no place in Belfast **for** that kid **to go**

F C F C / G F C - (4x)

A cafeteria line in Chicago / The fat man in front of me
Is calling black people trash to his children
And he's the only trash here I see
And I'm thinking this man wears a white hood
In the night when his children should sleep
But, they'll slip to their windows & they'll see him
And they'll think that white hood's all they need

It's a hard life...
And there ain't no place in Chicago **for** those kids **to go**

I was a child in the 60's / When dreams could be held thru TV
With Disney & Cronkite & Martin Luther
And I believed, I believed, I believed
Now I am a backseat driver from America
And I am not at the wheel of control
And I am guilty, I am war, & I am the root of all evil
Lord & I can't drive on the left side of the road

...there ain't no place in this world **for** these kids **to go**

— w & m: Nanci Griffith

© 1989 Irving Music, Inc. & Ponder Heart Music. All rights controlled & administered by Irving Music, Inc. On her *From a Distance*, & Emmylou Harris *At the Ryman*.

JESSE JAMES

Jesse James was a lad that killed many a man
He robbed the Glendale train
He stole from the rich & he gave to the poor
He'd a hand & a heart & a brain

`D - G D / - - A - / D - G D / - A D -`

Oh, Jesse had a wife to mourn for his life
3 children they were brave
But that dirty little coward that shot Mr. Howard
Has laid poor Jesse in his grave

`G - D - / " / " / " /`

It was Robert Ford, that dirty little coward
I wonder how he does feel
For he ate of Jesse's bread and he slept in Jesse's bed
Then he laid poor Jesse in his grave
  It was on a Wed. night and the moon was shining bright
  They robbed the Glendale train
  And the agent, on his knees, he delivered up the keys
  To those outlaws, Frank & Jesse James
It was on Sat. night, Jesse was at home
Talking with his family brave
Robert Ford came along like a thief in the night
And laid poor Jesse in the grave
  Now the people held their breath when they heard of Jesse's death
  They wondered how he ever come to fall
  Robert Ford, it was a fact, shot Jesse in the back
  While Jesse hung a picture on the wall
Jesse was a man, a friend to the poor
He'd never rob a mother or a child
He took from the rich & he gave to the poor
So they shot Jesse James on the sly
  Well this song was made up by Billy Gashade
  As soon as the news it arrived
  He said there was no man with the law in his hand
  Who could take Jesse James when alive

— trad. (US)

Beans, Bacon & Gravy

I was born long ago in 1894
I've seen many a panic I will own
I've been hungry, I've been cold & now I'm growin' old
But the worst I've seen is 1931

Oh those beans, bacon & gravy, they almost drive me crazy
I eat them 'til I see them in my dreams, in my dreams
When I wake up in the morning & another day is dawning
I know I'll have another mess of beans

Well we congregate each morning at the county barn at dawning
Everyone is happy, so it seems
But when our day's work is done & we file in one by one
And thank the Lord for one more mess of beans

We've Hooverized on butter & for milk we've only water
And I haven't seen a steak in many a day
As for pies, cakes & jellies, we substitute sow bellies
For which we work the county road each day

If there ever comes a time, when I have more than a dime
They will have to put me under lock & key
For they've had me broke so long, I can only sing this song
Of the workers & their misery

— w: anon. (US 1930's), m: trad. ("Jesse James")

"Jesse James" arr © 2015 by Hal Leonard Corporation. In *Amer Songbag*, on & in Pete Seeger *Amer Fav Ballads*, in *Coll Reprints fr SO!* V1-6. James & his bro Frank were Confederate guerillas during Civil War. Their gang was part of ex-Confederate insurgencies more than frontier lawlessness or Robin Hood type activity. He was shot by Bob Ford a member of his gang in 1882 most likely in hopes of a reward.

"Beans, Bacon & Gravy" arr © 2015 by Hal Leonard Corporation. On Cisco Houston *Sings S of the Open Rd*, Pete Seeger *Amer Industrial Ballads* & in Seeger *Carry It On*.

LEAVING EDEN

Hush now, don't you wake up, we'll be leaving at first light
Mama's buying you a mockingbird to lull you thru the night
We'll cross the Dan by morning, here's a blanket for you to share
They're building down in Georgia, Daddy hears we'll find work there

(in 3/4) `C Am C Am / Dm C Em F - :|`

And the mockingbird can't sing like the crying of a dove
And I can't tell my daughters all the things that I'm scared of
But I am not afraid of that bright glory up above
Dying's just another way to leave the ones you love
The ones you love

I: `F C Dm - / F C Am - / 1st / Dm C Em F / C Am C Am`

II: `F C Em F / Dm C Em Am :|` **(omits final line)**

No work for the working man, just one more empty mill
Hard times in Rockingham, hard times harder still
The crows are in the kitchen, the wolves at the door
Our fathers' Land of Eden is paradise no more

My sister stayed in Eden, her husband's got some land
The agent for the county thinks that they can make a stand
It's a hard life of working with nothing much to show
A long life of leaving with nowhere to go

— w & m: Laurelyn Dossett

© 2003 Laurelyn Dossett, Pleasant Garden Music (ASCAP). On Polecat Creek *Leaving Eden* (I: '04) & Carolina Chocolate Drops *Leaving Eden* (II: '12).

MEAN THINGS HAPPENING IN THIS LAND

There are mean [strange] things happening in this land (2x)
But the union's goin' on & the union's growing strong
There are strange things happening in this land

(orig Handcox:) Am Em Am - / | / Am - Em Am / 1st

(Cunninghams verses:)

There are strange things happening in this land (2x)
Oh the rich man boasts & brags, while the poor man goes in rags
There are strange things happening in this land

Insert: Oh the farmer cannot eat 'cos he's raised too much wheat
Too much cotton in our sacks so we have none on our backs
Lots of groceries on the shelves but we have none for ourselves
Oh we'll have even less to eat when the drums commence to beat

There are strange things happening in this land (2x)
But when working men refuse to put on their old war shoes
There'll be good things happening in this land

There'll be good things happening in this land (2x)
When the workers take a stand & unite in a solid band
There'll be good things...

(Seeger:) C G C - / | / C - - Am / 1st /

(Juravich verses:)

We sent our boys all off to war, now tell me what was it all for?
If you're black or brown or tan, you're in trouble with the man

(Juravich) Am E Am - / - C E - / Am - Dm - / Am E Am -

— trad. Gospel ("Strange Things...") adap. by John Handcox

© 1937 (renewed) Camellia Cook John Handcox was a tenant farmer from Arkansas, organizer for the Southern Tenant Farmers Union & political folksinger. Chick & Agnes "Sis" Cunningham, who were friends of Pete Seeger & Woody Guthrie & members of the Almanac Singers, adapted the song adding many v. Their version was in *Hard Hitting Songs for Hard Hit People*. Sis was also publisher of *Broadside* Magazine On Handcox Songs, *Poems & Stories of the So. Farmers Tenants Union* & YT (I). Sis Cunningham *Broadside Ballads V6*. Pete Seeger *Gazette V1* (II). Healy & Juravich *Tangled in Our Dreams* (III). Orig gospel version rec by Blind Joe Taggert & Blues Boy Willie ('20s) & Chas Haffer Jr (*The Land Where the Blues Began* rec in '40s). Blues Boy Willie ('89).

MORE THAN ENOUGH

There's always the money for missiles & tanks
There's always the money for generals & banks
There's always the money for new ways to kill
But a limited budget for you if you're ill
Yes there's always enough for a war
But **there's never enough for the poor**

D A G A / | / G - D G / 1st / D A G - / D A D -

There's always the money for tunnels & roads
For opera & ballet, but not jobs & homes
For MPs' expenses & fat subsidies
But there's never the money for nurseries
And the well-off they always take more / So **there's never...**

There's always the money for tests they can pass
Or fail you for not being white middle class
There's always the goodies for those with most greed
But never enough for those in most need
There's a pay-rise if you're on the board, but **there's...**

Consider the little of life that we know
We bring nothing, take nothing, pass thru & go
We're all of us poor when it comes to the night
In need of the darkness, in need of the light
If we learned to want less & love more
There'd be **enough for the poor**
(tag) If we learned to want less & love more / There'd be **enough...**
'Cos there's more than enough for us all

D A G A / | / G - D G / 1st / D A G - (5x)

— w & m: Robb Johnson

© 1993 Moose Music. On his *Heart's Desire* & Roy Bailey *Sit Down & Sing*. Orig. written for a campaign to stop Nursery closures in Hounslow, West London.

MR. BUSINESSMAN'S BLUES

Tell me, Mr. Businessman, how does your money grow?
How much sweat is on your brow? How weary are your bones?
And how much toil to dig this Earth, to slash, enslave, control?
When you've used up our great resource do you plan to work your gold?

E - A E / A E - B7 / 1st / A E E B7 E

Tell me, Mr. Businessman, is business going well?
Can you put your best foot forward as you walk your Earth-bound hell?
Well, dreams are bought & muscles knot & wishes don't come true
And you get rich upon my back, then say it's what I choose
  Tell me, Mr. Businessman, oh tell me what's so rough?
  What is it that you're giving up that seems to mean so much?
  And how many dollars can you spare, how many acres will divide?
  How many will be sacrificed before you're satisfied?
Tell me, Mr. Businessman, oh, tell me what's so hard?
Do you have to pay an army to guard the fence around your yd?
Or are you innocent by scale, you've only gardeners for your lawn?
But can you make it right 'cos it's the lesser of the wrongs?

— w & m: D.M. Lafortune

© 1983, 1998, 2011 D.M. Lafortune. On her *Beauty & Hard Times*.

NO BANKER LEFT BEHIND

My telephone rang one evening, my buddy called for me
Said the bankers are all leaving, you better come round & see
It's a startling revelation, they robbed the nation blind
They're all down at the station, **no banker left behind!**
No banker (x3) could I find
They were all down at the station, **no banker left behind!**

C - - - / F C - G / 1st / F C C G C / F C F C / - C F C G C

Well the bankers called a meetin', to the White House they went one day
They was going to call on the pres-i-dent in a quiet & a sociable way
And the afternoon was sunny & the weather it was fine
They counted all our money & **no banker** was **left behind**
No banker (x3) could I find / They were all down at the
  White House, **no banker** was **left behind**

Well I hear the whistle blowing, it plays a happy tune
The conductor's calling "All aboard!" we'll be leaving soon
With champagne & shrimp cocktails & that's not all you'll find
There's a billion dollar bonus & **no banker left behind**
No (x3) could I find / When the train pulled out
  next morning, **no banker** was **left behind** (2x)

— w & m: Ry Cooder

© 2011 Hi-Lo Shag Music (BMI). All rights administered by Wixen Music Publishing, Inc. On his *Pull Up Some Dust & Sit Down*. In *SO!* 54:4.

ONE MEATBALL

A little man walked up & down
To find an eating place in town
He read the menu thru & thru
To see what 15 cents could do
One meat ball (3x) / He could afford but **one…**

Am E / - Am / - Dm / E - // AmG FE / / / AmE Am

He told a waiter near at hand
The simple dinner he had planned
The guests were startled one & all
To hear that waiter loudly call:
"**One meat ball (3x)** This here gent wants **one…**"

The little man felt ill at ease
He said "Some bread, sir, if you please"
The waiter hollered down the hall:
"You gets no bread with **one…**! / **One…** / You gets…"

The little man felt very bad
One meat ball was all he had
And in his dreams he hears that call
"You gets no bread with **one meat ball**"…

— trad. (US)

Arr. © 2015 by Hal Leonard Corporation. Rec. by Dave Van Ronk, Josh White.
Early versions of this song, titled "The Lone Fish-Ball," date back to the 1850s.

A PLACE CALLED ENGLAND

I rode out on a bright May morning like a hero in a song
Looking for a place called England, trying to find where I belong
Couldn't find the old flood meadow or the house that I once knew
No trace of the little river or the garden where I grew

AE A DA AE / AE A DA EA / DA EA DA EA / /

I saw town & I saw country, motorway & sink estate
Rich man in his rolling acres, poor man still outside the gate
Retail park & burger kingdom, prairie field & factory farm
Run by men who think that England's only a place to park their car

But as the train pulled from the station thru the wastelands of despair
From the corner of my eye a brightness filled the filthy air
Someone's grown [sown] a patch of sunflowers tho' the soil is
    sooty black
Marigolds & a few tomatoes right beside the railway track

Down behind the terraced houses, in betw the concrete towers
Compost heaps & scarlet runners, secret gardens full of flowers
Meeta grows the scent of roses right beneath the big jets' path
Bid a fortune for her garden, Eileen turns away & laughs

So rise up George & wake up Arthur, time to rouse out from your sleep
Deck the horse with the sea-green ribbons, drag the old sword
    from the deep
Hold the line for Dave & Daniel as they tunnel thru the clay
While the oak in all its glory soaks up sun for one more day

Come all you at home with freedom whatever the land that
    gave you birth
There's room for you both root & branch as long as you love the
    English earth
Room for vole & room for orchid, room for all to grow & thrive
Just less room for the fat landowner on his arse in his four-wheel drive

England is not flag or Empire, it is not money, it is not blood
It's limestone gorge & granite fell, it's Wealden clay & Severn mud
Blackbird singing from the May tree, lark ascending thru the scales
Robin watching from your spade & English earth beneath your nails

So here's 2 cheers for a place called England, badly used [sore
    abused] but not quite dead
A Mr. Harding sort of England hanging in there by a thread
Here's 2 cheers for the crazy Diggers, now their hour shall come
    around
We shall plant the seed they saved us, commonwealth & common
    ground

— w & m: Maggie Holland

© 1999 Moose Music. On her *Getting There*, June Tabor *A Quiet Eye* & Simon
Jackson *Sailing the Ice*. Inspired by the bk & song "World Turned Upside Down"
about the Diggers, a 17th c. English movement attempting to reclaim common
land for the whole people from private ownership. *LS

RAGGEDY RAGGEDY ARE WE

<u>Raggedy</u>, <u>raggedy</u> **are we**
Just as <u>raggedy</u> as <u>raggedy</u> can be
We don't get nothin' for our labor
So <u>raggedy</u>, <u>raggedy</u> **are we**

C G C - / / - - G - / C - F - / 1st

Insert: hungry, homeless, landless

Union, union **are we** / Just as <u>union</u> as <u>union</u> can be
We don't get nothin' for our labor
We're <u>gonna</u> **get** something from **our labor**

— w & m: John Handcox

© 1967, 1982 by Sanga Music, Inc. All rights administered by Figs. D Music c/o
the Bicycle Music Company. On his *Songs, Poems & Stories of the So. Farmers
Tenants Union* & Pete Seeger *Amer Industrial Ballads & Gr Hits*. In Seeger *Carry It On*.

RICH GIRL

You're a rich girl & you've gone too far
'Cos you know it don't matter anyway
You can rely on the old man's money (2x)
It's a bitch girl but it's gone too far
'Cos you know it don't matter anyway
Say money but it won't get you too far
Get you too far

(↑5) C Em7 / Am7 C / F C / Dm7 G / 1st 3 / Dm7 -

Don't you know, don't you know
That it's wrong to take what is given you
So far gone, on your own
You can get along if you try to be strong
But you'll never be strong 'cos

Fmaj7 - Dm7 - / C - FEm7 Am7 / 1st / Dm7 Am7 / Dm7 FG

High & dry, out of the rain
It's so easy to hurt others when you can't feel pain
And don't you know that a love can't grow
'Cos there's too much to give, 'cos you'd rather live
For the thrill of it all, oh

— w & m: Daryl Hall

© 1976 (renewed) Unichappell Music Inc. & Hot-Cha Music Co. All rights
administered by Unichappell Music Inc. On Hall & Oates *Bigger Than Both of Us*.

THE RICH MAN'S HOUSE

Well I went down to the <u>rich man's house</u> & I took back
  what he *[they]* stole from me
(Took it back) **took back my dignity**, (took it back) **took back
  my humanity (repeat)**
Now he's – under my feet **(x4)**
Ain't gonna let the system walk all over me!

Am - - - / Dm - Am - :|| Am - - - / - Dm Am -

insert: landlord's house, welfare office, governor's house
— w & m: the Kensington Welfare Rights Union & Anne Feeney
© 2000 Anne Feeney. On Anne Feeney *Have You Been to Jail for Justice?*

ROLLING HOME

Round goes the wheel of fortune, be not afraid to ride
There's a land of milk & honey waits on the other side
There'll be peace & there'll be plenty, you'll never need to roam
  When we go rolling home **(x2)**

(in D) D - A D / G D Em A / G D - A / D - A G -

Rolling home (when we go) rolling home (when we go)
Rolling, rolling, when we go rolling home

D - G A / D G D A G -

The gentry in their fine array do prosper night & morn
While we unto the fields must go to plough & sow their corn
The rich may steal the power but the glory is our own

The summer of resentment, the winter of despair
The journey to contentment is set with trap & snare
Stand true & stand together, your labour is your own...

The frost is on the hedgerow, the icy winds do blow
While we poor weary labourers strive thru the sleet & snow
Our hopes fly up to glory up where the larks do go...

So pass the bottle round & let the toast go free
Here's a health to every labourer wherever they may be
Fair wages now & ever, let's reap what we have sown...

— w & m: John Tams
© 1987 by Umlaut Corporation, BVI (ASCAP). All rights administered by Wixen
Music Publishing, Inc. On Roy Bailey *What You Do with What You've Got*, Dave
Auld *Work & Leisure*, Beggars Velvet (self-titled).

SING ABOUT THESE HARD TIMES

Sing about these hard times
Sing all about these hard old times
Sing about these hard times
When will the good times roll?

(↑3) D - - - / A - D G / 1st / Em - A -

I worked hard, I played my part
That's what I did right from the start
But these hard times are gonna break my heart
When will the good times roll?

A - D - / G - - D / 1st / Em - A -

Life gets harder every year
Those with the least have the most to fear
Those with the most just don't care
When will the good times roll?

The big corporations got no home
And the men on the Hill got hearts of stone
They worry my life like a dog with a bone / **When will...**

They moved my job to Mexico
Where children slave & the pay is low
How I'm gonna live I just don't know / **When will...**

O the world is ill divided
Those who work most are the least provided &
When they got a war they want US to fight it...
— w & m: Peggy Seeger
© 2005 Peggy Seeger/Harmony Music Ltd. On her *Love Call Me Home* & *3 Score & 10*.

THEY'RE TAKING IT AWAY

Oh they're taking it away, yes they're taking it away
They are taking all the good things, you can hear
  the people say
And they'll take it all tomorrow if they don't take it today
From the poor & sick & helpless they are taking it away

(↑5) C G Am F / C - - G / 1st / F - G C

Oh our government's elected in the democratic way
[Oh Republicans elected in a gerrymandered way]
A-whining at the cost of all the things they have to pay,
And the bully-boys on Bay *[Wall]* St, you can hear the bastards say
"To hell with paying taxes, pull the safety-net away!"

G - C - / F C D G / C G Am F / C - G C

If you're down upon your luck & need to keep the wolf at bay
Just don't rely on welfare or the dole to pay your way
For the rich, they have decided not another cent to pay
You can whistle for your supper for they've **taken...**

If you're native, black, or Asian, if you're feminist or gay
If you're just a little different from the most of us today
If you want to make your point or if you want to have your say
You can spit into the wind because they've **taken...**

If you're battered by your husband & you need a place to stay
You'd best get down upon your knees & quickly learn to pray
For the women's center's phone was disconnected yesterday
And there's no one left to talk to, now they've **taken...**

If it's ever your misfortune in a hospital to stay
You'd best not be impatient for a bed on which to lay,
For your health ain't worth the taxes that the healthy have to pay
And the beds were too expensive, so they've taken them...

Oh there's those that have & those that don't & those who are OK
And there's those who understand that fairness is the only way
But there's those who are so comfortable they look the other way
And they vote for all the villains who would **take...**

So if you've health & wealth & wisdom, stop & spare a thought today
For those who don't & those who can't, there is no other way
Or we might as well give up the ghost & join the USA
For there won't be any difference when they **take...**

— w & m: Ian Robb
© 1990 Ian Robb. On his *From Different Angels* (in G ↑7), Keith Kendrick *Home
Ground*. In *SO!* 35:3. Alt "US" lyrics by Jim Luckett ("Fiscal Cliff").

TIME TO REMEMBER THE POOR

Cold winter is come, with its cold chilling breath
And the leaves are all gone from the trees
All nature seems touched by the finger of death
And the streams are beginning to freeze
When the young wanton lads o'er the river slide
When the flowers attend us no more
When in plenty you are sitting by a warm fireside
That's the time to remember the poor

(↑3) DmA Dm / FG A :‖ F G / Dm A / DA Dm / GmA Dm

The cold, feathered snow will in plenty descend
And whiten the prospect around
The keen, cutting wind from the North will attend
And cover it over the ground
When the hills & the dales are all candied with white
And the rivers are froze on the shore
When the bright twinkling stars they proclaim the cold night...

The poor timid hare thru the woods may be traced
By her footsteps indented in the snow
When our lips & our fingers are all dangling with cold
And the marksman a-shooting does go
When the poor Robin Redbreast approaches your cot
And the icicles hang at your door
And when your bowl smokes reviving & hot...

The time will come when our Saviour on Earth
All the world shall agree with one voice
All nations unite to salute the blest morn
And the whole of the Earth shall rejoice
When grim death is deprived of its killing sting
And the grave rules triumphant no more
Saints, angels & men Hallelujah shall sing
Then the rich must remember the poor

— trad. (English)

Arr. © 2015 by Hal Leonard Corporation. Lyrics are from 19th c. broadsides. Published in Frank Kidson *Traditional Tunes* (1891). On Waterson-Carthy *Holy Heathens & the Old Green Man*, Nowell Sing We Clear *Just Say Nowell*, Dave Townsend & the Mellstock Band *Tenants of the Earth*, Jennifer Cutting *S of Solstice*.

TOM JOAD

Tom Joad got out of the old McAlester Pen
There he got his parole
After 4 long years on a man killing charge
Tom Joad come a-walkin' down the road, poor boy
Tom Joad come a-walkin' down the road

(in D) G - D - / / /D - - - /D A D -

Tom Joad, he met a truck driving man
There he caught him a ride
He said, "I just got loose from McAlester Pen
On a charge called homicide" **(2x)**
     That truck rolled away in a cloud of dust
     Tommy turned his face toward home
     He met Preacher Casey & they had a little drink
     But they found that his family they was gone **(2x)**
He found his mother's old-fashioned shoe
Found his daddy's hat
And he found little Muley & Muley said
"They've been tractored out by the cats" **(2x)**

Tom Joad walked down to the neighbor's farm
Found his family
They took Preacher Casey & loaded in a car
And his mother said "We've got to get away" **(2x)**
     Now, the 12 of the Joads made a mighty heavy load
     But Grandpa Joad did cry
     He picked up a handful of land in his hand
     Said "I'm stayin' with the farm 'til I die" **(2x)**
They fed him short ribs & coffee & soothing syrup
And Grandpa Joad did die
They buried Grandpa Joad by the side of the road
They buried Grandma on the California side **(2x)**
     They stood on a mtn & they looked to the west
     And it looked like the promised land
     That bright green valley with a river running thru
     There was work for every single hand, they thought, there...
The Joads rolled away to the jungle camp
There they cooked a stew
And the hungry little kids of the jungle camp
Said "We'd like to have some, too" **(2x)**
     Now a deputy sheriff fired loose at a man
     Shot a woman in the back
     Before he could take his aim again
     Preacher Casey dropped him in his track, poor boy, Preacher...
They handcuffed Casey & they took him in jail
And then he got away
And he met Tom Joad on the old river bridge
And these few words he did say, poor boy, these few...
     "I preached for the Lord a mighty long time
     Preached about the rich & the poor
     Us workin' folkses, all get together
     'Cos we ain't got a chance anymore" **(2x)**
Now, the deputies come & Tom & Casey run
To the bridge where the water run down
But the vigilante thugs hit Casey with a club
They laid Preacher Casey on the ground, poor Casey, they...
     Tom Joad, he grabbed that deputy's club
     Hit him over the head
     Tom Joad took flight in the dark rainy night
     And a deputy & a preacher lying dead, 2 men, a deputy...
Tom run back where his mother was asleep
He woke her up out of bed
An' he kissed goodbye to the mother that he loved
Said what Preacher Casey said, Tom Joad, he said...
     "Ever'body might be just one big soul
     Well it looks that a-way to me
     Everywhere that you look, in the day or night
     That's where I'm a-gonna be, Ma, that's...
Wherever little children are hungry & cry
Wherever people ain't free
Wherever men are fightin' for their rights
That's where I'm a-gonna be, Ma, that's..."

— w & m: Woody Guthrie

WGP/TRO - © 1960 (renewed) & 1963 (renewed) Woody Guthrie publications, Inc. & Ludlow Music, Inc., New York, NY. All rights administered by Ludlow Music, Inc. Inspired by the 1939 novel by John Steinbeck & 1940 film. On his *Dust Bowl Ballads*, Country Joe McDonald *Thinking of Woody Guthrie*, Dick Gaughan *Outlaws & Dreamers*, YT video Andy Irvine. In *Coll Reprints fr* SO! V1-6.

WHEN THE RAIN COMES DOWN

When the r<u>a</u>in comes d<u>o</u>wn, **it** c<u>o</u>mes down on **every<u>o</u>ne** (2x)
No m<u>a</u>tter if you're r<u>i</u>ch or poor, no m<u>a</u>tter if you're gr<u>ea</u>t or **sm<u>a</u>ll** / When the r<u>a</u>in comes down, it c<u>o</u>mes down on us <u>a</u>ll!

A - - - / - - E - / A - D - / A E A -

When the sun shines down, it shines down on **every...** (2x)
No matter... / When the sun shines down, it shines down on us all

When a flower blooms, it blooms for **everyone...**
When a flower blooms, it's blooming for us all

When a baby smiles, she smiles for **everyone...**
When a baby smiles, she's smiling for us all

— w & m: Bob Devlin

© 1977 (renewed) Bob Devlin www.bobdevlinmusic.com. On his *When the Rain Comes Down*, Priscilla Herdman *Daydreamer*. Cathy Fink & Marcy Marxer *A Cathy & Marcy Collection for Kids*. Dan & Rachel *Plus One*. SongSisters *Room in This World for Everyone*.

WORLD IN THEIR POCKET

They've got the world in their pocket – pocket (x3)
They've got the world in their pocket & they're up there in control
They've got the world in their pocket, they can shake it, they can rock it / They can kick it for a goal
They've got the world in their pocket, but their pocket's got a hole!

A - D A / - - - E - / A - D - / A E / A - E A

There's inflation & pollution
Everything's been bought on credit in this rotten institution
And they waste the gentle people 'cos the system has no soul
They've got the world in their pocket, but their pocket's got a hole!
They've got the...

Dm - Am - /   / E7 - Am Dm / C G - Am - - -

Unemployment is their glory
If a million children starve, why that's an old familiar story
And there's rage & there's rebellion & there's grief from pole to pole....

Takes a war to keep them perking
And they have to bleed the world to keep their bloody system working
But the system's self-destructing while they play that gangster role...

— w & m: Malvina Reynolds

© 1974 (renewed) Schroder Music Company. On her *Held Over & Sings the Truth* (in G). In her *SB* & *SO!* 26:6.

The **Rich & Poor** chapter contains songs about economic justice & injustice including songs from the "Occupy" movement. For related songs see the **Farm**, **Struggle** and **Work** chapters. Others include **Earthcare**: Make it mend it, **Friendship**: Side by side, **Gospel**: There'll be no distinctions there, **Lullabies**: And we shall want no more, **Millennial**: If I had a $1,000,000, **Sing**: I want to sing that rock & roll.

Rock Around the Clock

ALL I HAVE TO DO IS DREAM

(intro) Dre-eam, dream dream dream (2x)

(↑3)   C Am F G /   /

When I want you in my arms
When I want you & all your charms
Whenever I want you, all I have to do is
Dre-eam dream, dream dream dream

C Am F G (4x)

When I feel blue in the night / And I need you to hold me tight
Whenever I want you, all I have to do is / **Dream**

C Am F G /   / / C F C -

(bridge) I can make you mine, taste your lips of wine
Anytime, night or day
Only trouble is, gee whiz / I'm dreamin' my life away

F - Em - / Dm G C - / 1st / D - G -

I need you so that I could die
I love you so & that is why...
Whenever I want you, all I have to do is
Dre-am dream (x3)   (repeat to fade)

— w & m: Boudleaux Bryant

© 1958 by House of Bryant publications, Gatlinburg, TN. Copyright renewed. All foreign rights controlled by Sony/ATV Music Publishing LLC. All rights for Sony/ATV Music Publishing LLC administered by Sony/ATV Music Publishing LLC, 424 Church Street, Suite 1200, Nashville, TN 37219. Rec by Everly Bros. David & Jenny Heitler-Klevans recorded a great parody called "All I Have to Do Is Scream" on their Two of a Kind *Family Album*. See their website for lyrics.

BOOK OF LOVE

Oh I w<u>o</u>nder, wonder wh<u>o</u> (mmbadoo-ooh)
Wh<u>o</u>, wh<u>o</u> wrote the Book of Love _?

(↑3)   G - / C - G -

T<u>e</u>ll me (x3) oh wh<u>o</u> wrote the Book of Love?
I've g<u>o</u>t to kn<u>o</u>w the <u>a</u>nswer: was it s<u>o</u>meone from ab<u>o</u>ve?

G Em C D /   /

Oh I wonder…
I love you darlin', baby, you know I do
But I've got to see this Book of Love, find out why it's true

(bridge) Chap.1 says to love her, you love her with all your heart
Chap. 2 you tell her you're never **(x5)** gonna part
In Chap. 3 remember the meaning of romance
In Chap. 4 you break up but you give her just 1 more chance

C - G - / C - D - / G - C D / | /

Baby, baby, baby, I love you, yes I do
Well it says so in this Book of Love, ours is the one that's true

— w & m: Warren Davis, George Malone & Charles Patrick

© 1957 (renewed 1985) EMI Longitude Music & Arc Music Corp. All rights for Arc Music Corp. administered by BMG Rights Management (US) LLC. Rec by The Monotones.

Bye Bye Love

Bye bye love, bye bye happiness
Hello loneliness, I think I'm gonna cry
Bye bye love, bye bye sweet caress
Hello emptiness, I feel like I could die
Bye bye my love goodbye

(in D) G D G D / G D D A D : | D A D

There goes my baby with someone new
She sure looks happy, I sure am blue
She was my baby 'til he stepped in
Goodbye to romance that might have been

A - D - / | / G - A - / 1st /

I'm thru with romance, I'm thru with love
I'm thru with countin' the stars above
And here's the reason that I'm so free
My lovin' baby is thru with me

— w & m: Felice Bryant & Boudleaux Bryant

© 1957 by House of Bryant Publications, Gatlinburg, TN. Copyright renewed. All foreign rights controlled by Sony/ATV Music Publishing LLC. All rights for Sony/ATV Music Publishing LLC administered by Sony/ATV Music Publishing LLC, 424 Church Street, Suite 1200, Nashville, TN 37219. Rec by Everly Bros 17, Roy Orbison *Lonely & Blue* ('60) & Simon & Garfunkel *Bridge Over Troubled Waters* ('70 14).

Can't Help Falling in Love with You

Wise men say
Only fools rush in
But I can't help falling
In love with you

(↑2) C Em Am C / F C G - / F G Am F / C G C -

Shall I stay? / Would it be a sin? / If **I can't…**

(bridge) Like a river flows surely to the sea, darling so it goes
Some things are meant to be

Em B7 **(x3)** / Em A7 Dm G

Take my hand / Take my whole life too / For **I can't…**

— w & m: George David Weiss, Hugo Peretti & Luigi Creatore

© 1961; renewed 1989 Gladys Music (ASCAP). All rights in the U.S. administered by Imagem Sounds. Sung by Elvis Presley in '61 film *Blue Hawaii* (1961). Tune based on "Plaisir d'Amour" (1784), a popular romance by Jean Paul Egide Martini.

Can't Take My Eyes Off of You

You're just too good to be true
Can't take my eyes off of you
You'd be like heaven to touch
I wanna hold you so much
At long last love has arrived
And I thank God I'm alive
You're just too good to be true
Can't take my eyes off of you

A - / Amaj7 - / A7 - / D - / Dm - / A - / B7 Bm / A -

Pardon the way that I stare
There's nothing else to compare
The sight of you leaves me weak
There are no words left to speak
But if you feel like I feel
Please let me know that it's real
You're just too good to be true
Can't take my eyes off of you

I love you baby & if it's quite all right
I need you baby to warm the lonely night
I love you baby, trust in me / When I say
Oh pretty baby, don't bring me down I pray
Oh pretty baby, now that I've found you stay
And let me love you baby **(2x)** Let me love you

Bm E / C#m F#m / Bm E / F#m F# / 1st 2 /
Bm - / F - / A -

— w & m: Bob Crewe & Bob Gaudio

© 1967 (renewed 1995) EMI Longitude Music & Seasons Four Music. Rec by Frankie Valli & 4 Seasons (in F 18), Letterman (medley w/ Goin' Out of My Head), Sinatra (in E 17), Overtones 14, Lauren Hill, film *Jersey Boys*.

Do Wah Diddy Diddy

There she was just a-walkin' down the street
Singin' do-wah diddy-diddy dum diddy-do
Snappin' her fingers & shufflin' her feet
Singin' do-wah diddy-diddy dum diddy-do
She looked good (looked good), she looked fine (looked fine)
She looked good, she looked fine & I nearly lost my mind

C - F C **(4x)**   C - - - / | /

Before I knew it she was walkin' next to me / **Singin' do-wah…**
Holdin' my hand just as natural as can be / **Singin' do-wah…**
We walked on (walked…) to my door (my…)
We walked on to my door, then we kissed a little more

(bridge) _ _ _ Whoa-oa / I knew we was falling in love _
_ _ _ Yes I did & so / I told her all the things I'd been dreamin' of

C - - - / Am - - - / F - - - / G - - -

Now we're together nearly every single day / **Singin' do-wah…**
We're so happy & that's how we're gonna stay…
Well I'm hers (I'm hers), she's mine, (she's mine)
I'm hers, she's mine, wedding bells are gonna chime

— w & m: Jeff Barry & Ellie Greenwich

© 1963 Trio Music Company & Universal-Songs of PolyGram International, Inc. Copyright renewed. All rights for Trio Music Company controlled & administered by Bug Music, Inc., A BMG Chrysalis Company. Orig rec by Exciters 13 & Manfred Mann 14. Sung by Bill Murray in '81 film *Stripes* & by Riders in the Sky in alb version of *Monsters Inc. Scream Factory* (in Bb).

Dᴏɴ'ᴛ Bᴇ Cʀᴜᴇʟ (To A Heart That's True)

You know I can be found sitting home all alone
If you can't come around, at least please telephone
Don't be cruel to a heart that's true

D - - - / G - D - / A7 - D -

Baby, if I made you mad for something I might have said
Please, let's forget my past, the future looks bright ahead
Don't be cruel…

    I don't want no other love, baby it's just you
    I'm thinking of

    G A7 G A7 / D -

Don't stop thinking of me, don't make me feel this way
Come on over here & love me, you know what I want you to say
Don't be cruel to a heart that's true

    Why should we be apart? I really love you baby
    Cross my heart
Let's walk up to the preacher & let us say I do
Then you'll know you'll have me & I'll know that I'll have you
Don't be… (to: I don't want no other love…**)**

    — w & m: Otis Blackwell & Elvis Presley

© 1956, renewed 1984 Elvis Presley Music (BMI). All rights for Elvis Presley Music administered by Songs of Imagem Music. Rec by Elvis.

Dᴜᴋᴇ ᴏꜰ Eᴀʀʟ

Duke, Duke, Duke, Duke of Earl
Duke, Duke, Duke of Earl **(repeat)**

C - Am - / F - G - :‖

As I walk thru this world / Nothing can stop the Duke of Earl
And you, you are my girl / No one can hurt you, oh no

Yes I, _ _oh I'm gonna / **Love you,** _ (oh oh) come on let me
Hold you, darlin' _ 'cos I'm the Duke of
Earl, _ so yeah yeah yeah yeah

C - - - / Am - - - / F - - - / G7 - - -

And when I hold you / You'll be my Duchess, Duchess of Earl
We'll walk thru my dukedom / And a paradise we will share

Yes I, oh I'm gonna / **Love you,** (oh oh) nothing can
Stop me now _ 'cos **I'm the Duke of…**

    — w & m: Earl Edwards, Eugene Dixon & Bernice Williams

© 1961 (renewed) Conrad Music (BMI). All rights administered by BMG Rights Management (US) LLC. Rec by Gene Chandler Ð6.

Eᴀʀᴛʜ Aɴɢᴇʟ

Earth angel, earth angel, will you be mine?
My darling dear, love you all the time
I'm just a fool, a fool in love / With you

C Am F G **(4x)** **(2nd v. ends: C F C C7)**

Earth angel, earth angel, the one I adore
Love you forever & ever more / **I'm just a fool, a fool in love**

(bridge) I fell for you & I knew
The vision of your love-loveliness
I hope & I pray that someday
I'll be the vision of your hap-happiness

F - C - / G - C C7 / 1st / D7 - G7 -

Earth angel, earth angel, _please_ be mine… **(ends: C F C -)**

    — w & m: Jesse Belvin

© 1954 (renewed) by Embassy Music Corporation (BMI). Orig rec by The Penguins (in Ab). Other recs Crew-Cuts ↑3, Marvin Berry & Starlighters, Temptations, Elvis (all three ↑5), Bobby Vee ↑4, Gloria Mann. In film *Back to the Future* & musical *Jersey Boys*.

Iᴛ'ꜱ Mʏ Pᴀʀᴛʏ

It's my party & I'll cry if I want to
Cry if I want to, cry if I want to
You would cry too if it happened to you

A - Aaug - / D - Dm - / A F#m Bm E A(D AE)

Nobody knows where my Johnny has gone
But Judy left the same time
Why was he holding her hand
When he's supposed to be mine?

A - C - / A - D - / F - A - / B7 - E -

Play all my records, keep dancing all night
But leave me alone for a while
Til Johnny's dancing with me
I've got no reason to smile

Judy & Johnny just walked thru the door
Like a queen with her king
Oh what a birthday surprise
Judy's wearing his ring

    — w & m: Herb Wiener, Wally Gold & John Gluck, Jr.

© 1963 (renewed) Chappell & Co., Inc. On Lesley Gore *I'll Cry If I Want To* ↑5 & in *DU*. The day after Ronald Reagan's election, in 1980, the University of Michigan student radio station played this song for 18 hours straight.

Lᴏᴠᴇ Mᴇ Tᴇɴᴅᴇʀ

Love me tender, love me sweet, never let me go
You have made my life complete, & I love you so

C D G7 C /   /

Love me tender, love me true, all my dreams fulfill
For my darlin' I love you, & I always will

CE7 AmC FFm C / CA7 D G7 C

Love me tender, love me long, take me to your heart
For it's there that I belong, & we'll never part
    Love me tender, love me dear, tell me you are mine
    I'll be yours thru all the yrs, till the end of time
When at last my dreams come true, darling, this I know
Happiness will follow you everywhere you go

    — w & m: Elvis Presley & Vera Matson

© 1956; renewed 1984 Elvis Presley Music (BMI). All rights in the U.S. administered by Imagem Sounds. Rec by Elvis in '56 ↑2. Tune is adap fr 1861 Civil War song "Aura Lee."

Lᴏᴠᴇ Pᴏᴛɪᴏɴ Nᴜᴍʙᴇʀ 9

I took my troubles down to Madame Ruth
You know that gypsy with the gold cap tooth
She's got a pad down at 34th & Vine
Sellin' little bottles of Love Potion #9

Am Dm /   / C CAm / Dm E Am -

I told her that I was a flop with chicks
I been this way since 1956
She looked at my palm & she made a magic sign
She said "Whatcha need is Love Potion #9"

232

(bridge) She bent down & turned around & gave me a wink
She said I'm gonna mix it up right here in the sink
It smelled like turpentine & looked like India ink
I held my nose, I closed my eyes, I took a drink!

Dm - / B7 - / Dm - / E -

I didn't know if it was day or night
I started kissing everything in sight
But when I kissed a cop down at 34th & Vine
He broke my little bottle of Love Potion #9

— w & m: Jerry Leiber & Mike Stoller

© 1959 Sony/ATV Music Publishing LLC. Copyright renewed. All rights administered by Sony/ATV Music Publishing LLC, 424 Church Street, Suite 1200, Nashville, TN 37219. Orig rec by The Clovers (in '73 film *Amer Graffiti*). Also by The Searchers, Coasters.

MONSTER MASH

I was working in the lab, late one night
When my eyes beheld an eerie sight
For my monster from his slab, began to rise
And suddenly to my surprise
    He **did the mash**, he **did the monster mash**
    The monster mash, it was a graveyard smash
    He **did the mash, it caught on in a flash**
    He **did the mash**, he **did the monster mash**

G - / Em - / C - / D7 - :‖

From my laboratory in the castle east
To the master bedroom where the vampires feast
The ghouls all came from their humble abodes
To get a jolt from my electrodes
    They **did the mash**...

(bridge) The zombies were having fun
The party had just begun
The guests included Wolfman / Dracula & his son

C - / D7 - :‖

The scene was rockin', all were digging the sounds
Igor on chains, backed by his baying hounds
The coffin-bangers were about to arrive
With their vocal group, "The Crypt-Kicker Five"
    They played **the mash**, they played **the monster**...

Out from his coffin, Drac's voice did ring
Seems he was troubled by just one thing
Opened the lid & shook his fist & said
"Whatever happened to my Transylvania Twist?"
    It's now **the mash**, it's now **the monster mash**...

Now everything's cool, Drac's a part of the band
And my Monster Mash is the hit of the land
For you, the living, this mash was meant too
When you get to my door, tell them Boris sent you
    Then you can mash, then you can monster mash
    The monster mash & do my graveyard smash!
    Then you can mash, you'll catch on in a flash
    Then you...

— w & m: Bobby Pickett & Leonard Capizzi

© 1962, 1963 (renewed) Reservoir 416, House of Paxton Music Press & Capizzi Music Co. All rights for Reservoir 416 & House of Paxton Music Press administered by Reservoir Media Management, Inc. (Publishing) & Alfred Music (Print). All rights for the world outside the US & Canada administered by Unichappell Music, Inc. Rec by Pickett.

NOT FADE AWAY

(intro) (_wa wa _ wa-wa) **(x2)**

AD A AD A

I'm a-gonna tell you how it's gonna be _ _
You're gonna give your love to me _ _
I wanna love you night and day
You know my love a-not fade away
A-well you know my love a-not fade away

(in A) (tacet) DG D / **(tacet)** AD A :‖ **2nd** /

My love a-bigger than a Cadillac
I try to show it & you drive a-me back
Your love for me a-got to be real
For you to know just how I feel
A love for real not fade away

I'm a-gonna tell you how it's gonna be
You're gonna give your love to me
A love to last a-more than one day
A love that's love − not fade away
A well, a-love that's love − not fade away

— w & m: Charles Hardin & Norman Petty

© 1957 (renewed) MPL Music Publishing, Inc. & Wren Music Co. Buddy Holly's band The Crickets rec this on same day as "Every Day." On Stones single ('67) & *Stripped* (live '09), James Taylor *Covers*, Sheryl Crow ad & YT conc. All but Crow in E 17. Beats are syncopated falling on 2nd, 4th, 6th & 7th beat of each phrase.

ROCK AROUND THE CLOCK

(intro) 1, 2, 3 o'clock, 4 o'clock, rock
5, 6, 7 o'clock, 8 o'clock, rock
9, 10, 11 o'clock, 12 o'clock, rock
We're gonna rock around the clock tonight

A - / / / E7 -

Put your glad rags on & join me, hon
We'll have some fun when the clock strikes one
We're gonna rock around the clock tonight
We're gonna rock rock rock til the broad daylight
We're gonna rock, gonna rock around the clock tonight

A - / A A7 // D7 - / A - / E7 - A -

When the clock strikes 2, 3 & 4
If the band slows down we'll yell for more /**We're**...

When the chimes ring 5, 6 & 7
We'll be right in 7th heaven...

When it's 8, 9, 10, 11 too
I'll be goin' strong & so will you...

When the clock strikes 12, we'll cool off then
Start a rockin' 'round the clock again...

— w & m: Max C. Freedman & Jimmy DeKnight

© 1953 Myers Music Inc., Kassner Associated Publishers Ltd. & Capano Music. Copyright renewed. All rights on behalf of Myers Music Inc. & Kassner Associated Publishers Ltd. administered by Sony/ATV Music Publishing LLC, 424 Church Street, Suite 1200, Nashville, TN 37219. Rec by Bill Haley.

A Teenager In Love

Each time we have a quarrel it almost breaks my heart
'Cos I am so afraid that we will have to part
Each night I ask the stars up above
Why must I be a teenager in love?

(↑6) G Em C D / / /(tacet)

One day I feel so happy, next day I feel so sad
I guess I'll learn to take the good with the bad

(bridge) I cried a tear for nobody but you
I'll be a lonely one if you should say we're thru

C D C D / /

Well if you want to make me cry, that won't be so hard to do,
If you should say goodbye, I'll still go on loving you

— w: Doc Pomus, m: Mort Shuman

That'll Be the Day

Well that'll be the day when you say goodbye
Yes that'll be… when you make me cry
You say you're gonna leave, you know it's a lie
'Cos that'll… when I die

(in G, ↑2) C - - - / G - - - / 1st / G - D7 G

Well you give me all your lovin' & your turtle dovin'
All your hugs & kisses & your money too
Well you know you love me baby still you tell me maybe
That someday, well I'll be thru

C - G - / / / A - D -

Well when Cupid shot his dart, he shot it at your heart
So if we ever part & I leave you
You sit & hold me & you tell me boldly / That someday, well I'll be blue

(tag) Well that'll be the day_ (hoo-hoo) (3x) Well that'll…day

C - - - / G - - - :‖

— w & m: Jerry Allison, Norman Petty & Buddy Holly

Wake Up Little Susie

Wake up little Susie, wake up (2x)
We've both been sound asleep, wake up little Susie & weep
The movie's over, it's 4 o'clock & we're in trouble deep
Wake up little Susie, wake up little Susie

D - - - / / G - - - / / A G A -

Well what're we gonna tell your mama? what're we gonna
tell your pop?
What're gonna tell our friends when they say "ooh la la"?
Wake up little Susie, wake up little Susie

A E A A E A / A E A (tacet) / D A D -

Well I told your mama that you'd be in by 10
Well, Susie baby, looks like we goofed again
Wake up little Susie (x2) / We gotta go home

D - - - / G - - - / A G A - / D (C G D C G D -)

Wake up little Susie, wake up (2x)
The movie wasn't so hot, it didn't have much of a plot
We fell asleep, our goose is cooked, our reputation is shot

— w & m: Boudleaux Bryant & Felice Bryant

When Will I Be Loved

I've been cheated, been mistreated
When will I be loved?
I've been pushed down, I've been pushed 'round / **When…**

D GA D GA / / / D GA D -

(bridge) When I find a new man [girl] that I want for mine
He [she] always breaks my heart in 2, it happens every time

G A G D / G A Bm A

I've been made blue, I've been lied to / **When…**
bridge to I've been cheated…

— w & m: Phil Everly

Why Do Fools Fall in Love

(intro) Oo wah, oo wah (3x) Why do fools fall in love?

(↑5) C Am F G (4x)

Why do birds sing so gay & lovers await the break of day?
Why do they fall in love? _
Why does the rain fall from up above? why do fools
Fall in love? why do they fall in love? _

C Am F G C Am F G (3x) C Am F G C -

Love is a losing game, love can be a shame
I know of a fool, you see - for that fool is me!
Tell me why? _ _ _ / _ _ **tell me why?** _

F - C - / F - G - / - - C - / - G C -

Why does my heart skip a crazy beat?
For I know it will reach defeat!
Tell me why, tell me why? / Why do fools fall in love?
Tell me why… / (tag) Why_ do fools fall in love?

F - G - C - - -

— w & m: Morris Levy & Frankie Lymon

Yakety Yak

Take out the papers & the trash _
Or you don't get no spendin' cash _
If you don't scrub that kitchen floor _
You ain't gonna rock & roll no more, **yakety yak** (don't talk back)

(↑2) G - / C - / D7 - / G -

Just finish cleanin' up your room
Let's see that dust fly with that broom
Get all that garbage out of sight
Or you don't go out Fri. night, **yakety…**

You just put on your coat & hat
And walk yourself to the laundromat
And when you finish doin' that
Bring in the dog & put out the cat…

Don't you give me no dirty looks
Your father's hip, he knows what cooks
Just tell your hoodlum friend outside
You ain't got time to take a ride…

— w & m: Jerry Leiber & Mike Stoller

The **Rock Around the Clock** chapter contains US rock 'n' roll fr the mid 50's thru the arrival of the Beatles in 1963. For later rock & pop songs see **British Invasion & Rock, Motown / R&B, Surfing USA.**

For the most part, rock 'n' roll music was innocent, fun music that didn't take itself seriously, music people could dance to. This was the era of Dick Clark's American Bandstand, where Philadelphia teenagers could strut their stuff on the dance floor on nationwide TV every weekday afternoon. One could argue forever about who started Rock 'n' Roll - was it Bill Haley, Elvis Presley, Buddy Holly, or maybe the Everly Brothers? More serious scholars might name Chuck Berry, Little Richard, Jerry Lee Lewis, & Bo Diddley. All of these learned their craft by listening to "race" records and attending performances of black blues and R&B performers. Rock 'n' roll was slow to recognize great women artists in the 1950s, but remarkable songwriters like Ellie Greenwich, Carole King, & Lesley Gore soon came on the scene.

Seas & Sailors

ADIEU SWEET LOVELY NANCY

Here's adieu sweet lovely Nancy, 10,000 times adieu
I'm a-going around the ocean, love, to seek for something new
Come change your ring with me, dear girl, come change your ring
   with me
For it might be a token of true love while I am on the sea

C FC C CG C /   / F C Am G / 1st

When I am far upon the sea, you know not where I am
Kind letters I will write to you from every foreign land
The secrets of your heart dear girl are the best of my good will
So let your body be where it might, my heart will be with you still

There's a heavy storm a-rising, see how it gathers round
While we poor souls on the ocean wide are fighting for the crown
There is nothing to protect us, love, or to keep us from the cold
On the ocean wide where we must bide like jolly seamen bold

There are tinkers, tailors, & shoemakers lie snoring fast asleep
While we poor souls on the ocean wide are plowing thru the deep
Our officers commanding us & them we must obey
Expecting every moment for to get cast away

But when the wars are all over there'll be peace on every shore
We'll return to our wives & families & the girls that we adore
We will call for liquor merrily, we will spend our money free
And when our money it is all gone, we will boldly go to sea

— trad.

BLOOD RED ROSES

Our boots & clothes are all in pawn
Go down, you blood red roses, go down
And it's flamin' drafty 'round Cape Horn / Go down, you…
O you pinks & posies / Go down…

D A / D Am D :| A - / D Am D

It's 'round that Cape we all must go
'Round Cape Horn in the frost & snow

My dear old mother she wrote to me
My dearest son, come home from sea

You've got your advance & to sea you'll go
To chase them whales thru the frost & snow

It's 'round Cape Horn you've got to go
For that is where them whalefish blow

It's growl you may, but go you must
If you growl too hard your head they'll bust

I thought I heard the old man say
Give her one good pull and then belay

— trad. (English halyard chantey)

CAN'T YOU DANCE THE POLKA?

As I walked down on Broadway one evening in July
I met a maid who asked me trade & a sailor John said I
Then away, you Santee, my dear Annie
O you New York girls, can't you dance the polka?

A D E A (4x)

To Tiffany's I took her, I did not mind expense
I bought her 2 gold earrings & they cost me 50 cents

Says she "You lime-juice sailor, now see me home you may"
But when we reached her cottage door, she this to me did say:

"My flash man he's a Yankee with his hair cut short behind
He wears a pair of long seaboots & he sails the Black Ball Line"

"He's homeward bound this evenin' & with me he will stay
So get a move on, sailor-boy, get crackin' on your way"

So I kissed her hard & proper afore her flash man came
An' fare-ye-well, me Bowery gal, I know yer little game

I wrapped me glad rags 'round me & to the docks did steer
I'll never court another maid, I'll stick to rum & beer

— trad. (US capstan chantey)

Arr © 2015 by Hal Leonard Corporation. Rec by Burl Ives as "You New York Girls."
In *Fireside Bk of Folk S.*

CLEAR AWAY IN THE MORNING

Take me back on the bay, boys
Clear away in the morning
I don't want to go ashore, boys
Oh bring her round

C - - - / Dm - G - / F Em Dm C / F - G -

Take me back on the bay, boys
Clear away in the morning
I don't want to spend my pay boys
Oh bring her round
　　Captain, don't you leave me / **Clear away...**
　　There's no one here that needs me / **Oh bring...**
Nancy, oh my Nancy...
She never played it fancy...
　　Bring me wine & brandy...
　　I'd only ask for Nancy...
Captain, don't let the main down...
Captain, don't let the chain run...
　　Captain, don't you need me?...
　　There's nothing I can do, boy...
Nancy, oh my Nancy
Clear away...
Nancy, oh my Nancy
Oh bring her...

— w & m: Gordon Bok

© 1970 (renewed) Timberhead Music. In his *Time & the Flying Snow* & on his *Peter Kagen and the Wind* (in Bb). Makem & Clancy *2 for the Early Dew.*

DOWN BY THE RIVER

I'll meet you down by the river, down by the river
Down by the river to see what we can see
Down by the river, by the Hudson River
Down by the river, that's where I want to be

A - - - / - - E - / A - D7 - / A - E A

You may be feeling cramped & crowded
You may be feeling restless & bored
I know a place can cure what ails you
Leave you refreshed, leave your mind restored

You never know what you might find there
You never know what the tide will bring
But I know you'll find peace of mind there
Something about it makes me want to sing

Just make your way down to the water
That river will bring the world to your feet
Might be something washed down from the mountains
Or dredged right up from the ocean deep

Once we got careless about our river
Let it fill up with pollution & trash
Now we're trying hard to protect it
Want to make sure that our river will last

— w & m: Jean McAvoy (of Betty & the Baby Boomers)

© 1997 Jean Mcavoy. On their *Where the Heron Waits* & *Tumbling thru the Stream of Days* ↑1. *LS

FINAL TRAWL

Now it's 3 long years since we made her pay
Sing haul away, my laddie-o
And the owners say that she's had her day
Sing haul away, my laddie-o

(in loose 3/4, ↑2) CCG Am / F C / AmAmG F / Dm FGG

So heave away for a final trawl
Sing haul away, my laddie-o
It's an easy pull, for the catch is small
Sing haul away, my laddie-o

Then stow your gear lads & batten down
Sing, haul away…
And we'll say farewell to the fishing grounds
Sing, haul away…

We'll join the 'Venture' & the 'Morning Star'
Riding high & empty beyond the bar

For I'd rather beach her on the Skerrie rock
Than to see her torched in the breakers dock

And when I die you can stow me down
In her rusty hold where the breakers sound

Then I'll make the haven of Fiddler's Green
Where the grub [*rum*] is good & the bunks are clean

For I've fished a lifetime, boy & man
And the final trawl scarcely makes a cran

— w & m: Archie Fisher

© 1983 Archie Fisher. On his *Windward Away*, Tannahill Weavers *Dancing Feet*, Bok Muir & Trickett *The Ways of Man*, Joe Keenan *The Best of the Vineyard Sound*. In *SO!* 37:2. A cran=37 gallons (about 750 herring).

FROBISHER BAY

Cold is the arctic sea
Far are your arms from me
Long will this winter be
Frozen in Frobisher Bay (2x)   (in 3/4)

`D - G D / - - G D / D A G D / - A Bm - / D A D -`

"One more whale," our captain cried
"One more whale, then we'll beat the ice"
But the winter star was in the sky
The seas were rough, the winds were high

`G - D - / G - D A / G - D - / Bm - - A`

Deep were the crashing waves
That tore our whaler's mast away
And dark are these sunless days
Waiting for the ice to break

Strange is the whaler's fate
To be saved from the raging waves
Only to waste away
Frozen in this lonely grave

— w & m: James Gordon

© 1990 Pipe Street Publishing (SOCAN). On his *Mining for Gold*, Tamarack *Frobisher Bay*, Kallet Epstein & Cicone *Heart Walk*, Anne Price *Hearth & Fire*.

THE HANDSOME CABIN BOY

It's of a pretty female as you may understand
Her mind being bent on ramblin' unto some foreign land
She dressed herself in sailor's clothes or so it does appear
And she hired with a sea captain to serve him for a year

`D - CG D / - - GC D / | 1st`

The captain's wife she being on board, she seemèd in great joy
To see her husband had engaged such a handsome cabin boy
And now & then she'd slip him a kiss & she would have liked to toy
But 'twas the captain found out the secret of **this handsome
    cabin boy**

Her lips they were like roses red & her hair hung in a curl
The sailors often smiled & said "he looks just like a girl"
But eating of the captain's biscuit her color did destroy
And the waist did swell of pretty Nell, **this handsome…**

It was in the Bay of Biscay our gallant ship did plow
One night among the sailors was a fearful flurry & row
They tumbled from their hammocks & their sleep it did destroy
And they swore about the groaning of **this…**

"O doctor, dear, o doctor" this cabin boy did cry
"My time has come, I am undone & surely I will die"
The doctor he came a-runnin' & a-smilin' at the fun
For to think a sailor lad should have a daughter or a son

The sailors when they saw the joke, they all did stand & stare
This child belonged to none of them, they solemnly did swear
The captain's wife she says to him "My dear I wish you joy
For it's either you or me has betrayed **this…**"

Now sailors, take your tot of rum & drink success to trade
And likewise to the cabin boy who was neither man nor maid
Here's hoping the wars don't rise again our sailors to destroy
And here's hoping for a jolly lot more like **this…**

— trad. (English)

Arr © 2015 by Hal Leonard Corporation. On *Sweeney's Men 1968*, Jerry Garcia & David Grisman *Shady Grove*, Ewan MacColl & AL Lloyd *Blow Boys Blow* & Martin Carthy. In *Coll Reprints fr SO!* V1-6.

JACK WAS EVERY INCH A SAILOR

Jack was every inch a sailor
5 & 20 yrs a whaler
Jack was every inch a sailor
He was born upon the bright blue sea

`C - G - / - - C - :‖`

Now 'twas 25 or 30 yrs since Jack 1st saw the light
He came into this world of woe one dark & stormy night
He was born on board his father's ship as she was lying to
'Bout 25 or 30 miles SE of Bacalhao

`C - - G / - - - C :‖`

When Jack grew up to be a man he went to the Labrador
He fished in Indian Harbour where his father fished before
On his returning in the fog he met a heavy gale
And Jack was swept into the sea & swallowed by a whale

O the whale went straight for Baffin's Bay 'bout 90 knots an hour
And every time he'd blow a spray he'd send it in a shower
O now, says Jack unto himself, I must see what he's about
He caught the whale all by the tail & turned him inside out

— trad. (Newfoundland sea song)

Arr. © 2015 by Hal Leonard Corporation. In *Folk Songs of Canada*. Rec. by Burl Ives, Ed McCurdy, Fred Penner, Sharon Lois & Bram. Prob derived fr a NY music hall song. Bacalhao (pronounced back-a-loo) is an island off the east coast of Newfoundland.

Jack Is Every Inch a Sailor

Jack is every inch a sailor
He'll see a pretty girl & hail 'er
He'll vow his love will never fail 'er
Then go sailing with his heart still free

When Jack steps down the gang-plank there's a quiver thru the
    town
And all the girls past 17 come gaily running down
They know that night that one of them has happiness in store
And each believes that if it's her, he'll never leave the shore

He's got a prize from every port to win a woman's heart
Brocade & silk & lace & pearls & oriental art
Somewhere he'll meet a girl whose kiss can keep him on the shore
But while he looks for her, he'll kiss at least a thousand more

— trad. (parody)

Arr © 2015 by Hal Leonard Corporation. Per *Folksinger's Wordbk*.

THE JEANNIE C.

Come all ye lads, draw near to me
That I be not forsaken
This day was lost the Jeannie C
And my living has been taken
I'll go to sea no more

(in 6/8 ↑2) Am – F C / Am G F C / Am G – F /
G – F – / G – C –

We set out this day in the bright sunrise
The same as any other
My son & I & old John Price
In the boat named for my mother / **I'll...**
    Now, it's well you know what the fishing has been
    It's been scarce & hard & cruel
    But this day, by God, we sure caught cod
    And we sang & we laughed like fools...
I'll never know what it was we struck
But strike we did like thunder
John Price gave a cry & pitched overside
Now it's forever he's gone under...
    Now a leak we've sprung, let there be no delay
    If the Jeannie C we're saving
    John Price is drowned & slipped away
    So I'll patch the hole while you're bailing...
But no leak I found from bow to hold
No rock it was that got her
But what I found made my heart stop cold
For every seam poured water...
    My God, I cried as she went down
    That boat was like no other
    My father built her when I was 9
    And named her for my mother...
And sure, I could have another made
In the boat shop down in Dover
But I would not love the keel they laid
Like the one the waves roll over...
    So come all ye lads, draw near to me
    That I be not forsaken
    This day was lost the Jeannie C
    And my whole life has been taken...

    — w & m: Stan Rogers

© 1978 Fogarty's Cove Music (SOCAN). On his *Turnaround* & in *Stan Rogers SB.*

LEAVE HER JOHNNY

I thought I heard the old man say
Leave her, Johnny, leave her
It's a long, hard pull to the next payday
And it's time for us to leave her

(↑2) G – – – / C – G – / C G D Em / G – DG G

Leave her, Johnny, leave her!
Oh, leave her, Johnny, leave her
For the voyage is done and the winds don't blow
And it's time for us to leave her!

D – G – / C – G – /   "   /   "   /

And the captain was bad but the mate was worse
Leave her, Johnny, leave her
He could blow you down with a sigh & a curse
And it's time for us to leave her

It was rotten meat and weevily bread
Leave her, Johnny...
You'd eat it or you'd starve to death
And it's time...

And the rats are all gone & we the crew...
Well it's time, by Christ, that we went too...

And a dollar a day is a Jack Shite's pay...
Well it's pump all night & it's work all day...

It was "pump or drown" the old man said...
Or else, by Christ, we'll all be dead...

Oh times were hard & the wages low...
I guess it's time for us to go...

    — trad. (US sea song)

Arr © 2015 by Hal Leonard Corporation. On Stan Rogers *Fr Coffee Hse to Conc Hall 17, Rogue's Gallery* (Lou Reed), Dave Van Ronk *Down in Washington Sq,* Makem & Clancy *Conc,* Dan Milner *Irish Ballads & S of the Sea.* In *Amer Songbag & S of Work & Protest.* Often used to close chantey sings.

THE LEAVING OF LIVERPOOL

Fare thee well, my own true love
I am going far away
I am bound for California
But I know that I'll return someday

G – C G / – C G D – / G – C G / – D G –

So fare thee well, my own true love
And when I return united we will be
It's not the leaving of Liverpool that grieves me
But my darling when I think of thee

D – C G /   "   /   "   /   "   /

I have shipped on a Yankee sailing ship
'Davy Crockett' is her name
And Burgess is the captain of her
And they say that she's a floating Hell

I have been with Burgess once before
And I think I know him right well
If a man is a seaman, he can get along
But if not, then he's sure in Hell

O the sun is on the harbor, love
And I wish I could remain
For I know it will be some long time
Before I see you again

    — trad. (English)

Arr © 2015 by Hal Leonard Corporation. Rec by Clancy Bros & Lou Killen, Dubliners, Corries, MacColl, Pogues, Gaelic Storm, High Kings, Luke Kelly. Adap by Dylan as "Farewell."

LOWLANDS AWAY

I dreamed a dream the other night
Lowlands, lowlands away, my John
I dreamed a dream the other night
Lowlands, my lowlands away

A – / – E / – D / E A

238

I dreamed I saw my own true love
Lowlands, lowlands away, my John
He stood so still, he did not move
Lowlands, my lowlands away

So dank his hair, so dim his eye / **Lowlands...**
I knew he'd come to say goodbye / **Lowlands...**

"I'm drowned in the lowland sea" he said...
"Oh you & I will ne'er be wed"...

"I'll never kiss you more" he said...
"Ne'er kiss you more, for I am dead"...

I will cut off my bonny hair...
No other man will find me fair...

(male version) I dreamed a dream the other night...
My love she came all dressed in white...

She came to me at my bedside...
All dressed in white like some fair bride...

And bravely in her bosom fair...
A red, red rose my love did wear...

She made no sound, no word she said...
And then I knew my love was dead...

  — trad. (English)

Arr. © 2015 by Hal Leonard Corporation. 1st variant is fr singing of Rika Ruebsaat of Vancouver BC. 2nd is fr *Fireside Bk of Folk S*. On Corries *Lads Among the Heather*, *Rogue's Gallery* (Rufus Wainwright & Kate McGarrigle), *The Waverleys*, Ragged Glory *Quiet Joys*, *Assassin's Creed 4* (*Sea Shanty Ed. V2*).

THE MERMAID

It was Friday morn when we set sail
And we were not far from the land
When our captain, he spied a mermaid so fair
With a comb & a glass in her hand

D - G D / G A D - :‖

And the ocean waves do roll
And the stormy winds do blow
And we poor sailors are skipping at the top
While the landlubbers lie down below, below, below
While the landlubbers lie down below

D - - - / - - A - / D - G D / G A D - /   /

Then up spoke the captain of our gallant ship
And a fine old man was he
This fishy mermaid has warned me of our doom
We shall sink to the bottom of the sea

Then up spoke the cabin boy of our gallant ship
And brave young lad was he
He said, I have a sweetheart in Salem by the sea
And tonight she'll be weepin' for me

Then up spoke the mate of our gallant ship
And a fine spoken man was he
Sayin', I have me a wife in Brooklyn by the sea
And tonight a widow she will be

Then up spoke the cook of our gallant ship
And a crazy old butcher was he
I care much more for my pots & my pans
Than I do for the bottom of the sea

Then 3 times around spun our gallant ship
And 3 times around spun she
3 times around spun our gallant ship
And she sank to the bottom of the sea

  — trad. (Child Ballad #289)

Arr. © 2015 by Hal Leonard Corporation. Rec by The Clancy Bros.

MINGULAY BOAT SONG

Heel y'ho, boys, let her go, boys
Bring her head round into the weather [now all together]
Heel y'ho, boys, let her go, boys
Sailing homeward to Mingulay

(in 3/4)   D - / A G / D - / A D

What care we tho' white the Minch is
What care we for wind and weather?
Let her go boys, every inch is
Wearing homeward to Mingulay

Wives are waiting on the hillside
Looking seaward from the heather
Pull her 'round, boys, and we'll anchor
Ere the sun sets at Mingulay

Ships return now, heavy laden
Mothers holdin' bairns a-cryin'
They'll return, though, when the sun sets
They'll return to Mingulay

  — w: Sir Hugh S. Roberton (1938), m: trad. (Gaelic)

Arr © 2015 by Hal Leonard Corporation. Roberton founded the Glasgow Orpheus Choir in 1906 & led it until 1951. On *Rogue's Gallery* (Richard Thompson), & recs by Clancy Bros, Gaelic Storms, Seamus Kennedy, Stan Hugill & Louis Killen, Dan Zanes. In Clancy Bros SB & SO! 19:4.

OLD ZEB

I'm not tired of the wind, I'm not weary of the sea
But she's prob'ly had a bellyfull of a damned old coot like me
I'm going ashore, she's gone for better days
But I'll see her topsail flyin' when I come down off the ways

C Am F C / F C Dm F / 1st / F C DmG C

Rosie, get my Sunday shoes, Gertie get my walkin' cane
We'll take another walk to see Old Alice sail again

C ↓ F CG / FEm CAm DmG C

I'd like to have a nickel for the men I used to know
Who could load 3 cord of lumber in half an hour or so
Who could put on sail by hauling, 'stead of donkeyin' around
Then I'd be the poorest coasterman this side of Edgartown

Any fool can work an engine, takes brains to work a sail
And I never seen no steamer make much good out of a gale
You can go & pay your taxes on the rationed gas you get
But at least to me, the wind is free, & they haven't run out yet

If I ever get back to her, you know I'll treat her just the same
I'll jibe her when I want to, boys & I'll sail in freezing rain
I'll park that old boat on the beach & go dancin' in the town
'Cos a man who's fit for hangin' prob'ly never will get drowned

  — w & m: Larry Kaplan

© 1976 (renewed), 1991 Hannah Lane Music. On his *Worth All the Telling* (Folk Legacy). Gordon Bok *Ensemble*. Kallet Epstein Cicone *Heart Walk*. Written for MA fisherman & coasterman Zebulon Northrup Tilton (1867-1952) about his daughters helping him ashore leaving his favorite vessel the "Alice Wentworth" for the last time.

PADDY WEST

As I was walkin' down Great Howard Street,
    I come to Paddy West's house
He gave me a plate of Amer. hash, he called it Liverpool scouse
He said "There's a ship & she's wantin' hands & on her you must sign
The mate's a bastard, the captain's worse, but she will suit you fine"

(in 3/4) D G A D / - GD D G /   / 1st

**Take off yer dungaree jacket & give yourself a rest
And we'll think on them cold nor'westers
    that we had at Paddy West's**

D GD D G / D G A D

When we had finished our dinner, boys, the wind began to blow
Paddy sent me to the attic, the main-royal for to stow
But when I got to the attic, no main-royal could I find
So I turned myself 'round to the window & I furled the window blind

Now Paddy he pipes all hands on deck, their stations for to man
His wife she stood in the doorway, a bucket in her hand
And Paddy he cries, "Now let 'er rip!"
    and she throws the water our way
Cryin' "Clew in the fore t'gan'sl, boys, she's takin' in the spray!"

Now seein' she's bound for the south'ard, to Frisco she was bound
Paddy he calls for a length of rope & he lays it on the ground
We all stepped over & back again & he says to me "That's fine
And if ever they ask were you ever at sea
    you can say you crossed the line"

To every 2 men that graduates, I'll give one outfit free
For 2 good men on watch at once, ye never need to see
Oilskins, me boys, ye'll never want, carpet slippers made of felt
I'll dish out to the pair o' you & a rope yarn for a belt

Paddy says "Now pay attention, these lessons you will learn
The starboard is where the ship she points,
    the right is called the stern
So look ye aft, to yer starboard port & you will find NW"
And that's the way they teach you at the school of **Paddy West**

There's just one thing for you to do before you sail away
Just step around the table, where the bullock's horn do lay
And if ever they ask "Were you ever at sea?"
    you can say "10 times 'round the Horn"
And bejesus but you're an old sailor man
    from the day that you were born

(last refrain)

Put on **your dungaree jacket** & walk out lookin' yer best
And tell 'em that you're an old sailor man
    that's come from **Paddy West**
    — trad. (English, tune "Tramps & Hawkers")

Arr. © 2015 by Hal Leonard Corporation. The story of an old salt, Paddy West, who kept a boarding house in Liverpool. Scouse=stew. On AL Lloyd & Ewan MacColl *Blow Boys Blow*, Lou Killen *50 Sailors Ships & Chanteys*. In *Shanties fr the 7 Seas*.

PAY ME MY MONEY DOWN

I thought I heard the Captain say, **pay me my money down**
Tomorrow is our sailing *[your salary]* day, **pay me my...**

C - - G / - - - C

**Pay me, oh pay me *[you owe me]*, pay me my money down
Pay me or go to jail *[Mr Stevedore]*, pay me my...**

The very next day we cleared the bar, **pay me...**
He knocked me down with the end of a spar, **pay...**

I wish I was Mr. Howard's son...
Sit in the house & drink good rum...

I wish I was Mr. Steven's son...
Sit on the bank & watch the work done...

*If I had-a known the boss was blind...
Oh wouldn't-a went to work until half past 9...*

*I heard them talkin' in the deck below...
If you don't pay me, this ship won't go...*
    — w & m: Lydia A. Parrish

TRO - © 1942 (renewed) Hollis Music, Inc., New York, NY. On Springsteen *We Shall Overcome: The Seeger Sessions*. Italicized lyrics are fr Revels rec *Blow Ye Winds in the Morning*. This version includes the reference to "Mr Stevedore" that Lomax collected fr Af-Amer workers in Savannah in 1944. Also rec by The Weavers, Kingston Trio, Dan Zanes. In *Coll Reprints fr SO!* V1-6.

ROUND THE BAY OF MEXICO

'Round that Bay of Mexico / **Way oh, Susianna!**
Mexico is the place that I belong in / **'Round the Bay of Mexico**

C - G C / - - F C / F Em Dm G / C - G C

Wind from the East & it's blowin' strong / **Way oh...**
Looks like a hurricane comin' along, well / **'Round...**

Wind will blow & that rain will pour
Better get the sugar boats up on the shore, now
    Why those young gals love me so?
    'Cos I don't tell ev'rything that I know
When I was a young man & in my prime
Court those young girls 10 at a time, boys
    Nassau girls ain't got no comb
    Comb their hair with a whipper back bone
When I leave the sea, I'll settle down
With a big, fat mama from Bimini town
    — Collected, adapted & arranged by John A. Lomax & Alan Lomax

TRO © 1941 (renewed) Ludlow Music, Inc., New York, NY. Rec by Belafonte, Weavers, Kingston Trio. In *Coll Reprints fr SO!* V1-6.

SANTA LUCIA

Sul mare luccica l'astro d'argento
Placida è l'onda, prospero è il vento (repeat)
    Venite all'agile barchetta mia
    Santa Lucia! Santa Lucia! (repeat)

(in 3/4) G D7 - G (4x) ‖: G C Edim G / - D7 - G :‖

Con questo zeffiro, così soave
Oh com'è bello star sulla nave! (repeat)
    Su passegieri, venite via! / **Santa...** (repeat)

O dolce Napoli, o suol beato
Ove sorridere volle il creato (repeat)
    Tu sei l'impero dell'armonia / **Santa...** (repeat)

Now 'neath the silver moon ocean is glowing
O'er the calm billows, soft winds are blowing
Here balmy breezes blow, pure joys invite us
And as we gently row, all things delight us

    Hark, how the sailor's cry joyously echoes nigh:
    Santa Lucia, Santa Lucia! (repeat)

When o'er the waters light winds are playing
Thy spell can soothe us, all care allaying
To thee sweet Napoli, what charms are given
Where smiles creation, toil blest by heaven

— Ital w: Teodoro Cottrau based on a Neapolitan folksong

Arr © 2015 by Hal Leonard Corporation. Borgo Santa Lucia is the beautiful waterfront district of Naples. In *Fireside Bk of Folk S*. There are 3 more Italian v. Cottrau transcribed the orig. Neapolitan lyrics, translated them into Italian & published them in 1849.

Schedar

I am the Schedar, the star-christened schooner
And I am the bridge 'tween the sea & the land
And my hull is wood as it was in the old days
I'm **out on the water again**

(↑2)   C - F G / C G F G / 1st / C G F -

Out where the whale-fishes roam
Where the stars still guide the way
I am the traveler's home
And on the waves I will play
The wind fills my sails with a poem

Dm - G - / C - Am - :‖ F - G -

We are the crew on the good schooner Schedar
And we are all handy, both woman & man
We are quite ready as soon as you want to
Go out on the water again

And we are the singers who sail on the Schedar
And if we're becalmed, well then we'll lend a hand
We fill the sails with the sound of our voices
We're off on our journey again

The crew is on board & we've taken on water
The gear is all stowed & we're ready to sail
It's back off the dock & then into the harbor
We're **out on the water...**

— w & m: Peter Fischman

© 1980 Peter Fischman. On his *Far East Kitchen* ↑4 & on The Beans' *2nd Hand Songs*. About a schooner the author crewed on. *LS

Shawneetown

Some rows *[poles]* up, but we floats down
Way down the Ohio to Shawneetown
Hard on the beech oar, she moves too slow
Way down to Shawneetown on the Ohio

D - D G D / - - A D :‖

Now the current's got her & we'll take up the slack
Float her down to... & bushwhack her back
    The whiskey's in the jug, boys, the wheat is in the sack
    We'll trade 'em down in... & bring the rock-salt back

I got a wife in Louisville & one in New Orleans
And when I get to..., gonna see my Indian Queen
    The water's mighty warm, boys, the air is cold & dank
    And the cursed fog it gets so thick that you cannot see the bank
Those keelboat boys call loud & long
Round as a barrel & they're twice as strong
    Oh I like to fight, I can take my knocks
    But not like last Sat. night at the Cave-in-Rock
The sun is mighty hot boys, got blisters on my feet
Drifting down to... to earn my bread & meat

— w & m: Dillon Bustin

© 1975 (renewed) Dillon Bustin. 1st verse & refrain adap fr historical printed fragments, additional by Dillon Bustin. On Martin Simpson *Collection*, Dalglish & Larsen *1st of Autumn*, Curley Maple *AthFest 2009*, Wintergreen Trio *Pass It On Down*, Sam Pascetti *Solitary Travel*, The Beans *2nd Hand Songs*. In *SO!* 41:3. Folklorist Bustin 1st learned this while working as a fisherman on the White River in Indiana. He coll. addl vs. fr travel logs & novels of keelboat era.

Shoals of Herring

(intro – freely) With our n<u>e</u>ts & gear we're f<u>a</u>ring
On the w<u>i</u>ld & wasteful oc<u>ea</u>n
It's th<u>e</u>re on the deep that we h<u>a</u>rvest & reap our bread
As we h<u>u</u>nt the bonny shoals of h<u>e</u>rring

(in 3/4) G - D G / - - D - / G C G D G - / - - C D G -

O it w<u>a</u>s a fine & a pleasant day
Out of Y<u>a</u>rmouth harbour I was f<u>a</u>ring
As a c<u>a</u>bin boy on a sailing l<u>u</u>gger
For to g<u>o</u> & hunt **the shoals of herring**

G - - - - - / - - - D - - / <u>G</u> D C D E<u>m</u> - / <u>G</u> - C D <u>G</u> -

O the work was hard & the hrs were long
And the treatment sure it took some bearing
There was little kindness & the kicks were many
As we hunted for the...

O we fished the Swarth & the Broken Bank
I was a cook & I'd a quarter-sharing
And I used to sleep, standing on my feet
And I'd dream about...

O we left the home grounds in the month of June
And to canny Shields we soon was bearing
With a hundred cran of the silver darlings
That we'd taken from...

Now you're up on deck, you're a fisherman
You can swear & show a manly bearing
Take your turn on watch with the other fellows
While you're following...

In the stormy seas & the living gales
Just to earn your daily bread you're daring
From the Dover Straits to the Faroe Islands
While you're following...

Well I earned me keep & I paid me way
And I earned the gear that I was wearing
Sailed a million miles, caught 10-million fishes
We was following...

— w & m: Ewan MacColl

© 1959 (renewed) Harmony Music Ltd. O/B/O Stormking Music Inc. Rec by Clancy Bros, Dubliners, Corries, Luke Kelly, Spinners, Leon Rosselson. In *Coll Reprints fr SO!* V1-6.

SONNY'S DREAM

Sonny don't go away, I am here all alone
And your daddy's a sailor who never comes home
And the nights get so long & the silence goes on
And I'm feeling so tired, I'm not all that strong

`G - - - / G - C G / D - - - / C - G D`

Sonny lives on a farm, on a wide open space
Where you can kick off your shoes & give up the race
You could lay down your head by a sweet river bed
But Sonny always remembers what it was his mama said
　　Sonny carries a load tho' he's barely a man
　　There ain't all that to do, but he does what he can
　　And he watches the sea from a room by the stairs
　　And the waves keep on rollin', they've done that for yrs
It's a hundred miles to town, Sonny's never been there
And he goes to the hwy & he stands there & stares
And the mail comes at 4 & the mailman is old
And he still dreams his dreams full of silver & gold
　　Sonny's dreams can't be real, they're all stories he's read
　　They're all stars in his eyes, and dreams in his head
　　And he's all hungry inside for the wide world outside
　　And I know I'll never hold him tho' I've tried & I've tried & I tried

— w & m: Ron Hynes

© 1976 (renewed) Ronald Hynes. On his cut on the *Singalong & Shanties* compilation, Christy Moore *Rise On*, Carl Peterson *Pirate S.*, Liam Clancy, YT video w/ Mary Black, Dolores Keane & Emmylou Harris.

SWEET ROSEANNA

Sweet Roseanne, sweet Roseanne / **Bye-bye, sweet Roseanna**
I thought I heard my baby say / **I won't be home tomorrow**
Sweet Roseanne, my darlin' child / **Bye-bye, sweet...**
Sweet Roseanne, my darlin' child / **I won't be...**

`D - / - A7 / - - / - D :‖`

Bye-bye (x4) / Bye-bye, sweet... / Bye-bye (x4) / I won't...

`D - / - A7 / - - / - D`

The steamboat comin' 'round the bend / **Bye-bye, sweet...**
She's loaded down with harvest men / **I won't be home...**
Don't you want to go home on your next payday? / **Bye-bye...**
Don't you want to go home... / **I won't...**

Sweet Roseanne, sweet Roseanne... / **Bye-bye...**
Sweet Roseanne, sweet.../ **I won't...**
I'm goin' away, but not to stay... / **Bye-bye...**
I'm goin'... / **I won't...**

　　— w & m collected: the Bright Light Quartette (Lawrence Hodge, Arnold
　　　　Fisher, James Campbell, Robert Beane, Shedrick Cain), & Alan Lomax

TRO © 1960 (renewed) Ludlow Music, Inc., New York, NY. Cain, Campbell, Fisher & Hodge were Afr-Amer fishermen in VA tidewater country rec by Lomax in 1960. On Lomax *So. Journey V. 1*. Rec by Holdstock & MacLeod, Eliz LaPrelle. In *Coll Reprints fr SO!* V7-12.

WE SAIL THE OCEAN BLUE

We sail the ocean blue & our saucy ship's a beauty
We're sober men & true & attentive to our duty
When the balls whistle free o'er the bright blue sea, we stand to
　　our guns all day
When at anchor we ride on the Portsmouth tide we have plenty
　　of time to play

`C - G C /　/ F C G C / F C B7 Em`

Ahoy! **(x2)** the balls whistle free, Ahoy! **(x2)** o'er the bright blue
　　sea / We stand to our guns, to our guns all day

`Em B7Em x2 / Em - G -`

We sail the ocean blue...
Our saucy ship's a beauty, we're attentive to our duty
We're sober men & true, we sail the ocean blue

`C - G C /　/ F C F C / F C G - C -`

　　— w: William S. Gilbert, m: Sir Arthur Sullivan

Arr. © 2015 by Hal Leonard Corporation. In *HMS Pinafore.*

WINDY OLD WEATHER

In this windy old weather, stormy old weather,
Boys, when the wind blows, we'll all go together
Up jumped the herring, the king of the sea
He sang out, old skipper, now you can't catch me

(in 3/4) `C - F - / G7 - - C - / C - F C / F C Dm G7`

Up jumped the mackerel with his striped back
He sang out, old skipper, come haul your main tack

Up jumped the sprat, the smallest of all
He sang out, old skipper, come haul your trawl haul

Up jumped the crab with his great long claws
He sang out, old skipper, you'll run us ashore

Up jumped the herring, right under the lee
He sang, drifting's finished, why bother catch me?

　　— trad.

Arr. © 2015 by Hal Leonard Corporation. On Harry Cox *What Will Become of England?* Ewan MacColl & Peggy Seeger *Now Is the Time for Singing*, Pete Seeger *Bitter & the Sweet* & rec by Clancy Bros & Tommy Makem, Dan Zanes & Bob Roberts.

WITH CAT-LIKE TREAD UPON OUR PREY WE STEAL

With cat-like tread upon our prey we steal
In silence dread our cautious way we feel
No sound at all, we never speak a word
A fly's foot-fall would be distinctly heard

`C - F C / - - G C / 1st / C G D G`

Tarantara, Tarantara
So stealthily the pirate creeps while all the household soundly sleeps

`Em - - - / EmB7 Em x2`

Come friends, who plough the sea
Truce to navigation, take another station
Let's vary piracy / With a little burglary (repeat)

`C - - - / G7 - - - / C - - - / Em D7 Em -`
`/　"　/　"　/ C - D7 F / C G C -`

(2nd bridge) Tarantara with cat like tread, tarantara in silence dread

`Em B7Em x2`

　　— w: William S. Gilbert, m: Sir Arthur Sullivan

Arr. © 2015 by Hal Leonard Corporation. Sung by Samuel & chorus in *Pirates of Penzance*.

The previous **Seas & Sailors chapter** includes sailors' work songs, often called shanties or chanteys (same pron.). Rhythms vary by work songs accompanied, e.g. halyards (hauling a rope to raise a sail), capstans (steady walking in a circle to raise an anchor), pumping (up & down) chanteys etc. Most are sung *a cappella*, usually as call-&-response led by a chanteyman. Off work, sailors sang forecastle (fo'c's'le) songs or forebitters accompanied by concertina, fiddle or any instrument that ight be handy.

There are more sea songs in **Pub Songs chapter**. Songs elsewhere include **Ballads**: Henry Martin **Earthcare**: Call me the whale, I am a dolphin, My dirty stream **Faith**: Nearer my God to thee **Golden**: Beyond the Sea, By the beautiful sea, Moonlight Bay, Old Cape Cod **Home**: River that runs both ways **Hope**: Ready for the storm **Love**: Bring me a boat **Motown**: The tide is high **Old-timey**: Handsome Molly, Sail away ladies, Storms are on the ocean, Waves on the sea **Peace**: Reuben James **Play**: Jenny Jenkins **Surfing**: Proud Mary.

Sing People Sing!

AMERICAN PIE

(intro) A long, long time ago, I can still remember
How that music used to make me smile
And I knew if I had my chance that I could make those people dance
And maybe they'd be happy for a while
But February made me shiver with every paper I'd deliver
Bad news on the doorstep, I couldn't take 1 more step
I can't remember if I cried when I read about his widowed bride
But smth touched me deep inside the day the music died

GD Em Am C / Em D7 - / 1st / Em Am D - /

Em Am x2 / C↓ Am C D / GD Em Am C / GD Em C D G -

So **bye-bye, Miss American Pie**
Drove my Chevy to the levee, but the levee was dry
Them good old boys were drinkin' whiskey & rye
Singin' "This'll be the day that I die
This'll be the day that I die"

G C G D / / / Em - A7 - / Em - D7 -

Did you write the book of love & do you have faith in God above
If the Bible tells you so?
Now do you believe in rock & roll, can music save your mortal soul
And can you teach me how to dance real slow?
Well I know that you're in love with him 'cos I saw you dancin' in the gym
You both kicked off your shoes, man I dig those rhythm & blues!
I was a lonely teenage broncin' buck with a pink carnation & a pickup truck
But I knew I was out of luck **the day the music died**, I started **singing**:

G Am C Am / Em D - / GD Em Am C / Em A7 D7 -
Em D Em D / C↓ Am C D /   "   / GD Em C D G -

Now for 10 yrs we've been on our own & moss grows fat on a rollin' stone / But that's not how it used to be
When the jester sang for the king & queen in a coat he borrowed from James Dean / And a voice that came from you & me

Oh & while the king was looking down, the jester stole his thorny crown
The courtroom was adjourned, no verdict was returned,
And while Lenin read a book on Marx, the quartet practiced in the park
And we sang dirges in the dark, **the day... we were singing**:

Helter skelter in a summer swelter, the birds flew off with a fallout shelter
8 miles high & falling fast
It landed foul on the grass, the players tried for a forward pass
With the jester on the sidelines in a cast
Now the halftime air was sweet perfume while the sergeants played a marching tune
We all got up to dance, but we never got the chance!
'Cos the players tried to take the field, the marching band refused to yield
Do you recall what was revealed, **the day... we started singin'**:

And there we were all in one place, a generation lost in space
With no time left to start again — so come on
Jack be nimble, Jack be quick, Jack Flash sat on a candlestick
'Cos fire is the devil's only friend
Oh & as I watched him on the stage, my hands were clenched in fists of rage
No angel born in Hell could break that Satan's spell!
And as the flames climbed high into the night to light the sacrificial rite
I saw Satan laughing with delight, **the day... he was singin'**:

(as intro) I met a girl who sang the blues & I asked her for some happy news / But she just smiled & turned away
I went down to the sacred store where I'd heard the music yrs before / But the man there said the music wouldn't play
And in the streets, the children screamed, the lovers cried & the poets dreamed
But not a word was spoken, the church bells all were broken
And the 3 men I admire most: The Father, Son & the Holy Ghost
They caught the last train for the coast, **the day... they were...**

— w & m: Don McLean

CALLING JOE HILL

Where are the languages we spoke, sparks from the anvil
When we were music-minded folk – **calling Joe Hill?**
Calling calling, calling Joe Hill (2x)

(↑2) CEm FC Am G / FG Am DmG FC :‖

Rhymes in the broken beechwoods ring, tuneless & chill
Into the darkness echoing, **calling...**
    Leaves in the wildernesses fall, fearing no ill
    Down to the deepest note of all...

Thru the archangel-haunted night, true songs may still
Quicken the dreamer's 2nd sight...
    Teller of elemental wrongs, teach me the skill
    Maker to maker, tongue to tongue...

Songs for the hopelessness of friends hauled thru the mill
Songs with a meaning in the end...
    These are the heart's imaginings when there's a will
    Even the broken beechwoods sing...

    — w & m: Ray Hearne

© 2001 Voice Publishing. On his *Broad St Ballads* & Roy Bailey *New Directions in the Old* ↑5.

CANCIÓN A VÍCTOR

Trigo‿y maíz era tu voz, mano de sembrador
Alma de cobre, pan y carbón, hijo del tiempo‿y del sol **(2x)**

(↑4) EmAm x2 Em Bm / AmD GAm EmB7 E /   /

Tu canto fue flor de metal, grito de multitud
Arma‿en el puño trabajador, viento del norte‿y del sur...

Caíste allí junto‿a‿otros mil cuando nació‿el dolor
Hoz y martillo tu corazón, rojo de vida se abrió...

El pueblo así te regará en su jardín de luz
Serás clarín de lucha y‿amor ¡Canto de Chile serás!...

    — w: Jorge Coulón, m: Horacio Salinas

© 1974 (renewed) Jorge Coulón & Horacio Salinas. On their (Inti-Illimani) *Hacia La Libdertad*

CHRISTMAS IN WASHINGTON
(Come Back, Woody Guthrie)

It's Christmastime in Wash., the Democrats rehearsed
Gettin' into gear for 4 more yrs of things not gettin' worse
The Republicans drank whiskey neat & thanked their lucky stars
They said, "He cannot seek another term, there'll be no more FDRs"
And I sat home in Tennessee just staring at the screen
With an uneasy feeling in my chest & I'm wonderin' what it means

(↑3) C - F - / G - FC :‖ (3x)

So come back Woody Guthrie, come back to us now
Tear your eyes from paradise & rise again somehow
If you run into Jesus, maybe he can help us out
Come back Woody Guthrie to us now

C - F - / G - FC / - - F - / GFC -

I followed in your footsteps once back in my travelin' days
But somewhere I failed to find your trail, now I'm stumblin'
    thru the haze
But there's killers on the hwy now & a man can't get around
So I sold my soul for wheels that roll, now I'm stuck here in this town

C - F - / G - FC :‖

There's foxes in the hen house, & cows out in the corn
The unions have been busted, & their proud red banners torn
To listen to the radio you'd think that all was well
But you & me & Cisco know, it's going straight to hell

(as cho) So come back Emma Goldman, rise up old Joe Hill
The barricades are goin' up, they cannot break our will
Come back to us, Malcolm X & Martin Luther King
We're marching into Selma as the bells of freedom ring

    — w & m: Steve Earle

© 1997 Sarangel Music. All rights administered by BMG Rights Management (US) LLC. On his *El Corazón*, Joan Baez *Bowery Songs.*

CIRCLE OF SONG

Come join with me in the circle of song
The young & the old, the weak & the strong
Singing with one voice tho' we may speak different tongues
In the circle of song, we are one

(↑3) G D Em C /   /   / G D G -

Some sing of the past, of battles lost & won
Some sing of their dreams of a new day in the sun
Some sing out for love & some sing just for fun
In the circle...

G D C G / - D C D / G D Em C / G D G - /

Some sing of this land, the country of their birth
Some sing of this land, of the beauty of the earth
Some sing of this land, for all that it is worth / **In...**

Each of us must leave this place, go back to our home
Each of us must walk a path that must be walked alone &
Each of us will bear the fruit of the seeds that we have sown...

(French cho) *Viens avec moi dans ce cercle d'amis*
Où jeunes et moins jeunes, où grands et petits
Chantent d'une seule voix à travers leurs différences
Dans ce cercle d'amis tous unis

(Span cho) *Vamos a juntarnos con esta canción*
Joven y viejo, débil y fuerte
En todas lenguas cantando con una voz
En esta canción somos unidos

    — w & m: Tony Turner

© 1994 Tony Turner. Fr cho: Lucie-Marie Castonguay-Power. Sp cho: Gwen Temmel. *LS

COMMON GROUND

Voices are calling 'round the earth
Music is rising in the sea
The spirit of morning fills the air
Guiding my journey home
Where is the path beyond the forest?
Where is the song I always knew?
I remember it just around the bend
In the village the music never ends
In a circle of friends, in the circle of sound
All our voices will blend when we touch common ground

(↑2) D - / C G / Am Bm / G D :‖ Am Bm G D /   /

Voices are calling… home
Here is path beyond… forest / <u>Here</u> is the song I always knew
I remember it just… bend / In the <u>music</u> the <u>village</u> never ends
In a circle…

— w & m: Ivan Lins, Ronaldo Monteiro DeSouza, Paul Winter, Harry
Guth and Michael Holmes

DID YOU HEAR JOHN HURT

It was a frosty night, it was beginning to snow
And down the city streets, the wind began to blow
We all came to the cellar, we all emptied the bar
To hear a little old fellow play his shiny guitar

(in G) C - G - / D - G - :‖

Did you hear John Hurt play the "Creole Belle"
The "Spanish Fandango" that he loved so well?
And did you love John Hurt? Did you shake his hand?
Did you hear him sing his "Candy Man"? (2x)

G - - - / D - G - / 1st / C G D G /   /

On a straight back chair with his felt hat on
He tickled our fancies with his "Avalon"
And everybody passing down MacDougal Street
Would cock their heads & listen to the tappin' feet

— w & m: Tom Paxton

EMMYLOU

Oh the bitter winds are coming in
And I'm already missing the summer
Stockholm's cold but I've been told
I was born to endure this kind of weather
When it's you I find like a ghost in my mind
    I am defeated & I gladly wear the crown

G Bm Em Cmaj7 (5x - v2: 7x) / G Bm D -

I'll be your Emmylou & I'll be your June
If you'll be my Gram & my Johnny too
No, I'm not asking much of you
Just sing, little darling, sing with me

G - Cmaj7 - / Em - D - / 1st / Em D G -

So much I know, that things don't grow
If you don't bless them with your patience
And I've been there before, & I held up the door
For every stranger with a promise
But I'm holding back, that's the strength that I lack
Every morning keeps returning at my window
And it brings me to you & I won't just pass thru
    But I'm not asking for a storm

(bridge) And yes, I might have lied to you
You wouldn't benefit from knowing the truth
I was frightened but I held fast
I need you now at long last

Em D Cmaj7 G (4x)

— w & m: Johanna Soderberg & Klara Soderberg ("First Aid Kit")

FOLK SONG ARMY

We are the Folk Song Army
Every one of us cares
We all hate poverty, war & injustice
Unlike the rest of you squares

(↑3) C - F - / G - C - / A - Dm - / C G C G

There are innocuous folk songs, yeah
But we regard 'em with scorn
The folks who sing 'em have no social conscience
Why they don't even care if Jimmy Crack Corn

C - F - / G - C - / A - Dm - / G - C -

(bridge #1) If you feel dissatisfaction
Strum your frustrations away
Some people may prefer action
But give me a folk song any old day

Em - Bm - /   / F - C - / Dm - E7 G7

(as v.2) The tune don't have to be clever
And it don't matter if you put a coupla extra syllables into a line
It sounds more ethnic if it ain't good English
And it don't even gotta rhyme – excuse me: "rhyne"

(bridge #2) Remember the war against Franco?
That's the kind where each of us belongs
Tho' he may have won all the battles
We had all the good songs

(in 3/4) B7 - C - /   - - B7 - / 1st / C - B7 (G7)

So join in the Folk Song Army
Guitars are the weapons we bring
To the fight against poverty, war & injustice
Ready! Aim! Sing!

— w & m: Tom Lehrer

Great Tom Is Cast

1. Great Tom is cast &
2. Christ Church bells ring <u>one</u>, two, three, four, five
3. <u>Six</u> & Tom comes last

— w & m: Matthew White (17th c.)

Arr © 2015 by Hal Leonard Corporation. Great Tom is the hour bell in Tom Tower, at Christ Church, Oxford. In Rounds Galore.

High Over the Hudson

The news came over the air tonight
Pete Seeger went sailing today
Set out on the Hudson 'bout 9 o'clock
Searching for new songs to play
    Passed by Bear Mountain, making great time
    As the water slapped hard on the bow
    At Storm King he turned that boat into the wind
    Set the old "Woody G" on the prow! Now he's:

(in 3/4) G - / Em - / Am - / F D :‖

High over the Hudson
Sails headed for home
Hard on the breeze as it cuts thru the trees
Pete, you're not sailing alone
    You're high over the Hudson
    You've got one hell of a view
    Your battles are won, a new journey's begun
    Pete, we're singing with you (last time: with you)

G - / Em - / Am F / Am D :‖ (last time add **G -**)

The troubadour's life has its ups & its downs
Of that, there's so much that's been said
Pete spoke out for justice, year after year
A leader who actually led
    He sang out for freedom, he sang out for peace
    Taught thru the power of song
    Ahead of his time in all seasons of life
    He kept us all singing along! And he's:

Odetta & Mary say "Welcome good friend!"
And Woody & Faith both agree
That you lived your passion for 94 years
And you lived it with integrity
    Now we as your children and we as your friends
    Take up your mission of song
    As Toshi yells out, with a smile on her lips
    "Hey, Peter, what took you so long!" And you're / **High over...**

— w & m: Reggie Harris

Huddie Ledbetter Was a Helluva Man

Huddie Ledbetter was a helluva man
Huddie got his music from the heart of the land
In his voice you could hear John Henry's hammering
While his hands would "buck & wing" upon the big 12-string
Sometimes a lion, sometimes a lamb
Huddie Ledbetter was a helluva man
He's a long time gone _ but his songs live on _ (2x)

(↑4) G - / / D - / G - / B7 E / A DG / D - G - / /

Down in Louisiana 1888
There was a Black baby born into a White man's state
He saw the cane & cotton stretch for miles around
He heard his mama's voice a-singing when the sun went down
Into a world where having dark skin was a crime
Huddie was born & started serving his time / **He's...**

Teenage Huddie went to Shreveport town
There he got in trouble, was jailhouse bound
The odds were slim that he would get out alive
But somehow Huddie & his music survived
He escaped just once, was put back again
He was called Leadbelly by the rest of the men...

A collector, name o' Lomax, brought a record machine
Huddie sang 'em sweet & high, he sang 'em low & mean
For yrs to come, they would tell the tale
Of how Huddie Ledbetter sang his way out-a jail
Sayin' "If I had you, Governor, like-a you got me
I'd awake up in the morning & I'd set you free"...

He got his farewell ticket back in '49
He caught the Midnight Special on the Rock Island Line
But I bet you when he wakened from his earthly dream
He was wakened by a kiss from a gal named Irene
Now millions of people the whole world around
Are taking Huddie's hammer up & swinging it down!...

— w & m: Peter Seeger & Lorre Wyatt

I Want to Sing That Rock & Roll

I want to sing that rock & roll
I want to 'lectrify my soul
'Cos everybody been making a shout, so big & loud, been
    drowning me out
I want to sing that rock & roll

G - C G / - - A D / G - C - / 1st

I want to reach that glory land
I want to shake my savior's hand, &
I want to sing...

Em - C G / D - A D

I been a-traveling near & far
But I want to lay down my old guitar, &...

— w & m: Gillian Welch & David Rawlings

In My Family's House

There'll be joy, joy, joy in my family's house
In my family's... (x2) / There'll be joy, joy, joy...
There'll be peace, sweet peace

D - G D / A - D - /   / D A D -

There'll be homemade music in my...
(insert: guitar pickin', banjo playin', fiddle playin', etc.)
And we'll play the spoons in... /And we'll sing along...

— w & m: Bruce O'Brien

© 1989 Bruce O'Brien. On his *In...*, Bonnie Lockhart *Dreams Drums & Green Thumbs* 12. *LS

Last Call

The Cowboys are winning, the bar is doing okay
They won't mind paying me to play
Well I'm 10 days out on a 2-week Texas tour
I hit San Antonio today

C - G - / Am C F - / 1st / F G C -

This is a genuine roadhouse on the outside of town
The newest old dance hall around
They like songs about Texas & most things by Willie
They let the kids & the dogs run around

There's a sign on the back wall behind the bottles & stools
Announcing the "closing time" rules – it says:

G - Am - / D - G -

"You don't have to go home, but you can't stay here
Leave your change for the waitress & finish your beer
We all hope you have somebody you can hold tight
When it's last call, that's it for the night"

F - C - / G - C - / F - C Am - / F G C -

There are one dollar bills stuck to the ceiling
The table legs wear boots & blue jeans
There's a cowboy in the corner who can't rope a cowgirl
His pickup spits dirt when he leaves

Here's 2-year old Ruby, she smiles at me while I'm playing
Runs away before her mom can catch her
Everyone works here, or knows someone who does
Before long, the bar is self-serve

Then the bartender asks me to make the last call
So I read from the sign on the wall – I say: / "You don't…"

— w & m: Jim Henry

© 2000 Money Sink Music. On his *The Wayback*.

Leader of the Band

An only child alone & wild, a cabinet maker's son
His hands were meant for different work & his heart was known
   to none
He left his home & went his lone & solitary way
And he gave to me a gift I know I never can repay

(↑2) C F C Em F / Dm Am Dm F G / 1st / Dm Am Dm G C

A quiet man of music, denied a simpler fate
He tried to be a soldier once, but his music wouldn't wait
He earned his love thru discipline, a thundering, velvet hand
His gentle means of sculpting souls took me yrs to understand

The leader of the band is tired and his eyes are growing old
But his blood runs thru my instrument & his song is in my soul
My life has been a poor attempt to imitate the man
I'm just a living legacy to the leader of the band

F Em F C / Dm Am F Bb G / 1st / Dm Am Dm G

My brothers' lives were different for they heard another call
One went to Chicago & the other to St. Paul
And I'm in Colorado when I'm not in some hotel
Living out this life I've chose & come to know so well

I thank you for the music & your stories of the road
I thank you for the freedom when it came my time to go
I thank you for the kindness & the times when you got tough
And Papa, I don't think I said "I love you" near enough

— w & m: Dan Fogelberg

© 1981 EMI April Music Inc. & Hickory Grove Music. All rights controlled &
administered by EMI April Music Inc. On his *Innocent Age* (in Eb 18). Written as a
tribute to his father who conducted bands on the HS & college level.

Like Woody Done

Well his name was Woody Guthrie & way back in 1912
He came into this world kicking & a-fussing
And we came to love him well for a life spent trying to tell
How we all could change the things that we'd been cussing

(↑2) C - F - / C - G - / C - F - / C G C -

We just gotta **do like Woody done, like Woody done**
We just gotta **do like Woody done**
When folks said you cannot change things, Woody said,
   oh yes I can
'Cos a man can make a difference & that difference made
   the man
A hero we can turn to when it's time to make a stand
And our lesser angels say to cut & run
We just gotta do like Woody done

F - C - / - - G - / C - F - /   / / Am - G - / - - C -

Well his name was Woody Guthrie, & way back in 1912
He commenced a life of holy rabble rousing
Now with beat-up guitar cases and them bound-for-glory faces
You can number his disciples by the thousand

They just wanna **do like Woody done, like Woody done**
They just wanna **do like Woody…**

(bridge) 'Cos there ain't much right with a mouth kept shut tight
When your duty just might be to shout
And they're there ain't much wrong that the soul in a song
Can't make better if you sing it out / Just sing it out!

Bb F C - / Bb F C - / Bb F C - / - - G - / - C -

His name was Woody Guthrie & some hundred years ago
He came into this world kicking and a-yelling
And he never really quit & we're better 'cause of it
And the brave & shining truth that he was telling

— w & m: John Flynn

© 2012 Flying Stone Music (ASCAP). On his *Poor Man's Diamonds*.

MUSIC IN MY MOTHER'S HOUSE

There were wind chimes in the window, bells inside the clock
An organ in the corner, & tunes on a music box
We sang while we were cooking or working in the yard
We sang because *[altho']* our lives were really hard

G - C - / G - - D / G - GEm C / G D C G

There was music in my mother's house
There was music all around
There was music in my mother's house
And my heart's still full with the sound

G - C G / - - D - / 1st / G D C G

She taught us all piano but my sister had the ear
She could play the harmony for any song she'd hear
Well I don't claim much talent but I've always loved to play
I guess I will until my dying day

Those days come back so clearly altho' I'm far away
She gave me the kind of gifts that I love to give away
And when my mother died & she'd sung her last song
We sat in the living room, singing all night long

(bridge) Singing, lala lala **(x2)**
Singing the front porch songs, singing the old torch songs
Singing, lala... / Singing the hymns to send her home

C - G - / D - G - :|

— w & m: Stuart Stotts

© 1985 Stuart Stotts (BMI). On his *One Big Dance* & *I Carried the News*. On
Prairie Orchid *New Day*, MUSE *Coming into Our Voice* & recs by Holly Near,
Ronnie Gilbert, Tom Hunter, Bev Bos. *LS

MY IMAGES COME

My images come from the people who do the work
From the people who sing the songs, from the people who live the life
From the people who get along
A bottle of rum for the demon what always lurk
For the demon what do me wrong, for the fury what is my wife
For the struggle what is my song

C - CG C / FG C F G / CG C :|

It get me down sometime, it get me down but only
A little look around & I find that I am not so lonely
We in the same boat brother, we in the same boat sister

C GC C FC / C G C G / C GC x2

My images come from the pleasures I had before
From the pleasure I'm still to know, from the pleasure my dreams
    provide / From the pleasure what I bestow
A bottle of rum for the trouble what's at my door
For the trouble where'er I go, for the misfortune what I abide
And for the courage I'm trying to show

My images come from the woman what's on my knee
From the woman what's in my head, from the woman out in the sun
From the woman what shares my bed
A bottle of rum for a broken love's misery
For a love what has grown so dead, expectations my life's undone
For illusions what I've been fed

My images come from the world in which I live
From the world I know so well, from the world of change & light
From the world of which I tell
A bottle of rum for the feelings I cannot give
For the feelings what fears impel, for the screams of a fraughtful
    night / And for the time what is spent in hell

— w & m: Don Cooper

© 1983 New Mutant Music. On Bok, Muir & Trickett *All Shall Be Well Again* &
Gordon Bok *Because You Asked*.

OH, MANDOLIN

Oh mandolin, sing me a song
Sweet & soft to soothe my soul
I want to dance til the night is gone
And the sun burns away this bitter cold

Am - / Dm Am :|

Moonlight slides across the cracks in my floor
North wind howls like a wolf at my door
How many times have we been here before
Just you & me again?

G Am / / F Am / F G

Bring love back in an old melody
Heal my heart, take this sadness from me
Leave me with only my best memories
And play like only you can

— w & m: Herb McCullough, Susanne Taylor & Deborah Nims

© 2000 Songs of Universal, Inc., Pecan Pie Music, Inc., Syncronims Music &
Walden Holler Music. On Taylor Pie *Jubal*, The Tuttles *Endless Ocean* & Valerie
Smith *Turtle Wings*.

PAUL ROBESON SONG (Powerful Voice)

Oh what a powerful voice
Ringing out all over the land
Oh Mr. Paul Robeson
Singing out & taking a stand

C - F - / C - G - / 1st / Em F C (G7)

About a hundred yrs ago, a baby boy was born
Over in Princeton town
And he grew up singing for freedom & justice
Oh what a glorious sound!
    On the stage, on the screen, on the football field
    Seemed like nothing that he could not do
    But it was singing the songs of freedom & struggle
    Where his spirit really rang true
He said "Everyone must make a choice
To be a slave or to walk free
You can go whichever way you want
But freedom is for me"
    Paul Robeson's gone, but his voice remains
    You can hear it ringing over the hills
    When you sing out for freedom & you fight for justice
    His spirit is living still!

— w & m: Kevin Slick

© 1998 Nu Vu Du Music. On 2 of a Kind *Connections* 15. *LS

RISE UP SINGING

If you are weary & trying to find your way home
Well don't give up my friend, 'cos you are not alone
In a world full of trouble, you know trouble may find you
But I've got your medicine baby, this is what you do

D G A D (4x)

You've got to rise up,_rise up singing_
In time this too shall pass
You've got to rise up, rise up singing
_You know trouble ain't built to last

D - G - / A - D - / 1st / Em A D -

And when you're left standing with no hope inside
'Cos at the end of the tunnel someone's been dimming out the light
Well you can lose your way & end up far from home
Till the day you lose your voice, you cannot lose your song

You know life ain't easy & life will make you cry, but
So long as you're breathing you know you are still alive, and
When you're standing at the station waiting for your train
Don't you think you'll be singing, oh that sweet refrain

— w & m: May Erlewine

© 2007 May Erlewine. On Seth & May *Mother Moon.* *LS

ROLL ON WOODY

You were born with the heart of a cowboy
Okemah, the place you began
But right from the start the road called to your heart
So you set out to discover the land
    You hitched & you rode & you rambled
    With a passion that burned to be free
    And you lifted the stories of all that you met
    From the dust bowl of humanity

(↑3) **C G C - / C - G - / Am G C F / C - G -**
Am G Am - /   "   /   "   /   "   /

So roll on, Woody – Woody, roll on
You taught us well **by singing your song**
And now we're here to carry it on
Roll on, Woody, roll on / Oh, roll on, Woody, roll on

Am G C F / C - - G - / 1st / C - G - / C G F - - - C -

From the farmers, the miners, the old & the young
To the refugee women & men
You made a name by exposing the games
That kept good folks facin' the wind!
    In all those years of hard travelin'
    You often said you had no choice
    Your words made it clear / Don't give in to fear!
    And speak out so they hear your voice

So roll on Woody, – Woody, roll on
You took a stand **by singing your song...**

From the pastures of plenty to Columbia's shores
From the mountains right down to the sea
You said this land was our land to have
It's a land made for you & for me!
    But now, dear Woody, the tables are turned
    As the forces of greed try to win
    But we're bound for glory & we're up to the fight
    We won't be denied in the end!

So roll on, Woody – Woody, roll on
You gave us hope **by singing your song**
And now we're here to carry it on
Roll on, Woody, roll on / Oh, roll on, Woody, roll on

— w & m: Reggie Harris

© 2012 Reggie Harris. On Kim & Reggie Harris *Resurrection Day.*

SING PEOPLE SING

When I was four I had a toy made of plastic & of joy
A magic, musical machine from a drum, a stick & strings
I couldn't know as I would play, I'd live to meet the man one day
Playing songs that shaped my life & taught the world to sing

(↑2) **G ↓ C G / C G C D / 1st / C G CD G**

Oh hear the banjo ring
Hear the people sing
Hope changes everything
Sing, people, sing!

D - C G / C D G - / D C G Em / C D G -

The summer of my 18th year in San Francisco he'd appear
I jumped onto a trolley car alone & wondering
The "grove" was full when I got there, people came from everywhere
I climbed a redwood by the stage to watch the reveling

Years went by, I got a call, a festival in early Fall
Along the Hudson River shore, a harvest gathering
Asking me to volunteer to keep the river clean & clear
To celebrate the river's life & all the gifts she brings

(bridge) You stood up to McCarthy's rage, rallied for a living wage
Rode with Woody, marched with Dr. King
You patiently brought us along, taught us each & every song
With Toshi by your side you could do most anything

Em - A - / C D G - / 1st / C - D -

You showed us how the world could be, living with integrity
Together we create a force beyond imagining
As I observed your dimming light I felt a spark in me ignite
But I would trade it all today to hear your banjo ring

— w & m: Pat Humphries & Sandy Opatow

© 2014 Pat Humphries & Sandy O. Written shortly following Pete's death in Feb. 2014. In *SO!* 55:4.

SINGER OF SONGS

Singer of songs, writer of rhymes
Righter of wrongs, changer of times
You've found your place, you've planted a seed
Right where your deepest love meets the world's greatest need

(in C ↑2) F - C - / F - G - / 1st / FG AmG C -

When you were a kid you picked up a guitar
Don't know why you did, it's just who you are
You looked around, saw a lot that was wrong
So you set out to change the world with the power of song

You blew into town 4 hrs ago
3rd stop on the tour, 5 more to go
You stood on the stage, opened your soul
If everyone lived that way we could make the world whole

So thank you for this, this beautiful time
Such moments of bliss so hard to find
The songs that you sing, the stories you tell
It's what you were born to do & you do it so well

— w & m: Pat Lamanna

SINGIN' IN THE RAIN

I'm **singin' in the rain**, just **singin'**...
What a glorious feeling, I'm happy again
I'm laughing at clouds, so dark, up above
The sun's in my heart and I'm ready for love

(↑2) G - - - / - - Am - / - - - - / - D G -

Let the stormy clouds chase everyone from the place
Come on with the rain, I've a smile on my face
I'll walk down the lane with a happy refrain
Just singin', **singin'**...

— w: Arthur Freed, m: Nacio Herb Brown

SPOON OF SAND

Spoon of sand can tip the balance
Drops of water turn a mill
Way out here over the rainbow
Someone's standing, singing still

(↑2) C - F - / G - C - / 1st / C G C -

You weathered the storm, you finished the race
We see by the weary smile upon your face
You've stumbled & risen, you sang up the dawn
You kindled the fire, you carried the torch, you're passing it on

G - C - /   / F - Em - / C G C -

Dark clouds on the mtn, dead fish on the shore
The bottom-line bandits *[bankers]*, the vultures of war
You turn & you face them & when push comes to shove
Somehow you believe hate has to surrender, surrounded by love

You charted the waters, saw the river run clear
You raised the sail when we thought the journey would end in despair
At the darkest hour on the edge of the dawn
You caught the 1st light & gave us the vision to carry it on

— w & m: Charlie King

UKULELE LADY

(intro) I saw the splendor of the moonlight on Honolulu Bay
There's smth tender in the moonlight on Honolulu Bay
And all the beaches are full of peaches who bring their ukes along
And in the glimmer of the moonlight they love to sing this song:

CEm AmC AbG C /   / Am - Em - / CEm AmC D7 G

If you like a ukulele lady, ukulele lady like-a you
If you like to linger where it's shady, ukulele lady linger too
If you kiss a ukulele lady while you promise ever to be true
And she see another ukulele lady fool around with you
  Maybe she'll sigh, maybe she'll cry
  Maybe she'll find somebody else by & by?
To sing to when it's cool & shady where the tricky wicky
  wackies woo
If you like a ukulele lady, ukulele lady like-a you

CEm AmC x2 / G - - C :| F - C - / D7 - G - / 1st 2

— w: Gus Kahn, m: Richard A. Whiting

WALKING IN MEMPHIS

_Put on my blue suede shoes & I boarded the plane
Touched down in the land of the Delta Blues in the
 middle of the pouring rain
_W.C. Handy, won't you look down over me?
Yeah I got a 1st class ticket, but I'm as blue as a boy can be

FG CAm x2 /   / FG CAm FG C

Then I'm walking in Memphis, _ walking with my feet 10
 feet off of Beale
Walking in Memphis,_ but do I really feel the way I feel?

FG CAm x2 / FG CAm FG Csus (C Csus C)

_Saw the ghost of Elvis on Union Avenue
Followed him up to the gates of Graceland,
 then I watched him walk right thru
Now security they did not see him,
 they just hovered 'round his tomb
But there's a pretty little thing waiting for the King
 down in the Jungle Room

(bridge) They've got catfish on the table _ _
They've got gospel in the air _ _
And Rev. Green be glad to see you when you haven't got a prayer
_ _But boy you've got a prayer in Memphis _ _ _

Csus C x2 /   / E7 F D7 G / (tacet) FG CAm x2

Now Muriel plays piano every Friday at the Hollywood
And they brought me down to see her & they asked me if I
     would
_Do a little number & I sang with all my might
And she said "Tell me are you a Christian child?" & I said "Ma'am I
     am tonight!"

— w & m: Marc Cohn

© 1991 Sony/ATV Music Publishing LLC. All rights administered by Sony/ATV Music Publishing LLC, 424 Church Street, Suite 1200, Nashville, TN 37219. On his self-titled alb. At 32 Cohn met Muriel Wilkins, a little known club singer at a restaurant. She talked to him for an hr & asked him up to sing. He says she changed his life. WC Handy was a blues composer & musician widely known as the "Father of the Blues."

WAY OVER YONDER IN THE MINOR KEY

I lived in a place called Okfuskee
And I had a little girl in a holler tree
I said, little girl, it's plain to see
Ain't nobody that can sing like me (2x)

C - - F - - - / - - - C - - - / 1st / F - - C / G - - Am - - -

     She said it's hard for me to see
     How one little boy got so ugly
     Yes, my little girly that might be, but there
     Ain't nobody that can sing like me (2x)

Way over yonder in the minor key (2x)
There ain't nobody that can sing like me

F - - C - - - / Dm - - C - - - / G - - Am - - -

We walked down by the Buckeye Creek
To see the frog eat the goggle eye bee
To hear that west wind whistle to the east
There **ain't nobody...**
     Oh my little girly will you let me see
     Way over yonder where the wind blows free
     Nobody can see in our holler tree & there / **Ain't...**

Her mama cut a switch from a cherry tree
And laid it onto she & me
It stung lots worse than a hive of bees but there / **Ain't...**
     Now I have walked a long long ways
     And I still look back to my tanglewood days
     I've led lots of girls since then to stray sayin' / **"Ain't...**

— w: Woody Guthrie, m: Billy Bragg

© 1965 (renewed), 1998, 1999 Woody Guthrie Publications, Inc./admin. by Bug Music, Inc., a BMG Chrysalis Company & Chrysalis Music/admin. by Chrysalis Music Group, Inc., A BMG Chrysalis Company. On Bragg & Wilco *Mermaid Avenue*, in *SO!* 43:3. Bragg & Wilco put melodies to several Woody Guthrie lyrics for which Guthrie had not written music himself.

WE'LL PASS THEM ON

When <u>you're</u> gone (who will sing?) (x2)
When <u>you're</u> gone who will sing your songs?
You have **planted the simple seed of singing** <u>in our hearts</u>
And we'll sing them with each other as we **pass them on**
     <u>We'll</u> **pass** (pass them on) them on (pass...)
     We'll **sing** (pass...) your songs (pass...)
     You have **planted the simple seed of singing** in our hearts
     And we'll sing them with each other as we **pass...**

D - G - / D - A - / D D7 G - / D - A D //

A - D - /   / 3rd-4th

When <u>we're</u> gone (who will sing?) (x2)
When <u>we're</u> gone who will sing our songs?
We will **plant the simple seed of singing** <u>in the world</u>
And we'll sing them with the children who will **pass...**
     They'll **pass** (pass...) **them on** (pass...)
     They'll **sing** (pass...) <u>our</u> songs (pass...)
     We will plant **the simple seed of singing** in the world
     And we'll sing them with the children who will...

When <u>they're</u> gone (who...?) (x2)
When they're **gone** who will sing their songs?
They will **plant the simple seed of singing** <u>on the wind</u>
And the children of the future, they will **pass...**
     They'll **pass** (pass...) **them on** (pass...)
     They'll **sing** (pass...) their songs (pass...)
     They will **plant the simple seed of singing** on the wind
     And the children of the future, they will...

— w & m: Sally Rogers

© 1993 Sally Rogers, Thrushwood Press Publishing. On her *We'll...* *LS

WOODSTOCK

I came upon a child of God, he was walking along the road
And I asked him, where are you going, & this he told me:
I'm going on down to Yasgur's farm, I'm going to join in a
     rock & roll band
I'm going to camp out the land, I'm going to try & get my soul free

Am - Dm7 - / - - Am - :|

We are stardust, we are golden
And we got to get ourselves back to the garden

Dm7 - - - / (2x in final cho)   Am G F D Am - - -

And can I walk beside you? I have come here to lose the smog
And I feel to be a cog in something turning
Well, maybe it is just the time of year, or maybe it's the time of man
I don't know who I am but life is for learning

By the time we got to Woodstock, we were half a million strong
And everywhere there was song & celebration
And I dreamed I saw the bombers riding shotgun in the sky
And they were turning into butterflies above our nation

(final cho) We are stardust, billion year old carbon
We are golden, we are caught in the devil's bargain
And we got to get ourselves back to the garden

— w & m: Joni Mitchell

© 1969 Crazy Crow Music. Copyright renewed. All rights administered by Sony/ATV Music Publishing LLC, 424 Church Street, Suite 1200, Nashville, TN 37219. On her *Ladies of the Canyon*, Crosby Stills Nash & Young Deja Vu, Eva Cassidy *Time After Time*.

WOODY'S CHILDREN

We are all Woody's children
We are all glory bound
When we smile, when we sing his songs
We show we know the truth he found

(in G) Am D G - / | / Am D G Em / 1st

In your Oklahoma home
A troubadour all set to roam
You & your family felt the Dust Bowl blow
You sang your songs & let us know
 You rode the rails as hobos do
 Saw hard-hit people scraping thru
 Took scattered voices feeling small
 You made a glorious chorus of us all
Every business man or woman in a suit
Every migrant farmer picking fruit
When they listen to your song
They know there's one family where we belong

You raised us well, so we became
Your children proud to share your name
Bound for glory – you showed the way
Bound together – that's how we'll stay
 Now we children know what to do
 It takes hard work to make a song come true
 The time has come to follow thru
 It's time to make this land for me & you

— w & m: Doug Mishkin

© 1987 Douglas B. Mishkin. On his *Woody's Children*. Seeger once said that all the folksingers who came after Woody Guthrie were "Woody's children." *LS

The **Sing People Sing** chapter contains songs celebrating singing, singers & influential songleaders, e.g.: Guthrie, Leadbelly, Mississippi John Hurt, Joe Hill, Seeger. See also: **Good Times** chapter (dancing, partying). Other songs include **Hope**: Lay down your weary tune **Jazz**: I got rhythm, **Musicals**: I whistle a happy tune **Rich**: Sing about these hard times, **Surfing:** Uncle John's Band

Struggle

AIN'T DONE NOTHIN' IF YOU AIN'T BEEN CALLED A RED

When I was just a little boy *[kid]* I used to love parades
With banners, bands, red balloons & maybe lemonade
When I came home one May Day my neighbor's father said
"Them marchers is all commies, tell me kid, are you a Red?"

G - A - / D - - G :|

Well I didn't know just what he meant, my hair back then
 was brown
Our house was plain red brick like many others in the town
So I went & told my daddy our neighbor called me red
My daddy took me on his knee & this is what he said

"Well ya ain't done nothing if ya ain't been called a Red
If you marched or agitated then you're bound to
 hear it said
So you might as well ignore it or love the word instead
'Cos ya ain't been doing nothing if ya ain't been…" (2x)

As I was growing up I had my troubles I suppose
When someone took exception to the contours of my nose
 [my face or to my clothes]
Or tried to cheat me on the job or hit me on the head
When I organized to fight back then those suckers called me Red

Then after I got married, one apartment that we had
Had a classic rotten rotten landlord, let me tell you he was bad
And when he tried to kick us out, I rubbed my hands & said
"You haven't had a struggle if you haven't fought a Red!"

So I kept on agitating, 'cos what else can you do?
Are you gonna let the sons-of-bitches walk all over you?
A friend said, "You'll get fired hanging with that Commie mob!"
I should only have such troubles, buddy, I ain't got a job!

So I been agitating now for fifty years and more,
For employment & equality & always against war,
And I'll keep doin' it forever, just as far as I can see,
And if that's what being Red is, then it's good enough for me!

— w & m: Eliot Kenin

© 1983 Eliot Kenin. On videos by him & by David Rovics & on Faith Petric *When Did We Have Sauerkraut*, Petric & Mark Ross *S of the IWW*.

CALL IT DEMOCRACY

Padded with power, here they come
International loan sharks backed by the guns
Of market-hungry military profiteers
Whose word is a swamp & whose brow is smeared
With the blood of the poor

D - / Bm G :| D - (G -)

Who rob life of its quality
Who render rage a necessity
By turning countries into labour camps
Modern slavers in drag as
Champions of freedom

Sinister cynical instrument
Who makes the gun into a sacrament
The only response to the deification
Of tyranny by so-called "developed" nations'
Idolatry of ideology

North, South, East, West
You kill the best & you buy the rest
It's just spend a buck to make a buck
You don't really give a flying f***
About the people in misery

(bridge) I.M.F. – dirty "M.F."
Takes away everything it can get
Always making certain that there's one thing left
Keep them on the hook with insupportable debt

A - / - GD :‖ (D G)

See the paid-off local bottom feeders
Passing themselves off as leaders
Kiss the ladies, shake hands with the fellows
And it's "Open for business" like a cheap bordello
And they call it democracy (4x)

D - / Bm G :‖(4x)

See the loaded eyes of the children, too
Trying to make the best of it the way kids do
One day you're going to rise from your habitual feast
To find yourself staring down the throat of the beast
They call the revolution   (to bridge)

(tag) And they call it democracy (4x)

D - Bm G (4x)

— w & m: Bruce Cockburn

© 1985 by Rotten Kiddies Music, LLC. On his *World of Wonders, Waiting for a Miracle.*
The International Monetary Fund (IMF) is blamed for many poorer countries'
problems & target of repeated protests around the world.

DANCE TO TOM PAINE'S BONES

As I dreamed out one evening
By a river of discontent
I bumped straight into old Tom Paine
As running down the road he went
He said, "I can't stop right now, my son
King George is after me
He'll have a rope around my throat
And hang me on the Liberty Tree"

C G Am F / C - G F :‖ (4x)   (2x on final verse)

And I will dance to Tom Paine's bones
Dance to Tom Paine's bones
Dance in the oldest boots I own
To the rhythm of Tom Paine's bones (repeat)

He said "I just spoke about freedom
Justice for everyone
Ever since the very first word I wrote
I've been looking down the barrel of a gun
They say I preached revolution
But let me say in my defense
All I did wherever I went
Was to talk a lot of Common Sense"

Well old Tom Paine he ran so fast
He left me standing still
And there I was, a piece of paper in my hand
Standing at the top of the hill
And it said "This is the 'Age of Reason'
These are the 'Rights of Man'
Kick off religion & monarchy"
It was written there in Tom Paine's plan

Old Tom Paine, there he lies
Nobody laughs & nobody cries
Where he's gone or how he fares
Nobody knows & nobody cares

— w & m: Graham Moore

© 1997 Graham Moore. On his *Tom...*, Roy Bailey *Coda*, Dick Gaughan *Outlaws &
Dreamers, Live!*, The Shee *Different Season*, Joe Solo *Forward Is Just Backwards*,
Stramash *The Uprising*. Paine's bones were brought back to his birthplace,
England, by William Cobbett. Paine (1737-1809) pamphlet *Common Sense* played
a key role in the Amer. Revolution. *Rights of Man* was written in defense of the
French Revolution. *The Age of Reason* attacked institutionalized religion.

DO YOU HEAR THE PEOPLE SING

Do you hear the people sing, singing a song of angry men?
It is the music of a people who will not be slaves again!
When the beating of your heart echoes the beating of the
**   drums**
There is a life about to start when tomorrow comes!

C - F C / Am D7 G - / 1st / Am DmG C - /

2nd & 3rd cho: G - C G / Em A7 D - / 1st / Em AmD G -

Will you join in our crusade?
Who will be strong & stand with me?
Beyond the barricade is there a world you long to see?
Then join in the fight that will give you the right to be free!

Em - Bm - / Am - Em - / C Am D -

Will you give all you can give so that our banner may advance
Some will fall & some will live, will you stand up & take your chance?
The blood of the martyrs will water the meadows of France!

— w: Alain Boublil, Jean-Marc Natel & Herbert Kretzmer

© 1980 by Editions Musicales Alain Boublil. English Lyrics © 1986 by Alain Boublil
Music Ltd. (ASCAP). Mechanical & publication rights for the US administered
by Alain Boublil Music Ltd. (ASCAP) c/o Joel Faden & Co., Inc., MLM 250 West
57th St., 26th Floor, New York, NY 10107, Tel. (212) 246-7203, Fax (212) 246-7217,
jfaden@joelfaden.com. In *Les Mis* 15. Victor Hugo's novel (which the musical is based
on) culminates in the anti-monarchist Paris Uprising that took place in June 1832.

EVE OF DESTRUCTION

The eastern world it is explodin'
Violence flarin', bullets loadin'
You're old enough to kill but not for votin'
You don't believe in war, but what's that gun you're totin?
And even the Jordan River has bodies floatin'
But you tell me over & over & over again my friend
Ah you don't believe we're on the eve of destruction

D GA (5x, v. 3 & 4: 7x) // D GA D Bm / G A D -

Don't you understand what I'm trying to say?
And can't you feel the fears I'm feeling today?
If the button is pushed, there's no running away
There'll be no one to save with the world in a grave
Take a look around you boy, it's bound to scare you boy...

Yeah my blood's so mad, feels like coagulatin'
I'm sittin' here, just contemplatin'
I can't twist the truth, it knows no regulation
Handful of senators don't pass legislation
And marches alone can't bring integration
When human respect is disintegratin'
This whole crazy world is just too frustratin' / And **you...**

Think of all the hate there is in Red China!
Then take a look around to Selma, Alabama!
Ah you may leave here for 4 days in space
But when your return, it's the same old place
The poundin' of the drums, the pride & disgrace
You can bury your dead, but don't leave a trace
Hate your next door neighbor, but don't forget to say grace...

— w & m: P.F. Sloan & Steve Barri

FREEDOM COME ALL YE

Roch the wind in the clear day's dawin
Blaws the cloods heilster-gowdie owre the bay
But there's mair nor a roch wind blawin
Thro the Great Glen o the warld the day
It's a thocht that wad gar oor rottans
Aa thae rogues that gang gallus fresh an gay
Tak the road an seek ither loanins
Wi thair ill-ploys tae sport an play   (in 3/4, ↑2)

GEmG CGC / G--- D--- / GEmG CGC / GGD GG(C)
GGC GEmC /   "   /   "   /   "   /

Nae mair will our bonnie callants
Merch tae war when oor braggarts crousely craw
Nor wee weans frae pitheid an clachan
Mourn the ships sailin doun the Broomielaw
Broken faimlies in lands we've hairriet
Will curse 'Scotlan the Brave' nae mair, nae mair
Black an white ane-til-ither mairriet
Mak the vile barracks o thair maisters bare

Sae come aa ye at hame wi freedom
Never heed whit the houdies croak for Doom
In yer hoos aa the bairns o Adam
Will find breid, barley-bree an paintit rooms
When Maclean meets wi's friens in Springburn
Aa thae roses an geans will turn tae blume
An the black lad frae yont Nyanga
Dings the fell gallows o the burghers doun

(singable transl) *Rough's the wind in the clear day's dawning*
Blow the clouds helter-skelter o'er the bay
But there's more than a rough wind blowing
Thru the Great Glen of the world today
It's a thought that would make our rodents
All those rogues that go cheeky fresh & gay
Take the road & seek other pasture
For their ill-ploys to sport & play

No more will our bonnie gallants
March to war when our braggarts saucily crow
Nor wee bairns from pithead & clachan
Mourn the ships sailing down the Clyde's flow
Broken families in lands we've harried
Will curse "Scotland the Brave" nae mair, nae mair
Black & white, one to another married
Make the vile barracks of their masters bare

So come all ye at home with freedom
Never heed what the carrion croak of Doom
In your house all the bairns of Adam
Will find bread, beer & brightly painted rooms
When MacLean meets with friends in Springburn
All the roses & trees will turn to bloom
And the Black lad from yon Nyanga
Tears the fell gallows of the burghers doon!

— w: Hamish Henderson

GOD'S COUNTING ON ME

When we look & we can see things are not what they should be
God's counting on me, God's counting on you
When we look & we see... / **God's counting...**

(↑5) C - Am - / F G C - / 1st / Dm G C -

Hopin' we'll all pull thru (3x), me & you

F G / CE Am / F G / C -

It's time to turn things around, trickle up not trickle down...
When drill baby drill turns to spill baby spill...
When there's big problems to be solved, let's get everyone involved...
Don't give up don't give in, workin' together we all can win...
What we do now, you & me, will affect eternity...
When we work with younger folks, we can never give up hope...

— w & m: Pete Seeger & Lorre Wyatt

HAVE YOU BEEN TO JAIL FOR JUSTICE?

Was it Cesar Chavez? maybe it was Dorothy Day
Some will say Dr. King or Gandhi set them on their way
No matter who your mentors are it's pretty plain to see
If you've been to jail for justice, you're in good company

(↑2) GC G C G / - Em A D / C G B7 Em / A7 - D -

Have you been to jail for justice? I want to shake your hand
Sitting in & lying down are ways to take a stand
Have you sung a song for freedom or marched that picket line?
Have you been to jail for justice? Oh you're a friend of mine!

GC G C G / - Em A D / C G B7 Em / GC G D G

You law abiding citizens, listen to this song
Laws were made by people & people can be wrong
Once unions were against the law, but slavery was fine
Women were denied the vote & children worked the mine
The more you study history the less you can deny it
A rotten law stays on the books 'til folks with guts defy it

GC G C G / - Em A D ‖: C G B7 Em / A7 - D - :‖

(as v1) The law's supposed to serve us & so are the police
And when the system fails, it's up to us to speak our peace
It takes eternal vigilance for justice to prevail
So get courage from your convictions, let them haul you off to jail!

— w & m: Anne Feeney

© 1999 Anne Feeney. On her *Have You…* & Peter Paul & Mary *In These Times*. In *SO!* 49:1.

I'M GONNA SAY IT NOW

Oh, I am just a student, sir & I only want to learn
But it's hard to read thru the risin' smoke from the books that
   you like to burn
So I'd like to make a promise & I'd like to make a vow, that
When I've got something to say, sir, I'm gonna say it now

C Am F C / Em Am D7 G / C Em F G / C Am FG C

Oh you've given me a number & you've taken off my name
To get around this campus why you almost need a plane
And you're supporting Chiang Kai-Shek while I'm supporting
   Mao, so / **When…**

I wish that you'd make up your mind, I wish that you'd decide
That I should live as freely as those who live outside
'Cos we also are entitled to the rights to be endowed &…

Ooh you'd like to be my father, you'd like to be my Dad
And give me kisses when I'm good & spank me when I'm bad
But since I left my parents, I've forgotten how to bow, so…

And things they might be different if I was here alone
But I've got a friend or 2 who no longer live at home
And we'll respect our elders just as long as they allow that…

I've read of other countries where the students take a stand
Maybe even help to overthrow the leaders of the land,
Now I wouldn't go so far to say we're also learnin' how but…

So keep right on a-talkin' & tell us what to do
But if nobody listens, my apologies to you
And I know that you were younger once 'cos you sure are older now &…

— w & m: Phil Ochs

© 1965 Barricade Music, Inc. Copyright renewed. All rights controlled & administered by Almo Music Corp. On his *There But for Fortune* ↑1.

IF YOU SAY YES

Somebody said "Gotta watch your step
Gotta close your eyes, gotta hold your breath"
Somebody said "If you say yes
Where will it lead (x2) / Where will it lead you?"
Somebody said "Gotta lock your car
Gotta draw the shades, gotta bolt the door"
Somebody said "If you say yes
Where will it lead (x2) / Where will it lead you?"   (↑5)

G - C D / G Em Am D / F C D Em / C - G D / Am D G - :‖

   But that fussy old crow's on the gutter again
   And a tufty little bird's in the backyard tree
   And I've worn holes in my blue jeans
   Down on my knees

   D G D G / Am - - Em / C D Em C / Em Am D -

Somebody said "If you sing too loud
Or you dance too wild, stick out in a crowd"
Somebody said "If you say yes
Where will it lead (x2) / Where will it lead you?"
Somebody said "If you rock the boat
If you climb too high, if you swim the moat"
Somebody said "If you say yes / Where…"

   But I ran outside in the howling rain
   And I thought, what have I got to lose
   For just a glimpse of some good news / **I'm down on…**

Somebody said "Don't act too smart
Don't start to cry, don't fall apart" / **Somebody…**
Somebody said "You aren't enough
Too soft & sweet, gotta just get tough" / **Somebody…**

   But I hear the beat of the strongest heart
   And I would walk a thousand miles
   For just the moment of your smile / **I'm down…**

Somebody said "You're so naive
To hope so hard, to just believe" / **Somebody…**
Somebody said "It'll stay the same
It's always been, it'll never change" / **Somebody…**

   But there's you now, a million strong
   And your voice there, a billion votes
   For just the smallest speck of hope / **I'm down…**

(last v.) Somebody said "Gotta watch your step
Somebody said "Gotta just get tough"
Somebody said "If you sing too loud
Or you rock the boat or you aren't enough"
Somebody said "If you say yes
Where will it lead, where will it lead / _ _ you?" _

G - C D (3x) / C D x2 / F C D Em / C - G D / Am D G -

— w & m: Cindy Kallet

© 2007 Cindy Kallet BMI. On her *Cross the Water* (w/ Grey Larsen ↑2) & in *SO!* 52:1.

JAILHOUSE DOOR

The jailhouse, the jailhouse it is an awful place
There was a time when only crime would merit such disgrace, but
Now if you should chance to say, you want to see a better day
You're liable to be put away with bars across your face

C - G C / G C F G / F - C - / D - G D G

Open up the jailhouse door (2x)
Open wide, open wide, for Democracy's inside
And we need her as we never did before

C G C - / F - C - / / F C G C -

The heroes **(x2)** who fight for peace & bread
They should be given glory but they're given chains instead
And if you want good company, for goodness sake don't look at me
They're all put under lock & key for fear they might be Red

It's lonely, it's lonely, within those prison gates
And Liberty's a prisoner, too, who languishes & waits
But when she hears our voices sound, she'll know we've got
    reaction downed
That wants to make a prison ground of these United States

Wisconsin, Wisconsin, Scott Walker's done you wrong
He says you need a permit just to sing a protest song
But if you'll join your voice with mine, we'll stand together &
    hold the line
And he can stick his permit where the sun don't shine,
    as we all sing along
    — w & m: Malvina Reynolds, new v by Paul Landskroener

© 1958 (renewed) Schroder Music Company (ASCAP). Verse 4 refers to a series of protest sings held at the state capitol in Madison in response to Gov. Walker's union-busting actions. Paul found this unrec song in a 1948 mimeographed Malvina SB. On Jan Hammerlund *Uncovered Malvina Reynolds* & YT video by Landskroener.

LET JUSTICE ROLL DOWN

There is no freedom, the wise man said
Let justice **roll down, roll down**
When the poor cry out for shelter & bread
Let justice **roll down like a mighty stream!**

C - F G / / / C Am G C -

Oh children, don't you get weary
Walk together, believe in that dream
When the way gets rough, we'll make a new way
Let justice **roll down like a mighty stream**

I: F - C G / C Am F G / 1st / C Am G C
II: F G Em Am / C Em F G / F G Em Am - / F Am G C -

Hatred will never drive out hate/ **Let** love...
Remember our hearts can make us great / **Let** love...

When brutality threatens our daughters & sons / **Let** peace...
May our voices ring out above the guns...

When fists rise up to strike a blow / **Let** songs...
May the poets remind us of what we know...

Step by step & one by one/**Let** justice...
They can kill the prophet but the dream lives on...
    — w & m: Aileen Vance

© 2004 Avenida Music. On Dean Steven *At Last* (cho II), Mystic Chorale (Nick Page) *20th Anniv* & YT by Kristen Lems & Joe Jencks. Cho I is author's: see *LS.

LONG KESH

I went down to Long Kesh **to see** Bobby Sands
He was not there but his spirit keeps on living
I could see his shining face on the men & on the women
And the children, they sang Freedom songs

C FC - G / FC FC G - / C FC FC Am / F G C -

I went down to Atlanta **to see** Martin King / **He was not...**
I... New York City to... Malcolm X / **He was**
I... Granada to... Maurice Bishop
I... El Salvador to... Oscar Romero
I went over **to** India **to...** Mahatma Gandhi / **He was not...**

I went down to Belfast **to see** Bernadette Devlin
She was **there & her spirit keeps on living**
I could see her **shining face on the men & on the women...**
    — w & m: Matt Jones

© 1983 Matt Jones (ASCAP), (c) 1997 Matt Jones (Wisdom Train). Matt Jones, freedom fighter & freedom singer/songwriter composed Long Kesh after a trip to N. Ireland in '82 w/ his friend Rev. Frederick Douglas Kirkpatrick (chronicled in the film *The Black & the Green*). Matt left a deep impression when he sang for people on the front-line of Irish Freedom. On the trip they visited the infamous prison, Long Kesh, where Bobby Sands & other Irish freedom fighters had been imprisoned. Sands died after a 66 day hunger strike protesting the conditions of IRA prisoners. When Matt returned to the US he made the cause of Irish Freedom an integral part of his message. On Magpie *Of Changes & Dreams*. Insert your own v. for those whose struggles & lives you remember & celebrate.

LOVE ME, I'M A LIBERAL

I cried when they shot Medgar Evers, tears ran down my spine
I cried when they shot Mr Kennedy as tho' I'd lost a father of mine
But Malcolm X got what was coming, he got what he asked for
    this time
So – love me (x3), I'm a liberal   (in 3/4)

CF CF C Am / CF C D7 G / CF C Em F / CAm FG C -

I go to civil rights rallies & I put down the old DAR
I love Harry & Sidney & Sammy, I hope every "colored" boy
    becomes a star
But don't talk about revolution – that's going a little bit too far
So love me...

I cheered when Humphrey was chosen, my faith in the system
    restored
I'm glad the commies were thrown out of the AFL-CIO board
I love Puerto Ricans & Negroes as long as they don't move next door
So – love me...

The people of old Mississippi should all hang their heads in shame
I can't understand how their minds work, what's the matter don't
    they watch Les Crane?
But if you ask me to bus my children, I hope the cops take down
    your name...

I read *New Republic & Nation*, I've learned to take every view
You know I've memorized Lerner & Golden,
    I feel like I'm almost a Jew
But when it comes to times like Korea there's no one more red,
    white & blue...

I vote for the Democratic Party, they want the UN to be strong
I attend all the Pete Seeger concerts – he sure gets me singing
    those songs
And I'll send all the money you ask for but don't ask me to come
    on along...

Sure once I was young & impulsive, I wore every conceivable pin
Even went to a socialist meeting, learned all the old union hymns
But I've grown older & wiser & that's why I'm turning you in...

— w & m: Phil Ochs

O GOD OF EARTH & ALTAR

O God of earth & altar, bow down & hear our cry
Our earthly rulers falter, our people drift & die
The walls of gold entomb us, the swords of scorn divide
Take not thy thunder from us, but take away our pride

Em B7 Em Am Em B7 / C D G C B7 Em
G D G B7 Em Am B7 / Em B7 Em C B7 Em

From all that terror teaches, from lies of tongue & pen
From all the easy speeches that comfort cruel men
From sale & profanation of honor & the sword
From sleep & from damnation, deliver us, good Lord!

Tie in a living tether the prince & priest & thrall
 [poor home & mighty hall]
Bind all our lives together, smite us & save us all
In ire & exultation, aflame with faith & free
Lift up a living nation a single sword to thee
 [with hearts knit one in thee!]

— w: Gilbert Keith Chesterton, m: trad. Welsh ("Llangloffan")

ONE VOICE IN THE CROWD

I've lived a life of privilege, I've never known what hunger is
I've never laboured with my hands except to play guitar
Middle class my middle name, life's been more or less a game
But in the end it's all the same, the buck stops where you are

G D G D / G D A D :‖

And **we are foolish people who do nothing**
Because we know how little one person can do
Yes, we are foolish people who do nothing
Because we know how little one can do

It's not my issue, not my scene, I've got to get my own house clean
I keep it neat & tidy just in case the queen should call
Come back to me another day & gladly I'll join in we say
And I'm just one voice anyway, just one brick in the wall

(bridge) One brick in the wall, you may be one voice in the crowd
But without you we are weaker & our song may not be heard
One drop in the ocean but each drop will swell the tide
So be your one brick in the wall, be one voice in the crowd

A - D A D / G D A - / 1st / G - - A

— w & m: Judy Small

THE RED FLAG

The People's *[workers']* flag is deepest red
It shrouded oft our martyred dead
And ere their limbs grew stiff & cold
Their life-blood dyed its every fold
Then raise the scarlet standard high!
Beneath its folds we'll live & die
Tho cowards flinch & traitors sneer
We'll keep the red flag flying here

(in 3/4) D - / A D :‖ D G / A D / 1st 2

Look 'round, the Frenchman loves its blaze
The sturdy German chants its praise
In Moscow's vaults its hymns are sung
Chicago swells the surging throng

It waved above our infant might
When all ahead seemed dark as night
It witnessed many a deed & vow
We will not change its color now

It suits today the meek & base
Whose minds are fixed on pelf & place
To cringe beneath the rich man's frown
And haul that sacred emblem down

It well recalls the triumphs past
It gives the hope of peace at last
The banner bright, the symbol plain
Of human right & human gain

With heads uncovered swear we all
To bear it onward 'til we fall
Come dungeons dark or gallows grim
This song shall be our parting hymn

— w: James O'Connell (1889), m:trad.

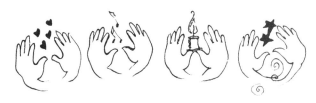

RISE AS ONE (Fowler)

We will march as one & we will stand as one
We will rise as one (repeat)

D - G - / D A D - :‖

We will rise as one (2x)
Working hand in hand / We will...

G A D - / / G A D Bm / G A D -

2. **We will** dance... sing...
3. **We will** laugh... cry...
4. **We will** fight... win...

— w & m: Aaron Fowler

RISE AS ONE (Jencks)

It is we who serve the lunches, we who sweep the floors
We who drive the buses with your children off to school
We keep the buildings warm in winter & cool when it's hot
And we will not let you play us for the fool
When we ask for better healthcare or an increase in our wage
You tell us that the township can't afford to pay the bill
But you found half a million dollars fr within those very coffers
To try & break the union's back & break our will

(↑2) G - C G / - - D - / 1st / G D G - :‖ (2x)

We will never give up, we will never give in
And we'll never, ever go away
We will build a brand new future for our daughters & our sons
We will work til all workers rise as one

G - C G / - - D - / 1st / G D G -

We believe in education & the future of our town
And the children that we serve from day to day
Whenever there's a need we always go the extra mile
God knows we do it for the love, not for the pay
But we have worked as hard as any for every inch of ground
That we've gained in the struggle for our rights
And we will not stand by idly as you try to tear us down
If we have to, we will organize a strike

Well we didn't have a penny in our strike fund, sad but true
And that made us all a little bit afraid
But the call went out to every other union in the state
And somehow all the workers' bills were paid
You see this isn't just our struggle & it isn't just our jobs
And it isn't just the schools within our town
When we dare to raise our voice in solidarity we stand
With every other worker all the world around

We held a rally at the fairgrounds to show them our resolve
And to drum up some support for our campaign
A thousand people hit the street & that's more than half our town
And after that you know things couldn't be the same
Now whoever would've guessed it when this whole thing began
We'd have the strength to hold out for so long
But 3 mos. have now gone by & the school board just gave in
On their demands, now we can sing our victory song!

— w & m: Joe Jencks

© 2002, 2005 Joe Jencks/Turtle Bear Music (ASCAP). On his *Rise As One & I Hear Your Voice*. *LS

SI ME QUIERES ESCRIBIR

Si me quieres escribir ya sabes mi paradero _ (2x)
En el frente de Gandesa primera línea de fuego
En el frente de Gandesa primera línea de fuego _

Em B7 Em (B7) /   / Em DC B7 / Em D* C B7 - (*1 beat only)

Si tú quieres comer bien barato y de buena forma _ (2x)
En el frente de Gandesa allí tienen una fonda
En el frente de Gandesa allí tienen una fonda _

En la_entrada de la fonda hay un moro Mojamed _ (2x)
Que te dice "Pasa, pasa qué quieres para comer"
Que te dice "Pasa, pasa qué quieres para comer" _

El primer plato que dan son granadas rompedoras _ (2x)
El segundo de metralla para recordar memorias
El segundo de metralla para recordar memorias _

— trad. (Span. Civil War)

Arr. © 2015 by Hal Leonard Corporation. Rec by Almanac Singers in 1941. Re-released on Folkways *S of the Span Civil War (V1)*. On *Spain in My Heart*. Also rec by Ronnie Gilbert & the Weavers.

SÓLO LE PIDO A DIOS

Sólo le pido_a Dios
Que_el dolor no me sea_indiferente
Que la reseca muerte no me_encuentre
Vacío y solo, sin haber hecho lo suficiente

C G Am - / F Em Dm - / C - G - / F Em Am -

Sólo le pido... / Que lo_injusto no me sea_indiferente
Que no me_abofeteen la_otra mejilla
Después que una garra me_arañó esta suerte

Sólo... / Que la guerra no me sea_indiferente
Es un monstruo grande_y pisa fuerte
Toda la pobre inocencia de la gente

Sólo... / Que_el engaño no me sea_indiferente
Si_un traidor puede más que unos cuantos
Que_esos cuantos no lo_olviden fácilmente

Sólo... / Que_el futuro no me sea_indiferente
Desahuciado_está_él que tiene que marchar
A vivir una cultura diferente

Sólo... / Que la guerra no me sea_indiferente
Es un monstruo grande_y pisa fuerte
Toda la pobre inocencia de la gente

— w & m: León Gieco

© 1979 SADAIC Latin Copyrights, Inc. Rec by Gieco, Mercedes Sosa, Ana Belén, Antonio Flores, Pibes Chorros, Mexicanto.

STILL LOOKING FOR FREEDOM

If you're looking for freedom, **you won't find it alone**
If we walk that road together, freedom**'s gonna light the**
way home

(insert:) justice, peace (sweet peace!), victory, the union, **etc.**

(last v:) If you're still looking for freedom...

(↑3) G D Em G / Am7 D G (D)

(tag) Freedom's gonna light the *[find a]* way (x2)
Freedom's gonna light the way home

Am7 D x2 / Am7 D G -

— w & m: Jon Fromer

© 2004 Jon Fromer (BMI). On his *We Do the Work* 13.

TALKIN' ABOUT A REVOLUTION

**_Don't you know they're talkin' about a revo-lution -
it sounds** (like a whisper) **(2x)**

`GC EmD GC EmD /   /`

While they're standing in the welfare lines,_ _
  _crying at the doorsteps of those armies of salvation
_Wasting time in the unemployment lines,
  _sitting around waiting for a promotion / **Don't...**

Poor people gonna rise up& get their share_ _ _
Poor people gonna rise up& take what's theirs _ _ _

_Don't you know, you better run **x4** run **x4** run **x3** run _ _ _
_Oh I said you better run **x4** run **x4** run **x3** run _ _ _

_Yes finally the tables are starting
  to turn, talkin' bout a revolution _ **(2x)**

**_Don't you know they're talkin' about a revo-lution -
it sounds** (like a whisper) **(2x)**

    — w & m: Tracy Chapman

WE ARE THE MANY

Ye come here & gather 'round the stage
The time has come for us to voice our rage
Against the ones who've trapped us in a cage
To steal from us the value of our wage
    From underneath the vestiture of law
    The lobbyists at Washington do gnaw
    At liberty, the bureaucrats guffaw
    And until they are purged, we won't withdraw

`(↑2) D A D - / A G Bm - :‖ (4x)`

**We'll occupy the streets, we'll occupy the courts
We'll occupy the offices of you
'Til you do the bidding of the many / Not the few** _

`G - A - / D - G - / A - GA / D - - -`

Our nation was built upon the right
Of every person to improve their plight
The laws of this republic they rewrite
And now a few own everything in sight
    They own it free of liability
    They own, but they are not like you & me
    Their influence dictates legality
    And until they are stopped we are not free / **We'll occupy…**

You enforce your monopolies with guns
While sacrificing our daughters & sons
But certain things belong to everyone
Your thievery has left the people none
    So take heed of our notice to redress
    We have little to lose, we must confess
    Your empty words do leave us unimpressed
    A growing number join us in protest / **We occupy…**

You can't divide us into sides
And from our gaze you cannot hide
Denial serves to amplify
And our allegiance you can't buy

Our govt is not for sale
The banks do not deserve a bail
We will not reward those who fail
We will not move 'til we prevail
We'll occupy…

(tag) We are the many, you are the few

`G - A - D - - -`

    — w & m: Makana

WE SHALL RISE

I have been a long time traveling thruout this mighty land
With my pack upon my back & this guitar in my hand
There are people, things & places I haven't ventured yet
For everything that I remember there's a dozen more that I forget

`D - DG D / - - - A / 1st / D DA D -`

I have known my share of trouble but one thing I've learned is true
That the times are like the people, it's the good ones see me thru
And there is a light that guides me when they both turn hard & mean
And by the flame of that small candle now let me tell you just
    what I've seen

I have seen the men & the women that make this old world turn
Seen their pride & seen their passion, felt the fire that
    makes them burn
I've watched them struggle with their demons, seen the angels fill
    their eyes / And their face as they discover we shall rise

**We shall rise (x2)
From the silence, from the shadows, we will stand & recognize
All the ones who've gone before us, the promise of the prize
Ever spoken, never broken, we shall rise**

`G A DG D / - - GA / D - - G / D A D -`

And I have seen the sweat of the farmer wrestle supper from the soil
Felt the muscle of the miner in the cool, dark day of toil
And in the office, the home & the factory, still I see to my surprise
Midst the trouble & the triumph we shall...

And I have heard the hounds of history ever baying at my door
Heard the cries & the curses as the dead shout ever more
And I have heard the quiet voice of truth 'midst the thunder of the lies
It's not a threat, it is a promise, **we...**

It will rattle the foundations, it will stop the hands of time
It will part the mighty oceans, it will wear the rainbow sign
It will be heard by even silent ears & seen by blinded eyes
It will happen without warning, **we...**

And the chains will all be broken, the locks will all fall free
The doors will swing wide open for the whole, wide world to see
And the powerful will understand as the scales fall from their eyes
It is not given, it is taken...

(tag) And when we finally stand in judgment before
    our children's eyes / Not a soul will be forgotten, **we...**

`D - - G / DG DA D -`

    — w & m: John McCutcheon

The **Struggle** chapter includes songs that have played a critical role in social change movements including Afr-Amer civil rights, struggles for labor unions, Irish resistance to British rule, the anti-apartheid movement in South Africa & struggles to end war, among many. The Peoples Music Network brings together activist singers in US & Canada.

See also **Dignity & Diversity**, **Earthcare**, **Freedom**, **Hope & Strength**, **Peace**, **Rich & Poor**, **Work**. Other songs include **Country**: Pancho & Lefty, **Gospel**: Soon & very soon (alt. lyrics in notes under song) **Home**: I am a patriot **Millennial**: Amer idiot **Sing**: Christmas in Washington, **Time**: Temps des cerises.

Surfin' USA

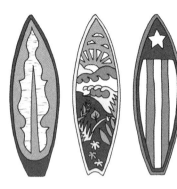

ANGEL OF THE MORNING

There'll be no strings to bind your hands
Not if my love can find your heart
And there's no need to take a stand
For it was I who chose to start
I see no need to take me home
I'm old enough to face the dawn

G C D C (4x) / Am C D - /   /

Just call me angel of the morning, angel
Just touch my cheek before you leave me, baby
Just call me… / Then slowly turn away / From me

G C D CD /   /   / C - - - / G (C D C)

Maybe the sun's light will be dim
But it won't matter anyhow
If morning's echo says we've sinned
Well, it was what I wanted now
And if we're victims of the night
I won't be blinded by the light
   — w & m: Chip Taylor

BAD BAD LEROY BROWN

Well the South Side of Chicago
Is the baddest part of town
And if you go down there, you better just beware
Of a man named Leroy Brown
Now Leroy more than trouble
You see he stand about 6 ft 4
All those downtown ladies call him "Treetop Lover"
All the men just call him "Sir"

G - / A7 - / B7 C / D G(D) :‖ (1x only on cho & last verse)

And he's bad, bad Leroy Brown
The baddest man in the whole damn town
Badder than old King Kong
Meaner than a junkyard dog

Now Leroy he a gambler / And he like his fancy clothes
And he like to wear his diamond rings / In front of everybody's nose
He got a custom Continental
He got a Eldorado too
He got a .32 gun in his pocket for fun
He got a razor in his shoe

Well Friday 'bout a week ago / Leroy shootin' dice
And at the edge of the bar sat a girl name of Doris
& ooh that girl looked nice
Well he cast his eyes upon her / & the trouble soon began
Leroy Brown, he learned a lesson 'bout messin'
With the wife of a jealous man

Well the 2 men took to fightin'
And when they pulled them from the floor
Leroy looked like a jigsaw puzzle
With a couple of pieces gone
   — w & m: Jim Croce

BAD MOON RISING

I see the bad moon a-risin'
I see trouble on the way
I see earthquakes & lightnin'
I see bad times today
Don't go around tonight, well it's bound to take your life
There's a bad moon on the rise

D AG D - (4x) // G - D - / A G D -

I hear hurricanes a-blowin'
I know the end is comin' soon
I fear rivers overflowin'
I hear the voice of rage & ruin

Hope you got your things together
Hope you are quite prepared to die
Looks like we're in for nasty weather__
One eye is taken for an eye
   — w & m: John Fogerty

BARBARA ANN

Ba-ba-ba, Ba-ba-bara Ann (2x)
Barbara Ann _ / Take my hand_ / Barbara Ann_
You got me rockin' & a-rollin', rockin' & a-reelin'
Barbara Ann Ba-ba, Ba-ba-bara Ann

E - /   /   / A - / E - / B7 A / E -

Went to a dance, lookin' for romance
Saw Barbara Ann, so I thought I'd take a chance
Barbara Ann / Take my hand
You got me rockin' & a-rollin', rockin' & a-reelin'
Barbara Ann, Ba-ba, Ba-ba-bara Ann

E - /   / A - / E - / B7 A / E -

Tried Peggy Sue, tried Betty Lou
Tried Mary Lou, but I knew she wouldn't do
Barbara Ann / Take my hand... (as v1)

— w & m: Fred Fassert

BROWN EYED GIRL

Hey where did we go, days when the rains came
Down in the hollow, playin' a new game
Laughing & a-running hey, hey, skippin' & a-jumpin'
In the misty morning fog with our hearts a-thumpin' &
You, my brown eyed girl
You, my brown eyed girl

G C G D (4x) // C D G Em / C D G (D)

Whatever happened to Tues. & so slow
Going down the old mine with a transistor radio
Standing in the sunlight laughing, hiding behind a rainbow's wall
Slipping & sliding all along the waterfall
With **you, my...**

Do you remember when we used to sing
"Shalala lalalala lalalala teda" – just like that:
"Shalala…"

D - / G C G D /   /

So hard to find my way now that I'm all on my own
I saw you just the other day, my how you have grown
Cast my memory back there, Lord, sometime I'm overcome
   thinking 'bout
Making love in the green grass behind the stadium with...

— w & m: Van Morrison

DON'T KNOW WHY

I waited til I saw the sun
I don't know why I didn't come
I left you by the house of fun
I don't know why I didn't come (2x)

Cmaj7 C7 Fmaj7 E7 / Am D7 G7 C :‖ Am D7 G7 C

   When I saw the break of day
   I wished that I could fly away
   Instead of kneeling in the sand
   Catching teardrops in my hand

   Cmaj7 C7 Fmaj7 E7 / Am D7 G7 C :‖

(bridge) My heart is drenched in wine
But you'll be on my mind forever

Am - D7 - G - - - / Am - D7 - G F Em Dm

   Out across the endless sea
   I would die in ecstasy
   But I'll be a bag of bones
   Driving down the road alone **(to bridge)**

Something has to make you run
I don't know why I didn't come
I feel as empty as a drum / **I don't know why... (3x)**

— w & m: Jesse Harris

DON'T STOP BELIEVIN'

Just a small town girl, livin' in a lonely world
She took the midnight train goin' anywhere
Just a city boy, born & raised in south Detroit
He took the midnight train goin' anywhere
A singer in a smoky room , a smell of wine & cheap perfume
For a smile they can share the night, it goes on & on & on & on

C G Am F / C G Em F :‖ (3x)

Strangers waiting, up & down the blvd
Their shadows searching in the night
Street lights, people, living just to find emotion
Hiding, somewhere in the night

F - C - /   /   / F - GC GF (C G Am F)

Working hard to get my fill„ everybody wants a thrill
Payin' anything to roll the dice just one more time
Some will win, some will lose, some were born to sing the blues
Oh the movie never ends, it goes on & on & on & on

C G Am F / C G Em F :‖

(tag) Don't stop believin', hold on to the feelin'
Street lights people

C G Am F / C G Em F

— w & m: Steve Perry, Neal Schon & Jonathan Cain

FRIEND OF THE DEVIL

I lit out from Reno, I was trailed by 20 hounds
Didn't get to sleep that night til the morning came around

Set out runnin' but I take my time, a friend of the devil
is a friend of mine
If I get home before daylight, I just might get some sleep
Tonight

`GD EmG CG AmG / / D - Am - / / D - - -`

Ran into the devil, babe, he loaned me 20 bills
I spent the night in Utah in a cave up in the hills

I ran down to the levee but the devil caught me there
He took my 20 dollar bill & he vanished in the air

(bridge) Got 2 reasons why I cry away each lonely night
The 1st one's named sweet Anne Marie & she's my heart's delight
The 2nd one is prison, babe, the sheriff's on my trail
And if he catches up with me, I'll spend my life in jail

`D - - - / C - - - / D - - - / Am - C D - - -`

Got a wife in Chino, babe & one in Cherokee
The 1st one says she's got my child, but it don't look like me

— w: Robert Hunter, m: Jerry Garcia & John Dawson

© 1970 Ice Nine Publishing Co., Inc. Copyright renewed. All rights administered by Universal Music Corp. On Grateful Dead *Amer Beauty*.

FUN FUN FUN

Well she got her daddy's car & she cruised thru the hamburger
stand now
Seems she forgot all about the library like she told her old man now
And with the radio blasting goes cruising just as fast as she can now

And she'll have fun fun fun til her daddy takes
the T-bird away

`C - F - / C - G - / 1st / CEm FG CF C(G)`

Well the girls can't stand her 'cos she walks, looks, & drives like
an ace now (you walk like an ace now, you walk like an ace)
She makes the Indy 500 look like a Roman chariot race now
(you look like an ace now, you look like an ace)
A lotta guys try to catch her, but she leads them on a wild goose
chase now (you drive like an ace..) / **And she'll have...**

Well you knew all along that your dad was gettin' wise to you
now (you shouldn't 've lied, now **x2**)
And since he took your set of keys you've been thinking that
your fun is all thru now (you shouldn't 've...)
But you can come along with me 'cos we gotta a lot of things to
do now (you shouldn't...)
And we'll have **fun fun fun** now that **daddy** took **that...**

— w & m: Brian Wilson & Mike Love

© 1964 Irving Music, Inc. Copyright renewed. Recs by Beach Boys ↑3, Carpenters, Jan & Dean.

HAPPY TOGETHER

Imagine m<u>e</u> & you, I d<u>o</u>
I think about you d<u>a</u>y & night, it's only r<u>igh</u>t
To think about the g<u>ir</u>l you love & hold her t<u>igh</u>t
So happy together

`(↑3) Am - / G - / F - / E -`

If I should c<u>a</u>ll you up, invest a dime
And you say you bel<u>o</u>ng to me & ease my mind
Imagine how the w<u>or</u>ld could be, so very fine / **So...**

I can't see me lovin' nobody but you for all my life
When you're with me, baby the skies'll be blue for all...

`A Em A C / /`

Me & you & you & me
No matter how they toss the dice, it had to be
The only one for me is you & you for me / **So...**

(tag) So happy together, how is the weather?
So happy..., we're **happy...** etc.

`Am E :‖ (as needed)  A`

— w & m: Garry Bonner & Alan Gordon

© 1966, 1967 by Alley Music Corp. & Trio Music Company. Copyright renewed. All rights for Trio Music Company controlled & administered by Bug Music, Inc., a BMG Chrysalis company. On The Turtles *Happy*... (in F#m ↑9).

HELPLESSLY HOPING

Helplessly hoping, her harlequin hovers
Nearby awaiting a word
Gasping at glimpses of gentle true spirit
He runs, wishing he could fly only to
Trip at the sound of goodbye

`Am - C - / G - D - :‖ Am7 C G - D -`

Wordlessly watching, he waits by the window
And wonders at the empty place inside
Heartlessly helping himself to her bad dreams
He worries did he hear a good-bye / Or <u>even_hello?_</u>
They are <u>1</u> person, they are <u>2</u> alone
They are <u>3</u> together, they are <u>4</u> for / Each other _ _

`Am - C - / G - D - :‖ Am7 C G C / G - - - /`
`- - - Dm7 / C - G -`

Stand by the stairway, you'll see something certain
To tell you confusion has its cost
Love isn't lying, it's loose in a lady
Who lingers, saying she is lost / And choking on hello
They are...

— w & m: Stephen Stills

© 1969 Gold Hill Music, Inc. Copyright renewed. On *Crosby, Stills & Nash*.

I FEEL THE EARTH MOVE

I feel the earth move under my feet
I feel the sky tumbling down
I feel my heart start to trembling
Whenever you're around

`(↑3) Am7 - - D7 / Am7 - - - / D7 - - - / Am7 - D6 -`

Ooh, baby, when I see your face
Mellow as the month of May
Oh darling, I can't stand it
When you look at me that way

`Cmaj7 - Fmaj7 - / Dm7 - G7 - / 1st / Dm7 - G7E7`

Ooh darling, when you're near me
And you tenderly call my name
I know that my emotions
Are smth I just can't tame (I've just got to have you, baby)

(tag:) I feel the earth move under my feet

I feel the sky tumbling down, tumbling down
I just lose control / Down to my very soul
I get a hot & cold / All over **(x4)** / **I feel the earth**, etc.

Am7 - D7 - :‖ **(as needed)**

— w & m: Carole King

© 1971 (renewed 1999) Colgems-EMI Music Inc. On her *Tapestry*.

I GOT A NAME

Like the pine trees lining the winding road
I got a name, I got a name
Like the singing bird & the croaking toad
I got a name, I got a name
And I carry it with me like my daddy did
But I'm living the dream that he kept hid

(↑4) C G Am - / F G C - / 1st / D - G - /
Em F C E / Am D G -

Moving me down the hwy, rolling me down the hwy
Moving ahead so life won't pass me by

Em F Em A7 / F G Bb - -

Like the north wind whistling down the sky
I've got a song, I've got a song
Like the whippoorwill & the baby's cry
I've got a song, I've got a song
And I carry it with me & I sing it loud
If it gets me nowhere, I go there proud

(bridge) And I'm gonna go there free

C - - -

Like the fool I am & I'll always be
I've got a dream, I've got a dream
They can change their minds but they can't change me
I've got a dream, I've got a dream
Well, I know I can share it if you want me to
If you're going my way, I'll go with you

— w: Norman Gimbel, m: Charles Fox

© 1973 (renewed) Warner-Tamerlane Publishing Corp. On Jim Croce *I Got a...* 14, Lena Horne *Lady & Her Music* & Helen Reddy *Love S for Jeffrey*. In '73 film *Last Amer Hero*.

IN MY ROOM

There's a world where I can go & tell my secrets to
In my room, in my room
In this world I lock out all my worries & my fears / **In my...**
     Do my dreaming & my scheming, lie awake & pray
     Do my crying & my sighing, laugh at yesterday
Now it's dark & I'm alone but I won't be afraid / **In my...**

(↑2) G - - -   G F G Em / Am F D -   G F G - :‖

Em - D - Em D Em D G - / Em - D - Am C - D / above 2

— w & m: Brian Wilson & Gary Usher

© 1964 Irving Music, Inc. Copyright renewed. Rec by Beach Boys on *Surfer Girl* 14, Linda Ronstadt on *Dedicated to the One I Love*, Wilson Phillips on *California*.

LOVE THE ONE YOU'RE WITH

If you're down & confused
And you don't remember who you're talking to
Concentration slips away
Because your baby is so far away, well

G Gsus Gsus - G (4x)

There's a rose in a fisted glove
And the eagle flies with the dove
And if you can't be with the one you love, honey
Love the one you're with / Love the one... (2x)

Em D C - / / / / G Gsus Gsus - G / /

Don't be angry, don't be sad
Don't sit crying over good times you've had
There's a girl right next to you
And she's just waiting for something to do, and...

(doo doo doo...)

Turn your heartache right into joy
'Cos she's a girl & you're a boy
Get it together, make it nice
You ain't gonna need any more advice / And...

— w & m: Stephen Stills

© 1970 Gold Hill Music, Inc. Copyright renewed. Orig solo '70 rec by Stills, often performed by Crosby Stills & Nash in conc.

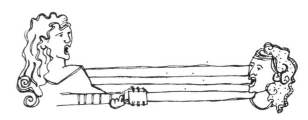

PEACEFUL EASY FEELING

I like the way your sparkling earrings lay
Against your skin, so brown
And I wanna sleep with you in the desert tonight
With a billion stars all around, 'cos

D G D G / D G A - :‖

I got a peaceful easy feeling
And I know you won't let me down
'Cos I'm already standing
On the ground

G - D - / G - Em A / D Em G A / D - - -

And I found out a long time ago
What a woman can do to your soul
Oh but she can't take you any way
You don't already know how to go, and

I get this feeling I may know you
As a lover & a friend
But this voice keeps whispering in my other ear
Tells me I may never see you again, 'cos **I get...**

— w & m: Jack Tempchin

© 1972 (renewed) WB Music Corp. & Jazz Bird Music. All rights administered by WB Music Corp. On *Eagles* 12 & Kate Wolf *Give Yourself to Love* 15.

PROUD MARY

Left a good job in the city
Workin' for the Man every night & day
But I never lost a minute of sleepin'
Worryin' 'bout the way things might have been

D - - - (4x)

**Big wheel keep on turnin' / Proud Mary keep on burnin'
Rollin', rollin' / Rollin' on the river**

A - - - / Bm - - - / D - - - / / /

Cleaned a lot of plates in Memphis
Pumped a lot of 'pane down in New Orleans
But I never saw the good side of a city
Til I hitched a ride on the riverboat queen

If you come down to the River
Bet you're gonna find some people who live
You don't have to worry 'cos you have no money
People on the river are happy to give

You get a job on the Clearwater
Better not mind about the kind of pay you get
It may sound funny, you make hardly any money
But you'll be richer by far than you ever been yet

— w & m: John Fogerty (new v. Pete Seeger)

RED RUBBER BALL

I should have known you'd bid me farewell
There's a lesson to be learned from this & I learned it very well
Now I know you're not the only starfish in the sea
If I never hear your name again it's all the same to me

G Bm C G / G Bm Am D / C D G Em / Am Bm C B7

**And I think it's gonna be all right, yeah the worst is over now
The morning sun is shining like a red rubber ball**

Em - Am - / D - C G

You never cared for secrets I'd confide
For you I'm just an ornament, smth for your pride
Always running, never caring, that's the life you live
Stolen minutes of your time were all you had to give

The story's in the past with nothing to recall
I've got my life to live, & I don't need you at all
The roller coaster ride we took is nearly at an end
I bought my ticket with my tears, that's all I'm gonna spend

— w & m: Paul Simon & Bruce Woodley (of The Seekers)

SURFIN' USA

If everybody had an ocean across the U.S.A.
Then everybody'd be surfing like California
You'd see 'em wearin' their baggies, Huarache sandals too
A bushy, bushy blond hairdo, **surfin' USA**

(in C) G - C - / / F - C - / 1st

You'd catch 'em surfin' at Del Mar, Ventura Co. Line
Santa Cruz & Trestles, Australia's Narrabeen
All over Manhattan & down Doheny way
Everybody's gone surfin', **surfin'**…

We'll all be planning out a route, we're gonna take real soon
We're waxing down our surfboards, we can't wait for June
We'll all be gone for the summer, we're on safari to stay
Tell the teacher we're surfin'…

At Haggerty's & Swami's, Pacific Palisades
San Onofre & Sunset, Redondo Beach, LA
All over La Jolla & Waimea Bay
Everybody's gone surfin'…

— w & m: Chuck Berry

SWEET CAROLINE

Where it began, I can't begin to knowin'
But then I know it's growin' strong
Was in the spring & spring became a summer
Who'd have believed you'd come along
    Hands, touchin' hands
    Reachin' out, touchin' me, touchin' you

(↑2) G - C - / G - D - :‖ G - Em - / D - C - D -

**Sweet Caroline,_good times never seemed so good_
I've been inclined_to believe they never would but now I**

G C - - D - / G C - - DC BmAm

Look at the night, and it don't seem so lonely
We fill it up with only 2
And when I hurt, hurtin' runs off my shoulders
How can I hurt when holding you?
    Warm, touchin' warm
    Reachin' out, touchin' me, touchin' you

— w & m: Neil Diamond

THESE BOOTS ARE MADE FOR WALKIN'

You keep saying you got something for me
Something you call love but confess
You've been a' messin' where you shouldn't 've been a-messin'
And now someone else is getting all your best

A - - - / / D7 - - - / A - - -

**Well, these boots are made for walking
   & that's just what they'll do
One of these days these boots are gonna walk all over you**

C A C A / C A tacet A

You keep lyin' when you oughta be truthin'
You keep losing when you oughta not bet
You keep samin' when you oughta be a-changin'
Now what's right is right but you ain't been right yet

You keep playing where you shouldn't be playing
And you keep thinking that you'll never get burned
Well I've just found me a brand new box of matches
And what he knows you ain't had time to learn

— w & m: Lee Hazlewood

TIME AFTER TIME

Lying in my bed I hear the clock tick & think of you
Caught up in circles, confusion is nothing new
Flashback, warm nights, almost left behind
Suitcase of memories, time after
    Sometimes you picture me I'm walking too far ahead
    You're calling to me, I can't hear what you've said
    Then you say, go slow, I fall behind
    The second hand unwinds

FC x4 /   / FG EmF FG Em / FG EmF FG

FC x4 /   / FG EmF FG Em / FG EmF

If you're lost you can look & you will find me, time after…
If you fall I will catch you, I'll be waiting, time… (repeat)

G Am FG C :‖ (4x)

After my picture fades & darkness has turned to gray
Watching thru windows, you're wondering if I'm OK
Secrets stolen from deep inside
The drum beats out of time

— w & m: Cyndi Lauper & Rob Hyman

UNCLE JOHN'S BAND

Well the 1st days are the hardest days, don't you worry any more
'Cos when life looks like easy street, there is danger at your door
Think this thru with me, let me know your mind
Wo-oh, what I want to know, is are you kind?
    It's a buck dancer's choice my friends, better take my advice
    You know all the rules by now & the fire from the ice
    Will you come with me? Won't you come with me?
    Wo-oh, what I want… will you come with me?

G - C* G /   / Am Em C D / CD G GD G :‖ (*3 beats)

Goddamn, well I declare, have you seen the like?
Their walls are built of cannonballs, their motto is don't tread on me
Come hear Uncle John's band playing to the tide
Come with me or go alone, he's come to take his
   children home

G GC AmEm D / C - GD CD :‖

It's the same story the crow told me, it's the only one he knows
Like the morning sun you come & like the wind you go
Ain't no time to hate, barely time to wait
Wo-oh… where does the time go?
    I live in a silver mine & I call it beggars' tomb
    I got me a violin & I beg you call the tune
    Anybody's choice, I can hear your voice
    Wo-oh… how does the song go?

Come hear Uncle John's band by the riverside
Got some things to talk about, here beside the rising tide
Come hear Uncle John's band playing to the tide
Come on along or go alone, he's come to take…

— w: Robert Hunter, m: Jerry Garcia (of Grateful Dead)

UP ON CRIPPLE CREEK

When I get off of this mountain, you know where I want to go
Straight down the Mississippi River to the Gulf of Mexico
To Lake Charles Louisiana, Little Bessie, girl that I once knew
She told me just to come on by if there's anything that she could do

G - C - / G - D - :‖

Up on Cripple Creek, she sends me
If I spring a leak, she mends me
I don't have to speak, as she defends me
A drunkard's dream if I ever did see one

G - / C - / D - / Em F - -

Good luck had just stung me, to the race track I did go
She bet on one horse to win and I bet on another to show
The odds were in my favor, I had 'em 5 to one
When that nag to win came around the track, sure enough
   we had won

I took up all of my winnings, and I gave my little Bessie half
And she tore it up & threw it in my face just for a laugh
Now there's one thing in the whole wide world I sure would
   like to see
That's when that little love of mine dips her donut in my tea

Now me & my mate were back at the shack, we had Spike Jones
   on the box
She said "I can't take the way he sings, but I love to hear him talk"
Now that just gave my heart a throb to the bottom of my feet
And I swore as I took another pull my Bessie can't be beat

There's a flood out in Calif. & up north it's freezing cold
And this living off the road is getting pretty old
So I guess I'll call up my big mama, tell her I'll be rolling in
But you know deep down I'm kind of tempted to go &
   see my Bessie again

— w & m: Robbie Robertson

WALK AWAY RENÉE

And when I see the sign that points one way
The lot we used to pass by every day
Just walk away Renée, you won't see me follow you back home
The empty sidewalks on my block are not the same
You're not to blame   (↑2)

G D F Am / Cm G C A / G Em C GD / G Em C Bm / C↓ G

From deep inside the tears that I'm forced to cry
From deep inside the pain that I chose to hide / **Just walk...**
Now as the rain beats down upon my weary eyes
For me it cries

Just walk... / Now as the rain beats down upon my weary eyes
For me it cries

G Em C GD / G Em C Bm / C↓ G

Your name & mine inside a heart upon a wall
Still finds a way to haunt me, tho' they're so small / **Just...**
The empty sidewalks on my block are not the same
You're not to blame

— w & m: Mike Brown, Tony Sansone & Bob Calilli

THE WEIGHT

_I pulled into Nazareth, was feeling 'bout half past dead
I just need someplace where I can lay my head
Hey, Mr., can you tell me, where a man might find a bed?
He just grinned & shook my hand, "No" was all he said

(↑2)   G Bm C G (4x)

_Take a load off Fanny, _take a load for free
_Take a load off Fanny _and _
You put the load (put the load) **right on me** _ _ _

GD C x2 / GD C - - / C* G(Em D C -)   *3 beats

I picked up my bags, I went looking for a place to hide
When I saw old Carmen & the Devil, walking side by side
I said, "Hey, Carmen, c'mon, let's go downtown"
She said "I gotta go, but my friend can stick around"

Go down, Miss Moses, ain't nothin' you can say
It's just old Luke, & Luke's waiting on the judgment day
Well, Luke, my friend, what about young Annalee?
He said "Do me a favor, son, won't you stay & keep Annalee company"

Crazy Chester followed me & he caught me in the fog
He said, "I will fix your rag, if you'll take Jack, my dog"
I said "Wait a minute Chester, you know I'm a peaceful man"
He said "That's OK boy, won't you feed him when you can"

Catch the Cannonball, now to take me down the line
My bag is sinking low & I do believe it's time
To get back to Miss Fanny, you know she's the only one
Who sent me here, with her regards for everyone

— w & m: J. Robbie Robertson

YOU'RE MY HOME

When you look into my eyes
And you see the crazy gypsy in my soul
It always comes as a surprise
When I feel my withered roots begin to grow
Well I never had a place that I could call my very own
But that's all right, my love, 'cos you're my home

(↑2) C - C7 - / F - G - :‖ Em - F - / - G C -

When you touch my weary head
And you tell me everything will be all right
You say, "Use my body for your bed
And my love will keep you warm thruout the night"
Well I'll never be a stranger & I'll never be alone
Wherever we're together, that's my home

(bridge) Home can be the Pennsylvania Tpk
Indiana's early morning dew
High up in the hills of California
Home is just another word for you

Am G C - / Am Em G - / 1st / Am Em G - C - - -

(instr 4 lines of v. to) **Well I never had a place...**

If I travel all my life
And I never get to stop & settle down
Long as I have you by my side
There's a roof above & good walls all around
You're my castle, you're my cabin & my instant pleasure dome
I need you in my house 'cos you're my home / You're my home.

— w & m: Billy Joel

YOUR MAMA DON'T DANCE

Your mama don't dance & your daddy don't rock & roll (2x)
When evening rolls around & it's time to go to town,
where do you go – to rock & roll?

C - - - / F7 - C - / G7 F7 C -

The old folks say that ya gotta end your date by 10
If you're out on a date & you bring it home late it's a sin
There just ain't no excuse & you know you're gonna lose & never
    win – I'll say it again (And it's all because your...)

You pull into a drive-in & find a place to park
You hop into the backseat where you know it's nice & dark
You're just about to move in, thinkin' it's a breeze
There's a light in your eyes & then a guy says "Out of the car,
    Longhair"
"Louise, you're comin' with me & no more movies"

F - - - (4x) G7 F C

— w & m: Jim Messina & Kenny Loggins

The **Surfin' USA** chapter contains US rock groups & artists from about 1963–95. For other rock songs see: **British Invasion & Rock**, **Motown and R&B** (Af-Amer), **Rock Around the Clock** (pre-Beatles rock 'n' roll). Also find Amer rock songs in **Dreams & Mystery** & **Good Times**

Other songs include **Dignity**: I kissed a girl, I will survive, True colors **Home**: Sweet home Alabama **Peace**: For what it's worth **Rich**: Down on the corner, Rich girl **Sing**: Leader of the band **Struggle**: Eve of destruction

Time & Changes

100 YEARS

_I'm 15 for a moment, _caught in between 10 & 20
And I'm just dreaming _counting the ways to where you are
_I'm 22 for a moment _& she feels better than ever
And we're on fire _making our way back from Mars

Dsus7

G C Am7 Dsus7 / G Em Am7 DsusD :‖

15: _there's still time for you, time to buy
And time to lose – 15: _there's never a wish better than this
When you only got a hundred yrs to live _

G DC x2 / G DC EmD C / tacet G(C EmD GC EmD)

I'm 33 for a moment, _still the man but you see
I'm a "They," a kid on the way, babe, a family on my mind
_I'm 45 for a moment, _the sea is high
And I'm heading into a crisis chasing the yrs of my life

(2nd cho) 15: there's still time for you, time to buy & time
To lose yourself within a morning star _
_15: I'm all right with you – 15: _ / There's never a wish better
   than this when you only got a hundred yrs
To live – half time goes by, suddenly you're wise,
   another blink of an eye
67 is gone, the sun is getting high, we're moving on _

G DC x2 / Em D C - / G DC GD / EmD C (tacet)
C D Em Fmaj7 / C DsusD G (C Am7 D7sus)

_I'm 99 for a moment _& time for just another moment
And I'm just dreaming, counting the ways to where you are
_15: there's still time for you – 22: I feel her too – 33: you're on
   your way – every day's a new day _ **(instrum to 1st cho)**

G C Am7 Dsus7 / G Em Am DsusD / G DC x4

    — w & m: John Ondrasik (Five for Fighting)

ACROSS THE GREAT DIVIDE

I've been walkin' in my sleep
And countin' troubles 'stead of countin' sheep
Where the yrs went, I can't say
I just turned around & they've gone away

G GC G - / Em - C - / G - Em - / C D G -

And I've been siftin' thru the layers
Of dusty books & faded papers
They tell a story I used to know
It was one that happened so long ago / It's...

It's gone away in yesterday
And I find myself on the mountainside
Where the rivers change direction across the Great Divide

G GC G - / Em - C - / GC G D G

Well, I heard the owl callin'
Softly as the night was fallin'
With a question & I replied
But he's gone across the borderline / He's **gone...**

The finest hour that I have seen
Is the one that comes between
The edge of night & the break of day
When the darkness rolls away / It's **gone...**

    — w & m: Kate Wolf

BREATHS

Listen more often, to things than to beings (2x)
'Tis the ancestors' breath when the fire's voice is heard
'Tis the ancestors' breath in the voice of the waters

Ah… chh… (2x)

(in 3/4 a capella) G - - - / / G - D G / / /

Those who have died, have never, never left
The dead are not under the earth
They are in the rustling trees, they are in the groaning woods
They are in the crying grass, they are in the moaning rocks
The dead are not under the earth / So I **listen...**

G - C G / C G D - / G - D G / / G - D -

Those who have died, have never never left
The dead have a pact with the living
They are in the woman's breast, they are in the wailing child
They are with us in the home, they are with us in the crowd
The dead have a pact with the living

    — w: adapted from the poem Birago Diop, m: Ysaye M. Barnwell.

CARRY ON

Well I woke up to the sound of silence, the cars were cutting like
  knives in a fist fight_

And I found you with a bottle of wine, your head in the curtains
  & heart like the 4th of July _

You swore & said we are not, we are not shining stars, this I know,
  I never said we are

Tho' I've never been thru hell like that, I've closed enough windows to know you can never look back_

(↑5) C F C F /   / C Dm Em Dm / C Dm C F(G)

**If you're lost & alone or you're sinking like a stone,
  carry on _**

**May your past be the sound of your feet upon the ground,
  carry on _**

C FG C FG /   /

So I met up with some friends in the edge of the night at a bar off 75 _

And we talked & talked about how our parents will die, all our
  neighbors & wives _

But I like to think I can cheat it all to make up for the times I've
  been cheated on

And it's nice to know when I was left for dead, I was found & now
  I don't roam these streets, I am not the ghost you want of me

(bridge) My head is on fire but my legs are fine, after all,
  they are mine_

Lay your clothes down on the floor, close the door, hold the
  phone, show me how, no one's ever gonna stop us now

(as 2nd half of v.) 'Cos we are, we are shining stars, we are invinci-
  ble, we are who we are

On our darkest day, when we're miles away, so we'll come, we will
  find our way home

FC G x2 / FC G FG C / C Dm Em Dm / C Dm C F(G)

— w & m: Jeff Bhasker, Andrew Dost, Jack Antonoff & Nate Ruess

CASIMIR PULASKI DAY

Goldenrod & the 4-H stone
The things I brought you when I found out
You had cancer of the bone___

D C / Am G / D C (Am G)

Your father cried on the telephone
And he drove his car into the Navy Yard
Just to prove that he was sorry
    In the morning, thru the window shade
    When the light pressed up against your shoulder blade
    I could see what you were reading
All the glory that the Lord has made
And the complications you could do without
When I kissed you on the mouth
    Tues. night at the Bible study
    We lift our hands & pray over your body
    But nothing ever happens

I remember at Michael's house
In the living room when you kissed my neck
And I almost touched your blouse
    In the morning at the top of the stairs
    When your father found out what we did that night
    And you told me you were scared
All the glory when you ran outside
With your shirt tucked in & your shoes untied
And you told me not to follow you
    Sun. night when I clean the house
    I find the card where you wrote it out
    With the pictures of your mother
On the floor at the Great Divide
With my shirt tucked in & my shoes untied
I am crying in the bathroom
    In the morning when you finally go
    And the nurse runs in with her head hung low
    And the cardinal hits the window
In the morning in the winter shade
On the 1st of March, on the holiday
I thought I saw you breathing
    All the glory that the Lord has made
    And the complications when I see His face
    In the morning in the window
All the glory when He took our place
But He took my shoulders & He shook my face
And He takes & He takes & He takes

— w & m: Sufjan Stevens

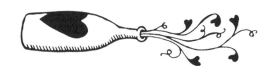

LA CHANSON DES VIEUX AMANTS

_Bien sûr nous eûmes des orages,_vingt ans d'amour,
  c'est l'amour fol
_Mille fois tu pris ton bagage,_mille fois je pris mon envol
_Et chaque meuble se souvient dans cette chambre sans berceau
  des éclats des vieilles tempêtes
_Plus rien ne ressemblait à rien, tu avais perdu le goût de l'eau et
  moi celui de la conquête

Am E - Am /   / C GBb F Am / C GBb F EsusE

Mais *[Oh]* **mon amour,_mon doux mon tendre,
  mon merveilleux amour – _ de l'aube claire**
Jusqu'à la fin du jour, _je t'aime encore tu sais, je t'aime

DmAm Am Dm E / AmC FAm AdimE

Moi, je sais tous tes sortilèges, tu sais tous mes envoûtements
Tu m'as gardé de pièges en pièges, je t'ai perdue de temps en temps
Bien sûr tu pris quelques amants, il fallait bien passer le temps, il
  faut bien que le corps exulte
Finalement finalement, il nous fallut bien du talent
  pour être vieux sans être adultes / **Oh mon amour…**

Et plus le temps nous fait cortège et plus le temps nous fait tourment
Mais n'est-ce pas le pire piège que vivre en paix pour des amants
Bien sûr tu pleures un peu moins tôt, je me déchire un peu plus
   tard, nous protégeons moins nos mystères
On laisse moins faire le hasard, on se méfie du fil de l'eau, mais
   c'est toujours la tendre guerre / **Oh mon amour…**

  — w & m: Jacques Brel & Gerard Jouannest

© 1967 (renewed) Editions Pouchenel S.P.R.L. All rights in the US & Canada administered by Unichappell Music Inc. On *Jacques Brel 67* up 3 & Judy Collins *Wildflowers* up 2, Placido Domingo *Songs* (w/ Zaz).

COMING INTO MY YEARS

Well, I'm a gray-haired woman & I'm comin' into my years
I'm a weathered woman & I'm comin' into my years
No more holding back, no more tryin' to please,
   got the will & the power to get off my knees
I'm an aging woman & I'm comin' into my years

Am Dm7 E7 Am - / Am Dm E7 - / Am - Dm7 - / Am E7 Am -

I'm a street-wise woman & I'm comin' into my prime
I'm a fight-back woman & I'm comin' into my prime
No more shrinking with fear when they whistle & jeer,
   I got a fist that's hard, a mind that's clear
I'm a night-walk woman & I'm comin' into my prime

And I'm a loud-mouthed woman & I'm comin' into my voice
I'm a talk-back woman & I'm comin' into my voice
Cause there's an ocean of words got caught in my throat, gonna
   let loose the waters & learn how to float
I'm a sing-out woman comin' into my voice

And I'm a fighting woman & I'm comin' into my strength
I'm a make-change woman & I'm comin' into my strength
I won't save the world, I won't drain my song, but I'll fight any
   battle that'll move us along
I'm a far-sighted woman comin' into my strength

I'm a loving woman & I'm comin' into my own
I'm a heart-beat woman & I'm comin' into my own
Well I'll go for passion, I'll go for strength,
   I'll go for the moment & I'll go for the length
I'm a give-take woman & I'm comin' into my own

  — w & m: Betsy Rose

© 1984 Betsy Rose. On her *Heart of a Child* & *Live from the Very Front Row*. Charlie King & Karen Brandow *Sparks & Tears* & MUSE – Cincinnati Women's Choir *Coming into Our Voice*. *LS

FARTHEST FIELD

There is a l<u>a</u>nd (there is a l<u>a</u>nd) high on a h<u>i</u>ll (high on…)
Where I am g<u>o</u>ing, there is a v<u>o</u>ice that calls to m<u>e</u> _
The air is sweet (The air is sweet) the grasses wave (the grasses…)
The wind is blowing away up in the farthest field

C CG C - / FCC* G C(F CG) :‖   (*extra beat)

Oh - walk with me & we will see the mystery revealed
When one day we wend our way up to the farthest field
F - C G / F - CG C

The sun will rise (the sun will rise) the sun will set (the sun…)
Across the mountains & we will live with beauty there
The fragrant flowers… the days & hours…
Will not be counted & peaceful songs will fill the air

I know one day… I'll leave my home…
Here in the valley & climb up to that field so fair
And when I'm called… & counted in…
That final tally, I know that I will see you there

Oh my dear friends… I truly love…
To hear your voices lifted up in radiant song
Tho' thru the years… we all have made…
Our separate choices, we've ended here where we belong

  — w & m: David Dodson

© 1995 David Dodson. On his *Weasel Rhythm* 12, Bok Muir & Trickett *Harbors of Home*, Kallet Epstein & Cicone *Heartwalk* & Dean Stevens *At Last*. *LS

FEEL SO NEAR

You'll find me sitting at this table
With my friend Fin & my friend John
My friend Murdaney tells us stories
Of things long gone, long gone
And we may take a glass together
The whisky makes it all so clear
It fires our dulled imaginations
And I feel so near, so near

(↑5) C Am G - /   / Em Am F - / C G - :‖

I feel so near to the howling of the winds
Feel so near to the crashing of the waves
Feel so near to the flowers in the fields
Feel so near

C - F - /   / Am FC F - / C (F C -)

The old man looks out to the islands
He says this place is endless thin
There's no real distance here to mention
We might all fall in, all fall in
   No distance to the spirits of the living
   No distance to the spirits of the dead
   And as he turned his eyes were shining
   And he proudly said, proudly said:

So we build our tower constructions
There to mark our place in time
We justify our great destructions
As on we climb, on we climb
   Now the journey doesn't seem to matter
   The destination's faded out
   And gathering out along the headland
   I hear the children shout, children shout:

  — w & m: Douglas Menzies MacLean

© 1996 Limetree Arts & Music. Sub-published by Fintage Publishing B.V. On his *Riof* (w/ Kathy Mattea 15), Sierra Hwy *Keep Your Heart Warm*, Oceans Apart *You Asked for It*, Michael Griffin *Ballads & Blues*, Caleigh *Branching Out*.

FOREVER YOUNG

May God bless & keep you always, may your wishes all come true
May you always do for others & let others do for you
May you build a ladder to the stars & climb on every rung
May you stay forever young
Forever young (x2) / May you stay…   (↑2)

G Bm / Am CG G - / 1st / C D G - // D - Em - / G D G -

May you grow up to be righteous, may you grow up to be true
May you always know the truth & see the lights surrounding you
May you always be courageous, stand upright & be strong…

May your hands always be busy, may your feet always be swift
May you have a strong foundation when the winds of changes shift
May your heart always be joyful, may your song always be sung…

‖: G - C G / G - D - / G - C - / G D G C / G D G -

— w & m: Bob Dylan

© 1973, 1985 Ram's Horn Music. He sings this w/ the Band in *Last Waltz* film 17. Also on Baez *Fr Every Stage* 12, Peter Paul & Mary *Reunion* (in E), The Pretenders *Last of the Independents*, Rhiannon Giddens & Iron & Wine on NBC's *Parenthood*, Norah Jones at the Celeb of Steve Jobs conc on YT 11. Dylan plays it faster w/ different chords (‖) on his *Planet Waves*, repeating last line of ea v. & omitting chorus.

GALILEO

Galileo's head was on the block
The crime was looking up the truth
And as the bombshells of my daily fears explode
I try to trace them to my youth

C G F G /   /   / Am Em F G

And then you had to bring up reincarnation
Over a couple of beers the other night
And now I'm serving time for mistakes
Made by another in another lifetime

How long 'til my soul gets it right?
Can any human being ever reach that kind of light?
I call on the resting soul of Galileo
King of night vision, king of insight

C G F G /   / Am Em D - / F G C - (G -)

And then I think about my fear of motion
Which I never could explain
Some other fool across the ocean yrs ago
Must have crashed his little airplane

(bridge) I'm not making a joke, you know me
I take everything so seriously
If we wait for the time 'til all souls get it right
Then at least I know there'll be no nuclear annihilation
In my lifetime I'm still not right

Am - F - / Adim - F - / 1st / G F G F / C G F G

I offer thanks to those before me
That's all I've got to say
'Cos maybe you squandered big bucks in your lifetime
Now I have to pay

But then again it feels like some sort of inspiration
To let the next life off the hook
But she'll say "Look what I had to overcome from my last life
I think I'll write a book"

How long 'til my soul gets it right?
Can any human being ever reach the highest **light**
Except for Galileo (God rest his soul)
King of night vision, king of insight
How long til my soul gets it right?
How long til we reach the highest light? / How long?

C G F G /   / Am Em D - / F G C - /
/   "   /   / C G F G C - -

— w & m: Emily Saliers

© 1992 Godhap Music. All rights controlled & administered by Songs of Universal, Inc. On Indigo Girls *Rites of Passage* 15.

A GARDEN OF MY OWN

There's a place where dreams are gathered, there's a place
   [soil] where seeds are sown
There's a light beyond the shadows where truths are known
In this light I reach for heaven, in this soil I root my soul
In this place I have a garden of my own

(↑) C Em F Dm / C Em F G / 1st / C F G C -

Time was I was up at dawn & eager for the field
Time was I was welded to the plough
Time was I would work as hard as flesh & bone allow
Til the glory of the harvest was revealed

G - C - /   / G - C↓ / DmEm FG C -

These days, I am on my knees with flowers in my hands
These days, I refuse to plant in rows
These days, I can feel a seedling tremble as it grows
And the heartland deep within me understands

Who knows whether time & quiet faith bring something new?
Who knows, if I learn to improvise?
Who knows if a flower never seen before will rise
And the world will be the richer for its hue?

— w & m: Patricia McKernon Runkle

© 1994 Patricia McKernon. On Annie Patterson *Deep Roots*. In *Worship in Song* hymnal. Choral versions available at halleonard.com & kallmancreates.com.

GOOD LUCK JOHN

John had a horse & the horse ran away – **bad luck** (x2)
John had a horse & the horse ran away – **bad, bad luck**

(↑2) Am F C G / Am F CG Am

Bad bad luck! the neighbors did say,
   bad luck, John, has come your way
Bad luck has come your way
He said maybe, it's hard to say (2x)

F C G Am / F C G - / Am F G - /   /

The horse came back with a wild mare – **good luck** (x2)
The horse came back with a pretty white mare – **good, good…**

Good good luck! the neighbors did say,
  good luck, John, has come your way
Good luck has come your way

He said maybe, it's hard to say (2x)

The mare kicked John & broke his leg – **bad luck…**
The pretty white mare broke John's leg – **bad, bad…**
Bad bad luck…

With a broken leg he missed the draft – **good…**
The army came & walked on past…

His leg grew worse & it would not heal – **bad…**
And the pain was all that John could feel…

The nurse she came to take care of – **good…**
And the 2 of them, they fell in love…

— w & m: Joe Crookston

© 2011 Joe Crookston. On his *Darkling & the Bluebird Jubilee* 15 & in *SO!* 54:4.

I Will Follow You Into the Dark

Love of mine,_someday you will die _
But I'll be close behind,_I'll follow you into the dark
No blinding light_or tunnels to gates of white_
Just our hands clasped so tight_waiting for the hint of a spark

C - Am - / F - C G :‖

If Heaven & Hell decide that they both are satisfied
Illuminate the no's on their vacancy signs
If there's no one beside you when your soul embarks
Then I'll follow you into the dark _

Am C F C / Am C G - / Am C E Am / F Fm C -

In Catholic school_as vicious as Roman rule
I got my knuckles_bruised by a lady in black
I held my tongue_as she told me, son
Fear is the heart of love,_so I never went back

You & me_have seen everything to see
From Bangkok to Calgary_& the soles of your shoes
Are all worn down,_the time for sleep is now
It's nothing to cry about,_'cos we'll hold each other soon
In the blackest of rooms   (Am F - -)

— w & m: Benjamin Gibbard

© 2005 EMI Blackwood Music Inc. & Where I'm Calling From Music. All rights controlled & administered by EMI Blackwood Music Inc. On Death Cab for Cutie *Plans* 15 & rec by Everclear & Daniel Andrade.

Mrs. Robinson

And here's to you, Mrs. Robinson
Jesus loves you more than you will know / Woah (x3)
God bless you, please, Mrs. Robinson
Heaven holds a place for those who pray / Hey hey hey (x2)

(↑2) G Em / G Em C - / D - / 1st 2 / Am - E - - -

We'd like to know a little bit about you for our files
We'd like to help you learn to help yourself
Look around you all you see are sympathetic eyes
Stroll around the grounds until you feel at home

E7 - - - - / A7 - - - / D G C Am - / E - D7 -

Hide it in a hiding place where no one ever goes
Put it in your pantry with your cupcakes
It's a little secret just the Robinsons' affair
Most of all you've got to hide it from the kids

Koo-koo-ka-choo, **Mrs. Robinson…**

Sitting on a sofa on a Sunday afternoon
Going to the candidates' debate
Laugh about it, shout about it when you've got to choose
Every way you look at it you lose

(as cho) Where have you gone, Joe DiMaggio?
A nation turns its lonely eyes to you / Woo woo woo
What's that you say, Mrs. Robinson?

Joltin' Joe has left & gone away / Hey hey hey (x2)

— w & m: Paul Simon

© 1968, 1970 Paul Simon (BMI). Copyright renewed. Rec by Simon & Garfunkel for film *The Graduate*.

Ne Me Quitte Pas

Ne me quitte pas, il faut oublier
Tout peut s'oublier qui s'enfuit déjà
Oublier le temps des malentendus
Et le temps perdu à savoir comment
Oublier ces heures qui tuaient parfois
À coups de pourquoi le coeur du bonheur
Ne me quitte pas, ne me quitte pas (2x)   (in 3/4, ↑3)

Em Em7 / Am - / D - / G - / Am B7
Em Em7 / Am B7 / Em -

    Moi je t'offrirai des perles de pluie
    Venues de pays où il ne pleut pas
    Je creuserai la terre jusqu'après ma mort
    Pour couvrir ton corps d'or et de lumière
    Je ferai un domaine où l'amour sera roi
    Où l'amour sera loi, où tu seras reine / **Ne me quitte…**

Em - / B7 Em / - - / D G / Em F / EmB7 Em / G Am / B7 -

Ne me quitte pas, je t'inventerai
Des mots insensés que tu comprendras
Je te parlerai de ces amants-là
Qui ont vu deux fois leurs coeurs s'embraser
Je te raconterai l'histoire de ce roi
Mort de n'avoir pas pu te rencontrer / **Ne…**
    On a vu souvent rejaillir le feu
    De l'ancien volcan qu'on croyait trop vieux
    Il est paraît-il des terres brûlées
    Donnant plus de blé qu'un meilleur avril
    Et quand vient le soir pour qu'un ciel flamboie
    Le rouge et le noir ne s'épousent-ils pas / **Ne…**
Ne me quitte pas, je ne vais plus pleurer
Je ne vais plus parler, je me cacherai là
À te regarder danser et sourire
Et à t'écouter chanter et puis rire
Laisse-moi devenir l'ombre de ton ombre
L'ombre de ta main l'ombre de ton chien / **Ne…**

— w & m: Jacques Brel

© 1961 (renewed) Tutti Intersong Editions Musicales SARL & Editions Jacques Brel. All rights in the U.S. & Canada administered by WB Music Corp. On his *La Valse à Mille Temps* 14, Edith Piaf 17, Nina Simone, Celine Dion. English lyrics ("If You Go Away") on recs by Barbra Streisand, Amy Grant.

PASSING THROUGH

We are passing this world on to our kids
From the day when they climb from their cribs
We'll try to teach them well, show them that they're loved
But in the end, all we can do is hope our best was good enough
'Cos they'll witness how this life can be so beautiful & cruel
We can't shelter them forever but if we show them all the tools
They might leave this world in a little better shape than me &
    you / **We are only passing thru**

(↓2) C F C - / F Em Dm - / G - - - / F - G - /
       C - C7 - / F - D7 - / G E7 Am F / C G C -

Passing thru (x2) / We are only passing thru (repeat)

C C7 F - / C D7 G - / 1st / C G C -

We are watching this world from our living rooms
40 yrs since we walked on the moon
This big blue ball is shrinking, I don't know if that's good
But for better or for worse now this whole world is our neighborhood
And there's no place left to run to stay above the fray
We'd better learn to get along & not just get our way
Not only for each other, but our children's children, too...

Now I wonder sometimes what will I pass on
How much can one voice do with just a song
Sometimes injustice & indifference are all that we see
But I refuse to let my hope become the latest casualty
So I'll sing of love & truth & try to practice what I preach
If I can't change the world, I'll change the world within my reach
What better place to start than here & now with me & you...

    — w & m: Catie Curtis & Mark Erelli
© 2006 Water Tower Music & Hillbilly Pilgrim Music. On her *Hello Stranger*. In SO! 51:1.

A QUESTION OF TEMPO

1. When I'm under pressure I get / speedy & tense up & then
Ironically I don't get as much / done as I could if I would
2. Slow down, _ breathe / deep, _ stay / centered, _ & / calm_
3. I try, but I can't! I'm / thinking of _ adding a
Relaxation class / _ into my schedule so
4. I can be more / steady even / tho' I'm adding / * more _ 'cos

Em - / D - / C - / B7 - :‖   coda: B7 - / / / E -

    * Last time thru Part 4 go to coda

(coda) More, more / more, more / more, more / more!
    — w & m: Joanne Hammil
© 1995 JHO Music. On her *Rounds & Partner S v1*, Short Sisters *Love & Transportation*, Acoustic Blender *Crazy Whirled*, *Rounds Galore & More v1*. *LS

STONES IN THE ROAD

When we were young, we pledged allegiance every morning of
    our lives
The classroom rang with children's voices under teacher's
    watchful eye
We learned about the world around us at our desks & at dinnertime
Reminded of the starving children, we cleaned our plates with
    guilty minds
And the stones in the road shone like diamonds in the dust
And then a voice called to us to make our way back home

(↑3) GD C D Am / GD C D G :‖ C D G D / Am Em CG D

When I was 10, my father held me on his shoulders above the crowd
To see a train draped in mourning pass slowly thru our town
His widow kneeled with all their children at the sacred burial ground
And the TV glowed that long hot summer with all the cities
    burning down
And the stones in the road flew out beneath our bicycle tires
Worlds removed from all those fires as we raced each other home

And now we drink our coffee on the run, we climb that ladder
    rung by rung
We are the daughters & the sons & here's the line that's missing
The starving children have been replaced by souls out on the street
We give a dollar when we pass & hope our eyes don't meet
We pencil in, we cancel out, we crave the corner suite
We kiss your ass, we make you hold, we doctor the receipt
And the stones... they fly out from beneath our wheels
Another day, another deal, before we get back home
And the stones... leave a mark from whence they came
A thousand points of light or shame, baby, I don't know

(↑3) GD C D Am / GD C D G :‖ (3x)
‖: C D G D / Am Em CG D :‖

    — w & m: Mary Chapin Carpenter
© 1992 EMI April Music Inc. & Getarealjob Music. All rights controlled & administered by EMI April Music Inc. On her *Stones...*

TANK PARK SALUTE

Kiss me goodnight & say my prayers, leave the lights on
    at the top of the stairs
Tell me the names of the stars up in the sky
A tree taps on a window pane, that feeling smothers me again
Daddy is it true that we all have to die?
At the top of the stairs is darkness **(2x)**

G D / Em C **(4x)** / EmD C x3 G -

I closed my eyes & when I looked, your name was in the memorial book
And what had become of all the things we planned
I accepted the commiserations of all your friends & your relations
But there's some things I still don't understand
You were so tall, how could you fall?

Some photographs of a summer's day, a little boy's lifetime away
Is all I've left of everything we'd done
Like a pale moon in a sunny sky, death gazes down as I pass by
To remind me that I'm but my father's son
I offer up to you this tribute
I offer up to you this Tank Park salute

— w & m: Billy Bragg

TEARS IN HEAVEN

Would you know my name **if I saw you in heaven**?
Would it be the same **if...**
I must be strong & carry on
'Cos I know I don't belong here in heaven

G D Em C G D / / Em B7 G7 E / Am D7 G(D Em C D G)

Would you hold my hand... / Would you help me stand...
I'll find my way thru night & day
'Cos I know I just can't stay here in heaven

(bridge) Time can bring you down, time can bend your knees
Time can break your heart, have you **begging please (2x)**

BbF GmC Dm(CF) / BbF GmC FC D

(lines 1 & 2 instr.) Beyond the door there's peace I'm sure
And I know there'll be no more tears in heaven

— w & m: Eric Clapton & Will Jennings

LE TEMPS DES CERISES

Quand nous chanterons le *[en serons au]* temps des cerises
Et gai rossignol et merle moqueur / Seront tous en fête
Les belles auront la folie en tête
Et les amoureux du soleil au cœur
Quand nous chanterons le temps des cerises
Sifflera bien mieux le merle moqueur   **(↑2)**

C Am Dm G / Em C F - / C G C - / F - C / Em D G
/   "   / C Em G C

Mais il est bien court le temps des cerises
Où l'on s'en va deux cueillir en rêvant
Des pendants d'oreille
Cerises d'amour aux robes vermeilles
Tombant sous la feuille en gouttes de sang
Mais il est bien court le temps des cerises
Pendants de corail qu'on cueille en rêvant!

Quand vous en serez au temps des cerises
Si vous avez peur des chagrins d'amour
Évitez les belles!
Moi qui ne crains pas les peines cruelles
Je ne vivrai pas sans souffrir un jour
Quand vous en serez au temps des cerises
Vous aurez aussi des peines d'amour !

J'aimerai toujours le temps des cerises
C'est de ce temps-là que je garde au cœur / Une plaie ouverte!
Et Dame Fortune en m'étant offerte
Ne pourra jamais fermer *[calmer]* ma douleur
J'aimerai toujours le temps des cerises
Et le souvenir que je garde au cœur!

— w: Jean-Baptiste Clément (1866), m: Antoine Renard (1868)

THAT'S THE WAY THE WORLD GOES 'ROUND

I know a guy that's got a lot to lose
He's a pretty nice fellow, kinda confused
Got muscles in his head ain't never been used
Thinks he owns half of this town
    He starts drinking heavy, gets a big red nose
    Beats his old lady with a rubber hose
    Then he takes her out to dinner, buys her new clothes
    That's the way that the world goes 'round
That's... / **You're up one day, the next you're down**
It's half an inch of water & you think you're gonna drown
That's...

E - / A - / E - / - B7 - / 1st 3 / B7 E //
/ " / " / " / E B7E

I was sitting in the bathtub, counting my toes
When the radiator broke, water all froze
I got stuck in the ice without my clothes
Naked as the eyes of a clown
    I was crying ice cubes, hoping I'd croak
    When the sun come thru the window, the ice all broke
    I stood up & laughed, thought it was a joke / **That's...**

— w & m: John Prine

THESE DAYS

Well I've been out walking _ _
I don't do that much talking **these days_** / **These days_ _ _**
These days I seem to think a lot about the things that I forgot
To do_ for you_ / And all the times_I had the chance to_ _ _ _ _

C ↓ F - /   / C - G - / F - - - / C - G E /
Am - F - / C ↓ F -

And I had a lover _ _
It's so hard to risk another **these days** / **These days**
Now if I seem to be afraid to live the life that I have made
In song / Well it's just that_I've been losing_so long _ _ _

Well, I'll keep on moving, moving on _
Things are bound to be improving **these...** / One of **these...**
These... I sit on corner stones & count the time in quarter tones
To ten _ my friend _
Don't confront me_with my failures_I had not forgotten them

— w & m: Jackson Browne

Tide and the River Rising (Oars)

Come on, get your oars & row, my darling
Come on, get your oars & row
We've got tide & the river rising
Come on get your oars & row

G - / D - / Am CEm / D -

Come up on your feet & walk, my baby
Rise up on your feet & walk
We've got arms reaching out to catch you
Haul up on those feet & walk

G - / D - / Am CEm / EmD D

In the morning call my name, my darling
In the morning call my name
We grow old, young, we birth, we die
And somehow rearrange

Some live & change the world with grace
And a vision & a strength of mind
Some rise from trouble, some lend a hand
And some keep trying to find

Watch that little boy go walking, my lover
And watch him as he learns to run
Watch him as he rounds the corner out of sight
Then tumbling back in our arms he comes

When it's time to say goodbye, my darling
When it's time to say goodbye_
We'll live on in the old & the young ones
Dreaming down a quiet line

— w & m: Cindy Kallet

© 1989 Cindy Kallet. On her *Dreaming Down a Quiet Line* 13. In *Cindy Kallet* SB.

To My Old Brown Earth

To my old brown earth & to my old blue sky
I'll now give these last few molecules of "I"

DDsus D DEm D / Em A DA D

And you who sing & you who stand nearby
I do charge you not to cry

DDsus D DEm D / G D Bm -

Guard well our human chain, watch well you keep it strong
As long as sun will shine

AG A x2 / Em - A -

And this our home keep pure & sweet & green
For now I'm yours & you are also mine

DDsus D DEm D / Em A Em A D -

— w & m: Pete Seeger

© 1964 (renewed) by Stormking Music, Inc. All rights administered by Figs. D Music c/o the Bicycle Music Company. Written in 1958 for the funeral of John McManus, co-editor of *The Guardian*, a radical newsweekly. On his *Pete & Broadsides* & in his *WHATFG*. Rec by Pat Humphries on *Seeds (S of Pete Seeger V3)*. In *SO!* 14.5, 55:4. Fine choral arrs by Paul Halley & by Steve Schuch.

Travelin' Shoes

Death came a knockin' on my mother's door
Singin' "Come on mother, ain't ya ready to go?"
And my mother stooped down, buckled up her shoes
And she moved on down by the Jordan stream
And then she shout "Hallelujah!! Done done my duty!
Got on my travelin' shoes"

Am - :‖ (6x)

insert: sister, brother, neighbor, preacher

(last v.) You know when death comes a-knockin' on my front door
Singin' "Come on sister, ain't ya ready to go?"
I'm gonna stoop right down, buckle up my shoes,
Gonna move on down by the Jordan stream, & then I'll shout...

— trad. (African-Amer spiritual)

Arr © 2015 by Hal Leonard Corporation. aka "Death Came A-Knockin'." On Ruthie Foster *Runaway Soul*, Maria Muldaur *Waitress in a Donut Shop* , Rani Arbo & Daisy Mayhem *Some Bright Morning*.

Twentieth Century Is Almost Over

Back in 1899 when everybody sang "auld lang syne"
A hundred yrs took a long, long time for every boy & girl
Now there's only one thing that I'd like to know:
   where did the 20th century go?
I'd swear it was here just a minute ago **all over this world**

G - C CG / - - - D / 1st / G - D -

The 20th century is – almost over (x3)
The 20th c. is almost over, all over this world
All over this world (x2)
The 20th c. is almost over, all over this world

G - C CG / - - GD G / G - GC G / 2nd

Does anyone remember the Great Depression,
   I read all about it in *True Confessions*
I'm sorry I was late for the recording session
   but somebody put me on hold
Has anybody seen my linoleum floors,
   petroleum jelly & 2 world wars
They got stuck in the revolving doors **all over...**

The winter's getting colder, summer's getting hotter, wishing
   well's wishing for another drop of water
And Mother Earth's blushin' cause somebody caught her
   making love to the Man in the Moon
Tell me, how you gonna keep 'em down on the farm
   now that outer space has lost its charm
Somebody set off the burglar alarm & not a moment too soon

Old Father Time has got his toes a tappin',
   standin' in the window, grumblin' & a-rappin'
Everybody's waiting for smth to happen,
   tell me if it happens to you
The Judgment Day is getting nearer,
   there it is in the rear view mirror!
If you duck down, I could see a little clearer **all...**

— w & m: Steve Goodman & John Prine

© 1970 (renewed) Big Ears Music, Inc. & Red Pajamas Music. On his *Say It in Private*, Johnny Cash *Rockabilly Blues*, The Highwaymen *Super Hits*.

WANTING MEMORIES

I am sitting here wanting memories to teach me
To see the beauty in the world thru my own eyes (repeat)
You used to rock me in the cradle of your arms
You said you'd hold me 'til the pains of life were gone
You said you'd comfort me in times like these
And now I need you, now I need you, & you are gone

(↑3) [G - / Am G :‖ DC G (3x) / D - G -]

I am sitting... (once only)
Since you've gone & left me / There's been so little beauty
But I know I saw it clearly thru your eyes
Now the world outside is such a cold & bitter place
Here inside I have few things that will console
And when I try to hear your voice above the storms of life
Then I remember all the things that I was told

I am sitting... (repeat) / I think on the things that made me feel
  so wonderful when I was young
I think on the things that made me laugh, made me dance, made
  me sing
I think on the things that made me grow into a being full of pride
I think on these things, for they are true

I am sitting... (once only)
I thought that you were gone, but now I know you're with me
You are the voice that whispers all I need to hear
I know a please, a thank you, & a smile will take me far
I know that I am you & you are me & we are one
I know that who I am is numbered in each grain of sand
I know that I've been blessed again & over again

— w & m: Ysaye M. Barnwell

WHAT WILL I LEAVE

Late in the evening as light fades away
In silence we gather together
Searching the faces of those who are here
For those who have left us forever

C G Am / F C - G / 1st / F C G C

What will I leave, what will I leave?
What will I leave behind?
When I am gone, who'll carry on?
What will I leave behind?

C - F - / C - G - / C - F̂ - / CF CG C -

Where are the ones who caught flame in the night
Fired up by the heat of devotion?
Measuring their lives by the light of the truth
They burned like a lamp on the ocean

Who will remember the words of the brave
That lifted us higher & higher?
Who will remember the price that they paid
For lives lived too close to the fire?

Hearts of the ones who inherit your lives
Will rest in the truth you have spoken
Memory will echo the trust that you kept
Like you, it will never be broken

— w & m: Si Kahn

WHEN I GO

Come, lonely hunter, chieftain & king
I will fly like the falcon when I go
Bear me, my brother, under your wing
I will strike fell like lightning when I go

(↑3) Am - C G / Am [Dsus2] FG Am - :‖

I will bellow like the thunder drum, invoke the storm of war
A twisting pillar spun of dust and blood up from the prairie floor
I will sweep the foe before me like a gale out on the snow
And the wind will long recount the story, reverence & glory,
  when I go

C - G - / Dm - Am - / 1st / Dm - F G Am

Spring, spirit dancer, nimble & thin
I will leap like coyote when I go
Tireless entrancer, lend me your skin
I will run like the gray wolf when I go
I will climb the rise at daybreak, I will kiss the sky at noon
Raise my yearning voice at midnight to my mother in the moon
I will make the lay of long defeat & draw the chorus slow
I'll send this message down the wire & hope that someone wise is
  listening when I go

(1st 4 lines instr.) And when the sun comes, trumpets from his
  red house in the east
He will find a standing stone where long I chanted my release
He will send his morning messenger to strike the hammer blow
And I will crumble down uncountable in showers of crimson
  rubies when I go

Sigh, mournful sister, whisper & turn
I will rattle like dry leaves when I go
Stand in the mist where my fire used to burn
I will camp on the night breeze when I go
And should you glimpse my wandering form out on the borderline
Betw death & resurrection & the council of the pines
Do not worry for my comfort, do not sorrow for me so
All your diamond tears will rise up & adorn the sky beside me
  when I go

— w & m: Dave Carter

WHO KNOWS WHERE THE TIME GOES

Across the evening *[purple, morning]* sky all the birds are leaving
But how can they know it's time for them to go?
Before the winter fire, I will still be dreaming
I have no thought of time
For who knows where the time goes? / Who knows…

(↑2) C Dm Em Dm / C Dm Em F / Dm Em F Em / F - C -
GF F / C F C - - -

Sad, deserted shore, your fickle friends are leaving
Ah but then you know it's time for them to go
But I will still be here, I have no thought of leaving
I do not count the time…

And I am not alone while my love is near me
And I know it will be so until it's time to go,
So, come the storms of winter & then the birds in spring again
I do not fear the time
For who knows how my love grows? / **Who knows where…**

II: C F C F / / DmEm FAm Em / F C - //
GF C / F↓ C (F…)

— w & m: Sandy Denny

© 1969 Winckler Musikforlag. Copyright renewed. All rights controlled & administered by Irving Music, Inc. On orig home '67 demo on YT ↑1, rec w/ The Strawbs *All Our Own Work* (rel. '73), II: Judy Collins '68 title track ↑3. Fairport Convention '69 *Unhalfbricking* ↑4, Nina Simone '70 live *Black Gold*. Denny died in '78 after a fall.

WON'T YOU COME & SING FOR ME

I feel the shadows now upon me
And fair angels beckon me
Before I go, dear sisters & brothers *[dear Christian brother]*
Won't you come & sing for me?

(in G) D - C G / C - G D / C - G - / D - C G

Sing the hymns we sang together
In that plain little church with the benches all worn
How dear to my heart, how precious the moments
We stood shaking hands & singing a song

C - G - / D - C G :|

My burden's heavy, my way has grown weary
I have traveled the road that was long
And it would warm this old heart, my brother
If you come & sing one song

In my home beyond that dark river
Your dear faces no more I'll see
Until we meet where there's no more sad parting
Won't you come & sing for me?

— w & m: Hazel Dickens

© 1973 Happy Valley Music. Copyright renewed. On Alice Gerrard & Hazel Dickens *Pioneering Women of Bluegrass*, Hot Rize *Untold Stories*, Joe Hickerson *Drive Dull Care Away*. In *Real Bluegrass Bk*.

YOU CAN'T ALWAYS GET WHAT YOU WANT

I saw her today at the reception
A glass of wine in her hand
I knew she was going to meet her connection
At her feet was her footloose man

C F (4x)

You can't always get what you want (3x)
But if you try sometime, you just might find
You get what you need

C F / / / D F / C (F C F)

And I went down to the demonstration
To get my fair share of abuse
Singing "We're gonna vent our frustration
If we don't, we're gonna blow a 50-amp fuse"
   I went down to the Chelsea drugstore
    To get your prescription filled
    I was standin' in line with Mr. Jimmy
    And man, did he look pretty ill
We decided that we would have a soda
My favorite flavor, cherry red
I sung my song to Mr. Jimmy
And he said one word to me, & that was "Dead"
   And I saw her today at the reception
    In her glass was a bleeding man
    She was practised at the art of deception
    Well, I could tell by her blood-stained hands

— w & m: Mick Jagger and Keith Richards

© 1969 (renewed) ABKCO Music, Inc., 85 Fifth Avenue, New York, NY 10003. On Rolling Stones *Honky Tonk Women* ↑1, Luther Allison *Paint It Blue* ↑4, Glee '09 episode (in G), Bette Midler *Divine Madness*, Aretha rec.

YOUR LONG JOURNEY

God's given us years of happiness here / Now we must part
And as the angels come & call for you
The pangs of grief tug at my heart

D - A - / G D - / D - A D / A D G D

Oh my darling, my darling
My heart breaks as you take your long journey

Â - D̂ - / A D G D

Oh the days will be empty, the nights so long / Without you my love
And as God calls for you I'm left alone
But we will meet in heaven above

Fond memories I'll keep of the happy days
That on earth we trod
And when I come we will walk hand in hand
As one in heaven in the family of God

— w & m: Doc Watson & Rosa Lee Watson

© 1963 (renewed) Downtown DMP Songs (BMI) on behalf of Budde Songs Inc. (BMI) & Hillgreen Music (BMI). On Doc Watson *My Dear Old Southern Home*, Alison Krauss & Robert Plant *Raising Sand*.

Time chap contains songs about the seasons of life & songs about death & dying. See also: **Dignity** (AIDS), **Family**, **Gospel**, **Healing & Letting Go** (threshold/comfort songs), **Outdoors** (seasons of the year). Other songs include **Ballads**: Three ravens **British**: Fields of gold, Julia (author missing mother who died) **Country**: The gambler **Dignity**: At seventeen **Dreams**: Time in a bottle, Wondering where the lions are **Faith**: Nearer my God to thee, Swimming to the other side **Friendship**: Closer to fine, Gathering of spirits, Old friends, Parting song, **Funny**: Always look on the bright side **Hope**: Fast car, Lay down your weary tune **Musicals**: Aquarius, Matchmaker **Outdoors**: Red-wing blackbird Peace: These hands **Sea**: Old Zeb **Sing**: Amer pie, Leader of the band, We'll pass them on **Struggle**: Long Kesh, **Surfing**: Time after time **Travelin**: Been all around this world

Travelin'

BEEN ALL AROUND THIS WORLD
(Hang Me O Hang Me)

Hang me, oh, hang me & I'll be dead & gone (2x)
I wouldn't mind the hanging, Lord, it's laying in jail *[the*
   grave] **so long**
I've been all around this world

`A - - - / E - D A / D - A - / E A`

Working on the new RR, mud up to my knees (2x)
Working for John Henry & he's mighty hard to please
Been all around this world

Went up on the mtn, there I took my stand (2x)
Rifle on my shoulder, 6-shooter in my hand / **Been...**

Lulu, oh Lulu, come & open that door (2x)
Before I have to open it with my old .44...

Mama & papa & baby sister makes 3 (2x)
Take me down to the gallows, boys, that's the last they'll see of me...

Now if you meet a rich girl, boys, send her down the line (2x)
If you meet a poor girl, bet she's a friend of mine...

— trad. (bluegrass)

BICYCLE SONG

Everybody's wondering what they're gonna do
Everything's a mess, folks are feeling blue
If your troubles got you down so much you can't abide
Get on that bicycle & ride

`C - G C / - - D G / 1st / F G C -`

Yeah, get on that bicycle & ride
'Neath the sunny skies or along the oceanside
Just ride, ride ride, ride, ride

`F G C - / F - G - / F G C -`

They're doing it in Eugene, Havana & Shanghai
Even folks in Boston town are giving it a try
Throwin' out their gas tanks, the clean air by their side / Just **get**
   on that bicycle...

It's good for your heart & it's good for your brain
Those fluorescent lights are drivin' you insane
Your toes will tingle in your shoes when to the pedal they're applied
Just get...

You're having troubles with your lovers, the tandem's made for that
You'll work together wonderfully or else you'll just go splat
Gonna shut down Main Street, make the bike paths far & wide
And get...

— w & m: David Rovics

CAREY

The wind is in from Africa, last night I couldn't sleep
Oh you know it sure is hard to leave here, Carey,
   but it's really not my home
My fingernails are filthy, I got beach tar on my feet
And I miss my clean white linen & my fancy French cologne

`D - A - / G D A - :|`

Oh Carey get out your cane & I'll put on some silver
Oh you're a mean old Daddy, but I like you fine

`A D - A / G D A D -`

Come on down to the Mermaid Cafe & I will buy you a bottle of wine
And we'll laugh & toast to nothing & smash our empty glasses down
Let's have a round for these freaks & these soldiers, a round for
   these friends of mine
Let's have another round for the bright red devil who keeps me
   in this tourist town / Come on **Carey...**

Maybe I'll go to Amsterdam or maybe I'll go to Rome
And rent me a grand piano & put some flowers 'round my room
But let's not talk about fare-thee-wells now, the night is a starry
   dome
And they're playin' that scratchy rock & roll beneath the Matala
   Moon / Come on **Carey...**

The wind is in from Africa... not my home
Maybe it's been too long a time since I was scramblin' down in
   the street
Now they got me used to that clean white linen & that fancy
   French cologne

(last cho) Oh **Carey...** cane, I'll put on my finest silver
We'll go to the Mermaid Cafe, have fun tonight
I said, Oh you're a mean old Daddy, but you're out of sight

`A D - A / G D A D - / / /`

— w & m: Joni Mitchell

Don't Give Your Heart to a Rambler

Don't fall in love with me darling, I'm a rambler
Altho' you're the sweetest sweetheart in this world
It's all for your sake, dear, that I'm leaving
Don't give your heart to a rambler, little girl

A D / E A :|

I handed you a line dear & I'm sorry
You're just a little sweeter than the rest
Believe me when I say I don't want to hurt you
Or do anything to mar your happiness
    Don't be blue when I say that I don't love you
    I've said it all so many times it seems
    I'm just a guy whose restless mind keeps wandering
    I guess that I was born to drift & dream
If I'd never had the blues, my little darling
Or the lure of the road, dear, on my mind
But I'm bound to hear the whistle of a freight train
And the boxcars as they rattle down the line

    — w & m: Jimmie Skinner

Follow That Road

If you're coming in the summer, you'd be better to split off on 35
There's the Starlight Drive-In Movie on your left, just beyond the
    county line
Right after that you'll see 2 silos, one is silver, one is blue
'Bout a quarter mile further, make a left onto Hwy 42
Then **follow that road**, cornfields just as far as you can see
Follow… back thru time, back thru distance, back to me

A - D - /   / D - A - / - - D (E) // 1st /   /

If you're drivin' by in autumn, you should follow up the river to
    Bear Lake
That's the time to see the colors, there's an old covered bridge
    you'll want to take
Late at night, be careful, just be sure to watch for deer out on the road
And if it's early in the morning, sometimes it gets foggy, take it slow
But **follow…** sugar maples far as you can see / **Follow…**

If you get the notion in December to drop by for just a day
There's that tiny little road that no one knows about, it's safe to
    go that way
It's up between 2 fields, so the sunlight melts the ice by afternoon
You'll see 2 houses by the fields, someone's always there, if not,
    they'll be back soon
So **follow…** snowdrifts just as far as you can see / **Follow…**

You'll remember in the springtime how the puddles look like
    pieces of the sky
Fallen down by the roadside to delight any stranger passing by
The softness of the grass on Raven Hill where we counted
    stars all night
You must know how much I miss you & that any way you get
    here is all right
Just **follow…** wildflowers just as far as you can see…

    — w & m: Anne Hills

Freeborn Man (I'm a Freeborn Man)

I'm a freeborn man of the travelling people
Got no fixed abode, with nomads I am numbered _
Country lanes & byways were always my ways
I never fancied being lumbered

A - Bm - [D E] / E7 - A - / E7 E7A DA A / BmA BmG A -

Oh we knew the woods & the resting places
And the small birds sang when wintertime was over _
Then we'd pack our load & be on the road
They were good old times for a rover

There was open ground where a man could linger
Stay a week or 2 for time was not your master_
Then away you'd jog with your horse & dog
Nice & easy, no need to go faster

Now & then you'd meet up with other Travellers
Hear the news or else swap family information
At the country fairs, you'd be meeting there
All the people of the travelling nation

O I've known life hard & I've known it easy
And I've cursed the times when winter days were dawning
But I've danced & sang thru the whole night long
Seen the summer sunrise in the morning

I've made willow creels & the heather besoms
And I've even done some begging & some hawking_
[Lifted tatties, pu'd the berrie, & gaed hawkin']
And I've lain there, spent, happed up in the tent
And I've listened to the old folks talking

All you freeborn men of the travelling people
Every tinker, rolling stone & Gypsy rover _
Winds of change are blowing, old ways are going
Your travelling days will soon be over

I am a freeborn man of the travelling people
Got no fixed abode, where no man is your master _
Country lanes & byways were always my ways
I never fancied going faster

    — w & m: Ewan MacColl

Girl from the North Country

If you're travelin' in *[to]* the north country fair
Where the winds hit heavy on the borderline
Remember me to one who lives there
For she once was a true love of mine

I: G Bm D7 G - - / Em - D7 G - - / G Bm C G - - / 2nd

Well, if you go when the snowflakes storm *[fall]*
When the rivers freeze & summer ends
Please see if she's wearing a coat so warm
To keep her from the howlin' winds

Please see for me if her hair hangs *[is hanging]* long
If it rolls & flows all down her breast
Please see for me if her hair hangs long
That's the way I remember her best

I'm a-wonderin' if she remembers me at all
Many times I've often prayed
In the darkness of my night / In the brightness of my day

‖: G Bm C G (4x)

— w & m: Bob Dylan

GREAT AMERICAN BUM (The Bum's Song)

Come all you jolly jokers If you want to have some fun
And listen while I relate the tale of the Great American Bum
From E & W & N & S, like a swarm of bees they come
They sleep in the dirt & they wear a shirt that's dirty & full of crumb*
I am a bum, a jolly old bum & I live like a royal Turk
And I have good luck & I bum all my chuck & to heck
with the man that works!

D - - A / - - - D :‖ (3x)

It's early in the mornin', when the dew is on the ground
The bum arises from his nest & gazes all around.
While goin' east they're loaded & goin' west, sealed tight
I reckon we'll have to ride aboard the fast express tonight!

Well, I met a man the other day that I never met before
And he asked me if I wanted a job a-shovelin' iron ore
I asked him what the wages was, he said 10 cents a ton
I said "Old fellow, go scratch your neck , I'd rather be on the bum!"

Oh lady, would you be kind enough to give me smth to eat?
A piece of bread & butter & a 10 ft slice of meat
Some apple pie & custard, just to tickle me appetite
For really I'm so hungry, I don't know where I'll sleep tonight!

— w & m: Cisco Houston

I AM A WANDERER

I am a wanderer, feet on the ground
Heart on my sleeve & my head in the clouds
I own the star above some distant shore
Wandering ever more

C - - Dm / F Am F G / 1st / F G C -

I am a refugee torn from my land
Cast off to travel this world to its end
Never to see my proud mountains again / But I still remember them

I am a laborer, sign 'round my neck:
"Will work for dignity, trust & respect"
Stand on this corner so you don't forget / I haven't had mine yet

I am a prisoner pacing my cell
Three steps & back in my corner of hell
Lock me away & you swallow the key / But someday I shall be free

And I'll be a wanderer, feet on the ground
Heart on my sleeve & my head in the clouds
I own the star above some distant shore / Wandering evermore

— w & m: Steve Earle

I'M ON MY WAY

I'm on my way, and now I'm going
Back to a place that I know well
Folks I tell may say I'm crazy
But all my friends, they wish me well

C - FC C / F - C - / F - Am F / C CG C -

I've been favoured at your table
Where I have feasted as your guest
But there's a hunger in me burning
Like a fire in my breast

"   /   "   /   "   / C CG F -

We are like a rolling river
For years been flowing deep and strong
While the waters have been changing
And forever moving on

Now a restless soul, set to wander
And weary feet that are bound to roam
Leave a heart forever yearning
For the body knows no home

— w & m: Mark Haines

LEAVING ON A JET PLANE

All my bags are packed, I'm ready to go
I'm standin' here outside your door
I hate to wake you up to say goodbye
But the dawn is breakin', it's early morn
The taxi's waitin', he's blowin' his horn
Already I'm so lonesome I could die

(↑2) C F / / C Am Dm G :‖

So kiss me & smile for me
Tell me that you'll wait for me
Hold me like you'll never let me go
'Cos I'm leavin' on a jet plane
Don't know when I'll be back again
Oh babe, I hate to go

There's so many times I've let you down
So many times I've played around
I tell you now, they don't mean a thing
Every place I go, I'll think of you
Every song I sing, I'll sing for you
When I come back, I'll bring your wedding ring

Now the time has come to leave you
One more time, let me kiss you
Close your eyes, I'll be on my way
Dream about the days to come
When I won't have to leave alone
About the times I won't have to say / Oh, **kiss…**

— w & m: John Denver

ME & BOBBY MCGEE

Busted flat in Baton Rouge, waitin' for a train
When I's feeling near as faded as my jeans
Bobby thumbed a diesel down, just before it rained
And rode us all the way to New Orleans
I pulled my harpoon out of my dirty red bandana
I's playin' soft while Bobby sang the blues
Windshield wipers slapping time, I's holding Bobby's hand in mine
And we sang every song that driver knew

`C - / - G / - - / - C / - - / CC₇ F / - C / G C`

Freedom's just another word for nothing left to lose
Nothing, I mean nothing, honey, if it ain't free
Feeling good was easy, Lord, when he sang the blues
You know feeling good was good enough for me
Good enough for me & my Bobby McGee

`F C / G CC₇ / F C / G - / - C`

From the Kentucky coal mines to the California sun
Bobby shared the secrets of my soul
Thru all kinds of weather, thru everything we done
Bobby baby kept me from the cold world
One day near Salinas, Lord, I let him slip away
He's lookin' for that home & I hope he finds it
But I'd trade all of my tomorrows for one single yesterday
To be holdin' Bobby's body next to mine

Freedom's... / Nothing & that's all that Bobby left me...

— w & m: Kris Kristofferson & Fred Foster

© 1969 (renewed 1997) TEMI Combine Inc. All rights controlled by Combine Music Corp. & administered by EMI Blackwood Music Inc. Orig rec by Roger Miller. Also rec by Gordon Lightfoot, Grateful Dead, Kristofferson & Janis Joplin (on her *Pearl*).

MUSS I DENN (Muß I Denn)

Muß i denn, muß i denn zum Städtele hinaus
Städtele hinaus, und du, mein Schatz, bleibst hier
Wenn i komm, wenn i komm, wenn i wieder wieder komm
Wieder wieder komm, kehr i ein, mein Schatz, bei dir
Kann i gleich net allweil bei dir sein
Han i doch mein Freud an dir

(repeat lines 3 & 4:) Wenn i komm...

`D G D - / - - A - D - :‖A - D - / G - D - / - - A D / 2nd`

Wie du weinst, wie du weinst, daß i wandere muß
Wandere muß, wie wenn d'Lieb jetzt wär vorbei
Sind au drauß, sind au drauß der Mädele viel
Mädele viel, lieber Schatz, i bleib dir treu
Denk du net, wenn i ein andre seh
No sei mein' Lieb vorbei
Sind au drauß...

Übers Jahr, übers Jahr, wenn mer Träubele schneid'
Träubele schneid't, Stell i hier mi wiedrum ein
Bin i dann, bin i dann dein Schätzele noch
Schätzele noch, so soll die Hochzeit sein!
Übers Jahr, do ist mei Zeit vorbei
Do g'hör i mein und dein
Bin i dann...

— trad. (German folksong)

Arr. © 2015 by Hal Leonard Corporation. Rec by Martha Schlamme ('54) & Marlene Dietrich ('58) & in *Fireside Bk of Folk S.*

Wooden Heart

Can't you see, I love you? Please don't break my heart in 2
That's not hard to do, 'cos **I don't have a wooden heart**
And if you say goodbye, then I know that I would cry
Maybe I would die, 'cos **I don't have a...**
There's no strings upon this love of mine
It was always you from the start
Treat me nice, treat me good, treat me like you really should
'Cos I'm not made of wood, & **I don't...**

`D G D - / - - A - D - :‖A - D - / G - D - / 1st 2`

— w & m: Ben Weisman, Fred Wise, Kay Twomey and Berthold Kaempfert

© 1960 Gladys Music, Inc. Copyright renewed, assigned to Chappell & Co., Erika Publishing & Sinless Music. All rights for Erika Publishing controlled & administered by BMG Rights Management (US) LLC. Eng sung by Elvis in '60 film *GI Blues*. On Elvis *Dinner at 8* & on Tom Petty *Nobody's Children*. Same melody as Muss I Denn.

MYSTERY TRAIN

Train I ride, 16 coaches long **(2x)**
Well that long black train carried my baby from home

(in E, ↑5) `B₇ - E - / | B₇ A E -`

Train train, comin' on 'round the bend **(2x)**
Well it took my baby, it's gone do it again

Train train, comin' on down the line **(2x)**
Well it's bringin' my baby 'cos she's mine all, all mine

— w & m: Sam Phillips & Herman Parker, Jr.

© 1953, 1955 (copyrights renewed) Hi Lo Music & Mijac Music. All rights for Hi Lo Music administered by Unichappell Music, Inc. All rights for Mijac Music administered by Sony/ATV Music Publishing LLC, 424 Church Street, Suite 1200, Nashville, TN 37219. The song was written by Junior (Herman) Parker, with a credit later given to Sun Records owner Phillips. Rec by Junior Parker, Elvis Presley, The Band, Vince Gill, Paul Butterfield Blues Band. All these recs are played in E but it may be easier to sing in A.

ROUTE 66

If you ever plan to motor west
Travel my way, take the hwy that's the best
Get your kicks on Route 66
It winds from Chicago to LA
More than 2,000 miles all the way / **Get your...**

`G C G - / C C₇ G - / Am₇ D₇ G - :‖`

(bridge) Now you go thru Saint Looey & Joplin MO & Oklahoma City is mighty pretty
You'll see Amarillo, Gallup, New Mexico
Flagstaff AZ, don't forget Winona, Kingman, Barstow, San Bernardino

`G C₇ G G₇ / C C₇ G - / Am₇ D₇ GC₇ Am₇D₇`

Won't you get hip to this timely tip:
When you make that California trip / **Get your... (repeat)**

— w & m: Bobby Troup

© 1946, renewed 1973, assigned 1974 to Londontown Music. All rights outside the U.S.A. controlled by Edwin H. Morris & Company, a division of MPL Music Publishing, Inc. Rec by Nat & Natalie Cole, Chuck Berry, The Rolling Stones, Asleep at the Wheel.

ROVING GAMBLER

I am a roving gambler, I gamble all around
Wherever I meet with a deck of cards, I lay my money down
I lay my money down **(x2)**

`A - - - / D A D A / - - E A`

I had not been in Frisco many more weeks than 3
I met up with a pretty little gal, she fell in love with me
She fell in love with me (x2)

She took me to her parlor, she cooled me with her fan
She whispered low in her mother's ear, "I love that gambling man..."

"Oh daughter, dear daughter, how can you treat me so?
To leave your dear old mother & with a gambler go? To leave..."

"O mother, O dear mother, you cannot understand
If you ever see me coming back, I'll be with a gambling man..."

I left her there in Frisco & I wound up in Maine
I met up with a gambling man, got in a poker game...

We put our money in the pot & dealt the cards around
I saw him deal from the bottom of the deck &
   I shot that gambler down...

Well now I'm in the jailhouse, got a number for my name
The Warden said as he locked the door, you've gambled your
   last game...
   — trad. (US)

RUSTY OLD AMERICAN DREAM

Well, I don't look all that ragged for all the time it's been
But I'm weakened underneath me where my frame is rusted thin
And this year's state inspection, I just barely passed
Won't you drive me 'cross the country, boy?
   This year could be my last

D - G D / - - Em A / 1st /   /

I'm a tailfin road locomotive
From the days of cheap gasoline
And I'm for sale by the side of the road going nowhere
A rusty old American dream

G - D - / A - D - / G - D Bm / G A D -

I rolled off the line in Detroit back in 1958
Spent 3 days in the showroom, that's all I had to wait
I've been good to all who owned me, so have no fear
C'mon, boy, put your money down & get me out of here!

(bridge) Now, this car needs a young man to own him
One who will polish the chrome
I will give you the rest of my lifetime
But don't let me die here alone
Just jump me some juice to my battery
Give that old starter a spin
Hear me whir, sputter, backfire thru the carburetor
And roar into life once again

D - - - / - - G - / - - D Bm / Em - A - / 1st 3 / G A D -

I am a tailfin road locomotive
You can polish my chrome so clean
We can fly off into the sunset together
A rusty old Amer. dream, still runnin'! / A rusty...
   — w & m: David Wilcox

SIX DAYS ON THE ROAD

Well, I pulled out of Pittsburgh rolling down the Eastern seaboard
I've got my diesel wound up & she's running like never before
There's a speed zone ahead but all right, I don't seen a cop in sight
6 days on the road & I'm a-gonna make it home tonight

G D G - / - - D - / C D G C / G D G -

I got me 10 forward gears & a Georgia overdrive
I'm takin' little white pills & my eyes are open wide
I just passed a Jimmy & a White, I've been a-passin' everything in sight
6 days on the road &...

Well it seems like a month since I kissed my baby goodbye, &
I could have a lot of women but I'm not like some of the guys
I could find one to hold me tight, but I could never make believe
   it's all right / 6 days...

ICC is a-checkin' on down the line
I'm a little overweight & my log book's way behind
But nothing bothers me tonight, I can dodge all the scales all right...

Well my rig's a little old, but that don't mean she's slow
There's a flame from my stack & that smoke's blowin' black as coal
And my hometown's coming in sight, if you think I'm happy,
   you're right / 6 days...
   — w & m: Earl Green & Carl Montgomery

WAGON WHEEL

Headed down south to the land of the pines
And I'm thumbin' my way into North Caroline
Starin' up the road & pray to God I see headlights
I made it down the coast in 17 hours
Pickin' me a bouquet of dogwood flowers
And I'm a hopin' for Raleigh, I can see my baby tonight _

G D / Em C / G D C - :|

So rock me mama like a wagon wheel
Rock me mama any way you feel
Hey mama rock me
Rock me mama like the wind & the rain
Rock me mama like a south-bound train / Hey mama...

Runnin' from the cold up in New England
I was born to be a fiddler in an old-time stringband
My baby plays the guitar, I pick a banjo now
Oh the north country winters keep a gettin' me now
Lost my money playin' poker so I had to up & leave
But I ain't a turnin' back to livin' that old life no more _

Walkin' to the south out of Roanoke
I caught a trucker out of Philly, had a nice long toke
But he's a-headed west from the Cumberland Gap to
   Johnson City, Tennessee
And I gotta get a move on before the sun,
I hear my baby callin' my name & I know that she's the only one
And if I die in Raleigh at least I will die free _
   — w & m: Bob Dylan & Ketch Secor

WELL MAY THE WORLD GO

Well may the world go, the world go, the world go
Well may the world go when I'm far away

D G D A / D G D A D

Well may the skiers turn, the swimmers churn, the lovers burn
Peace may the generals learn **when I'm far away**

Sweet may the fiddle sound, the banjo play the old hoe-down
Dancers swing round & round **when…**

Fresh may the breezes blow, clear may the streams flow
Blue above, green below **when…**

— w: Pete Seeger, m: trad. (English "Weel May the Keel Row")

The **Travelin'** chapter contains songs about being "on the road again" (about cars, trucks, RRs, airplanes & bikes). See also: **Blues, Country, Home & Roots** (immigration, exile). Other songs include **Ballads**: I live not where I love **Country**: Folsom prison blues (RR) **Farm**: Don't fence me in, Night rider's lament, Tumbling tumbleweed **Hope**: Fast car **Jazz**: Chatanooga choo choo, Let's get away fr it all **Love**: Beeswing **Rich**: Tom Joad **Old-timey**: Train on the island **Sing**: Amer pie (car), Last call (traveling musician).

Work

BALLAD OF THE CARPENTER

Jesus was a working man, a hero you shall hear
Born in the slums of Bethlehem at the turning of the year
Yes, the turning of the year

(↑5) Am - AmG Am / CG AmEm Am Dm / E Am

When Jesus was a little lad, the streets rang with his name
He argued with the aldermen & he put 'em all to shame / He put…

His father he apprenticed him, a carpenter to be
To plane & drill & work with skill in the town of Galilee / In…

He became a roving journeyman & he wandered far & wide
He saw how wealth & poverty live always side by side / Live…

He said "Come all you working men, you farmers & weavers, too
If you will only organize, the world belongs to you / The…

So the fishermen sent 2 delegates, the farmers & weavers too
And they formed a working committee of 12 to see the struggle thru…

When the rich men heard what the carpenter had done, to the
   Roman troops they ran
Saying "Put this rebel Jesus down, he's a menace to God & man…

The commander of the occupying troops, he laughed & then he said
"There's a cross to spare on Calvary Hill, by the weekend he'll be dead…

Now Jesus walked among the poor, for the poor were his own kind
And they wouldn't let the cops get near enough to take him from
   behind…

So they hired a man of the traitor's trade & a stool pigeon was he
And he sold his brother to the butcher's men for a fistful of
   silver money / A fistful of money

Jesus lay in the prison cell & they beat him & offered him bribes
To desert the cause of his own poor folk & work for the rich
   men's tribe / Yes, work for…

The sweat stood out upon his brow & the blood was in his eye
And they nailed his body to the Roman cross & they laughed as
   they watched him die
Yes they laughed…

2000 yrs have passed & gone & many a hero, too
And the dream of this poor carpenter, at last it is coming true
[it's time it is coming true]…

— w & m: Ewan MacColl

BRING BACK THE 8 HOUR DAY

My job makes me crazy, I'm always behind,
   even tho' I am not one to shirk
And some fuzzy folksinger repeats in my mind
   that my life should be more than my work
Well I like the work that I do, I don't mind earning my pay
But there's so much to do when the workday is thru:
   bring back the 8 hour day

C GC FC / F C - G / CG C FC / F C G C

Say you work at a white collar job,
   you get paid at a fixed monthly rate
But you come in for mtgs a half hour early,
   you're working a full hour late
Then you sit for an hour in traffic
   with the rest of the overtime drones
There's a latchkey kid you must chase off to bed
   'fore you eat a cold supper alone, oh:

Bring back the 8-hr day, when did we give it away?
 There's so much to do when the work day is thru, bring…

C G C FC / F C G C

When I was a kid, mom stayed home
  & we lived on dad's blue-collar pay
Our standard of living was decent & sweet,
  just as good as what I've got today
Now my wife has a good-paying job & me, well, I'm doing OK
But we're putting out 99 hrs a wk,
  tell me who the hell's getting my pay? hey:

They've got cellular phones for your car,
  they've got notebook PC's for your lap
If you crawl off to sleep you stay close to your beeper,
  now why do we stand for this crap?
They tell you you gotta to compete
  No! we're tired from footing the bill
8 hrs for work, 8 hrs for rest & 8 hrs for what we will

In 1886 in Chicago in Haymarket Square
They gathered from shipyard, from mine & from mill
  just to march in the sun & the air
They'd been slaving from dawn until dusk
  but not on the 1st of May
'Cos you can't smell the flowers when you're working 12 hrs,
  so they struck for an 8-hr day

Hey, **bring back** that 8..., bring back the 5-day week
When did we give it away? How'd it become an antique?
I like the work that I do, I don't mind earning my pay
But there's so much to do when the work day is thru, **bring...**

  — w & m: Charlie King

© 1994 Pied Asp Music (BMI). On his *Inside Out* & *So Far So Good.*

BYKER HILL

If I had another penny I would have another gill
I would make the piper play "The Bonny Lass of Byker Hill"
Byker Hill & Walker Shore, collier lads forever more (2x)

Am - C Em / G - Am Em / 1st / Am Dm G Am

The pitman & the keelman trim, they drink bumble made from gin
Then to dance they do begin to the tune of "Elsie Marley"

When 1st I went down to the dirt I had no cowl nor no pit shirt
Now I've gotten 2 or 3, Walker Pit's done well by me

Geordie Charlton, he had a pig, he hit it with a shovel & it
  danced a jig
All the way to Walker Shore to the tune of "Elsie Marley"

  — trad. (English)

Arr. © 2015 by Hal Leonard Corporation. Collier lads are coal miners. Byker Hill and Walker Shore are names of coal pits near Newcastle. Rec by Young Tradition †2, The Cottars, Martin Carthy, Chanticleer, The Tempest. In *Coll Reprints fr SO!* V7-12.

CALL THE CAPTAIN

Call up the captain, tell him I ain't comin' in
He can dig his own coal, something else is happening
This living that I'm making is doing us in
He's broken the lives of too many good men

C Em Am - / / / G - - -

Been hauling coal since I was big enough to fight
Some 30-odd shifts without a glimpse of daylight
The corporation likes to say that everything's all right
Dig yourself a hole, get outta sight

There's a dark cloud above me that's blocking out the sun
Burn another hunk of coal, listen to the engines run
One half is starving while the other's having fun
So – call the captain **(x4)**

_ _ Melinda _ close the door
I ain't going down to the mines today
I want clear blue skies & whole lot more
I ain't going down to the mine

C Em Am - G - / - - Am - / C Em G - / - - Am -

There's a hole in this bucket I've been carrying around
I fill it up to the top & watch it spill on the ground
I go down to the mines & when I come back out
I got nothin' to show but the sweat on my brow
  These hills are my own flesh & bones
    They're all that I love & they're all that I've known
    So please don't ask me to destroy my home
    I'm not gonna choose btw my heart & my soul, so
Call up the Captain, tell him I ain't coming in
He can dig his own coal, something else is happening
This living that I'm making is doing us in
So – call the captain **(x4)**

(bridge) Hear the whistle blow this morning
Hear the whistle blow today
Hear the whistle blow this morning

Am - - - / C - Am - /   /

  — w & m: Graham Sharp

© 2006 Enchanted Barn Publishing. On Steep Canyon Rangers *Lovin' Pretty Women* †4.

COAL TOWN ROAD

We get up in the black **down the coal town road**
And we hike along the track **where the coal trains load**
And we make the ponies pull till they nearly break their backs
And they'll never see again **down the coal town road**

D - GA D / G - Em A / D - G - / 1st

We hear the whistle call **down the coal town road**
And we take our towels & all **where the coal trains load**
In the cages then we drop till there's nowhere else to fall
And we leave the world behind us **down the ...**

We never see the sun **down...**
At a penny for a ton **where...**
When the shift comes up on top we're so thankful to be done
We head home to sleep & dream about **the coal town road**

There's miners' little sons **down...**
Playing with their cowboy guns **where...load**
But they'd better make the best of their childhood while it runs
There's a pick & shovel waitin' **down...**

If there's a God for us **down...** / All the miners He can bless **where...**
For we're sweatin' in the hole, suckin' down the devil's dust
Just to keep the fires a-blazin' **down...**

We get up in the black **down...** / And we hike along the track **where...**
And we make the ponies pull till they nearly break their backs
And they'll never see again **down...**

  — Allister MacGillivray

© 1978 Cabot Trail Music. Represented in the U.S. by Morning Music (USA) Inc. On The Barra MacNeils *Rock in the Stream* (14), Cockersdale *Doin' the Manch*, Woods Tea Co. *The Passage*, Fraser Union *Hello, Stranger* & Ryan's Fancy.

DIGNITY

We're talkin' about dignity, we're talkin' about self-respect
We're sayin' that unity is the way to get it
Don't tell me that times are tough, you know that I've
    heard that stuff
This union ain't gonna bust – you can just forget it!

CF C x2 / CF C G - / 1st / CF CG C -

They tell us tighten up your belt that's what we need
In this recession smth's got to go
Well if they want to do away with waste & greed
Don't tell the union, tell the CEO!

G - C - / / / D - G -

They tell us that we've got to be competitive
We can't afford these unions any more
Well take a look around the world & you will see
That unions never made a nation poor

They say we'll lose a lot of jobs if we hold out
Well, under slavery everyone's employed
We just can't compromise on solidarity
What good's a job if unions get destroyed!

    — w & m: Bonnie Lockhart

DUMP THE BOSSES OFF YOUR BACK

Are you cold, forlorn, & hungry? Are there lots of things you lack?
Is your life made up of misery? Then **dump the bosses off your back!**
Are you clothes all torn & tattered? Are you living in a shack?
Would you have your troubles scattered? / Then **dump the...**

D G D A / D G D A D / A D G D A / 2nd /

Are you almost split asunder? Loaded like a long-eared jack?
Boob [chump], why don't you buck like thunder & **dump...**
All the agonies you suffer, you can end with one good whack
Stiffen up, you orn'ry duffer &...

Did you find your factory's closed down?
  Are your neighbors all on crack?
Bud, let me give you the lowdown: **Dump**…
Did you find your pension looted? Are your buddies in Iraq?
Would you see those rascals booted? / **Dump**…

    — w & m: John Brill (1916), m: trad. ("What a Friend We Have in Jesus")

HANDS

I've seen the hands of the laborer lifting all the loads
Granite stuck to their fingers as they built the canals & the roads
Now they're cleared & the bridges span, the river's paused by a
    power dam
And now the hand of the laborer **is reaching out to you**

(↑2) G Bm C D / / Em Bm C D [Ochs: Em Bm] / 1st

**Oh the hands hands hands that worked to build the
Land, land, your land, the labor of the
Woman & the man workin' with their hands**

G Em Am D / / G Em Am D G (C G -)

I've seen the hands of the miner digging out the coal
Black dust stuck to their fingers as they live their lives in a hole
Now the rock, it's still under the ground & the mine is closin' down
And now the hand of the miner **is reaching...**

Well **I've seen the hands of th**e lumberjack,
    forests swaying in the breeze
Splinters stuck to their fingers as the lumber was torn from the trees
Now the wood from the timbers tall built your
    buildings from wall to wall
And now the hand of the lumberjack...

And **I've seen the hands...** farmer plowin' across the fields
Topsoil stuck to their fingers as the earth was split by the steel
Growing all that they could grow to fill your tables row after row
And... of the farmer...

    — w & m: Phil Ochs

HILLCREST MINE

Down in the mines of the Crowsnest Pass
It's the men that die in labour
Sweating coal from the womb of the pit
It's the smell of life they savour
And in that mine, young man, you'll find
A wealth of broken dreams
As long & as dark & as black & as wide
As the coal in the Hillcrest seam

D - / / G D / A G :|

They say you don't **go** (say you don't go)
Say you don't go down in the Hillcrest Mine (repeat)
'Cos it's one short step
You might leave this world behind
And they say you don't go
Say you don't go down in the Hillcrest Mine _

D - / G D / A - / G A / D A / G D / A G / A D

I've heard it whispered in the light of dawn
That mountain sometimes moves
That bodes ill for the morning shift
And you know what you're gonna lose
Don't go, my son, where the deep coal runs
Turn your back to the mine on the hill
'Cos if the dust & the dark & the gas don't getcha
Then the goons & the bosses will

Well, son, I'm gonna open up, I'm gonna have my say
You'll get no peace from the Hillcrest Mine
'Cept the peace of any early grave
Go out & work for the workers' rights
Go work for the workers' needs
Don't stay down here to toil for your buck
To be a tool for the owner's greed

    — w & m: James Keelaghan

IF IT WEREN'T FOR THE UNION

Our union's story is there to be seen
We've won many victories & we've suffered defeats
But as I turn thru the pages & look back thru time
There's one single question stands out in my mind
Today we may prosper, today we live free
But **if it weren't for the union, where would we be?**

D - - G / D - A - / 1st / D G A D / A - - - / D G A D

It's our union, our union that defends our rights
But our union's as strong as our will is to fight
For the union is you & the union is me
So stand up & stand by our union!

A - - - / D G A - / D - - G / D G A D

From its humble beginnings our union has grown
So no working person need struggle alone
But no gain that's been made has been made without cost
And together we'll see that no gain's ever lost
Take a look at those countries where workers aren't free / **If...**

Would you choose to go back, working 12 hrs a day
Would you choose to toil more & a pittance be paid?
Will you stand in the union against the new right
Or do you think on your own you can withstand their might?
The answer is written in our history / **If...**

They say we've got problems & the unions they blame
Well, Franco & Pinochet, they said the same
If our union they weaken, if our union they break
Then where's our defense from becoming enslaved?
So would you choose bondage above liberty? / And **if...**

— w & m: Geoff Francis & Peter Hicks

© 1991 Geoff Francis & Peter Hicks. On their *Union Is Strength*. *LS

MINIMUM WAGE STRIKE

When I awoke one morning, there was a feeling in the air
Everything was quiet, things were different everywhere
The Wobblies were back again with Joe Hill at the mike
When all the minimum-wage workers went on strike

(in G, ↑2) C G D G / C G A D / G E7 C D / G↓ D C G

There was no one pumping gasoline, no one driving from
    town to town
No one at the registers, all the hwys were shut down
The cars were stuck in the garage, businessmen *[CEOs]* on bikes
When all the minimum-wage workers ...

There was no one flipping burgers. All the grills were cold
Onion rings were in their bags, fries were growing mold
There were no baristas at Starbucks asking "How many shots
    would you like?" / **When...**

The fruit was falling off the trees, no one to load the truck
Corn was rotting on the stalks, no farm hands to shuck
The workfare workers were hanging at home spending the day
    with their tykes...

Yuppie parents were housebound, their nannies left the job
Wal-Mart workers said enough of our labor has been robbed
The Foot Locker was locked up, the boss had to take a hike...

When I awoke one morning... **(1st 2 lines of v.1)**
The Wobblies were back again with T-Bone at the mike...

— w & m: David Rovics

© 1998 David Rovics. On his *We Just Want the World, Behind The Barricades*. In *SO!* 55:4. *LS

NINE POUND HAMMER

This 9 lb. hammer is a little too heavy
For my size, honey, for my size
Roll on buddy, don't you roll so slow
Baby, how can I roll when the wheels won't go

G - C - / G D G - ://

Take this hammer, take it to the captain
Tell him I'm gone, tell him I'm gone
    I'm goin' on the mtn just to see my honey
    Never coming back, Lord, I ain't coming back
It's a long way to Hazzard, a long way to Harlan
Just to get a little brew **(x2)**
    Ain't one hammer in this tunnel
    That can ring like mine **(x2)**
Rings like silver & shines like gold
It rings like silver & it shines like gold
    Somebody stole my 9 lb. hammer
    They took it & gone **(x2)**
This 9 lb. hammer killed John Henry /
Ain't gonna kill me **(x2**
    Asheville Junction, Swannanoa Tunnel
    All caved in, baby, all caved in
When I die, make my tombstone / Out-a No. 9 coal **(x2)**

— trad. (US)

Arr. © 2015 by Hal Leonard Corporation. Rec. by Merle Travis, Doc Watson, Tony Rice, Bill Monroe, Brothers Four, Monroe Bros.

PEG & AWL

In the days of 18 & one, **peg & awl (2x)**
In the days of 18 & one peggin' shoes was all I done
Hand me down **my pegs, my pegs, my pegs & my awl**

D - - - / / D - - G / D A D -

In the days of 18 & 2, **peg & awl (2x)**
In the days of 18 & 2 peggin' shoes was all I'd do
Hand me down **my pegs, my pegs...**

In the days of 18 & 3, **peg & awl (2x)**
In the days... peggin' shoes was all you'd see / Hand me down **my...**

In the days of 18 & 4, **peg & awl (2x)**
In the...I said I'd peg those shoes no more / Throw away **my...**

They've invented a new machine, **peg & awl (2x)**
They've... prettiest little thing I ever seen / Throw away **my...**

Makes 100 pairs to my one, **peg... (2x)**
Makes 100 pairs to my one peggin' shoes it ain't no fun
Throw away **my pegs...**

— trad. (US)

Arr © 2015 by Hal Leonard Corporation. On Pete Seeger *Am. Industrial Ballads*, Hobart Smith *Trad. Appalach S & Tunes*, Eliz Laprelle *Lizard in the Spring*. In Lomax *FolkS of N. America, SO!* 6:4, *Carry It On.*

SILKEN DREAMS

This here loom is 50 years old – me & Mary, we're a little older
We've been here since 1918, now the factory's closing down
This loom came from another mill that was falling into a river
Me & Mary, we came here from Austria together

C Dm F CDm / C Dm F CG / Dm F C Dm / F CDm Dm G

And on a hot summer night you could hear these looms,
　　they never shut them down
Weavin' & spinnin' the silken dreams of the workers
　　in Allentown

G C - F / DmG CF CG C

Back in the days when I moved here to try my hands as a weaver
We made silk that could circle the world more than 30 times around
We made silk for the Navy flags of the finest Bemberg thread
We made silk that could beat the best, that's what we always said

Now me & Mary & all these looms, we're the last ones at the factory
Sick or expired or just plain tired, all those weavers come & gone
Young folks now they don't see the sense of a skill whose time is run
Stop the clock & close up shop, this silk mill's day is done

　　— w & m: Anne Hills

© 1990 Anne Hills. On Hills, Mangsen & Kallet *Voices* & her *Paradise Lost* 14 &
Found (w/ Michael Smith) & in *SO!* 36.2.

TAKE 'EM DOWN

When the boss comes callin' he'll put us down, **when…** gotta
　　stand your ground / …don't believe their lies
When… he'll take his toll, …don't you sell your soul
…we gotta organize

(↑2)　G C G C / G - D - :‖

Let them know: we gotta take the bastards down / Let them
　　know: …smash 'em to the ground / ..take the bastards down!

D - C G /　/ D - C - G (C G C)

…you'll be on your own …will you stand alone?/ …will you let them in?
…will you stand & fight? …we must unite /…we can't let them win!

　　— w & m: Alexander Barr, Timothy Brennan, Kenneth Casey, Jeff
　　DaRosa, Matthew Kelly & James Lynch (Dropkick Murphys)

© 2011 Boston Scally Punk Publishing. All rights administered by Scion Four Music
LLC. On their *Going Out in Style* (in G)

TALKING UNION

Now, you want higher wages, let me tell you what to do
You got to talk to the workers in the shop with you
You got to build you a union, got to make it strong
But if you all stick together, folks, 'twon't be long
　　You'll get shorter hrs, better working conditions
　　Vacations with pay, take the kids to the seashore

G C / D - :‖ (as needed 2-4x)　G - C - / D - G -

It ain't quite that simple, so I better explain
Just why you got to ride on the union train
'Cos if you wait for the boss to raise your pay
We'll all be waiting til Judgment Day
　　We'll all be buried, gone to heaven
　　St. Peter'll be the straw boss then, boys

Now, you know you're underpaid, but the boss says you ain't
He speeds up the work til you're 'bout to faint
You may be down & out, but you ain't beaten
You can pass out a leaflet & call a meetin'
　　Talk it over, speak your mind
　　Decide to do something about it

'Course the boss may persuade some poor damn fool
To go to your meeting & act like a stool
But you can always tell a stool, tho, that's a fact
He's got a yeller streak running down his back
　　He doesn't have to stool, he'll always make a good living
　　On what he takes out of blind men's cups

Well, you got a union now, you're sitting pretty
Put some of the boys on the steering committee
The boss won't listen when one guy squawks
But he's got to listen when the union talks
　　He'd better, he'll be mighty lonely
　　Everybody decide to walk out on him

Suppose they're working you so hard it's just outrageous
And they're paying you all starvation wages
You go to the boss & the boss would yell
"Before I'd raise your pay I'd see you all in Hell!"
Well, he's puffing a big ci-gar & feeling mighty slick
He thinks he's got your union licked
'Til he looks out the window & what does he see
But a thousand pickets & they all agree
　　He's a bastard, unfair, slave driver / Bet he beats his own wife

Now, boys, you've come to the hardest time
The boss will try to bust your picket line
He'll call out the police, the National Guard
They'll tell you it's a crime to have a union card
They'll raid your meeting, they'll hit you on the head
Call every one of you a goddamn Red
　　Unpatriotic, Moscow agents /Bomb throwers, even the kids

Well, out in Detroit *[at Ford]* here's what they found
And out in Frisco *[at Vultee]* here's what they found
And down in Pittsburgh *[at Allis-Chalmers]* here's what they found
And down in Bethlehem here's what they found
That if you don't let red-baiting break you up
If you don't let stool pigeons break you up
If you don't let vigilantes break you up
And if you don't let race hatred break you up
　　You'll win! What I mean:
　　Take it easy – but take it! **(Seeger does last refrain tacet)**

　　— w & m: Lee Hays, Millard Lampell & Pete Seeger

© 1947 (renewed) by Stormking Music, Inc. All rights administered by Figs. D Music
c/o the Bicycle Music Company. On Almanac Singers *Talking Union* & Pete Seeger
If I Had a Hammer. S of Hope & Struggle. In Seeger *WHATFG, S of Work & Protest.*

THERE IS POWER IN THE UNION (Hill)

Would you have freedom from wage slavery
Then join in the Grand Industrial Band
Would you from mis'ry & hunger be free
Then come, do your share, lend a hand! *[like a man]*

D - G - / A - D - :‖

There is power (x2) in a band of working folk *[men]*
When they stand hand in hand
That's a power (x2) that must rule in every land:
One industrial union grand

D - G D / A - D - :‖

Would you have mansions of gold in the sky
And live in a shack, way in the back?
Would you have wings up in heaven to fly
And starve here with rags on your back?

If you've had 'nuff of "the blood of the lamb"
Then join in the Grand Industrial Band
If, for a change, you would have eggs & ham
Then come, do your share, lend a hand! *[like a man]*

If you like sluggers to beat on *[off]* your head
Then don't organize, all unions despise
If you want nothing before you are dead
Shake hands with your boss & look wise

Come, all ye workers, from every land
Come join in the Grand Industrial Band
Then we our share of this earth shall demand / Then come...

— w: Joe Hill (1913), m: Lewis E. Jones (1899 "There Is Power in the
   Blood")

Arr © 2015 Hal Leonard Corporation. Utah Phillips (who was a huge Hill fan) called
this Hill's best song. On Joe Glazer *Songs of Joe Hill.* In *Coll Reprints fr SO!* V1-6.
In *The Little Red Songbook: S to Fan the Flames of Discontent,* which was 1st pub by
the Industrial Workers of the World in 1909. The IWW (aka "Wobblies") believed
that revolution could be accomplished by persuading all workers to join one large
union. Hill was executed in Utah by a firing squad for a trumped-up murder charge.

THERE IS A POWER IN A UNION (Bragg)

There is power in a factory, power in the land
Power in the hands of a worker
But it all amounts to nothing if together we don't stand
There is power in a union

D - G - / D - A - / 1st / D - A D

Now the lessons of the past were all learned with workers' blood
The mistakes of the bosses we must pay for
From the cities *[factories]* & the farmlands to trenches full of mud
War has always been the bosses' way, sir

The union forever defending our rights
Down with the blackleg, all workers unite
With our brothers & our sisters from many far-off lands
   [together we will stand] / **There is power in a union**

D DG D - / D DG D A / D - G - / D - A D

Now I long for the morning that they realise
Brutality & unjust laws can not defeat us
But who'll defend the workers who cannot organise
When the bosses send their lackies out to cheat us?

(as cho) Money speaks for money, the devil for his own
Who comes to speak for the skin & the bone?
What a comfort to the widow, a light to the child
There is power in...

— w & m: Billy Bragg

© 1986 Chrysalis Music. All rights administered by Chrysalis Music Group Inc., a BMG
Chrysalis company. On his *Talking with the Taxman about Poetry* (15) & *The Internationale.*
Tune is "Battle Cry of Freedom" by Geo Frederick Root in 1862 w/ chorus: "The Union
forever! Hurrah, boys, hurrah! / Down with the traitors, up with the stars / While we rally
'round the flag, boys, we rally once again / Shouting the battle cry of freedom!"

WE WERE THERE

We have plowed, we have planted, we have gathered into barns
Done the same work as the men with babies in our arms
But you won't find our stories in most history books you read
We were there, we're still here fighting for the things we need

(↑5) G Em C D / / Bm - C Em / Am C D -

We were there in the factories, we were there in the mills
We were there in the mines & came home to fix the meals
We were there on the picket line, we raised our voices loud
It makes me proud, just knowing we were there

G - D - / Em - C D / Bm C Em G / Am D G (Bm C D)

From the textile mills in Lawrence, to the sweatshops in New York
From the fields in California where our children had to work
We fought to make a living, "bread & roses" was our cry
Tho' they jailed & beat our bodies, our spirits never died

We were Polish, we were Irish, we were African & Jew
Italian & Latina, Chinese & Russian too
They tried to use our differences to split us all apart
But the pain we felt together touched the bottom of our hearts

We are teachers, we are doctors, we are cooks & engineers
Letter carriers, truck drivers, conductors & cashiers
We operate machinery, we fly the big airplanes
And we help to build our unions, we got struggle in our veins

— w & m: Bev Grant

© 1997 Beverly Grant. On her *We Were There,* Brooklyn Women's Chorus *Power
of Song,* Pat Humphries *Hands* (all 12). In *SO!* 37:1.

WHICH SIDE ARE YOU ON?

This govt had an idea & parliament made it law
It seems like it's illegal to fight for the union anymore
Which side are you on, boys? Which side are you on? (2x)

Am G Am F Am / Am G Am F tacet // 1st / /

We set out to join the picket lines, for together we cannot fail
We got stopped by police at the county line, they said "Go home
   boys or you're going to jail!"

Well, it's hard to explain to a crying child why her daddy
   won't go back
So the family suffer but it hurts me more to hear a scab say
   "Sod you, Jack!"

Well, I'm bound to follow my conscience & I'll do whatever I can
But it'll take much more than a union law to knock the fight out
   of a working man

— w & m: Billy Bragg & Florence Reese

© 1987 Sony/ATV Music Publishing Ltd. UK & Stormking Music, Inc. All rights on
behalf of Sony/ATV Music Publishing Ltd. UK administered by Sony/ATV Music
Publishing LLC, 424 Church Street, Suite 1200, Nashville, TN 37219. On his *Back to
Basics, Brewing Up With.*

The **Work** chapter contains songs about working people & the
unions that defend & expand their dignity & rights. See also: **Farm
& Prairie, Seas & Sailors, Rich & Poor.** Other songs include
Dignity: Annie **Earthcare:** There goes the mtn **Good:** Whistle
while you work **Lullaby:** Duerme negrito **Peace:** Betw the wars **Pub
songs:** Calton weaver **Struggle:** Red flag.

Artist Index

This is an Artist Index, *not* a Composer Index. Use this index to find songs by artists you are familiar with. Many of the songs listed under each artist (or group) were composed by that artist. However, some of the songs listed may indicate recordings of traditional songs or cover songs written by other artists. In all three indices song titles that are italicized are alternative titles or songs using the same tune as a song directly above it. The arrow indicates where you can find this song alphabetically in the chapter indicated. For space reasons we could not list all composers or artists here. You can find a complete composer index or search for songs by first line, topic, etc. in the editor's online song database at: www.riseupandsing.org/songs.

Cultures Index *(& Special Music Genres)*

Titles Index